Latin America

*Social Policy in a Development Context*

General Editors: **Thandika Mkandawire and Huck-ju Kwon,** both at UNRISD

Social Policy in a Development Context is a new series which places social policy at the centre of research while maintaining the United Nations Research Institute for Social Development (UNRISD)'s unified approach to social development. The series provides a new and exciting contribution to the literature in economic development and social policy. In economic development, social policy has been recognized as an integral part of development, but the literature often falls short of elaborating social policy for a unified approach to economic and social development. In social policy, analysis has concentrated mainly on European and North American countries, and studies on developing countries often lack comparative rigour. The bridge between economic development and social policy will not only contribute to the academic research but also inform the policy debate at the international and national levels.

*Titles include*:

'Jìmí O. Adésínà (*editor*)
SOCIAL POLICY IN SUB-SAHARAN AFRICAN CONTEXT
In Search of Inclusive Development

Giovanni Andrea Cornia (*editor*)
PRO-POOR MACROECONOMICS
Potential and Limitations

Olli Kangas and Joakim Palme (*editors*)
SOCIAL POLICY AND ECONOMIC DEVELOPMENT IN THE NORDIC COUNTRIES

Massoud Karshenas and Valentine M. Moghadam (*editors*)
SOCIAL POLICY IN THE MIDDLE EAST
Political, Economics and Gender Dynamics

Huck-ju Kwon (*editor*)
THE DEVELOPMENTAL WELFARE STATE AND POLICY REFORMS IN EAST ASIA

Maureen Mackintosh and Meri Koivusalo (*editors*)
COMMERCIALIZATION OF HEALTH CARE
Global and Local Dynamics and Policy Responses

Thandika Mkandawire (*editor*)
SOCIAL POLICY IN A DEVELOPMENT CONTEXT

Shahra Razavi and Shireen Hassim (*editors*)
GENDER AND SOCIAL POLICY IN A GLOBAL CONTEXT
Uncovering the Gendered Structure of 'the Social'

Manuel Riesco (*editor*)
LATIN AMERICA
A New Developmental Welfare State Model in the Making?

---

**Social Policy in a Development Context**
**Series Standing Order ISBN 1–4039–4295–1 (hardback) 1–4039–4296–X (paperback)**
(*outside North America only*)

You can receive future titles in this series as they are published by placing a standing order. Please contact your bookseller or, in case of difficulty, write to us at the address below with your name and address, the title of the series and the ISBN quoted above.

Customer Services Department, Macmillan Distribution Ltd, Houndmills, Basingstoke, Hampshire RG21 6XS, England

---

# Latin America

## A New Developmental Welfare State Model in the Making?

Edited by

Manuel Riesco

palgrave macmillan

UNRISD
United Nations Research Institute for Social Development

First published 2007 by
PALGRAVE MACMILLAN
Houndmills, Basingstoke, Hampshire RG21 6XS and
175 Fifth Avenue, New York, N.Y. 10010
Companies and representatives throughout the world

PALGRAVE MACMILLAN is the global academic imprint of the Palgrave Macmillan division of St. Martin's Press, LLC and of Palgrave Macmillan Ltd. Macmillan® is a registered trademark in the United States, United Kingdom and other countries. Palgrave is a registered trademark in the European Union and other countries.

ISBN-13: 978–0–230–00788–8 hardback
ISBN-10: 0–230–00788–0 hardback

This book is printed on paper suitable for recycling and made from fully managed and sustained forest sources.

A catalogue record for this book is available from the British Library.

Library of Congress Cataloging-in-Publication Data
Latin America:a new developmental welfare state model in the making?/edited by Manuel Riesco.
p. cm. — (Studies in development economics and policy)
Includes bibliographical references and index.
ISBN 0–230–00788–0 (cloth)
1. Latin America—Social policy. 2. Latin America—Economic policy. 3. Welfare state—Latin America. I. Riesco, Manuel.
HN110.5.A8L382 2007
361.6′5098—dc22 2006049424

10 9 8 7 6 5 4 3 2 1
16 15 14 13 12 11 10 09 08 07

Transferred to Digital Printing 2011.

# Contents

*List of Tables* vii

*List of Figures* x

*Foreword* xii

*Preface, or 'Out of the Fog of History'* xiv

*List of Abbreviations and Acronyms* xvi

*Notes on the Contributors* xix

Introduction 1
*Sônia M. Draibe and Manuel Riesco*

**Part I: Latin America: Modernizing on the Threshold of the Twenty-First Century**

1 Latin America: A New Developmental Welfare State in the Making? 21
*Sônia M. Draibe and Manuel Riesco*

**Part II: In the Highlands of Ancient American Empires**

2 Mexico's Welfare State: Birth, Growth and Retrenchment (1822–2002) 117
*Viviane Brachet-Márquez*

3 Social Policy in a Development Context: The Case of Peru 148
*Francisco Sagasti, Fernando Prada and Mario Bazán*

**Part III: On the Rich Shores of Late Immigrants**

4 Social Policy and Economic Regime in Argentina: Crisis and Retrenchment of Social Protection 187
*Alberto C. Barbeito and Laura Goldberg*

5 Uruguay's Social and Economic Challenges and Its Policy Responses 217
*Maria Bonino, Huck-ju Kwon and Alexander Peyre Dutrey*

**Part IV: In the Imperial Immensities, and the Revolutionary Island, of Former American Slavery**

6 The Brazilian Developmental Welfare State: Rise, Decline and Perspectives 239
*Sônia M. Draibe*

7 Social Policies in Cuba within the Context of Development (1902–2002) 282
*Dr Julio A. Díaz Vázquez and Dr Julio Carranza Valdés*

**Part V: On the Meagre Fringes of Early American Settlers**

8 Social Policy and Social Reform 'Costa Rican Style': A Paradigmatic Case of Heterodoxy in the Context of a Peripheral Economy 327
*Manuel Barahona, Ludwig Güendel and Carlos Castro*

9 Developmentalism and Social Change in Chile 378
*María Angélica Illanes and Manuel Riesco*

*Index* 425

# List of Tables


| | | |
|---|---|---|
| 1.1 | Population and GDP in Latin America and the Caribbean, by demographic transition groups | 24 |
| 1.2 | Urbanization and salaried workers in Latin America and the Caribbean, by demographic transition groups | 27 |
| 1.3 | Public social expenditure in Latin America and the Caribbean, by demographic transition groups | 29 |
| 1.4 | Human development and income distribution in Latin America and the Caribbean, by demographic transition groups | 30 |
| 1.A1 | Latin American and the Caribbean countries, by demographic transition groups | 93 |
| 1.A2 | Population and GDP: Latin America and the Caribbean countries, by demographic transition groups | 94 |
| 1.A3 | Urbanization: Latin America and the Caribbean countries, by demographic transition groups | 96 |
| 1.A4 | Structure of the economically active population: Latin America and the Caribbean countries, by demographic transition groups | 98 |
| 1.A5 | Non-farm occupational structure: Latin America and the Caribbean countries, by demographic transition groups | 100 |
| 1.A6 | Human development: Latin America and the Caribbean countries, by demographic transition groups | 102 |
| 1.A7 | Total public social expenditure: Latin America and the Caribbean countries, by demographic transition groups | 104 |
| 1.A8 | Public expenditure in education and health: Latin America and the Caribbean countries, by demographic transition groups | 106 |
| 1.A9 | Public expenditure in social security, housing and others: Latin America and the Caribbean countries, by demographic transition groups | 108 |
| 1.A10 | Income distribution: Latin America and the Caribbean countries, by demographic transition groups | 110 |
| 1.A11 | Population growth for different countries, 1900–95 | 112 |
| 3.1 | The traditional approach to social policy and the changes underway in Peru | 154 |
| 3.2 | Social expenditures 1993–2000 (US$ million) | 165 |

| | | |
|---|---|---|
| 3.3 | Social policy, economic development, and social structures | 167 |
| 4.A1 | Federal public sector debt (US$ million) | 213 |
| 4.A2 | Educational system indicators (annual variation rates) | 213 |
| 4.A3 | Coverage of the social security system in year 2000 | 214 |
| 4.A4 | Resources of the public social security system | 214 |
| 4.A5 | External trade 1993–2002 (US$ million) | 214 |
| 5.1 | Public social expenditure in Uruguay (percentage of GDP) | 222 |
| 5.2 | Public pension programmes in Uruguay | 223 |
| 6.A1 | Brazil: demographic indicators, 1940–2003 | 279 |
| 6.A2 | Brazil: GDP annual growth rate, 1980–2003 | 279 |
| 6.A3 | Brazil: some labour market indicators, 1990–2002 | 280 |
| 6.A4 | Brazil: household goods and public facilities, 1960–2002 | 281 |
| 7.1 | Structure of Cuban exports, 1902–58 (thousands of pesos; proportions) | 288 |
| 7.2 | Cuban exports by areas, 1902–58 (thousands of pesos; proportions) | 288 |
| 7.3 | Immigrants arriving in Cuba, 1902–34 | 289 |
| 7.4 | Students registered in primary schools (public and private) by provinces, population proportion, 1932 | 290 |
| 7.5 | Amount of doctors per provinces in 1934 | 291 |
| 7.6 | State and municipal hospital services in 1934 | 292 |
| 7.7 | Introduction of insurance and social security programmes in Cuba, 1902–33 | 293 |
| 7.8 | Cuban foreign commerce, 1932–58 | 296 |
| 7.9 | Evolution of state social property in Cuba, 1961–77 (percentage) | 303 |
| 7.10 | Structure of employment by type | 303 |
| 7.11 | Structure of Cuban exports (percentage) | 306 |
| 7.12 | Distribution of arable lands according to use (in thousand ha.) | 308 |
| 7.13 | Social expenses in the budget (millions of pesos) | 310 |
| 7.14 | Social security expenses (α) (millions of pesos) | 311 |
| 7.15 | Selected economic indicators, 1994–99 | 311 |
| 7.16 | Workers occupied in the national economy (thousands of workers) | 313 |
| 7.17 | Indicators of public health services | 315 |
| 7.18 | Trends in life expectancy at birth | 315 |
| 7.19 | Evolution of health indicators | 316 |
| 7.20 | Budget expenses in health care | 317 |
| 7.21 | Budget expenses in education | 317 |
| 7.22 | Levels of enrolment in relation to population of school age (in percentage) | 318 |
| 7.23 | Network of educational centres | 318 |

7.24 Coverage for drinking water and sewage at the end of 1999 (percentage) 318
8.A1 Costa Rica: Human Development Index 2003 356
8.A2 Costa Rica: basic demographic indicators, 1941–2002 357
8.A3 Costa Rica: child mortality per groups of causes, in percentages, 1970–2001 358
8.A4 Costa Rica: child malnutrition among school-age children, 1966–2000 359
8.A5 Costa Rica: indicators of the population's educational levels, in percentages, 1953–2000 360
8.A6 Costa Rica: economic indicators for the foreign sector, 1991–2002 361
8.A7 Costa Rica: balance of public foreign debt and debt servicing, 1991–2002 362
8.A8 Costa Rica: workforce participation rates, by sex, 1987–2002 363
8.A9 Costa Rica: employed population per sector and area of activity, in percentages, 1987–2001 364
8.A10 Costa Rica: rates of open unemployment, underemployment and workforce total under-utilization, 1990–2002 365
8.A11 Costa Rica: indicators of evolution of the monthly minimum wages and average monthly income, nominal and real rates, 1991–2002 366
8.A12 Costa Rica: indicators for distribution of household income by decils and quintiles of per capita income, 1990–2002 367
8.A13 Costa Rica: poor household percentages by poverty level, 1990–2002 368
8.A14 Costa Rica: indicators of consolidated social public expenditure, 1991–2002 369
8.A15 Costa Rica: social expenditure by sector as a percentage of GDP, 1991–2002 370
8.A16 Costa Rica: alternative management models in health care services, 2001 371

# List of Figures


| | | |
|---|---|---|
| 1.A1 | Population for different countries, 1900–95 | 113 |
| 3.1 | GDP per capita and total population (1950–2002) | 151 |
| 3.2 | Average consumption per deciles in Metropolitan Lima and rural sierra (US$) | 172 |
| 3.3 | Urban and rural population and cohorts, 1970–2050 | 177 |
| 4.A1 | Labour market indicators 1993–2003 | 215 |
| 4.A2 | Poverty rate 1993–2003: Larger Buenos Aires | 215 |
| 4.A3 | Economic activity growth rates | 216 |
| 5.1 | Real wage index development in Uruguay | 220 |
| 5.2 | Performance of the Uruguayan economy (GDP growth rate) | 221 |
| 5.3 | Unemployment rate in Uruguay | 224 |
| 5.4 | Employment in the manufacturing sector in Uruguay | 227 |
| 5.5 | Uruguay: recipients of unemployment benefits | 229 |
| 8.A1 | Costa Rica: child mortality rate, 1941–2002 (per 1,000 live births) | 372 |
| 8.A2 | Costa Rica: coverage of the social security system and maternity scheme, 1950–2002 | 372 |
| 8.A3 | Costa Rica: primary and secondary education, gross coverage rate, 1957–80 | 373 |
| 8.A4 | Costa Rica: primary and secondary education, gross rate of coverage, 1980–2002 | 374 |
| 8.A5 | Costa Rica: GDP per capita in US dollars, 1940–2002 | 374 |
| 8.A6 | Costa Rica: domestic production structure per sector of the economy, in percentages, 1960–2000 | 375 |
| 8.A7 | Costa Rica: GDP real annual variation rate, 1984–2002 | 375 |
| 8.A8 | Costa Rica: public sector consolidated deficit as a percentage of GDP, 1984–2002 | 376 |
| 8.A9 | Costa Rica: internal public debt as a percentage of GDP, 1990–2001 | 376 |
| 8.A10 | Costa Rica: workforce under-utilization rates, 1990–2002 | 377 |
| 9.A1 | Chile: social and political change, 1900–1995 | 415 |
| 9.A2 | Chile: GDP and fiscal expenditure (million pesos at the 1995 rate) | 416 |
| 9.A3 | Chile: social fiscal expenditures, 1900–1999 (millions 1995 CH$) | 417 |

9.A4 Chile: main economic cycles (peaks) (yearly % change) 418
9.A5 Chile: growth during main political cycles (average % yearly change) 419
9.A6 Chile: social indicators and political cycles (average yearly % change) 420
9.A7 Chile: public expenditure on education and health (% GDP) 421
9.A8 Chile: per capita public expenditure on education and health, 1970–2000 ($2,000/person-year) 422
9.A9 Chile: occupied and unemployed workforce, 1960–1997 423
9.A10 Chile: wages adjusted by inflation, 1960–2000 424

# Foreword

This book is part of the UNRISD series, *Social Policy in a Development Context*. The research on which the series is based asked how social policy could perform a transformative role in economic development while maintaining its intrinsic goal of social protection and equity.

Latin America has exerted an important influence on thinking about development. The much-maligned 'import-substitution strategies' led to profound changes in the Latin American economic and political landscape, and ushered in the first phase of serious industrialization. They also brought to centre stage the 'social question' of 'late industrialization' and a number of social policies, albeit segmented – labour market policies, industrial protection, pensions, etc. – were introduced to address the new social problems of industrialization.

Social policy and import substitution were among the elements of Latin America's development experience that were blamed for the region's crisis of the late 1970s. Not surprisingly, in the more reactionary reform programmes, precisely these social policies and the social pacts behind them were targeted. The authoritarian regimes implementing structural adjustment programmes had more than *sotto voce* support from the western powers. They were the type of 'strong' government able to make recalcitrant populations swallow the bitter pill that was ultimately for their own good.

The welfare system that had grown over the years and gradually extended to cover more groups was dismantled on the pretext that it was exclusive. But all welfare systems were initially segmented systems, and have been extended gradually. The problem with the Latin America case was therefore not the segmentation but the slow pace of the extension of the social rights. The solution should have been a modification of the existing systems and the extension of rights to hitherto excluded social groups and not simply the dismanling of existing welfare arrangements. The orthodox solution of 'segmentation' caused much social damage without improving the lives of those who had previously been left out.

In the early phases of democratization in the 1980s and 1990s, the new democratic governments were at great pains to demonstrate that they too – and perhaps better than military regimes – could carry out orthodox reforms. They were under enormous pressure to prove they were fiscally responsible and would not succumb to popular pressure to resort to 'macroeconomic populism'. Although some of the new democracies tried to use any available space to address the pent-up demands of the electorate without disturbing the macroeconomic balances established through orthodox economic policies, it became increasingly clear that the marginal role attached to social policy was not only politically unsustainable, but also that it denied social policy its transformative role.

There is lively debate today in Latin America surrounding the socioeconomic model to be pursued after the 'two lost decades' of orthodox adjustment and in light of the demands of newly empowered social groups. The acceptance of a more developmental role for the state has implications for social policy. This collection of papers, together with the other volumes in the UNRISD series, is a contribution to the great challenge of formulating and implementing policies that are developmental and socially inclusive in a democratic context and in the context of globalization.

The papers in this volume were presented and discussed at a workshop in Santiago, Chile in November 2003. UNRISD would like to take this opportunity to thank the National Centre for Alternative Development Studies (CENDA) for hosting this workshop.

UNRISD is grateful to the Swedish International Development Cooperation Agency (Sida), the United Kingdom Department for International Development (DFID) and the Ford Foundation for their financial support for the research on which this volume is based. As is the case with all UNRISD projects, work on the Social Policy in a Development Context project would not have been possible without the core funding provided by the governments of Denmark, Finland, Mexico, Norway, Sweden, Switzerland and the United Kingdom. Let me once again take this opportunity to express our gratitude.

THANDIKA MKANDAWIRE
Director, UNRISD
April 2006

# Preface, or 'Out of the Fog of History'

This work is a call upon history for help to better understand the present state and future paths of Latin American social policies, in a development context. However, can history be expected to say anything on the matter? Rubens Ricupero tried to answer this question in a recent dissertation about the history of the United Nations Conference on Trade and Development (UNCTAD), delivered when he forwarded the command post of this organization. He recalled the apparent accuracy of G.K. Chesterton, who once said 'History teaches us that history teaches us nothing'. Certainly, the world has evolved in a direction that seems amazingly different from what was expected four decades ago. Unexpected, paramount, historical events have completely changed our perception regarding where the world is heading during this epoch.

But should this acknowledgement make us forget history as a useful guide for action? Ricupero recalled what is possibly the most carefully planned of all human engagements, which is none other than war – and the example is brought to our attention daily, as it is also the most damaging, uncivilized and cruel of human engagements, but sadly recurrent. Commanders before battle, as Ricupero recalled, try to consider every possible element, aspect and outcome. They account for terrain and climate, international and local political environments, the mood and state of mind of enemy forces and their own. Nevertheless, every general knows that always, in the midst of battle, out of the fog of war, will emerge the unexpected, which will completely change all of their planning. Moreover, they know that true commanding capabilities will be tested on how they adapt to the unexpected emerging out of the fog of war.

It is the same with history, said Ricupero, which we should carefully try to understand and take into account for its quite definitive and momentous patterns. Nevertheless, at the same time, we should always be aware that out of the fog of history would emerge the unexpected, that would both change and determine future paths. The new directions, on the other hand, will always follow the course of historical patterns in one way or another. Moreover, he said, without ever abandoning our best purposes or surrendering our most enlightened inspirations, we should always be prepared to change the way we view and act upon things, quite radically and promptly, in order to take account of a reality that is always, simultaneously, predictable and unpredictable.

I would like to acknowledge the contributors to this book, and to the authors and research coordinators of the other books on the same subject matter that are simultaneously being produced in other regions of the world, within the same UNRISD project. Particular thanks go to Huck-ju Kwon, Research Coordinator at UNRISD, who put everything together, and Thandika Mkandawire, UNRISD Director, who created the project altogether. These acknowledgments are also addressed very especially to Nina Torm and Jenifer Freedman, at UNRISD. We do know how hard and how many hours and days Nina has put into formatting the manuscripts and making sure it was all very nice and presentable to send to Palgrave, and how conscientious both she and Jenifer have been in ensuring that the papers were perfect. They also extend to all the staff at UNRISD and to each of the countries involved, who have made this book possible.

MANUEL RIESCO
Valparaiso, Chile
April 2006

# List of Abbreviations and Acronyms

| | |
|---|---|
| AFJP | Administrators of Pensions and Retirement Funds |
| AFORES | Retirement Fund Administrators |
| ANFE | National Association of Economic Promotion |
| APRA | Peruvian Aprista Party |
| AWI | Average Wage Index |
| BDWS | Brazilian Developmental Welfare State |
| BPS | Social Security Bank |
| BWI | Breton Woods Institutions |
| CAC | National Confederation of Campesinos |
| CAEM | Peruvian Center of Advanced Military Studies |
| CAIF | Children and Family Care Centre |
| CAUCE | Convenio Argentino-Uruguayo de Cooperación Económica |
| CCSS | Costa Rican Social Security System |
| CELADE | UN Latin American Demographics Centre |
| CEPAL | Comisión Económica para America Latina y el Caribe (ECLAC) |
| COAP | Comité de Asesoramiento de la Presidencia |
| CODESA | Costa Rican Corporation of Development |
| COMECON | Council for Mutual Economic Assistance |
| COOPOP | Oficina Nacional de Cooperación Popular |
| COPARMEX | Mexican employers' association |
| COPLAMAR | General National Plan Coordinator for Depressed Zones and Marginalized Groups |
| CORDES | Departmental Development Corporations |
| CORETT | Commission for the Regularization of Land Ownership |
| CT | Labour Congress |
| CTM | Confederation of Mexican Workers |
| EAP | Economically Active Population |
| EBAIS | Basic Teams for Integrated Attention |
| ECLAC | Economic Commission for Latin America and the Caribbean |
| ESSALUD | National Institution of Social Security for Health |
| EU | European Union |
| FAO | Food and Agriculture Organization of the United Nations |
| FNDE | National Fund for Economic Development |
| FODESAF | Social Development and Family Allowance Fund |
| FONCODES | Fondo de Compensación Social y Desarrollo |

| | |
|---|---|
| FOVISSSTE | Housing Fund of the ISSSTE |
| FTA | Free trade agreement |
| FTAA | Free Trade Agreement of the Americas |
| GATT | General Agreement on Tariffs and Trades |
| GDP | gross domestic product |
| GNP | gross national product |
| GSP | global social product |
| HDI | Human Development Index |
| IADB | Inter-American Development Bank |
| ILO | International Labour Organization |
| IMF | International Monetary Fund |
| IMM | Municipality of Montevideo |
| IMSS | Mexican Social Security Institute |
| INA | National Institute of Learning |
| INDECO | National Institute for Community Development |
| INEGI | National Institute of Geographic Statistics |
| INFONAVIT | National Worker Housing Fund |
| INP | National Planning Institute |
| IRIC | Industrial and Commercial Income Tax |
| IS/ISI | import substitution industrialization |
| ISSSTE | Institute for Security and Social Services for State Workers |
| LA | Latin America/Latin American |
| LAD | Latin American Developmentalism |
| LADWS | Latin American Developmental Welfare State |
| LAIA | Latin American Integration Association |
| LSS | Social Security Law |
| MERCOSUR | Southern Common Market formed by Brazil, Argentina, Uruguay and Paraguay. Chile and Bolivia hold a special associate status. |
| MIVIVIENDA | Fondo Hipotecando de Promoción de la Vivienda |
| MNS | Minimum National Salaries |
| MP | Member(s) of Parliament |
| MWI | minimum wage index |
| NAFTA | North American Free Trade Agreement |
| NGO | non-governmental organization |
| NLSS | New Social Security Law |
| NSSO | New Social Security Orthodoxy |
| NSSS | National Social Security System |
| OAS | Organization of American States |
| PAN | National Action Party (Mexico) |
| PAN | National Food Program (Argentina) |
| PASSPA | Support Program of Health Services for the Uninsured |
| PEC | Protocolo de Expansión Comercial |

| | |
|---|---|
| PJJHD | Programme for Unemployed [Female and Male] Heads of Households |
| PB | Basic Health Package |
| PFL | Party of the Liberal Front |
| PMDB | Party of the Brazilian Democratic Movement |
| PRI | Partido Revolucionario Institucionalizado |
| PROCAL | Labour Qualification Programme |
| PROGRESA | Education, Health, and Food Program |
| PRONASOL | Mexico National Solidarity Program |
| PSD | Social Democratic Party |
| PSE | Public Social Expenditure |
| PT | Party of the Workers |
| PTB | Labour Party |
| PUC | Pontificia Universidad Católica de Chile |
| SAM | Mexican Food System |
| SAR | Retirement Savings System |
| SISBEN | System of Social Policy Beneficiary Selection |
| SINAMOS | National System of Mobilization |
| SIPO | Target Population Information System |
| SNS | National Health Service |
| SUS | Integrated Health System (Sistema Unificado de Saúde) |
| SP | Social Protection or Social Policies, usually meaning all such policies, including education, health, pensions, unemployment protection, poverty alleviation, etc. Social Policies usually include labour legislation as well. |
| SPS | Social Policy System, Social Protection or Social Policies System, usually meaning all such policies, including education, health, pensions, unemployment protection, poverty alleviation, etc. Social Policies include labour legislation as well. |
| SSF | Social Security Fund |
| TNC | Transnational corporation |
| UBPC | Basic Units of Cooperative Production |
| UNIDO | United Nations Industrial Development Organization |
| UNDP | United Nations Development Programme |
| UNESCO | United Nations Educational, Scientific and Cultural Organization |
| UNRISD | United Nations Research Institute for Social Development |
| US | United States |
| USSR | Union of Soviet Socialist Republics |
| WS | welfare state |
| WTO | World Trade Organization |
| WWI | First World War |
| WWII | Second World War |

# Notes on the Contributors

**Manuel Barahona** is a professor at the School of Economics of the National University, and co-editor of the electronic journal *Democracia Digital,* in San José, Costa Rica. He has worked as a consultant in the area of social development, social policy and sociodemographic indicators for several governmental institutions and international organizations. He obtained his degree in sociology from the University of Costa Rica.

**Alberto Barbeito** is an economist and a lead researcher at the Centro Interdisciplinario para el Estudio de Políticas Públicas (CIEPP) in Buenos Aires, Argentina. Previously, he was general coordinator of the Oficina de Promoción y Desarrollo Urbano (OPDU).

**Mario Francisco Bazán Borja** is an economist at the Pontificia Universidad Católica del Perú. At present, he works as a researcher at the FORO Nacional/Internacional, and he is also general coordinator of Ophèlimos, an association specialized in the dissemination of economy-related information.

**María Bonino** is a sociologist and an associate researcher at the Centro de Investigación Económica y Social del Uruguay (CIEDUR). She does research and evaluation projects in the areas of poverty, social policies and gender issues for various national and regional NGOs, government institutions and multilateral agencies.

**Viviane Brachet-Márquez** is a professor of sociology at El Colegio de México. Her recent publications in the area of social policy include 'Gendering the Debate on the Welfare State in Mexico: Women's Employment and Welfare Entitlements in the Globalized Economy' (with Orlandina de Oliveira, in *Globalization, Export Oriented Employment and Social Policy: Gendered Connections,* 2004). She is a coauthor of *La reforma de la salud y la seguridad social en América Latina: Argentina, Brasil, Chile y México en perspectiva comparativa* (2006).

**Julio Carranza Valdés** is Specialist and Regional Adviser for Social and Human Sciences for Latin American and the Caribbean at the United Nations

Educational Scientific and Cultural Organization (UNESCO), Regional Office for Science in Latin America and the Caribbean, Montevideo, Uruguay. He has been professor of economics at the University of Havana, and guest professor at several other universities in Latin America, the United States and Europe, as well as the vice director of the Centro de Estudios sobre America in Havana. His book *Los Desafios de la Globalizacion en el Caribe* (co-author) was awarded the Caribbean Thought Prize in 2003 in Mexico.

**Carlos Castro Valverde** is affiliated with the Institute of Social Research at the University of Costa Rica. Recent publications include 'Déficit en la generación de oportunidades y medios de vida sostenibles: Salud, educación y vivienda' (with Manuel Barahona, in Jorge Nowalski (ed.), *Asimetrías económicas, sociales y políticas en Costa Rica*, 2003); and 'Inserción laboral y remesas de los inmigrantes nicaragüenses en Costa Rica' (in Abelardo Morales and Carlos Castro (eds), *Redes transfronterizas*, 2002).

**Julio A. Diaz Vazquez** is a researcher, professor and president of the scientific board of the Centro de Investigación de Economia Internacional at the University of Havana, Cuba. The author of numerous articles and essays in Cuban and international journals, he was previously editor of *Revista Economía y Desarrollo* and is editor or coauthor of several books, among them, *Cuba y el CAME* (1988); *La Integracion Economica Socialista* (1989).

**Sônia M. Draibe** is an associate professor at the Institute of Economics, State University of Campinas (Unicamp), Brazil, senior researcher in the Unicamp Group on Public Policies (NEPP), and director of the Social Capacity Building Association. Her areas of interest and publication include public policy, social protection systems in Latin America, and poverty reduction initiatives.

**Laura Goldberg** is a member of the research team at the Centro Interdisciplinario para el Estudio de Políticas Públicas (CIEPP) in Buenos Aires, Argentina and a professor of economics at the University of Buenos Aires. She has been a junior advisor for the ministries of finance and of labour in Argentina. Currently researching and writing her PhD thesis, she has authored and coauthored several CIEPP working papers and articles in Argentine journals.

**Ludwig Güendel** is the director of Centro de Estúdios para la Acción Social (CEPAS) in San José, Costa Rica, and is a professor at the School of Sociology at the Universidad Nacional de San José.

**María Angélica Illanes** is the director of the School of History and Social Sciences at Universidad ARCIS in Santiago, Chile and a professor of Social History at the University of Santiago. She has published several articles and books on the history of social policies, including *La batalla de la memoria:*

*Ensayos históricos de nuestro siglo* (2002) and *Chile descentrado: Formación socio-cultural republicana y transición capitalista, 1810–1910* (2003).

**Huck-ju Kwon** is a professor at Sung Kyun Kwan University in Seoul, Korea and was the overall coordinator of UNRISD research on Social Policy in a Development Context. His publications include *Transforming the Developmental Welfare State in East Asia* (2005) and *The East Asian Welfare Model: the State and Welfare Orientalism* (1998).

**Alexander Peyre Dutrey** was a research assistant for the UNRISD project, Social Policy in a Development Context, with a focus on inequality in Latin America. He obtained his MA in Social Sciences at the University of Amsterdam, and previously worked for a Swedish NGO in southern Mexico and in Sweden as a political campaign coordinator.

**Fernando Prada** is an associate researcher at FORO Nacional/Internacional in Lima, Peru. He has been an advisor in the office of the prime minister in Peru, and a research assistant at the Institute of Development Studies in Sussex, United Kingdom. He is currently studying toward a Masters in Public Policy at the University of Michigan, Ann Arbor, United States.

**Manuel Riesco** is Vice President of the National Centre for Alternative Development Studies (Centro de Estudios Nacionales de Desarrollo Alternativo/CENDA) in Santiago, Chile, and of the Foundation for Poverty Elimination. He has held administrative and teaching positions at universities in Chile and the United States, and has been a senior advisor to the Chilean government and parliament. He has written widely on Chilean development, and is the editor of *Revista Encuentro XXI.*

**Francisco Sagasti** is the president of FORO Nacional/Internacional in Lima, Peru, and director of its Agenda: PERU programme on development strategy, institutional reform and democratic governance. His recent publications (both with Keith Bezanson) include *A Foresight and Policy Study of the Multilateral Development Banks* and *Financing and Providing GlobalPpublic Goods: Expectations and Prospects* (2001).

# Introduction

*Sônia M. Draibe and Manuel Riesco*

The subject of this book is the *Latin American Developmental Welfare State* (LADWS), its origins, rise, peak and decline, also its recent Neoliberal form, and present-day perspectives. Drawing on long time series of empirical data, comparative literature, and detailed case studies, it examines its century-old history, the changing conditions, and institutional configurations, of the social policies systems across the region. The study considers Latin America in general terms, and also offers case studies of eight selected countries – Brazil, Argentina, Uruguay, Mexico, Peru, Costa Rica, Cuba, and Chile.

The core argument of this volume is that LADWS was the original historical form that drove forward social and economic development in the particular conditions of the region during the twentieth century. From the 1930s approximately up to the 1980s, under a peculiar form of developmental welfare state, late-industrializing LA countries managed to transform their social and productive structures, against a backdrop of large numbers of peasants becoming salaried workers, and being incorporated into the dynamics and structures of urban market economies.

Since the 1980s, in a framework of globalization and the promotion of pro-market reforms, the structural transformation of LA economies has entered a new phase. As is well known, Neoliberal policies have introduced considerable growth instability, and have also adversely affected employment and social protection. Nevertheless, they have also promoted substantial alterations in economic and state structures in the region, including the decline of the LADWS and the kind of socioeconomic development they had promoted.

It may be asserted that this second policy prevails to the present day, with minor modifications, in most countries throughout the region. Nevertheless, the first years of the twenty-first century have already witnessed changes and movements that, affecting economies, political life, and ways of thinking, seem to be pointing, if not towards the end, at least to a significant inflexion of Neoliberal ideology and orientations. It is not coincidental that a resumption of the path of development has regained the centre of attention of the new governments, some of whom have been elected on an explicitly anti-Neoliberal platform. Likewise, and in this case beyond the LA borders, academic debate has again conferred legitimacy and importance on theories of economic development. Will these changes lead to new alternatives of economic development for LA? If that were the case, what would be the role assigned to social policies in a new expansive cycle in the region?

*New LADWS in the Making?* has assembled a group a set of LA scholars under the framework of the project *Social Policy in Late Industrializers: A Comparative Study of Latin America,* coordinated by Manuel Riesco (Riesco 2003). It is part of a wider research programme, *Social Policy in a Development Context,* coordinated by Huck-ju Kwon, by the United Nations Research Institute for Social Development, UNRISD, directed by Thandika Mkandawire (UNRISD, www.unrisd.org). Organized into two strands – thematic and region-centred, comparative researches – this overarching programme has been conducting similar studies in late industrializers in East Asia, Africa, the Middle East and North Africa, and Northern Europe.[1]

Rooting the various studies in the common ground of the forms and types of welfare states, related to the patterns of modernization and economic development, this line of research has stimulated a productive confrontation of general concepts and typologies on the one hand, and historical circumstances and determinations on the other. The traditional concept of *Welfare State* has been unfolded into new, middle range, conceptual categories, such as the *East Asian Developmental Welfare State* (Kwon 1999; Goodman *et al.* 1998) and now the *Latin American Developmental Welfare State,* advanced in this book.[2]

## Subjects, theories, and methods: an integrated historical perspective

The theoretical-analytical framework of the overall UNRISD project is oriented by the integrated approach of economic and social policies, and a historical method of analysis. The first positions social policies within their political and economic contexts, with special attention being paid to the links between macroeconomic performance and the fundamental goal of improving human well-being. Prospectively, in the countries and regions under study, it tries to explore the possibilities of building *a state–society nexus that is developmental, democratic, and socially inclusive,* as well as highlighting the role played by social policy in securing this goal.

The historical perspective suggests that processes of economic and social transformation should be studied in all of their complexity, and over long periods of time. In addition, it stimulates the identification of patterns, or routes of development, that different countries or groups of countries have followed, with the purpose of understanding their specificities. For this purpose, it considers it crucial to confront history and theory persistently, to analyse historically determined processes and general concepts, and the intellectual effort to construct new categories and concepts such as the above mentioned middle range welfare state regimes.

The unified approach between economic and social policy is certainly nothing new. For example, in the 1930s, the 'Keynesian virtuous circle' tried to comprehend the peculiar dynamics of social and economic growth achieved by nascent welfare states (Offe 1984). Nevertheless, mainstream economic thought continues to treat these two dimensions quite separately, at most considering social policy under the perspective of factors of production.

Certainly, the UN system and agencies may deserve considerable credit for recovering, reconceptualizing, and disseminating a unified approach of economic and social policy with regard to economic development. Since the 1960s, under the concept of *Social Development*, UN agencies have asserted that social policy is a necessary condition for economic development. In addition, it is considered preferable for this process to be oriented by clear ethical and normative principles – so that no segment of the population is excluded from development and social change, and the process is participative and oriented equally towards the joint goals of equity and efficiency. In addition, it gives priority to the development of human potential, especially that of children (Kwon 2003: 5).

The concept of *Social Development* evolved successfully over the following decades, adding new contents such as *Human Development* and *Investment in People*, and emphasizing the imperatives of *Inclusion* and *Social Cohesion*. This concept has managed to become the strategic reference of other agencies and systems in many successive international forums, starting with the *Copenhagen Summit on Social Development* in 1995, the *Millennium Development Declaration* in 2000 or the *Social Agenda* defined at the UE Summit of Lisbon, in 2000 (Midgley 1999, 2003).

More recently, under the unified approach, developmentalist conceptions of economic and social policies have re-entered the international debate. However, showing many different emphases, such a conception has tended to be strongly committed to sustainable and people-centred development. In addition, these viewpoints value macroeconomic policies that promote employment, raise incomes, and achieve other 'people-centred' economic outcomes. Finally, to prefer social programmes that are 'productivist', and investment oriented, that is, social programmes that promote economic participation, and generate positive rates of return to the economy (Midgley 1999; Midgley and Sherraden 2000).[3]

The UNRISD's integrated approach has certainly advanced further than other currents of the unified approach, since it considers social policy as a starting point, whereas others begin with economic policy (UNRISD 2003a, 2003b, 2002). In this sense, it suggests an audacious radicalization of the Keynesian argument. Furthermore, from a theoretical point of view, here it registers an additional and significant change of direction, towards a concrete, historical approach to social policy analysis. Moreover, it moves further away from all too abstract, 'one-size-fits-all' schemes, which have predominated in the subject during recent decades. In LA, such a new theoretical base seems to support the emergence of a new developmentalist thought, whose main lines are presented in Chapter 1.

Is there such an entity as a Latin American Welfare State? Have LA social policy systems managed to meet, in some way, the minimum institutional characteristics that could make them worthy of being understood under the concept of welfare state? If that were the case, which would be their *diferentia specifica, vis à vis* the *welfare states* in developed countries, or even in other late industrializers in other regions of the world? Finally, if it were possible to talk in meaningful terms about a LA welfare state, how could such a concept comprehend the wide internal diversity in the region, which so sharply distinguishes the different countries and localities, among themselves?

LA studies on social protection, with few exceptions (Mesa-Lago 1978, 1989; Draibe 1989, 1995; Draibe and Aureliano, 1989), have traditionally avoided the concept of Welfare State, and, likewise, the concept of *System of Social Policies*. This has also happened in other late-developing countries, and has usually been as a result of the historical specificity of each region and its countries. Nevertheless, recent comparative studies on welfare states seem to offer incentive to break with this tendency.

In effect, historical research on the origins and trajectories of welfare states has advanced significantly since the 1980s, driven largely by studies of European Welfare States. In the mid-1980s, the monumental work of Peter Flora, *Growth to Limits* (Flora 1986) was of great significance. Since the beginning of the 1990s, *The Three Worlds of Welfare Capitalism* (Esping-Andersen 1990) has led this fertile current. These new developments have also been encouraged by two processes, mainly the European Union.[4] (Théret 1995; MIRE 1990, 1995, 1996, 1997, 1999; Cochrane *et al.* 1997), and the movement to reform and change the social protection systems (Pierson 1994, 1998, 2001).

As has often been noted, the effort to identify different *patterns* or types of welfare states in widely differing national experiences has been peculiar to this theoretical production. Its purpose has been less to classify countries according to 'general' scales and variables that may be indicative of the degrees of social and economic development – which were typical in comparative studies during the 1980s. Rather, they have intended to group them according to similarities or typical historical configurations, captured by concepts such as *welfare state regimes* (Esping-Andersen 1990) and *families of nations* (Castles 1993).

The widely disseminated distinction made by Esping-Andersen of the three *regimes* that have configured Western European welfare states – liberal, conservative-corporatist and social-democratic – has provided a fertile methodology for the assessment of such systemic variations. Among the criteria used, the following may be underlined as especially relevant: the composition of social provision,[5] the degrees of autonomy of families and persons in relation to the market (de-commoditization), and the family system (de-familization), the interests and resources of power and the values of different social stratum and categories. In addition, the different political and institutional histories,[6] dynamically considered (Esping-Andersen 1990, 1996, 1999; Gough 1999, 2001; Orloff 2003a; Pierson 2004; Sabel and Zietlin 2004).

The intellectual trajectory followed by the 'welfare regimes approach'[7] (Abrahamson 1999) has been remarkable. One of its merits is to have established contemporary terms of reference for comparative and historical research in the field of welfare states. Such terms are distant from the formalism of pioneering works (Tittmuss 1958; Briggs 1961; Rimlinger 1971; Wilenski 1975), as well as later studies centred in the specificities of national social protection systems (Flora and Heidenheimer 1981; Flora 1986; Orloff 1988; Skocpol 1992).

In addition, middle-range type theorizations have contributed to avoid two frequent biases of historical analysis. On the one hand, the mechanical application of concepts under the assumption that all countries should travel the same development stages and, on the other hand, the so-called historicist risk, which tends to consider each particular history as a unique case, refractory to fit into any general pattern (Gough 2001).

Nevertheless, typologies are always limited, and the welfare regimes approach has not been exempt from strong criticism (Powell and Barrientos 2004; Gough 2001; Orloff 2003a,b).[8] Frequently, literature underlines the difficulty of applying such categories to countries other than Western Europe. Ironically, the arguments are sometimes contradictory. Some criticize the Euro-centred bias of the historical association of the welfare regimes, which supposedly impairs their use outside the region.[9] Others, by contrast, criticize the limited historicity, or inadequate generalization, of the welfare regimes. In this view, the three classic regimes of Esping-Andersen, based on the characteristics of only a small group of countries, would be insufficient to apprehend even the characteristics of other European countries, such as Italy and Spain.[10]

In a certain sense, the concept of *families of nations* (Castles 1993) tries to amplify and deepen the historical categorization of welfare regimes. In addition to the features listed above, this concept considers the historical-cultural conditions, especially variables related to values and traditions shared by groups of countries. Such wider perspectives have identified, for example, peculiar features of countries in Southern Europe, through concepts such as the *Southern Model of Welfare* or the *Mediterranean Welfare State* (Ferrera 1996, 1997). This conceptualization, in turn, has been accused of considering the cases of Southern Europe only as a sub-species of the welfare regimes (Flaquer 2000),[11] and to present their particularities only as expression of the embryonic or insufficiently developed character of their forms.

As an alternative to establishing limits such as those detailed above, there has been a movement to consider more deeply, the knowledge of the origins and the processes of emergence, development, and consolidation of the welfare states. This may be viewed as a way to 'impregnate' with history, so to say, the categories with which their different welfare configurations are comprehended. A similar path seems to be followed by scholars who look back at theories of modernization and economic development, in an attempt to uncover concepts and analytical instruments that may be adequate for the historical and integrated treatment of the processes of socioeconomic transformation, including the welfare state. Research into the origins and types of welfare states in LA as advanced in this book share the basic assumptions of modernization theory, enhanced with the critical revision to which it has been subjected during recent decades.

For some considerable time, sociological criticism has pointed out the limits which *Modernization Theory* has experienced in explaining the movement, development, and maturity of societies.[12] This critique is addressed not so much to the general direction assumed by this theory, which the real processes that have taken place during the 1990s have tended to confirm dramatically (Riesco 1995). Rather, it aims towards other postulates under which social change was thought about, such as, among others, unilateralism, linearity, uniformity of sequences, and convergence of phases and directions.[13] Based on such assumptions, it seemed natural to 'measure' the different levels of development among countries through a few variables, with the metrics of the traditional–modern, rural–urban, or other, *continuum*.

Trying to capture the relative level of socioeconomic development of a region, a country, or a zone within a country, is certainly very useful. Moreover, there is probably no other single factor that is more significant than this one, when trying to understand a specific society. Nevertheless, in the final analysis, it is concrete, historically determined processes, political outcomes, which shape the nature of societies, institutions and certainly social policy regimes among them. In those processes, many factors, apart from the socioeconomic structure, have to be taken into account. These factors are certainly conditioned, act over, and are determined by, the relative development of the underlying socioeconomic structure, and its relative level of development. However, such determination seems quite light, and never definitive.

In addition, usually events that were completely unaccounted for, which emerge out of the 'fog of history',[14] in the most unexpected moments, in the end determine the concrete outcomes of these processes, which are always, to a large degree, uncertain. Because of this, it is very difficult to predict even the simplest sociopolitical event, let alone the course of the most complex outcomes of human activity, such as economic development, the evolution of institutions, the outcome of political events, and, certainly, social policy. Socioeconomic structures and the degree of development they testify to, even past historical patterns and the course of current historical processes themselves, may be considered only as guidelines, conditions, historical legacies that may be changed. Nevertheless, no other approach seems to provide a richer insight than these, regarding the comprehension of current socioeconomic and political structures, institutions, and events, and the charting of their probable future developments. It certainly seems unnecessary to further argue about the usefulness of this charting.

Incorporating these critiques, recent researches recover the thematic of development and construction of modernity, and bring them forward to the comparative studies on welfare states. Two works, the seminal study of Therborn (1995) and the more recent one by Ian Gough (1999), offer clear examples of this fertile research approach, specifically highlighting its strong potential for elaborating intermediate-level, historically circumstanced, categories. These authors try to identify from their origins the diverse paths to modernity (Therborn 1995, 2002) taken by different countries and groups of countries. These studies operate under the basic assumption that advances in terms of modernization of socioeconomic structures, which they recover as useful and probably the single most relevant explanatory factor, were nevertheless made through richly differing paths, and diverse sociopolitical, institutional, cultural, and other configurations.[15]

This kind of approach certainly seems fruitful in terms of offering an understanding of the widely different contemporary societies that have resulted in LA from apparently similar origins. Moreover, would it be possible to establish relations between development patterns thus defined, and the characteristics of the social policies later developed in LA states in the north and the south?[16]

This book broadly follows this line of historical investigation, while remaining conscious of its limitations.

## Worldwide ideological sea change?

'Something tantamount to a paradigmatic shift' (Mkandawire 2001: 14) seems to be taking place in the consideration of social policy in relation to economic policy, within a development context.[17] While the theoretical critique of Neoliberal ideology becomes increasingly comprehensive in the fields of economic and social policy, it is also becoming increasingly assertive, thus ending decades when it was on the defensive (Standing 2002). Economists who have been in the mainstream for years, will now agree that social policy and economic policy must be blended in a context of increased social spending, to counter globalization-induced inequities and insecurities that affect a majority of citizens in the region and other developing regions (Stallings 2002).

As is well known, during recent decades, the prevailing methodology of economic and social policies, and their interrelationships, as well as many other disciplines in science, seem to have been subject of excessive influence from one particular school of economic thought – so-called Neoliberalism. In the case of social and economic policies, this influence has in fact frequently been exerted to the outright exclusion of almost all other points of view. This phenomenon has manifested itself in academic and specialized circles in LA, and has had a considerable impact on public opinion and governmental policies. As this book will argue, the rise of the referred school of thought to the hegemonic pedestal it still holds today, can probably be explained mainly because of reasons that are rooted quite deeply in the then prevailing needs of the socioeconomic structures, and the historical evolution of the different countries that have applied them to greater or lesser degrees. Nevertheless, this ascent has also benefited from the enthusiastic backing that such theories have received from powerful patrons. Such support has been strategically conceived, efficiently organized, and implemented, by the BWI, among other deep-pocketed organizations.

Because of the afore-mentioned conceptual hegemony, the economic and social policies implemented in the LA region have managed to advance considerably in those aspects that such a school of thought privileges. Such has been the case for macroeconomic equilibriums, the privatization of state enterprises, and the opening up to foreign investment and trade in general. In the field of social policies, this hegemony has resulted, among other phenomena, in the development of a strong industry of private social services. However, socioeconomic analysis has tended to be oversimplified, and reduced to a just few variables. 'One-size-fits-all' approaches have been recommended and quite forcefully applied throughout the region. Meanwhile, little attention has been paid to the complexities and particularities of each concrete situation. The results of such policies certainly have not always been successful with respect to the objectives pursued. Rather, on the contrary, the results have often been negative and quite painful in many cases, at least in the short run, for wide sections of the affected populations. This has occurred especially when the policies have been inspired by extremist versions of this school – as has been the case, for example, with fixed exchange rates.

After more than two decades of such hegemony over LA social sciences, it seems time to engage seriously in a critical evaluation of its limits, at least in the realm of social policies in a development context. The main thrust of criticism seems to point towards their excessively abstract character, that is, as mentioned before, their tendency to reduce the analysis to a few variables. As is well known, this school is based on the results of mathematical optimizing procedures, applied over axiomatically assumed behaviours of individuals, regardless of their socioeconomic environment. The variables considered may sometimes prove to be quite relevant, but in most situations, they do not seem to capture some of the predominant features and determinants of the social objects under study.

In this sense, it seems legitimate to suggest, that an alternative, or rather complementary, methodology should address some of these complexities, appreciating it in more concrete terms, and considering as many determinations and aspects as possible. From this point of view, the essays presented in this book return to those social sciences that try to study total social subjects in their concrete and real movement, and in the interaction among them, in each determined epoch. As has been emphasized, the research has nourished itself from theoretical orientations based on the integrated approach to economics and social policy, on the historical-structural insights of contemporary modernization theories, on the contemporary debate over the patterns of the welfare state, and especially upon history as a methodology.

Moreover, if history can teach us something about the predominance of determined schools of thought, it is that they are never eternal, but are rather ephemeral when considered in a longer time span. A cyclical form of movement, familiar from many natural phenomena, seems also to apply to the succession of schools of thought. It is well known, for example, that the hegemony of classical liberalism in economic theory during the nineteenth and first part of the twentieth century gave way to Keynesianism in the wake of the 1930s world economic crisis. In the case of LA, the school of thought that replaced classic liberalism, and presided over twentieth-century state-led development, was given the precise label LA Developmentalism, and was formalized as a development theory by ECLAC, around the mid-century (Ricupero 2004). By the end of the century, Neoliberalism and the Washington Consensus had replaced Developmentalism as the theoretical paradigm for LA development. Could then perhaps something like Neo-Developmentalism be in the making in LA, as a replacement for Neoliberalism in the wake of the current world economic crisis? The studies undertaken by the project *Social Policy in a Development Context*, and in particular those referring to LA presented here, have suggested some of the possible determinations of such a concept. They also suggest, as argued in this book, that such a possibility may occur, or, more accurately that the chances for such an occurrence seem to be increasing.

This theoretical and political 'counter-counter revolution' (Mkandawire 2001: 21), evolves against the backdrop of turmoil that erupted over the world economy, starting with the Asian crisis in 1997. Since then, as is well known, economic turbulence has been increasing, with still no clear end in sight. Since the Asian crisis, as has been repeatedly pointed out (see, for example, Stiglitz 2003), mainstream economic predictions, as well as their recipes, no longer seem accurate, or even effective. This has been particularly the case with the Bretton Woods Institutions (BWI), as well as local economic authorities throughout LA.[18]

However, economic crises of the magnitude of the current one do not only promote the emergence of theoretical and political movements, and currents, that may be considered as broadly-based, rational, democratic and progressive. While in the end such tendencies seem more likely to prevail, in the short run fear and uncertainty also stimulate the opposite. Extremist tendencies attempt to confront crisis through the exacerbation, sometimes up to the point of aggressive irrationality, of the same kind of policies that caused the crisis in the first place. Historical experience, as well as dangerous international events that are presently developing, point to this frightening alternative possibility.

## Research questions

Following the above-described theoretical and analytical lines, suggested by the research framework proposed by UNRISD in *Social Policy in a Development Context*, the regional project *Social Policy in Late Industrializers: A Comparative Study of Latin America* (Riesco 2003) tried to focus the general questions of the overall UNRISD framework (Kwon 2002, 2003; MacDermott *et al.* 2003) into the context of Latin America. It identified five groups of questions and hypothesis for LA, to be addressed at a country level.

The first group refers to the kind of relationship that has been established in Latin America, between social policy, economic development, and the underlying social structures. Asserting the hypothesis that a particular form of welfare state has appeared since the mid-twentieth century in many countries throughout Latin America, it would be legitimate to ask: What was the relationship between state-led industrialization of the time and welfare state development in LA? In what kind of society did this peculiar institution develop? What were its underlying social structures? What social groups did it address? How do the different stages of development of social policy in the continent correlate with the underlying social structures that prevailed at the same time? How do different historical patterns present in LA correlate with the evolution of the Latin American Welfare State?

A second group of questions refer to the limits and crisis of welfare state and developmentalist experience in LA, during the last decades of the twentieth century. Focusing on the transformations in the social structure, and in processes such as globalization, it advances questions such as: What were the main determinants of the crisis and decline of the LA welfare state experience? What can be said now, about the momentous policy shift in the region, away from Developmentalism and towards Neoliberalism, experienced during the latter part of the twentieth century?

A third group of questions refer to the Neoliberal experiences in LA during the last two decades of the century. Assuming that Neoliberal experiences have not followed a unique pattern, the key questions in this case are: Which determinants and characteristics distinguish the different kinds of experiences? And: What were the characteristics of the social policy reforms in them?

A fourth group of questions refer to the differences between LA countries. Why are the countries and regions in LA so different from one another? Why are their levels of economic development so diverse? Why is it that they present such a wide range of differing social policies? What is the relationship between democracy and social policy in LA? Is it true that LA experienced a sort of Bismarckian period, during which welfare states were sometimes developed by authoritarian regimes? What were those authoritarian regimes like? Did they differ in their political constituency? What were the characteristics of those welfare states that may be related to the kind of regimes that implemented them? What was the role of social organizations and movements, and progressive parties, of the recurrent periods of massive political turmoil, in the development of the LA welfare states, regardless of the kind of governments that actually implemented them? In addition, in the Neoliberal experiences, what was the relationship between social policy and democratic representation? What was the effect of democratization over social policy in the different countries? Up to what point did democratization in the 1990s influenced Neoliberal social policy then implemented?

The final set of questions refer to the present situation, and the possibility of building in LA a state–society nexus that, in UNRISD terms, is economically developmental, politically democratic, and socially inclusive; in other words, social policy that may be at the heart of a new wave of LA developmental economic policy. Could social policy be an answer to some of the current economic problems? Can such a new relationship between social and economic policy, during the present period, open the way to a new wave of inclusive developmentalist policy in LA? Could it, in turn, reinforce the continued democratization process in the continent? What are the main economic and SP issues in LA today? Regarding social policies, upon which legacies and institutional capacities may the different countries count, in order to address the economic and political challenges of growth and consolidation of democracy?

The following studies have tried to answer some of these questions, exploring the general regional tendencies, exposed in Part I, and the particularities of each of the eight national cases, presented in Parts II, III, IV and V.

## Notes

1. In addition to the Latin American Project, the regional comparative strand encompass the following other projects: *Social Policy in Late Industrializers: The Nordic Experience; Social Policy in Late Industrializers: Transforming the Developmental Welfare State in East Asia; Social Policy in Late Industrializers: Outcomes in the Middle East*

*and North Africa; Social Policy in Late Industrializers: Sub-Saharan Africa and the Challenge of Social Policy*. The thematic comparative research includes the following four projects: *Macroeconomics and Social Policy; Democratization and Social Policy; Commercialization of Health Care: Global and Local Dynamics and Policy Responses;* and *Gender and Social Policy*. The literature produced by the projects is already quite voluminous and may be accessed at the UNRISD website (www.unrisd.org).

2. Certainly, the concept is inspired mainly by the East Asian Developmental Welfare State. Kwon first used the term 'developmental welfare state' in 'Welfare Changes and Future Challenges in the Republic of Korea', *International Social Security Review*, 55 (4), 23–38. However, the most comprehensive discussion of the concept is to be found in Kwon (ed.) (2005), in particular the chapter entitled 'An Overview of the Study: The Developmental Welfare State and Policy Reforms in East Asia' (pp. 1–23).
3. The *productivist* conception, shared by many authors in its different versions of *Social* and *Human Capital Investment, Workfare* or *Welfare to Work, New Welfarism, Positive Welfare* or yet the concept of *Active Welfare*, seems to be a special derivation of *developmentalism*. As a general case, these conceptions consider that, in addition to redistributive purposes, social policy should enhance economic participation and make a positive contribution towards economic growth. This is achieved through programmes that enhance social and human capital and capacities to participate in the productive economy. The *Productivist* conception is often associated with 1990s European social democratic parties, especially the 'third way' trend and its prospects of an 'active welfare state', one that emphasizes the reduction of the social risks by means of education and training, aiming to transform citizens from the passive recipients of insurance benefits into independent co-producers of their own security. Well-known slogans of this school, used by Blair, Clinton, Giddens, and others, illustrate the different *productivist* trends in social policy: *No rights without responsibilities*! *Making work pay*! *Work for those who can; security for those who cannot*! *Ending the welfare as we know it*! *Less to the fathers, more to the sons*! (Sen 1999; Taylor-Gooby, 1998, 2001; Holliday 2000; Giddens 2001; Sabel 2004).
4. This is clearly the case of the extensive programme *Comparing Social Welfare System in Europe* by MIRE – Mission Recherche of the Ministere du Travail et des Affaires Sociaux of the French government. This programme has commissioned over one hundred researchers and works presented in four large international colloquiums, the Rencontres de Oxford (1995), Berlin (1996), Florence (1997) and Copenhagen (1999).
5. That is to say, the different 'welfare mix' that results from variations in the relative participation in social provision of the state, the market, families and NGOs.
6. In common with the tradition of historical institutionalism of Esping-Andersen and his followers, they emphasize the path-dependent nature of the institutional development of welfare states, affected by their institutional legacy and policy feedback, and also, likewise, by international dissemination of institutions, and policy learning.
7. The typological effort has multiplied in innumerable works, in the midst of an intense and endless intellectual debate, so vivid that it has been referred to as 'the welfare modeling business'.
8. The feminist criticism of the *male breadwinner model* implicit in the welfare regimes has been quite relevant in this respect. Esping-Andersen has acknowledged such criticism, and added a gender dimension to his analytical tables, with domestic/family economics as a crucial sphere of social reproduction, together with other institutions of social policy.

9. The widespread thesis of inapplicability of welfare regimes to countries outside Western Europe is based on the criticism that only that region was considered in the theoretical elaboration of the regimes. Nevertheless, this critique may be reflecting a limited grasp of these concepts, considered as ideal types, disregarding the the effort of authors such as Esping-Andersen and the followers of historical institutionalism precisely to try and capture historical characteristics and configurations that establish qualitative differences between groups of countries in Western Europe (Orloff, 2003b).
10. In this case, the criticism points to supposed insufficiencies and gaps in the variables considered to determine the welfare regimes.
11. The argument of 'degree of development' is recurrently used in comparative literature about welfare states, to avoid the use of perhaps more clear wording such as 'embryonic development', 'incompleteness', 'low coverage and extension of social programmes', 'hybridism', and so on.
12. In classical terms, the nucleus of modernization theory is, roughly, the process of transition from one model of society to another, specifically the process by which simple, rural societies change into modern complex, industrial types of societies. Modernization theory postulates that this is the unique and only direction of evolution and development of societies. In this sense, through the imperatives of industrialization, societies would converge and turn alike. Social, cultural and political changes move along together in this general process: urbanization, an increase in social mobility, and educational levels; the substitution of religious and conservative values by laic mentality and permanent innovation; the substitution of oligarchic power by mixed political systems, based on the circulation of elites and the mediation of institutions and bureaucracies.
13. Wide and diversified literature – mainly historical, sociological, and economic – has pointed out that modernization theory has not adequately considered the importance of non-structural endogenous factors, as well as exogenous conditioning, in the origin and development of the industrialization process. In addition, it has pointed out the variations of the process in accordance to the different social groups who lead the process, as well as the impact of urbanization, education, and communications in the modernization of societies, even in the relative lag in industrialization itself. In addition, it has considered the possible overlaying and composition, rather than outright rupture and opposition, between the traditional and modern sectors in the course of modernization, as well as social struggle, contradictions, differences and inequalities, as 'normal' characteristics regarding the results of modernization.
14. See editor's foreword.
15. In his overarching study 'European Modernity and Beyond. The Trajectory of European Societies 1945–2000' (Therborn 1995), Goran Therborn postulates that the origins of contemporary regional characteristics should be re-examined in terms of four different routes to modernity: (i) the endogenous European path; (ii) the settler societies of the New Worlds, including both North and South America; (iii) the Colonial Zone of Africa and much of Asia; and, finally, (iv) the challenged countries of Reactive Modernization or countries with externaly-included modernization (Therborn 1995, 1999, 2002). Of direct interest to the LA thematic is his proposal that certain original marks colonization have defined the peculiarity of the route ovserved in countries of the New World and South Africa in their later transition to modernity. This path, argues the author, is characterized by establishing simultaneously against the local indigenous populations and

against the traditionalism in the settlers' mother countries. According to how this variable behaves, this pattern unfolds in others: settler colonialism and genocide societies. This will be considered in Chapter 1, below (Therborn 1995,2002).

16. This has been considered by Ian Gough (Gough 1999, 2001), who suggests two types of welfare regimes according to the path to modernity proposed by Therborn. In his characterization, he adds to the criteria of Therborn, the different colonial legacies of Britain, France, Holland, Spain, Portugal, and others in the establishment of different settings for the emergence of the indigenous systems of social protection (Gough 1999: 10). Considering such variables, the first step of this author has been to identify two types of welfare regimes, building upon the four paths to modernity advanced by Therborn. A first type is formed by the groups Therborn labels the Endogenous but uneven modernization (including central Europe, Russia, south-eastern Europe) and the Externally-induced modernization (e.g. Japan, China, Thailand, Turkey). The second type comprehends the Settler Societies (Latin America, South Africa) and the countries of the Colonial Zone (India and much of South and South East Asia and Africa) (Gough, 1999 10).
17. Such a theoretical shift has been extensively documented by UNRISD, according to whom renewed interest in social policy stems from 'the rediscovery of poverty in national and international policy discourse. And the realization that it is not a biologically given, but instead a socially constructed capacity or potential resulting from deliberate investment in human capital or institutional arrangements, that determines the participation of individuals from different social groups in labour markets.' Other factors mentioned by UNRISD are 'the revival of interest in growth economics and the emergence of so-called "new growth theories", which recognize that social development contains crucial instrument for economic development'. Also, 'interest in social equity, both as an instrument for the promotion of growth and as an end in itself; an interest in social security, in light of the greater economic volatility of economies in the context of globalization and the greater vulnerability of ever-larger groups of people.' And, finally 'historical lessons of the importance of social policy in the late industrializers.' (Mkandawire 2000a: i).
18. In LA, for example, economic growth virtually stopped between 1997 and 2004. GDP growth slowed down from 3.6 per cent a year between 1991 and 1997 to 1.8 per cent from 1998 to 2001. Mean GDP growth of Argentine, Brazil, Mexico, and Chile taken as a whole slowed down from 4.9 per cent to 1.9 per cent, over the same period, with all four countries experiencing at least one year of null or negative growth during the last period (ECLAC 2002). In Chile, aggregate demand was still 6 per cent lower in 2003, than it had been in 1998 (Fazio 2003).

## References

Abrahamson, P. (1999). 'The Male Breadwinner Model Under Change The Case of Germany Towards the 21st Century'. Copenhagen Draft.

Briggs, A. (1961). 'The Welfare State in Historical Perspective'. *Archives Européennes de Sociologie* 2, 228.

Castles, F. (1993). *The Welfare State Reader.* Cambridge: Polity Press.

Cochrane, A., Clarke, J. and Sharon, G. (1997). *Comparing Welfare States.* London: Sage.

Draibe, S. M. (1995). 'América Latina: O Sistema de Proteção Social na Década da Crise e das Reformas, Cadernos de Pesquisa'. Sao Paulo: NEPP/UNICAMP.
Draibe, S. and Aureliano, L. (1989a). 'A especificidade do Welfare State Brasileiro. A Política Social em Tempo de Crise'. *Economia Desenvolvimento* 3. Brasília: MPAS/CEPAL.
Draibe, S. and Aureliano, L. (1989b). 'An Overview of Social Development in Brazil'. *CEPAL Review* 39, 47–61.
ECLAC (2002). *Statistical Yearbook*. http://www.cepal.cl. Accessed on 17 November 2004.
Esping-Andersen, G. (1999). *Social Foundations of Post-Industrial Economies*. Oxford: Oxford University Press.
Esping-Andersen, G. (ed.) (1996). *Welfare States in Transition: National Adaptations in Global Economies*. London: Sage.
Esping-Andersen, G. (1994). 'Equality and Work in the Post-Industrial Lifecycle', in D. Miliband (ed.), *Reinventing the Left*. Cambridge: Polity.
Esping-Andersen, G. (1990). *Three Worlds of Welfare Capitalism*. Princeton: Princeton University Press.
Fazio, H. (2003). *Quienes Gobiernan America Latina?* Santiago: LOM Ediciones.
Ferrera, M. (1997). 'General Introduction', in U. Ascoli, D. Bouget, M. Ferrera, M. Maravall, Y. Mény and M. Rhodes (eds), *Comparer les systèmes de protection sociale en Europe du SUD*. Paris: MIRE.
Ferrera, M. (1996). 'The Southern Model of Welfare in Social Europe'. *Journal of European Social Policy*, 6 (1), 17–37.
Flaquer, L. (2000). 'Family Policy and Welfare State in Southern Europe'. Working Paper 185. Barcelona: Institut de Ciencias Politicas i Socials.
Flora, P. (1986). *Growth to Limits*. Berlin: Praeger.
Flora, P. and Heidenheimer, A. J. (eds) (1981). *The Development of Welfare States in Europe and America*. New Brunswick: Transaction Books and the HIWED Project.
Giddens, A. (ed.) (2001). *The Global Third Way Debate*. Cambridge: Polity Press.
Goodman, R., White, G. and Kwon, H.-J. (1999). *The East Asian Welfare Model: Welfare Orientatism and the State*. London: Routledge.
Gough, I. (2001). 'Globalization and Regional Welfare Regimes: The East Asian Case'. *Global Social Policy*, 1 (2), 163–89.
Gough, I. (1999). 'Welfare Regimes: Some Initial Notes on Adapting the Framework to Developing Countries'. European Forum Conference Paper WS/95, European University Institute.
Holliday, I. (2000). 'Productivist Welfare Capitalism: Social Policy in East Asia'. *Political Studies*, 48, 706–23.
Kwon, H.-j. (2005). *Transforming the Developmental Welfare State*. Basingstoke: Palgrave Macmillan.
Kwon, H.-j. (2003). *Social Policy in a Development Context*. Draft. Geneva: UNRISD.
Kwon, H.-j. (2002). 'Transforming the Developmental Welfare State: A Comparative Study of the East Asian countries'. A Project within the UNRISD Research Area 'Social Policy in a Development Context'. Geneva: UNRISD. http://cep.cl/CENDA/Proyectos/UNRISD/References/Project Proposal Kwon.doc.
Kwon, H.-j. (1999). *The Welfare State in Korea: The Politics of Legitimation*. London: St Martin's Press.
MacDermott, J., Karshenas, M., Kwon, H.-J. and Valentine, V. (2003). 'Social Policy in a Development Context: Social Policy and Economic Development in the Middle East and North Africa'. Geneva: UNRISD.
Mesa-Lago, C. (1989). *Ascent to Bankruptcy*. Pittsburgh: University of Pittsburgh Press.

Mesa-Lago, C. (1978). *Social Security in Latin America*. Pittsburgh: University of Pittsburgh Press.
Midgley, J. and Sherraden, M. (2000). 'The Social Development Perspective in Social Policy', in J. Midgley, B. Martin, T. Livermore and M. Livermore (eds), *Handbook of Social Policy*. London: Sage. pp. 435–46.
Midgley, J. (2003). 'Assets in the Context of Welfare Theory: A Developmentalist Interpretation'. Washington DC: Center For Social Development Working Paper No. 03–10.
Midgley, J. (1999). 'Growth, Redistribution and Welfare: Toward Social Investment'. *Social Service Review* (March), 3–21.
MIRE-DRESS (1999). *Comparing Social Welfare Systems in Nordic Europe and France*. Edited by P. Abrahamson, D. Blancher, A. Hatland, N. Lefaucheur, J. Palme and H. Uutisalo. Paris: MIRE-CNRS.
MIRE-DRESS (1997). *Comparer les systèmes de protection sociale en Europe du SUD*. Edited by U. Ascoli, D. Bouget, M. Ferrera, M. Maravall, Y. Mény and M. Rhodes. Paris: MIRE.
MIRE-DRESS (1996). *Comparer les systèmes de protection sociale en Europe*, vol. 2. Edited by W. Abelshauser, R. Delorme, B. Jobert and F. X. Kaufmann. Paris: MIRE.
MIRE-DRESS (1995). *Comparer les systèmes de protection sociale dans l'Europe*, vol. 1. Edited by A. M. Guillemard, J. Lewis, S. Ringen and R. Salis. Paris: MIRE.
MIRE-DRESS (1990). 'Les comparaisons internationales des politiques et des systèmes de sécurité sociale'. Paris: Association Internationale de Sécurité Sociale.
Mkandawire, T. (2001). *Social Policy in a Development Context*. Geneva: UNRISD.
Offe, C. (1984). *Contradictions of the Welfare State*. Cambridge, MA: MIT Press.
Orloff, A. S. (2003a). 'Systems of Social Provision and Regulation'. Paper presented at the Annual Meeting of the Canadian Political Science Association. Halifax, 31 May.
Orloff, A. S. (2003b). 'Social Theory, Modernity, and the Three Waves of Historical Sociology'. Working Paper 206. New York: Russell Sage Foundation.
Orloff, A. S. (1988). 'Understanding American Social Politics', in M. Weir, A. S. Orloff and T. Skocpol (eds), *The Political Origins of America's Belated Welfare State*. Princeton: Princeton University Press. pp. 37–80.
Pierson, P. (2004). *Politics in Time: History, Institutions and Social Analysis*. Princeton: Princeton University Press.
Pierson, P. (ed.) (2001). *The New Politics of the Welfare State*. Oxford: Oxford University Press.
Pierson, P. (1998). 'Irresistible Forces, Immovable Objects: Post-Industrial Welfare States Confront Permanent Austerity'. *Journal of European Public Policy*, 5 (4), 539–60.
Pierson, P. (1994). *Dismantling the Welfare State? Reagan, Thatcher and the Politics of Retrenchment*. Cambridge: Cambridge University Press.
Powell M., and Barrientos, A. (2004). 'Welfare Regimes and the Welfare Mix'. *European Journal of Politics* 43 (1), 83–105.
Ricupero, R. (2004). Farewell speech as director of UNCTAD, Geneva, September 12, 2004. http://cep.cl/UNRISD/References/UNCTAD/Ricupero.pdf. Accessed on 17 November 2004.
Riesco, M. (2003). 'Social Policy in Late Industrializers: A Comparative Study of Latin America'. UNRISD Project. Geneva: UNRISD. http://cep.cl/UNRISD/Papers/LA_Research_Questions/UNRISD_Paper.doc. Accessed on 17 November 2004.
Riesco, M. (1995). 'Honour and Glory to the Jacobins!' *New Left Review*, 212, 55–67.
Rimlinger, G. V. (1971). *Welfare Policy and Industrialisation in Europe, America, and Russia*. New York: Wiley.

Sabel, C. F. and Zeitlin, J. (2004). 'Active Welfare, Experimental Governance, Pragmatic Constitutionalism: The New Transformation of Europe'. Revised draft of a paper presented at International Conference of the Hellenic Presidency of the EU, 'The Modernisation of the European Social Model & EU Policies and Instruments', Ioannina, Greece, 21–2 May 2003.

Sen, A. (1999). *Development as Freedom*. New York: Alfred A. Knopf.

Skocpol, T. (1992). *Protecting Soldiers and Mothers*. Cambridge, MA: Harvard University Press.

Stallings, B. (2002). 'Social Protection in an Insecure Area: A South–South Exchange on Alternative Social Policies Responses to Globalization'. Inter-Regional Workshop, Santiago, Chile, 14–17 May. http://videos.cep.cl/sw2002/SW2002_Movies.html. Accessed on 17 November 2004.

Standing, G. (2002). 'Globalisation: The Eight Crises of Social Protection'. UNDP Inter-Regional Workshop, Santiago, Chile, 14–17 May 2002.

Stiglitz, R. (2003). Press clippings in CENDA Cuadernos de Información Económica de Prensa. http://cenda.cep.cl.

Suleiman, E. (2003). *The Dismantling of Democratic States*. Princeton: Princeton University.

Taylor-Gooby, P. (2001). 'The Silver Age of the Welfare State: Resilience and Contingency'. Presented at the Hellenic Social Policy Association Inaugural Conference, 10–13 May.

Taylor-Gooby, P. (ed.) (2000). *Risk, Trust and Welfare*. Basingstoke: Macmillan Press.

Taylor-Gooby, P. (1998). 'Convergence and Divergence in European Welfare States', in R. Jowell, J. Curtice, L. Brook and A. Park (eds), *European Social Attitudes: The 3rd ISSP Report*. Aldershot: SCPR.

Therborn, G. (2002). 'Between Sex and Power. The Family in the World of the 20th Century'. Yale Colloquium on Comparative Social Research. New Haven, CT: Yale Papers.

Therborn, G. (ed.) (1999). *Globalizations and Modernities*. Stockholm: FRN.

Therborn, G. (1995). *European Modernity and Beyond: The Trajectory of European Societies, 1945–2000*. London: Sage.

Théret, B. (1995). 'De la comparabilité des sistémes nationaux de protection sociale dans les sociétés salariales'. Paris : Université Paris Dauphine.

Tittmuss, R. (1958). *Essays on the Welfare State*. London: Allen and Unwin.

UNRISD (2003a). 'Late Industrializers and the Development of the Welfare State'. Draft paper. Geneva: UNRISD.

UNRISD (2003b). 'Sub-Saharan Africa and the Challenge of Social Policy'. Report of the UNRISD Methodology Workshop, Social Policy in a Development Context, 27–8 February, Rhodes University, South Africa.

UNRISD (2002). 'Social Policy in a Development Context: East Asia, Latin America and Sub-Saharan Africa'. Project Proposal. Ford Foundation. http://cep.cl/UNRISD/References/unrisd_ford.doc.

Wilenski, H. L. (1975). *The Welfare State and Equality*. Berkeley: University of California Press.

# Part I

# Latin America: Modernizing on the Threshold of the Twenty-First Century

# 1

# Latin America: A New Developmental Welfare State in the Making?

*Sônia M. Draibe and Manuel Riesco*

## Chapter overview

As the new century begins, LA seems to be approaching yet another historical crossroads, where a new development strategy could be evolving. Far from a nostalgic return to past models, the strategy that today defines the region seems original, in at least three important dimensions: its new contents, the international geometry over which it is projected and, in particular, the complexity of the historical inheritance from which it develops. Social policy has acquired a renewed importance, integrated together with economic policy, in a way that may become similar to what UNRISD has summarized as socially inclusive, economically developmental, and democratic. The geopolitical dimension of the new strategy seems to be a wider, integrated, multinational LA region.

The new strategy has its roots in the successive experience of Developmentalism and Neoliberalism, which most of the region lived through during the twentieth century. Such development strategies presided over, and stimulated, the radical socioeconomic changes that have occurred in the region during that period, certainly an ongoing process, which gave birth to modern social actors. As a result, the new strategy is based on a new public–private alliance, where strong, state-led developmental policy now relies for its implementation mainly on aggressive, emerging, regional entrepreneurs. In turn, the leadership of political institutions and the focus of social policies seem to be increasingly addressing itself towards the new, widely ranging, massive, popular, mainly salaried, middle classes. Both of these rather recent newcomers, together with a renewed role for state bureaucracy, which was so important during the twentieth century, seem destined to lead the region and its peoples through this developing process. If they manage the transition successfully, the region could become a relevant actor in the emerging world of the twenty-first century.

This opening chapter tries to present evidence in support of this thesis, with abundant data that provide an overview of the present socioeconomic condition of the region and its evolution. The salient feature is that, while huge advances have been already achieved, enormous differences may still be perceived among the countries of the region, as well as between regions within each country, and the region as a whole seems to be still in a process of widespread socioeconomic transition. Possible historical patterns of development are sketched, that may help to explain some of these differences. The argument then goes to the heart of the subject, reviewing the history of social policies in a development context in LA during the twentieth century. The *Latin American Developmental Welfare State* (LADWS) is presented as the salient institution that has presided over most of the process. LADWS is viewed as the main actor in both economic development and social change. The chapter then studies the decline and fall of LADWS, and its replacement by the *Washington Consensus* as a development paradigm towards the end of the century. The suggestion is that perhaps the success of LADWS in transforming the socioeconomic structure of the continent, somehow created the conditions for its own demise, as the new social actors whose interests it had advanced, were now able to support the new policies.

The Neoliberal phase is seen as a direct consequence of the LADWS period and part of the overall transformation process. This period is viewed as a sort of unilateral and distorted advance of the new times, in the sense that it rushed to create a sort of 'dream' short-term economic environment for both local and foreign capital, and to provide high-quality goods, including differentiated social services, to the high-income consumers among the emerging middle classes. Nevertheless, it was achieved at the expense of the population at large, and through unsustainable exploitation of natural resources and the environment. In many cases, even state institutions created during the previous period were severely dismantled as well.

The chapter ends with reflections about the main conceptual determinations of the development paradigm that is postulated as possibly emerging, which is called Neo-LADWS. As summarized in the opening paragraph, these determinations refer to the contents of this strategy where social policy moves centre stage, its wider, regional, geopolitical space, and the complex terrain in which it is rooted, a result of the above described historical process as a whole.

## LA – ongoing transition, different stages, varying speeds

Don Timoteo Inquiltupa, in his seventies, cares for his Llamas and Alpacas from sunrise to sunset, at the foot of the 6,000-metre-high, perfect cone, of *Volcán Parinacota*. In a beautiful, remote, Andean highland, where other rare species such as Guanacos, Vicuñas, Ñandúes, Vizcachas and Andean Flamingos roam at will. His day seems no different from those of his 'old ones', as he calls them, who inhabited that very place centuries ago, long before it became the (disputed) border of Peru, Bolivia, and Chile.

He certainly speaks the same language as they did, although his granddaughter will pride herself on the fact that she is learning Aymara, Spanish, and English at the same time at the local school. The same day under the sun, will see Dr Fernando Macías, in his thirties, write some of the best software in the world, in Puebla, Mexico, in the elegant setting of a seventeenth-century seigniorial *hacienda* building, now recovered with glass and aluminium panes, and decorated with tasteful, modern art and furniture. Dr Macías studied in neighbouring Austin, Texas, and worked for Intel in computer chip design, before establishing his own company that now processes vouchers for Avis rent-a-car and other companies in the US.

A cross-section of LA today seems to encompass almost the entire panorama of societies and development stages that have been recorded throughout history. Similarly, LA's present situation regarding both social policies and economic development illustrates an amazing range of differences, both between countries, and between regions within countries. Considered as a whole, LA seems to be a region still in a process of profound socioeconomic transition.[1]

## Transition in the mirror of demography

Considering a wide set of demographic variables, the UN Latin American Demographics Centre (CELADE) classified the LA population into four categories, showing their relative positions in a scale of demographic transition. Of 556 million inhabitants in LA and the Caribbean today, 18 million live in Haiti and Bolivia, countries that are considered by CELADE to be in a state of *early transition*. Another 40 million live in Central America and Paraguay, countries that may be considered to be in *moderate transition*. The bulk of the LA population, around 430 million people, live in countries that are in *full transition*. These include the most populated countries, Brazil, Mexico, and Colombia, as well as Peru and other countries. Finally, 80 million people live in countries that may be considered in a state of *advanced transition*. This group includes the Argentina and Uruguay, as well as Chile, Cuba, and Puerto Rico among other smaller countries (see Table 1.1 and Appendix Table 1.A1).

In the tables presented in the Appendix to this chapter, all of the countries in LA and the Caribbean have been ordered according to these demographic categories. Then, a large set of other socioeconomic indicators, including many related to social policies, was added alongside population data. For each indicator, weighted averages[2] were calculated – both for each category and for the region as a whole. Most socioeconomic indicators are remarkably similar within each group, suggesting that CELADE categories seem to capture not only the degree of advance of the different LA countries along the demographic transition scale, but also seem quite useful, perhaps even better, more comprehensive, and accurate, than other individual variables,

*Table 1.1* Population and GDP in Latin America and the Caribbean, by demographic transition groups

| *Classes of demographic transition* | *Population (2005)* | *Population growth (Annual %, 2000–10)* | *GDP (ppp) 2002 (millions, international dollars)* | *Per capita GDP (ppp) 2002 (international dollars per inhabitant)* | *Position in per capita GDP ranking 2002 (175 countries)* | *GDP growth 1960–2002 (average % per year)* |
|---|---|---|---|---|---|---|
| Group I. Early Transition | 18,361 (3.3%) | 1.9 | 34,996 (0.9%) | 2,081 | 145 | 1.6 |
| Group II. Moderate Transition | 39,293 (7.1%) | 2.3 | 138,102 (3.5%) | 4,109 | 112 | 3.6 |
| Group III. Full Transition | 418,623 (75.3%) | 1.3 | 2,968,667 (75.7%) | 7,164 | 73 | 4.2 |
| Group IV. Advanced Transition | 79,926 (14.4%) | 0.9 | 779,478 (19.9%) | 10,262 | 61 | 2.6 |
| Total Latin America and the Caribbean | 556,203 (100.0%) | 1.4 | 3,921,243 (100.0%) | 7,050 | 73 | 3.8 |

*Source*: CELADE, UNDP, ECLAC, Table 1A.1.

in their use as a proxy for the degree of the overall socioeconomic development of different countries.

Certainly, these country averages may be misleading in more than one respect. For example, they do not capture the fact that socioeconomic development varies widely within each country, especially the largest ones. The regional giants, Brazil and Mexico, represent roughly just over one-third and one-fifth of LA, respectively, according to population and economic output (Brazil also represents over 40 per cent of the region's area), and these two countries reproduce the whole of LA within themselves, in many aspects. For example, the most advanced LA industrial zones are located in Brazil and Mexico; however, these countries fall into the intermediate class of *full transition* according to this classification, which is probably accurate on the average.

Regardless of these and other limitations, the CELADE classification seems useful for the purposes of this investigation. It seems quite reasonable to assert that with respect to the evolution of their socioeconomic structures, from traditional up to modern, today about 10 per cent of Latin Americans are still in *early* or *moderate transition,* 75 per cent are in *full transition,* and about 15 per cent have already reached a stage of *advanced transition.* These proportions result of the country groupings described above (see Table 1.1), but are probably quite accurate as well, if applied to the individual populations of the largest countries, and even some smaller ones.

The relative degree of advance of the different countries and regions along this path seems to explain many of the enormous differences that may be seen in LA, certainly including those related to social policies. Population growth is twice as fast in those regions still in the early or moderate stages of transition than in those more advanced ones, which have reduced theirs considerably. Nevertheless, a rapid mean population growth will propel LA to almost a billion inhabitants by the mid-century.[3] Conversely, economic performance,[4] as measured by per capita GDP, adjusted by purchasing power parity,[5] is five times higher in the latter group.[6] However, over the course of the last four decades the highest economic growth rates have been attained by the group in full transition, led by Brazil, with rapid average growth rates of 4.5 per cent a year from 1960 to 2002, and as high as 8.5 per cent a year during the 1970s.[7] In this way, LA seems to confirm the familiar 'S-shaped' pattern of economic development, according to which slow growth in traditional agrarian countries, becomes very fast during the transition process, only to slow down again, as the new socioeconomic structure becomes increasingly mature[8] (Table 1.1, Appendix Table 1.A1).

## Urbanization: mother of transition

Urbanization, and the myriad ways in which it affects how millions live and work, seems to be the main process underlying transition, and the region has been urbanizing rapidly in recent decades. In 1960, more than one in every two Latin Americans was a peasant, while today more than three-quarters already live in cities and towns.[9] By 2015, this figure will have risen to 80 per cent. Nevertheless, in the *early* and *moderate transition* groups, the proportion of urban dwellers is much lower, and similar today to what LA as a whole looked alike four decades ago, as measured by this indicator. Conversely, if preferred, the socioeconomic picture of LA forty years ago was similar to these countries today, in this aspect. Meanwhile, at the other end of the scale, countries in *advanced transition* had already reached the present urbanization rate of LA in 1960, and are now approaching 90 per cent urbanization,[10] with Argentina and Uruguay being the earliest developers in the region, according to this indicator. However, even as the continent advances rapidly towards full urbanization, it will be several decades before LA, as a whole, attains these levels.

The urbanization process has been so fast that a good part of the LA population has migrated from the countryside in the course of the last four decades, or belong to the first urban generation. As present-day immigration from other continents is negligible, the above figures suggest that between 100 and 200 million Latin Americans have lived through this quite traumatic process. The proportion of rural to total inhabitants has decreased by over one per cent a year on average during the last four decades, which is amazingly fast, representing over 5 million people a year. The speed of urbanization slows down sharply as transition advances, and is decreasing in the region as a whole; however, it remains at top speed, and is still increasing in some countries[11] (see Table 1.2 and Table 1.A2).

Most of LA's population have already adopted the forms of life and work that characterize modern cities. The economically active population (EAP) in agriculture fell by nearly half between 1970 and 1990, and the reduction has continued since then. Nevertheless, in LA as a whole, still around one-quarter of the EAP remains in the countryside, a figure that rises to around 40 per cent in countries in *early transition*. However, in countries in *advanced transition*, this variable is nearing 10 per cent (Table 1.2 below and Appendix Table 1.A3). In the cities, they have become mainly salaried workers for private employers, usually in short-term jobs, activity that they frequently alternate with self or informal employment, and periods of unemployment in between[12] (INP 2004) (see Table 1.2, and Appendix Table 1.A4).

## Social policies in transition

Public social policies in the region also show a wide variation, which, in general terms, shows a high correlation with the previously displayed categories. This may be appreciated by considering public social spending, both per capita and as a percentage of GDP, as a proxy variable to measure the overall evolution of social policies in the different countries.

Those countries where transition has reached a more advanced stage are higher public spenders in social policies than those in earlier stages. A lot

*Table 1.2* Urbanization and salaried workers in Latin America and the Caribbean, by demographic transition groups

| *Demographic transition classes* | *Urban population (percentage)* | | *Average urbanization rate (percentage of total population per year)* | | *Economic active population (EAP) in Agriculture (percentage)* | | *Non-farm occupational structure, 2000 (percentage of total occupied workforce)* | | |
|---|---|---|---|---|---|---|---|---|---|
| | *1960* | *2005* | *1960–2005* | *1980–2005* | *1970* | *1990* | *Total formal Sector* | *Public sector* | *Private firms over five workers* |
| Group I. Early Transition | 26.2 | 55.2 | 0.6 | 0.8 | 63.2 | 39.3 | NA | NA | NA |
| Group II. Moderate Transition | 33.4 | 50.9 | 0.4 | 0.4 | 58.2 | 43.9 | 39.3 | 10.1 | 29.2 |
| Group III. Full Transition | 47.4 | 78.4 | 0.7 | 0.5 | 43.3 | 23.1 | 52.4 | 13.2 | 39.3 |
| Group IV. Advanced Transition | 69.3 | 86.5 | 0.5 | 0.3 | 20.5 | 12.4 | 54.2 | 12.4 | 41.7 |
| Total Latin America and The Caribbean | 48.9 | 76.7 | 0.6 | 0.5 | 41.8 | 23.6 | 53.1 | 13.0 | 40.1 |

*Notes*: NA = Not available.
*Source*: CELADE, UNDP, ECLAC, Appendix Tables 1.A–A4.

more indeed, because the group of countries in *advanced transition* spend over 12 times as much on this item as countries in earlier stages of the transition process, expressed in dollars per capita (2000–01).[13] Nevertheless, there are also significant deviations, as some countries that rank median or lower, according to other indicators, focus considerable efforts on their social policies.[14] Similar behaviour is observed in the region regarding education (6.6 times), with other significant deviations as well,[15] some of them probably originated in different accounting methods.[16] Public expenditure in health also displays follows a similar pattern (12.3 times).[17] The largest differences are found in public expenditure in social security, where differences among groups reach almost 30 times, and some countries do not spend in this item. Additional differences may be appreciated as well, as countries that privatized their social security are large public expenders in this item[18] (see Table 1.3 and Appendix Tables 1.A1–8).

## Human development in wanting

As shown, socioeconomic indicators in LA seem to vary widely across the region, and most of them roughly follow the logic established by the progress of the transition process. However, most LA countries seem to be equal regarding one particular indicator: the region as a whole, with only a couple of notable exceptions, shares one of the most inequitable income distributions in the world. Furthermore, the elites of three countries in the region enjoy the dubious privilege of belonging to the top group in the world ranking of worst income distribution: Brazil, Chile, and Colombia. On the other hand, only Cuba,[19] Uruguay, and Costa Rica show income distributions that may be considered acceptable. In the region as a whole, the richest 10 per cent receive 40 per cent of overall income, while the poorest 40 per cent get little more than 10 per cent. The middle half of the population receives roughly the remaining half of income, but most of it goes to the 20 per cent that comes after the richest 10 per cent[20] (see Table 1.4 and Appendix Table 1.A8).

To be fair, and not completely hopeless, there seems also to be certain improvement in this indicator, as the transition process advances. However, its pattern seems not in the least straightforward, and perhaps, sometimes, this indicator may even tend to worsen before it improves, as transition advances[21] (see Table 1.4, Appendix Tables 1.A8 and Chapter 9). On the other hand, if all indicators in general certainly seem to be highly dependent on the different historical patterns of development, and on the political institutions and events that each country has built and experienced, this seems especially true regarding income distribution (see the next section in this chapter).

All the above-described transitions in process in LA socioeconomic structures are also reflected in the Human Development Index (HDI) elaborated

*Table 1.3* Public social expenditure in Latin America and the Caribbean, by demographic transition groups

| *Demographic transition classes* | *Public Social Expenditure 2000–01* | | | | | | | | |
|---|---|---|---|---|---|---|---|---|---|
| | *Total* | | | *Education* | | *Health* | | *Social Security* | |
| | *1997 per capita dollars* | *percentage of GDP* | *percentage of public budget* | *1997 per capita dollars* | *percentage of GDP* | *1997 per capita dollars* | *percentage of GDP* | *1997 per capita dollars* | *percentage of GDP* |
| Groups I–II. Early and Moderate Transition | 114 | 9.8 | 44.2 | 51 | 4.4 | 25 | 2.4 | 22 | 1.6 |
| Group III. Full Transition | 618 | 14.2 | 54.3 | 161 | 3.9 | 111 | 2.7 | 320 | 7.1 |
| Group IV. Advanced Transition | 1,445 | 20.2 | 65.1 | 335 | 4.7 | 308 | 4.3 | 653 | 9.2 |
| Total Latin America and The Caribbean | 686 | 14.8 | 55.1 | 175 | 4.1 | 130 | 2.9 | 338 | 6.8 |

*Source*: ECLAC, Tables 1A.6–A8.

*Table 1.4* Human development and income distribution in Latin America and the Caribbean, by demographic transition groups

| *Demographic transition classes* | *Human Development Index (HDI) 2001* | | | *Share of total income (per cent)* | | | |
|---|---|---|---|---|---|---|---|
| | *Relative position in HDI ranking of 175 countries* | *Life expectancy at birth (years)* | *Adult literacy rate* | *Poorest 40 per cent* | *Medium 50 per cent* | *Richest 10 per cent* | $D^{10}$ $/D^{(1a4)(\text{per capita})}$ |
| Group I. Early Transition | 132 | 56.2 | 68.5 | 10.1 | 50.8 | 39.3 | 25.0 |
| Group II. Moderate Transition | 110 | 68.3 | 75.8 | 13.2 | 49.6 | 37.2 | 20.1 |
| Group III. Full Transition | 65 | 70.3 | 89.6 | 12.4 | 47.5 | 40.1 | 24.0 |
| Group IV. Advanced Transition | 41 | 74.8 | 96.4 | 14.7 | 47.7 | 37.7 | 16.6 |
| Total Latin America and The Caribbean | 65 | 70.3 | 89.2 | 12.7 | 47.8 | 39.5 | 23 |

by UNDP.[22] According to the HDI, LA occupies place 65 among 175 countries considered worldwide, that is to say, LA is over the median country worldwide, but still far from the upper quartile of those countries with the highest human development. Moreover, the countries in early transition, are within the fifth of countries with the worst human development, while LA countries in advanced transition, on the other hand belong to the first quartile of countries with the highest human development, worldwide.[23]

## The course of transition

All of the above figures, and many others that could be displayed, illustrate the ongoing transition process that has been taking place in LA throughout the past century. They indicate that the transition in LA is due to continue well into the twenty-first century. This process is rapidly transforming a region where traditional agrarian structures predominated well into the second half of the twentieth century in most countries, to one where modern urban social structures are beginning to become widespread.

As is well known, as countries consolidate the latter kind of structure, rural population is reduced to a minimum.[24] On the other hand, most of the urban population end up working as salaried employees in private sector firms, and the rest become engaged in commodity production in one way or the other. This kind of socioeconomic structure consolidated in England since the mid-nineteenth century, and in zones of Western Europe, as well as the US, during the late nineteenth century and early twentieth century. In other parts of Western Europe, and in the so-called 'white colonies', Canada, Australia, and New Zealand, this kind of socio-economic structure had consolidated as well by the mid-twentieth century. In Japan and the so-called Asian 'Tigers', as well as other countries, this same kind of social structure has consolidated during the second half of the twentieth century. On the other hand, in large urban centres within many countries, this kind of socioeconomic structure evolved long before the rest of each respective country (Hobsbawm 2000, 1995, 1989, 1988). However, 2005 is a landmark year in this process: according to UN data,[25] for the first time in human history, the number of urban dwellers will equal rural inhabitants, worldwide.

The first half of the twenty-first century should, in all probability, be the time when the same kind of socioeconomic structure will extend to the most populated regions of the world, including China, India and LA. This should result in momentous changes in the world balance of economic power, as those regions that are developing to modern social structures rapidly catch up with the present world leaders. Recent publications by leading financial institutions have calculated that the so-called BRIC groups of countries, an acronym that stands for Brazil, Russia, India and China, which now represent 15 per cent of the G6 economies,[26] will represent half of the economic power of the latter group by 2025, and will surpass them by 2040, in dollar terms (Goldman-Sachs 2003).

The historical pattern stamped by the above-described transition process over world events that have taken place during the last two centuries seem quite clear by now, especially after the fall of the communist regimes in the ex-Soviet Union and most socialist countries, and the changes that are taking place in the rest of them (Riesco 1995). Probably, this same pattern will persist over a good part of the new century as well, as said. Nevertheless, as will be argued in what follows, the transition from traditional to modern socioeconomic structures, however relevant it may be, represents only one dimension of the overall historical process.

## Myriad colours in the many rich paths towards modernity

In the case of the subject matter of this book, certainly this evident transformation from traditional to modern lies behind the evolution of LA social policies in a development context. However, the sole acknowledgement of general transition, however important, only explains a small part of the myriad differences that may be appreciated today in LA countries and their social policy institutions. In order to better understand some of these realities, as well as their probable evolution, additional conceptualization layers, of higher-level, historical, more concrete, must be constructed over the backdrop of the above-described transition process. A tentative approach to some of these new analytical levels is presented in the following sections, in the field of interest of this book.

Interesting attempts have been made to classify LA countries from the point of view of their social policy systems.[27] Nevertheless, these approaches seem to be still work in progress, and remain at a rather formal level.[28] The intent that follows, which draws on recent theoretical developments in this direction (see Introduction, Therborn 1995, 2002), suggests that taking into account the overall, historically determined, socioeconomic evolution of the different countries and regions in LA may well enrich these classification efforts. A relevant question seems to be: Why do LA countries, which apparently share such a common historical background, exhibit such diversity? The design of adequate and specific development strategies and social policies for the region requires both the full acknowledgement of these differences, as has been argued above, but also the answer to the question of why they came to be.

There seems to be evidence that suggests that LA countries show these differences today, in part, because the historical processes that have conformed each one of them are also themselves of a quite different nature. It seems possible to distinguish at least some historical development patterns in LA, which seem foreign from one another. This text advances four patterns that could be labeled tentatively: *classical colonial, early developers upon late immigration, slave-based colonial,* and *early settlers.*

It seems important to mention that although these patterns seem to predominate in some countries as a whole, they are also quite visible, each of them, in zones within individual LA countries. This holds true especially in the case of the largest nations. However, even small Ecuador, for example, looks like three totally different countries, whether you visit magnificent colonial-rich Quito, up in the Sierra, where the Indian population predominates, lively coastal Guayaquil, where the African-American population is highly visible, or the tropical jungles down on the other side of the Andes, which resembles none of the here described patterns.

### Over ancient American empires

The *classical colonial* LA development pattern developed over the ancient American empires that flourished along the Andes from Mexico to Peru. This pattern originates in highly developed pre-Columbian social formations, with large, sedentary, native-American populations.[29] Ancient American empires evolved towards colonial societies of great richness in every aspect, which prolonged after independence.[30] The latter coincided with the generalization of *latifundia*[31] throughout LA, as the protection of the Spanish king over lands occupied by indigenous American was abolished (Lipschutz 1955). In these regions, *latifundia*-based societies became very rich and powerful as well during the nineteenth century with important religious and state institutions, as the rich architecture from those times proves to any visitor today. Therefore, in many countries and zones within many countries, traditional agrarian social order went on for a long time, long past its prime, well into the second part of the twentieth century, causing a serious delay in transition to modern socioeconomic organization. This seems quite evident in countries such as Peru, for example.

The region of ancient empires shares a basic historical feature that seems to be common in Europe, as well as in Asia, India, and most certainly in Africa: the fact that mostly anyone in any small town may eventually trace up his ancestors – in that same place or nearby tribes, perhaps all the way up to the Neolithic period. A relevant characteristic of societies evolved through this pattern seems to be their highly distinct, complex, structured, and stratified societies (Anderson 1974). Very large indigenous American populations, and a strong presence of their physical characteristics, remain today, even in the elites sometimes, in these countries. They show very rich cultural inheritances, including original languages, as well as food, music, dances and many other forms of art. Religion, mainly the Catholic Church, but some indigenous American religions that have been preserved as well, continues to play a very significant role in these regions. As has been highlighted in the case of other continents, because of these deep roots, it seems not at all improbable that in the future, as these societies move on into modernity, it will be here that the most complex and original LA culture will flourish. It should come as no surprise that sometime in the future, the zones of ancient

American empires would again become the important centres of economic and institutional power they have been formerly. Some features of this future are clearly foreseeable in Mexico today.

On another analytical dimension, the complete range of socioeconomic development phases may be found among the countries that have followed the classic pattern. Mexico on one end and Bolivia and Peru on the other, stand in opposite extremes, not only of the Andean region, but also of the socioeconomic development scale. The former harbours one of the two main poles of industrial development in LA, and is one of the two giant economies in the region. Meanwhile, Bolivia on the other end, as well as Peru, and Ecuador, or Guatemala in Central America, all at different levels of development within this same historical pattern, are living through the midst of tribulations that characterize the more turbulent periods of transition (see the previous section and Chapters 2, 3). Furthermore, as in the case of Mexico, most stages of socioeconomic development are present *within* the countries that follow this historical pattern, in all their rich variety, perhaps more than any other cases. It still maintains a large peasant population, and presents enormous differences among different regions. The political institutions and their evolution, including social policies, also seem highly complex in these countries, as is clearly exemplified by Mexico, the most evolved within the pattern (Chapters 2, 3).[32]

### Late immigrants, early developers

An opposite historical pattern of development may found in LA *early developers*, which emerged in Rio de la Plata by the end of the nineteenth century. This pattern may also be recognized in distinct zones within many countries in LA, such as Sao Paulo in Brazil, or even in Chilean Patagonia, for example. The Rio de la Plata region witnessed the earliest modern socioeconomic development in LA, following a pattern that shows more resemblances to contemporary developments in the US, and the so-called 'white colonies',[33] than to the rest of LA. Until the mid-nineteenth century, this region resembled an important provincial trading and military post, which even suffered periodical attacks from indigenous American tribes whose frontier lay no more than a few hundred kilometres away. In the case of Buenos Aires, it did not even form part of Argentina until the second part of the nineteenth century. Most of the inhabitants of present-day Argentine – 1.1 million by 1850[34] (Chapter 9) – lived and worked in the interior provinces, which had followed a *latifundia*-based development pattern that resembled the one above described, or rather, perhaps, that of neighbouring Chile. Cordoba, whose economy was oriented in large part towards providing the rich mining-based colonial Bolivia and Peru, led the Argentinean provinces at the time.

Nevertheless, during a few decades in the late nineteenth and early twentieth centuries, the Rio de la Plata region exploded into a huge, bustling, modern metropolis. By itself, it had nearly two million inhabitants as early as 1900, living and working in the twin urban poles of Buenos Aires and Montevideo, on opposite sides of the river mouth. A huge migratory wave, mainly from Europe, that peaked at over 500,000 immigrants per year by the turn of the century flowed into this region.[35] The twin cities developed modern social-relations and bustling capitalist economies early on, and exerted determinant influence over Argentina and Uruguay, respectively. They quickly expanded towards the interior, conquering of the *pampas húmedas* for raising cattle, activity that in turn fuelled the economic explosion of the region. This was accomplished thanks to the twin advance into the *pampas* of new railroads and the army, in a pincer movement that practically exterminated indigenous American inhabitants, all the way south to Patagonia. Much in the same way as the US expanded to the west, around the same time.

Nevertheless, the so-called 'cow oligarchies' that traditionally dominated the interior provinces of both countries and now dominated the *pampas húmedas,* continued to wield political and economic power throughout most of the twentieth century. Argentinean and Uruguayan politics and institutions, including their early and quite advanced social policies, have resulted mostly out of the interaction, sometimes the violent clash, of these forces, among others (Chapters 4 and 5).

## A giant empire and a socialist revolution over a past of slavery

Brazil represents an original pattern in itself. It includes and combines many of the other patterns but, in addition to the fact it was colonized by Portugal, presents another peculiar and determinant historical form: slavery. In the case of Brazil, the sheer magnitude of the country makes a difference of quality by itself. As shown in the previous section, Brazil represents one-third of LA, as measured by surface, population, or GDP, among other possible measures. In this continent-sized country, the internal variety of patterns and levels of development means that the dimensions of each distinct region within Brazil may perfectly be similar to whole other countries, and sometimes larger, even by one order of magnitude. The Sao Paulo region, for example, is not much smaller than Argentina by many measures, including population, and GDP, their levels of development, and even their historical development patterns. In addition, this region generates over ten times the GDP of Bolivia.

The Portuguese conquest and colonization of Brazil, which prolonged until the eve of the twentieth century, distinguishes this country significantly from the rest of LA, including a different language.[36] It is relevant, for example, that in 1806, when the French menaced Portugal, the Lusitanian crown and court established themselves in Brazil for years. Another relevant feature of Lusitanian conquest was that Portugal dominated slave world trade during the sixteenth century, which was probably decisive in making

Brazil a slave-based economy. To make things worse in this sense, the Dutch invaded the Recife region in the 1730s and held it for some decades. This invasion took place during the period when the Dutch were successfully wrestling the dominance of world slave trade from the Portuguese.[37] In Brazil, slaves imported from Africa replaced the relative scarcity of a rather primitive indigenous American population. It was the largest importer of African slaves in the world, by far, with 40 per cent of the total.[38] Even after 1860, when the British had outlawed the slave trade they had dominated for two centuries, and Secession War freed slaves in the US,[39] of two million slaves that remained worldwide in 1870, Brazil had 1.4 million, and the rest were mostly in Cuba[40] (Blackburn 1997).

Brazil's historical trajectory also shows some interesting political-institutional and timing peculiarities. The Brazilian Empire (1822–89) was established after independence and was only abolished at the end of the century. When the new republic was proclaimed in 1891, solid and exclusive hegemony was attained by liberal-leaning regional agrarian oligarchies, based mainly on coffee exports, and the corresponding merchants and financers. The acute federalism of what is known as the Oligarchic Republic delayed the consolidation of centralized state structures, a process that was completed only after the 1930 revolution.

Over the large differences of structures and social systems, in a country that is known for its heterogeneity, its modern social policies institutions, built during the twentieth century, show the patronage, authoritarian, and conservative features that molded basic social relations in Brazil and remain until today. In the Brazilian case, twentieth-century state developmentalism reached its maximum expression in LA.

Cuba may be presented as an outstanding example of how diverse historical development patterns, together with landmark political events, may shape unique outcomes in present political and social policy institutions. It certainly presents a peculiar historical development pattern, where it shares with Brazil the fact that the early liquidation of indigenous American population was followed by its replacement by African slaves, upon which the economy was based until the late nineteenth century. On the other hand, Spain did not relinquish its rule over Cuba until the eve of the twentieth century. And then, only to be replaced by a US invasion, followed by the overt or covert dominance by this too close and giant power, which lasted throughout large part of the twentieth century (Chapter 8). Cuba represents a very peculiar case with respect to the rest of LA, even though it shares many of the regional features in other senses. It has reached an advanced stage of socioeconomic transition, according to most indicators presented in the previous section. Its social policies present a high degree of development, and income distribution is very good as well. On the other hand, Cuba has lived through recurrent economic crisis since the 1960s, all its markets are highly distorted, and its social structure notoriously lacks a modern bourgeoisie (Chapter 8).

It seems quite clear that in the case of Cuba, it was a landmark political event, the 1959 socialist revolution led by Fidel Castro, which has shaped its present reality in a decisive manner. In this sense, concrete analysis in a higher level, where even more aspects are considered, seems to be needed in order to understand the main features of present-day Cuban socio-economic structure, as well as its political and social policy institutions. This is the case everywhere, of course, but especially in countries that have undergone forceful external interventions, such as Panama or Puerto Rico, for example. This approach is advanced in part in the following section, where Cuba is presented as a border case LA Developmentalism, where the state was forced by purely political events to assume, not some, but all economic functions, during the last half century (see the following section and Chapters 6 and 7).

## Poor settlers on the fringes of ancient empires

Costa Rica, as is well known, has become one of the most advanced countries in LA with respect to social policies, income distribution, and human development. In fact, as mentioned in the previous section, Costa Rica, which occupies 42nd place in the world ranking of UNDP Human Development Index (HDI) (2001), disputes the third place in LA with Chile (43), after Uruguay (40), and Argentina (34), according to this indicator (see Appendix Table 1.A5). Costa Rica has achieved this high standard even though it does not rank in the group of countries in advanced socioeconomic transition in LA according to most variables. Furthermore, Costa Rica has become a sort of anomaly located in the Central American isthmus, where most countries instead are still struggling through moderate stages of socioeconomic transition, with the exception of Panama (Tables 1.A1–9 in Appendix). How can the peculiar evolution of Costa Rica be explained?

It seems probable that, as is usually referred to by Costa Rican analysts[41] (Chapter 8), in part, the exceptional behaviour of Costa Rica may be rooted in its peculiar socioeconomic history, where weak *seigniorial* structures on the one hand, and a notorious relevance of small farmers, seem to have been recurrent. This has been a secular presence since pre-Columbian times, but poor Spanish settlers reproduced it since the sixteenth century. As is usual in other regions of the world, such kinds of secular socioeconomic structures tended to prevail in zones where agricultural or mining productivity were not very high in the past, and consequently surplus product was never large enough to support powerful *seigniorial* structures. A similar kind of relation has been mentioned, for example, in the case of the Nordic European countries (Anderson 1974; Therborn 1995). This kind of independent settler-based colonization is a peculiar historical pattern that may also be found in many other parts of LA, in limited zones within different countries.[42] However, in no other LA country this particular kind of development pattern seems to attain the determinant weight it seemingly exerts in Costa Rica.

On the other hand, the peculiar present political institutions – where there is no army, for example – and their seamless democratic workings under wide consensus during half a century, may seem misleading regarding their past evolution. In effect, the present political arrangement of Costa Rica was largely established after a civil war in 1948. It confronted the communist party against the social democrats, both allied to different fractions of the upper classes, and the latter side won. After that civil strife, a new social pact, and a new constitutional arrangement, were established under the 'Second Republic', many of whose main features remain in place until today, under the guidance, mostly, of successive Social democrat and Christian democrat governments (Chapter 8).

Chile may represent another kind of development pattern based on poor early Spanish settlers, who established themselves on the fringes of the Inca Empire during the sixteenth century. They conformed a closely-knit elite of small *seignori*,[43] which remained throughout the following five centuries, as it successfully co-opted successive settler waves who enriched as merchants, some of them turned into bankers, miners, and finally, during the twentieth century, industrialists (Jocelyn-Holt 1999). Even today, and after being shaken by the reforms of the 1960s and the revolution of the early 1970s, this elite has mutated once more, to become the core of the modern entrepreneurial class that was bred by the Pinochet dictatorship (Chapter 9).[44]

## Rise and pinnacle of the Latin American Developmental Welfare State: holding the rudder through the great tectonic change

The course of transition seems to be the general process underlining and determining the region's main socioeconomic phenomenon, including its social policies, throughout the twentieth century – and the relative degrees of advance clearly explain many of their differences. On the other hand, varied paths to modernity, deeply rooted in centuries of quite remarkably diverse historical routes of the distinct countries and regions, seem to have stamped many characters in each of them – and also to have exerted decisive influence upon the form and relative degree of advance in their transition process. To emphasize the methodological relevance of this often disregarded aspect, the country studies in this book have been grouped according to these historical development patterns, instead of, for example, their relative positions in the transition process. Nevertheless, as emphasized by the social sciences, finally it is events and institutions, social and political actors, and the strategies they adopt, which for the most part concentrate in them the resulting vectors of such general and particular economic, social and historical forces. In return, in this concrete, complex and vital sphere, their unique interactions, and the somewhat random outcome of their conflicts, shape the way through which the more general determinations find their course in each country, time, and place. Consequently and in what follows, this text is centred on the study of the latter, highlighting the institution that stands above the rest during the twentieth century: the Developmentalist State. Nevertheless, in doing so, it seems to illustrate that social policies have constituted not a secondary aspect of the process. Instead, they appear as the main instrument through which this institution exerts its decisive direct intervention upon the core of social relations in transition.

During the twentieth century, many LA countries coincided in building a peculiar form of welfare state – regardless, to a certain extent, of their quite different levels, and patterns of development. This institution, which was quite original in more than one sense, was to play a leading role in modernizing the region. The building of a welfare state in LA takes place mainly during the middle part of the twentieth century, in the wake of the 1930 world economic crisis, and up to the 1980s, coincidentally with the widespread implementation of state-led development strategies, model that was theoretically formulated by ECLAC around the 1950s, and is known as *LA Developmentalism (LAD)*.

This period mostly coincides with the so-called *Golden Age* (Hobsbawm 1995) of the *Welfare State* in pioneering industrial countries. Nevertheless, since the nineteenth century, those regions had consolidated underlying social structures where modern urban bourgeoisie and salariat had become predominant figures. Social landscapes observed in LA looked completely different. With the notorious exception of the Rio de la Plata region, the developmentalist experience took place in the backdrop of widespread traditional agrarian social relations, which were deteriorating rapidly, as masses of peasants migrated into exploding mega cities. Throughout a continent, which received the twentieth century mostly in peasant garments, meanwhile no small part of it welcomed the twenty-first century dressed quite modestly, but rather like modern citizens.

As formulated by UNRISD,

> it is often said that 'late industrializers' were likely to evolve different institutional forms in order to exploit their 'lateness' and to 'catch up'. More specifically the State, in such a context, was bound to play a more active role in the process of industrialization (through State control of finance as the conduit of industrial policy) than in the 'pioneer' countries. This part of the story – the patterns of articulation between State and business – has been well documented and theorized in the literature. What has not been so extensively analysed and theorized is that among the institutions adapted for such 'late industrialization' were those dealing with social policy. (UNRISD, 2002: 2)

What was the role of social policy in LA developmentalism? To answer this question, this book advances the concept of the *Latin American Developmental*

*Welfare State (LADWS).* It suggests that social policies were an integral part of the developmentalist project, which in fact included them as an essential, although not always explicit, part of itself. It will be argued that LADWS was the basic institutional form that the continent developed, as a 'late industrializer' in relation to first world, in order to exploit its 'lateness' and to 'catch up'. The basic determinations of this concept are described below.

**Building what infant social actors couldn't**

As is well known, where the modern salariat cannot be found in massive proportions, neither exists its complement, a modern entrepreneurial class. In a predominantly peasant society, so-called LA 'entrepreneurs' of the nineteenth and a good part of the twentieth century, were more likely to be traditional landowners, masters of export crop plantations and mining outposts. In addition, there were merchants, some of whom had turned into bankers. They exerted hegemony over LA societies throughout the nineteenth and well into the twentieth century, just as their ancestors had done for centuries, they dominated the political scene, built *seigniorial* hacienda mansions and city palaces for themselves, which they filled with arts and crafts bought during their spendthrift tours of Europe, which could last years. They erected imposing public buildings and even some public libraries, indulging in a few 'enlightened' enterprises, such as short railways, irrigation canals, and small electricity plants. Mostly, they ran servitude-based haciendas and other ventures, rather than modern industrial complexes, at least none based on then almost inexistent, or very rare, free salaried labour. Rather, traditional agrarian servitude relations, and even slavery, predominated throughout LA until the end of the nineteenth century, decaying slowly during good part of the twentieth century.

Some of the largest worker concentrations in the early twentieth century were export-oriented enclaves, such as *ingenios* and *cafetales* in Brazil or Cuba, or nitrate *oficinas* in Chile. The former had recently freed the slaves who had provided their labour force since the seventeenth century and up to 1879, and replaced them with a kind of servitude system sometimes called *colonato*.[45] The latter operated with *enganchados*, that is, peasants who were drafted out of their traditional *haciendas* and villages, and into the heart of the Atacama Desert 2,000 kilometres to the north, where they ended up in mining *oficinas* or *campamentos*. There, the *hacienda* regime to which they were accustomed was more or less reproduced. Everything was provided by the *oficina*, from housing up to salary payment in tokens which could be exchanged for food and wares in the *pulpería* or store. Such transitional labour relations predominated also in *enclaves* owned by foreign capitalist firms, many of them listed on the London, Paris, or Amsterdam stock exchanges (Chapters 6 and 9).

The above notwithstanding, labour unions, leftist political parties, and the LA workers' movement, who would play a significant role in the modernization of the continent, were also born there. *Ingenios* and *cafetales,* mining *oficinas* and *campamentos*, as well as railroads and other early state-run enterprises, were the hub out of which the modern LA salaried working class developed. Early welfare institutions were also born out of these large early worker concentrations.[46]

Since the mid-nineteenth century, merchants, miners, and financiers, as well as other 'liberal' members of traditional LA elites, disputed leadership with the more conservative landowners, in many countries. The conflict was quite violent and, in several instances, led to civil wars. From Mexico's *Positivistas* down to Chilean *Liberales*, governments headed by these factions confronted the conservative Catholic Church, and in many cases managed to separate it from the state, and engaged in educational and sanitary campaigns. Public works were also initiated, some of relating to infrastructure, such as running water and sewerages in the main capital cities, which were built around the turn of the century in many countries. Remarkably, as has been mentioned, during this period long railroad networks were built by the state in most LA countries. Many of them covered the whole territory, and in some cases were built surmounting amazingly difficult landscapes, thousands of metres high through the Peruvian Andes or across the rugged deserts of northern Chile. Sometimes, these networks, which included telegraph networks alongside, even introduced variant development patterns, as when railroads spearheaded the fast army and cattle expansion over the pampas. Railroads were a notorious early expression of developmentalism (Chapters 2, 6 and 9).

Social policy was also assumed by traditional LA elites, come what may, including limited public educational systems and sanitary campaigns stemming from colonial or early independence times. *Beneficiencias Públicas* (public welfares) for the poor, *Gotas de Leche* (drops of milk) for the infant-poor, or the likes, hospitals, and other private charity institutions, developed everywhere. Later on, by the mid-1920s, many of the new public social services were to be born consolidating many of these originally private institutions (Chapter 9). The Catholic Church also played a significant role in these early social protection initiatives. Towards the end of the nineteenth century, liberal-republican leaning elites conferred large importance to basic education and, in the other end, to universities[47] (Chapters 2, 6 and 9).

This development pattern continued into the 1920s, when the last export boom of the traditional LA economic structure took place (Chapters 4 to 7 and 9).[48] During the 1920s, both a new kind of state and a new set of social policies and institutions took shape in some LA countries. In several cases, including Argentina, Brazil, and Chile, the birth of a new kind of state was under the guidance of the military. In other countries, such as Uruguay and Costa Rica, elected governments guided the process. Furthermore, in early developing Argentina and Uruguay, quite comprehensive social protection institutions were already in place by the first decades of the century. In Mexico, in turn, the modern state consolidated in the 1920s, following the long revolutionary struggle that erupted in 1912. The new state engaged immediately in ambitious educational, health, and other social programs (Chapters 2 to 9).

Thus, the infancy – or pre-history – of LADWS may be traced back to the late nineteenth and early twentieth century. However, it came of age in the wake of the world economic crisis in 1929. The impact of the crisis on traditional exports was catastrophic. To mention just one example, by 1932 Chile's overall export income had collapsed to 8 per cent of their 1929 levels (Chapter 9). The new economic situation forced states to change their export-oriented, liberal-inspired, economic policies, and replace them with protectionist measures, and policies to stimulate internal production. LA states had been quite moderate or restrictive in their expenditures during previous decades and even during the crisis itself, with aggravating results. Now, on the contrary, they adopted quite expansive fiscal and monetary policies, including generous credit policies offered to nascent local industrialists.[49]

During this period and up to the 1980s, throughout LA, governments built electric power-generating[50] and national transmission networks, thousands of kilometres of roads and highways, telephone and telecommunications networks, steelworks and agro-industrial complexes,[51] oil exploration and extraction. They enlarged existing universities, created new ones, and promoted science and technology. Towards the peak of the developmentalist period, the most advanced LA states had developed complex industries, including aerospace. State-run business accounted for a substantial part of overall production and employment, although its significance varied widely between countries. *Early developers* Argentina and Uruguay, or regions such as Sao Paulo, on the one hand, showed the strongest private sectors. Meanwhile, on the other end, socialist Cuba concentrated all economic activities in the State. Other LA countries rested in between (Chapters 2 to 9).

## Social policy: an integral part of LADWS

Social policy was a key component of the LADWS project from its very beginning. It developed during the period, as public social expenditure increased year after year.[52] Most social policy institutions were also created during this period. Social legislation, regulating aspects such as working hours and others, which had been first enacted around the 1920s in some countries, expanded considerably, especially since the mid 1960s, and by the 1980s, most LA countries had quite comprehensive labour legislations in place (Chapters 2 to 9).

Public schools and universities, which had been created almost everywhere during the nineteenth century, expanded rapidly, especially after the 1960s, and accounted for most of the enrolment. Nevertheless, educational coverage remained quite low everywhere up to the 1980s, even for basic levels of education, with the exception of Argentina and Uruguay, and a few other countries such as Chile, Costa Rica, and Cuba (Table 1.A5 in Appendix). Health care networks were created everywhere as well, although they were not based on large public infrastructure in all countries (Chapters 2 to 9).[53]

Pension systems were created almost[54] everywhere, with Argentina and Uruguay again leading the continent in this matter. By the mid-century, both countries had developed comprehensive schemes, based on union-administered funds, which covered most of the economically active population (EAP) (Chapters 4 and 5). Other countries combined social security funds, sometimes called *Cajas de Previsión,* for each relevant worker group, with a centralized, state-run, social security system, usually called *Servicio de Seguro Social,* mainly for blue-collar workers. The first kind of system began at the beginning of the century, with members of the military, high-level government officials, and teachers, and expanded successively to include increasingly large worker groups, and even the whole of the EAP, as in the aforementioned cases of Argentina and Uruguay. In other countries, the centralized, state-run *Servicio de Seguro Social* extended faster. Later on, both kinds of systems were to be unified in some countries (Chapters 4, 5, 6 and 9).

Housing and poverty alleviation policies, such as family allowances and limited unemployment subsidies, were also developed in most countries. In many cases, housing programmes were a side effect of the *Cajas* type of pension funds, as the huge surpluses that they produced during the initial decades of their functioning were invested in such programmes for their beneficiaries (Chapters 2 to 9).

Nevertheless, social policy during LADWS was mainly available for urban workers, meanwhile peasants, who constituted the bulk of the population in most LA countries, were mostly excluded, at least until the 1960s. In Chile, for example, social legislation, such as the right to form labour unions, which had developed throughout the century to cover most of the urban and mining workers, was not extended to peasants until the mid-1960s. With the exception of the more advanced countries, illiteracy remained high throughout LA, as educational coverage remained low, even at primary levels, still by the end of the century. Health indicators remained quite poor until the 1980s, with high levels of malnutrition, poor sanitary conditions, and frequent epidemics (Chapters 2 to 9).

In addition, even as LADWS reached its peak in the 1980s, poverty remained high throughout the continent and, as a rule, income distribution was among the worst in the world. Again, only the continent's *early developers* Argentina and Uruguay, as well as Cuba and Costa Rica for different historical reasons, showed better performances in most social indicators by the end of the period, and other countries such as Chile followed closely behind. Meanwhile, most countries showed very poor social results. Including giant Brazil, which nevertheless, at the same time, had been able to develop considerably in economic terms (Chapters 2 to 9).

Nevertheless, regardless of its varied results and coverage, social policy was an integral part of this strategy because it was one of its main instruments to promote social change, which increasingly became a central objective as the project advanced towards its climax.

### A major actor of social change

In the wake of the 1930s economic crisis, new, progressive, political forces appeared, and in many cases assumed office throughout LA,[55] while in other cases they exerted decisive influence from the opposition.[56] As stated, some of them emerged from military movements. The new governments fostered LADWS as their explicit programme, throughout the continent. The new political alliances marked, for the first time, the ascent to power of nascent LA middle classes, as social change and mobility began to remove a previously unyielding social landscape. Furthermore, the state became a mayor actor of social change in the continent throughout the century (Chapters 2 to 9).

The 1930s economic crisis by itself had played a huge role in accelerating social change across the continent, as it closed many export enclaves and sent hundreds of thousands of workers back to the countryside from where they had been evicted years before, or into the expanding cities. In Chile, for example, 5 out of 6 nitrate workers suffered this plight (Chapter 9). Ever-accelerating internal migration surrounded LA capitals with vast popular constituencies the renowned *favelas, villas miseria, poblaciones callampas* of the 1950s and 1960s, which provided support for the new strategy and also became its clients. By the 1960s and before, social policies had by themselves engendered another noisy and highly restive social actor, in the thousands of students that frequently took to the streets in political protests, coming mainly from public-supported universities, secondary and even primary schools, became a familiar scene in LA cities.

Modern entrepreneurial classes were formed and grew up during this period. As mentioned, such processes started at the turn of the century in Río de la Plata and other regions within LA countries that received massive immigration. Across the rest of the continent, this process ran in parallel to urbanization, which, as said, accelerated greatly during the 1930 crisis and its aftermath. Starting out with small family shops and workshops, usually in their immigrant homes, small enterprises grew up, manufacturing and distributing textiles, shoes, furniture, food, and other products, mostly consumer-oriented. In the wake of the crisis, these nascent industries got a big push from the ISI-inspired policies. At the same time, they found a generous supply of free salaried workers, out of the ever-increasing migration into the cities, of peasants, and workers expelled from export enclaves ruined by the crisis, whom many times landed in the same neighbourhoods where immigrants established themselves. By the 1960s, and under the protection and stimulus of developmentalism, the new entrepreneurial classes had become quite powerful, especially in the early developing regions, but elsewhere as well, as in Mexico, in Chile, and other countries throughout the continent.

Traditional LA landowning elites tried to involve nascent industrialists in their secular expertise in the art of successively co-opting all those who got rich.[57] In this way, as mentioned, by this time their kin included merchants, financiers, miners, and others. Such procedures also seemed to be successful to a certain extent regarding twentieth-century entrepreneurs, up to the point that the mere existence of a LA bourgeoisie, capable of genuine independence from the traditional oligarchies, was a major controversy in LA social science during the 1960s.[58] Nevertheless, nascent modern LA bourgeoisie seems to have played a rather independent role, and centrist political parties and military regimes that built upon the new strategy drew strong support from these new classes, which were nurtured in return.

State employment has risen quickly since the 1930s, both in traditional state bureaucracy, as well as in new state companies. As has been mentioned, the first large enterprises by the turn of the twentieth century were state-owned railroads. In many countries, state firms and public social services, such as education and health, were also among the largest worker concentrations. They inaugurated a new kind of salaried workers, employed in large numbers by the state for producing goods or services. Not quite a modern proletariat, but no longer traditional state bureaucrats either, this peculiar labour relation would play a relevant role throughout the twentieth century. As the strategy reached its zenith in the 1970s and 1980s, the state accounted for over one-fifth of the overall occupied workforce in most countries, and, even now, it remains in the 15–20 per cent range in most countries, including a vast social protection sector (Tables 1.A4–5 in Appendix).[59]

New bureaucratic elites, both civil and military, were nurtured by LADWS. Mostly, they came from the nascent middle classes and not from the traditional oligarchies.[60] Most of the bureaucratic cadres were formed in the best public schools and universities, and made lifelong careers. Public service at its best in terms of professionalism became a distinctive part of the LA elites.[61] In addition, the new elites included politicians from progressive and even leftist parties, who accessed to power through elections, or who belonged to rather progressive military movements.

The old oligarchies do not seem to have been quite successful either, in co-opting these bureaucratic newcomers. Rather on the contrary, they became increasingly independent, and even defiant, as they grew and became more powerful. In alliances with other emerging classes, such as nascent industrial bourgeoisies and working classes, as well as peasants later on, increasingly they were to confront the oligarchies (Chapters 2 to 9).[62]

Land reform became a keyword in LA politics during the 1960s, early 1970s, and even into the 1980s in regions such as Central America[63] and still today, agrarian reform is a relevant term in many countries' politics.[64] Land reform posed a serious threat to traditional LA oligarchies, and was furiously resisted by them everywhere, even leading, in some instances, military coups and civil war.[65] Nevertheless, it proved irreversible wherever it was applied, because nowhere was the old servitude-based agrarian system reinstated.[66] Proportionally to its radicalism, agrarian reform proved the most effective intervention of LADWS, in terms of changing traditional LA social structures, thus becoming one of its paramount modernizing legacies (Chapter 9).

A wave of nationalizations also swept through LA, as states assumed control of natural resources and the largest private industrial complexes that exploited them. Until then, many, if not most, of them were in foreign – mainly US – hands.[67] State companies also developed natural resources from the beginning in many countries[68] (Chapters 2 to 9). LADWS initiatives regarding the national appropriation of ground rent associated with natural resources constitutes another one of the most relevant legacies of the period. Many survived the privatization wave of the Neoliberal period, and are still in place. Nevertheless, as the result of this, significant natural resources have been privatized again, and no few are once more in foreign hands. This seems to be one of the main challenges facing the continent at present, as will be mentioned below.

The state did not become an actor of social change in isolation, or exclusively thanks to the progressive stance of the bureaucratic elites. The rapid social changes it set in movement led to widespread social unrest, reformist movements, and even revolutions, during the 1960s and early 1970s. Mostly since the Cuban revolution, although in some of the main countries, such as Mexico, and in a certain way in Argentina, these processes took place decades earlier. Reformist and revolutionary political processes consolidated the ongoing social transformations, accomplishing agrarian reform, and nationalization of natural resources and important industrial complexes. These transformations proved irreversible, even in the wake of quite brutal rightist military regimes that took over most of the continent during the 1970s and 1980s, and earlier in Brazil.[69] Moreover, social transformations achieved by reformist and revolutionary regimes of the 1960s and 1970s seem to have laid, in no small part, the foundations for the rapid development of capitalism during the following decades.[70] Although social actors in the background of reform and social change seem to be roughly the same throughout LA, their protagonist roles in the resulting political processes vary widely (Chapters 2 to 9).[71]

All of the above has been extensively documented. Nevertheless, the way the social policy component inherent of LADWS played an all-important role in promoting social change and economic development has perhaps not been highlighted enough. Education and health policies, as well as labour legislation, among others, were key to transforming LA peasantry into modern citizens. An inclusive strand of thinking in social policy, which placed equal emphasis on economic development and social protection, became widespread in LA, especially during the 1960s, at the peak of reformist-revolutionary activity. During this period, universal welfare, mainly state-provided, was regarded as good economic policy, according to the demand sideline of economic argumentation that is well described in developmental economics.

Important social policy objectives were attained during this period – among them, drastic reduction of malnutrition, massive literacy programmes, rapid expansion of higher education, and others. Unlike their peasant parents, popular masses in LA today see few of their newborn die at birth, or their mothers. They live considerably longer lives and have increased access to better health services, including better sanitary conditions such as running water. Quite many, if not most of them in some countries, live in houses they own. Mostly they know how to read, write, and have completed primary education, with a considerable number having finished secondary level. Some have even managed to complete university (Table 1.A8 in Appendix).

Even if they do not read much in fact, they do listen to radios all day long and watch a lot of TV. In contrast to their peasant fathers, they are quite free to move around and take many jobs throughout their lifetime, much as some perhaps have better remembrances of the more secure jobs enjoyed by some of their parents during LADWS. That seems to hold true, however poor, precarious, and insecure their lifestyle may still be – no matter how much hunger or cold they might still suffer at times, perhaps sometimes even more than their peasant parents did. No matter how insulting the enormous differences in riches and incomes may result. Most of these social achievements were attained during this period, and have been maintained and developed upon, during the following decades.

LADWS seems to have been the decisive political institution of socioeconomic change, which by the end of the century had generated a completely new social, economic, and political landscape throughout the continent. At its best in this aspect, it managed to lead reforms and revolutionary changes that drastically transformed the traditional LA social structure. Nevertheless, even in its most conservative versions, it achieved social and economic changes that provided lasting and solid bases for subsequent economic and social modernization throughout the continent. Moreover, the social policy component of this strategy is much to be credited for it.

## Decline and fall of LADWS: victim of its own success?

The above notwithstanding, strong criticism of LADWS grew and had become widespread as it peaked, by the end of the 1960s and early 1970s. Criticisms sprung from both left and right, the former emphasizing its more radical aspect of promotion of social change, while the other recommended what would later be known as the Neoliberal model.[72] As developmentalism entered a period of decline, the two main lines of criticism had their chance to put their policies into practice. Its fall did not arrive before it was effectively tested to the limit in many countries, and gave out of itself what it possibly could. In the end, though, the latter strategy prevailed.

The intervention of BWI and other powerful and deep-pocketed, institutions, in order to stimulate, and in some cases enforce, such policy change has been extensively documented. Nevertheless, by the end of the twentieth century, such deliberate sowing efforts seem to have found fertile and well-prepared soil in LA.

The fall of LADWS has been attributed to economic stagnation. Nonetheless, regarding economic growth, the period in fact holds a record that has not yet been equalled in most LA countries, nor in the continent as a whole.[73] On the other hand, its fall certainly unfolded in the wake of the world economic recession of the early 1980s, which hit LA especially hard,[74] as many of the countries in the region, including giants Brazil and Mexico, were still under this paradigm. Nevertheless, the crisis was quite evidently of foreign origins. Moreover, the most seriously affected country was Chile, which had of course initiated Neoliberal reforms almost a decade before, while the least affected countries, such as Costa Rica, were those who resisted the emerging model most effectively (Chapters 2 to 9).[75] Therefore, it is not clear that LADWS replacement may have been induced by reasons related to economic stagnation. If it were, anyway, the ensuing period may well be accused of a far more disappointing record in this matter, certainly worse, and in fact the worst in the whole of the twentieth century in most countries (Table 1.A2 in appendix, and Figures 9.A4–6 in Appendix to chapter 9).

Neoliberal policies were also justified sometimes, as a reaction against what has been labelled *macroeconomic populism in LA* (Dornbusch and Edwards 1991).[76] Nevertheless, were mounting fiscal deficits and debt, as well as hyperinflationary episodes, some of which, but not the worst ones, occurred during this period, really caused by excessive social or state expenditure? At least from one point of view, such phenomena seems to have little to do with social policy or social spending: Even at its pinnacle, social expenditure, and state expenditure as a whole, rarely reached levels that could be considered excessive in LA. Quite the opposite, both items achieved magnitudes that seem distant even from present levels of public expenditure in most LA countries (Tables 1.A7–9 in the Appendix, and Figure 9.A3 in Appendix to Chapter 9). Moreover, they were certainly very far away from what countries in the first world would consider reasonable public spending. The above notwithstanding, public deficit management did seem rather too expansive throughout LADWS experience as a whole, and outright freewheeling in some late periods, in many countries, as inflation rates suggest. Nevertheless, this does not seem to explain but some LA hyperinflations periods.[77] Other hyperinflation episodes seem to relate more to high-tension political periods during which opposition parties approved government expenditures while denying financing at the same time (Haslam 2004). In most cases, these episodes originated in debt-liquefying schemes.[78] Moreover, in some countries,[79] the worst hyperinflation episodes occurred under governments already influenced by Neoliberalism.

Rather, the severe limitations of economic, social, and human development seem to be more relevant in creating widespread dissatisfaction with developmentalism that led to FFA and its replacement.[80] Nevertheless, such limitations had always been there, and indeed LADWS may surely be credited for making quite an inroad towards their improvement.

Something else must have happened in order to generate a change. Sober overall reassessment of twentieth-century LA developmentalism should provide new insights for alternative approaches to explain its decline. It can be argued that the decline may be due to its own success in changing the underlying social structure. The above-mentioned limitations, for example, only became political problems after LA masses began to awake from their secular peasant *siesta*, because of processes that were strongly stimulated by state policies. At the same time, modern LA entrepreneurs and high-income middle classes were coming of age, and becoming increasingly assertive, in large part, as stated, bred and nurtured by developmentalism. They provided the possibility, and the political support in the case of the former, for privatizations and market policies. Affluent LA middle classes were quite satisfied with the opening of borders to globalization, because they could obtain better-quality goods at cheaper prices than ISI-protected local industries could provide. They were receptive to Neoliberal discourse, in part because it offered them differentiated, good quality, social services, sooner than universal public social policies could deliver. Perhaps, later on, the Neoliberal period will be seen as a unilateral initial moment, when these privileged minorities anticipated long sought and hard fought LA modernity, for their exclusive benefit, passing over the vast majority of the population.

## The legacy of Neoliberalism

Following the demise of LADWS, and building on the new realities that were its legacy, a new set of policies were put into practice throughout the continent, in lesser or greater extent, which would be called the Washington Consensus.[81] Starting with the Chilean 'Chicago boys' experiment in the mid-1970s, one LA country after another abandoned developmentalist concepts and initiated liberal reforms. Some were undertaken under the authoritarian regimes that seemed to plague LA during the 1970s and 1980s. However, most of them occurred under democratic governments that replaced the former, during the late 1980s and 1990s. In the case of Mexico, as mentioned, these reforms were also implemented by PRI governments. During the last two decades of the century, Neoliberal-inspired policy was put in place everywhere in LA, both as a new development strategy and a new social policy paradigm.

In short, the new model promoted the establishment of the best possible short-term environment for private business,[82] in a framework of openness to foreign trade and investment, in an international economic environment that was then dominated by a booming globalization process. However, it was characteristically extreme in pursuing these purposes, due to its Neoliberal theoretical support as well as its political and socially excluding practices. Nevertheless, the degree of unilateralism with which the model was adopted varied widely from one country to another[83] (Chapters 2 to 9).

The above notwithstanding, *Washington Consensus* policies have exerted a hegemonic influence over LA policy making over the last decades and, although seemingly on the decline, continue to do so up to the present day. Such policies in effect significantly improved the general climate for private business in the region. This was particularly true for foreign investors, as LA economies were effectively opened to overseas commerce and investment, although to varying degrees. At the same time, the cyclical behaviour of LA economies was severely accentuated. In the course of acute cycles, financial and economic crises occurred during this period, of a violence that had not been experienced since the 1930s. This resulted in high unemployment and a significant slowdown in rates of average economic growth. LA GDP growth fell from 5.5 per cent and 6 per cent a year during the 1960s and 1970s, respectively, to 1.4 per cent during the 1980s and 3.2 per cent during the 1990s, the worst performance in the region since the 1930s (Table 1.A2 in Appendix to this chapter and Figure 9.A2 in the Appendix to Chapter 9).

On the other hand, the unilateral emphasis of *Washington Consensus* policies had generally negative implications, although to varying degrees in different countries, depending perhaps, in part, on the advance of their respective socioeconomic transition processes. The most extreme policies proved harmful everywhere, such as weakening state regulatory systems, particularly those regarding financial flows, or fixed exchange rate schemes, or 'structural adjustments' that resulted in pro-cyclical fiscal and monetary policies (Ffrench-Davis 2002, 2003). In addition, orthodox ground rent economic theory was overlooked, and natural resources were handed out again to private, mostly foreign, firms at no charge (Fazio 2000). Negative effects were felt as well out of Neoliberal dismantling of the LA public bureaucracies that had been formed with sustained effort along a century (Fukuyama 2004; Suleiman 2004). Then again, transferring state firms to the private sector may have made sense where the latter had already attained the age and size required to manage these enterprises themselves, and become stronger in the process. Additionally, success required relatively strong states, enabled to impose reasonable regulations and avoid corruption in the process. However, in countries where this had not happened yet, states were simply weakened, corruption was an extended practice during privatization processes, which resulted in severe market distortions. In addition, privatizations resulted in no significant gain for national entrepreneurs, because firms ended up mostly in foreign hands. Even the contrary may have happened, because foreign ownership has proved suboptimal in areas such as banking, with regard to local business, particularly small and medium sized (Ffrench-Davis 2003).

At the same time, socioeconomic changes in the region were accelerated during this period, as the main modern social actors consolidated their presence in some countries, and the socioeconomic transition process was accelerated everywhere by globalization, in a remarkably painful manner. The general legacy of Neoliberalism is highly disputed and its results mixed, but its massive impact on the transition process at this structural level can hardly be denied. In this classic sense of primitive accumulation, the *Washington Consensus* certainly meant a huge boost to capitalist development in LA, even though generally this did not show itself in faster economic growth.

Regarding social policies, Neoliberal policies placed a unilateral emphasis on privatization of public social services, and protecting the private social services industry. In parallel, such policies targeted constrained public spending into creating social 'safety nets' for the extremely poor. These policies ended up providing differentiated private social services for the affluent few. Meanwhile, an insufficient amount of public social spending was only enough to slightly alleviate the living conditions of the extremely poor. The vast majority of the population, meanwhile, including the majority of the emerging LA salaried classes, saw their social protection seriously deteriorate, and become more expensive, at the same time that their job insecurity was augmented due to globalization. Nevertheless, as said, these kinds of policies were applied to different degrees in the different countries and in different periods. In the case of Brazil, for example, the social policies applied during the 1990s rather perfected the universal-oriented, public services-based social policies of the previous period.

During the 1990s, on the other hand, the unilateral emphasis of 'structural reforms' on short-term business-friendly policies resulted in a serious deterioration of the already shameful income distribution of the region (Table 1.A9 in the Appendix), when targeted and other public social expenditure are not taken into account. Nevertheless, when social expenditure is considered, income distribution maintained more or less the same inequality that most countries in LA had attained by the 1980s. Furthermore, in some exceptional LA countries, such as Uruguay, increased expenditure in pensions during the 1990s further improved an already fair income distribution, as it managed to balance the deterioration experienced by autonomous incomes.

### Successive waves of Neoliberal reforms

Neoliberal economic experiments were first implemented in Chile during the 1970s by the dictatorship that had put an end to the revolutionary agitation of the previous period. Neoliberal social policies were also pioneered in Chile during the 1980s, as this country seems to have adhered to the *Washington Consensus* long before it became consensual. In the rest of LA, Neoliberal economic reforms started during the 1980s in some countries, in the wake of the debt crisis. However, Neoliberal social policies were not generally implemented in most countries until the 1990s.

There are at least two significant differences between the pioneering reforms of the 1970s and 1980s, and those implemented later. While the former were implemented by dictatorships, in conditions of economic crisis or stagnation, the latter were usually implemented mostly by democratic regimes, and, with respect to social policies, during the generally expansive 1990s. As a result, there are significant variations in the outcomes, in relation to both the general economic structure and social policies, and also in the degree of subordination of the latter to the former. In the end, each country has its own story to tell, and there also seem to be historical patterns for different regions, as commented above. However, the differences between pioneering Neoliberal reforms and those which came later seem to prove the relevance of democratic environments in this respect.[84]

During the pioneering wave of Neoliberalism, Chile introduced 'the most radical example of the Neoliberal market model, particularly under the Pinochet regime (1973–89)' (Mesa-Lago 2002: 3). Under the first generation of Neoliberal social policy reforms, implemented in Chile during the 1980s, pensions were almost completely privatized, under a widely known scheme, which most of the workforce was forced to join after 1981. Public education was privatized almost in half. In addition, a national, private, health insurance scheme was instituted. On the other hand, a social 'safety net', non-contributory, welfare scheme, was put in place for the poorest (Chapter 9). Less well known, though, is the fact Pinochet had previously slashed public social spending by more than half during the 1970s, in the midst of a massive state reduction and stabilization programme, with the resulting serious deterioration of the public SP network (Chapter 9).

Neoliberal reforms of SP during the 1990s followed a quite diverse path to that followed in the 1970s and 1980s, and the differences seem to stem in particular from the fact that, as stated, such reforms were introduced not under dictatorships but the ensuing democratic governments. There was an increased awareness during the 1990s of the importance of social policy, not just as a moral issue but also as contribution to the economic and political future of the countries (Stallings 2002). Expansive overall economic conditions during the 1990s certainly contribute their part as well. As a result, the second wave of reforms rode over rapidly increasing social spending, which added up to about 50 per cent along the decade, on the average, on a per-capita basis (see Tables 1.A7–9 in the Appendix). Such spending was reflected in important increases in school enrolment in all levels, reaching full coverage in basic and near-full coverage in medium levels, while university enrolment increased quite dramatically. Poverty reduction was also significant in the decade, although most of it may be attributable to economic growth, which, as said, was important up to 1997 (Tables 1.A6–10 in the Appendix).

The impact of Neoliberal social policy in overall economic development during this period should not be minimized, as the Chilean experience seems to illustrate. In a negative way, it has already been mentioned how the drastic reduction of social spending was significant in the stabilization programmes of the 1970s. It has been noted as well that the privatization of pensions, although not significant in increasing overall savings rate, due to the accompanying public pension deficit, has nonetheless helped capital markets, a no small economic objective (Mkandawire 2001). In addition, the reforms drastically reduced the employers' contributions, transferring them almost completely to the employees. Even though this reform is probably minor in relation to overall salary-related costs, because salaries were raised more or less in the same proportion, it nonetheless may have had an important psychological impact regarding general investment conditions. Last, but not least, Neoliberal reforms have resulted in the rise of an important private social protection industry, which sells services previously provided by the government at no charge. Because of this, the same activities now appear adding value to the national accounts, as part of an increased services sector.

Brazil has experienced two reform cycles of its own regarding social policies, but with significant differences from the ones described above. The first, in the 1980s, was highly influenced by the democratization process, while the second occurred in the second half of the 1990s, when economic adjustment takes place. The newly elected democratic governments of the 1980s opened a wide reform agenda, oriented by goals of universal coverage, the strengthening of public provision, and the decentralization of management. In a certain sense, it tried to revert to the strong authoritarian centralization experienced during the military regime. On the other hand, it reversed the market-driven tendencies towards the development of private SP systems, experienced in this country during the booming 1970s, that were geared to satisfy the demand of the high-income segments of the burgeoning new urban middle classes.

The second reform cycle in Brazil was implemented during the 1990s. Although it was carried out within the framework of a fiscal adjustment process and market-oriented institutional reforms, the social policy reform goals aimed, on the contrary, to reinforce the public social systems. The reforms tried to correct some of the mistakes that had been made during the implementation of previous policies, without changing the basic orientations of universal coverage and public provision of services. A good example of the former is health policy. The 1988 democratic constitution created a Swedish-style free public health system whose target population numbered 170 million people. This system continued to be implemented during the 1990s, and fiscal resources earmarked for health have increased systematically, while, simultaneously some reforms have made it more equitable and redistributive. Other areas also reflect these tendencies. For example, Brazil did not privatize its public pension, educational, and health services, during the 1990s, in spite of the Neoliberal model – previous public–private combinations have been was maintained. Indeed, even a return to the public schools by children of the middle class took place to some extent during the 1990s because of impoverishment of these sectors. Obviously, governmental orientations have influenced the direction of reforms, as well as the general support for the maintenance of the democratic orientation of the first wave of reforms, coming from actors who benefited out of the same. In other words, there was no power – liberal, or conservative – capable of retrenching these systems; instead, they perfected them (Chapter 7).

During the 1990s, the Argentinean welfare state was severely retrenched, ironically, by an elected and re-elected government of the same Peronista party that had originally established the welfare state in this country. Universal programmes, such as public health, were decentralized almost entirely to provincial governments. Wage contributions were drastically reduced – from over 33 per cent to less than 18 per cent. On the other hand, an important part of wage contributions were redirected to the new AFJP private pension system. On the other hand, VAT tax was generalized and significantly increased, and a greater proportion of it was redirected to the central government. Thus, a high burden was passed on to the provinces, which bear most of the cost of universal programmes and lost much of the contributions to finance them. Other results have included a deterioration of union-dependent *Obras Sociales* (social works), as employment contributions decreased due to an increase in informality and a decrease in employers' contributions, and thus a growing number of workers drifted to the public hospitals. Even though public social expenditure increased significantly during the decade, it was not enough to absorb the additional pressure on the public system. In part, the resulting deficit was covered directly by contributions from the families to education and health, which increased significantly (Chapter 3).

As a rule, the objectives of Neoliberal reforms in the 1990s were tilted towards objectives of greater efficiency through partial privatization, and heavily towards fiscal moderation in those countries that had not implemented fiscal adjustments at an earlier stage. These objectives prevailed over outright dismantling and privatization of public social services, which had prevailed during the first wave of Neoliberal reforms. Nevertheless, the latter objectives were present and relevant as well during the 1990s in many cases (UNDP 2002). However, deterioration and dismantling of public services – exception made for the effects of the catastrophic Argentinean crisis of 2001, which was overcome in a short time –, and privatization of social policy institutions, were everywhere and in almost every case lesser than in the Chilean 1980s reform. In other countries, these effects were either slight or virtually nonexistent – as in the cases of Uruguay or Costa Rica (Chapters 5 and 8). The newly created SP institutions, such as private pension schemes, were in most cases complementary to the old public ones. In many cases, the new institutions were also public, as in the case of the largest Uruguayan, Bolivian, and Mexican pension administrators. The old public systems, as a general case, remained fully or at least partially in place (Mesa-Lago 2002). Even in Chile, during the last decade, the previous 'imbalance has been gradually corrected since 1990, by democratic administrations that, although maintaining the essence of the previous economic model, have placed a stronger accent on social policy under the more balanced approach' (Mesa-Lago 2002: 3).

During the 1990s substantial efforts were made to restore the standing of undermined and underfunded welfare institutions. However, and despite the above mentioned efforts, the levels of public spending remains very low in LA – as per capita, or related to GDP (Tables 1.A7–9 in the Appendix). In some countries such as Chile, it has not yet recovered the levels reached during the LADWS period (Chapter 9). This probably remains to be the main problem of the sector and its workers, even considering the urgent need for rebuilding and modernizing public social protection institutions.

## Continued social change under Neoliberal reforms

Why was the anti-state aspect of Neoliberal discourse assumed, to a lesser or greater extent, by the LA elites? This particular aspect of Neoliberalism seems quite obviously inadequate in LA, considering the state is the main – and sometimes the only – cohesive national institution in many LA countries. Moreover, its size and influence are everywhere minimal in relation to First World countries, and evidently inadequate relative to general requirements in most areas, as stated earlier. In addition, a strong backlash against this extreme aspect of Neoliberalism is occurring at present in advanced countries, as it is accused of dismantling democratic states (Suleiman 2003) and even fomenting terrorism (Fukuyama 2004). Furthermore, LADWS was originally, and mostly, a project created and sustained by LA elites. Nevertheless, by the end of the twentieth century, this bourgeois-anarchist (Hobsbawm 1995) feature of Neoliberalism fell into willing ears of those same elites, especially in some countries.

Perhaps the emerging LA elites turned against the state they had originally formed, because LADWS bureaucracies had ended up confronting their ancestors, the traditional LA elites? In Chile, this seems to be the case. As said, LADWS exerted a leading role in the revolution that expropriated traditional landowners. Small wonder then, their brethren, now turned modern entrepreneurs, have been the most fervent and true believers in Neoliberalism in LA. This phenomenon is receding in this country, but then only very slow, and seems bound to persist long past the time of this ideology.[85] Moreover, in all LA countries, this particularly damaging aspect of Neoliberal ideology may also have been adopted by opportunistic reasons. Namely, because of the succulent enrichment opportunities privatizations offered, both for those who acquired state firms as for state functionaries who privatized them.

It is a fact that LA elites were greatly empowered by privatizations. It is true that many of the largest privatized firms and services ended up in the hands of foreign capital, mainly Spanish this time. Nevertheless, other privatized companies and banks went to LA entrepreneurs, and multiplied the assets of the main private economic conglomerates throughout the continent. In some cases, state functionaries in charge of privatizations built these conglomerates up from nothing, as they kept the firms they privatized for themselves (Fazio 2002, 2003). This seems to have also happened elsewhere, as the conformation of new entrepreneurial elites in the ex-socialist countries seems to show. However, regardless of them being benefited or not by direct transferral of state property, modern LA entrepreneurial elites have mostly come of age, in no small part due to the myriad stimulus offered to them by Neoliberal reforms. If LADWS was instrumental in weakening or even liquidating the traditional elites, Neoliberal reforms have been decisive in consolidating the new entrepreneurial elite. This is but one of the relevant social changes occurred during the Neoliberal period.

Peasant migration and urbanization accelerated almost everywhere, reaching breakneck speed towards the millennium, as has been mentioned, although it now seems that secondary cities growing even faster than capitals in many countries (Tables 1.A1–3 in Appendix to this chapter, and Figures 9.A1–6 in Appendix to Chapter 9). This was not only the result of purely economic forces. In many countries, it was in part the result of violent expulsion of peasants out of their traditional dwellings.[86]

Powerful forces have also further changed the character of the urban workforce during recent decades. Neoliberal reforms, including tariff reductions and free trade agreements, strongly promoted competitiveness. This in turn generated massive relocations of the workforce, among different industrial sectors and from manufacturing towards services (Tables 1.A4–5 in Appendix). Usually, new jobs are far less stable than the former. In fact, lifelong employment, which had been the norm during LADWS, has become quite a rarity today. Meanwhile, most of the modern urban workforce seems to be constantly shifting from short-term, low pay, salaried jobs, to informal occupations or outright unemployment (INP 2004). Generalized stagnation, and even reduction of overall state employment in some countries, both in privatized industries and services, as in the bureaucracy at large, has taken its toll on the urban workforce as well (Tables 1.A1–5 in the Appendix, and Chapter 9). These processes have resulted in much higher unemployment rates than was the norm. This tendency has seriously affected social protection systems that were built on the assumption of full, stable employment, especially in the early developers Argentina and Uruguay, but has also damaged the new pension systems based on individual savings, which have become quite ineffectual for the vast majority of the population (Tables 1.A4–5 in the Appendix, and Chapters 3, 4 and 9).

Nevertheless, greater job instability should not be confused with the reduction of salaried jobs. Countries such as Chile, for example, where the quality of jobs today is noted for its precariousness, has at the same time more than doubled its salaried and overall employment over the last three decades (Tables 1.A4–5 in the Appendix, and Chapter 9). Even some statistics that point towards a reduction, such as the increase of self-employment as a proportion of the occupied workforce that occurs in determined periods of the economic cycle, are usually compensated in other periods of the same cycle. Self-employment itself seems to be more a result of job rotation between salaried and independent employment, rather than a stable condition in itself, as the book shows, at least in some countries (Chapter 9). As a whole, the proportion of the workforce employed in private firms with over five employees seems to have increased significantly in LA, during the Neoliberal period, as mentioned before (Tables 1.A4–5 in the Appendix).

As in the aforementioned case of peasant migration, these changes have not occurred only because of economic tendencies, but also as forced results of Neoliberal reforms. State reduction, as said, but also the privatization of social services, have resulted in massive job changes, in some countries. In the case of Chile, for example, no fewer than half of the teachers, as well as an important proportion of doctors,[87] and other health personnel, social security administrators and clerical personnel, etc. that were public servants 20 years ago, are presently employed in the burgeoning private social services industry (Chapter 9). The same has occurred massively in privatized firms. As mentioned before, the labour relation that prevailed in state-owned companies, and modern private LA employment, even in the same firms, is clearly not the same thing.

In addition to the above, as stated, there has been a continued reduction of illiteracy, and a rapid and significant heightening of the educational level of the LA population, as well as its general health indicators and life expectancy (Table 1.A1–6 in the Appendix). These processes, as stated earlier, had been evolving during the LADWS period, and in some countries suffered during the first wave of Neoliberal reforms. Nevertheless, they continued in force during the 1990s, even during the second wave of reforms. When weighted by the population, the average increase in total LA per capita public social expenditure was 40 per cent during the 1990s, equivalent to 2.7 percentage GDP points. The equivalent figure for increase in per capita education expenditures was 49 per cent (1.0 GDP percentage point). In the case of health, per capita expenditures increased 15 per cent during the decade (0.1 GDP percentage points), and 59 per cent in social security (2.0 GDP percentage points) (Tables 1.A6–9 in the Appendix).

It is worthwhile noting that although 'structural adjustments' of overall public expenditure played a negative role in LA (Ffrench-Davis 2002, 2003), public social expenditure showed moderate anti-cyclical behaviour even after the 1997 crisis started, as it continued to grow in LA by 1.4 GDP percentage points[88] (Tables 1.A7–9 in the Appendix).

All of the above changes had a strong impact on the LA workforce, but more so on their overall productivity, which has increased significantly, and less in their general living conditions, which continue to be destitute in the general case, and miserable for tens of millions (Tables 1.A1–2 in the Appendix).

**Better times for the modern LA affluent few**

Under the hegemony of this way of thinking, a strong shift of mentalities has taken place in the LA masses, away from traditional, agrarian-based, communitarian ideas, and towards liberal, individualistic thinking. In addition, the *Washington Consensus* has introduced modern living standards into LA, including differentiated social services, for the affluent few that can afford them. Afford they may, because as said, the richest 10 per cent of LA population seize over 40 per cent of total LA income, and even more in three countries. Sadly, these feats were attained mostly at the expense of the poorest 40 per cent of the LA population, as well as the middle 50 per cent that lie in between the two extremes. The latter experience increased job insecurity and has been largely left aside by newly privatized social services. Meanwhile, the former have to survive with only 13 per cent of overall income, and even less than 10 per cent in Brazil, and continue living everywhere in conditions of extreme poverty (Table 1.A1–9 in the Appendix).

As the century came to its end, LA population had certainly advanced a long way from the generalized idiocy, word that etymologically means ignorant isolation (Hobsbawm 1998), of peasant life at the dawn of the twentieth century. At that time, the overwhelming majority of LA population shared this fate, with the sole exception of the land-based oligarchies and their small entourage of high state functionaries and politicians, liberal professionals, and other privileged members of the traditional LA elite. Even for the latter, though, life had been quite hard and unimposing as well in most of LA, except in the lands of ancient LA empires or former slavers, where truly rich elites could be found in the old times, as contemporary architecture witnesses.[89]

LA middle classes, including the nascent salariat, began to emerge as relevant actors by the mid-twentieth century. During the LADWS period, they improved their lot and differentiated themselves from the peasants, which remained as always during a good part of the century, while traditional oligarchies slowly declined. Only as developmentalism approached its climax, during the second part of the century, did overall living conditions improve significantly for the mass of the LA population, while the old oligarchies definitively phased out, or were forcefully liquidated by revolutionary processes. At the same time, entrepreneurs emerged in command of the new elite in LA societies, together with their relatively wider entourage of very high-income, upper middle classes. During the Neoliberal period in LA, the latter groups asserted their general well-being, and that of business in the first place, for the most part disregarding the rest of society.

## Neo-LADWS in the making?

*Washington Consensus* policies began to show signs of exhaustion in LA as the twentieth century ended. However, at present Neoliberal ideas are still largely hegemonic in several areas of LA policy making, and the move away from them could advance very slowly. Nevertheless, any sober assessment of the matter will conclude that Neoliberalism is no longer consensual in LA, and that it is past its heyday.

Moreover, the Neoliberal pretence of being the only true development paradigm – it has been widely referred to as *the only way of thinking* – is today under severe assault in LA, as serious alternative policies begin to surface, and gain public acceptance, and even attention from LA governments, in increasingly wide areas. Many elements seem to point towards the emergence of a new development strategy in LA, which looks increasingly coherent. The emergent development strategy suggests a new relation between economic development and an inclusive, universal kind of social policy, as well as a new relation between public policies and private business, all within the framework of constructing a wider regional economic space.

In what follows, some of these new approaches are summarized, emphasizing alternative social policy. Even though a new development strategy is still in the making, and far from completion, drawing on the historical approach, such an emerging strategy may perhaps begin to look something like a *Neo-Latin American Developmental Welfare State*, or *Neo-LADWS*.

### A *New Deal* for LA?

Assessing Lula's election as president of Brazil, *The Economist* magazine concluded that it marked an 'unambiguous shift of direction', away from the centre-right trend that has dominated Latin American (LA) politics over the last two decades (*The Economist* 2002: 1). A few months later, the same shift of direction resulted out of the apocalyptic events that marked the collapse of the political system in Argentina, soon to be followed by the election of President Kirchner, closely identified, as well, with Lula's discourse. Both presidents have run through a good part of their mandates enjoying huge public support, and, in the case of Lula, his figure has become a symbol throughout the region and even around the world, of a new set of policies that address the needs of the poor. Tabaré Vázquez, leader of the leftist Frente Amplio, was elected president of Uruguay with over 50 per cent of the vote. As will be underlined below in the case of Lula's PT, Frente Amplio is no latecomer either into Uruguayan politics, as it endured a long march up to power, which started back in 1971, which included resisting a cruel dictatorship and, later, exercising the local government of Montevideo for a number of periods.

A good part of the continent seems to be riding a wave of political agitation. In Venezuela, President Chávez, who comes from the military, was deposed by a widespread, US-supported, middle-class revolt against his reform-oriented policies, only to be restored to office two days later, by a popular upheaval, supported by the military. Recently, a plebiscite confirmed that a wide majority of citizens support his reform-oriented policies. Popular revolts in Bolivia forced the resignation of President Sánchez de Losada, and, later on, his successor, President Mesa, and a plebiscite and successive legislation regarding natural resources confirmed that the overwhelming majority of Bolivians support moving away from Neoliberal policies. All this culminated in the 2006 Election of President Evo Morales, the first authentic indigenous American to become president in LA, and closely identified with the emerging policy trend. The situation is not stable either in bordering Peru, where President Toledo, a social democrat who replaced authoritarian President Fujimori, has nonetheless been accused of continuing some of the Neoliberal policies and corrupt practices of his predecessor. His current approval ratings are very low, even though the economic performance of his government has been rather good. Colombia's decades-long civil war does not seem to abide under a rightist government, as the country undergoes increased US military presence, justified on the war against terrorism and drug trafficking.

Nevertheless, turmoil is certainly not generalized, and most countries in LA enjoy relatively stable situations. Even countries that are overcoming severe crises, or undergoing significant political shifts, have managed to do so in a remarkably peaceful and democratic way, such as the aforementioned Brazil and Argentina. Mexico, the other regional giant together with Brazil, just a few years ago put an end to the 70-year dominance of the *Partido Revolucionario Institucionalizado* (PRI), a paramount event for this country, with a certain parallel to the end of the Communist Party's rule over Russia. Nevertheless, it was achieved without a breakdown of the Mexican political system, and has proceeded in a remarkably peaceful way. Chile has undergone 16 years of transition out of the Pinochet dictatorship, and in 2005 will hold its fourth successive democratic presidential election during this period. Many may feel frustrated by the slow pace of democratic transition, but no one can dispute its stability. Economic perspectives that suggest better times ahead, coming as good news after six years of recession and crisis that started in 1998, should further reinforce political stability in LA.

Everybody is aware of the paramount difficulties which Presidents Lula and Kirchner must surmount to implement the kind of policies they promote – including corruption. Not least, the resistance of the Bretton Woods Institutions (BWI). Dissident voices within Lula's own *Partido dos Trabalhadores*, and other opposition figures in Brazil, even question his willingness to implement alternative policies, pointing to the continuity of economic policies during his first years in office. In Chile, socialist Ricardo Lagos was elected president in 1999, in an election that reflected a deep desire for change among voters.[90] President Lagos' government has been very effective in developing the transport infrastructure throughout Chile, and the country has finally approved its first divorce law. Nevertheless, a balance of Lagos' administration suggests no serious attempt to change the prevailing policy model, even if timid reforms have been initiated, regarding social protection, mining policy, and other issues, as new presidential elections approach.[91]

Nevertheless, the above-cited assertion by *The Economist* in relation to Brazil may hold true in a wider sense throughout the continent. The proposal of a 'New Deal', explicitly inspired by Franklin D. Roosevelt, where increased social protection (SP) is considered a basic component of new economic policies, is central to President Lula's programme. The PT programme calls for 'the implantation of an alternative model of development, with the social issue as its axis... accompanied by the democratization of the State and social relations... ' (PT 2002: 1). Similar propositions may be found in the discourse of Presidents Kirchner and Vasquez, as well as in alternative government proposals across the continent. Such proposals may be heard in assemblies such as Forum Social Mundial de Porto Alegre and other alternative regional assemblies, which are becoming increasingly representative, as leaders of political parties now in power in the main countries in LA continue to participate in them.

The same kind of propositions may be heard coming from institutions such as UNDP and other UN agencies and leaders (Ocampo 2002). Voices that promote significant policy changes are becoming increasingly authorized within organizations such as ECLAC (Ffrench-Davis 2001, 2002, 2003). Even the flagship institutions of Neoliberal policies, such as the Inter-American Development Bank (IDB) and even the World Bank (WB), have recently insinuated timid exploratory openings to the possibility of a different kind of policies (Gill *et al.* 2004).

Most importantly, the emerging, progressive reform agenda, of an increasingly wide assortment of political, academic and social actors, may be now resting quite solidly over the current moment of the historical development of LA, as this book will argue quite extensively.

## A young giant in the making

In a longer historical perspective, interesting options seem to be opening up for LA. There is a growing awareness that by the mid twenty-first century, and even long before that, the present balance of economic power in the world will have changed quite dramatically. As mentioned before, when assessing the course of the LA transition process, the region is considered as one of the emerging economic powers of the twenty-first century (Goldman-Sachs 2003).

The building of such an economic LA giant, how it will look, and what its main features will be regarding economic and social policy, are questions that largely depend on the development strategies of the continent's three largest countries – Brazil, Mexico and Argentina. The development strategies of the other LA countries will exert some influence, but this encompassing process will largely determine them. The strategy of the US in relation to the region will certainly play a significant role as well. However, its influence will be offset, at least in part, by the increasing presence in the region of the EU and other large international powers.

To date the Brazilian development strategy has privileged creating a wider economic space, jointly with Argentina, who have followed a similar path. Together with Uruguay and Paraguay, they have founded Mercosur. Mercosur has been developing already for more than a decade, and has recently shown itself capable of surviving quite severe economic and political crises in its main partners. Mexico, in turn, has privileged integrating itself into the US market through NAFTA, together with Canada. Nevertheless, at the same time, Mexico has been pursuing an independent path, which includes FTA with the EU and rapprochement to the south (Fazio 2004), including the possibility of fully joining Mercosur as well (CENDA 2004a).

On the contrary, smaller Chile has privileged unilateral opening of its economy since the 1970s, while trying to pursue rapprochement on the one side to Mercosur, as a special associate that keeps arm's-length distance, and to the US on the other, while at the same time actively seeking openings both to the EU and Asia. Chile has signed FTAs with the EU, the US, and Korea during 2003, before that with Canada, Mexico and other LA countries, and is presently negotiating FTAs with Japan, China, and India, among several other countries. Nevertheless, such a strategy seems to be overstretching itself, as its neighbours show increasingly hard feelings about it. Recent problems with natural gas provision from its neighbours, on which Chile depends for 30 per cent of its overall energy needs, seems to prove the limits of such a unilateral approach (Fazio 2004; CENDA 2004b).

The Andean countries, including Colombia and Venezuela, which are the continent's fourth and fifth largest economies (Table 1.A1 in the Appendix), together with Ecuador, Peru, and Bolivia, have established a regional Andean Pact since the 1960s to which Chile also belonged until the mid-1970s. All these countries are living through rapid and difficult social and economic transitions, as well as violent political struggles. Even though their future strategy does not yet seem to be clearly defined, they seem to privilege rapprochement with Mercosur, particularly the Chávez government in Venezuela, who formally joined in 2006, and Bolivia, who has already achieved a special associate status.

Central America and the Caribbean is a region where civil wars in many countries during the 1980s underline how fast they are presently undergoing the social and economic changes that have marked LA as a whole throughout the past century. US influence has always been and remains determinant in this region, more than elsewhere in LA. Many of these countries have recently signed FTAs with the US. Nevertheless, as the remarkable example of Cuba has proven throughout almost half a century, an independent development path is possible even in such close proximity to the US, whichever hardships it may carry. The Costa Rican experience also supports this. Recently, for example, Costa Rica refrained from signing a FTA that was offered to them by the US. Difficult as it seems, some countries in this region may choose to seek rapprochement with the southern block led by Brazil, as Cuba has been doing for a long time. It is possible that some of them will achieve this purpose, overcoming US pressures against it.

The US has been following a strategy for LA that was defined by George H. Bush in 1994, when he announced the *Free Trade Agreement of the Americas* (FTAA), a free trade region that by 2005 would encompass America from Alaska to Tierra del Fuego. The FTA recently signed by Chile and three Central American countries underline the main points pursued by the US through FTAA. These FTA have established a rather slow calendar for free trade itself, with long adjustment periods for those goods that are sensitive to specific US constituencies. Sensitive trade items for the US are not included in the FTA pacts, such as reducing farm subsidies and limiting anti-dumping legislation. Quite the opposite, the minor partners have accepted to include non-trade matters that interest the US, such as government purchases, investments, and intellectual property rights (Fazio 2004). Meanwhile, the US military Southern Command has been pursuing a less outspoken, though no less clearly defined strategy for LA, which includes securing US military presence in Paraguay, Bolivia, and Colombia, under the cover of war against drug traffic and terrorism.

Nevertheless, LA seems recently to have been asserting its independence progressively. Mercosur, headed by Brazil, has resisted imbalances – such as those accepted by LA countries who have signed FTAs with the US – from being incorporated into in FTAA. Mercosur has stated that they will accept to include non-trade matters of interest to the US, but only if this country will in turn accept including trade-related issues as the ones mentioned above. As the US has refused to do this, FTAA talks are currently stalled and its original timetable seems to have been abandoned. Over the same argument, Brazil, together with India and China, led a group of countries including Chile, which walked out of the WTO meeting in Miami in 2003 (Fazio 2004). It seems clear that the new LA strategy outlined here, though drawing heavily on twentieth-century LADWS experience, also has essential differences from it. Mainly, the new strategy may probably only happen in an enlarged, multinational, LA space, if indeed it is meant to happen at all. The sub-regional redefinition of the international economic insertion of LA countries, which has been referred to above, points to the kind of space and actors where such international definitions are being shaped.

The magnitude of the developmentalist programmes facing Neo-LADWS seems to exceed both the capacity and the space of individual countries, even the continental giants, Brazil and Mexico. National security in fields such as energy may only be achieved in optimal conditions within an increasingly solid integrated environment. On the other hand, the economic advantages of solving such problems with LA resources are so huge that they constitute a significant incentive towards economic integration. In the above-cited example, the provision of over one-third of Chilean energy requirements with cheap LA gas generates economic benefits that exceed by far those that may be obtained by the sum of all marginal trade benefits rendered by all the FTA agreements recently signed by this country, including those with the US and the EU (CENDA 2004b). Other developmentalist programmes facing LA countries in coming decades include such huge engagements as building a science and technology base that may be able to compete with the other large international players such as the US, EU, China, India, and Russia. Full development of the aerospace industry is another engagement to be mentioned. A continental network of superhighways and modern railway connections such as is already available in EU and the US should certainly be built in LA. Finally, yet importantly, the building of a competitive defence industry could also be added. Many more areas could be mentioned that by sheer size require a larger space than may be provided by individual countries.

When Chile signed a FTA with the US recently, its fans hailed it as the moment when the country joined the 'big leagues'. Similar expressions were used in Honduras, Guatemala, and El Salvador, when those small countries signed their own FTA with the US shortly afterwards. The above-mentioned list of challenges facing the alternative Neo-LADWS project may perhaps closer resemble what really playing the 'big leagues' is all about in LA during the twenty-first century.

The shape of the continent in the future seems to be strongly dependent upon the fate of the subregional integration efforts now being developed. Unlike similar intents that have been successively frustrated in the past, this time it seems possible that the dream of Simón Bolivar may prevail in the near future.

### A new developmental relation between state and business

In addition, and perhaps more relevant from a factual point of view, economic integration in LA simply seems to be happening, engaged by LA entrepreneurs, following purely economic forces. Horst Paulman, owner of the Chilean *Jumbo* supermarket chain, which holds a significant market share in both Chile and Argentina, has recently declared, 'Entrepreneurs who do not take advantage of investing in Argentina are simply being foolish' (CENDA 2004a). Argentina accounts for more than half of Chilean foreign direct investment since 1990, with Brazil and Peru coming in second place.[92] In addition to the gas connection, which has been mentioned, all these previously unthinkable cross-border private ventures have occurred during the last decade.

A recent invitation by Mexican Carlos Slim, LA's biggest entrepreneur, to his kin in the rest of LA countries, to a meeting that took place in Mexico in 2004 and lasted for several days, seem to point in this strategic direction (CENDA 2004a). The new strategy points towards a state–business relation that is quite different to the one established under the old developmentalism. Unlike its ancestor, the state is now able to rely mainly on the new LA entrepreneurial class, which simply did not exist but in infant form during the old times, and the new strategy seems oriented towards further strengthening such an actor.

The Neo-LADWS project seems rooted not only in the twentieth-century experience, from which it will probably draw inspiration, but also over the inheritance of Neoliberalism in LA. The emerging paradigm implies a radical change of direction away from Washington Consensus-style policies, and, in fact, it is being conceived over the criticism of that model. Nevertheless, the new project seems to inherit quite a lot from the Neoliberal period as well. It should rely on new LA entrepreneurial classes, as said, which in their present form are certainly a part of the Neoliberal inheritance, as much as the latter model inherited them from the old developmentalism, at least in infant form. Complementary, the new strategy is to be built upon the new salaried middle classes, both over their productive power, as well as their present demands of wider and better SP as will be mentioned below. Such a new salariat has also sprung up from both the Neoliberal period, as well as from developmentalism before that.

Many other inheritances from the Neoliberal period will probably be built into the conceptualization of the new development paradigm that seems to be emerging. For example, strong voices are demanding more active monetary and fiscal policies than those accepted under *Washington Consensus* policies, especially under recession. Nevertheless, few would support any kind of fiscal irresponsibility, and fear of hyperinflation remains high, perhaps too high as has been said, across every level of LA elites. In addition, governments throughout LA have started to consider putting into place stronger regulations on business practices, to ensure competitiveness, transparency, and tax compliance. Nevertheless, maintaining an economic and regulatory environment that looks attractive to business seems to gather wide consensus as well. Regarding social policies, a new relation between the public and private sectors seems to be in the making as well, as will be argued below, in which both sectors play complementary roles.

Nevertheless, the main shift in direction in this relation seems to point towards the need to rebuild and reinforce the public sector. After decades of unilateral emphasis on creating optimal conditions for business, a change seems to be in the making in LA, towards emphasizing the public sphere. This is not viewed as a way of constraining entrepreneurial initiative, but rather, on the contrary, as a way of reinforcing it through better regulatory frameworks and a strong complementary public sector. The rebuilding of strong, well-trained, efficient, and non-corrupt professional civil services seems to be one of the main points in this shift away from decades of trying to transform the public sector in the image of private business. This seems also to be an international current (Suleiman 2003; Fukuyama 2003).

## Recovering ground rent of natural resources

Regulations over natural resource exploitation, including conservationist and ecological concerns, as well as royalty charges for minerals and other resources, are now receiving due attention from LA governments, as such policies enjoy high support among their public opinions.

As is well known, a good part of national income in developing countries, including LA countries, comes from the exploitation of natural resources, which have high ground rents associated with them. The high labour productivity, and the comparative advantages of these industries, derives not only from up-to-date technology, and workforce qualification, which are normally present as well in these sectors – at least relative to other industries in the same countries. Most of these advantages really arise out of the high ground rent associated with the valuable natural resources in which these industries are based upon. That is the case in industries such as mining, export-oriented plantations, fisheries, etc., among others.

On the other hand, it is also well known that over the last few decades, under the inspiration of *Washington Consensus* economic policies, LA countries have lured foreign investment by adopting highly generous and permissive taxing systems, which in fact allow foreign investors to avoid paying any relevant taxes to the governments of their host countries. In addition, in the case of industries that are natural resources-based, the taxing systems currently in use in developing countries have generally abandoned the orthodox economic policy recommendation of charging royalties, and using other instruments of state appropriation of the significant ground rent associated with these resources. In addition, state companies that in some cases exploited these resources themselves have been privatized in some countries (UNRISD 2005; Riesco 2004; CENDA 2004d).

The ground rent of natural resources in developing countries is thus appropriated by the private investors in these industries, and becomes the equivalent of a high subsidy to investors in these areas – nothing less than enjoying free raw materials in many cases. As a result, there is significant over-investment in natural resources-based industries in developing countries, which results in the overexploitation of these resources in the short run, with severe consequences for the environment. Overinvestment and overproduction of natural resource-based industries in developing countries has also resulted in periodic gluts in world markets for some of these products, with severe price falls. Even the theoretical border case of 'inmiserizing growth', where an expanded output is sold for a lower overall price, has been experienced in determined natural resources-based markets during certain periods (UNRISD 2005; Riesco 2004; CENDA 2004d).

The above-described situation has been studied thoroughly in the case of mining companies operating in certain developing countries, where a strong movement is in the making, to reform taxing schemes in natural resources-based industries, introducing royalties and other ground rent appropriation mechanisms by the state (UNRISD 2005; Riesco 2004; CENDA 2004d).

In brief, the disregard of ground-rent-related policies in the taxing schemes currently prevailing in developing countries has resulted in a severe reduction of state revenues in developing countries, as well as having a negative impact on employment and environment, among other negative consequences. All these consequences have had a severe negative impact over social policies and social development. This process has resulted in a serious loss of the capabilities for ground rent appropriation acquired by developing nations during the nationalization wave of the 1960s and 1970s.

Nevertheless, and although prosecuting the same goals, the present movement is based mainly on defining sound and effective ground rent appropriation taxing schemes, instead of having the state directly assuming all production in these industries, as was the general case in the previous wave of nationalizations. In this way, the appropriation of ground rent may cohabit in harmony with emerging local entrepreneurs, who desire to participate in the business together with foreign capital. Nonetheless, state enterprises continue to play an important role in the new schemes, as long-term regulators in these industries.

Strictly speaking, from a theoretical point of view, ground rent appropriation by host states in developing countries is the equivalent of a transfer of value from developed countries towards developing countries. Consumers in developed countries usually make the bulk of the demand for products of natural resources-based industries, and thus pay most of the higher price that results from the scarcity of these resources, which in turn originates ground rent. In this sense, promoting the reintroduction of orthodox ground rent appropriation policies in developing countries, is the equivalent of redirecting part of the income of the developed world to developing nations, only in this case this transferal takes place by the action of purely economic forces.

All the above, of course in addition to the overall gain in economic efficiency that results from re-establishing sound economic policies in natural resources-based markets, of which not the least are those related to the rational protection of environment.

## New, enhanced, inclusive, social policies: binding for neo-LADWS

Regarding social policies, criticism and dissatisfaction over private social protection schemes applied during the Neoliberal period runs high across public opinion, and governments are also taking charge of them throughout LA (UNDP 2002; Riesco 2002a, 2002b; Gill *et al.* 2004). Nevertheless, few would support going back to the old schemes. Rather, alternative SP proposals suggest multiple tiered schemes, where reinforced and better public systems will attend the needs of the majority of the population, and private schemes will be kept in place whether as complements of the latter, or as differentiated SP alternatives for higher-income groups (CENDA 2004c; Chapters 2 to 9 below). Thus the new project to seems to be taking shape in this critical area.

Rivalries, border conflicts, and even armed skirmishes between neighbouring countries are quite frequent in LA. Recent conflicts for example have confronted Chile against Bolivia, Peru, and Argentina, and serious problems aroused between Argentina and Brazil when the latter depreciated its currency a few years ago. Serious tensions leading to border skirmishes have occurred in recent decades between Ecuador and Peru, Chile and Argentina, and Venezuela and Colombia. In effect, strong chauvinist sentiments that are deeply rooted within populations of bordering countries readily erupt, poising one against the other. Obviously, apart from all other ethical considerations, this kind of incidents result in border closures and other problems that are very bad business, and may seriously hamper or delay the integration project. They underline the need of building up public support for the integration project.

There seems no better way of securing public support for the integration project than embedding it into the Neo-LADWS project itself. In this sense, the social policy component of LA integration has been present since its conception, at least in Mercosur. Following the EU model, Mercosur has devised three party commissions, where workers are represented, together with employers and governments. Even though advances in this area have not been great to date, inroads have been made in many matters, and some common ground is already in place. Presently Mercosur is discussing many subjects related to social policies, among them, cross-border retirement and health benefits, educational equivalences between university degrees, labour legislation, etc., among others.

In terms of other aspects of social policies, the liberal reforms have resulted, as said, in the rise of an important private social protection industry. This industry mostly cares for the needs of families belonging to the upper-income brackets, financed in an important part directly by them. Nevertheless, as mentioned, serious deficiencies may be found in the regulatory framework of the private systems and in their relation with the public system. Important market distortions, high costs for the users and associated global inefficiencies stem from these problems. However, there seems to be enough accumulated evidence on which a different approach may be built, regarding the coexistence of the public and private systems. These new approaches consider overcoming not only the imperfections of the traditional public system, but also the serious failures of the private sector in the funding and the provision of the welfare benefits. The idea that prevailed during past decades, that privatization is the master key to solve all problems, has seemingly proven inaccurate. Growing voices suggest advancing now towards a more regulated and harmonic development of both the public and private sectors, with a continued strong recovery and improvement of the public sector, aiming to develop a universal, more equitable and good quality social protection system for all (UNDP 2002; CENDA 2004c; Gill *et al.* 2004).

It seems inevitable to link the issue of the size of public spending dedicated to social protection, of which a major part goes to financing the deficit resulting from the privatization of pension schemes in several countries. This discussion, in the longer term, leads inevitably towards a revision of the level of public expenditure as a whole, because social spending already absorbs the greater part of government budgets. This in turn points towards a revision of the taxation system. As asserted recently by the Chilean Minister of Finance: 'With the current tax rate it is only possible to provide a social policy for the poorest quintile, yet the second quintile is also horribly poor . . . also middle class has to be satisfied [in their needs], but that is impossible with the current tax rates. For full university grants, adequate pension retiring schemes, a different tax rate is needed' (Riesco 2002a: 3). It has been suggested in this respect, along with other progressive taxation proposals, that it would be nice if transnational corporations operating in LA would pay their taxes (UNDP 2002).

In the short term, another quite pressing issue relates social spending to economic policy. Increased social spending has been argued strongly as a way to provide an efficient and just way of reactivating the LA economy, which remained stagnated or in recession from 1998 up to 2003 (Stiglitz 2003; Ffrench-Davis 2003). Of course, the historical precedent is well known, since many of the main SP programmes were initiated in the US in the wake of the 1930s crisis. The East Asian experiences reviewed in the present project show that countries like Korea and Taiwan, for example, increased their public social expenditure from around 16 per cent in the 1980s up to 30 per cent today, while they extended health care and pensions universally, and created comprehensive unemployment protection systems. Many of these changes were implemented during the Asian crisis started in 1997, and financed in part through significant though temporary fiscal deficits they played a strong role in economic recovery (Wong 2003). In the long term, such an eventual new relationship between social policy and economic policy opens the way for a renewed interest in developmental economic policy.

These developments notwithstanding, and drawing again on the historical method of this book, the main challenge confronting the Neo-LADWS project seems to be addressing the same kind of improvements in their SP systems which other regions succeeded in implementing, when those regions went through to the development moment that LA is presently confronting. That would suggest looking now to the SP systems that Europe, the US, and white colonies such as Australia, or New Zealand, managed to construct during the twentieth century. A more recent and nearby example for LA may be drawn from the East Asian experience mentioned before.

## Removing impediments

The question of the possibility of taking advantage of the present window of opportunity brings the debate back to the impediments confronting the possibility that these insights translate into policy measures. According to UNRISD's Thandika Mkandawire, such impediments are threefold: (i) 'the persistence of economic policy making based on a "leader/follower" model, where macroeconomic policy (stability and growth) is determined first and social policy is left to address the social consequences' (ii) 'the complexity and ambiguity of the policy implications' of renewed developmental economics; and (iii) recalcitrant political and ideological impediments, 'social policy is a highly political process, touching upon power relations, access to resources and ideological predilections about the role of State and markets' (Mkandawire 2001: 23).

Academic research and debate seems to be able to accomplish a great deal in LA, in the direction of partially removing at least the first two of these impediments and, through this, aspiring to be modestly influential with regard to the third one. The simple review of old and new theories and insights in developmental economics, in the light of studying social policy in relation to social and economic history in LA, may prove to be, by itself, not in the least unimportant. Certainly, the consideration of social policy in conjunction with economic policy in a development context seems especially fruitful,

Systematic dialogue and interchange between researchers and studies of these matters in the different LA countries, under a critical perspective and with the sponsorship of UN institutions, may also prove fruitful, beyond the specific thematic involved. One of the main questions to be addressed is how social (and economic) policy measures are in fact decided, as of now, in LA countries. What are the implications and ramifications of the BWIs and other transnational entities in this process? How do they accomplish such a high degree of influence? Such processes need to be countered, starting from the theoretical background and through the preparation and grooming of elite technocrats and up to the ramifications of their closely-knit community with government, academy, media, and business. How can this decision making process may be made more transparent and accountable to democratic institutions?

Addressing the former against the backdrop of the political trends that seem to be emerging in LA may reasonably support a not overly pessimistic stance regarding the possible outcomes.

## Notes

1. The discussion over the concept of socioeconomic transition is presented in the introduction to this book. The authors use this concept in the same sense as the theory of modernization, summarized there. That is to say, that there is obviously

a progression from the traditional agrarian, peasant-*latifundia* owners, oligarchic, etc. socioeconomic and political structures that prevailed in LA a century ago, towards the modern, urban, salaried-entrepreneurial, democratic, etc. socioeconomic and political structures, which are beginning to prevail today. In that progress, some LA countries as a whole, and some regions within countries, are clearly ahead of others. As said in the introduction, full reckoning of this fact not only makes sense, furthermore, it seems to be the main aspect to be taken into account, when studying social and economic phenomena, as well as political events and institutions, in developing countries. By contrast, in developed countries, this aspect seems quite irrelevant, because it refers to processes that took place and were completed long ago – which may be the reason why many studies tend to overlook this significant fact. Nevertheless, at the same time, the authors also acknowledge a critical approach to modernization theory, and try to avoid mechanisism, structuralism, linearity, using fixed stages, and many other unilateral approaches to this theory, which have proved quite misleading. In particular, the authors try to complement and confront this kind of structural approach, with historical analysis. In this sense, the present section represents a unity with the following sections, where different historical patterns and concepts are introduced, which explain and make up for a more complex approach to the subject.

2. Normally, the averages were calculated by weighting the variables according to the population in each country.
3. Population is growing in LA as a whole at a rate of 1.4 per cent a year (2000–10), and growth is faster in countries in early and moderate transition, where it is higher than 2 per cent a year, considering both groups as a whole. It diminishes to 1.3 per cent a year in countries in full transition, and drops to 0.9 per cent a year in those in advanced transition. At these rates, the continent will top 595 million inhabitants by 2010, will surpass 698 million in 2025, and will reach 900 million by 2050 (Table 1.A1 in appendix). As a reference, the US today has slightly less than 300 million inhabitants, and the European Union neared 450 million inhabitants after it was recently enlarged to 25 members. As the growth rates in these two regions is significantly slower, LA will increasingly exceed them in population, as the century advances.
4. Gross Domestic Product (GDP) adjusted by purchasing power parity (ppp) of LA is slightly under US $4 trillion. By contrast, US GDP is in the order of US $10 trillion (ppp 2002). However, the group of countries in early and moderate transition, taken together, represent only 4.4 per cent of regional GDP. The group of countries in full transition generates about three-quarters, and the group of countries in advanced transition taken as a whole, about one-fifth, of regional GDP. In relation to their respective populations, the first groups generate far less output than their share of regional population, and the opposite takes place. In the latter group, meanwhile, the proportion of GDP generated by the middle group is roughly equivalent to its share of the population. Brasil generates about one third of regional GDP by itself, and Mexico about one fifth (see Table 1.1 and Appendix Table 1.A1).

   According to per capita GDP, adjusted by purchasing power parity (2001), LA, as a whole, as well as the full transition group of countries, occupies place number 73 in the worldwide ranking of 175 countries according to per capita GDP. That is to say, both LA as a whole, and the group of countries in full transition, is slightly above the median country in the world, according to this indicator. Alternatively, the group of countries in early transition belongs to the last quintile worldwide. Conversely, the group of LA countries in advanced transition fall within the second quintile. Regional leaders according to this indicator, Argentina and Chile, occupy places 49 and 57, respectively, meanwhile the regional laggard, Haiti, is in place 153 and the highest GDP per capita in LA are generated in Bahamas (place no. 38 worldwide) and Barbados (40). (See Table 1.1 and Appendix Table 1.A1).

5. As is well known, the World Bank calculates a correction to nominal exchange rates, called 'purchasing power parity (ppp)', based on the cost of acquiring a comparable set of goods in each country. Originally, this was undertaken by *The Economist* magazine, which corrected local exchange rates according to the price in each country of a Big Mac hamburger. The resulting prices are expressed in 'international dollars', that is, after correcting the exchange rate. All figures in dollars in the 'economic growth' section are expressed in international dollars – that is, dollars corrected by ppp.
6. Per capita GDP (ppp) is one of the *proxy* variables used to measure per capita productivity. It is a crude measure of the level of training in the workforce, in addition to both the proportion of inhabitants, and the proportion of the working day dedicated by each of them, to commodity production. That is to say, to work on products and services to be sold in the market, and because of that are reflected in national accounts. By the same reason, this indicator is a good *proxy* variable to measure the predominant social relations, because, as is known, peasant economies dedicate most of the working day to self-consumption, and comparatively little to the production of commodities. By contrast, the urban economy and modern economy in general is predominantly and increasingly oriented towards commodity production. *Business Week* magazine has recently calculated that in China, for example, the economy of a peasant family of five, amounts approximately to US $200 a year, roughly equivalent to the salary of one of its members who migrates to Shanghai, whom is most surely paid a fraction of the actual value added to his or her produce. This shows the huge importance of social relations regarding economic performance. Nevertheless, per capita GDP is greatly influenced by ground rent-generating economic activities, particularly in less developed countries, where these industries weigh heavily in overall GDP. Because of this, per capita GDP in oil-producing less developed countries appear highly inflated, and this is almost entirely due to oil ground rent. In the case of LA, this ground rent factor significantly increases per capita GDP in countries such as Venezuela and Ecuador (oil) and Chile (copper), for example. In developed countries, ground rent originating in sky-high urban rent greatly increases per capita GDP when measured in current dollar prices (it amounts to around 30 per cent of prices), but this factor is quite completely corrected when international dollars (ppp adjusted) are used.
7. The fastest economic growth during the last half-century was experienced by the countries that belong today to the full transition group, which as a whole grew at a rate of 4.2 per cent a year between 1960 and 2002. The group was pulled by Brazil, which grew at the record average rate of 4.5 per cent a year during the whole period, and at a record 8.5 per cent a year during the 1970s. The countries in early transition, for their part, grew at a yearly rate of 1.6 per cent during 1960–2002; meanwhile the moderate transition group grew 3.6 per cent during the same period. The countries in the advanced transition group grew 2.6 per cent a year during the 1960–2002 period. Chile however, grew 4.2 per cent a year during

this whole period, similar to the group in full transition, thanks to an accelerated growth of 6.5 per cent a year during the 1990s (see Appendix Table 1.A1).

8. An explanation for this kind of evolution seems quite straightforward, when the relative stages of socioeconomic transition are taken into account. As commented above, traditional peasants contribute very little value to GDP, simply because most of their work is dedicated to self-consumption. By contrast, when they migrate to cities, most of their work becomes necessarily devoted to producing goods and services that are sold in the market – the fact that they may be hired as salaried workers or that they work on their own or informally, are quite irrelevant for this purpose. Once in the cities, they will still work as before in the countryside, from sunrise to sunset, exhaustingly past the inflexion point of diminishing returns. Nevertheless, now they seem to have acquired the Midas touch, as the products or services they deliver turn into gold, and suddenly appear in the national accounts. Alas, very little of that gold is left for themselves. Therefore, when masses of peasants start to migrate into cities, their new commodity-producing labour adds quite a number of percentage points to national GDP, and countries experience decades-long sprees of very high economic growth, which then slow down when the migration process slows and ends.
9. All urbanization figures in this section are based on UN sources (see Appendix Table 1.A2). The methodology used by the UN to compile its urbanization figures is based on the ones accepted by each of the individual countries, which are not necessarily the same. Recently, the World Bank recalculated urbanization data applying to every country the methodology used by the OECD. The resulting urbanization figures are much lower in the case of LA. If, according to UN sources, only 25 per cent of LA population is still rural, that figure increases to 42 per cent according to the WB study (World Bank 2005).
10. The respective urbanization figures for Chile were 67.8 per cent in 1960, 86.9 per cent today, and a projection of 88.5 per cent in 2015. That is to say, in 1960 Chile had the degree of urbanization that LA reached in 1985. Furthermore, in Chile, urban population surpassed peasant population back in 1930 (Chapter 9); meanwhile it was not until 1960 that LA as a whole achieved this landmark. Argentina and Uruguay had urban populations of 73.6 per cent and 80.1 per cent, respectively, already in 1960; they have 90 per cent and 93 per cent today, respectively; and are projected to reach 92 per cent and 93.9 per cent in 2015, respectively.
11. It has slowed from 1.1 per cent a year in 1960–85, to 0.7 per cent a year from 1985–2005, and halved in Brazil, Peru and Venezuela but increased in Bolivia, Haiti, El Salvador, and Paraguay, among other countries, during the same periods (see Appendix Table 1.A1).
12. In Chile, for example, at a given moment, private firms of five or more employees, hire 51.2 per cent of the non-farm-occupied workforce, and an additional 10.8 per cent are salaried public employees. In addition, 5.9 per cent of the occupied urban workforce is made up of salaried domestic servants. On the other hand, 12.5 per cent are employed in micro-firms of fewer than five employees, and finally, 19.7 per cent of the urban workforce work on their own, as 'self-employed'. This accounts for about two-thirds in salaried jobs and one-third in informal occupations. However, in another moment, these figures may remain the same, but with the exception of State employees and others that hold secure jobs, many of the workers will have shifted from one category to another (Chapter 10, INP 2004). The respective figures for LA as a whole show a higher proportion

of non-farm workers in informal jobs, but only in early or moderate transition countries, they make up a majority.

13. The group of countries in early and moderate transition are very low spenders in public policies, with less than $100 per capita in the latter case, equivalent to 8 per cent of GDP and about 40 per cent of total public expenditure, on the average. On the other end, the group of countries in advanced transition have a public social expenditure of $1,445 per capita, which is equivalent to 20.2 per cent of GDP, and 65.1 per cent of total public expenditure. The average for the region is $686 per capita, which is equivalent to 14.8 per cent of GDP (2000–01) (see Appendix Table 1.A6).
14. It is interesting that Bolivia, for example, which is otherwise classified as a country in early transition, has a total public social expenditure of $183 per capita, which corresponds to 17.9 of GDP and 60 per cent of total public expenditures. This is higher than all countries in moderate transition, and higher than the expenditure of Ecuador, Peru, and the Dominican Republic, which may be considered countries in full transition by other concepts. The countries with the highest public social expenditure in the region are, by far, Uruguay (1454 US$/pc – 23.5 per cent of GDP) and Argentina (1650 US$/pc – 21.6 per cent of GDP). Cuba, which is also classified in the advanced transition group according to other variables, is also a large public social spender (Chapter 9). Another country classified in this group, Chile (936 US$/pc – 16.0 per cent of GDP), is also a relatively high spender in dollars per capita. Nevertheless, it ranks lower than Brazil (936 US$/pc – 18.8 per cent of GDP). Additionally, in relation to GDP, Chile spends less than Panama (25.5 per cent of GDP), Costa Rica (18.2 per cent of GDP), and even Bolivia (17.9 per cent). On the other side, the laggards in the region according to this indicator are Salvador (82 US$/pc – 4.2 per cent of GDP), Guatemala (109 US$/pc – 6.2 per cent of GDP), Honduras (77 US$/pc – 10.0 per cent of GDP), and Nicaragua (61 US$/pc – 13.2 per cent of GDP). In addition, Ecuador (131 US$/pc – 8.8 per cent of GDP), the Dominican Republic (170 US$/pc – 7.6 per cent of GDP), Peru (187 US$/pc – 8.0 per cent of GDP), and Colombia (337 US$/pc – 13.6 per cent of GDP) (2000–2001) (see Appendix Table 1.A6).
15. As mentioned in relation to total public social expenditures, the group of countries in early and moderate transition are very low spenders in education, with the moderate transition group spending $48 per capita, equivalent to 3.9 per cent of GDP. The group of countries in full transition spend $161 per capita, which also corresponds to 3.9 per cent of GDP. At the other end, the group of countries in a state of advanced transition have a public expenditure in education of $335 per capita, which is equivalent to 4.7 per cent of GDP. The largest public spender in education in the region by far is Argentina (385 US$/pc – 5.0 per cent of GDP), followed by Chile (238 US$/pc – 4.1 per cent of GDP) and Uruguay (213 US$/pc – 3.4 per cent of GDP). In addition, Panama (199 US$/pc – 6.0 per cent of GDP), Costa Rica (189 US$/pc – 5.0 per cent of GDP), and Brazil (185 US$/pc – 3.8 per cent of GDP) are also big spenders in education. It is significant that Mexico (190 US$/pc – 4.1 per cent of GDP) appears within the group of countries with the largest expenditures in education (2000–01). Some countries that appear in lower stages of transition are nevertheless making a larger effort in education than other countries that are more advanced in the transition process overall. Bolivia (66 US$/pc – 6.5 per cent of GDP) is again spending more in education than all the countries in the moderate transition group (48 US$/pc – 3.9 per cent of GDP). Although very low in absolute terms, public expenditure in education

as a percentage of GDP in Nicaragua (28 US$/pc – 6.1 per cent of GDP), and Honduras (45 US$/pc – 5.8 per cent of GDP), is higher than the LA average (175 US$/pc – 4.1 per cent of GDP) (2000–2001) (See Appendix Table 1.A7).

16. The figures of public social expenditure for Mexico published by ECLAC appear with some differences in relation to other countries in LA that may be misleading. In public social expenditure as a whole Mexico appears as a very low spender (2000–2001), with $456 per capita and 9.8 per cent of GDP, which are far below the LA average (686 US$ /pc – 14.8 per cent of GDP). On the contrary, it appears to be targeting 61.5 per cent of its public expenditure in social policies, above the LA average of 55.1 per cent for this figure. On the other hand, Mexico is a high spender on education (190 US$/pc – 4.1 per cent of GDP), at least above the LA average (175 US$/pc – 4.1 per cent of GDP). The same case for public expenditures in housing and others, where Mexico (50 US$/pc – 1.1 per cent of GDP) appears above the LA average (44 US$/pc – 1.0 per cent of GDP). The contrary may be appreciated in public expenditure in health, where Mexico (86 US$/pc – 1.9 per cent of GDP) appears far below the LA average (130 US$/pc – 2.9 per cent of GDP). This figure does not seem to be coherent with physical health indicators such as medicine doctors per capita or hospital beads per capita, where Mexico appears to be well above over the LA average. The same case for public expenditure in social security, where Mexico (131 US$/pc – 2.8 per cent of GDP) appears far below the LA average (338 US$/pc – 6.8 per cent of GDP) (Tables 1.A7–9 in the Appendix). Could this be a consequence of statistical methodology used in this case? In the case of Mexico, ECLAC confirmed to the authors that it only considers the central government expenditures for some of these figures. This is not the case in other countries, where regional and local governments are considered as well in the expenditure figures published by ECLAC.
17. The group of countries in early and moderate transition are very low spenders in health, with the moderate transition group spending $22 per capita, equivalent to 2.1 per cent of GDP. The group of countries in full transition spend $111 per capita, which corresponds to 2.7 per cent per cent of GDP. At the other end, the group of countries in advanced transition have a public expenditure in health of $308 per capita, which is equivalent to 4.3 per cent of GDP. Within this group, Chile (165 US$/pc – 2.8 per cent of GDP), as well as Uruguay (175 US$/pc – 2.8 per cent of GDP), appear to have a low public expenditure in health, below Panama (274 US$/pc – 8.2 per cent of GDP), and Costa Rica (199 US$/pc – 5.3 per cent of GDP). The latter two countries are the largest spenders in health in the region, together with Argentina (379 US$/pc – 5.0 per cent of GDP), which in this indicator is again the leader in the region, by far (2000–01) (see Appendix Table 1.A7).
18. The group of countries in early and moderate transition are very low spenders in social security, with the moderate transition group spending $16 per capita, equivalent to 1.0 per cent of GDP. The group of countries in full transition spend $320 per capita, which corresponds to 7.1 per cent per cent of GDP. On other end, the group of countries in advanced transition have a public expenditure in social security of $653 per capita, which is equivalent to 9.2 per cent of GDP. The largest public spenders in social security in the region are Argentina (705 US$/pc – 9.2 per cent of GDP), and Brazil (588 US$/pc – 11.8 per cent of GDP), together with Uruguay (1075 US$/pc – 16.2 per cent of GDP), by far the leader in the region according to this indicator. It is interesting to note that Chile (435 US$/pc – 7.4 per cent of GDP), and Bolivia (47 US$/pc – 4.6 per cent of GDP), which are

countries that have fully privatized pension systems, appear as high spenders in this item as well, in relation to GDP (2000–01) (see Appendix Table 1.A8).

19. It is well known that Cuba is the country that probably leads the region in this indicator, as is the case with many other social indicators such as health, education, and others (Chapter 9). Regrettably, Cuba is not considered by ECLAC and other sources, in many of the comparative data presented in the tables in the Appendix to this chapter.

20. The poorest 40 per cent of the population receives only 13 per cent of overall income in LA as a whole. Nevertheless, this segment seem to slightly increase their share of overall income as countries move along the transition process, but the path is nowhere smooth, and many countries seem to be special cases. One of the worst countries in the region according to this indicator is Bolivia, where the poorest 40 per cent of the population receive only 10.1 per cent of the overall income. In the group of countries in moderate transition as a whole, the poorest 40 per cent of the population receive 13.2 per cent of the income. The group of countries in full transition fares even worse according to this indicator (12.4 per cent), but that is because Brazil (9.9 per cent) pulls the group down. In the other end, in countries in advanced transition the poorest 40 per cent of the population receive 14.7 per cent of overall income (see Table 1.4).

    However, there are large deviations within each group. Within the moderate transition group, Paraguay (15.3 per cent), and El Salvador (14.5 per cent) allocate a larger part of overall income to this segment of the population than Chile (13.4 per cent), and a similar amount to Argentina (14.7 per cent), both the latter countries in the advanced transition group. Within the group of countries in full transition, in Colombia, the poorest 40 per cent receive 11.7 per cent of income, only slightly more than Brazil (9.9 per cent). On the contrary, in countries such as Ecuador (15.9 per cent), Costa Rica (15.8 per cent), and even Venezuela (15.1 per cent), which also belong to this group, the poorest 40 per cent receive larger portions of overall income than the LA average (13 per cent), and larger than in the advanced transition group taken as a whole (14.7 per cent). Within this last group, Uruguay, the country in the region with the best distribution of income, allocates 21.3 per cent of overall income to this segment of the population (2000–01) (See Appendix Table 1.9).

    On the other extreme, the richest 10 per cent of the population receives 40 per cent of income in LA as a whole. Nevertheless, large deviations may also be appreciated in all groups, and the overall average is again heavily weighted in by Brazil, where the richest 10 per cent of the population receive 46 per cent of overall income. Chile (40.4 per cent), together with Colombia (40.1 per cent), shares with Brazil the shameful distinction that the richest 10 per cent of the population receive more than 40 per cent of overall income. Furthermore, many other countries in the different transition groups have similar figures. Such is the case for Bolivia (39.3 per cent), Guatemala (38.8 per cent), Honduras (39.2 per cent), and Nicaragua (39.9 per cent), all countries in the early and moderate transition groups. In the full transition group, apart from Brazil (46.0 per cent), and Colombia (40.3 per cent), already mentioned, the Dominican Republic (38.6 per cent) also shows a high-income concentration. Most countries in this group, however, exhibit a better performance in this indicator. Such is the case of Costa Rica (28.1 per cent), already mentioned, but also Ecuador (33.3 per cent), Mexico (35.5 per cent), Panama (34.8 per cent), Peru (34.4 per cent), and Venezuela (31.1 per cent). Within the advanced transition group, in Uruguay the richest 10 per cent receive only 27.8 per cent of overall income, but Argentina (37.4 per cent) together with the already mentioned case of Chile show high-income concentrations (2000–2001) (See Appendix Table 1.A9).

21. In LA as a whole, the richest 10 per cent of the population receives 23 times more income than the poorest 40 per cent, on a per capita basis. In Bolivia this ratio is 25 times, in the moderate transition group as a whole the ratio is 20.1 times. In the full transition group the ratio grows up to 24 times, but mainly because of Brazil (31 times). In the advanced transition group the income ratio between the richest 10 per cent and the poorest 40 per cent of the population again falls to 16.6 times (see Table 1.4).

    Nevertheless, deviations within each group are also very wide in this indicator as well. Within the moderate transition group, countries such as Salvador (15.1 times) and Paraguay (15.9 times) show much better performance than the LA average in this indicator (23 times), and even the advanced transition group as a whole (16.6 times). Within the full transition group (24 times), again Brazil (31.9 times), as said, and Colombia (23.9 times) weigh heavily into this ratio. Meanwhile, Mexico (16.9 times) Venezuela (14.1 times), Ecuador (14.0 times), and certainly Costa Rica (11.8 times) present ratios that are equal or better than those in Chile (18.4 times) and Argentine (16.5 times), both the latter countries belonging to the group in advanced transition. In this last group, however, Uruguay again shows the best behaviour in the region, as in this country per capita income of the richest 10 per cent is only 9.1 times that of the poorest 40 per cent of the population (2000–01) (see Appendix Table 1.A9).

22. This index, as is well known, considers other variables in addition to per capita GDP adjusted by purchasing parity (ppp). These variables are life expectancy, literacy rate, and school enrolment.

23. Bolivia and Haiti rank 132 in this indicator. The LA countries in moderate transition, that is to say, most of Central America and Paraguay, rank 110 according to this indicator, which is just slightly away from the worst quartile of countries worldwide. LA countries in full transition, including the most populated countries, Brazil, Mexico, Colombia, and Peru, among others, rank 65 according to this indicator, the same as LA as a whole. LA countries in advanced transition rank 41 according to this indicator, Argentine, the regional leader by far according to this indicator, occupies place 34, and is the sole LA country that belongs to the upper fifth of countries with the highest human development worldwide (see Appendix Table 1.A5).

24. As is well known, advanced countries have rural populations that are insignificant, in the range of 2–5 per cent, as a proportion to overall populations.

25. As mentioned in a note above, recent World Bank data shows that this landmark may still be some years away in the future.

26. The G6 economics are US, Japan, Germany, France, UK, Italy.

27. Draibe (1989b, 1995), for example, has used Esping-Andersen categories to analyse some LA cases, recognizing in many of them some of the characteristics of the corporativist-conservative type. However, it has proved insufficient to capture the strongly historically rooted differences within countries in the region. More recently, Mesa-Lago (1994, 2002) has correlated the economic performance of different LA countries with the way they have mixed their economic and social objectives. He distinguishes three groups of such policy combinations, with Chile representing the extreme case of social policy being subordinated to economic development, Cuba the opposite case, and Costa Rica representing a better

equilibrium between both policy objectives. His conclusion is that Costa Rica presents a better economic and social performance than the two other cases considered, over the last few decades (Mesa-Lago, 2002).

28. Draibe (2004) has recognized that even though the commented approach seems useful, it remains at a very high level of generality.
29. They were based on highly productive crops such as maize, and others, which generated a sequence of highly structured seigniorial societies, ancient empires, for centuries before the Christian era. According to the acute thesis formulated by Alejandro Lipschutz, the Spanish conquest transplanted peninsular feudalism over pre-existing American seigniorialisms. According to Lipschutz, small teams of Spanish conquerors acted like a sort of condotierri that inserted themselves in the wars that Aztec or Inca lordships constantly waged against one another. As a result, the condotierri-conquerors became the new lords themselves, ruling over thousands of indigenous Americans. Lipschutz proves his thesis by opposition, showing Spaniards were only able to conquest those regions where ancient empires had ruled, or their fringes at most. On the contrary, they were fought out from, and never able to submit, those regions of America where original peoples still lived as nomads, or in early tribal organizations. This happened, for example, in the North American Great Plains that are today the US, or in the southern parts of Argentina and Chile, among other regions (Lipschutz, 1955).
30. Independence took place around 1810, and countries throughout LA became republics, with the exception of Brazil, which itself became, an empire in 1822, and Cuba, which remained a Spanish colony until the end of the nineteenth century.
31. *Latifundium* was a unique LA kind of seigniorialist agrarian formation, which, in many aspects, resembles similar social relations in many parts of the world. According to this system, roughly, the landowner provided peasants – who were free men according to the law, and usually meztizos or descendants of poor Spanish settlers – with land for them to live in and cultivate for themselves, in exchange for work from the peasant and his family in the *hacienda. Latifundia* developed in symbiosis, as well, with independent small peasants who who concentrated in poor lands in the interstices of the haciendas, who worked for the landlords in harvest or other labour-intensive periods, and on their own plots for the rest of the year. The *latifundia* or *hacienda* system, as it is usually called, had its golden age during the nineteenth century throughout LA, but endured until the 1960s in some countries, although in a decaying form, as it was being slowly transformed into a modern, salary-based social relation. Agrarian reform accelerated this transformation in many countries.
32. Mexican history shows great complexity during the nineteenth century – it even formed a Napoleonic empire at one time, but then, only until they executed the Austrian-born emperor – including the evolution of its social policy institutions (Chapter 1). During the twentieth century, the political transition to modernity has also been remarkable in Mexico, even by world historical standards. The first great revolution of the twentieth century worldwide took place in Mexico in 1912. Moreover, it led to a seventy-year period where the state bureaucracy that was the offspring of the triumphant revolutionary process played the leading role it has only recently, rather unwillingly, relinquished in favour of a more democratic system. The bureaucracy ruled Mexico, mostly supported through an intricate and remarkably successful and enduring system of political alliances,

mainly with peasants and workers, in which social policies and state patronage played a relevant role (Chapter 1).

33. Australia, New Zealand and Canada.
34. By 1850, Chile had 1.4 million, and Peru and Colombia 2 million each. Meanwhile, Mexico had 7.6 million inhabitants, and Brazil 7.2 million (PUC 2000).
35. By 1925, Argentina's population had topped 10 million inhabitants, almost ten times the population it had by the mid-nineteenth century. Meanwhile, during the same period, Chile multiplied its population only 2.8 times (to 4 million inhabitants), Peru 2.5 times (to 5 million inhabitants), Colombia 3.4 times (to 7 million); Mexico only duplicated its population (to 15.8 million), and finally Brazil quadrupled its population (up to 30.3 million). The growth of the Rio de la Plata region during this period was unrivalled worldwide. It was even faster than the US, which quintupled its population (up to 116 million inhabitants), or Canada, which quadruped its own (up to 9.5 million). Significantly, the growth of Argentina during this period was surpassed only by countries such as Australia, which multiplied its population 15 times over during this same period, (to 5.9 million inhabitants). Moreover, during the first two decades of the twentieth century, Argentina increased its population at a rate of 3.2 per cent a year, even faster than Australia (2.2 per cent) and Canada (2.4 per cent), during that period. The immigration-fuelled high population growth rate of LA early developers maintained full speed until the end of the 1930s, but then started to slow down sharply. Argentina grew at 1.7 per cent a year during the following decades until the 1960s, based now mainly in internal population growth, much slower than Mexico (3.1 per cent), Colombia (2.8 per cent), Brazil (2.7 per cent), Peru (2.5 per cent) and even Chile (2.1 per cent). During the 1970s and 1980s, the population growth of Argentina slowed further, down to 1.5 per cent, compared to Mexico (2.6 per cent), Peru (2.5 per cent), Brazil (2.4 per cent), and Colombia (2.1 per cent) (PUC 2000, Table 1A11 and Figure 1.A12 in appendix). Presently (2000–2010), population in Argentina is growing at 1.1 per cent a year, similar to Chile and slower than all the rest of LA countries except Uruguay (0.7 per cent) and Cuba (0.3 per cent) (see Appendix Table 1.A11 and Figure 1.A10).
36. The inheritance of the Portuguese colonization overall, for its part, has been characterized more exploitation-oriented than settler colonies, and conferred a peculiar character to the national formation (Buarque de Holanda 1936) In his masterpiece *Raizes Do Brasil*, Sergio Buarque de Holanda notes the difference between Spanish and Portuguese colonizations: 'If the bricklayer characterizes the long run, rational, implantation of the Spanish settler, the sewer better pictures the urgency of the predatory character of the Portuguese colonizer.'
37. The architecture of Recife still shows many traces of Dutch dominion, The Dutch were to be displaced as well from slave trade dominance by the British, who would dominate such market during the eighteenth and nineteenth centuries (Blackburn 1996).
38. Of a total of 10.5 million African slaves imported from 1451 to 1860, over four million went to Brazil, equivalent to 39 per cent of the total. During the same period, British West Indies imported 1.6 million, and the French West Indies 1.8 million. North America, by contrast, appears importing only around 560,000 African slaves, the Atlantic Islands 115,000, and Europe 50,000 (Blackburn 1997).
39. African slave imports to the US totalled around 560,000 persons, according to the latest estimates (Herbert Klein, *The Atlantic Slave Trade*, Cambridge, 1999, p. 211, cited by Blackburn in 2005), which represented around 5 per cent of the

total African traffic from 1452 to 1860. Nevertheless, large imports from the West Indies, in addition to better living conditions that made possible a large number of US born slaves, raised their total number to nearly four million in 1860, the largest slave population in the world at that time.

40. Spanish America was a large slave importer as well, as it accounted for 1.6 million African slaves, 15 per cent of the total trafficked from 1541 to 1860, and most of them arrived to Cuba (Blackburn 1997). Nevertheless, many other LA countries received large numbers of African slaves as well, as is quite visible today at plain sight, from LA countries with Caribbean coasts, down to specific regions in Ecuador, Peru, or even elsewhere, as in Uruguay, for example. Nevertheless, in Spanish America with the exception of Cuba, slave-based economies nowhere acquired even near the importance it had in Brazil.
41. Ms Roxana Víquez Salazar, by then president of the Costa Rican Institute of Social Aid (IMAS), explained the Costa Rican exception using this argument in UNDP Seminars *Social Protection in an Insecure Era, South–South Dialogues.* Held in Beirut, Lebanon, in 2001, and in Santiago, Chile in 2002. (See http://videos.cep.cl/sw2002.)
42. Many aspects of this pattern may be recognized for example, in *Isla Grande de Chile*, in southern Chile.
43. The Spanish conquerors of the Aztec and Inca empires became rulers over tens of thousands of indigenous Americans who lived in large cities with monumental buildings. By contrast, the Spanish conquerors of Chile found relatively small and scattered concentrations of original peoples, who lived in the fringes of the Inca Empire, in the narrow valleys of the north and centre of Chile. In 1557, the *Oidor*, Fernando de Santillan, was sent by the king of Spain to assess the way in which Indians were being treated by their new masters in the valleys of La Serena and Santiago. He reports that less than 5,000 Indians were distributed in about 80 *Encomiendas* to the Spanish conquerors. Most of them were in charge of around 30 to 50 Indians, and no one had more than 300. He also reported horrible treatment of Indians in most cases (*Visita y Tasa del Oidor de Santillan*, published in full in 2004 by Professor Hernán Cortés, cited by Professor Erika Zúñiga Fuentes, Universidad de la Serena, La Serena, in a seminar in June 2004).
44. After independence from Spain (1810), the Chilean elite consolidated its hold over lands that the Crown had protected for Indian communities, and generalized the peculiar LA form of lordship known as *latifundia* (Lipschutz 1955). By the mid-nineteenth century they had already built a strong, centralized state, which made possible the expansion of Chilean territory 1500 kilometres to the north at the expense of much richer Peru, and Bolivia, which Chile defeated in two wars during the nineteenth century (1836–39 and 1879–81). After the second war in the north, and without pausing, they redirected their winning armies, and 'pacified' the Mapuche territory to the south of the Bio-Bio river, which had remained unconquered for three centuries. A few years later, in 1891, a civil war confronted different fractions of the elite, in part over the issue of mining property in the nitrate-rich north (Ramirez Necochea 1972). By the end of the nineteenth century, this settler elite had effectively consolidated its control over the present Chilean territory, which the State had already linked for the most part through an extensive railway network (Jocelyn-Holt 1999).

    The ruling of this elite was not effectively questioned until well into the twentieth century, and then only quite partially. In 1925, a military coup enforced a new constitution, as well as all the social policy laws that a populist government had been unsuccessfully trying to approve in a parliament dominated by the oligarchy. The basic institutions of what is defined in this book as Latin American Developmentalist Welfare State (LADWS) (see next section) were laid then. After that, LADWS bureaucracy, supported by emerging urban middle classes, increasingly by workers, and, finally, by peasants, became increasingly independent, and even confrontational, with the oligarchic elite. This process climaxed in their revolutionary showdown during the early 1970s. It was not before the Allende government had effectively and irreversibly deprived old oligarchy of most of their land, and all their dependant peasants, that the 1973 military coup put an end to revolutionary agitation. The ensuing military dictatorship was headed this time by a brutal general of conservative convictions, and occurred in the hateful political climate of counter-revolution. Pinochet relied on the younger descendants of the old elite, who had been formed in the ideas of Milton Freedman. As is known, such lessons inspired the well-groomed 'Chicago Boys' with fervour, and they put them into practice ruthlessly, with a vengeance (Chapter 9).

45. On the other hand, modern urban worker concentrations in industry also became important at the beginning of the century in the Río de la Plata region, as said, as well as other early developing LA zones such as Sao Paulo in Brazil. European immigrants flowed into these new industries, and brought with them the new revolutionary ideas, such as anarchism, and they led the first general strike in Brazil, in 1917, for example. Nevertheless, in the case of Brazil, these urban industries grew as a part of the export complex, which was based on traditional, based plantation products, mainly coffee. In 1920, for example, 38 per cent of urban industrial workers were in food related industries, while 25 per cent were in textiles and 9 per centin minerals, metallurgy chemicals, and others.
46. With the exception of Río de la Plata and other early developing regions, as said, where modern salariat and social policy institutions is of predominantly immigrant-urban origins.
47. In Brazil, after the Portuguese Crown and court were transferred to Rio de Janeiro in 1806, a few innovations in social policy matters were initiated, including the creation of the first university, for example. A limited primary educational system was organized later on by the empire, and then developed autonomously by the provincial states of the old republic in a quite fragmentary manner. Towards the 1930s, municipalities implemented modest social assistance and public health programmes, especially in regions around ports through which exports flowed
48. As has been mentioned, Uruguay and Argentina, the continent's *early developers*, experienced booming growth and expansion by the end of the nineteenth century and during the first decades of the century. Something similar took place in Chile, and in Cuba, for example, the sugar industry reduplicated its output during that decade (Chapters 4 to 7 and 9)
49. They adopted such Keynesian economic policies so enthusiastically in fact, that high inflation would become almost a trademark of LA economics during many decades, including a few hyperinflation episodes in some countries. All these processes have been extensively documented, and Neoliberal critics of the LADWS experience have vastly exaggerated the latter.
50. Including Itaipú, giant hydroelectric complex built in the *triple* frontera of Brazil, Argentina and Paraguay, where the *Iguazú* waterfall is located, which was the largest such plant in the world until the *Three Gore* Dam in China overtook it in 2004.

51. Such as the sugar beet and cellulose industries in Chile, for example, built during the 1950s, 1960s and 1970s, which also had a huge impact on agriculture, where they generated demand, financing and technological change.
52. In Chile, for example, public social expenditure, which was not significant before 1930, has expanded quite fast since then, and by the beginning of the 1970s, had reached levels that even today seem quite substantial (Figure 9A.3 in Appendix to Chapter 9).
53. Argentina and Uruguay based their health care systems mainly in *Obras Sociales*, and other union-administered health plans, financed by payroll discounts (Chapters 2, 3). These countries also developed a complementary public system, as a first-tier, universal access system. Chile, on the other hand, starting in the 1950s, built a centralized national public health system. This system, called *Servicio Nacional de Salud*, built a network of hospitals, emergency wards, and primary-level *Consultorios*, which by the early 1970s had encompassed the whole territory of the country, and even now cares for over 80 per cent of the population (Chapter 9). Only by the end of the 1980s, Brazil built a national health service that is public, and free at all levels. Nevertheless, the private sector continues to participate widely within this system (Chapter 6).
54. According to their lack of public expenditure in this item, some countries, such as El Salvador, Guatemala, Honduras and Nicaragua, still do not seem to have serious pension systems (Table 1.A8 in Appendix).
55. In Mexico, the revolutionary government took a new spin after the election of President Lázaro Cárdenas, who engaged in land reform, nationalized oil, and initiated wide social protection programmes. In other countries, such as Argentina and Brazil, progressive authoritarian governments came to power, headed by military leaders in the likes of Juan Domingo Peron (1943–55) and Getúlio Vargas (1930–45). In some cases such as Chile, popular fronts won elections (1938). In Costa Rica the Figueres governments led this process after the 1948 civil war (Chapters 2 to 9).
56. This is the case with Víctor Raúl Haya de la Torre's APRA, in Peru (Chapter 3).
57. Marriages played a not in considerable role in this game; quite conveniently, as it was common that newcomers happened to be more affluent, especially in cash terms.
58. *The theory of underdevelopment* in fact seemed to deny even the possibility of such outcome.
59. In Chile state employment has been lowered to around 10 per cent, meanwhile in Cuba, it accounts for most formal employment in the country.
60. Although the latter employed one or two sons – usually not very bright ones – in foreign ministries or other privileged bureaucratic niches.
61. These included the Military, Foreign Service, Central Banks, and other services, together with the executive and professional echelons of state enterprises, and public services such as education, including public universities, health services, and others. In Brazil, for example, it has been noted that state enterprises occupied dynamic spaces and positions within society. Even the idea of a 'cosmopolitan' state bourgeoisie has been advanced by some authors such as Lucian Martins, which have also underlined that together with the military, they were able to look beyond the walls of their factories where private entrepreneurs were, by contrast, confined.
62. In some countries, such as Brazil, such confrontation was mostly muted, as conservative military regimes headed LADWS for long periods. Nevertheless, they

confronted traditional elites all the same, as General Vargas – who was led to suicide by a conservative coup – and the Brazilian developmentalist military cadres of the 1960s demonstrate. In Argentina, Perón confronted oligarchies, which finally ousted and sent him in to exile. In other countries, such as Cuba and Chile during the 1960s and early 1970s, this confrontation assumed the character of full-blown popular revolutions, which ended up wiping out the traditional elites altogether, with a brutal retaliation in the case of Chile, which led President Allende to suicide. Mexico seems to follow almost a classic path in this matter, as a peasant revolution that erupted in 1912, followed by years of war, opened the way to the 70-year dominance of the bureaucratic-based *Partido Revolucionario Institucionalizado* (PRI). PRI presided over the rise, decline, and fall of the Mexican LADWS experience, and also over Neoliberal reforms. Irrespective of its revolutionary origins and self-proclaimed ideology, PRI seems to have presided over Mexican social and economic development in a remarkably consensual way, holding both traditional classes such as peasants, and also new emerging entrepreneurs and workers, within its constituency (Chapters 2 to 9)

63. Following the Cuban revolution, the US Kennedy Administration fostered land reform throughout the region, as part of its *Alliance for Progress* response to the Cuban challenge. LADWS had assumed land reform since its origins, as in the 1930s Lázaro Cárdenas practiced in Mexico, and the programmes of *APRA* and *Frente Popular* proposed for Peru and Chile, among others. However, little or nothing had in fact been achieved in the matter in most countries until the late 1960s. Then, under the bizarre twin impulse of the Cuban revolution and *Alliance for Progress*, land reform programmes were put into practice almost everywhere throughout LA. The Chilean parliament approved a strong agrarian reform law in the mid-1960s, and Salvador Allende put it into practice at the beginning of the 1970s, drastically expropriating most of country's cultivated land in less than two years. In Peru, the progressive Velasco Alvarado military government also carried out a significant agrarian reform, during the same years. Cuba, of course, had nationalized all land back in the early 1960s. In Brazil, the military dictatorship that took power in 1964 extended labour rights to the peasants, stimulating the modernization of rural social relations all the same, but without agrarian reform. In this sense, Brazil followed a conservative way out of the agrarian problem that is characteristic of transitions to modernity.
64. Notably, Venezuela, Colombia – where the land problem underlies the secular civil war, some countries in Central America, Bolivia and Paraguay, but even in Brazil it remains important, as the 'Sin Tierra' movement highlights.
65. From Chile in 1973, to El Salvador, after the Duarte government tried to implemented agrarian reform there in the 1980s.
66. Even the murderous Pinochet regime could not recreate *latifundia* after the coup, as much as it would have desired to. Rather, even though it did not show much respect for Chilean laws at large, it did comply with the Agrarian Reform law quite to the letter.
67. Cuba started in the 1960s, when it nationalized US property in 1962, following the *Bahía de Cochinos* (Bay of Pigs) failed US invasion, and followed suit with the property of traditional Cuban elites, as they confronted the revolution in bulk, and ended in exile in Miami. Much earlier, Mexico had nationalized oil companies during the Cárdenas government. Costa Rica had nationalized the banking system and the Instituto de Defensa del Café or Institute for Coffee Advocacy, in the wake of the 1948 civil war. Argentina had nationalized the oil

industry under President Frondizi (1958–62). In 1971, Chilean President Salvador Allende (1970–73) nationalized the US companies who had exploited most of the copper and other minerals throughout the twentieth century. He did so with the unanimous approval of the Chilean parliament where the opposition to his government was in majority, which points out to the widespread support that nationalizations enjoyed in LA at the time. Allende's nationalizations also included the banking system, and the textile and other large industries that had grown under ISI protection (Chapters 2, 3, 7, 8 and 9).

68. In Brazil, this started after the 1930 military coup headed by General Vargas, but especially during the 1964–85 military dictatorship, where military planners assigned great importance to this aspect. During this period, huge firms such as Petrobras, Vale do Rio Doce (steel), and others, were formed. In Chile, state firms pioneered electricity generation, oil, sugar, cellulose, iron, and steel industries, among others related to natural resources (Chapters 6, 9).
69. Even Pinochet's regime in Chile complied mostly not only with the agrarian reform law, as mentioned, but also with copper nationalization.
70. Much in the same way as massive land reform that took place in South East Asian countries during the 1950s, in the wake of war, was decisive for their latter economic performance.
71. As mentioned, it was mainly the Brazilian and Argentinean military who created LADWS in those countries in the first place, widely supported by rising entrepreneurs as well as urban workers, particularly in the Argentinean case. Authoritarian governments also pushed the concept to its peak in those countries, while the democratically elected governments that replaced them led to Neoliberal reforms. In Chile, LADWS may trace its origins to a military regime as well during the 1920s, but grew of age during *Frente Popular* democratic governments during the 1930s, and reached its peak during the reformist presidency of Frei Montalva and especially during the revolutionary government of President Salvador Allende, both of them widely supported by uprising workers and peasants. Pinochet, the military dictator that assassinated him, in turn inaugurated Neoliberal reforms in LA. It seems ironical that the Chilean experience of LADWS started with a military coup on 9/11/1924, and ended brutally in the 9/11/1973 coup. In Mexico, as said, PRI governments presided over both processes, as democratic governments did in Costa Rica and other counties. In Cuba the limit case of LADWS, this peculiar LA form of state is still in place, a result of popular uprising, revolution, and reaction against US intervention, and business friendly market reforms have not been yet implemented as in the rest of LA.
72. The former formulated the *Theory of Underdevelopment*, which signalled insufficiencies and distortions in LA development, and its great social inequalities. This theory attributed problems mainly to the persistence of an obsolete social structure, dominated by traditional oligarchies and foreign capital. It postulated independent national development, even faster social change, and greater state intervention, including an enhanced universal social protection system (Furtado 1964, 1965; Cardoso and Falleto 1973). In a certain sense, this line of thought postulated testing LADWS to its limit, modelled after socialist Cuba (Dos Santos 1972). On the contrary, opposition to LADWS coming from the right attributed problems to an exaggerated state presence in the economy, both for its widespread economic regulations as its direct involvement in production, as well as to high, protectionist, trade barriers. On the other hand, rightist criticism emphasized labour legislation and social security as additional culprits for economic

problems. It postulated state reduction, privatization, and a market economy based on private enterprise, open to world competition, together with the deregulation of labour markets and reform of social security.

73. Growth rates between the 1930s and the beginning of the 1980s were very high in most countries, and tended to accelerate during the 1960s and the early 1980s. Some countries such as Brazil attained record growth rates during that period – 6.1 per cent a year from 1960 to 1970 and 8.5 per cent a year from 1970 to 1980 – that only resemble what countries such as China is experiencing nowadays. Many countries, including big players Brazil, Mexico, and Argentina, have not achieved those growth rates ever since. In the case of Chile, they were only surpassed during the booming 1990s (Table 1.A2 in appendix, and Figures 9.A4-6 in Appendix to chapter 9).
74. It was named the *debt crisis*, as countries in the region stumbled into it after freewheeling lending by foreign banks during the late 1970s ended abruptly in 1982, and interest rates shot up. The damage was so severe that ECLAC called the 1980s the 'lost decade' for LA (Table 1.A2 in Appendix) (Ffrench-Davis 2003).
75. Unemployment in Chile surpassed one-third of the workforce during the worst years of the 1980s crisis, including over 10 per cent of the workforce that was hired by the *empleo mínimo* or minimum employment programmes. In contrast, in Costa Rica, where LADWS institutions and policies were maintained far more than other countries in the region, unemployment never exceeded 10 per cent of the workforce during the same period (Chapters 9 and 10).
76. Even today, policy makers in LA seem overcautious in fiscal matters, and overwilling to subordinate social spending to anti-inflationary restrictions, in good part, because they are still afraid of being pinned by Wall Street analysts with the populist label.
77. Peru under President Alan Garcia (1985–90) may be one example.
78. Notorious schemes were as the ones implemented by Minister Cavallo in Argentina.
79. Argentine and Chile, among others.
80. In the case of Brazil, for example, by the end of the period, exclusion remained quite high, coverage of the educational system was low even at the basic level, and the operation of the enormous social protection machinery was crossed by clientage, resource appropriation, and other bad practices. The authoritarian governments had also accentuated the conservative-corporate features that Brazilian experience had evidenced since the beginning. As a result, the model was subject of widespread criticism on the part of democratic and social movements at the onset of the liberalization and democratization period in the mid-1980s (Draibe 1989, 2002).
81. It was in effect put in place by force.
82. Everywhere, though in a more or less comprehensive manner, Neoliberal reforms promoted fiscal restraint, privatization and market-oriented policies, as well as more or less full openness and integration to the trends of globalization, together with deregulation of labour markets and social policy reform, as a way for both economic development and social policies.
83. Chile represented one extreme, pioneering the experience, and applying the model with extreme unilateralism. This may be explained, in part, by the particular historical origins of the Chilean elite and the characteristics of the Pinochet dictatorship. Brazil may represent the opposite face of the Neoliberal experience in LA. In this giant country, out of particular historical circumstances as well,

democratic governments did not buy the *Washington Consensus* wholesale and neither did the elite, which never became too enthusiastic with Neoliberalism. In the Argentinean case, a *Peronista* government, democratically elected and re-elected during the 1990s, made frequent and strident allegiances to the *Washington Consensus*, and reforms inspired in this paradigm were certainly enforced to a certain extent, in this country as well as Uruguay, which culminated in a cataclysmic crisis in 2002. Nevertheless, the significantly better overall condition of this region regarding social policies could not be entirely disregarded by Neoliberal reformists, and in practical terms, such policies were applied in lesser degree than in the Chilean case. Costa Rica, for its part, applied a very moderate version of the new model, meanwhile Cuba has skipped it altogether (see previous section and Chapters 2 to 9 and Tables 1.A1–9 in appendix).

84. Even in pioneering Chile, the transitional democratic governments that succeeded the military dictatorship during the 1990s were themselves responsible for a good part of Neoliberal implementations. Nevertheless, they certainly marked strong differences with their predecessor, especially regarding social policies.
85. Perhaps this may explain why Chile became the only LA country where Neoliberal reforms implied a quite brutal reduction of the state during the Pinochet dictatorship. Particularly within the realm of social policy, where public spending was slashed in the wake of the coup, as said, and public social policy institutions have yet to recover their pre-coup level (Figure 9A.3 in Appendix to Chapter 9).
86. In Chile, for example, Pinochet's ruthless manner of complying with the Chilean agrarian reform law threw peasants out to the roads by the hundreds of thousands in the wake of the 1973 coup, meanwhile other 'loyal' peasants and the old landowners' sons were assigned the small farms that they were entitled by the law (Chapter 9). Civil wars that raged through Central America and Peru during recent decades, and that still go on in countries like Colombia, have provoked the same kind of forceful expulsion of peasants.
87. In Brazil, it has been estimated that due to these changes, the personal income of medical doctors, for example, has been reduced by as far as 20 per cent, which may introduce some ambiguity in their demands, no longer for differentiated market provided social services but for universal high quality public services as well.
88. The only LA country that lowered its public social expenditure during the crisis was Colombia (−1.7 GDP percentage points), while Ecuador stagnated.
89. Maria Graham, a friend of Charles Darwin who lived in Chile for a few years in the 1850s, was a keen observer of the lifestyles of the Chilean 'upper' classes at the time. She wrote that more comforts could be found in a fisherman's hut in Scotland, that in the 'mansions' of the Chilean elite.
90. In fact, 'change' was the central campaign motto of Joaquin Lavin, the rightist candidate narrowly defeated by Lagos. Lavin rarely, if ever, mentioned traditional Neoliberal slogans, such as privatization or reduction of the state, during his campaign, being quite aware of their unpopularity.
91. Public social expenditure indeed slowed the fast growth pace experienced during the previous democratic governments, and Lagos' finance minister remained quite deaf to calls from ECLAC to increase the public expenditure and deficit in order to overcome the long recession (Ffrench-Davis 2001, 2002, 2003). Free trade agreements (FTA) continue to be signed all around, including with the US

and the EU. Meanwhile, relations with bordering countries show worrying strains that had not been experienced for several decades.

92. Following a pattern that has been followed for much of the last decade, the main destiny for Chilean direct investment abroad during the first quarter of 2004 was Argentina, country that accounted for 70 per cent of operations. Countries that followed were Peru (5.4 per cent), Colombia (3.8 per cent) and Ecuador (3.8 per cent). Accumulated figures show Argentina accounts for slightly over half of foreign direct investment by Chilean entrepreneurs between 1990 and 2004, with a figure of over US $ 14,000 million. Brazil, even though less active during the last quarter, retains second place, with 14.5 per cent of the overall total, closely followed by Peru (13.8 per cent) (CENDA 2004: 04/04).
93. Tables in the Appendix are available for download in Excel format at:http://cep.cl/UNRISD/Papers/Introduction/Introduction.xls.

## References


Abrahamson, P. (1999). *The Male Breadwinner Model under Change: The Case of Germany Towards the 21st Century* (Draft). Copenhagen: University of Copenhagen.

Anderson, P. (1974). *Lineages of the Absolutist State*. London: Verso.

Blackburn, R. (1997). *The Making of New World Slavery*. London: Verso.

Briggs, A. (1961). 'The Welfare State in Historical Perspective'. *Archives Européennes de Sociologie* 2, 228.

Cardoso, F. and Falleto, E. (1973). *Dependency and Development in Latin America*. Berkeley: University of California Press.

Castles, F. G. (1993). *The Welfare State Reader*. Cambridge: Polity Press.

CELADE/BID (Centro Latinoamericano de Demografía/Banco Interamericano de Desarrollo) (1996). *Impacto de las tendencias demográficas sobre los sectores sociales en América Latina; contribución al diseño de políticas y programas*. Serie E (45), CELADE: Santiago de Chile.

CENDA (2004a). *Centro de Estudios Nacionales de Desarrollo Alternativo. Base de Datos Cuadernos de Información Económica de Prensa*. Santiago: CENDA.

CENDA (2004b). 'Propuesta para una Nueva Política de Integración Regional'. http://cep.cl/CENDA/Proyectos/Minsegpres/Propuesta_Integracion.doc. Accessed on 17 November 2004.

CENDA (2004c). 'Propuesta para una Reforma del Sistema de AFP'. http://cep.cl/CENDA/Cen_Documentos/Indice_AFP_CENDA/Varios_CENDA_AFP/Propuesta_Reforma.doc. Accessed on 17 November 2004.

CENDA (2004d). 'Propuesta para un Nuevo Esquema de Royalty e Impuestos para la Minería'. http://cep.cl/CENDA/Cen_Documentos/Cobre/Impuestos_Mineria_0408.doc. Accessed on 17 November 2004.

Chang, Ha-Joon (2002). 'The Role of Social Policy in Economic Development. Some Theoretical Reflections and Lessons from East Asia'. Background paper for the UNRISD Project on Social Policy in a Development Context. Geneva: UNRISD.

Cochrane, A., Clarke, J. and Sharon, G. (1997). *Comparing Welfare States*. London: Sage.

Dornbusch, R. and Sebastian, E. (eds) (1991). 'The Macroeconomics of Populism in Latin America'. National Bureau of Economic Research Conference Report. Cambridge, MA: NBER.

Dos Santos, T. (1972). *Socialismo o Facismo, El Dilema de América Latina*. Buenos Aires: Editora Periferia.

Draibe, S. M. (2003). 'A política social do governo FHC e o sistema de proteção social', in B. Sallum, (ed.) *Revista Tempo Social*, 15 (2).
Draibe, S. M. (2002). 'Brasil 1980–2000: Proteção e insegurança sociais em tempos difíceis' in 'Social Protection in an Insecure Era: A South–South Exchange on Alternative Social Policy Responses to Globalization', Draft Report on the SU/TCDC, UNDP Inter-Regional Workshop. Santiago: UNDP. http://videos.cep.cl/sw2002. Accessed on 17 November 2004.
Draibe, S. M. (1995). 'América Latina: O Sistema de Proteção Social na Década da Crise e das Reformas, Cadernos de Pesquisa'. Sao Paulo: NEPP/UNICAMP.
Draibe, S. M. and Aureliano, L. (1989a). 'A especificidade do Welfare State Brasileiro. A Política Social em Tempo de Crise'. *Economia Desenvolvimento*, 3. Brasilia: MPAS/CEPAL.
Draibe, S. M. and Aureliano, L. (1989b). 'An Overview of Social Development in Brazil'. *CEPAL Review*, 39, 47–61.
ECLAC (2002). *Statistical Yearbook*. Santiago: ECLAC.
Esping-Andersen, G. (2002). *Why We Need a New Welfare State*. Oxford: Oxford University Press.
Esping-Andersen, G. (1999). *Social Foundations of Post-Industrial Economies*. Oxford: Oxford University Press.
Esping-Andersen, G. (ed.) (1996). *Welfare States in Transition: National Adaptations in Global Economies*. London: Sage.
Esping-Andersen, G. (1994). 'Equality and Work in the Post-Industrial Lifecycle' in Miliband, D. (ed.) *Reinventing the Left*. Cambridge: Polity.
Esping-Andersen, G. (1990). *Three Worlds of Welfare Capitalism*. Princeton: Princeton University Press.
Fazio, H. (2004). *Cartas Económicas*. http://cep.cl/CENDA/Cen_Documentos/Cartas_Economicas. Accessed on 17 November 2004.
Fazio, H. (2003). *Quienes Gobiernan America Latina?* Santiago: LOM Ediciones.
Fazio, H. (2000). *La transnacionalización de la economía chilena: Mapa de la extrema riqueza al año 2000*. Santiago: LOM Ediciones.
Ferrera, M. (1997). 'General Introduction', in U. Ascoli, D. Bouget, M. Ferrera, M. Maravall, Y. Mény and M. Rhodes (eds), *Comparer les systèmes de protection sociale en Europe du SUD*. Paris: MIRE.
Ferrera, M. (1996). 'The Southern Model of Welfare in Social Europe'. *Journal of European Social Policy*, 6 (1), 17–37.
Ffrench-Davis, R. (2003). Press clippings in CENDA Cuadernos de Información Económica de Prensa and interventions in panels in CENDA. http://www.cenda.cep.cl.
Ffrench-Davis, R. (2002). *Economic Reforms in Chile from Dictatorship to Democracy*. Michigan: Michigan University Press.
Ffrench-Davis, R. (ed.) (2001). *Financial Crises in 'Successful' Emerging Economies*. Washington DC: Brookings Institution Press/ECLAC.
Flaquer, L. (2000). 'Family Policy and Welfare State in Southern Europe'. Working Paper, 185. Barcelona: Institut de Ciencias Politicas i Socials.
Flora, P. (1986). *Growth to Limits*. Berlin: Praeger.
Flora, P. and Heidenheimer, A. J. (eds) (1986). *The Development of Welfare States in Europe and America*. New Brunswick: Transaction Books and the HIWED Project.
Fukuyama, F. (2004). *State-Building: Governance and World Order in the 21st Century*. Ithaca, NY: Cornell University Press.
Furtado, C. (1965). *Dialéctica del desarrollo*. Mexico: Fondo de Cultura Económica.
Furtado, C. (1964). *Desarrollo y subdesarrollo*. Buenos Aires: EUDEBA.
Giddens, A. (ed.) (2001). *The Global Third Way Debate*. Cambridge: Polity Press.

Giddens, A. (1998). *The Third Way: The Renewal of Social Democracy*. Cambridge: Polity Press.
Giddens, A. (1994). *Beyond Left and Right*. Cambridge: Polity Press.
Gill, S., Truman, P. and Juan, Y. (2004). *Keeping the Promise of Old Age Income Security in Latin America: A Regional Study of Social Security Reforms*. Washington DC: World Bank. http://wbln1018.worldbank.org/LAC/LAC.nsf/0/146EBBA3371508E785256CBB005C29B4?Opendocument. Accessed on 17 November 2004.
Goldman Sachs (2003). 'Dreaming With BRICs. The Path to 2050'. *Global Economics Paper, 99*. Economic Research from the GS Financial Workbench.
Gough, I. (2001). 'Globalization and Regional Welfare Regimes: the East Asian Case'. *Global Social Policy*, 1 (2), 163–89.
Gough, I. (1999). 'Welfare Regimes: Some Initial Notes on Adapting the Framework to Developing Countries'. European Forum Conference Paper WS/95, European University Institute.
Haslam, J. (2004). 'The Death of Allende's Chile: A Case of Assisted Suicide'. Manuscript. London: Verso.
Hobsbawm, E. (2000). *The Age of Capital*. London: Weidenfeld & Nicolson.
Hobsbawm, E. (1998). *The Communist Manifesto*. Modern Edition. London: Verso.
Hobsbawm, E. (1995). *The Age of Extremes*. Maine: Abacus.
Hobsbawm, E. (1989). *The Age of Empire*. Maine: Abacus.
Hobsbawm, E. (1988). *The Age of Revolutions*. Maine: Abacus.
Holliday, I. (2000). 'Productivist Welfare Capitalism: Social Policy in East Asia'. *Political Studies*, 48, 706–23.
INP (Instituto de Normalización Provisional) (2004). 'Chile: Proyección Previsional de la Población Afiliada y Cotizante a las AFP'. Santiago: INP. http://cep.cl/Cenda/Proyectos/INP/INP.htm.
IRES (Institut de recherche économique et sociale) (1984). *Protection Sociale dans le Monde*. Paris: IRES.
Jocelyn-Holt, A. (1999). *La Independencia de Chile*. Santiago: Planeta.
Kuhnle, S. (2002). 'Productive Welfare in Korea: Moving Towards a European Welfare State Type?'. Paper ECPR Joint Sessions of Workshops. Torino: ECPR.
Kwon, H-j. (2003). *Social Policy in a Development Context*. Draft. Geneva: UNRISD.
Kwon, H.-j. (2002a). 'Transforming the Developmental Welfare State: A Comparative Study of the East Asian countries'. A Project within the UNRISD Research Area 'Social Policy in a Development Context'. Geneva: UNRISD. http://cep.cl/CENDA/Proyectos/UNRISD/References/Project_Proposal_Kwon.doc.
Kwon, H.-j. (2002b). 'The Economic Crisis and the Politics of Welfare Reform in Korea'. Background paper for a Project within the UNRISD Research Area 'Social Policy in a Development Context'. Geneva: UNRISD.
Kwon, H.-j. (1999). *The Welfare State in Korea: The Politics of Legitimation*. London: St Martin's Press.
Lipschutz, A. (1955). 'El Problema Racial en la Conquista de América y el Mestizaje', in J. Cademártori (1972) *La Economía Chilena*. Santiago: Cormorán.
MacDermott, J., Karshenas, M., Kwon, H-J. and Valentine, V. (2003). *Social Policy in a Development Context: Social Policy and Economic Development in the Middle East and North Africa*. Geneva: UNRISD.
Mesa-Lago, C. (2002). 'Models of Development, Social Policy and Reform in Latin America'. Background paper for the UNRISD Project 'Social Policy in a Development Context'. Geneva: UNRISD.

Mesa-Lago, C. (1994). *La reforma de la seguridad social en America Latina y el Caribe.* Santiago: Ciedess.

Mesa-Lago, C. (1989). *Ascent to Bankruptcy.* Pittsburgh: University of Pittsburgh Press.

Mesa-Lago, C. (1978). *Social Security in Latin America.* Pittsburgh: University of Pittsburgh Press.

Midgley, J. (2003). 'Assets in the Context of Welfare Theory: A Developmentalist Interpretation'. Working Paper 03–10, Center for Social Development. Washington D.C.: University of Washington Press.

Midgley, J. and Sherraden, M. (2000). 'The Social Development Perspective in Social Policy', in J. Midgley, B. Martin, T. Livermore and M. Livermore (eds), *Handbook of Social Policy.* London: Sage, pp. 435–46.

Midgley, J. and Sherraden, M. (1999). 'Growth, Redistribution and Welfare: Toward Social Investment', *Social Service Review* (March), 3–21.

Midgley, J. and Sherraden, M. (1995). *Social Development: The Developmental Perspective in Social Welfare.* London: Sage.

MIRE-DRESS (1999). *Comparing Social Welfare Systems in Nordic Europe and France.* Edited by P. Abrahamson, D. Blancher, A. Hatland, N. Lefaucheur, J. Palme and H. Uutisalo. Paris: MIRE-CNRS.

MIRE-DRESS (1997). *Comparer les systèmes de protection sociale en Europe du SUD.* Edited by U. Ascoli, D. Bouget, M. Ferrera, M. Maravall, Y. Mény and M. Rhodes. Paris: MIRE.

MIRE-DRESS (1996). *Comparer les systèmes de protection sociale en Europe,* vol. 2. Edited by W. Abelshauser, R. Delorme, B. Jobert and F. X. Kaufmann. Paris: MIRE.

MIRE-DRESS (1995). *Comparer les systèmes de protection sociale dans l'Europe,* vol. 1. Edited by A. M. Guillemard, J. Lewis, S. Ringen and R. Salis, Paris: MIRE.

MIRE-DRESS (1990). 'Les comparaisons internationales des politiques et des systèmes de sécurité sociale'. Paris: Association Internationale de Sécurité Sociale.

Mkandawire, T. (2002). 'Courrier de la Planète: Développement, environnement, les défis d'un monde solidaire'. Draft country papers on Social Policy in LA in a Development Context 67 (1).

Mkandawire, T. (2001). *Social Policy in a Development Context.* Geneva: UNRISD.

Mkandawire, T. and Virginia, R. (2000). 'Globalization and Social Development after Copenhagen: Premises, Promises and Policies'. Project entitled 'Geneva 2000: The Next Step in Social Development'. Geneva: UNRISD. http://www.unrisd.org/unrisd/website/document.nsf/(httpPublications)/DEA5491C2B61C47980256B67005B74CB?OpenDocument.

Ocampo, J. (2002). 'Globalization and Development'. Paper presented at the International Seminar on 'New International Trends for Economic Development'. Rio de Janeiro: BNDES.

Offe, C. (1984). *Contradictions of the Welfare State.* Cambridge: MIT Press.

Orloff, A. S. (2003). 'Systems of Social Provision and Regulation'. Paper presented at Annual Meeting of the Canadian Political Science Association. Halifax, 31 May.

Orloff, A. S., Clemens, E. and Adams, J. (2004). *Remaking Modernity: Politics, History and Sociology.* Durham, NC: Duke University Press.

Orloff, A. S., Clemens, E. and Adams, J. (2003). 'Social Theory, Modernity, and the Three Waves of Historical Sociology'. Working Paper 206. New York: Russell Sage Foundation.

Orloff, A. S., Clemens, E. and Adams, J. (1988). 'Understanding American Social Politics', in M. Weir, A. S. Orloff and T. Skocpol (eds), *The Political Origins of America's Belated Welfare State.* Princeton: Princeton University Press, pp. 37–80.

Pierson, P. (2004). *Politics in Time: History, Institutions and Social Analysis*. Princeton: Princeton University Press.

Pierson, P. (ed.) (2001). *The New Politics of the Welfare State*. Oxford: Oxford University Press.

Pierson, P. (1998). 'Irresistible Forces, Immovable Objects: Post-Industrial Welfare States Confront Permanent Austerity'. *Journal of European Public Policy*, 5 (4), 539–60.

Pierson, P. (1994). *Dismantling the Welfare State? Reagan, Thatcher and the Politics of Retrenchment*. Cambridge: Cambridge University Press.

Powell M., and Barrientos, A. (2004). 'Welfare Regimes and the Welfare Mix'. *European Journal of Politics* 43 (1), 83–105.

PT (Partido dos Trabalhadores) (2002). 'Programa de Governo'. http://www.pt.org.br/.

Ramirez, H. (1972). *Balmaceda y la contrarevolución de 1891*. Santiago: Editorial Universitaria.

Ricupero, R. (2004). Farewell Speech as Director of UNCTAD, Geneva, September 12, 2004. http://cep.cl/UNRISD/References/UNCTAD/Ricupero.pdf. Accessed on 17 November 2004.

Riesco, M. (2004). 'Pay Your Taxes! Corporate Social Responsibility in the Mining Industry in Chile'. Paper prepared for UNRISD. http://cep.cl/UNRISD/UNRISD_CSR/Mining_CSR_Chile.doc.

Riesco, M. (2003). 'Social Policy in Late Industrializers: A Comparative Study of Latin America'. UNRISD Project. Geneva: UNRISD. http://cep.cl/UNRISD/Papers/LA_Research_Questions/UNRISD_Paper.doc. Accessed on 17 November 2004.

Riesco, M. (2002). 'Chile: 20 Years of Liberal Experiences in Social Protection'. Brief of the Report to UNDP Inter-Regional Workshop, Santiago, Chile, May 14-17, 2002. http://videos.cep.cl/sw2002/Informe_Chile/SW2002_Chile_Brief.html. Accessed on 17 November 2004.

Riesco, M. (1995). 'Honour and Glory to the Jacobins!' *New Left Review*, 212, 55–67.

Rimlinger, G. V. (1971). *Welfare Policy and Industrialisation in Europe, America, and Russia*. New York: Wiley.

Sabel, C. F. and Zeitlin, J. (2004). 'Active Welfare, Experimental Governance, Pragmatic Constitutionalism: The New Transformation of Europe'. Revised draft of a paper presented at International Conference of the Hellenic Presidency of the EU, 'The Modernisation of the European Social Model & EU Policies and Instruments', Ioannina, Greece, 21–22 May 2003.

Skocpol, T. (1992). *Protecting Soldiers and Mothers*. Cambridge, MA: Harvard University Press.

Sen, A. (1999). *Development as Freedom*. New York: Alfred A. Knopf.

Stallings, B. (2002). 'Social Protection in an Insecure Area: A South–South Exchange on Alternative Social Policies Responses to Globalization'. Inter-Regional Workshop, Santiago, Chile, 14–17 May 2002. http://videos.cep.cl/sw2002/SW2002_Movies.html. Accessed on 17 November 2004.

Standing, G. (2002). 'Globalisation: The Eight Crises of Social Protection'. UNDP Inter-Regional Workshop, Santiago, Chile, 14–17 May.

Stiglitz, R. (2003). Press clippings in CENDA Cuadernos de Información Económica de Prensa. http://cenda.cep.cl

Suleiman, E. (2003). *The Dismantling of Democratic States*. Princeton, NJ: Princeton University Press.

Taylor-Gooby, P. (2001). 'The Silver Age of the Welfare State: Resilience and Contingency'. Presented at the Hellenic Social Policy Association Inaugural Conference, 10–13 May.

Taylor-Gooby, P. (ed.) (2000). *Risk, Trust and Welfare*. Basingstoke: Macmillan Press.

Taylor-Gooby, P. (1998). 'Convergence and Divergence in European Welfare States', in R. Jowell, J. Curtice, L. Brook and A. Park (eds), *European Social Attitudes: The 3rd ISSP Report.* Aldershot: SCPR.

*The Economist* (2002). 'Brazil's Presidential Election: The Meaning of Lula for Latin American Democracy. How Good for Brazil?', 5 October.

Therborn, G. (2002). 'Between Sex and Power: The Family in the World of the 20th Century'. Yale Colloquium on Comparative Social Research. New Haven, Yale Papers.

Therborn, G. (ed.) (1999). *Globalizations and Modernities.* Stockholm: FRN.

Therborn, G. (1995). *European Modernity and Beyond: The Trajectory of European Societies, 1945–2000.* London: Sage.

Théret, B. (1995). 'De la comparabilité des systémes nationaux de protection sociale dans les sociétés salariales'. Paris: Université Paris Dauphine.

Tittmuss, R. (1958). *Essays on the Welfare State.* London: Allen and Unwin.

UNDP (2002). 'Social Protection in an Insecure Area: A South–South Exchange on Alternative Social Policies Responses to Globalization'. Final Report. Inter-Regional Workshop, Santiago, Chile, 14–17 May 2002. http://videos.cep.cl/sw2002/Informe_Final/SW2002_Final_Report.html. Accessed on 17 November 2004.

UNRISD (2005). 'The Pay Your Taxes Debate!' http://www.corporate-accountability.org/docs/UNRISD_taxes-Chile_Riesco.pdf. Accessed September 2005.

UNRISD (2003a). 'Late Industrializers and the Development of the Welfare State'. Draft paper. Geneva: UNRISD.

UNRISD (2003b). 'Sub-Saharan Africa and the Challenge of Social Policy'. Report of the UNRISD Methodology Workshop, Social Policy in a Development Context, 27–8 February 2003, Rhodes University, South Africa.

UNRISD (2002). 'Social Policy in a Development Context: East Asia, Latin America and Sub-Saharan Africa'. Project Proposal. Ford Foundation. http://cep.cl/UNRISD/References/unrisd_ford.doc

Wilenski, H. L. (1975). *The Welfare State and Equality.* Berkeley: University of California Press.

Williamson, J. (2002). 'Did the Washington Consensus Fail? Institute for International Economics'. Outline of remarks at the Center for Strategic & International Studies, 6 November 2002. http://www.iie.com/publications/papers/williamson1102.htm.

World Bank (2004). 'Urban Population in World Bank Regions by City Size'. http://www.worldbank.org/urban/env/population-regions.htm. Accessed on 11 January 2006.

# Appendix 1.A: Tables and Figures[93]

*Table 1.A1* Latin American and the Caribbean countries, by demographic transition groups

| *Classes of Demographic Transition: CELADE Definition* | *Countries* |
|---|---|
| *Group I. Early transition*<br>Countries with high birth rate and mortality, with moderate natural growth, around 2.5 per cent. Countries in this group have a very young age structure, and a high dependency ratio. | Bolivia and Haití |
| *Group II. Moderate transition*<br>Countries with high birth rate, but moderate level of mortality. Because of this, their natural growth natural is still high, around 3 per cent. Lowering of mortality, especially during the first year, has caused a rejuvenation of the age structure, which also causes a high dependency ratio. | El Salvador, Guatemala, Honduras, Nicaragua and Paraguay |
| *Group III. In full transition*<br>Countries with moderate birth rates and low or moderate mortality, which determines a moderate natural growth rate, around 2 per cent. As lowering of fecundity is recent, the age structure is still relatively young, even though the dependency ratio has already decreased. | Brasil, Colombia, Costa Rica, Ecuador, México, Panama, Peru, Dominicana Republic, Venezuela, and Guyana, Surinam and Trinidad and Tobago in the Caribbean |
| *Group IV. Advanced transition*<br>Countries with low birth rates and low or moderate mortality rates, which translates in low natural growth rates, around one per cent. | Argentina, Chile, Cuba and Uruguay; Bahamas, Barbados, Guadalupe, Jamaica, Mastirique and Puerto Rico, in the Caribbean. |
| Two sub-groups may be defined:<br>Countries that have had low fecundity and mortality for a long time (Argentina, Uruguay and, in lesser terms, Cuba) and consequently, have growth and age structures that are similar to developed Countries;<br>Countries that, although having recently attained very low fecundity and mortality rates, still have higher growth rates because their population is relatively young. | |

*Source*: CELADE, 1992; CELADE/BID 1996.

*Table 1.A2* Population and GDP: Latin America and the Caribbean countries, by demographic transition groups

| *Transitional categories / countries* | *Total population (thousands)* | | | *Total population growth 2000–2010 (% per year)* | *GDP (ppp), 2002 (millions of international dollars)* | *GDP per capita (PPP US$) 2001* | *GDP per capita (ranking) 2001* | *GDP growth (average % per year)* | | | | |
|---|---|---|---|---|---|---|---|---|---|---|---|---|
| | *2005* | *2010* | *2025* | | | | | *1960–2002* | *1960–1970* | *1970–1980* | *1980–1990* | *1990–2000* |
| *Early transition* | *18,361* | *20,223* | *25,650* | *1.9* | *34,996* | *2,081* | *145* | *1.6%* | *1.5%* | *4.1%* | *– 0.1 %* | *1.3%* |
| Bolivia | 9,219 | 10,229 | 13,131 | 2.1 | 21,650 | 2,300 | 138 | 2.6% | 2.7% | 3.9% | 0.1% | 3.7% |
| Haiti | 9,141 | 9,994 | 12,519 | 1.8 | 13,346 | 1,860 | 153 | 0.6% | 0.2% | 4.3% | –0.4% | –1.3% |
| *Moderate transition* | *39,293* | *44,078* | *57,955* | *2.3* | *138,102* | *4,109* | *112* | *3.6%* | *5.4%* | *4.8%* | *0.9%* | *3.7%* |
| Belize | 266 | 294 | 370 | 2.0 | 1,539 | 5,690 | 90 | 5.4% | 5.2% | 7.3% | 4.9% | 4.5% |
| El Salvador | 6,840 | 7,441 | 9,062 | 1.7 | 31,378 | 5,260 | 97 | 3.0% | 5.6% | 2.3% | –0.4% | 4.6% |
| Guatemala | 12,932 | 14,631 | 19,816 | 2.5 | 48,908 | 4,400 | 106 | 3.9% | 5.5% | 5.7% | 0.9% | 4.1% |
| Honduras | 7,286 | 8,203 | 10,656 | 2.4 | 17,701 | 2,830 | 128 | 3.9% | 4.8% | 5.4% | 2.4% | 3.3% |
| Nicaragua | 5,771 | 6,529 | 8,696 | 2.5 | 13,190 | 2,450 | 135 | 2.4% | 6.8% | 0.3% | –1.4% | 4.1% |
| Paraguay | 6,199 | 6,980 | 9,355 | 2.4 | 25,386 | 5,210 | 99 | 4.2% | 4.3% | 8.9% | 2.8% | 2.0% |
| *Full transition* | *418,623* | *447,502* | *520,995* | *1.3* | *2,968,667* | *7,164* | *73* | *4.2%* | *6.0%* | *6.8%* | *1.7%* | *3.0%* |
| Brazil | 181,109 | 192,240 | 220,509 | 1.2 | 1,354,997 | 7,360 | 69 | 4.5% | 6.1% | 8.5% | 1.5% | 2.7% |
| Colombia | 45,876 | 49,665 | 59,758 | 1.6 | 278,562 | 7,040 | 73 | 4.1% | 5.3% | 5.5% | 3.6% | 2.5% |
| Costa Rica | 4,421 | 4,857 | 5,929 | 1.9 | 34,855 | 9,460 | 55 | 4.7% | 6.1% | 5.6% | 2.4% | 5.2% |
| Ecuador | 13,762 | 14,899 | 17,796 | 1.6 | 45,921 | 3,280 | 121 | 3.8% | 4.3% | 7.0% | 2.0% | 1.8% |
| Guyana | 891 | 923 | 1,045 | 0.7 | 3,261 | 4,690 | 103 | 1.5% | 3.5% | 1.3% | –3.4% | 4.9% |

| | | | | | | | | | | | | |
|---|---|---|---|---|---|---|---|---|---|---|---|---|
| Mexico | 105,831 | 112,891 | 130,196 | 1.3 | 904,570 | 8,430 | 62 | 4.4% | 6.7% | 6.7% | 1.8% | 3.5% |
| Panama | 3,062 | 3,266 | 3,779 | 1.3 | 18,127 | 5,750 | 89 | 4.4% | 7.9% | 4.1% | 1.4% | 5.1% |
| Peru | 27,741 | 29,885 | 35,518 | 1.5 | 134,079 | 4,570 | 105 | 3.0% | 5.3% | 3.6% | –0.8% | 4.0% |
| Dominican Republic | 9,101 | 9,708 | 11,165 | 1.3 | 57,190 | 7,020 | 74 | 5.2% | 5.8% | 6.9% | 2.6% | 5.9% |
| Suriname | 434 | 452 | 525 | 0.8 | 1,998 | 4,599 | 104 | | | | | |
| Venezuela | 26,395 | 28,716 | 34,775 | 1.7 | 135,107 | 5,670 | 91 | 2.3% | 5.1% | 2.7% | 0.8% | 2.0% |
| *Advanced transition* | *79,926* | *83,718* | *93,617* | *0.9* | *779,478* | *10,262* | *61* | *2.6%* | *4.1%* | *2.9%* | *0.4%* | *4.7%* |
| Antilles Dutch | 227 | 237 | 257 | 0.9 | | | | | | | | |
| Argentina | 39,266 | 41,474 | 47,160 | 1.1 | 412,666 | 11,320 | 49 | 1.9% | 3.9% | 3.0% | –1.5% | 4.5% |
| Bahamas | 330 | 354 | 415 | 1.4 | 5,089 | 16,270 | 38 | 3.9% | 8.2% | 2.8% | 2.9% | 1.8% |
| Barbados | 276 | 282 | 297 | 0.4 | 4,114 | 15,560 | 40 | 2.8% | 6.6% | 2.8% | 1.2% | 1.5% |
| Chile | 16,105 | 17,010 | 19,548 | 1.1 | 153,086 | 9,190 | 57 | 4.2% | 4.1% | 2.9% | 3.8% | 6.5% |
| Cuba | 11,345 | 11,516 | 11,798 | 0.3 | 59,662 | 5,259 | 98 | | | | | |
| Guadalupe | 483 | 510 | 569 | 1.1 | | | | | | | | |
| Jamaica | 2,693 | 2,816 | 3,245 | 0.9 | 10,421 | 3,720 | 117 | 1.8% | 4.8% | -0.8% | 2.5% | 0.7% |
| Martinique | 409 | 421 | 450 | 0.6 | | | | | | | | |
| Puerto Rico | 4,015 | 4,158 | 4,478 | 0.7 | 95,811 | 23,860 | | 4.9% | 7.9% | 4.3% | 3.6% | 4.1% |
| Trinidad and Tobago | 1,334 | 1,374 | 1,493 | 0.6 | 12,299 | 9,100 | 59 | | | | | |
| Uruguay | 3,444 | 3,566 | 3,907 | 0.7 | 26,330 | 8,400 | 63 | 1.4% | 1.4% | 3.0% | 0.0% | 3.0% |
| *Latin America & Caribbean* | *556,203* | *595,521* | *698,217* | *1.4* | *3,921,243* | *7,050* | *73* | *3.8%* | *5.5%* | *6.0%* | *1.4%* | *3.2%* |

*Sources*: CELADE, UNDP, ECLAC, ILO, WB. Calculations based on data sheets available at http://cep.cl/UNRISD/Papers/Introduction/Introduction.xls. Classification criteria was established by CELADE, based on demographic data.

*Table 1.A3* Urbanization: Latin America and the Caribbean countries, by demographic transition groups

| *Transitional Categories/Countries* | | | | | *Population of the two main Metropolitan Areas* | | | | |
|---|---|---|---|---|---|---|---|---|---|
| | *Percentage of urban population* | | | | *Percentage of total population* | | | *Average annual growth rates* | |
| | *1960* | *1985* | *2005* | *2015* | *1970* | *1980* | *1990* | *1970–1980* | 1980–1990 |
| *Early transition* | *26.2* | *38.9* | *55.2* | *61.0* | *12.6* | *17.5* | *28.3* | *3.4* | *4.5* |
| Bolivia | 36.8 | 50.5 | 68.2 | 73.1 | | 19.3 | 28.3 | 3.4 | 4.5 |
| Haiti | 15.6 | 27.2 | 41.8 | 48.4 | 12.6 | 15.6 | | 3.5 | |
| *Moderate transition* | *33.4* | *42.5* | *50.9* | *54.7* | *19.4* | *22.1* | *22.9* | *3.7* | *3.3* |
| Belize | 54.0 | 48.7 | 48.2 | | | | | | |
| El Salvador | 38.3 | 46.9 | 57.8 | 62.6 | 16.7 | | 23.1 | | |
| Guatemala | 32.4 | 37.5 | 39.9 | 41.2 | 20.6 | 20.9 | 20.7 | 2.2 | 2.4 |
| Honduras | 22.7 | 37.7 | 52.1 | 59.5 | 10.2 | 16.0 | 19.1 | 6.1 | 4.7 |
| Nicaragua | 39.6 | 51.4 | 56.7 | 59.4 | 24.2 | 24.2 | 21.7 | 4.4 | 3.0 |
| Paraguay | 35.6 | 44.9 | 59.7 | 65.7 | 26.5 | 29.9 | 32.7 | 3.1 | 4.0 |
| *Full transition* | *47.4* | *68.7* | *78.4* | *81.2* | *19.7* | *21.2* | *20.9* | *3.7* | *2.1* |
| Brazil | 45.6 | 71.0 | 81.7 | 84.2 | 15.7 | 16.4 | 16.9 | 3.6 | 1.4 |
| Colombia | 49.1 | 66.9 | 76.6 | 80.0 | 21.1 | 21.9 | 22.6 | 3.4 | 2.1 |
| Costa Rica | 34.3 | 44.8 | 52.3 | 56.1 | 23.8 | 27.5 | | 3.7 | |
| Ecuador | 34.4 | 51.3 | 65.8 | 70.7 | 22.2 | 25.6 | 27.0 | 4.5 | 2.9 |
| Guyana | 29.0 | 31.7 | 41.5 | 48.0 | | | | | |

| | | | | | | | | | |
|---|---|---|---|---|---|---|---|---|---|
| Mexico | 50.8 | 68.6 | 77.2 | 80.2 | 21.5 | 24.2 | 22.1 | 4.2 | 1.1 |
| Panama | 41.3 | 51.7 | 59.5 | 62.9 | 36.6 | 39.3 | 40.5 | 2.7 | 3.2 |
| Peru | 46.3 | 66.3 | 73.5 | 75.5 | 26.7 | 28.5 | 30.6 | 3.0 | 9.6 |
| Dominican Republic | 30.2 | 52.3 | 62.9 | 67.3 | 20.6 | 28.2 | 27.1 | 6.2 | |
| Suriname | – | 60.4 | 77.3 | 81.4 | | | | | |
| Venezuela | 61.2 | 81.6 | 88.8 | 90.8 | 26.6 | 24.9 | 22.5 | 2.4 | 1.8 |
| *Advanced transition* | *69.3* | *84.2* | *86.5* | *89.0* | *36.7* | *37.4* | *36.8* | *1.7* | *1.3* |
| Antilles Dutch | | | | | | | | | |
| Argentina | 73.6 | 84.9 | 90.6 | 92.0 | 39.1 | 39.2 | 38.2 | 1.7 | 1.2 |
| Bahamas | 74.3 | 79.7 | 90.0 | 91.5 | | | | | |
| Barbados | 35.4 | 42.3 | 52.9 | 58.3 | | | | | |
| Chile | 67.8 | 81.1 | 86.9 | 88.8 | 38.3 | 41.1 | 40.7 | 2.6 | 1.7 |
| Cuba | 54.9 | 71.6 | 81.9 | 84.7 | 24.0 | 23.4 | 23.4 | 0.9 | |
| Guadalupe | – | | | | | | | | |
| Jamaica | 33.8 | 49.2 | 58.5 | 63.5 | 28.3 | 28.1 | 28.1 | | |
| Martinique | – | | | | | | | | |
| Puerto Rico | 44.5 | 69.2 | 75.9 | | | | | | |
| Trinidad and Tobago | – | 66.2 | 76.1 | 79.3 | 37.3 | 38.4 | 38.4 | | |
| Uruguay | 80.1 | 89.2 | 93.1 | 93.9 | 50.9 | 52.3 | 53.3 | 0.8 | 0.5 |
| *Latin America & Caribbean* | *48.9* | *68.1* | *76.7* | *79.3* | *21.7* | *23.3* | *23.5* | *3.4* | *2.1* |

*Sources*: CELADE, UNDP, ECLAC, ILO, WB. Calculations based on data sheets available at http://cep.cl/UNRISD/Papers/Introduction/Introduction.xls. Classification criteria was established by CELADE, based on demographic data.

*Table 1.A4* Structure of the economically active population: Latin America and the Caribbean countries, by demographic transition groups

| *Transitional categories/countries* | *Structure of the economically active population by sector of economic activity, 1970–1980–1990* | | | | | | | | |
|---|---|---|---|---|---|---|---|---|---|
| | *Agriculture* | | | *Industry* | | | *Services* | | |
| | *1970* | *1980* | *1990* | *1970* | *1980* | *1990* | *1970* | *1980* | *1990* |
| *Early transition* | *63.2* | *57.7* | *39.3* | *13.6* | *14.0* | *16.8* | *23.2* | *27.8* | *42.2* |
| Bolivia | 52.1 | 45.5 | 39.3 | 20.0 | 19.7 | 16.8 | 27.9 | 33.8 | 42.2 |
| Haiti | 74.4 | 70.0 | | 7.1 | 8.2 | | 18.5 | 21.8 | |
| *Moderate transition* | *58.2* | *52.3* | *43.9* | *16.3* | *17.7* | *18.3* | *25.5* | *30.0* | *35.5* |
| Belize | | | | | | | | | |
| El Salvador | 56.0 | 43.2 | 36.1 | 14.4 | 19.3 | 20.5 | 29.6 | 37.5 | 41.4 |
| Guatemala | 61.2 | 56.9 | 52.5 | 17.1 | 17.1 | 19.4 | 21.7 | 26.0 | 27.8 |
| Honduras | 64.9 | 60.5 | 43.9 | 14.1 | 16.2 | 15.9 | 21.0 | 23.3 | 33.1 |
| Nicaragua | 51.5 | 46.5 | 43.2 | 15.5 | 15.8 | 14.0 | 33.0 | 37.7 | 42.8 |
| Paraguay | 52.6 | 48.6 | 35.4 | 20.2 | 20.6 | 20.5 | 27.2 | 30.8 | 41.2 |
| *Full transition* | *43.3* | *33.1* | *23.1* | *22.3* | *25.9* | *25.8* | *34.4* | *41.1* | *50.1* |
| Brazil | 44.9 | 31.2 | 22.7 | 21.8 | 26.6 | 27.8 | 33.3 | 42.2 | 49.5 |
| Colombia | 39.3 | 34.2 | 26.9 | 23.3 | 23.5 | 21.9 | 37.4 | 42.3 | 51.2 |
| Costa Rica | 42.5 | 30.8 | | 20.0 | 23.1 | | 37.5 | 46.1 | |
| Ecuador | 50.6 | 38.6 | 30.8 | 20.5 | 19.8 | 17.9 | 28.9 | 41.6 | 48.3 |
| Guyana | 31.9 | 26.8 | | 28.5 | 25.8 | | 39.6 | 47.4 | |

| | | | | | | | | | |
|---|---|---|---|---|---|---|---|---|---|
| Mexico | 44.1 | 36.6 | 22.6 | 24.3 | 29.0 | 27.8 | 31.6 | 34.4 | 47.7 |
| Panama | 41.6 | 31.8 | 28.8 | 17.6 | 18.2 | 14.8 | 40.8 | 50.1 | 55.1 |
| Peru | 47.1 | 40.0 | 26.7 | 17.6 | 18.3 | 15.9 | 35.3 | 41.7 | 50.3 |
| Dominican Republic | 54.7 | 45.7 | 21.3 | 14.2 | 15.5 | 28.3 | 31.1 | 38.8 | 50.4 |
| Suriname | 24.8 | 19.9 | | 20.9 | 19.8 | | 54.3 | 60.3 | |
| Venezuela | 26.0 | 16.1 | 13.3 | 24.8 | 28.4 | 25.1 | 49.2 | 55.5 | 61.6 |
| *Advanced transition* | *20.5* | *16.3* | *12.4* | *31.1* | *30.3* | *25.9* | *48.4* | *53.5* | *60.8* |
| Antilles Dutch | | | | | | | | | |
| Argentina | 16.0 | 13.0 | 11.0 | 34.3 | 33.8 | 25.3 | 49.7 | 53.2 | 62.7 |
| Bahamas | | | | | | | | | |
| Barbados | 18.2 | 9.9 | | 26.0 | 20.8 | | 55.8 | 69.3 | |
| Chile | 23.2 | 16.5 | 15.8 | 28.7 | 25.2 | 27.4 | 48.1 | 58.3 | 55.8 |
| Cuba | 30.3 | 23.8 | | 26.7 | 28.5 | | 43.0 | 47.7 | |
| Guadalupe | | | | | | | | | |
| Jamaica | 33.2 | 31.3 | | 18.1 | 16.4 | | 48.7 | 52.3 | |
| Martinique | | | | | | | | | |
| Puerto Rico | | | | | | | | | |
| Trinidad and Tobago | 18.6 | 10.2 | | 35.2 | 38.6 | | 46.2 | 51.2 | |
| Uruguay | 18.6 | 18.8 | 11.9 | 29.1 | 29.2 | 25.2 | 52.3 | 55.0 | 63.0 |
| *Latin America & Caribbean* | *41.8* | *32.8* | *23.6* | *22.8* | *25.5* | *25.0* | *35.4* | *41.7* | *50.3* |

*Sources*: CELADE, UNDP, ECLAC, ILO, WB. Calculations based on data sheets available at http://cep.cl/UNRISD/Papers/Introduction/Introduction.xls. Classification criteria was established by CELADE, based on demographic transition. Such criteria was established by CELADE, based on demographic data.

*Table 1.A5* Non-farm occupational structure: Latin America and the Caribbean countries, by demographic transition groups

| *Transitional categories/countries* | *Non-farm occupational structure, formal jobs, 2000 (% of total occupied workforce)* | | | *Non-farm occupational structure, informal jobs, 2000 (% of total occupied workforce)* | | | |
|---|---|---|---|---|---|---|---|
| | *Total* | *Public Sector* | *Small, medium and large private firms* | *Total* | *Self-employed* | *Domestic service* | MICRO-FIRMS |
| *Early transition* | | | | | | | |
| Bolivia | | | | | | | |
| Haiti | | | | | | | |
| *Moderate transition* | *39.3* | *10.1* | *29.2* | *60.7* | *39.6* | *5.5* | *15.6* |
| Belize | | | | | | | |
| El Salvador | | | | | | | |
| Guatemala | | | | | | | |
| Honduras | 39.3 | 10.1 | 29.2 | 60.7 | 39.6 | 5.5 | 15.6 |
| Nicaragua | | | | | | | |
| Paraguay | | | | | | | |
| *Full transition* | *52.8* | *13.3* | *39.6* | *47.2* | *25.2* | *6.5* | *15.5* |
| Brazil | 52.9 | 14.2 | 38.8 | 47.1 | 24.0 | 9.4 | 13.7 |
| Colombia | 44.4 | 7.0 | 37.3 | 55.6 | 32.2 | 5.3 | 18.1 |
| Costa Rica | 54.8 | 16.4 | 38.5 | 45.2 | 19.7 | 6.0 | 19.5 |
| Ecuador | 48.4 | 17.6 | 30.7 | 51.6 | 31.0 | 5.3 | 15.3 |
| Guyana | | | | | | | |

| | | | | | | | |
|---|---|---|---|---|---|---|---|
| Mexico | 60.8 | 14.5 | 46.4 | 39.2 | 18.3 | 3.7 | 17.2 |
| Panama | 0.0 | 0.0 | 0.0 | 0.0 | 0.0 | 0.0 | 0.0 |
| Peru | 40.8 | 7.8 | 33.0 | 59.2 | 36.4 | 5.4 | 17.4 |
| Dominican Republic | | | | | | | |
| Suriname | | | | | | | |
| Venezuela | 49.4 | 16.1 | 33.3 | 50.6 | 34.5 | 2.3 | 13.8 |
| *Advanced transition* | *54.2* | *12.4* | *41.7* | *45.8* | *21.9* | *6.3* | *17.7* |
| Antilles Dutch | | | | | | 0.0 | 0.0 |
| Argentina | 50.7 | 12.7 | 38.0 | 49.3 | 22.7 | 6.4 | 20.3 |
| Bahamas | | | | | | | |
| Barbados | | | | | | | |
| Chile | 62.0 | 10.8 | 51.2 | 38.0 | 19.7 | 5.9 | 12.5 |
| Cuba | | | | | | | |
| Guadalupe | | | | | | | |
| Jamaica | | | | | | | |
| Martinique | | | | | | | |
| Puerto Rico | | | | | | | |
| Trinidad and Tobago | | | | | | | |
| Uruguay | 56.9 | 17.1 | 39.8 | 43.1 | 22.5 | 7.5 | 13.1 |
| *Latin America & Caribbean* | *53.1* | *13.0* | *40.1* | *46.9* | *24.6* | *6.7* | *15.6* |

*Sources:* CELADE, UNDP, ECLAC, ILO, WB. Calculations based on data sheets available at http://cep.cl/UNRISD/Papers/Introduction/Introduction.xls. Classification criteria was established by CELADE, based on demographic transition. Such criteria is established by CELADE, based on demographic data.

*Table 1.A6* Human development: Latin America and the Caribbean countries, by demographic transition groups

| *Transitional categories/countries* | *HDI ranking, 2001 (a)* | *Human development index (HDI) value 2001* | *Life expectancy at birth (years) 2001* | *Adult literacy rate (% age 15 and above) 2001* | *Combined primary secondary and tertiary gross enrolment ratio (%) 2000–01* |
|---|---|---|---|---|---|
| *Early transition* | *132* | *0.57* | *56.2* | *68.5* | *68.1* |
| Bolivia | 114 | 0.67 | 63.3 | 86.0 | 84.0 |
| Haiti | 150 | 0.47 | 49.1 | 50.8 | 52.0 |
| *Moderate transition* | *110* | *0.68* | *68.3* | *75.8* | *61.6* |
| Belize | 67 | 0.78 | 71.7 | 93.4 | 76.0 |
| El Salvador | 105 | 0.72 | 70.4 | 79.2 | 64.0 |
| Guatemala | 119 | 0.65 | 65.3 | 69.2 | 57.0 |
| Honduras | 115 | 0.67 | 68.8 | 75.6 | 62.0 |
| Nicaragua | 121 | 0.64 | 69.1 | 66.8 | 65.0 |
| Paraguay | 84 | 0.75 | 70.5 | 93.5 | 64.0 |
| *Full transition* | *65* | *0.78* | *70.3* | *89.6* | *82.9* |
| Brazil | 65 | 0.78 | 67.8 | 87.3 | 95.0 |
| Colombia | 64 | 0.78 | 71.8 | 91.9 | 71.0 |
| Costa Rica | 42 | 0.83 | 77.9 | 95.7 | 66.0 |
| Ecuador | 97 | 0.73 | 70.5 | 91.8 | 72.0 |
| Guyana | 92 | 0.74 | 63.3 | 98.6 | 84.0 |
| Mexico | 55 | 0.80 | 73.1 | 91.4 | 74.0 |
| Panama | 59 | 0.79 | 74.4 | 92.1 | 75.0 |
| Peru | 82 | 0.75 | 69.4 | 90.2 | 83.0 |
| Dominican Republic | 94 | 0.74 | 66.7 | 84.0 | 74.0 |
| Suriname | 77 | 0.76 | 70.8 | 94.0 | 77.0 |
| Venezuela | 69 | 0.78 | 73.5 | 92.8 | 68.0 |

| | | | | | |
|---|---|---|---|---|---|
| *Advanced transition* | *41* | *0.83* | *74.8* | *96.4* | *83.0* |
| Antilles Dutch | | | | | |
| Argentina | 34 | 0.85 | 73.9 | 96.9 | 89.0 |
| Bahamas | 49 | 0.81 | 67.2 | 95.5 | 74.0 |
| Barbados | 27 | 0.89 | 76.9 | 99.7 | 89.0 |
| Chile | 43 | 0.83 | 75.8 | 95.9 | 76.0 |
| Cuba | 52 | 0.81 | 76.5 | 96.8 | 76.0 |
| Guadalupe | | | | | |
| Jamaica | 78 | 0.76 | 75.5 | 87.3 | 74.0 |
| Martinique | | | | | |
| Puerto Rico | | | | | |
| Trinidad and Tobago | 54 | 0.80 | 71.5 | 98.4 | 67.0 |
| Uruguay | 40 | 0.83 | 75.0 | 97.6 | 84.0 |
| *Latin America & Caribbean* | *65* | *0.78* | *70.3* | *89.2* | *81.0* |

*Sources*: CELADE, UNDP, ECLAC, ILO, WB. Calculations based on data sheets available at http://cep.cl/UNRISD/Papers/Introduction/Introduction.xls. Classification criteria was established by CELADE, based on demographic transition. Such criteria was established by CELADE, based on demographic data.

*Table 1.A7* Total public social expenditure: Latin America and the Caribbean countries, by demographic transition groups

| *Transitional categories/countries* | *Total social public expenditure* | | | | | | |
|---|---|---|---|---|---|---|---|
| | *2000–2001 Period* | | | *Change since 1996–1997* | | *Change since 1990–1991* | |
| | *per capita 1997 dollars* | *% of GDP* | *% of fiscal Budget* | *per capita 1997 dollars* | *GDP percentage points* | *per capita 1997 dollars* | *GDP percentage points* |
| *Early transition* | *183* | *17.9* | *60* | *36* | *3.3* | – | – |
| Bolivia | 183 | 17.9 | 60 | 36 | 3.3 | | |
| Haiti | | | | | | | |
| *Moderate transition* | *97* | *8.0* | *40.4* | *20* | *1.6* | *53* | *3.2* |
| Belize | | | | | | | |
| El Salvador | 82 | 4.2 | 30.9 | 12 | 0.4 | 82 | 4.2 |
| Guatemala | 109 | 6.2 | 45.6 | 36 | 1.9 | 57 | 2.8 |
| Honduras | 77 | 10.0 | 38.7 | 21 | 2.8 | 17 | 2.1 |
| Nicaragua | 61 | 13.2 | 38.4 | 14 | 1.9 | 13 | 2.1 |
| Paraguay | 148 | 8.5 | 43.8 | (2) | 0.5 | 91 | 5.4 |
| *Full transition* | *618* | *14.2* | *54.3* | *70* | *1.1* | *156* | *2.6* |
| Brazil | 936 | 18.8 | 61.6 | 93 | 1.5 | 150 | 0.7 |
| Colombia | 337 | 13.6 | 33.5 | (66) | (1.7) | 179 | 6.8 |
| Costa Rica | 689 | 18.2 | 40.5 | 121 | 1.4 | 220 | 2.6 |
| Ecuador | 131 | 8.8 | 29.8 | (3) | 0.6 | 43 | 3.3 |
| Guyana | | | | | | | |
| Mexico | 456 | 9.8 | 61.5 | 104 | 1.3 | 197 | 3.3 |
| Panama | 853 | 25.5 | 49.7 | 200 | 4.6 | 356 | 6.9 |

| | | | | | | | |
|---|---|---|---|---|---|---|---|
| Peru | 187 | 8.0 | 46.8 | 21 | 0.9 | 111 | 4.0 |
| Dominican Republic | 170 | 7.6 | 45.2 | 62 | 1.6 | 110 | 3.3 |
| Suriname | | | | | | | |
| Venezuela | 402 | 11.3 | 37.9 | 85 | 3.0 | 82 | 2.8 |
| *Advanced transition* | *1,445* | *20.2* | *65.1* | *110* | *2.0* | *464* | *3.1* |
| Antilles Dutch | | | | | | | |
| Argentina | 1, 650 | 21.6 | 62.4 | 66 | 1.6 | 439 | 2.3 |
| Bahamas | | | | | | | |
| Barbados | | | | | | | |
| Chile | 936 | 16.0 | 69.7 | 218 | 3.0 | 495 | 4.3 |
| Cuba | | | | | | | |
| Guadalupe | | | | | | | |
| Jamaica | | | | | | | |
| Martinique | | | | | | | |
| Puerto Rico | | | | | | | |
| Trinidad and Tobago | | | | | | | |
| Uruguay | 1, 494 | 23.5 | 75.0 | 104 | 2.2 | 606 | 6.6 |
| *Latin America & Caribbean* | *686* | *14.8* | *55.1* | *71* | *1.4* | *194* | *2.7* |
| | 7.9 | | | | | | |

*Sources*: CELADE, UNDP, ECLAC, ILO, WB. Calculations based on data sheets available at http://cep.cl/UNRISD/Papers/Introduction/Introduction.xls. Classification criteria was established by CELADE, based on demographic transition. Such criteria was established by CELADE, based on demographic data.

*Table 1.A8* Public expenditure in education and health: Latin America and the Caribbean countries, by demographic transition groups

| *Transitional categories/countries* | *Public expenditure on education* | | | | | | *Public expenditure on health* | | | |
|---|---|---|---|---|---|---|---|---|---|---|
| | *2000–2001 period* | | *Change since 1996–1997* | | *Change since 1990–1991* | | *2000–2001 period* | | *Change since 1996–1997* | |
| | *per capita 1997 dollars* | *% of GDP* | *per capita 1997 dollars* | *GDP percentage points* | *per capita 1997 dollars* | *GDP percentage points* | *per capita 1997 dollars* | *% of GDP* | *per capita 1997 dollars* | *GDP percentage points* |
| *Early transition* | *66* | *6.5* | *7.0* | *0.6* | – | – | *38* | *3.7* | *4.0* | *0.3* |
| Bolivia | 66 | 6.5 | 7.0 | 0.6 | | | 38 | 3.7 | 4.0 | 0.3 |
| Haiti | | | | | | | | | | |
| *Moderate transition* | *48* | *3.9* | *11.7* | *1.1* | *22.4* | *1.7* | *22* | *2.1* | *4.1* | *0.4* |
| Belize | | | | | | | | | | |
| El Salvador | 51 | 2.6 | | | | | 29 | 1.5 | | |
| Guatemala | 46 | 2.6 | 18.0 | 0.9 | 22.0 | 1.1 | 19 | 1.1 | 6.0 | 0.3 |
| Honduras | 45 | 5.8 | 17.0 | 2.3 | 12.0 | 1.5 | 24 | 3.1 | 7.0 | 0.9 |
| Nicaragua | 28 | 6.1 | 8.0 | 1.1 | 10.0 | 1.8 | 22 | 4.8 | 5.0 | 0.5 |
| Paraguay | 70 | 4.0 | (4.0) | 0.2 | 47.0 | 2.9 | 19 | 1.1 | (4.0) | (0.1) |
| *Full transition* | *161* | *3.9* | *22.8* | *0.4* | *43.0* | *0.8* | *111* | *2.7* | *9.1* | *0.2* |
| Brazil | 185 | 3.8 | 28.0 | 0.6 | 23.0 | 0.1 | 151 | 3.0 | 13.0 | 0.2 |
| Colombia | 97 | 3.9 | (30.0) | (0.9) | 34.0 | 1.2 | 107 | 4.3 | 21.0 | 1.1 |
| Costa Rica | 189 | 5.0 | 41.0 | 0.6 | 76.0 | 1.2 | 199 | 5.3 | 40.0 | 0.6 |
| Ecuador | 45 | 3.0 | (11.0) | (0.4) | – | 0.1 | 16 | 1.1 | (2.0) | |
| Guyana | | | | | | | | | | |
| Mexico | 190 | 4.1 | 37.0 | 0.4 | 86.0 | 1.6 | 86 | 1.9 | (4.0) | (0.3) |
| Panama | 199 | 6.0 | 19.0 | 0.3 | 75.0 | 1.4 | 274 | 8.2 | 64.0 | 1.5 |

| | | | | | | | | | | |
|---|---|---|---|---|---|---|---|---|---|---|
| Peru | 58 | 2.5 | 1.0 | – | 28.0 | 0.8 | 41 | 1.8 | 7.0 | 0.3 |
| Dominican Republic | 67 | 3.0 | 26.0 | 0.7 | 51.0 | 1.8 | 42 | 1.9 | 17.0 | 0.5 |
| Suriname | | | | | | | | | | |
| Venezuela | 178 | 5.0 | 59.0 | 1.9 | 49.0 | 1.5 | 50 | 1.4 | 8.0 | 0.3 |
| *Advanced transition* | *335* | *4.7* | *52.5* | *0.8* | *152.4* | *1.5* | *308* | *4.3* | *22.2* | *0.4* |
| Antilles Dutch | | | | | | | | | | |
| Argentina | 385 | 5.0 | 49.0 | 0.8 | 159.0 | 1.4 | 379 | 5.0 | 17.0 | 0.4 |
| Bahamas | | | | | | | | | | |
| Barbados | | | | | | | | | | |
| Chile | 238 | 4.1 | 69.0 | 1.0 | 151.0 | 1.7 | 165 | 2.8 | 37.0 | 0.5 |
| Cuba | | | | | | | | | | |
| Guadalupe | | | | | | | | | | |
| Jamaica | | | | | | | | | | |
| Martinique | | | | | | | | | | |
| Puerto Rico | | | | | | | | | | |
| Trinidad and Tobago | | | | | | | | | | |
| Uruguay | 213 | 3.4 | 16.0 | 0.4 | 84.0 | 1.0 | 175 | 2.8 | 12.0 | 0.3 |
| *Latin America & Caribbean* | *175* | *4.1* | *25.8* | *0.5* | *57.7* | *1.0* | *130* | *2.9* | *10.5* | *0.2* |

*Sources*: CELADE, UNDP, ECLAC, ILO, WB. Calculations based on data sheets available at http://cep.cl/UNRISD/Papers/Introduction/Introduction.xls. Classification criteria was established by CELADE, based on demographic transition. Such criteria was established by CELADE, based on demographic data.

*Table 1.A9* Public expenditure in social security, housing and others: Latin America and the Caribbean countries, by demographic transition groups

| *Transitional categories/ countries* | *Public expenditure on social security* | | | | | | *Public expenditure on housing and others* | | | |
|---|---|---|---|---|---|---|---|---|---|---|
| | *2000–2001 period* | | *Change since 1996–1997* | | *Change since 1990–1991* | | *2000–2001 period* | | *Change since 1996–1997* | |
| | *per capita 1997 dollars* | *% of GDP* | *per capita 1997 dollars* | *GDP percentage points* | *per capita 1997 dollars* | *GDP percentage points* | *per capita 1997 dollars* | *% of GDP* | *per capita 1997 dollars* | *GDP Percentage points* |
| *Early transition* | *47* | *4.6* | *19.0* | *1.8* | – | – | *33* | *3.2* | *7.0* | *0.7* |
| Bolivia | 47 | 4.6 | 19.0 | 1.8 | | | 33 | 3.2 | 7.0 | 0.7 |
| Haiti | | | | | | | | | | |
| *Moderate transition* | *16* | *1.0* | *4.4* | *0.3* | *10.0* | *0.6* | *12* | *1.2* | *1.5* | *0.0* |
| Belize | | | | | | | | | | |
| El Salvador | 2 | 0.1 | | | | | 1 | | | |
| Guatemala | 19 | 1.1 | 7.0 | 0.4 | 7.0 | 0.3 | 26 | 1.5 | 6.0 | 0.3 |
| Honduras | 2 | 0.2 | 1.0 | 0.1 | 1.0 | 0.2 | 7 | 0.9 | (4.0) | (0.6) |
| Nicaragua | 1 | 0.2 | 1.0 | 0.2 | | | 10 | 2.2 | 2.0 | 0.2 |
| Paraguay | 56 | 3.2 | 6.0 | 0.6 | 36.0 | 2.1 | 3 | 0.2 | (2.0) | (0.1) |
| *Full transition* | *320* | *7.1* | *34.6* | *0.5* | *127.0* | *2.4* | *27* | *0.7* | *5.1* | *0.0* |
| Brazil | 588 | 11.8 | 52.0 | 0.8 | 187.0 | 2.6 | 12 | 0.2 | 2.0 | |
| Colombia | 109 | 4.4 | (52.0) | (1.8) | 49.0 | 1.8 | 26 | 1.0 | (5.0) | (0.2) |
| Costa Rica | 235 | 6.2 | 40.0 | 0.5 | 88.0 | 1.4 | 67 | 1.8 | 1.0 | (0.2) |
| Ecuador | 68 | 4.6 | 17.0 | 1.5 | 41.0 | 2.9 | 3 | 0.2 | (7.0) | (0.4) |
| Guyana | | | | | | | | | | |

| | | | | | | | | | | |
|---|---|---|---|---|---|---|---|---|---|---|
| Mexico | 131 | 2.8 | 56.0 | 1.0 | 120.0 | 2.6 | 50 | 1.1 | 16.0 | 0.2 |
| Panama | 192 | 5.7 | 10.0 | (0.1) | 37.0 | (0.1) | 188 | 5.6 | 107.0 | 3.0 |
| Peru | 77 | 3.3 | 13.0 | 0.5 | 52.0 | 2.0 | 13 | 0.6 | 2.0 | 0.1 |
| Dominican Republic | 31 | 1.4 | 19.0 | 0.7 | 26.0 | 1.0 | 33 | 1.5 | 3.0 | (0.2) |
| Suriname | | | | | | | | | | |
| Venezuela | 128 | 3.6 | 19.0 | 0.7 | 55.0 | 1.6 | 46 | 1.3 | – | 0.1 |
| *Advanced transition* | *653* | *9.2* | *32.4* | *0.7* | *173.4* | *0.7* | *151* | *2.1* | *4.4* | *0.1* |
| Antilles Dutch | | | | | | | | | | |
| Argentina | 705 | 9.2 | 1.0 | 0.4 | 136.0 | 0.1 | 183 | 2.4 | 2.0 | 0.1 |
| Bahamas | | | | | | | | | | |
| Barbados | | | | | | | | | | |
| Chile | 435 | 7.4 | 100.0 | 1.4 | 198.0 | 1.1 | 99 | 1.7 | 11.0 | 0.1 |
| Cuba | | | | | | | | | | |
| Guadalupe | | | | | | | | | | |
| Jamaica | | | | | | | | | | |
| Martinique | | | | | | | | | | |
| Puerto Rico | | | | | | | | | | |
| Trinidad and Tobago | | | | | | | | | | |
| Uruguay | 1,075 | 16.9 | 75.0 | 1.6 | 485.0 | 5.8 | 31 | 0.5 | 1.0 | – |
| *Latin America & Caribbean* | *338* | *6.8* | *31.6* | *0.6* | *125* | *2* | *44* | *1.0* | *4.8* | *0.1* |

*Sources*: CELADE, UNDP, ECLAC, ILO, WB. Calculations based on data sheets available at http://cep.cl/UNRISD/Papers/Introduction/Introduction.xls. Classification criteria was established by CELADE, based on demographic transition. Such criteria was established by CELADE, based on demographic data.

*Table 1.A10* Income distribution: Latin America and the Caribbean countries, by demographic transition groups.

| *Transitional categories/countries* | *Income distribution* | | | | | | |
|---|---|---|---|---|---|---|---|
| | *Mean income (number of poverty lines)* | *Participation in overall income of* | | | *Relation of mean per capita income* | | |
| | | *Poorest 40%* | *Following 30%* | *20% before richest 10%* | *Richest 10%* | $D^{10}/D^{(1a4)}$ | $Q^5/Q^1$ |
| *Early transition* | *6.3* | *10.1* | *22.3* | *28.4* | *39.3* | 25.0 | 37.1 |
| Bolivia | 6.3 | 10.1 | 22.3 | 28.4 | 39.3 | 25.0 | 37.1 |
| Haiti | | | | | | | |
| *Moderate transition* | *6.0* | *13.2* | *22.6* | *27.0* | *37.2* | 20.1 | 23.2 |
| Belize | | | | | | | |
| El Salvador | 6.4 | 14.5 | 24.7 | 28.0 | 32.8 | 15.1 | 18.2 |
| Guatemala | 6.6 | 13.4 | 21.6 | 26.2 | 38.8 | 20.8 | 21.9 |
| Honduras | 4.2 | 11.5 | 21.7 | 27.7 | 39.2 | 23.6 | 26.8 |
| Nicaragua | 5.6 | 11.0 | 22.1 | 27.1 | 39.9 | 25.0 | 32.7 |
| Paraguay | 6.9 | 15.3 | 24.2 | 26.6 | 34 | 15.9 | 18.1 |
| *Full transition* | *9.3* | *12.4* | *20.8* | *26.7* | *40.1* | 24.0 | 27.0 |
| Brazil | 11.0 | 9.9 | 17.8 | 26.4 | 46.0 | 31.9 | 36.4 |
| Colombia | 7.4 | 11.7 | 21.7 | 26.4 | 40.3 | 23.9 | 28.6 |
| Costa Rica | 10.7 | 15.8 | 26.4 | 29.8 | 28.1 | 11.8 | 14.6 |
| Ecuador | 6 | 15.9 | 24.3 | 26.5 | 33.3 | 14.0 | 14.9 |
| Guyana | – | – | – | – | – | – | – |

| | | | | | | | |
|---|---|---|---|---|---|---|---|
| Mexico | 8.5 | 15.4 | 22.9 | 26.3 | 35.5 | 16.9 | 17.1 |
| Panama | 11.4 | 13.8 | 23.8 | 27.7 | 34.8 | 17.5 | 20.3 |
| Peru | 7.5 | 13.4 | 24.1 | 28.1 | 34.4 | 18.3 | 20.6 |
| Dominican Republic | 7.2 | 11.7 | 22.4 | 27.3 | 38.6 | 20.2 | 25.9 |
| Suriname | – | – | – | – | – | – | – |
| Venezuela | 7.8 | 15.1 | 24.9 | 29 | 31.1 | 14.1 | 16.1 |
| *Advanced transition* | *11.2* | *14.7* | *21.6* | *26.0* | *37.7* | *16.6* | *17.1* |
| Antilles Dutch | – | – | – | – | – | – | – |
| Argentina | 10.9 | 14.7 | 21.7 | 26.3 | 37.4 | 16.5 | 17.1 |
| Bahamas | – | – | – | – | – | – | – |
| Barbados | – | – | – | – | – | – | – |
| Chile | 12 | 13.4 | 20.7 | 25.6 | 40.4 | 18.4 | 18.7 |
| Cuba | – | – | – | – | – | – | – |
| Guadalupe | – | – | – | – | – | – | – |
| Jamaica | – | – | – | – | – | – | – |
| Martinique | – | – | – | – | – | – | – |
| Puerto Rico | – | – | – | – | – | – | – |
| Trinidad and Tobago | – | – | – | – | – | – | – |
| Uruguay | 10.5 | 21.3 | 25.4 | 25.4 | 27.8 | 9.1 | 9.6 |
| *Latin America & Caribbean* | *9* | *13* | *21* | *27* | *40* | *23* | *26* |

*Sources*: CELADE, UNDP, ECLAC, ILO, WB. Calculations based on data sheets available at http://cep.cl/UNRISD/Papers/Introduction.xls. Classification criteria was established by CELADE, based on demographic data.

*Table 1.A11* Population growth for different countries, 1900–95

| *Country* | *Growth rate (yearly %)* | | | | | |
|---|---|---|---|---|---|---|
| | *1900–1995* | *1900–1920* | *1920–1938* | *1938–1973* | *1973–1989* | *1989–1995* |
| UK | 0.45 | 0.6 | 0.5 | 0.5 | 0.1 | 0.5 |
| USA | 1.32 | 1.7 | 1.1 | 1.4 | 1.0 | 1.0 |
| India | 1.45 | 0.3 | 1.1 | 1.8 | 2.2 | 2.2 |
| Indonesia | 1.60 | 1.1 | 1.3 | 1.7 | 2.2 | 1.6 |
| *Chile* | *1.65* | *1.3* | *1.4* | *2.1* | *1.6* | *1.5* |
| Australia | 1.68 | 1.8 | 1.4 | 1.9 | 1.4 | 1.4 |
| Canada | 1.84 | 2.4 | 1.5 | 1.9 | 1.1 | 2.7 |
| Peru | 1.97 | 1.0 | 1.5 | 2.5 | 2.5 | 2.2 |
| Mexico | 2.06 | 0.5 | 1.6 | 3.1 | 2.6 | 1.9 |
| Argentina | 2.11 | 3.2 | 2.5 | 1.7 | 1.5 | 1.1 |
| Colombia | 2.31 | 2.2 | 1.9 | 2.8 | 2.1 | 1.7 |
| Brasil | 2.36 | 2.1 | 2.0 | 2.7 | 2.4 | 1.9 |

*Source*: Universidad Católica (2000, Table 91a).

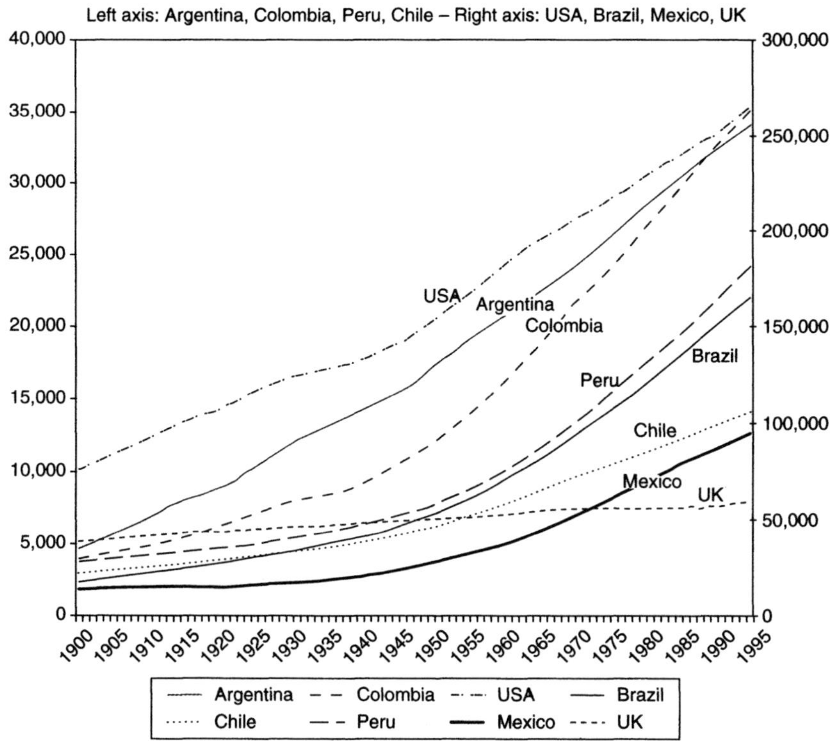


*Figure 1.A1* Population for different countries, 1900–95
*Source:* Universidad Católica (2000).

# In the Highlands of Ancient American Empires

# 2

# Mexico's Welfare State: Birth, Growth and Retrenchment (1822–2002)

*Viviane Brachet-Márquez*

## Introduction

In north-western Europe, the Welfare State (WS) grew out of the struggles of subaltern groups (workers, peasants, women) within states that had been consolidated for centuries and were slowly opening up to these groups as a consequence of the protests, social movements, strikes and other types of collective actions these organized (Esping-Andersen, 1990; Hicks, 1999; Huber and Stevens, 2001). After they achieved universal male suffrage in the early twentieth century, these groups began to constitute power centres of their own within the dynamics of democratic politics, and to obtain, in alliance with others (mainly peasants and middle sectors), public services and rights to welfare programmes. Of course, this pattern differed between liberal democracies, such as the United Kingdom, and countries with a state-led tradition such as France, Germany, and Italy, or social democratic Scandinavian countries (Huber, Ragin and Stevens, 1993). But without following Marshall's lead, it can be asserted that in Western Europe, a more or less continuous line may be drawn between the granting of basic civic rights and the adoption of public policies designed to reduce social inequalities and protect families from the vagaries of the labour market.

The birth of the WS was markedly different in those Ibero-American countries that had been formed by Spanish colonialism and who had been late in entering the international market. Although industrialization started in the last quarter of the nineteenth century, with railroad construction and the growth of the international market, these processes occurred on a far smaller scale than in Europe, and, more often than not, took place in militarist, authoritarian contexts. Therefore, far from having pushed for a WS from below, the young Ibero-American republics seem to have followed a trajectory of industrialization and WS building impelled from above and based, to all appearances, on purely productive grounds. In such contexts, the popular alliances likely to push for social legislation either failed to appear, or, where they did appear, during the short-lived populist period, were often blamed for slowing down the process owing to their alleged tendency to awaken unrealistic expectation of redistribution in the masses.

For Latin America, therefore, industrial development did not coincide with democratization, so that the explanations offered for the development of the WS in Europe are inapplicable in this instance. Are we then left, as the only explanation to account for the growth of WS in Latin America, with the 'logic of industrialism', according to which every process of industrialization requires and contains within itself the conditions for WS growth (Huber and Stevens, 2000)? The problem is that, faced by the great diversity in the trajectories of industrial development followed by individual Latin American countries, or by countries in other regions of the Third World, the validity of a single universal logic of industrialism appears doubtful.

A different perspective can be outlined if we start from the premise that there is not one, but many trajectories of industrialization, and none with an overriding universal 'logic', but, rather, a variety of them according to the internal and external factors that have historically constructed the reality of each country. In other words, the *why* and the *how* of this phenomenon, in all its variations, should be considered to be part of the dynamic of the formation and transformation of these nations.

This chapter examines the case of Mexico, and argues that Mexico's WS was in large part the product of the process of formation of the post-independent state, and subsequently the consolidation and eventual transformation of the state that was born with the 1910 Revolution. This process is divided into four periods: (1) Independence, Reforma and Restored Republic (1822–76); (2) Porfiriato (1877–1910); (3) post-revolutionary rising WS (1917–82); and (4) retrenched post-revolutionary WS (1982–2003). The arguments presented are based on the historical sources substantiating the main stages of the development of social legislation on the one hand, and those focusing on the transformation of the Mexican state, on the other. Therefore, the value of the work presented does not consist in unearthing new facts, but in offering a new reading of established facts by connecting the construction of the WS with that of the state.

## From independence to Reforma and restored republic (1822–77)

Independent Mexico was born in a state of bankruptcy with an economy fashioned by Spanish corporatist colonial structures (Staples, 1981), yet without the international connections to support them. As a result of Napoleon I's war on Spain, the Spanish Crown had to withdraw the capital that guaranteed public charity expenditures, although it promised to continue to send the corresponding amount of interest. In spite of this assurance, all payments stopped after 1813.

At the onset of independence, the only institution still capable of pursuing any coherent political project likely to be approved both by landowning elites and the masses was the Catholic Church. Its power was such that obligatory submission to its dogmas was included in the Cadiz Constitution of 1812.[1] Mexican independence therefore started with a fundamental contradiction between a formal declaration of national sovereignty and de facto recognition of ecclesiastical authority over politics (Villaseñor, 1978: 32).

This contradiction would soon find its primary arena of conflict in the social policies of the young republic, particularly education. Liberals and conservatives alike considered that elementary education should be open to the 'whole people', and even agreed that such term should include *mestizo* city dwellers, but exclude the indigenous population, the rural masses (80 per cent of the population), and city paupers.[2] However, most conservatives wanted to preserve the old ways of education under ecclesiastical authority, while liberals wanted education to be independent of the Church and formative of citizenship. This projection on education of an antithetical vision of the National State was at the core of the recurrent civil war that would wrack the country until the 1870s, but also at the very heart of the formative process of the new state that saw in education an indispensable constitutive element of its project for a nation. For Mora (1949), architect and ideologue of the liberal view on education, 'The nation's prosperity could only be achieved when the majority of the population could be counted upon to construct the democratic state in its republican form [which meant] a clear knowledge of their duties and obligations toward the mother land' (quoted in Villaseñor, 1978: 515).

In August 1821, when a war-weary Spain finally conceded Mexico's independence, barely 0.6 per cent of the 4,800,000 adults in the population were literate (Martínez Jimenez, 1973). University education was reduced to two conciliary seminars – the University of Guadalajara, the University of San Carlos and the Colegio de Minería. There were no teachers, schools, or textbooks to meet the new perceived need for educating the population. Yet, the Lancaster method of literacy teaching[3] had been diffused throughout the national territory.[4] Twenty years later, 1,310 schools had been opened, all of them Lancasterian, with a total of 58,744 students (Martínez Jimenez, 1973). The Lerdo de Tejada law of June 1856, and subsequently the *Manifesto of the Nation's Constitutional Government* of 1859, legally defined the project of creating a state independent of the Church with secular, free, and mandatory education. In addition to reducing the power of the Church, it was hoped that secular education would assimilate the indigenous population and put Mexico on an equal footing with more advanced nations. For good measure, all Church properties (except places of worship) were confiscated, which simultaneously weakened the adversary and brought urgently needed funds to the nation's coffers.

It was hoped that such policies would make education into an instrument capable of strengthening the state while simultaneously distancing the population from the Church (Vázquez Zoraida, 1967: 201). Yet the dearth of funds and the chaos in which the country found itself after the war against the French invasion made the implementation of such a programme highly problematic. In 1867, the government of the Restored Republic reasserted the principle of free, secular education, and created the *Escuela Nacional Preparatoria*.[5] These actions, although taken by several states, were nevertheless constitutionally limited to the Federal District and the Territories (Baja California and Tepic). By then, liberals had turned positivist, and had become the self-appointed custodians of 'liberty, order and progress'. By 1874, the number of schools had reached 8,103 with 349,999 students, 65 per cent financed by the municipalities, 7 per cent by the federation and 28 per cent privately (both religious and nonreligious) (Martínez Jimenez, 1973).

What about the generalized poverty the war had left behind? Moreover, what about the grave epidemics suffered throughout the whole country?[6] Although the history of the Reforma and Restored Republic untiringly analyses the alleged great conflict between Church and state, the latter appears to have mainly manifested itself in education and the registration of demographic data. We find surprisingly little evidence of its presence in other social programmes. For example, although religious hospitals had been expropriated at the same time as other Church property, they went on functioning very much as in the past. Whether because of the difficulty in founding new institutions in the middle of a civil war, or through lack of interest for the indigent sick on the part of the new state, the Church remained at the head of the hospitals and dispensaries created during the colonial period. This continued from the Independence period to the end of the Porfiriato, apparently with no opposition on the part of the state authorities (Kretschmer, 2000: 124). Nevertheless, in 1833, Gomez Farias had created the so-called Scientific Establishments, including a medical facility, where medical education began to move away from the old colonial traditions, and to follow French leadership. The French invasion even brought French military physicians who, along with their Mexican colleagues, founded the present-day Academy of Medicine (Kumate, 2000: 245). We may conclude, therefore, that what displeased the liberals was not the role of the Church in general so much as its pretence to dominate an activity which they considered crucial to the strengthening of the new Republic.

In the social realm the actions and decisions of the Reforma government did not invariably lead to improvements in the population's welfare. For example, the decision to create a new 'farmer' class, in order to follow the US model, resulted in the pauperization of the peasantry and municipalities alike (Martínez Jimenez, 1973). The *Ley de Terrenos Baldios*[7] enacted for that purpose constituted the legal instrument through which the *ejidos*[8] could be dismantled, and untilled land sold. However, in practice, it provided legal cover for the wholesale theft of peasant land by the haciendas (Womack, 1970).

## The Porfiriato (1877–1910)

The dictatorship of Porfirio Díaz (1877–1910), otherwise known as the Porfiriato, marked the triumph of social Darwinism that considered social inequality and poverty to be natural mechanisms for the elimination of the unfit. Social Darwinism advanced the notion that the poor were destitute because they were lazy and ridden with vices, and workers would soon follow suit if they were granted the wage increases they requested. During this era there was, therefore, no perceived moral obligation to alleviate social injustice via individual charity (as in the conservative model), and even less so via redistributive policies. Therefore, if the Porfiriato performed poorly in social policy, it was not because of an absence of financial or administrative means, as usually assumed, but out of the conviction that prosperity would be a natural product of progress. The role of the state was to make such progress possible, albeit not through social policies.

These attitudes, although widely held among the bourgeoisie and secularized middle classes, paradoxically, no longer corresponded to the Church of Leon XIII. The latter untiringly denounced inequality and social injustice, declaring itself in favour of the right to work, the legal stipulation of a minimum daily wage and the social protection of workers associations, all of which were denigrated by the elites in power and the educated public. In 1878, for example, the daily *La Voz de México* 'repudiated legal charity on the grounds that it multiplied the causes of poverty (laziness, improvision, vices) . . . [and] *La Libertad* . . . could not accept that the rich should be reminded of their obligations, as this could only end up stimulating the hatred of the poor toward their betters' (González Navarro, 1979: 372). Likewise, *El Imparcial* published in 1895 the view that to advocate a minimum wage was to confuse factories with welfare associations, and would amount to equalizing the apt and the inept (González Navarro, 1979: 374). Even Justo Sierra, the great ideologue and creator of secular education, opined that there was no difference between Catholic doctrinaires and 'the most fanatical socialists', as they both used the language of Marx and Bakunin (González Navarro, 1979: 373).

Despite such doctrinaire positions, the Díaz dictatorship de facto made its peace with the Church by simply allowing the states and municipalities to implement anti-clerical laws (or, more exactly, not implement them), in conformity with the otherwise little respected Constitution of 1857. Although a position of secularization was maintained in the Federal District and Territories, private schools, almost all of them religious, were allowed to flourish again, reaching 2,499 in number by 1907 (Vaughan, 1982).

During the Porfiriato, the expropriation of communal and municipal land continued. Municipalities also lost revenues following the outlawing of *Alcabala* taxes.[9] The consequence was a general slowdown in the expansion of education towards the end of the period (Martínez Jiménez, 1973).

Between 1895 and 1910, literacy rose from 14.4 per cent to 19.7 per cent of the adult population. Yet with 55.8 per cent of the federal budget spent in the Federal District and Territories, the distribution of expenditure was so unequal that the states suffered a setback, in absolute as well as relative terms: by 1910, while the Federal District spent 6.9 pesos per capita on education, the equivalent figure for the states was 36 cents (Vaughan, 1982). Breaking down these amounts reveals even greater inequality: in 1900 elementary education only received 20 cents per student, while secondary education received 104.79 pesos, and university education 126.42 pesos. In sum, progressive though the Porfiriato's educational policies may have appeared, they aggravated existing inequalities, especially between urban and rural areas.[10]

Health policy (if we may use such a term) followed along the same lines. More hospitals were built, most of them in the Federal District: the Juárez hospital, the National Bacteriological Institute, the General Hospital of México, and the Castañeda insane asylum,[11] to which were added the private hospitals of foreign communities such as the French Hospital, the Anglo-American Hospital, the American Hospital and the Sanatorio Español. Rather than being intended to cure the sick, public hospitals were now 'designed to recruit the elite in any given scientific field who, under the direct supervision of the 'emperor' [worked] toward nothing less than excellence' (Kretschmer, 2000). Rather than a health policy, this was some kind of scientific policy.

The slowness in the efforts to improve public health was due, in great part, to the far higher costs involved in relation to education. Contrary to railroads, the sanitary infrastructure required to provide drinkable water and drainage had little attraction for foreign capital. Even in Mexico City, where streets were periodically flooded by a mixture of rain water and organic waste, deep drainage works were not undertaken until the end of the century, so that the so-called 'city of palaces' should also have been labelled the 'city of typhus' (González Navarro, 1994). In the rest of the country, yellow fever, dengue, malaria and cholera were endemic.[12]

During the last five years of the Porfiriato, the usual humble entreaties of wounded or sick workers for their bosses' benevolent 'help' changed to insistent demands for shorter working days and compensation for accidents and occupational diseases (Rajchenberg, 1996). This 'magonist' movement[13] was harshly repressed in 1905–06, leaving as its only positive result the creation (yet not the implementation) of insurance against work accidents in the states of Nuevo León and México. Nevertheless, on 1 July 1906, The Liberal Party, headed by Madero, a future candidate for the presidency, published a programme in the United States that incorporated the magonist demands of eight-hour working days and a minimum daily wage of 1 peso. During his campaign, Madero would also repeatedly assert his commitment to institute social insurance (González Díaz Lombardo, 1973), a project he forgot as soon as he was elected.

## From revolution to Cardenism (1910–39)

The government of the 'apostle of democracy', as Madero was called, lasted for barely two years before he was assassinated on the orders of Victoriano Huerta who then assumed power as a neo-Porfirian dictator. Nevertheless, the first democratically elected president did have the time to create a Department of Labour through which labour conflicts were mediated. He also managed to send Congress a minimum wage bill that met with little opposition despite protest by the defenders of the law of supply and demand considered 'as legitimate as the force of gravitation that moves the celestial bodies' (González Navarro, 1979: 392).

During the first few years of armed struggles that followed Madero's assassination, nothing could be legislated, excluding Victoriano Huerta's interim (and failed) efforts to win labour support. However, even during this turbulent period, the partial reforms (especially land distribution) launched by several revolutionary caudillos helped to create strong expectations of institutional change. Consequently, labour conflicts and worker demands for sickness and accident insurance multiplied.

This period also saw the gestation of the social reforms of the future post-revolutionary regime in the hard bargaining over the drafting of a new constitution. The losers in that process would be the Zapatistas and Villistas, and the old-time liberals. The first because they had done little to attract labour support, while their proposal to expropriate all haciendas horrified the moderates as much as the liberals. The second because they merely sought a return to the 1857 Constitution, to which the reformist centre headed by Obregón, and now strengthened by considerable popular support, was vehemently opposed. The Constitution of 1917, finally approved by the assembly gathered in Querétaro, is a crucial document in the creation of the WS in Mexico: it dealt with the policy areas of land redistribution, the regulation of relations between capital and labour, social insurance, education (free, secular and mandatory), profit sharing and housing. Although post-revolutionary Mexico would take decades to carry out this programme effectively, the text of the Constitution became a legitimate blueprint of social demands and state responses alike. In short, the revolution had given birth to the WS, and the latter would play a crucial role in the stabilization and legitimating of the new regime.

From the 1920s onwards, once the country had returned to peace and the new regime was established on solid institutional bases, the most innovative (and at the time really revolutionary) feature was the transformation of the poor and/or indigenous peasant into a visible subject with rights: first to land and education, and later to health. As Palacios (1998: 244) observes, 'already during these years, post-revolutionary intellectuals were constructing indigenous poverty as a political concept to join other implicit subconscious causes in the revolutionary movement'. But if peasants were an implicit cause for intellectuals, for politicians they were a very concrete problem: that of distancing the rural masses from Zapatism and their enduring attachment to the Church. To achieve this, the Mexican *campesino* had to become part of the national culture via an educational programme that presented the history of the country as a triumphant march toward the Revolution (Palacios, 1998). The distribution of land, conceived as a fundamental right, also had to be promoted (yet needed to be implemented only moderately).

The Calles government (1924–28) and the 'Maximato' (1928–34)[14] saw the continuation of the concern for inculcating, through education, those values which would consolidate the regime. It also saw the end of the truce between Church and state, which Obregón had maintained.[15] To prevent *campesinos* from following the *Cristeros* in revolt,[16] education would impart the values of free enterprise (which led to the creation of agricultural schools teaching industrial agriculture), and a nationalist spirit (Arce Gurza, 1981). Between 1922 and 1932, while *Cristeros* were being repressed, the number of rural schools rose rapidly, from 309 to 6,796, and the number of students from 17,925 to 593,183 (Arce Gurza, 1981). In these were deployed the best efforts to transform revolutionary history into a patriotic narrative (Palacios, 1998: 250). Among them, private schools were still predominant: 640 public primary non-rural schools vs 1,270 private schools in 1928 (ibid.), but many finally had to close down following the outlawing of religious orders and religious content in education.

During the Calles period, the education budget was at its lowest level since the revolution, despite the emphasis on education in the official discourse, declining from 15 per cent in the Vasconcelos era to 7 per cent of the federal budget.[17] Yet, it would rise again to 14 per cent during the Maximato under the leadership of education minister Narcisso Bassols. The short administrations of Ortiz Rubio (1930–32) and Abelardo Rodriguez (1932–34) also saw the birth of the concept of 'socialist education', as proclaimed in 1933 at the annual convention of the recently created National Revolutionary Party (PNR). This doctrine stipulated that: 'education (would) have to follow the principles and postulates of the socialist doctrine which the Revolution sustains' (from Villaseñor, 1978: 160). Nevertheless, the policy became official only during the following presidential term (1934–39).

Throughout the 1920s and until as late as 1934, the debate on social insurance re-emerged, but the economic crisis of 1926–27 and business opposition to the government's labour code proposal, finally adopted in 1930, prevented much progress in that direction.[18] It was therefore limited to the creation in 1925 of social insurance programmes for public servants and the armed forces, which had not been requested by these groups. Three years later, following a prolonged series of strikes, teachers were also included. Futhermore, in 1928, a new proposal for social insurance was presented (with the support of the recently created ILO), but, once again, business was opposed, and the project abandoned.

Despite the defence of his government by the labour unions against Calles' two attempted coups, Cárdenas was first and foremost a pro-*campesino* president. He distributed 50 per cent more land than all of the presidents that preceded him; reconstituted the *ejido* system based on a system of credit designed for small farmers (through the *Banco Ejidal*); and built an extensive network of health centres on a cooperative model shared between the Department of Social Medicine, rural municipalities and Banco Ejidal (González Block, 1989). The Cárdenas government also undertook projects that favoured private enterprise, such as irrigation in the northern states, bridge and road construction, and the introduction of low import tariffs. Yet its insistence on the unionization of the labour force consistently damaged its relations with capitalists and the right, so that it repeatedly had to resort to debt financing of its social reforms. After the 1938 expropriation of the oil companies, the opposition to Cardenism grew to the point of building an electoral alliance between the extreme right and extreme left unions behind Andréu Almazán's candidacy. Should the latter win, the social revolutionary experiment would be in serious jeopardy.

## The ascending phase of the welfare state (1940–82)

The 1940 election of Avila Camacho, in the midst of a notorious electoral fraud, ushered in a new era of social reform, during which the greatest beneficiaries of public welfare would be workers (as organized and controlled by the Confederation of Mexican Workers (or CTM)), and the urban population. Peasants were also formally incorporated into the official party (as the reformed and renamed Revolutionary Institutional Party (PR) in 1946) via the National Confederation of Campesinos (or CNC), yet they were given only a marginal position within this body, losing even the programmes that had protected them in the previous era, now considered dangerous hotbeds of Cardenists. In any case, as the golden period of industrial 'take-off' via import-substitution industrialization (ISI) opened, the interests of peasants were of little concern. Year after year, most of them would have to leave the countryside in search of food and employment opportunities.

After Cardenism, the state would limit its quest for social justice to ensuring, in principle, universal access to education (Loaeza, 1998: 189), while permitting regional differences in the school network to continue reproducing accumulated social inequality. But following the end to the endemic war between state and Church that had prevailed since the 1920s, President Ávila Camacho profoundly changed the terms in which this process would proceed towards the future. The state of 1940 would successfully consolidate its institutional base, due, among other reasons, to the now extensive network of public schools built by previous administrations. The rules and laws that barred the Church from public education were by now unquestioned, as was the position occupied by private education, whether religious or nonreligious.

The CTM's reward for having voted for Ávila Camacho was the Labour Pact, which nevertheless failed when manufacturing companies refused to implement profit sharing or the principle of union incorporation into decisions.[19] This failure would lead various groups within the labour movement to leave the CTM, which threatened the regime as transformed from the 1940s onwards (Brachet-Márquez, 1994). The president's reaction to this situation of potential destabilization was, on the one hand, to control workers through a more stringent version of the Labour Code, and, on the other, to enact a system of social insurance.[20]

In 1944, the Mexican Social Security Institute (IMSS), created in the previous year, had little to offer to the 103,046 workers it covered exclusively in the Federal District (Zertuche Muños, 1960). Yet its symbolic value was very high, first because it breathed new life into the tripartite principle that had died with the Labour Pact, and secondly because it was to cover the whole of the workforce in the future. Social Security Law (LSS) covered workers and their families for health, maternity, disability, old age, unemployment for those 60 and over, and death, in addition to work accidents and child care.[21] In contrast to European and American social insurance, it did not include unemployment, on the grounds that this contingency was covered by employers' obligation to pay three months' wage and one month per year of employment to discharged employees. However, unlike the American system, it included health insurance for workers and their families, as well as retired workers.

In the years that followed, such was the general satisfaction about the growing incorporation of the workforce into social insurance that the ill-advised ways in which pension funds were being spent, for example, to build the hospital infrastructure of the system without any compensation for the fund, went largely without comment. This would become one of several time bombs to explode in the 1990s. The implications of the segmentation of the health sector (and, consequently, the population) into public health institutions of unequal endowments and benefits also went unnoticed. On the one hand, formally employed labour receiving benefits financed in part through general taxation, and therefore paid by the whole population, and, on the other, the so-called 'open population' covered by the Ministry of Health, but with benefit levels far lower than those enjoyed by the insured, due to the budgetary poverty of this institution. This segmentation, in turn, would create serious obstacles to all future attempts to reform the health or pension systems.

From 1946 on, the prosperity brought by the Second World War began to disappear – among other reasons because the capital that had taken refuge in Mexico gradually withdrew. Mexican governments began the construction of a model of unequal development: low wages, sustained by low agricultural prices, low taxes, total tariff protection, and total submission of industrial proletariat to the PRI's iron control. The 1940s were the era of *charrismo,*[22] or the repression of any movement that was not directly under the official party's control.

In the late 1950s, following the Cuban Revolution, a new era of social welfare legislation began. The government of Lopez Mateos (1958–64) witnessed a new period of economic prosperity and social progressivism, during which social expenditures began to be financed in part via external debt (instead of inflation) and loans from the Alliance for Progress. In 1959, LSS was modified to include agricultural day workers and *ejido* members, and more land was distributed to *campesinos*, so that Lopez Mateos came only second after Cárdenas for land distribution. The Institute for Security and Social Services for State Workers (or ISSSTE), equivalent to IMSS for the public sector, was created the same year, at the same time as the social security plans for oil, electricity and railroad workers were upgraded. Growing prosperity made possible the spectacular expansion of IMSS, doubling the number of its affiliates between 1959 and 1964.[23] Finally, in 1961, to the total surprise of business leaders (Kaufman, 1975), the constitutional obligation to provide profit sharing became mandatory. Lopez Mateos was also the first president to act more than symbolically with respect to housing. Although the preceding governments had offered low interest credit (mostly to the middle sectors and labour elite), such efforts had been limited. Between 1959 and 1967, ISSSTE built 4,279 housing units per year (Aldrete Haas, 1991; Puebla Cadena, 2002).[24] In addition, large housing developments were built and rents in downtown Mexico City frozen.

In sum, the Lopez Mateos government represented a second reformist moment that proved crucial to the construction of Mexico's WS. By 1964, when the successor government assumed office, the working class had recouped its postwar wage losses, and was enjoying a relatively well-developed network of public services and benefits. Still waiting for inclusion were the majority of the agricultural population (especially among the indigenous population) whose poorly paid work had sustained the industrial and social development of the country.

The following presidential period (1964–70) would illustrate the limits of this model of 'stabilizing development', mostly because of the insuperable political obstacles to expanding the fiscal base that financed social policies.[25] Owing to the authorities' severe repression of the physicians' strike in 1964 and the unprecedented repression of the student movement in 1968, President Diaz Ordaz's term (1964–70) is remembered as a dark period in Mexico's contemporary history. Yet despite the relative stagnation of social policy during that period, institutions established by preceding governments continued to grow. The expansion of the educational system followed the accelerated demographic growth experienced during the 1950s,[26] and IMSS kept admitting an ever-growing number of affiliates (from 6,228,700 to 9,496,400 between 1964 and 1970), in tune with the even-greater growth rate of the economy (Spalding, 1978: 202).

Relative inactivity in relation to social policy suddenly changed in 1972, when 'shared development' and its ambitious programme of fiscal, structural and social reforms were introduced, despite raging stagflation, in order to re-launch flagging economic growth, and improve the social conditions of the masses. The cornerstone of this ambitious programme was fiscal reform, which was nevertheless abruptly cancelled only a few months after it had been launched, after a violent confrontation with business leaders that was to affect the relation between state and capital for the rest of the presidential term. In any case, this programme became increasingly problematic, as recession yielded to inflation. A number of labour conflicts broke out, fuelled by the increasing gap between wages and the cost of living.[27] Nevertheless, the government managed to maintain the peace, in part by the creation, in 1972, of the National Worker Housing Fund (or INFONAVIT), to be administered in tripartite fashion, following the social insurance and profit-sharing models. Business did not oppose the additional 5 per cent contribution from wages, despite their animosity towards President Echeverría. Experience had taught them that under a regime of tariff protection, the cost of social policies could be passed on to the end-consumer. Nevertheless, due to its eagerness to build new (and therefore expensive) housing, this programme de facto failed to include the majority of the working class that earned only 1 to 1.5 minimum wages.[28]

The middle sectors of society also received additional benefits during the Echeverría era, first with the extensive campaign to expand education to the declared 10 million (but probably nearer 15 million) people who had no access to education,[29] leading the government to double the number of teachers. Half of this expansion was devoted to elementary education, and the other half to the creation of a wide network of technical schools, understood as alternatives to university education. Additionally, public employees were granted (without having requested it) a 35-hour working week, despite the additional fiscal cost involved. Finally, FOVISSSTE, ISSSTE's housing fund, built 14,655 housing units destined to civil servants (Aldrete Haas, 1991: 87).

The poor also found a modest place within this reform scenario. The National Institute for Community Development (or Indeco) was created to build housing for the poor, while the Commission for the Regularization of Land Ownership (CORETT) undertook the regularization of the countless illegal settlements scattered around Mexico City. Four years after its creation, Indeco had built 28,000 housing units (Aldrete Haas, 1991: 87), which may seem quite modest in comparison with INFONAVIT's 154,626 units or FOVISSSTE's 14,655, yet doubtless represented an important first step. Finally, the urban poor (and middle sectors) benefited from the system of price controls for basic food and their sale in a network of stores incorporated to Conasupo, the government agency that imposed agricultural prices. Campesinos also benefited from this programme, with the creation of self-administered rural stores. Nevertheless, the network was left unfinished before it could be completed in 1976, and would even be partially dismantled by the following government (Fox, 1992).

With the creation of the Programme of Social Solidarity, a final effort was made in 1973 to incorporate the uninsured urban and rural population into social security. IMSS would finance 40 per cent of the programme through invalidity and pension funds (that were already being used to finance the growing deficit in health and maternity insurance). Together with the improvements in the heretofore poorly funded Health Ministry's health services, this reform was supposed to triple health coverage in the rural areas. Nevertheless, faced with the opposition of business, union leaders, and social insurance experts who feared for the financial health of the pension fund, this programme was soon abandoned (Spalding, 1981). In the end, the only universal health services that emerged from the Echeverría term were hospital emergency and family planning services.

At the end of the Echeverría term, neither INFONAVIT nor the efforts to freeze food prices or sustain wages could stop the tide of protest by workers as inflation kept eroding the value of their wages in real terms. Consequently, the government could not count on support from below in its showdown with business, or to mitigate the hostility of union leaders angry about the government's tolerance of democratic tendencies in unions. Months before the end of the term, the government was caught in the middle of two devaluations, an uncontrollable inflation spiral, rumours of a pending self-coup, and verbal battles between the president and business leaders. The government announced the expropriation of about 300,000 acres of irrigated land in the North, to be distributed among *campesinos* who had already taken it by force unopposed by public authorities. The final weeks of the government were characterized by mutual recriminations between the main partners in a regime that, for the first time, faced the limits to growth of the model of unequal development it had chosen.

Despite opposition to the implementation of its social reforms, Echeverría's term substantially advanced Mexico's WS, particularly for the unions, who still held the greatest bargaining power within the official party. Yet the government also had to mend its fences with the middle sectors of society, so that it was practically forced to declare a 'political opening' and to carry out a first electoral reform.

The social programmes of the following six-year term (1976–82), mainly aimed at the poorest in society, owe their origin to the political urgency of resolving the *impasse* in which the Echeverría era had left its successor, José Lopez Portillo. In addition to having to rebuild his relations with virtually every one of the politically active groups (capitalists, union leaders, small and medium-sized farmers), the incoming president had to redefine social welfare, create new types of action and find new interlocutors.

Carefully avoiding the term *campesino*, which was associated with Echeverría populism, the new official discourse talked of the 'marginalized', a term created by social scientists that would not offend business susceptibilities, and had the merit of explicitly including (for the first time) the truly marginalized indigenous population. From 1979 onwards, while the all-too-brief oil boom permitted it, the new government began to build an ambitious and innovative anti-poverty programme whose main features have survived to this day, although under different names, and with different programmes and intensity.

The social policies either begun or expanded during the preceding period (in areas such as education, housing and food price control) were continued, but with important innovations. These included the creation of the National Pedagogical University to improve the standards of teacher education (as well as the levels of salaries), and the transformation of INFONAVIT into a financing organization that left to contractors (generally in the hands of union leaders) the task of doing the building, thereby finding a way to conciliate state and union leaders' interests. The fringe benefits included in wage contracts (mainly transportation and food) were also increased, along with other kinds of benefits such as exempting supermarkets from the 15 per cent sales tax for IMSS and ISSSTE affiliates, and credits for the purchase of furniture. Simultaneously, business managed to end the price controls on 140 price controlled products.

The two major social policy innovations, both targeting the 'marginalized', were the General National Plan Coordinator for Depressed Zones and Marginalized Groups (better known as COPLAMAR) and the Mexican Food System (SAM). The first was conceived as a financial package composed of a number of different programmes but administered by institutions that were already in existence: the CONASUPO-COPLAMAR system for the supply of staple products to marginalized zones; the SAHOP-COPLAMAR system for rural housing, the distribution of drinkable water and road construction; the SEP-COPLAMAR system for the construction of rural schools; and IMSS-COPLAMAR, the most important, to bring health services to areas not covered by the Health Ministry.[30] COPLAMAR's first task was to gather statistical information on the satisfaction of basic needs, a term made fashionable at the time by the World Bank, in housing, nutrition, health and education, leading to the construction of a Basket of Essential Needs (CNSE) used to establish the first official definition of poverty (Hernández Laos, 2001).[31]

SAM, an even more innovative programme, but also one that was potentially more threatening to established commercial markets and regional bosses, sought to ensure the country's food independence by creating a systemic network connecting small producers with the consumers of food products.[32] Although initially promising, in terms of both its productive and its redistributive implications, this programme was discontinued in 1982 when the principle of food autonomy was replaced by that of comparative advantages in the minds of the world's leading economists.

Retrospectively, the end of the Lopez Portillo term marked the culmination of the construction and expansion of Mexico's WS, finally including the peasantry and indigenous people, after which time it would begin to decline and shrink. The end of the Lopez Portillo term was not exempt from turbulence, crises of confidence or devaluations. Still, had it not been for the brutal and unexpected fall of the international price of oil between 1981 and 1982, which brought down the economy,[33] Lopez Portillo would have been remembered as one of the most active, innovative and successful presidents in social policy. During his term, the war on poverty was won for the first time: whereas the Echeverría era had seen a decline of poverty's growth rate from 13.6 to 9.8 per cent, from 1977 to 1981 poverty declined in absolute terms.

Despite these achievements, Mexico's WS was far from complete in 1982, and what had been constructed was ripe with inequalities and anomalies: the rural population served by IMSS-COPLAMAR received, in financial terms, ten times less than IMSS affiliates, but still more than those served by the Health Ministry, while oil workers received more than any of the other insured groups. The indigenous population, marginalized within the marginalized, still received scarce and lower quality education and health services, and no benefits at all in housing or food.

## The declining welfare state (1982–2000)

The year 1982, departure point of the 'lost decade', is generally thought to have coincided with the onset of decline in Mexico's WS. Yet, although the economy unquestionably entered an acute crisis that same year, the WS was slower to decline, due to the efforts of Miguel de la Madrid's government (1982–88) to protect existing programmes as far as possible, in some cases even expanding them, as in the case of social insurance.[34] Nevertheless, the commitment with the IMF to cut public spending necessarily implied the reduction of some social expenditures, resulting in the generalized worsening of quality and working conditions in the educational and health sectors, intensified by the population's lesser ability to turn to the private sector, as in the past. Simultaneously, the policy to unfreeze basic food prices was immediately followed by a steep rise in the cost of living.

From 1982 to 1983, per capita social expenditures fell from $179 to $124, and it kept falling thereafter, reaching $99 per capita in 1986 (as compared with an average fall from $152 to $148 for the rest of Latin America). Additionally, the decentralization to the states of health and education, now part of the Neoliberal agenda, initially turned out to be more costly than the status quo, while creating administrative chaos and higher costs for users.

The solemn declaration in 1984 of the constitutional right to health notwithstanding, the population using Health Ministry services had to pay for medicines as well as consultations.[35] Even so, the damage to public services was less serious than that to wages: while the first fell by 12.5 per cent, going from 6.53 to 5.71 per cent of the GNP, the second plummeted by 57 per cent (Brachet-Márquez and Sherraden, 1994).

Although no reform of IMSS's pension system was carried out during the de la Madrid government (1982–88), its subsequent financial collapse can be traced to the economic crisis that began in 1982. With no reserves, because of the previous uses of the pension fund, IMSS functioned as a system of direct transfers between active and retired workers. As the level of unemployment rose, the capacity to pay pensioners automatically fell. In addition, the normal maturing of the system meant that the relation between the numbers of contributing and retired workers was bound to deteriorate from the 1980s onwards (Bertranou, 1995). During the 1980s tax evasion and the under-registration of the workforce by employers also began to increase dramatically. All of these factors combined to lower the level of pensions by 60 per cent between 1980 and 1988, leaving pensioners with only 35 per cent of the minimum wage. Following protests by the pensioners' association, pensions were increased to 70 per cent of the minimum wage in 1989, yet still remaining below the poverty threshold.

The de la Madrid period is generally understood to have established the legal bases and laboratory experiments for the future transformations of the Mexican economy, and hence its WS. In particular, the legal recognition – in the health law of 1984 – of private health institutions as part of the health sector was the first step in the reformulation of the relation between the private and public realms in Mexico, something that would subsequently evolve towards proposals to subcontract public services to private enterprises. By contrast, the right to health remained on a rhetorical level with no jurisdictional mechanisms to make it mandatory.

By the end of 1988, dissatisfaction and public protest, now backed by strong electoral opposition, had reached the point when it seemed possible that the state, as created and transformed since 1917, was about to undergo profound transformation. If the right won (that is, the National Action Party or PAN), the WS would shrink further, whereas if the left won (that is, the National Democratic Front), it would probably survive, but was unlikely to remain the same. These possibilities, however, were postponed by the proclamation of PRI's candidate Carlos Salinas de Gortari as the winner, despite flagrant electoral fraud.[36]

Carlos Salinas de Gortari (1988–94) took office with little electoral legitimacy and with multiple pressures being exerted by business leaders, the middle classes, the popular sectors, and external creditors. From such apparently contradictory and irreconcilable demands emerged a peculiar combination of political reformism, economic Neoliberalism, and populist welfarism, which preserved the political status quo for another ten years. In the political realm, the government did all it could to destroy and divide its most visible enemies (particularly opposition parties, but also recalcitrant union leaders). In the economic realm, it strengthened and institutionalized the pact with business that had made the control of inflation possible, renegotiated external debt, and signed the North American Free Trade Area treaty (NAFTA) with the United States and Canada. In the social realm, it revived the idea, shelved since 1973, of social solidarity, and now backed by the infrastructure and experience accumulated by COPLAMAR.

Following the COPLAMAR model, the National Solidarity Programme (PRONASOL) was a financial package administered by various established public agencies. In addition to refurbishing the regime's popularity (Bailey, 1993; Dresser, 1993; Molinar and Weldon, 1994), PRONASOL was meant to demonstrate the advantages of focused over unfocused anti-poverty programmes.[37] It offered urban services (water, drainage, electricity and street paving) in the slums on the periphery of cities (which had previously been performed by the Ministry of Public Services and Transportation). In addition, the programme encouraged the self-construction of housing (Puebla Cadena, 2002), continued the services provided by the health care centres and hospitals inherited from COPLAMAR, and offered credits to rural communities (substituting for Banrural). To these programmes were added a few more, of crucial political importance if only restricted funds, such as scholarships for school attendance and financial aid to micro-businesses.

PRONASOL was an expanded version of COPLAMAR as much as a new formula for popular participation, this time not through the official party (in other words, not under the control of union bosses), a fact that would have unanticipated consequences for the survival of the authoritarian political regime which Salinas tried to 'modernize' (Davis and Brachet-Márquez, 1997). As Lustig (1994: 88) points out, as an anti-poverty programme, PRONASOL would have been more efficient if the funds spent had been distributed among the poor (as would later be the case). During the Salinas era, the only initiative in health policy for the uninsured was the devolution to the states of vertical disease control programmes such as the measles and malaria programmes, despite there being insufficient state funds to carry them out effectively.[38] Simultaneously, the policy of decentralization started in the 1980s, and continued during the Salinas era, was beginning to produce a differentiation between poor and rich states in terms of education and health.[39] In 1991, a partial (and temporary) remedy to the problem – a $250 million international loan – was distributed to Chiapas, Oaxaca, Guerrero, Hidalgo, and the Federal District (for services to the marginalized population) through the Support Programme of Health Services for the Uninsured (PASSPA).

IMSS did not escape the Salinas regime's will to reform. For months, a reform project for the institution was secretly debated between the governmental team (chiefly the Treasury), insurance companies, COPARMEX (the employers' association), and union bosses. While the pensioners' association was formally excluded, it was able to advance its claims through the press and various protests (Brachet-Márquez, 2001). For the government, the importance of the project was not exclusively a question of alleviating IMSS's difficulties, but of promoting growth via internal savings, something that was indispensable after years of capital hemorrhaging. In mid-1991, the government formally presented the Labour Congress (CT)[40] with a project to create a complementary system of individual savings and the gradual privatization of the pension system. CT's response was no to privatization and yes to the additional insurance, which did not change the status quo. In view of the proximity of parliamentary and presidential elections (respectively in 1991 and 1994), for which labour support was crucial, the government did not insist. Thus was officially created, in February 1992, the Retirement Savings System (SAR), and immediately extended to ISSSTE, where it is still in existence. SAR, paid in full by employers and initially deposited in individual banks of their choice, represented 2 per cent of the payroll, and was under legal obligation to yield an interest of 2 per cent in real terms.

By the end of 1993, Salinas seemed to have renewed the bases of the PRI's hegemony and smoothed over the popular protests that had been the lot of his predecessors. But in the course of a few months in 1994, a new financial crisis, triggered by a combination of the Zapatista rebellion in Chiapas, the double assassination of the PRI's presidential candidates and its general secretary, and the so-called 'error of December',[41] destroyed the whole complex edifice of these political strategies. Even so, both elections were still won by the PRI, at the cost of a few concessions to old corporatist bosses for their collaboration and the loyal electoral efforts of their affiliates.

In social welfare, Salinism had been building on sand. PRONASOL's financial base – the sale of state enterprises – had disappeared while poverty had continued to grow (from 64 to 66 per cent between 1989 and 1992, according to Boltvinik, 1994) under the impact of re-structuring and stabilization policies. Among the poorest, which still had not attracted the state's attention, were the indigenous people, whose existence began to be politically perceived after the Zapatista rebellion, yet too late to be included in a fast-dwindling WS. Finally, the funds deposited in the SAR system, far from having re-launched economic growth, had disappeared in the December 1994 financial crash, yet had to be reimbursed to account holders.

Zedillo (1994–2000), the last president of a declining regime, rather than the first president of a new rising one, started his term with a financial crisis that required a $50 billion international rescue package, and with no extra funds to continue his predecessor's 'social neoliberalism'. He was indeed a 'social' president (as claimed in his campaign propaganda), but in the sense of cutting many health benefits and reducing anti-poverty expenditures through stricter targeting. The Health Sector's Reform Programme (Poder Ejecutivo Federal, 1997) formalized the segmentation between the paying population and the non-paying poor for whose exclusive benefit the State recognized its responsibility. For them, the health care centres for the uninsured would dispense the services included in a Basic Health Package (PB) consisting of only 12 interventions, selected according to cost-effectiveness and weight of illness criteria.[42] Yet, as for the right to health, strict implementation of the PB did not constitute a legally established obligation for the states. For the 10 million people living too far away from health care centres, mobile units were created,[43] financed by yet another loan from the World Bank. The regions still under IMSS-Solidarity jurisdiction were included in the reform, in principle, but administration of the PB was de facto carried out separately by IMSS and by the states.

Although the changes that were introduced solidified the division that had always existed between social insurance and services for the uninsured, some innovations were introduced: social insurance was made more inclusive through the creation of voluntary insurance tapping the prosperous portion of the informal sector, while the subsector intended to address the needs of the poor was 'integrated' under state government authority. In that way, the so-called National Health System functioned as a 'catch-all' symbol behind which old-time divisions persisted, as modified and modernized by these reforms.

After three years of almost no action on poverty, Zedillo's government created the Education, Health, and Food Programme (PROGRESA) to benefit 2.6 million households in extreme poverty, a modest target in comparison with PRONASOL that had reached approximately half of the estimated 24.2 million indigents (Heredia, 2003), according to the official poverty line.[44] PROGRESA addressed only extreme rural poverty, leaving out urban areas to the point of dismantling the distribution to the poor of subsidized tortillas and milk that had existed since the 1970s. In this new targeting formula, communities or community participation and organization were no longer the units of action or the push factors for demands from below, as had been the case in PRONASOL. The programme directly dispensed food and health care (through the PB), and distributed scholarships to encourage continuous school attendance. In parallel, PROCAMPO provided some subsidies for small-scale agriculture.[45]

More than a social policy, the 1996 reform of social security that privatized the pension system and opened it up to relatively prosperous non-wage workers seems a strategy designed to pull the country out of economic stagnation (Madrid, 2003). With the change from a redistributive to a capital principle, reformers hoped to create a solid instrument of national savings capable of making the country less dependent on foreign capital. To everyone's surprise, especially that of the governmental team, CT did not oppose the reform bill presented in the Chamber of Deputies in September 1995. IMSS' own union and the two main opposition parties, whose voices had increasingly been heard since the electoral reforms of the 1970s and 1980s, opposed the reform instead (Ulloa Padilla, 1996).

After protest had died down and the period of bargaining had ended, the pension system left standing was a privatized capital system that retained some predistributive aspects. In the new Social Security Law (NLSS), compensations for Disabling and Death, and Health Care to the Retired (invariably in the red) remained predistributive, while Retirement and Discharge in Advanced Age[46] were deposited in individual accounts managed by Retirement Fund Administrators (AFORES), the latter private financial institutions separate from banks in order to insure the safety of deposits. Insurance companies were to be in charge of paying pensions. At the end of this complicated financial maze, barely 70 to 75 per cent of the initial deposits would be left (depending upon the commissions charged by AFORES and insurance companies). There was little commitment toward account holders except that of a life pension of one minimum wage guaranteed by the government, which was no different from the level reached in the old system after 1987, but required a far longer period of active life.

For the great majority of workers (especially women) engaged in precarious non-wage work, the jump from 500 to 1,250 weeks of active status required by NLSS (at age 60 for Discharge in Advanced Age or 65 for retirement) was the most punishing change, although the impact of this change would not be felt until the possibility of opting for the old system for those affiliated before 1997 had elapsed. The great winners under the reforms were employers, whose contributions had been lowered from 95 to 74 per cent, while the state's contribution had risen from 5 to 13.85 per cent. Workers' contributions were apparently unchanged, but lasted much longer and lost 20–25 per cent in commissions. Additionally, voluntary affiliation was available for those capable of paying three minimum wages yearly in one single payment.[47]

In 2000, when the first non-PRI government headed by Vicente Fox took office, the situation was far from encouraging. Economic growth and employment generation were too low to validate the social reforms of the 1990s. Extreme rural poverty had not been abated despite PROGRESA, and extreme urban poverty, and poverty *tout court*, had been left untouched. Finally, the American recession, started in 2000 and aggravated by the 2001 terrorists attacks, backfired on the Mexican economy tied to that of the US through NAFTA. Consequently, savings levels reached in AFORES were disappointing.

Despite two failed attempts to expand his government's fiscal base, President Fox intensified the fight against poverty, concentrating first on extreme rural poverty, and then, from 2003 onwards, on urban poverty. This meant increasing the PROGRESA budget by 85 per cent, now renamed Oportunidades. Anti-poverty programmes now covered 4.6 million households, almost doubling the figure for PROGRESA, but still working on the principle of targeting families in extreme poverty. By providing adequate food, health care, and schooling, Oportunidades was concentrating all of its efforts on preventing the next generation from being trapped in poverty. More than attacking poverty, therefore, the programme aimed to break the intergenerational transmission of poverty. In July 2003, a decline in the extremely poor from 22 to 20 million was announced.[48]

Although there is to date no evaluation of the programme (apart from the frequency of school attendance and reception of food), Oportunidades is being criticized by some for its postulate that its beneficiaries will overcome poverty simply by virtue of growing up healthy and attending school. There is also a need, the argument goes, for the creation of economic opportunities. In other words, it is feared that the programme may not have the expected long-term effects unless employment for its 'graduates' is generated, something that cannot be planned within the six-year horizon of presidential terms.

Fox's term is also innovative in health policy for its initiative to launch, in 2004, the so-called 'popular insurance' for the uninsured, a programme jointly financed by the states, the federal government and beneficiaries. It aims to restructure the services to the uninsured on the basis of prepayments calculated according to recipients' capacity to pay, while offering a much wider variety of interventions than those contained in the PB. States may enter the programme at their own request.

Lastly, IMSS announced, in its 2003 financial report, first the 'grave situation' of its pension fund,[49] and secondly that should present conditions continue, Health and Maternity insurance would have only enough to pay salaries by 2020 (*Reforma*, July 2 2003). The report reveals that IMSS' growth has regressed, with fewer clinics and hospitals in 2002 than in 2000,[50] making it increasingly difficult to meet growing demand. For the informed public, however, this was hardly news. Without employment or growth, the pension fund could hardly grow. Health and Maternity, on the other hand, had always run at a deficit, and consequently depended on the surplus from pensions. With the latter's privatization, therefore, it could not fail to become insolvent, an eventuality of which the public had not been apprised in 1995–96 when the government had presented the pension reform as the perfect solution.

It is still too early to draw any conclusions regarding the performance in social policy of Vicente Fox's administration. Yet it is clear that the presidential term has contributed some important innovations within existing financial opportunities. However, it is equally clear that if the economic situation does not improve, his social policies will remain limited in scope, not unlike what has happened to his predecessors since 1982.

## Conclusion

This chapter has attempted to show how the regional, social and institutional inequalities of present-day Mexico have been constructed since the birth of the Mexican nation, first under the imperatives of the formation of a national state, and later in order to consolidate, reproduce and eventually transform the state born from the Revolution of 1910. This process witnessed the creation of a fragmented, unequal and incomplete welfare system, that has included the rural population, especially the indigenous population, too little and too late. The trajectory followed cannot be attributed to the policies of any particular president, as often argued in works limited to a short time span. Neither can it be attributed to a particular period or conjuncture, but to the general dynamic, shared by all social policies, of unequal development that, decade after decade, has generated inequality between rural and urban, between wage and non-wage, between agricultural and industrial, in short, between those favoured and those not favoured.

Of all the social policies analysed in this chapter, the least fragmented, unequal or incomplete, and that which has been most central to national policy since the birth of the Mexican state, is education. Today, practically the whole of the population has access to education. Even so, the national average of six years of education is still low in comparison with several countries that have achieved better results with the same or lower budgetary resources, sometimes in worse political conditions than Mexico. Moreover, although the problem of quality has not been discussed here, specialists agree that Mexican public education has not given quality a high priority, so that today, as in the nineteenth century, the country's elites give their children high-quality private education, most of it foreign. This means that long before Neoliberalism came to reduce social expenditures, one government after another has de facto divided the country between those who can afford quality education and those who have to study in public schools. From such a starting point, universities have had no other option than to select through entrance examinations that exclude a large number of high school graduates, or admit them less selectively, but then fail to offer study plans compatible with the levels required by the labour market.

Health policy, slower to be developed and less politically central than education, but no less crucial for the population's welfare, has divided the country into not two, but five categories with unequal services and benefits. Those who can afford private care, social insurance affiliates are, in turn, divided between oil workers, the private sector, IMSS, the Armed Forces, and ISSSTE affiliates. In addition, there are the uninsured serviced by IMSS health clinics, the uninsured serviced by the Health Ministry, and the 15+ million people who have nothing but will soon receive PB through mobile units, or are already receiving it through Oportunidades.

As for housing, a latecomer among social policies, this has also divided the population into unequal groups: those who can purchase their housing without credit; those who have access to private credit to do the same; those using INFONAVIT credit; those using ISSSTE credit; those who have neither, but may benefit from occasional governmental bounties (e.g.,

Indeco, PRONASOL, etc.); and, finally, those who have nothing, and are still in the majority.

Finally, anti-poverty policy also divides the population, in this case by priority rather than privilege. The low-income non-poor and the poor from whom food and transportation subsidies have been gradually withdrawn since 1982, and who have no access to social insurance or school subsidies.[51] In addition, the varying proportion of the extremely poor selected by PRONASOL and/or PROGRESA and/or Opportunities whose children are allowed to grow up healthy and with longer than average schooling.

What explains such fragmentation and inequality throughout Mexico's contemporary history? Three overlapping explanations may be suggested: fiscal penury, the primacy of corporate groups in the adjudication of services, and targeting. With the exception of a few brief periods of abundance, fiscal penury characterizes the whole period under analysis. It is primarily due to the difficulties, shared by all other countries on the capitalist periphery, of extracting surplus from the productive sector through taxation. However, among these, Mexico has been, is, and will probably continue to be, a country that easily exports capital, and where the state has shown itself to be unable, government after government, of effectively cashing in what little tax it has been able to legislate. Now as before, this situation reflects a consensus among the elites to reduce social expenditures to a minimum, contrasting with countries like Uruguay, Korea or Singapore, that have traditionally and consensually spent a large proportion of their public revenues in social policy, particularly health and education.

The amply commented and universally observed primacy of corporate groups in the adjudication of public services has generally – and correctly – been interpreted as reflecting the perceived imperative for post-revolutionary governments to secure the support of the best organized groups (workers and teachers). This was sometimes associated with the idea (retrospectively questionable) that this was the only way to reach the *El Dorado* of industrialization and urbanization. The second, less common but complementary interpretation argues that workers and public employees have repeatedly been favoured with earlier and superior social benefits not out of some inherent preventive rationality, but in order to resolve the periodic crises of hegemony of the one-party state, in which rewarding 'loyal' against dissident unions was necessary to the regime's survival (Brachet-Márquez, 1994). Whichever is the strongest explanation, it has led to the construction of a social insurance system based almost entirely on contributions from wages, which explains its fragility in the face of economic downturns.

After decades of penalizing the rural population (via low agricultural prices, low credit, low infrastructure, low education and poor health plans) with the consequent mushrooming of poverty in the countryside, the policy of equalizing minimum living standards through targeting has been the last and slowest to emerge in Mexico's welfare state model. It has channelled scarce fiscal resources towards those most urgently in need, admittedly the most effective policy. However, this targeting has been at the expense of high administrative costs of household-by-household selection and consequently high probabilities of type 2 error (rejecting those who should be included). In addition, it has inevitably created intra-community and intra-family divisions between the succoured poor and those left out (Escobar and González de la Rocha, 2003) that threaten with destruction the culture of solidarity that had traditionally sustained the poor in Mexico.

As long as social policies could be financed through debt, international loans or economic growth, these problems did not altogether prevent the construction of the WS, although they did reduce its scope and also made it non-egalitarian, fragmentary, and incomplete. From the moment that debt could no longer fuel social expenditure, the growth and extension of the welfare system ended, and the bureaucratic systems erected to manage it began to deteriorate. This is demonstrated in the crisis of social insurance witnessed since 1982, and in the strenuous, but always insufficient efforts to reverse poverty, which, after decades of systematic neglect, has reached today's morally unacceptable levels.

The incomplete, fragmentary and non-egalitarian nature of the WS forged since independence, especially since the 1910 Revolution, and presently in a state of extreme erosion, has as its counterpart the profound and multiple social injustices to which Mexico's '*olvidados*'[52] have been subjected despite the initial revolutionary thrust that had propelled the country towards more equality. As we close this general, panoramic view of the birth, growth and decline of Mexico's WS, we must accept that the social policies implemented since the revolution have been effective to some extent, but that they have never been comprehensive enough to counteract the persistent tendencies towards social injustice inherited from the colonial period and reproduced thereafter through strategies of unequal development. Although this chapter must be limited to offering a general diagnosis, there is no doubt that the situation it has described calls for more coordination, in the future, between economic and social policy, and for adapting to local conditions the more efficacious strategies implemented in countries comparable to Mexico in most respects but the tolerance and perpetuation of extreme inequality.

## Notes

1. Under the 1812 Cadiz Constitution, Catholicism was the only admissible religion. Heresy and apostasy were punishable by the loss of citizenship. Although this document was never enforced in Mexico, it was very influential. Subsequently, art. 40 of the Apatzinga Constitution would proclaim the freedom of the press and the freedom of expression, except in cases of 'attack[ing] the Dogma' (Villaseñor, 1978).
2. The wealthy hired private tutors for their children, so that they did not have to be included.

3. Joseph Lancaster launched the method in England at the beginning of the nineteenth century: it was a system in which the most advanced students instructed the beginners (Estrada, 1973; Staples, 1981).
4. The country's south-east was poorly covered (except for Mérida, Valladolid and Oaxaca), and so was the north. While the first (with high indigenous population) would stay behind in the future, the north (sparsely populated and with no indigenous population) would soon catch up with the Federal District.
5. Corresponding to years four to six of secondary education.
6. Typhoid fever, typhus, smallpox, malaria, cholera, tuberculosis, tetanus, whooping cough, diphtheria, and yellow fever were endemic during most of the nineteenth century (see Florescano and Malvido, 1982). There was even an epidemic of bubonic plague and pneumonic plague in 1903 (Kumate, 2000: 247).
7. This law called for the public sale of all untilled land.
8. Traditional communal farms.
9. In addition to pushing up the price of traded goods with their passage through each state, this tax was also used by state governors to finance private armies, a factor of destabilization which Porfirio Diaz wanted to do away with.
10. Bazant (1993) disagrees with Martínez Jimenez and others regarding the Porfiriato's alleged failure to create rural schools. He argues that some states (particularly Zacatecas, San Luis Potosi and Tamaulipas) exerted great efforts to disseminate elementary education in the countryside, and that at least half of the 6,000 haciendas must have had their own schools as legally required. But he admits that if the number of rural schools had been proportional to the rural population, they should have reached 40,000 instead of the estimated 2,500–3,000.
11. For more details, see Kretschmer (2000).
12. For more details on epidemics, see Florescano and Malvido (1982).
13. The name is derived from the Magon brothers who headed the movement and were inspired by anarchism.
14. This term refers to the period covering the three presidential terms that followed from that of Plutarco Elías Calles (1924–28): Emilio Portes Gil (1928–30), Pascual Ortiz Rubio (1930–32) and Abelardo Rodriguez (1932–34), who are said to have taken orders from Calles, dubbed 'Máximo Jefe', who removed them from office at will.
15. Nevertheless, the separation of Church from state, the laicity of education and the outlawing of religious orders were incorporated into the 1917 Constitution. Not surprisingly, Pope Pius XI condemned the measures.
16. See Meyer (1974) on this *Chouan* type of peasant rebellion.
17. Vasconcelos was minister of education during Obregón's administration (1920–24).
18. For a summary of this process, see Brachet-Márquez (1994).
19. For a summarized account of the events that marked the constitution, and finally dissolution of the Labour Pact, see Brachet-Márquez, 1994.
20. To make this measure palatable to employers, state spokesmen argued that productivity would rise as labour conflicts became less frequent (Spalding, 1978: 149). According to ILO's calculations, the additional production cost would be 1.14 per cent only, and introduced gradually. The workers' contribution was to be 3 per cent of their already depressed wages, which inevitably triggered labour opposition, at least from outside the CTM.

21. IMSS's childcare installations were de facto restricted to its employees, and were not even sufficient to cover all of them, so that they became a privilege of the few. The 2 per cent Retirement Savings System (SAR) would be introduced in 1992, as explained later.
22. The name originates in 1947 with the imposition of Diaz de León (informally called *charro*, or cowboy, for the way in which he dressed) as the head of the railroad workers' union.
23. The number of affiliates went from 2,657,200 to 5,448,700 (Spalding, 1978: 202).
24. IMSS's housing programme was cancelled as part of the agreement on profit sharing.
25. In the 1970s, the general tax only covered 8.2 per cent of federal expenditures (Brachet-Márquez, 1994: 175).
26. According to INEGI, between 1950 and 1970, the Mexican population almost doubled, going from 25,791,017 to 48,225,238.
27. Mainly a conflict between the democratic tendency, and its rival, the pro-government tendency. See Brachet-Márquez (1994).
28. The minimum wage, although a socially progressive measure when adopted in 1912, was subsequently used as an instrument of monetary and wage policy: the first consisted in letting the minimum wage lag behind inflation so as to slow down the latter, and the second to maintain low wage levels as part of the package of incentives offered to foreign investors. In the 1970s, it was no secret that those who earned only 1 to 1.5 minimum wages were poor.
29. We should note that obtaining 100 per cent coverage for health or education is a great achievement in a mountainous country with a dispersed rural population some of who live in locations that are, connected to other places only by horse trails.
30. 60 per cent of IMSS-Coplamar was financed through public funds, and 40 per cent by IMSS itself. Once again, the pension fund was called in to finance the construction of the infrastructure necessary to provide the health services, without any counterpart for pensioners: more than 3,000 rural clinics were built (in part with donated labour from rural communities), in addition to a network of rural hospitals. For details on the programme, see Barajas (2002).
31. For more details, see Coplamar (1983a, 1983b, 1983c, 1983d) and Fox and Gordillo (1989).
32. For more details on food policy during this period, see Austin and Esteva (1987); Brachet-Márquez and Sherraden (1994); Fox (1992); Luiselli (1985); Redclift (1981) and Spalding (1985).
33. In 1982, international banks suspended their loans to Mexico, and the country had to pay a debt service of $13.3 billion per year (47.5 per cent of its exports). Economic growth fell from 8 to −0.5 per cent and inflation reached 60 per cent. Public sector debt reached 18 per cent of GNP. The country ended up with a $87.6 billion external debt, 61 per cent higher than during the previous two years (Urquidi, 1988).
34. Various groups were admitted into social security during this period, among them university students with no contributions, bringing coverage from 46 to 52 per cent of the population, but with few changes in resources. To close the financial gap, employers' contributions were increased to 95 per cent and the state's share reduced to 5 per cent. In addition, the period of health coverage after discharge was reduced from six to three months.

35. Patients had to pay for consultation, with the amounts calculated on the basis of their declared income. To further reduce costs, the Health Ministry ensured that pharmaceutical laboratories would lower the prices of the 300 drugs most often used in public hospitals.
36. To be able to declare him the winner in the 1989 election, the computers that had been counting votes were shut down.
37. Some analysts of the period (such as Barajas, 2002 and Aguilar Villanueva, 1996) report that Salinas de Gortari attributed the generalized poverty of 40 million Mexicans (as measured by COPLAMAR in 1988) not to adjustment or open market policies, but to the non-targeted nature of his predecessor's social programmes.
38. Some analysts, among them Lopez Arellano (1992: 175), contend that the hasty transformation of these programmes into horizontal ones is responsible for the measles epidemic of 1988–89 and for the rise in malaria, acute respiratory diseases, enteritis and other intestinal infections.
39. The deep disparities in fiscal resources among the states are exposed in Laurell and Ruiz (1996).
40. An umbrella organization that brings together most of the country's unions.
41. This term refers to the announcement in December 1994 of a change in the peso's flotation range, which precipitated the financial panic that ruined the country and created the so-called 'Tequila effect' on international financial relations.
42. The PB which the Fundación Mexicana para la Salud had originally proposed to the government contained 24 basic interventions, out of which only 12 were selected.
43. Twenty years earlier, the same initiative had given disappointing results, owing to the difficulty for the mobile units to respect their schedules, on the one hand, and for health problems to wait for the (timely or untimely) arrival or these units, on the other.
44. The CEPAL/INEGI measure was based on a per capita basic food basket approximately corresponding to US$2.2 per day (Hernández Laos, 2001). According to COPLAMAR's poverty line, only 25 per cent of the population in extreme poverty (estimated to 48.9 million in 2000) was receiving Progresa.
45. See de Vries (1994).
46. According to this section, workers 60 years old and over who are fired may retire.
47. Presently about US$450.
48. In view of changes in the official definition of poverty (Sedesol, 2002) that distinguish between *food poverty* (or the inability to purchase the minimum food basket with a household's total income), *capacity poverty* (or the inability to cover food, health and education minima), and *patrimonial poverty* (or the inability to purchase the INEGI/Cepal basket), some experts argue that these results are not altogether clear, given that they are only statistically significant for food poverty in rural areas, and for capacity poverty in urban areas (Cortés, 2005).
49. Simultaneously, ISSSTE has been gestating its own reform since 2000, but to date without revealing the content of its internal debates or decisions.
50. 1,784 in 2000 against 1,771 in 2002.
51. Elementary education is free (although replete with 'voluntary' contributions), and provides free books, but not free (mandatory and multiple) uniforms, school supplies or transportation to school; above primary education, books must also be purchased.
52. *Los olvidados* (or the forgotten) is the title of a movie by director Buñuel.

## References

Aguilar, L. (1996). 'El federalismo mexicano: funcionamiento y tareas pendientes'. *Revista Mexicana de Sociología*, 58 (3), 3–37.

Aldrete Haas, José A. (1991). *La Deconstrucción del Estado mexicano: políticas de vivienda 1917–1988*. Mexico: Nueva Imagen.

Arce Gurza, F. (1981). 'En busca de una educación revolucionaria: 1924–1934', in Z. Josefina, E. Dorothy, S. Anne and F. Arce (1981), *Ensayos sobre historia de la educación en México*. Mexico: El Colegio de México, pp. 171–224.

Austin, J. and Gustavo, E. (eds) (1987). *Food Policy in Mexico: The Search for Self-Sufficiency*. Ithaca: Cornell University Press.

Barajas, Gabriel (2002). *A Las Politicas de administración de la pobreza en México: ayer y hoy @ Foro Internacional* 42 (1), 63–98.

Bazant, M. (1993). *Historia de la educación*. Mexico: El Colegio de México.

Bertranou, J. (1995). 'La política de la reforma a la seguridad social en México. Análisis de la formulación del Sistema de Ahorro para el Retiro.' *Estudios Sociológicos* 13 (37), 3–24.

Boltvinik, J. (1994). 'La satisfacción de las necesidades esenciales en México en los setentas y ochentas', in P. Montayo and J. Woldenberg (eds), *Desarrollo, desigualdad y medio ambiente*. Mexico: Cal y Arena, pp. 99–176.

Brachet-Márquez, V. (2002). 'Elementos para investigar la capacidad estatal político-administrativa en materia de salud pública. Los casos de Guanajuato, Oaxaca y Sonora.' *Estudios Sociológicos* 20 (58), 239–52.

Brachet-Márquez, V. (2001). 'La reforma de los sistemas de salud y previsión social en México, 1982–1999'. *Reflexiones sobre Política Social Social* 5, 103–30.

Brachet-Márquez, V. (1994). *The Dynamics of Domination: State, Class, and Social Reform in Mexico (1910–1990)*. Pittsburgh: Pittsburgh University Press.

Brachet-Márquez, V. (ed.) (1985). 'Salud para todos en el año 2000'. *Estudios Sociológicos* 2 (5–6), 417–62.

Brachet-Márquez, V. (1984a). 'La planificación familiar en México: proceso de elabouración de una política pública'. *Revista Mexicana de Sociología* 46 (2), 285–310.

Brachet-Marquez, V. (1984b). 'El proceso social en la formación de políticas: el caso de la planificación familiar'. *Estudios Sociológicos* 2 (5–6), 51–70.

Brachet-Márquez, V. and Sherraden, M. (1994). 'Political Change and the Welfare State: The Case of Health and Food Policies in Mexico (1970–1990)'. *World Development* 22 (9), 1295–1312.

COPLAMAR (1983a). *Macroeconomía de las necesidades esenciales en México. Situación actual y perspectivas al año 2000*. Mexico: Siglo Veintiuno Editores.

COPLAMAR (1983b). *Educación*. Mexico: Siglo Veintiuno Editores.

COPLAMAR (1983c). *Salud*. Mexico: Siglo Veintiuno Editores.

COPLAMAR (1983d). *Vivienda*. Mexico: Siglo Veintiuno Editores.

Cortés, F. (2005). *'La caida de* la pobreza? México 2000–2004.' Documento de trabajo, Centro de Estudios Sociológicos. México: El Colegio de México.

Davis, D. and Brachet-Márquez, V. (1997). 'Rethinking Democracy: Mexico in Historical Perspective.' *Comparative Studies in Society and History* 27, 86–119.

De Vries, P. (1994). 'Procampo and the Politics of Intervention: A Case Study and a Direct Subsidies Programme', Paper presented at the 28th Congress of the Latin American Studies Association, Atlanta, Georgia.

Dresser, D. (1993). 'Bringing the Poor back In: National Solidarity as a Strategy of Regime Legitimation', in W. Cornelius, A. Craig and J. Fox (eds), *Transforming State–Society Relations in Mexico: The National Solidarity Strategy*. La Jolla, CA: University of California, pp. 143–65.

Esping-Andersen, G. (1990). *The Three Worlds of Welfare Capitalism*. Princeton, NJ: Princeton University Press.

Estrada, D. (1973). 'Las escuelas lancasterianas en la ciudad de México, 1822–1842'. *La educación en la historia de México* 22 (4), 494–513.

Florescano, E. and Malvado, E. (eds) (1982). *Ensayos sobre la historia de las epidemias en México*. Mexico: IMSS.

Fox, J. (1992). *The Politics of Food in Mexico*. Ithaca: Cornell University Press.

Fox, J. and Gustavo, G. (1989). 'Between State and Market: The Campesino's Quest for Autonomy', in W. Cornelius, J. Gentleman and P. Smith (eds), *Mexico's Alternative Political Futures*, Research Monograph Series 30. La Jolla, CA: University of California. pp. 131–72.

González-Block, M. (1989). *Economía política de las relaciones centro-locales de las instituciones de salud*. Doctoral Thesis. Mexico: El Colegio de México.

González-Block, M., Angel, M. Gutierrez-Calderon, E. and Bardales, L. (1997). 'Las cuentas estatales de salud: el gasto de las entidades federativas', in J. Frenk (ed.), *Observatorio de Salud*. Mexico: Funsalud, pp. 143–71.

González Diaz Lombardo, F. (1973). *El derecho social y la seguridad social integral*. Mexico: El Colegio de México.

González Navarro, M. (1994). *Sociedad y cultura en el Porfiriato*. Mexico: Conaculta.

González Navarro, M. (1979). 'El primer salario mínimo'. *Historia Mexicana* 28 (3), 370–400.

Heredia, J. (2003). 'Distributive Justice and Poverty Alleviation in Mexico (1992–2000)'. Unpublished Doctoral thesis. Warwick: University of Warwick.

Hernández Laos, E. (2001). 'Retos para la medición de la pobreza en México'. Paper presented to the International Conference 'Poverty: Concepts and Methodology', Mexico City, 28–9 March.

Hicks, A. (1999). *Social Democracy and Welfare Capitalism: A Century of Income Security Politics*. Ithaca, NY: Cornell University Press.

Huber, E. and Stevens, J. (2001). *Development and Crisis of the Welfare State: Parties and Policies in Global Markets*. Chicago: University of Chicago Press.

Huber, E. and Stevens, J. (2000). 'Partisan Government, Women's Employment and the Social Democratic Service State'. *American Sociological Review* 45, 323–42.

Huber, E., Ragin, C. and Stephens, J. (1993). 'Social Democracy, Christian Democracy, Constitutional Structure and the Welfare State'. *American Journal of Sociology* 99, 711–49.

Kaufman, S. (1975). *The Profit-Sharing Decision: Politics in an Authoritarian Regime*. Princeton: Princeton University Press.

Kretschmer, R. (2000). 'La medicina institucional en México', in H. Aréchiga and L. Bribiesca (eds), *Un siglo de ciencias de la salud en México*. Mexico: Fondo de Cultura Económica, pp. 118–60.

Kumate, J. (2000). 'La investigación clínica en México', in H. Aréchiga and L. Bribiesca (eds), *Un siglo de ciencias de la salud en México*. Mexico: Fondo de Cultura Económica, pp. 244–86.

Laurell, A. Cristina and L. Ruiz (1996) *¿Podemos garantizar el derecho a la salud?* Mexico DF: Fundación Friedrich Ebert.

Loaeza, S. (1998). 'La Iglesia y la educación en México. Una historia en episodios', in P. Aizpuru (ed.), *Historia de la educación y enseñanza de la historia*. Mexico: El Colegio de México, pp. 173–93.

López Arellano, O. (1992). 'La política de salud en México' in A. Laurell (ed.), *Estado y políticas sociales en el neoliberalismo*. Mexico: Fundación Friedrich Ebert, pp. 165–183.

Luiselli, C. (1985). *The Route to Self-sufficiency in Mexico: Interaction with the US Food System.* Monograph Series 17. La Jolla, CA: University of California.
Lustig, N. (1994). 'Solidarity as a Strategy of Poverty Alleviation' in, W. Cornelius, A. Craig and J. Fox (eds), *Transforming State–Society Relations in Mexico: The National Solidarity Strategy.* La Jolla, CA: University of California Press, pp. 79–96.
Madrid, Raúl L. (2003). *The Politics of Pension Privatization in Latin America and Beyond.* Stanford: Stanford University Press.
Martínez Jimenez, A. (1973). 'La educación elemental en el Porfiriato.' *Historia Mexicana* 22 (4), 514–52.
Meyer, J. (1974). *El conflicto entre la Iglesia y el Estado.* Tomo 2 de '*La cristiada*', vol. 21. Mexico.
Molinar, J. and Weldon, J. (1994). 'Programa Nacional de Solidaridad: determinantes partidistas y consecuencias electorales'. *Estudios Sociológicos* 12 (34), 155–82.
Mora, L. (1949). *El clero, la educación y la libertad.* Mexico: Empresas Editoriales. *Opportunidades,* (2000). Mexico DF: Sedesol.
Palacios, G. (1998). 'Una historia para campesinos: el maestro rural y los inicios de la construcción del relato historiográfico posrevolucionario, 1932–34', in P. Aizpuru (ed.), *Historia de la educación y enseñanza de la historia.* Mexico: El Colegio de México, pp. 237–62.
Poder Ejecutivo Federal (1997). *Plan Nacional de Desarrolo.* Mexico DF: Secretaria de Hacienda.
Puebla Cadena, C. (2002). *Del intervencionismo estatal a las estrategias facilitadoras. Cambios en la política de vivienda en México.* Mexico: El Colegio de México.
Rajchenberg, S. (1996). 'Las enfermedades profesionales en el México revolucionario',in E. Malvado and M. Morales (eds), *Historia de la salud en Mexico.* Mexico: INAH, pp. 53–64.
Redclift, M. (1981). 'Development Policy Making in Mexico: The Sistema Alimentario Mexicano'. Working Paper in US–Mexican Studies. La Jolla, CA: University of California.
Sales Heredia, J. (2003). 'Distributive Justice and Poverty Alleviation in Mexico (1992–2000)'. Doctoral Thesis, University of Warwick.
Sales Sarrapi, C., F. S. Soberón and A. V. Amezcua (1997). 'La reforma al sistema de pensioner: el case Mexicano', *Gazeta de Economía,* supplements 2(4), 11–61.
Salinas de Gortari, C. (1991). *III Informe de Gobierno.* Anexo estadístico. Mexico: Gobierno Federal.
Sedesol/Comité Ejecutivo para la medición de la pobreza (2002). *Medición de la pobreza. Variantes metodológicas y estimación preliminar.* Mexico DF: Sedesol.
Spalding, R. (1985). 'El Sistema Alimentario Mexicano: ascenso y decadencia.' *Estudios Sociológicos* 3 (8), 4141–438.
Spalding, R. (1981). 'State Power and its Limits. Corporatism in Mexico.' *Comparative Political Studies* 14 (2), 414–38.
Spalding, R. (1978). 'Social Security Policy Making. The Formation and Evolution of the Mexican Social Security Institute'. Doctoral Thesis. Carolina: University of North Carolina.
Staples, A. (1981). 'Panorama educativo al comienzo de la vida independiente', in J. Vazquez, D. Tanck de Estrada, A. Staples and F. Gurza (eds), *Ensayos sobre historia de la educación en México.* Mexico: El Colegio de México, pp. 117–70.
Ulloa Padilla, O. (1996). 'Nueva Ley del Seguro Social: la reforma previsional de fin de siglo.' *El Cotidiano* 78, 27–52.
Urquidi, Victor (1988). 'Perspectivas de la economía Mexicana con especial referencia a la dueda externa', *Revista de El Colegio de Sonora,* 1(1), 70–85.

Vaughan, M. (1982). *The State, Education and Social Class in Mexico, 1880–1928*. Illinois: Northern Illinois University Press.

Vázquez Zoraida, J. (1967). 'La República Restaurada y la educación', *Historia Mexicana* 17 (2), 200–11.

Vázquez, J. (1965). 'Historia de la educación'. *Historia Mexicana* 15 (2–3), 291–309.

Villaseñor, G. (1978). *Estado e Iglesia en el caso de la educación*. Sociología Investigaciones. Mexico: Editorial Edicol.

Womack, J. (1970). *Zapata and the Mexican Revolution*. New York: Vintage Books.

Zertuche Muñoz, F. (1960). *Historia del IMSS: los primeros años*. Mexico: IMSS.

# 3
# Social Policy in a Development Context: The Case of Peru

*Francisco Sagasti, Fernando Prada and Mario Bazán*

## Introduction

During the last half century ideas of how to bring about development have changed and evolved.[1] Over the course of the past twenty years, development theory and practice has stressed institutional and social aspects, including poverty reduction, the efficiency of public policies, democratic governance, and conflict prevention and resolution. The World Bank dedicated its 1990 World Development Report to poverty, and the following year, in an evaluation of the development experience of the preceding forty years (World Bank, 1991), it established new concerns for multilateral development banks about the relation between social development and social policies in opposition to 'structural adjustment policies'. UNDP proposed the concept of 'sustainable human development' as an attempt to integrate economic growth, social development, and environment conservation (Speth, 1994). More recently, Amartya Sen has conceived development as a process of expanding human capacities, thereby reintroducing moral and ethical aspects to development policies. From this perspective, access to goods and services are intermediate means of exercising human freedom and choosing different ways of living (Sen, 1999).

What has been the result of five decades of attempts to promote development? A handful of low-income countries, particularly in Southeast Asia, have achieved standards of living comparable to those in industrialized countries in only one generation. Life expectancy and educational levels have increased in most developing countries, and per capita income has doubled in countries like Turkey, Brazil, South Korea and China in less than a third of the time it took to do so for the United Kingdom or the United States a century or more earlier. Despite this, the absolute number of poor people has increased in almost all regions in the last twenty years, the environment has suffered marked deterioration, and income disparities have noticeably increased (Sagasti *et al.*, 1999: 27–8).

How far has Peru advanced towards implementation of a social policy that is *developmental* (facilitating and promoting economic growth and structural transformation), *democratic* (deriving its legitimacy from popular participation and an electoral process), and *socially inclusive* (pursuing social policies that provide equal opportunities for all citizens to realize to a substantial degree their capacities for a decent inclusion in societal affairs)?

During the last sixty years, Peruvians have experienced a wide range of economic, political, and ideological swings – liberalism, authoritarianism, and populism – as well as profound social transformations. However, these various political and economic systems were never consolidated, leading to the creation of an unstable path for economic and social development.

Other Latin American countries began to apply policies to consolidate their internal markets after the Great Depression. However, the emergence of a developmental state did not fully materialize in Peru until the 1950s. On the contrary, Peruvian commercial regulations exemplified orthodox economic policies, creating two disconnected economies: one 'traditional', related to the agrarian sector, and located mainly in the Highlands; and an incipient 'modern sector', characterized by exports, international markets and foreign investment. This 'dual' economy was related to a fragmented social fabric, in which much of the population suffered from social, political, and economic exclusion. In this context, the design of public policies was identified with the elite group; it provided social services mainly to wage-earning workers, the bureaucracy, and the more well-established urban social groups.

As the modern sector developed and expanded in the 1960s and 1970s, cities were flooded with thousands of migrants, seeking better job opportunities and education. The emergence of the *barriadas* – or *Pueblos Jóvenes* – around Lima and other Peruvian cities brought about a new relationship between the urban poor and the government. The challenge then was how to extend the provision of social services and the benefits of economic growth, from which the State incurred large external debts financing this expansion.

When General Juan Velasco Alvarado took power in 1968, he initiated radical social and political reforms, with a national aim of creating a developmental state.

Nevertheless, the military government failed to maintain macroeconomic equilibrium, and the fragile Peruvian public finances could not sustain such a project. The democratic governments that followed could not maintain the levels of welfare spending because of fiscal limitations and economic crises (especially those that occurred in 1983 and 1988). During the 1990s, President Fujimori executed Neoliberal policies, promoting targeted programmes to fight against poverty instead of the universal social policies that had characterized previous decades.

Considering these political fluctuations, it is difficult to conclude how well Peru has advanced towards development, and towards the establishment of inclusive and democratic social policies. Peruvians are faced with difficult challenges in the twenty-first century: How to overcome a situation in which more than half the population lives below the poverty line, and almost 25 per cent exist in extreme poverty; and how to tackle social, political and economic exclusion, while promoting citizen rights and accumulating wealth to sustain the development process.

As Jorge Basadre stated five decades ago, independence carried a promise of prosperity and well-being for all Peruvians, which Peru has not yet honoured (Basadre, 1958), and which, furthermore, has caused widespread pessimism about Peru's future. Less than twenty years before the bicentenary of independence, the 'Peruvian promise' remains unfulfilled, largely because of lost opportunities by political leaders when the international situation became favourable for the Peruvian economy, and when democratic governments – which initially had legitimacy and widespread popular support – did not take advantage of such propitious conditions.

One of the main consequences of half a century of lost opportunities is illustrated in Figure 3.1. Gross domestic product (GDP) per capita reached its highest level in 1975; from then on, and for the next 25 years, the overall trend has been downwards, with only occasional upturns. This reduction in levels of prosperity is the result of not having adopted appropriate measures from 1950 onwards, and of the internal difficulties of the last quarter-century, which have been aggravated by violence, terrorism, economic mismanagement, and corruption. As a result, the 55 per cent of Peruvians who were born after 1975 have experienced declining levels of prosperity throughout their lifetimes.

In this chapter, we argue that Peru has failed to overcome its structural problems over the last six decades. Recurring economic crises, public financial problems and changes of political regimes, have led to the failure of designed social policies, funded and executed from above, to increase the welfare of most Peruvians. The recent recuperation of democracy has revived the debate about social and development policies; however, there is less clarity regarding how to implement them, and the challenges ahead are pressing.

This chapter is divided into four sections. The first briefly addresses some of the conceptual developments geared towards achieving a more inclusive and integral view of social policies. The second section offers a background description of past and present Peruvian social policy. The third section identifies the main challenges for social policies in Peru for the next twenty years. The final section presents a proposal for designing and implementing social policy in Peru, building on the consultation processes regarding development strategies that Agenda: PERU carried out during the last decade.

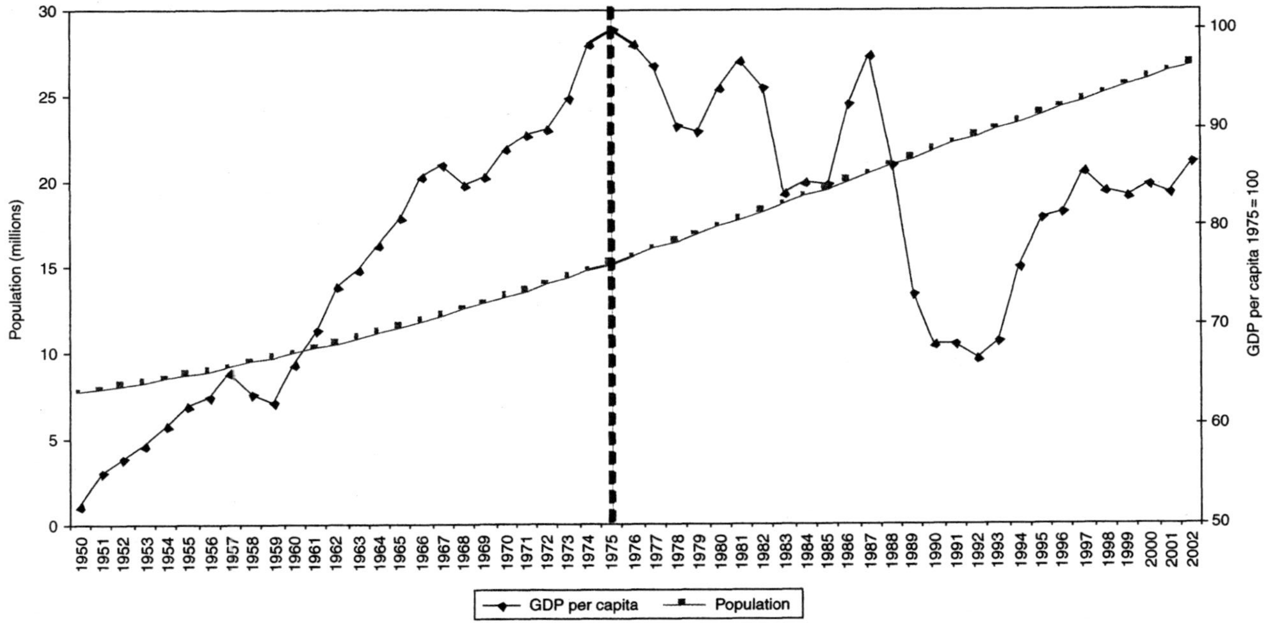


*Figure 3.1* GDP per capita and total population, 1950–2002

*Source*: Agenda: PERU, 2001 (actualized to 2002).

## Social policy and development in context: changes underway for Peruvian social policy

Theorists and political leaders have continuously occupied themselves with questions such as the following: (i) How can a society move towards development with a social policy that can be economically sound, while at the same time maintaining social objectives? (ii) How can we integrate excluded groups within the social, economic, and political spheres? (iii) How can we organize the provision of public services? And (iv) How can we establish controls and counterbalances for the exercise of economic and political power? These issues have now assumed greater importance as a result of the widespread adoption of democratic practices throughout the world, the increased role of popular and civil society participation, the process of decentralization and regionalization, and the recent attempts to articulate a long-term vision for Peru in the context of regional integration and globalization. In addition, during the past few decades, those concepts which have driven poor countries to improve their living conditions have evolved and changed. These changes in thinking about development have signalled a transition from a 'traditional' approach to social policies to a renewed set of changes, which have aimed to improve the results of social policies.

What can be called the 'traditional approach' to social policy in Latin America is based on rigid state control of the design, funding and implementation of social programmes – which are centrally managed and standardized, whether in the areas of education, health, nutrition, population, or sanitation services (Sagasti, Iguíñiz and Schuldt, 1999). These ideas were heavily influenced by the theories of social organization, which in various industrialized countries in the post-Second World War period led to the emergence of the 'welfare state'. They were adopted in Latin America on a limited scale because of fiscal restrictions. Social policies in Latin America, with the relative exceptions of Costa Rica, Uruguay, and Chile, were oriented towards the universal provision of social services, with marked differences in coverage and considerable deficiencies in most countries. This approach was prevalent in the region until the mid-1980s and the beginning of the 1990s, when most countries initiated structural adjustment reforms (Franco, 1996; Maurás and Minujin, 1998). The limitations and criticism of the traditional approach can be summarized as follows (Schuldt, 1998):

- Social dimensions are treated separately, in isolation from most government policies, especially macroeconomic policy.
- There is little awareness of the ways in which economic policies have an impact on social policies, and in particular on how economic policies may encourage social development if designed integrally.
- There is limited scope for the private sector and civil society in the design, implementation, and evaluation of social policies.

- Social policies rarely take into account local conditions; they are often designed and work on a broad national scale and heavily influenced by international organizations.
- Social policy is generally formulated from the viewpoint of mitigating the effects of economic policies such as adjustment or stabilization.
- There is a strong bias towards a paternalistic approach, instead of improving the human capacities of a local population. In the long term, this approach could generate rent-seeking and passive attitudes, distorting the impact of social policies.
- Specific activities and programmes in the field of social policy are designed to meet short-term needs that arise primarily from political calculations.

Despite the extensive criticism of this approach, some of its characteristics persist in the design and practice of present-day social policies. Peru is currently in the process of implementing several reforms in the execution and design of social policies. The public sector continues to be the main actor in the execution of social policies; their design is centralized in a small group of ministries whose policies are largely disconnected from economic policies. Table 3.1 describes the main features of the traditional approach in contrast to changes in social policy currently underway in Peru. These changes and what drives them are described in the following section.

## Social policy in Peru: economic development and the evolution of the underlying social structures and social policies from 1940 to 2000

Despite the deterioration of per capita GDP, the traditional approach to social policies has achieved some long-term results in terms of improving the living conditions of Peruvians. Life expectancy rose from 35.7 years in 1940 to 68.5 years sixty years later, whereas similar improvements took more than double the time in some developed countries. In the case of education, the rate of illiteracy has dropped from 60 per cent in 1940 to 7 per cent in 2000 (similar figures for both males and females). For the same period, the adult population that lacked any formal education was reduced from almost 58 per cent to 8 per cent, and the proportion of the population with higher education rose from 0.9 per cent to 20.1 per cent. Improvements in health and education indicators were also associated with the improvement of other social services access indicators.[2] Despite these achievements, today more than half of the Peruvian population lives in poverty, but the extent varies significantly between regions and population cohorts. Political, social, and economic exclusion are amongst the main structural problems, phenomena whose roots can be traced back several decades.

*Table 3.1* The traditional approach to social policy and the changes underway in Peru

| *Dimension* | *Traditional approach* | *Changes underway* |
|---|---|---|
| Institutional and organizational structure | • Controlled by the state with limited inputs from the private sector and civil society<br>• Centralization<br>• Vertical: ministries, agencies and programmes act in an isolated manner | • Controlled by the state but with more room for the private sector and civil society for manoeuvring<br>• Decentralization and elections of regional governments<br>• Ministries, agencies, and programmes coordinate with one another. Attempts to merge most important social programmes |
| Operating criteria | • Standardized supply of social services and programmes<br>• Comprehensive coverage with standard programmes and services<br>• Beneficiaries have no voice in the design and implementation of social programmes, nor are they allowed to choose services ('government knows best')<br>• Availability of private sector services. They are generally better in terms of quality, but are more costly and have limited coverage | • Differentiated supply of social services and programmes<br>• Comprehensive coverage, but adapted to local conditions<br>• Beneficiaries have more say in the design and implementation of social programmes, and are given a limited choice of services<br>• The public sector, the private sector and civil society join forces to improve the quality of services and offer them at a reasonable cost |
| Funding | • Almost entirely state funded through the national budget<br>• Centralized allocation of resources according to administrative criteria<br>• No allowances made for differences in purchasing power of users | • Mostly state funded with supplementary co-financing<br>• Decentralized allocation of resources according to social impact criteria<br>• Allowances made for differences in purchasing power of users |

*Sources*: Adapted from Rolando Franco, 1996; Maurás and Minujín, 1998; Sagasti, Iguíñiz y Schuldt, 1999.

## The 1940s: social and political transformations in the context of a dual economy

The early 1930s were decisive years in Peruvian republican history. Various conflicts converged because of the Great Depression, and the changes that had been affecting Peruvian society since the end of the war with Chile in the previous century. The once-buoyant economy, founded mainly on agricultural and livestock exports such as cotton, sugar, and wool, collapsed as commodity prices tumbled. While most Latin American countries succeeded in strengthening their industrial base and internal markets as a response to the economic crisis of the 1930s, Peru enjoyed only limited success in this area due both to the structure of its economy, which was composed mainly of mining and agricultural foreign enclaves and also the political domination of a landowning elite. In contrast to many Latin American countries, where the 1930s and onward was characterized by the emergence of a developmental state, this did not fully materialize in Peru until two decades later (Abugattas, 1987).

One important limitation to the emergence of a development state in Peru was the disconnection between traditional and incipient modern sectors, described as the 'dual structure' of the Peruvian economy (Fitzgerald, 1976). For example, 6 per cent of all corporations controlled 65 per cent of nationwide sales and exports during this decade. Twenty years later, this characteristic still persisted. In 1968, the 'modern' sector still generated 67 per cent of GDP, but it employed only 35 per cent of the population. Large modern capital-intensive enterprises coexisted within the same economic branch with 'traditional' small-scale non-corporate units which were characterized by low productivity (Thorp and Bertram, 1978: 9).

Around this incipient 'modern' sector, some political movements fought for the establishment of a number of political and social rights during the 1930s, such as the eight-hour working day, the establishment of a universal social health system and the establishment of women's right to vote. During the 1940s, the social reformist American Popular Revolutionary Party (APRA) consolidated its social base around middle-class workers. Along with other less influential leftist movements, APRA organized trade unions within the mining and agricultural sectors and formed a focus of opposition to the political control exercised by the elite class. In general, the bourgeoisie and the urban working middle class were relatively weak in Peru, where more than 70 per cent of the population lived in rural areas, in poor living conditions, with practically no access to public services and with little opportunity for political participation.[3] Even though it is not possible to describe their government measures as social policy, both Manuel Prado (1939–45) and José Luis Bustamante (1945–48) supported the type of interventions that prevailed during the following decades. These included: (i) price controls to protect urban population income; (ii) the provision of social services for organized urban employees, such as health, education, and unemployment assistance; and (iii) sporadic interventions in rural areas, specially funded by international organizations. State intervention and nationalist economic policies were launched in this period in an attempt to promote industrialization, supported by the APRA party's majority in the Congress. The Industrial Promotion Law in 1940 allowed Manuel Prado's government to grant special incentives, though some of them benefited his family's enterprises (Peruvian Times, 15 January 1943: 1).

To protect the urban population's level of income and to promote the interests of industry, the government increased controls over prices, land allocation and the distribution mechanisms of agricultural products, while at the same time lowering and reducing import tariffs. For example, President Bustamante introduced several bills requiring that sugar and oil producers should supply the local market at fixed prices during periods of inflation. At this time, the government adopted foreign exchange controls, carried out legislative measures to raise wages for organized labour, and also continued to increase public employment. These mechanisms were the expression of new economic and social forces that had emerged during the 1930s and 1940s, in which the political support for the middle class, headed by the APRA party, was central. To finance price controls and growing middle-class demands, government spending grew 4.6 times from 1939 to 1948. This increase was financed by export taxes, which grew from 4 to 14 per cent of total earnings in the same period (Thorp and Bertram, 1978: 185–8). During this decade, the indicators of public health were improved by the introduction of medical technology to combat the main transmissible diseases – such as malaria, typhus, bubonic plague, and yellow fever. The Rockefeller Foundation funded an extensive vaccination programme in coordination with health authorities to decrease the infant and women mortality in high-risk rural areas. The impact of this programme was enormous, in large part because of its contrast with the former policy of complete neglect of public health in rural areas (Aramburu *et al.*, 1983: 35). In the case of education in rural areas the results were disappointing, despite the increased awareness of public authorities influenced by the *indigenismo*. An ambitious and innovative programme of peasant schools was introduced in 1944. Although it did provide a curriculum designed to match the interests of the rural population, such as agricultural education, health instruction, etc.), the classes were still given in Spanish (Drysdale and Myers, 1975).

## The 1950s: *laissez-faire* and the foundation of a new state–society relationship

General Manuel Odría (1948–56) assumed power through a military coup. He was supported by the economic elite who were interested in ending the social movement led by the APRA party. President Odría quickly reversed import controls, liberalized the exchange rate, and installed a *laissez-faire* export-led growth regime with a low priority being given to import-substituting industry[4] and an increased emphasis on foreign direct investment and transnational companies. The second Prado government (1956–62), elected with the support of the APRA party, also followed this trend. This period is known as the *Convivencia,* as APRA returned to active political life after being banned by General Odría. By the first half of the 1950s, the Peruvian commercial regulations were the most 'free-trade' oriented in Latin America and an example of orthodox economic policies (Thorp and Bertram, 1978: 205). As Hunt states: 'In a continent that was witnessing ever-increasing state intervention in economic life in country after country, Peru (. . .) turned around to begin a march in the other direction that continued for the next 18 years' (Hunt, 1974).

This period was characterized by a rapid economic and exports growth in a context of favourable terms of trade. The volume of exports rose 6 per cent a year from 1948 to 1951, 10 per cent from 1952 to 1959, and 21 per cent from 1959 to 1962; and gross national product, in real terms, experienced average annual growth of 4.7 per cent from 1950 to 1959. This expansion meant that during this period per capita income grew at a rate of 2.4 per cent per year (Thorp and Bertram, 1978: 261). Nevertheless, the expansion accented the unequal income distribution: average annual income of workers in the modern sector of the economy increased by 4.1 per cent from 1950 to 1966, while rural sector workers' average annual income increased by only 1.3 per cent (Webb, 1973).

Several processes which took place in the 1950s became influential driving forces for social transformations in subsequent decades. As the manufacturing sector developed and expanded and the agricultural sector became increasingly mechanized, cities were flooded with thousands of migrants, seeking better job opportunities and education. The emergence of the *barriadas* around the Peruvian capital and other cities in the Coast – later called *Pueblos Jóvenes* or human settlements – initiated a new relationship between the urban poor and the government. This trend was reinforced by the increase of the annual population growth rate. From 1.9 per cent in 1941, it increased to 2.2 per cent in 1950 and reached 2.7 per cent in 1961. Urbanization, understood as the number of people residing in cities with more than 2,500 inhabitants, rose from 18 per cent in 1940 to 39 per cent in 1961.[5]

This situation brought about the design of explicit social policies for the first time in Peru. These were largely focused on providing basic social services to the new urban population, and increased attention was paid to the social demands of the organized urban middle class. At this point, the concentration of social services in Lima became notorious, reinforcing a process of massive migration. According to Collier, Odría's involvement in the formation of settlements was a response to a strategy to offer an alternative to the kind of social mobilization that APRA was promoting, centred on the lower classes rather the on the middle class (Collier, 1975: 134). President Odría established public work boards in several departments with the aim of improving the local infrastructure in response to a range of local problems (sanitation, housing, rural roads, small irrigation plants, among others[6]). These were coordinated and supervised by a central authority from the Ministry of Production and Public Works. Prado's second administration strengthened this mechanism and in 1956 it also created the *Fondo Nacional de Desarrollo Económico* (FNDE), which allocated public investment equally between Lima and the rest of Peru. To invest these funds at a sub-national level, several Departmental Development Corporations (CORDES) were created, and these continued in operation until 1968 (Schmidt, 1989: 204–6). During this decade, social services in urban areas improved to a great extent, as did the main social indicators. For example, Odría's government is known for its effort to implement social infrastructure, especially the construction of large hospitals and the *grandes unidades escolares* (scholars' units) in the main Peruvian cities, mainly financed with international cooperation and foreign debt. Between 1950 and 1961, the illiteracy rate decreased from 53 to 39 per cent, primary school enrolment increased by 51 per cent and secondary and university enrolment by almost 200 per cent. During the same period, government expenditure in education doubled from 1.6 to 3.2 per cent of GNP (Drysdale and Myers, 1975).

### The 1960s: continuity of social policy mechanisms and increasing pressures in support of more state intervention

By the early 1960s, pressures for policy reforms that would give the state an increased role in managing the economy had accumulated. The promulgation of the Industrial Promotion Law in 1959 and the establishment of the National System of Economic and Social Planning in October 1962 were clear signs indicating the developments in this direction. Raúl Prebisch, director of the Economic Commission for Latin America and the Caribbean (ECLAC), played an important role in the establishment of the National Planning Institute (INP). Although INP was established during a short-lived military government initiated in 1962,[7] its architect Fernando Belaúnde elected in 1963 furthered the reforms towards a more determined state intervention in the economy.

Fernando Belaúnde followed the application of the import substitution industrialization (ISI) model, which rapidly increased the fiscal deficit and the level of external debt. The latter grew from US$158 million in 1962 to US$737 million in 1968 (Paredes and Pascó-Font, 1991). The adjustment policy, put into effect in 1967 as a response to the balance of payments crisis and the government's inability to address social problems adequately, was the alleged justification for the *coup d'état* in 1968 by a leftist military government headed by General Juan Velasco, who ruled until 1975. The implementation of ISI policies during this period was related to the expansion of transnational corporations and foreign enterprises, furthering the trends of the previous decade. More than 200 major manufacturing corporations made investments from 1940 to 1969, nearly 80 per cent of them during Fernando Belaúnde's presidential term (Anaya, 1975). The process of industrialization changed the structure of the Peruvian economy: agriculture, manufacturing and the provision of services accounted respectively for 23, 14 and 12 per cent of real GNP in 1950, but by 1968 the proportions were 15, 20 and 15 per cent, respectively. In spite of these important developments, Thorp and Bertram made this conclusion about Peru:

> Industrialization came late. [It] was externally-induced and controlled, relied heavily on artificial props to its profitability, was not subject to carefully-designed planning procedures or clearly-defined priorities, quickly encountered problems of scale, and failed to create a new class of dynamic local industrial capitalists. (...) Despite the context of export growth and a rich natural-resource base, most of the new manufacturing sectors did not represent a clear-cut step towards a more integrated, autonomous economy. (Thorp and Bertram, 1978: 273–4)

The political context was highly confrontational. The middle class pressed for an increase of public expenditures in social services and for mechanisms to maintain its purchasing power. They also expressed concerns about foreign participation in economic sectors, while a growing awareness about land reform converged with the demands of some peasant movements. Although Fernando Belaúnde initiated this period by taking significant steps towards democratization – municipal elections were held for the first time, even though they had been was mandated by the 1933 Constitution, the most pressing issues during his government were land reform and foreign participation in economic activity. The Congress, controlled by the coalition APRA-UNO (the latter being Manuel Odría's political party), blocked several initiatives for reforms and investment projects.

President Belaúnde's social policies were was characterized by two types of interventions, which were similar to those used by the previous governments. Most of his measures were made explicit within National Plans developed by ministries and the INP:[8] (i) massive investment in urban infrastructure, targeting specially the urban middle-class population; and (ii) social programmes to construct and maintain infrastructure in rural and low-class urban areas, promoting also social mobilization to obtain political support.

During his first 90 days in office, Belaúnde launched an ambitious housing programme for white-collar employees: San Felipe was a vast complex consisting of 30 buildings with almost 2,000 apartments. Similar complexes were constructed in Lima, backed up by public funds and offered at low rates of interest. However, these programmes benefited the urban poor, whose creditworthiness was low, implying that these programmes were biased against the self-employed. In urban areas, inhabitants of *Pueblos Jóvenes* had the most pressing housing problems: In 1967, a survey revealed that

58 per cent of their homes had no water pipes, 61 per cent had no sewers and 87 per cent were located in areas with unpaved streets (Tapia, 1971). The health sector was also a good example of this bias: while per capita expenditures in health in 15 cities were $15, only $1 was spent in the rest of the country. The health system in the 15 major cities grew from the pressure of three well-organized groups: the military, the police and white-collar workers, which separately organized their specific health arrangements (Webb, 1975: 115). President Belaúnde continued the improvements in education coverage and government expenditure in education rose to 5 per cent of GNP during the period 1964–67. Primary enrolment increased by 46 per cent from 1962 to 1968, secondary enrolment by 136 per cent and university enrolments by 130 per cent (Drysdale and Myers, 1975: 257). It is worthwhile noting that the expansion of universities also accelerated – from ten in 1959 to thirty in 1968.

On the other hand, some special programmes were created with the express intention of improving living conditions in rural and low-class urban areas. *Cooperación Popular* (COOPOP) was launched as a temporary employment programme, but became a fund dedicated to the construction of small and productive infrastructure. COOPOP was supported by a voluntary workforce and promoted the birth of incipient communal organizations, aimed mainly at providing food to the poorer sectors of the population. During its first year, COOPOP built 2,600 kilometres of roads, 500 schools, and 2,000 community buildings (Bourque and Palmer, 1975: 196). Central government transfers of US$4 million per year were necessary to provide monetary subsidies to local governments (Bourque and Palmer, 1975: 194). Nonetheless, COOPOP competed with the CORDES at the local level. The main difference, and a reason for duplication, was that CORDES was mainly funded by specific taxes levied at the local and regional level. Because of that, CORDES resisted several attempts both to bring such taxes under the INP jurisdiction and to increase coordination at the local level (Schmidt, 1989: 207).

### The 1970s: the Peruvian revolution?

The social and political reforms implemented by the military government are widely regarded as marking a watershed in contemporary Peruvian history. General Juan Velasco Alvarado took power in October 1968, and soon after he launched radical reforms that sought to develop what was labelled 'national capitalism'. In a broad sense, the government believed in a strong state and in an interventionist approach to the economy. Unfortunately, it failed to maintain macroeconomic equilibrium in a context of diminishing terms of trade (Wise, 1994).

By 1968, Peru lagged considerably behind most of the other medium-sized Latin American countries, not just in terms of per capita income, but also on measures of urbanization, literacy, exposure to mass media and other aspects of social development. Army officials[9] shared the assessment of the Peruvian situation with like-minded middle-class civilian groups and prepared the '*Plan Inca*'. After the coups most of the officers that had participated in the Plan Inca became members of the *Comité de Asesoramiento de la Presidencia* (COAP) – the president's key advisory body.

General Velasco's measures were later codified into the National Plan of Development 1971–1975 (INP, 1971). This included several reforms and policy objectives, such as the following: (i) distributional policies, which included land reform in order to transform the 'feudal-class' structure and convert the landowning class into an efficient industrial bourgeoisie, along with public–private property schemes for major enterprises; (ii) increased state intervention in the economy through public enterprises to capitalize the country;[10] (iii) social mobilization to ensure the sustainability of policies; and (iv) expansion of social public services and reform to guarantee universal coverage in urban and rural areas.

The most important distributional policy was land reform. Nevertheless, its extent was very limited, lacking technical training for the new peasant owners, and it was affected by insufficient agro-industrial development, and a lack of inputs due to import market restrictions. Public–private property schemes were the other explicit measure used to redistribute wealth. However, the proposed schemes for shared property in the industrial, mining, and fishing sectors benefited only 12 per cent of the economically active population (Collier, 1975). Paradoxically, the inherent economic structure and dualism were the most difficult barriers to extending the benefits of shared property and land reform. At the same time, the military government launched a number of reforms in the areas of education, health, and the pensions system, with the objective of ensuring universal coverage and improving quality standards. For example, the education system was extended to include *Quechua* and other Peruvian languages; mass media were utilized as a mean of guaranteeing better access to universal education; the health system was decentralized to cover rural areas; and great efforts were made to implement sanitation, housing and transport infrastructure programmes.[11]

Nevertheless, political rights were suppressed and the level of social mobilization was reduced. In 1971, Velasco's government launched the *Sistema Nacional de Movilización Social* (SINAMOS) in order to create its own social and political base. This was based on the experience of CORDES and COOPOP, which were centralized and managed by the military. It was redefined to be in accordance with policies made by public agencies and to support government programmes dealing with economic, social, and cultural development (Decree Law 19400).

The growing social demands erupted as the economic and social models lost their effectiveness due to fiscal restrictions. Francisco Morales Bermúdez took power in 1975 and sought to reduce the high fiscal deficit created by the previous government. The subsequent five years, from 1974 to 1979, were characterized by steep declines in purchasing power and a rise in inflation, which exacerbated social conflict. From this point onwards, Velasco's short-lived reforms were gradually dismantled, from land reform to the expropriation of mass media, among other things, and the level of state intervention diminished as a proportion of GDP (González de Olarte, 1992; González de Olarte and Samamé, 1991). Rising social pressures motivated the military government to call for elections to a new Constituent Assembly. The Constituent Assembly, which properly represented the broad range of political parties, wrote the 1979 Constitution, which called for presidential elections the following year. The election brought Fernando Belaúnde to power for a second term.

### The 1980s: democracy, populism, economic failure and internal war (a Peruvian version of the 'lost decade')

President Belaúnde, whose government continued to reverse Velasco's reforms, launched a relatively successful programme of economic liberalization and IMF adjustment policies. Growth rates soared in the first two years (to 4.4 and 5.1 per cent of growth in 1980 and 1981 respectively). However, the economy was exposed to two external shocks: the collapse of international prices of Peruvian exports as a consequence of the Latin American debt crisis and the *El Niño* climatic phenomenon. The result was an economic contraction of 11 per cent, inflation of around 100 per cent per year, and a 15 per cent reduction in per capita social spending (Flores, 1991). Economic policies implemented during this time with the aim of mitigatins impacts made by the economic downturn, such as price controls on petrol, food, bank interests and foreign exchange, and the subsidization of public enterprises' production, became unsustainable.

Dualism continued to be the major characteristic of the economic structure: traditional informal sectors (both rural and urban) still comprised 75 per cent of the total workforce, but contributed only 36 per cent to the value-added of GDP (Wise, 1994). Moreover, large parts of rural and Andean areas remained disconnected from major cities with little state presence. Some of these towns were occupied by armed guerrilla groups, who faced stiff resistance from the Peruvian Army. Nevertheless, the surging of 'Shining Path', a dogmatic and organized armed group, initiated an internal war that lasted for more than a decade. The internal war against terrorism made impossible any attempt to consolidate democracy and further social welfare for Peruvians.

Alan Garcia, a member of the APRA party, became president in 1985. Garcia promised economic reform under a programme of economic heterodoxy. At the beginning of his term, his discourse on 'equality and social justice' made him very popular. Garcia imposed price controls to cope with inflation and launched state development programmes to expand aggregate demand, which could be considered the central elements of Garcia's social policy (Vasquez *et al.*, 2001). Thus, for instance, the control of the price of petrol was meant to be a redistributive measure due to its relationship to food and transportation prices, which were the main components of the goods and services of the household. Other controlled prices included interest rates charged on loans to poor agricultural workers, which proved to be more extensively used by better-informed peasants and not necessarily the poorest. On the other hand, the *Programa de Apoyo al Ingreso Temporal* (the social programme for temporary income) was designed to provide temporary income to poor people (Parodi, 2000).

The requirement to have foreign currency to import capital goods for the still-protected national industries, led the Garcia government to announce unilaterally that debt service repayments would be limited to a maximum of 10 per cent of export earnings, causing the cancellation of important credit sources from international donors.

Despite various attempts to compensate for the slide of nominal wages with the emission of 'inorganic liquidity', real wages were reduced to half between 1980 and 1989 and inflation had reached 60 per cent per month by July 1990. Price controls and subsidies deepened the already distorted relative price structure. The crisis was deeply felt by Peruvians: tax revenues fell to 4.8 per cent of GDP and economic activity contracted for three consecutive years (Figure 3.1). At the same time, the balance of payments registered a huge deficit and international reserves in the Central Bank were negative. The room for social spending narrowed in this context, because of what Richard Webb has called 'de facto privatization': from 1988 to 1990, government spending contracted by 70 per cent.

In this troubled economic environment, two important social programmes emerged, mainly supported by local governments and civil society: the *Comedores Populares* and the *Vaso de Leche* programmes were designed to ensure a minimal level of nutrition for the population (especially children) at a low cost. Despite the popularity of such programmes, from 1986 to 1990 the absolute number of population below the poverty line surged from 7.5 million to 12 million; and the number of people living in extreme poverty rose from 3 million to 5 million.

## The 1990s: technical approach to social policies or populism?

Economic distortions and imbalances inherited from the government of Alan Garcia and the social and economic impact of terrorist violence, led President Alberto Fujimori (elected in 1990) to implement a drastic stabilization programme with the intention of correcting macroeconomic problems and reintegrating Peru into the international financial community. As a reaction to state interventionist policies, the main objectives of the reforms were to make competitive markets the main mechanism for allocating resources. Private investment was aimed to be the main source of capital accumulation, assuming the role formerly played by public investment. Although these reforms were the cause of high rates of economic growth from 1993 to 1998, the Peruvian economy was affected by two external shocks: the *El Niño* phenomenon and the international financial crisis, which increased the deficit of the current account and aggravated a recession – which lasted until mid-2001. The downsizing of the state apparatus and the weakening of labour legislation are crucial to forming an understanding of what happened to employment during the 1990s. The privatization of public sector companies and, in particular, the closure of a series of non-profitable government agencies reduced public expenditures and significantly reduced the state's presence in production. However, after the reduction in the number of public employees, the impact of private investment on formal levels of employment was not significant. Various authors indicate that employment in Peru has become more precarious: from 1991 to 2000, the 'unstable' wage-earning workers in the private sector have increased from 38 to 77 per cent. In addition, seven of every ten jobs created in urban areas during the 1990s were informal (Saavedra, 2000; Verdera, 2000).

On the other hand, the revenue generated from the privatization process had reached nearly US$6.4 billion as of December 1998, when the process came to an end. Some of these resources, and those from international donors, were used for the implementation of social programmes.[12] Social policy aimed at alleviating poverty was also focused on institutional reforms to increase the efficiency of social expenditure. The strategies and policies of the social sectors during Fujimori's term can be found in policy documents such as *Estrategia nacional de alivio a la pobreza* for the 1993–1995 period and *Estrategia focalizada de lucha contra la pobreza* for 1996–2000. However, the strategies were never executed according to the principles described. Instead, several social programmes were established and executed mainly by two ministries, the Ministry of Presidency and the Ministry for the Promotion of Women and Social Development.[13] There is a wide consensus among authors about the lack of coordination and targeting of these programmes, the political use of public resources and the centralization of programmes' design (UNDP, 2002; Francke and Mendoza, 2001; Vásquez *et al.*, 2001). Nevertheless, during the 1990s, social expenditure rose from 3.4 to 5.3 per cent of GNP. For example, the social programmes to alleviate extreme poverty multiplied its resources three times over in the 1990s (Table 3.2).

One of the most successful programmes between 1995 and 1998 was the *Fondo de Compensación Social y Desarrollo* (FONCODES). Unlike other social programmes, FONCODES acted as a financial intermediary for local projects. It channelled funds from the central government to communities, using sophisticated poverty maps and optimization models to direct its funding (Afuso, 2002). FONCODES set out to evaluate the projects, undertake follow-ups, and to monitor the programmes to be better able to respond to local population demands. Its projects covered different areas, such as basic social services (health, nutrition, sanitation and education), roads, electrification, irrigation systems, community support, and employment generation.

*Table 3.2* Social expenditures 1993–2000 (US$ million)

| *Total* | *1993* | *1994* | *1995* | *1996* | *1997* | *1998* | *1999* | *2000* |
|---|---|---|---|---|---|---|---|---|
| | 1,462 | 1,999 | 3,575 | 3,646 | 3,707 | 4,048 | 4,051 | 4,346 |
| *1 Education and health* | 1,104 | 1,455 | 2,511 | 2,460 | 2,391 | 2,589 | 2,265 | 2,445 |
| Education | 795 | 1,033 | 1,799 | 1,648 | 1,667 | 1,854 | 1,623 | 1,743 |
| Health | 309 | 422 | 712 | 812 | 723 | 735 | 642 | 702 |
| *2 Extreme poverty alleviation programmes* | 318 | 503 | 1,006 | 1,051 | 1,000 | 1,090 | 1,026 | 1,057 |
| FONCODES | 189 | 205 | 223 | 187 | 244 | 217 | 215 | 237 |
| PRONAA | 29 | 45 | 95 | 81 | 72 | 67 | 88 | 86 |
| Vaso de leche | 58 | 77 | 102 | 96 | 90 | 97 | 90 | 93 |
| Special programmes and others | 41 | 176 | 587 | 687 | 594 | 708 | 633 | 640 |
| *3 Other social expenditures* | 40 | 41 | 58 | 135 | 317 | 369 | 760 | 845 |

*Source*: Cuánto, Anuario Estadístico 2000.

FONCODES was successful because of the high level of interaction with the local population and also because projects were placed under the direction of an autonomous team for implementing the programmes, which was endowed with autonomous decision-making capacity (Afuso, 1996; Sagasti *et al.*, 1999).

Nevertheless, during Alberto Fujimori's second term, FONCODES and other social programmes were used for the sole purpose of winning elections and generating social support. Several studies have found that almost 70 per cent of households in the six poorest deciles continuously received food assistance to complete their daily consumption. As a result, between 1995 and 2001, the presidential approval rating in the poorest sectors was around 30 to 35 per cent (Peruvian Government, 2003). Despite increases during the 1990s, social expenditures in Peru have been amongst the lowest in Latin America. For example, total expenditure in education per student was US$150 in 1999. In terms of GNP, Peru spends only 2.4 per cent in education, while comparable public expenditures are 4.0 per cent of GDP in Chile, and nearly 5.0 per cent in Brazil. This situation causes households to contribute around 41 per cent of public education experditure (in textbooks, transportation, clothes, etc.): In terms of GNP per capita, Peruvian families spend more on education than families in developed countries (World Bank, 2000). In general, during this period the Peruvian government continued some of the ineffective policy choices of previous decades. The shortcomings included: the design of policies employing little statistical information, the regressive nature of public social spending, a centralized design and management of social programmes and resources, a lack of coordination between departments of the public sector, a lack of continuity in sector policies, the use of social programmes for political ends, and a lack of transparency in public sector management.

## Recent developments in Peruvian social policy

Table 3.3 presents a comparative summary detailing sixty years of interaction between social policies, economic development, and the underlying social and political structures for the period 1940–2000. However, the policy context once again changed with the transition to democracy in 2001, introducing and reinforcing some elements, most of them already proposed or in the process of being implemented. New elements of social policy are: the establishment of the *Mesa de Concertación de Lucha contra la Pobreza*; the beginning of the decentralization process with the election of regional governments for the first time in history of the republic; and the signing of the '*Acuerdo Nacional*' by most political parties, private sector institutions and representatives of civil society (Sagasti and Prada, 2002). The latter is intended to consolidate democratic governance, to help to achieve higher levels of competitiveness and to strengthen public sector institutions to promote equality and social justice.

Recently, the government has launched the document 'Strategy for Poverty Reduction and Creating and Economic Opportunities for the Poor' (Peruvian Government, 2003), which complements a previous document called 'Social Policy Chart' (Peruvian Government, 2002). Both documents point to the necessity of a change of perspective regarding the design and execution of social policies, proposing an impartial view of the experience of Fujimori's presidential term. This change of perspective is related to the changes currently underway, indicated in Table 3.1. The main proposals for social policy contained in those documents are:

- Optimization and integration of major social programmes, establishing a social management group in order to increase efficacy and cost-effectiveness.
- Greater consideration of the link between economic growth and poverty alleviation.
- Decentralization of management and decision-making capacities to subnational levels.
- Increased investment in the capacity and organization of the poorer parts of the population.

*Table 3.3* Social policy, economic development, and social structures

| | | *1940s* | *1950s* | *1960s* | *1970s* | *1980s* | *1990s* |
|---|---|---|---|---|---|---|---|
| • *Social policy* | • Main benefi-ciaries | – Urban organized employees, mainly white-collar. | – Urban population | – Focussed on recently urbanized across | – Middle class and peasants | – Poor peasants and rural areas | – Attempts to focus social intervention to poor people |
| | | – High-risk rural population | – Poor populations from the *Barriadas* | | | – Urban middle class | |
| | • Main charac-teristics | – Provision of some social services, but did not constitute an integrated social policy. | – Social policy for political mobilization | – Provision of social services to the working middle class and new *Barriadas* | – Introduction of welfare state, education reform and health system. | – Based on price controls and temporal employment programmes | – Radical increases of public resources devoted to social policies |
| | | – Social programmes aimed at attending high-risk populations | – Increased expenditures to provide social service infrastructure | – Public works institutions specified most rural investment. | – Explicit income distribution policies | – At the end of the decade: state failure providing social services (de facto privatization) | – Technical approach turned to populism |
| | | | – Infrastructure construction through public work institutions. | – Expansion of public services infrastructure (schools, universities) | – Centralization of social policies under military control | | – Creation of several social programmes |

*Table 3.3* (Continued)

| | | *1940s* | *1950s* | *1960s* | *1970s* | *1980s* | *1990s* |
|---|---|---|---|---|---|---|---|
| *Economic development* | • Employment patterns | – Mainly in mining and agricultural. | – Mainly in mining and agricultural. | – Mainly in mining and agricultural. | – Industrialization for import substitution | – Growing informality as 'modern' sector could not create labour for the growing population. | – Growing informality and self-employment |
| | | – Importance of public sector employment | – Increasing industrialization oriented to export sectors<br>– Growing industrialization | – Growing public employment | | | |
| | • Underlying economic model | – Promotion of industrialization | – Liberalism and openness: *laissez-faire* export-led growth | – Liberalism and openness: *laissez-faire* export-led growth | – Import-substitution industrialization, with great participation of the public sector | – Expansion of internal markets through increase of demand. | – Neoliberalism and Washington Consensus policies |
| | | – Price control for agricultural products | | – From 1968: import-substitution industrialization | – From 1975: Return to economic orthodoxy | – Promotion of industrialization | |

| | | | | | | | |
|---|---|---|---|---|---|---|---|
| | • Economic characteristics | – Dual structure: Modern and traditional sector | – Export-oriented (agricultural and mining). | – Mainly export-oriented, but several measures are introduced to strengthen domestic markets. | – State intervention through public enterprises | – State intervention through public enterprises and price controls of main products. | – Private sector initiative |
| | | – Internal market protectionism: price and exchange controls | – Diversification | – Foreign investment grows in importance | – From 1975: Progressive decrease of state's intervention. | | – Export oriented economy |
| | | | – Importance of foreign capital investment | | | | – Deindustrialization |
| *Social and political structures* | • Migration and demographic changes | – Migration from rural to urban areas begins | – Increasing annual population growth (2.2%) | – Annual population growth reached 2.7%. | – Growing of the economically active population | – Growing of the economically active population | – Growing of the economically active population |

*Table 3.3* (Continued)

| | *1940s* | *1950s* | *1960s* | *1970s* | *1980s* | *1990s* |
|---|---|---|---|---|---|---|
| | – Moderate annual population growth (1.9%) | – Migration to Lima | – Consolidation of centralization in Lima. | | – Brain drain to foreign countries | – Migration to Lima stagnated. |
| | | | | | | – Brain drain to foreign countries |
| • Political regime and political rights | – Democratic rule. Great influence of APRA party | – From 1948: Authoritarian rule (APRA party banned) | – Democratic rule. | – Authoritarian rule and creation of an alternative social mobilization system (SINAMOS) | – Democratic rule | – Democratic rule turned to authoritarian rule |
| | | – From 1956: Democratic rule | – From 1968: Authoritarian rule | | | |

- Creation of a social protection network in order to guarantee universal access to basic social services.
- Conduction of an ethical and morally guided process for social development, where the creation of wealth is linked with human rights.

Although the Peruvian government is introducing institutional reforms – the process of decentralization and consolidation of subnational governments, and the reorganization of social programmes to facilitate their posterior devolution – the challenges ahead are enormous. The next section offers a summary of the main challenges facing social policy over the next twenty years, drawing on the consultation processes regarding development strategies that Agenda: PERU carried out during the last decade (Agenda Peru, 2001: chapter 4).

## Main challenges for Peruvian social policy in the next twenty years

### Point of departure

During the second half of the twentieth century, Peru has been unable to maintain stable growth rates or to improve living standards. In a recent report, the Economic Commission for Latin America and the Caribbean (ECLAC) announced that Peru would not be able to achieve the Millennium Goal of halving extreme poverty by 2015 (Paes de Barros *et al.*, 2003).

Hence, the main challenge for social policy for the next few decades is

> how to overcome the situation in which more than a half of the Peruvian population is below the poverty line, and almost 20 per cent are extreme poor; while tackling social, political and economic exclusion, promoting citizen rights and accumulating wealth to sustain the development process.

In 1993, the accumulated social deficit – the aggregate difference between the actual consumption and the necessary one to complete the minimum basic basket of consumption – was calculated to be US$15 billion (Abugattas, 1993). Moreover, recent calculations for necessary investment only in water and sanitation infrastructure reach US$ 5.4 billion. It is clear that public expenditure will not be enough, taking into account that the total annual budget is about US$10 billion. Private sector and civil society resources will also need to be included.

Raising living standards and eradicating extreme poverty are means of fighting economic, social, and political exclusion. Although income disparities are only one dimension of exclusions, Figure 3.2 is a proxy of the persistence of inequalities in Peruvian society.

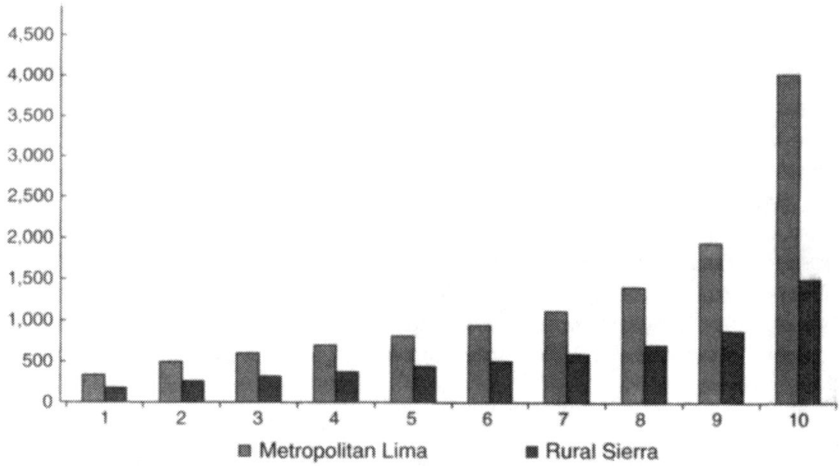


*Figure 3.2* Average consumption per deciles in Metropolitan Lima and rural sierra (US$)
*Source*: República del Perú, 2003.

## Main challenges for the provision of basic social services

The provision of basic social services (improving education, nutrition, health and sanitation) will allow for the inclusion of a significant proportion of the population in economic activities. For the next few decades, 'social and development policies must overcome the appalling situation of the bad quality of education, poor access to health services, and high infant mortality rates, when compared to other Latin-American countries'.

### *Education*

The Peruvian education system is still far from securing equal opportunities, providing continuous productivity increment and adopting democratic values. The educational system does not meet local or regional needs, nor is it based on any consensus between education experts and the community.

Access to primary education has improved enormously in recent decades and is presently at 92 per cent. However, the education system still requires huge improvements in terms of efficiency (internal and external), in quality and equality. In 2001, the average number of schooling years was just 8.8 years (INEI, 2002). In addition, 8.5 per cent of Peruvians older than 15 years of age received no education, only 50.4 per cent of children between three and five years of age attended the first level of formal education and 65.5 per cent of children between 12 and 16 years old attended the second level of schooling. According to an UNESCO test Peru has one of the lowest scores in Latin America in terms of quality of education (Benavides, 2002). There is also a wide gap in terms of opportunities between poor and non-poor, and this is even wider when accounting for geographical differences, urban or rural. The average number of years of schooling in Peru of the population above the poverty line was 10.7 years in urban areas and 7.7 years in rural areas, while for the population under the poverty line, the average was 8.2 years in urban areas and 2.3 years in rural areas (INEI, 2002).

*Health*

The main challenge is to ensure universal access to health care, placing an emphasis on prevention, sanitation, and nutrition services at low costs. The progress in this matter heavily depends upon improving access to drinking water and sanitation services. On the other hand, even when the incidence of acute respiratory and infectious intestinal diseases remains as one of the main causes of an early death, health services should be prepared to respond to more complex diseases as health and sanitation indicators improve.

Public and private services and local health networks should be better integrated when designing national health policies.[14] They must also be closely coordinated with other social programmes in the areas of nutrition, sanitation, and education in order to provide comprehensive care, especially to the most vulnerable groups, the social protection network. In 2001 only 43.8 per cent of the population had access to some kind of health insurance, although this situation was slightly improved following the introduction in 2002 of the Integral Health Insurance – a programme implemented to guarantee universal access to basic health services.

*Housing*

Most Peruvian families live in inadequate housing, overcrowded or lacking sanitation. These houses lack access to basic services such as water, sanitation or electricity, and they are built with inadequate materials, allowing for stark differences between rural and urban housing (INEI, 2002). Despite this, the ownership of a house is generally considered to be the main investment made by poor families. The promotion of self-construction and the provision of property titles could boost the demand for housing and promote the construction industry, generating positive externalities in other economic sectors, as the MIVIVIENDA programme has proved.

*Pension system*

Peru has a mixed pension system featuring both public and private schemes. The main challenge is to ensure the viability of the public pension system as the main option available to the majority of the population, guaranteeing its sustainability and the progressive decrease of the gap of actuarial debt. Under the present scheme, the private pension system is a more attractive alternative for the higher-income sectors, with only two million workers affiliated out of a working population of 12 million, while the public scheme is practically bankrupt.[15] Both the private and the public systems require strengthening and need to consider the effects of demographic changes. Furthermore, an urgent issue to be tackled is to provide access to the pension system for the large numbers of self-employed, small, and micro-business owners – including workers in the informal sector – by giving them the possibility of choosing between the public and private pension systems. In the end, these measures will have a huge impact on well-being of the population and help to boost the level of internal savings.

It is particularly important to ensure that the pension system is able to cover the needs of senior citizens, who will comprise an increasing proportion of the Peruvian population over the next few decades. For this reason, it will be necessary to promote saving mechanisms in order to enable people of working age to enjoy a decent income after retirement.

*Poverty reduction*

From the majority of poor people in Peru, it is possible to identify more vulnerable groups, which have greater difficulty than others in gaining access to a minimum basket of goods and services, in participating actively in national politics, and, generally speaking, in designing and realizing their own life plans. Those Peruvians who have been persistently excluded urgently require the support and solidarity of the rest of society, in order to access living conditions that are compatible with basic standards of human dignity.

Endemic poverty (the result of social, political and economic exclusion) has a variety of related causes like the subjacent economic development models, unequal power relations, and inefficient social policies (Sagasti *et al.*, 1999). In order to eradicate endemic poverty it is necessary to adopt integrated economic, social, environmental, and infrastructure development measures that must be designed and put into practice at the regional and local level, in order to respond to local priorities.

The notion that people generally access basic goods and services through income from stable and formal employment has prevailed since the early twentieth century. However, in recent decades the reality has been quite different for most of the young working-age population in Peru. Labour instability is a feature of the new global economic and financial climate. In terms of social policy, this implies the development of and effective coordination between employment policies and educational policies, taking into account *generational expectations*.

*Employment generation*

Peru faces the challenge of absorbing a still-rising number of new workers into the labour market and, simultaneously, tackling the problems of widespread unemployment and underemployment. This means that the economy needs to create 300,000 annual jobs in the short to medium term solely to absorb new workers. Furthermore, labour productivity also needs to improve to make the labour force more competitive in the global economy.

During recent decades, the vast majority of Peruvians have been unable to secure a decent and stable job. In a context of rapid demographic growth, the modern sectors of the economy have been incapable of providing employment to the increasing labour force and the incipient welfare state has been unable to achieve universal social protection for workers. This situation has compelled many people to look for alternative ways to make a living in the informal economy, mainly as self-employed workers in jobs with low productivity that barely satisfy their basic needs. The emergence of these low-quality jobs generally reflects a need for survival rather than entrepreneurial drive, even at the cost of self-exploitation. It is thus important to devise social policies to raise the quality of these jobs, to provide training, access to micro-credit, technical services to expand business, and to guarantee schemes to promote fusions of micro-enterprises, among other things.

## Towards an inclusive state: elements for a strategic framework for social policy

The experiences of previous years, both successes and failures, provide valuable lessons for how to improve social conditions and better face the challenges previously described:

- Perhaps the most important lesson refers to the role of institutions in the development process. Together, they make up the fabric of society, create relations of confidence, allow the establishment of shared commitments, and provide a basis for collective action. We have learned that institutions which are flexible, participative, decentralized, pluralist and capable of taking into account different opinions and viewpoints, have a greater chance of responding adequately to the growing and changing demands.
- In the political arena, institutions associated with democratic governance have proved the most effective for channelling, processing and responding to a varied range of social demands, primarily through intermediary institutions, which act as links between citizens and centres of political power. In addition, a well-functioning democracy allows for the stable change of government through regular elections, while avoiding the excessive concentration of power by establishing controls and counterbalances to the exercise of authority and political influence.
- In the economic field, institutions associated with markets, and competition, have proved the most effective in encouraging economic growth and in improving behaviour in many areas of human activity. However, societies which are capable to achieve a balance between competitive pressures on the one hand, and social solidarity on the other have better

possibilities of raising the living standards of the entire population and avoiding the exclusion of the weakest and most vulnerable.

There is a strong interrelation between democratic governance, economic growth, the reduction of extreme inequalities and the existence of networks of civic and social and political wide consensus and commitments. Beyond requirements for basic survival, men and women are guided by ethical and moral impulses. Non-material values and aspects of human activity are fundamental for the affirmation of the capacity for action of both the individual and the group, for the creation and running of institutions and for the success or failure of efforts to achieve prosperity and well-being in society.

Three elements should be taken into account when designing social policies for Peru in the next decades: demographic changes and generational expectation; regional and local diversity; and the participation of private sector and civil society in conjunction with public sector in the design, funding and implementation of social policies.

**Demographic changes and generational expectations**

During the second half of the twentieth century, the population in Peru grew 3.4 times (from seven million to 26 million inhabitants between 1950 and 2002). Almost half of the population lives on the coast, and 30 per cent of habitants are concentrated in Lima. The National Institute of Statistics expects there to be an increase in life expectancy over the next few decades – from 69.8 years in 2002–05 to 78.1 years in 2050 (INEI, 2001). This would mean that the population is projected to grow from 33.7 million in 2002–05 to 42.8 million in 2050. Furthermore, by this date, 20 per cent of the population will be less than 14 years of age and 16 per cent will be over 65 years of age. Urban population is expected to rise from 72 per cent in 2000 to 75 per cent in 2050 (see Figure 3.3).

The changes observed in recent decades in both the structure and the size of the population require the introduction of a temporal perspective in social policy design. Social policy needs to take into account the periods associated with the anticipated displacement of large numbers of the population. For example, over the next two decades, the increase in the working-age population will have a direct impact on training needs. Although workers should help to design measures for reducing unemployment, the state is responsible for providing workers with training – particularly for young people – and by encouraging the private sector to provide employment for graduates of training programmes.

This demographic process offers an opportunity for the country, since, with more people in employment, there will be, on average, fewer dependents: this may have a favourable impact on the savings rates and spending levels that generate increased economic demand. Nonetheless, it is necessary to prevent labour conditions from deteriorating any further. Increased

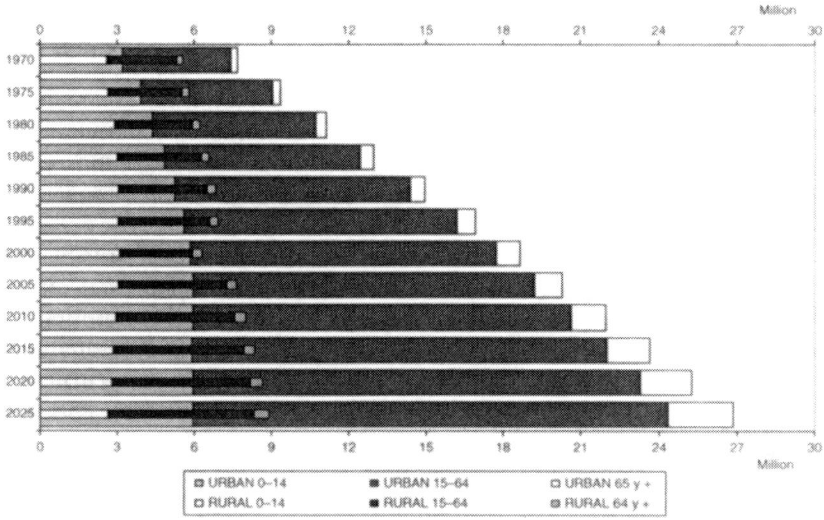


*Figure 3.3* Urban and rural population and cohorts, 1970–2050
*Source*: INEI, 2001

flexibility helps to generate lower-quality jobs under short-term contracts, unstable employment conditions, and low wages.

## Regional and local development: reducing internal gaps

Peru is characterized by great diversity in its geography. Traditionally, the country is divided into three natural regions: Coast (*Costa*), Mountain (*Sierra*), and Jungle (*Selva*). The distribution of poverty is unequal between these three regions: In the *Costa* region, 4 out of 10 Peruvians are considered poor; and in the *Sierra*, more than 7 out of 10 inhabitants are poor, with almost 50 per cent living in conditions of extreme poverty. In the *Selva* region, almost 7 out of 10 people are considered poor and 40 per cent live in conditions of extreme poverty. Futhermore, there is a strong relationship between the centralization of economic activity in Lima and the geographical distribution of poverty: Lima generates almost 55 per cent of the national income and 48 per cent of GNP, and almost 80 per cent of credit loans are disbursed there.

The difference between per capita incomes in Lima, the highest, is more than four times that of Huancavelica, which is the poorest region/city. The absolute poverty index developed in the UNDP human development report shows that the difference between the poorest district (Choropampa, province of Chota, department of Cajamarca) and the wealthiest of the districts (Miraflores, in Lima) is equivalent to 78.8 percentage points in the quality of living standards (UNDP, 2002).

Rural areas are also characterized by a special pattern of geographical dispersion, with small groups of families living apart from each other. This poses some difficulties for the provision of social services, and there is insufficient statistical information about their needs and specific requirements. In that situation, monitoring, implementing and evaluating social programmes and policies demand important financial and human resources. But policy makers are aware that the most severe and most endemic level of poverty is located in these towns.

A useful way to coordinate activities among different public, private, and community organizations is to design local development plans that can be articulated at the regional level at a later stage. In this way, communities can put forward their needs, while public institutions can channel programmes and project funds in a decentralized manner. Another means of fostering local development is to implement programmes that generating jobs and provide for basic social services in areas of extreme poverty. Local outreach workers can be recruited and provided with training, technical, and administrative support using telecommunications and modern information systems.

## The growing role of the private sector and civil society organizations in the design, funding, and implementation of social programmes: beyond the welfare state

The Peruvian social deficit will exceed the amount of public resources, especially if a considerable part is still channelled through inefficient institutions that lack transparency and do not coordinate with each other. Institutional reforms must lead to transparency in the formulation of policies, greater coordination, and coherence among such policies, increased accountability in public spending, and permanent monitoring of their impact.

Bearing in mind the budgetary limitations of the Peruvian state and the magnitude of the internal neglect of social needs that has built up over recent decades, it will not be possible to correct the country's poor social conditions using an approach under which only government entities provide social services. In addition to involving the private sector to boost the efficiency of government agencies, it is essential to pave the way for broader and more active participation by civil society organizations. Private involvement may be stimulated through contracts or concessions, instituting new forms of service delivery; through private administration of pension funds; and by promoting a greater sense of social responsibility in the corporate sector, for example, by offering tax incentives in return for philanthropy.

Peru should advance towards a scheme that guarantees a basic minimum level of social services for the whole population, at low cost and with the participation of beneficiaries. Volunteer work can bring significant savings in the cost of undertaking some social services. For example, the amount of time that women devote to the communal kitchens programmes in various regions of Peru represents around 25–30 per cent of the total cost of a meal. Although some evidence of corruption and inefficacy has been found (Alcázar, Cáliz and Wachtenheim, 2003), civil society organizations participating in a massive, systematic, and open manner, and organized in a way that precludes their political manipulation by government agencies and local government, could significantly increase total resources available for providing basic social services.

## Concluding remarks

During the second half of the twentieth century, several social, economic, and political changes have occurred. In the social field, the composition of the Peruvian population has changed from rural to urban, a demographic explosion has concentrated most of the inhabitants in the capital and main cities in the Coast region and structural social problems – poverty, social exclusion, labour informality – have been aggravated. On the other hand, different economic models have been applied without finding an adequate path for economic growth and capital accumulation. Political changes have seen the country lurch forwards and backwards between democratic and dictatorial governments. The result of these phenomena has been that per capita GDP has spiralled downwards, and since 1975 it has actually fallen. In present-day Peru half of the population lives below the poverty line, significant gaps between regions and population cohorts have been aggravated, and political, social, and economic exclusion are related to a fragmented social fabric. In this context, social policy has often responded to political considerations – both social mobilization and electoral support. It has also been biased towards middle-class sectors and mainly designed, executed and implemented by the public sector. However, a 'welfare state' has not yet been consolidated mainly because of fiscal restrictions and the recurrence of financial crises.

On the other hand, during the last 60 years there have also been important achievements that have helped to improve the living conditions of Peruvians: life expectancy has risen and illiteracy rates have dropped; health and education indicators have both improved. Nonetheless, Peru has failed to overcome its structural problems. At present, social policy faces a major challenge: how to overcome a situation in which more than half of the Peruvian population is still below the poverty line, and almost 20 per cent are classified as extremely poor, while tackling social, political and economic exclusion, promoting citizen rights and accumulating wealth to sustain the development process. In this economic and political context, are there conditions for a rebirth of a new LADWS model in Peru? The recent recuperation of democracy is giving Peruvians the opportunity to introduce new elements into social policies, and to enhance the participation of different social actors – civil society, political parties, and government – in the search for a consensus.[16]

The strategy to follow over the next decades must take demographic changes and generational expectations into account, recognising the new regional order that considers the geographical and biodiversity characteristic of Peru, and including a new role for the private sector and civil society organizations in the design, funding, and implementation of social policies. Meanwhile the government has the task of building a coherent institutional system balancing the needs of governance and the improvement of the quality of life, capable of economic development and avoiding social exclusion, in order to make possible the reconstruction of the social fabric.

## Notes

1. For example, at different times between the late 1940s and the early 1970s, development thinking and practice was based on concepts such as the need for a 'big push' of investment and capital to initiate self-sustaining economic growth, as advocated by Paul Rosenstein-Rodin and Ragnar Nurkse. The priority of investments in human capital, whose main proponents were Theodore Schultz and Hans Singer, was also sustained. Raul Prebisch and Albert Hirschman argued for the importance of fostering import-substitution industrialization, and exploiting backward and forward linkages respectively. In addition, Walt W. Rostow's imperative of advancing through a well-established sequence of stages that lead to 'take-off into self-sustained growth'. Over time, other notions were used to interpret the reality of developing countries and to offer policy recommendations.
   Among these concepts may be found: 'unlimited supply of labour' (Arthur Lewis); 'deterioration of the terms of trade' (Hans Singer, Raúl Prebisch); 'poles of development' (Francois Perroux); 'development planning' (P. Mahalanobis, Jan Tinbergen, among others); 'unbalanced growth' (Albert Hirschman); 'dependence theory' (Femando Henrique Cardoso, Osvaldo Sunkel); 'structural underdevelopment' (Celso Furtado); 'unequal exchange' (Emmanuel Aghiri); 'redistribution with growth' (Hollis Chenery); 'basic needs approach' (Paul Streeten, Manfred Max-Neef, Richard Jolly); 'export-oriented industrialization' (Ann Krueger, T. N. Srinivasan); 'another development' (Marc Nerfin); 'eco-development' (Ignacy Sachs, Maurice Strong).
2. For this section, it is worth noting that there are no comprehensive studies about the design, implementation, and use of public resources for social policies before the 1980s (for a long-term perspective on demographic and social indicators in Peru before 1980s, see Aramburu, *et al.* 1983). Nevertheless, reliance upon social data – and even some economic data – is quite uncertain for long-term series, due to several methodological changes that make comparative analyses difficult.
3. During the 1940s, an incipient peasant movement encouraged by leftist groups fought for a fair distribution of agricultural land. This movement grew over the next decades, and the case for land reform was also assumed by the medium-class and their political representatives.
4. Industrialization was not halted, although much of the expansion of the industrial sector was in export processing rather than in production for the local market.
5. 1940 and 1961 correspond to census years.

6. Another major regional development organization was set up to coordinate recovery tasks after the 1950 earthquake in Cuzco. It was called the Reconstruction and Promotion Board or JRYF and was funded by a United Nations agency.
7. The *Junta Militar de Gobierno*, presided over by General Godoy, took power in order to annul APRA's victory in the 1962 elections, and its possible alliance with Manuel Odría. After one year and three presidents, the *Junta* called for elections.
8. Several plans were introduced with the aim of ordering central government intervention in specific areas. See, for example, the first five-year education plan, República del Peru, Plan de Desarrollo Educativo 1964–1969, Lima, 1964.
9. The leading military were grouped together in the Centro de Altos Estudios Militares (CAEM).
10. During this period, the government increased its involvement in the economy, and controlled up to 30 per cent of the GDP because of the increasing number of state-owned enterprises. However, in sectors like mining and petroleum, large and profitable companies such as Belco and Southern Peru Copper Corporation were left under private ownership in orders to guarantee large inputs of foreign capital.
11. Most of these measures were included in the National Plan 1971–1975 (INP, 1971).
12. However, in 2002 the Peruvian Parliament calculated that during Fujimori's presidential term some US$2 billion was tied to illegal spending, including, among other things, purchases of armaments.
13. For example, there were seven food assistance programmes for children between 0 and five years of age and five programmes for children between six and 14 years of age.
14. The health network comprises ESSALUD, private scheme, Armed Forces and Police insurance.
15. A great share of internal public debt corresponds to public sector pensions. In 2003, public sector expenditures in pensions were approximately 20 per cent of yearly budget, and it will increase over the years.
16. Mainly through: *Mesa de Concertación para la Lucha contra la Pobreza*, the *Acuerdo Nacional* and the *Strategy for Poverty Reduction and Creating and Economic Opportunities for the Poor.*

## References

Abugattas, J. (1993). 'La política social para 1994', in J. Portocarrero (ed.), *Ataque a la pobreza*. Lima: Foro Económico.

Abugattas, L. (1987). 'Populism and After: The Peruvian Experience', in J. Malloy and M. Seligson (eds), *Authoritarians and Democrats: Regime Transition in Latin America*. Pittsburgh: University of Pittsburgh Press.

Afuso, A. (2002). *Aplicación de modelos de la investigación de operaciones en organismos de desarrollo social*. Lima: Agenda.

Afuso, A. (1998). *Proyectos de apoyo a la producción*. Mimeo. Lima: FONCODES.

Agenda Peru (2001). *Development Strategies for the 21st century*. Lima: Agenda.

Alcázar, L., Lopez Cáliz, J., Wachtenheim H. (2003). *Las Pérdidas en el Camino*. Fugas en el Gasto Público: Transferencias Municipales, Vaso de Leche y Sector Educación. Lima: Instituto Apoyo.

Anaya, F. E. (1975) *Imperialismo, industrialización y transferencia de tecnología en el Peru*. Lima: Editorial Horizonte.

Aramburu, C., Gonzales-Vigil, J., Wendorff, C., Fernandez, H. and Brito, P. (1983). *Población y políticas de desarrollo en el Peru*. Lima: INADEP.

Basadre, J. (1963). *Historia de la República del Perú. Editorial Historia* 11 (fifth edn). Lima: Editorial Historia.

Basadre, J. (1958). *La promesa de la vida peruan*. Lima: Ministerio de Educación.

Benavides, M. (2002). 'Para explicar las diferencias en el rendimiento en matemáticas de cuarto grado en el Peru urbano: análisis de resultados en base a un modelo básico'. Documento de Trabajo 13. *Análisis y resultados de las pruebas CRECER 1998*. MECEP. Lima: Ministerio de Educación.

Bourque, S. and Palmer, D. (1975). 'Transforming the Rural Sector', in A. Lowenthal (ed.), *The Peruvian Experiment: Continuity and Change under Military Rule*. New Jersey: Princeton University Press.

Collier, D. (1975). 'Squatter Settlements and Policy', in A. Lowenthal (ed.), *The Peruvian Experiment: Continuity and Change under Military Rule*. New Jersey: Princeton University Press.

Drysdale, R. and Myers, R. (1975). 'Continuity and Change: Peruvian Education', in A. Lowenthal (ed.), *The Peruvian Experiment: Continuity and Change under Military Rule*. New Jersey: Princeton University Press.

Fitzgerald, E. V. K (1976). *The Search for National Development: The Political Economy of Peru 1956–1976*. Cambridge: Cambridge University Press.

Flores, R. (1991) *El gasto social en la década de los ochenta*, in *Moneda* 36. Lima: Banco Central de Reserva del Peru, pp. 55–7.

FONCODES (2002). *Desafíos de las políticas sociales: Superación de la pobreza e integración social en América Latina*. Lima: FONCODES.

Francke, P. (2001). *Políticas sociales: balance y propuestas*. Documento de Trabajo CISEPA 194. Lima: Pontificia Universidad Católica del Peru.

Francke, P. and Mendoza, W. (2001). *El grado de orientación pro-pobre de las políticas económicas peruanas: una revisión bibliográfica*. Documento de Trabajo CISEPA 198. Lima: Pontificia Universidad Católica del Peru.

Franco, R. (1996). *Los paradigmas de la política social* in Revista de la CEPAL 58, 9–22.

Gonzales de Olarte, E. (1992). *Reforma del estado y políticas de estabilización económica 1979–1992: El Peru, un caso especial*. Documento de Trabajo No. 41. Lima: Instituto de Estudios Peruanos.

Gonzales de Olarte, E. and Samamé, L. (1991). *El péndulo peruano. Políticas económicas, gobernabilidad y subdesarrollo, 1963–1990*. Lima: Instituto de Estudios Peruanos.

Hunt, S. (1974). *Direct Foreign Investment in Peru: New Rules for an Old Game*. Woodrow Wilson School Research Program in Economic Development, Discussion paper 44. Princeton: Princeton University Press.

Instituto Nacional de Estadística e Informática (INEI) (2002). *Condiciones de Vida en el Peru: Evolución 1997–2001 – Encuesta nacional de Hogares*. Lima: INEI.

Instituto Nacional de Estadistica e Informatica (INEI) (2001). *Proyecciones de Población 1950–2050 – Urbana y Rural 1970–2025*. Boletín de Análisis Demográfico 35. Lima: INEI.

Instituto Nacional de Planificación (INP) (1971). *Plan Nacional de Desarrollo 1971–1975*. Lima: INP.

Koshla, A. (1997). *Sustainable Livelihoods: The Central Issue of Human Security and Sustainable Development*. New Delhi: Development Alternatives.

Maurás, M. and Minujin, A. (1998). *Derechos a inclusión social: desafíos para el siglo XXI, ponencia presentada en la reunión de la Comisión Sudamericana de Paz, Seguridad y Democracia*. Antigua, Guatemala, 6–9 September.

Paes de Barros, R. *et al.* (2003). *Hacia el Objetivo del Milenio de Reducir la Pobreza.* Santiago: CEPAL, IPEA, UNDP.

Palmer, D. (1973). *Revolution from the Above: Military Government and Popular Participation in Peru, 1968–1972.* Dissertation series, Latin America Studies Program. New York: Cornell University.

Paredes, C. and Pascó-Font, A. (1991). 'The Behaviour of the Public Sector in Peru: A Macroeconomic Approach', in F. Larraín and M. Selowsky (eds), *The Public Sector and the Latin America Crisis.* San Francisco: International Center for Economic Growth (ICS) Press.

Parodi, C. (2000). 'Política económica y social en el Peru: 1980–2000', in F. Portocarrero (ed.), *Políticas sociales en el Peru: Nuevos aportes.* Lima: Red para el desarrollo de las ciencias sociales en el Peru.

Peruvian Government (2003). *Documento de bases para la estrategia de superación de la pobreza y oportunidades económicas para los pobres.* Published in El diario oficial 04 January.

Peruvian Government (2002). 'Carta de Política Social'. *Desafíos de las políticas sociales: Superación de la pobreza e integración social en América Latina.* Lima: FONCODES, pp. 19–37.

Prebisch, R. (1981). *Capitalismo periférico: crisis y transformación.* Mexico: Fondo de Cultura Económica.

Saavedra, J. (2000). 'Generación de empleo y evolución de los ingresos y la productividad en el Peru: 1990–1998', in P. Egger (ed.), *Apertura económica y empleo.* Lima: OIT.

Sagasti, F. (1997). 'Pobreza, exclusión y estrategias de desarrollo: una aproximación preliminar', in *AGENDA: Peru, Pobreza, exclusión y política social: algunas ideas para el diseño de estrategias de desarrollo.* Lima: AGENDA.

Sagasti, F., Iguíñiz, J. and Schuldt, J. (1999). *Equidad, integración social y desarrollo: Hacia un nuevo enfoque para la política social en América Latina.* Centro de Investigación de la Universidad del Pacífico. Lima: Agenda.

Sagasti, F. and Prada, F. (2002). *Social Dialogues in Peru.* Report prepared for the seminar 'Social Dialogues and Social Policy' organized by CEPALC–Inter-American Development Bank. Santiago: IADB.

Schmidt, G. (1989). 'Political Variables and Governmental Decentralization in Peru: 1949–1988'. *Journal of Inter-American Studies and World Affairs* 31 (1/2), 193–232.

Schuldt, J. (1998). *Hacia un enfoque sinérgico de la política social.* Working paper. Lima: AGENDA.

Sen, A. (1999). *Development as Freedom.* New York: Anchor Books.

Speth, J. G. (1994). *Human Development Report.* New York: UNDP.

Tapia, A. (1971). *Acción de las instituciones de crédito especializadas en el financiamiento del sector vivienda en el Peru.* Lima: Imprenta del Hogar de Dios.

Thorp, R. and Bertram, G. (1978). *Peru 1890 1977: Growth and Policy in an Open Economy.* London: Macmillan Press.

UNDP (2002). *Informe sobre Desarrollo Humano: Aprovechando las Potencialidades.* Lima: UNDP.

Vásquez, H., Enrique, C., Aramburu, L., Figueroa, C. and Parodi, T. (2001). *Los Desafíos de la Lucha con la Pobreza Extrema en el Peru.* Centro de Investigación de la Universidad del Pacífico. Lima: International Development Research Centre.

Verdera, F. (2000). *Cambio en el modelo de relaciones laborales en el Peru, 1970–1996.* The Japan Center for Area Studies Occasional Papers. Osaka: JCAS-IEP.

Webb, R. (1991). 'Privatización de facto'. Prologue to Carlos Paredes and Jeffrey Sachs, *Estabilización y crecimiento en el Peru.* Lima: GRADE.

Webb, R. (1975). 'Government Policy and Distribution of Income', in Abraham Lowenthal (ed.), *The Peruvian Experiment: Continuity and Change under Military Rule*. New Jersey: Princeton University Press.
Webb, R. (1973). *Trends in Real Income in Peru, 1950–1966*. Discussion paper 41, Research Program in Economic Development. Princeton, NJ: Princeton University.
Wise, C. (1994). 'The Politics of Peruvian Economic Reform: Overcoming the Legacies of State-led Development'. *Journal of InterAmerican Studies and World Affairs* 36 (1), 75–125.
World Bank (2000). *Peru: Education at the Crossroads*. Washington DC: World Bank.
World Bank (1991). *World Development Report 1991: The Challenge of Development*. New York: Oxford University Press.

# Part III

# On the Rich Shores of Late Immigrants

# 4
# Social Policy and Economic Regime in Argentina: Crisis and Retrenchment of Social Protection

*Alberto C. Barbeito and Laura Goldberg*

## Introduction

This chapter traces the process of construction, maturation and retrenchment of Argentina's social protection system, and links this process to ongoing changes in the state's development strategies and the roles played by the key social actors. It then analyses the impact of economic and social protection reforms during the 1990s on both people's welfare and their life opportunities. Finally, it discusses the features of policies oriented towards reversing the negative consequences of those 1990 reforms. This chapter addresses three specific areas of social policy that, taken together, demonstrate the predominant orientation of each stage of the development of the welfare state (WS): education, social security, and income maintenance. The latter area primarily addresses protection policies related to problems in the labour market.

The hypothesis guiding our analysis holds that the reforms of public policy institutions in Argentina during the 1990s modified the very organizational principles of the traditional WS. In other words, during this period, changes in the objectives of the policy system's institutional arrangements altered the foundations of the welfare system's organizational principles.

An integral analysis of these processes requires a broad perspective that encompasses the functioning of the entire system. As such, we consider both the overall environment in which reforms were made and the specific characteristics of the transformations in the three above-mentioned social sectors.

The chapter is organized as follows: First, from a historic perspective, we briefly present the process of construction and maturation of the social institutions of the Argentine WS. In particular, we look at the nature and forms of the WS in terms of its origins, its relationship to the development of import-substitution industrialization and the role of social organizations and different power groups. Using the same focus, we then describe the guiding principles and salient characteristics of the social security, education, and income maintenance policies implemented up to the 1990s.

We then address the limits of Argentina's WS in terms of the crisis and retrenchment of traditional institutions. In particular, we analyse the role of different social actors in the crisis and the retrenchment of those institutions and the ideological framework that justified the reforms. We also outline the principal changes in the labour market environment and the distribution of income, since these are central to the capacity for income maintenance and the possibility of accessing social security institutions. Finally, we review institutional transformations during the last decade in the three areas studied, and consider their impact on people's life opportunities and the social system as a whole. We conclude by suggesting some general guidelines for the reconstruction of Argentina's social protection institutions and indicate the principal questions and challenges in each of the three areas.

## Construction and maturation of the system of social protection in Argentina

The 'embryonic' stage of the Argentine WS occurred during the second half of the nineteenth century and the beginning of the twentieth century. During this time, the state concentrated its efforts on making basic education universal and on constructing the infrastructure and communications networks necessary for the development of the agro-export model. This embryonic stage of social policy ended with Peronism taking power in the mid-1940s, an event which greatly spurred the process of urbanization and import-substitution industrialization (ISI).

The development of typical WS institutions was an essential element of the process of economic growth and social integration in Argentina. Like Europe, Argentina saw rapid growth in social spending, the expansion of social programmes, and the expansion of the regulation of the overall economic process. However, in contrast to the European experience, social and economic development was not accompanied by political stability: Military dictatorships, democratic regimes with authoritarian practices, the outlawing of political groups, and political violence characterized the expansion of Argentina's WS (Barbeito and Lo Vuolo, 1998: 17–18).

Economic policy during the ISI period assumed the existence of certain 'virtuous and mechanical circles' in markets that would guarantee full employment and uninterrupted growth in aggregate income. Based on this assumption, the system of social policies was constructed as an institutional hybrid, inspired principally in the 'Bismarckian' regime. The heart of the system – pension programmes, *obras sociales* (union-administered health plans) and family allowances – was established as a series of autonomous social security entities financed by payroll taxes. Combined with the full employment of the workforce, this type of institutional arrangement guaranteed that practically the entire population had access to these social benefits (Barbeito and Lo Vuolo, 1998: 34).

In addition, the logic of other social policies (such as education and public health) was identified with principles of the so-called social democratic regime, financed, and offered on a universal basis. Finally, this scheme included a 'residual liberal' policy component, characterized by targeted social assistance programmes, predominantly *clientelista* or 'favour-for-vote', and designed to 'rescue' those unable to achieve stable participation in the formal labour market.

The institutional hybrid constructed under Perónism was based on a paternalistic and favour-for-vote relationship between the state and society, defined by the interaction between the government and representatives of unions and professional organizations.[1] The government's corporate interests and ISI's 'industrial-meritocracy' logic supposed that once formal universal coverage was achieved in the majority of social policies, expansion would operate vertically. The search for and achievement of differential benefits became normal practice and defined different groups' relative position *vis-à-vis* the government and society.

The complex network of actors constructed during the 1940s and 1950s around the WS institutions endured during the WS's maturation stage and was the WS's principal long-term legacy. In the words of O'Donnell (1977), this network reflects 'a state apparatus extensively colonized by civil society, clung to by economically dominant sectors, middle classes and fractions of popular sectors'. This mode of functioning relegated both the legislature and beneficiaries to appendices of the public policies – and helps to explain why, after Perón fell in 1955 (and the military assumed control), different groups continued to veto attempts at state reform. This occurred despite an entirely weak system of political parties and a scant tradition of neo-corporative agreements.

## Social policies in the stage of creation and maturation of the Argentine Welfare State

### The National Education System

Argentina's first educational institutions arose as the result of government initiatives. Between the end of the nineteenth and the beginning of the twentieth centuries the government created a 'National Education System' whose objective was to expand basic education that was obligatory, secular and free. This system also aimed to promote the social integration of the various nationalities represented in the intense inflows of immigrants (Torrado 2003). The results were impressive: between 1869 and 1914, illiteracy fell from 80 per cent to less than 25 per cent.

The national government played a major role in the management and financing of the educational system. An uneven expansion of educational opportunities resulted from poor coordination between the national and provincial governments, and from weak links between the public sector and those private groups that participated (marginally) from the outset. Indeed, public and private establishments coexisted in the same territory, some dependent on the national government and others supervised and regulated by the provinces according to their respective laws and regulations (Repetto *et al.* 2001).

Although from the beginning the national educational project was to include development of secondary and tertiary institutions, the country's agro-export profile demanded neither special labour qualifications nor skills that could not be acquired 'on the job'. As such, the function and expansion of higher education was limited to elite urban leaders, administrative staff for the incipient state and commercial bureaucracies, and teachers to cover the expansion of basic education.[2]

From the 1930s onwards, shifts towards an ISI model of accumulation implied a significant increase in the number of enrolled students, especially those in secondary education and oriented towards technical and commercial studies. New occupational roles now demanded more complex, technical-professional, skills, as well as a work discipline that was nurtured by participation in the educational system. In this sense, and in contrast to the situation of basic education, the expansion of educational opportunities at the secondary level was, at least initially, gradual and strongly associated with the educational demands of the productive sector. The system's expansion continued to be poorly organized due principally to the absence of a legal framework to regulate its global structure and link the operations of different public and private actors.

Towards the end of the 1950s, a new stage in the development of the educational system coincided with the first symptoms of the slowing of the expansive dynamic of ISI: recurrent crises in the external sector, decreasing rates of growth, and a diminished level of incorporation of labour into the industrial sector.

Around this time, secondary education began to lose influence as a factor in upward social mobility. The reduced absorption of labour by modern sectors of the economy generated an excess labour supply that progressively expanded the informal sector (principally self-employment in low-skilled activities and small businesses with low productivity). This process became more pronounced in the following decades, as a growing number of those who finished high school were overqualified for the occupations they performed.

On the other hand, under President Arturo Frondizi (1958–62) the national government initiated a gradual process of educational decentralization.[3] Although the government argued that the main goals of decentralization were operational efficiency and managerial autonomy, decentralization consistently appeared to be aimed at meeting the national government's fiscal balance objectives. The flipside of this policy was lower public spending, and, in particular, a decrease in the real levels of teachers' salaries.

At the end of the 1980s, the national government had forfeited its central role in financing and managing education. The increasing number of actors providing educational services – including the national and provincial governments, municipalities, and the private sector – exacerbated the fragmentation of the system. Above all, this fragmentation was aggravated by the lack of coordination among these actors.[4]

## The national social security system

The first pension systems in Argentina date from the nineteenth century, but at this time the scheme was intended only for members of the military, high-level government officials, and teachers in the state sector. The first steps towards labour and social security legislation at the beginning of the twentieth century were a state initiative rather than a response to any specific demand from the labour movement. It was no coincidence that some of labour's best-positioned sectors in the agroexport economy (public services, banks, etc.) were the first to demand access to retirement benefits. In contrast, in most of the labour movement, demands were related to salaries, improved working conditions and a reduction in the length of the working day.

Perón's tenure as Secretary of Labour and Welfare (1943–45) and later as president (1946–55) heralded a new stage in the development of social security. His tenure also marked changes in the model of accumulation and in the peculiar link between the government and unions. During this period, the social security system expanded rapidly. This dynamic, which persisted as a legacy of Perónism, was sustained by the 'cumulative aggregation' of the pressure of union demands and the government's strategy of legitimizing its own power. Until 1956, the year following Perón's fall, the entire economically active population (EAP) enjoyed the legal right to social security.

Initially, the system generated a financial surplus because of a high ratio of assets to liabilities. This surplus was channelled toward other ends (such as the construction of low-income housing), which added to the loss of accumulated capital in real terms, resulting from inflation and a lack of investor rationality. In addition, financial problems deepened due to permissive access mechanisms and repeated moratoria. Growing financial difficulties led to the abandonment of the original collectively funded structure accumulation, accelerating the transition towards a simple distribution between income and payments ('pay-as-you-go'). This did not prevent the National Social Security savings system from registering financial deficits, beginning in 1966. In 1967, the military government of 1966–73 created the National Social Security System (NSSS), whose goals were to unify and centralize social security policy, displacing the union's presence in the governance of the social security cash desks, control evasion, and to standardize contributions and requirements for obtaining retirement benefits.

Participation in the NSSS was compulsory for all paid workers. The following legal retirement ages were established: (i) for salaried workers, 60 years for men and 55 for women; and (ii) for self-employed workers, 65 and 60 years, respectively. Likewise, 30 years of service were required, though social security contributions only had to be paid for 15 of these. For formally employed workers, retirement income was estimated as a percentage (between 70 and 82 per cent) of the average remuneration over their working life. For self-employed workers, retirement income was calculated based on the income bracket to which the workers had contributed during their period of activity.

The reform failed to correctly evaluate the potential imbalances created in the system over time and no long-term measures were designed to avoid a recurrence of the system's deficit. As such, the original problems that had justified the 1967 reforms soon re-emerged. Evasion was especially severe, in particular among self-employed workers. Additional problems included 'administrative' evasion due to under-declared income; contributions being retained by employers; delays in transfers from the state as an employer; the incorporation of 'non-remunerative' components in salaries[5] (particularly in the public sector); and policies that facilitated access to benefits for ample sectors that had failed to make the requisite contributions.

Towards the end of the 1980s, the system's growing financial imbalance obliged the government to introduce sustained increases in income taxes. At the same time, resources were incorporated from other sources, as were transfers from other social programmes. Despite these measures, the real purchasing power of the benefits deteriorated and the system accumulated an oversized debt owed to its members.[6]

### Social assistance and employment policies

Social assistance policies have traditionally been considered 'residual' by virtue of their separateness from more systematic and organized policies and the relatively low level of resources involved. The main characteristics of these policies included the diversity and discontinuity of social assistance programmes, the programmes' undefined nature, and their favour-for-vote management. By the mid-1980s, regardless of the progressively precarious labour market and the rise in the levels of poverty, total spending in this area did not exceed 0.5 per cent of GDP.

Notably, the Argentine WS had no unemployment insurance, nor policies to promote employment. The first programmes of this kind emerged by the end of the 1980s, but were quite limited.

On the other hand, the first massive assistance programme (the *Programa Alimentario Nacional* or National Food Programme, PAN) dates from 1984, a year after Argentina's return to democracy. This programme consisted of the distribution of boxes of basic foodstuffs for family consumption, and represented the first explicit acknowledgement of the growing phenomenon of hunger among the poorest in the country.

## Crisis and retrenchment of the Argentine Welfare State and its social actors

During the first half of the 1970s, the Argentine WS showed clear symptoms of a lack of rationality.[7] Attempts to resolve major macroeconomic aggregate instability after 1972, and mostly after the first debt crisis, were extremely conflictive. First, the government had to decide whether to scale back consumption or investment, and also which economic agents should bear the consequences of that adjustment. On the other hand, pressures to devalue the currency affected fiscal accounts and inflation levels. In this context, the decrease in wages and per capita income affected the collection of payroll taxes, which financed the bulk of the social policies. Furthermore, budget cuts resulted in a decrease in the real value of contributions, restrictions in coverage, and pressure on other sources of complementary financing. When the Argentinian economy finally collapsed into the traumatic bouts of hyperinflation in 1989 and 1990, it was clear the country had begun to experience a deepening crisis of social integration.[8]

At this time the notion that the state was the major cause of this crisis became quite popular, especially after the failure of the economic stabilization plan which was in operation from 1984 to 1988. Various dominant sectors of the economy began to suggest – and later to insist on – the need 'once and for all' to introduce the 'deep reforms' that the country was supposed to need, to recover from a permanent state of crisis and instability.[9]

These reforms finally occurred under President Carlos Menem (1989–99). From the outset, Menem shared the dominant economic sectors' understanding of the crisis and he incorporated much of their rhetoric into his discourse. He constructed a hegemonic alliance among the most concentrated economic groups in the country, transnational capital, and the bureaucracies of the international credit organizations. The 'structural reforms' implemented in Argentina in the 1990s were primarily inspired by the so-called *Washington Consensus* proposals.[10]

In terms of social policy, these reforms aimed to impose a narrow vision, which assumed a single, almost exclusive objective: to offer assistance only to those groups in extreme poverty. This vision abandoned other objectives such as universal coverage, a reduction in the unpredictability or unreliability of benefits, a progressive distribution of income, and upward social mobility.

The first result of the economic reforms was to reduce in the inflation rate practically to zero. The 'income effect' was key to improving the purchasing power of sectors with fixed income and to expanding economic activity.

In addition, a 'wealth effect' resulted from modifications to the exchange rate and an increase of the value in dollars of domestic real and financial assets. However, after an initial stabilizing effect, the imbalances provoked by overvalued currency and loss of external competitiveness soon became apparent.

The growth of both public and private external debt was an endogenous element of this economic model, a necessary condition for financing external imbalances and sustaining the convertibility regime and fixed exchange rate regime over time (see Appendix, Table 4.A1).

Meanwhile, the social and productive structures changed radically, including intense processes of de-industrialization, concentration and the transnationalization of production. The loss of competitiveness exerted downward pressure on labour costs, led to a deterioration in work conditions, and eliminated jobs. As a result, the unemployment rate increased from 7 per cent of the EAP in 1991 to 14.7 per cent at the end of the decade (after reaching 18.4 per cent in 1995). Unregistered salaried employment grew significantly: from 26 per cent to 38 per cent in the same period. Finally, involuntary hourly underemployment showed a similar evolution: from 8.6 per cent of the EAP in 1991 to 14.6 per cent in 2000 (see Appendix, Figure 4.A1 1).

In this context of labour market deterioration, the government promoted the decentralization of collective bargaining at a business-by-business level. New contracts tended to incorporate clauses that affected worker remuneration: (i) annual limits on the number of hours worked, which restricted overtime and reduced total remuneration; (ii) variability in salaries via components linked to criteria for output, productivity, etc.; and (iii) reduction in or elimination of additional benefits for attendance or time on the job. The weakness in decentralized collective bargaining is a result of a combination of three factors: (i) the high levels of unemployment in the global labour market; (ii) weakness in the representation of workers' interests;[11] and (iii) the state's passive role as guide and mediator in negotiations, even ratifying agreements with clauses that violated legal norms (for example, the number of the annual working days) (Beccaria and Galín 2002). Changes in the labour market clearly correspond to changes in the distribution of income (see Appendix, Figure 4.A2). Between 1994 and 2000, per capita family income decreased by almost 10 per cent. Still, the fall was uneven across social groups: the mean income of the poorest 10 per cent of the population fell by more than 30 per cent. At the same time, workers' incomes became more volatile: the study cited previously shows that for 57 per cent of those employed, their remuneration was totally or partially variable. Job insecurity did not only affect personal income. It also limited access to social security institutions, in particular to *obras sociales*, the payment of family allowances and the right to receive a pension. At the same time, a reduction in the registered salary base and salary deductions affected the sources of financing and the level of these services.[12] As part of this new 'adjustment', the regime of family allowances was altered to eliminate spousal benefits and create a sliding scale of benefits per child for monthly salaries up to 1,500 pesos (approximately double the average salary).

During the 1990s, the dominant political framework reversed the ascending dynamic that had characterized the previous stage of maturation of the Argentine WS. Expansion controlled by favour-for-vote practices eventually gave way to exclusion, either controlled or not. The result was an anarchic withdrawal of the government from areas in which it had traditionally played a major role, which led different interest groups to attempt to find individual solutions and to secure a specific part of public funding for them.

## Programmatic reforms of social policies in the 1990s

### Educational reform

Transformations in education were made through two principal instruments: (i) Law 24.049/92 that completed the process of secondary education decentralization to the provinces; and (ii) the Federal Educational Law (24.195/93), which had the goal of redesigning the education system.

The resources transferred from the federal government to the provinces were less than to the financial cost of the services transferred – and were clearly insufficient to cover the expansion of those services (even more if one considered the expansive dynamics of school assistance). The principal objective of the transfer was to reduce the pressure on the national finances, shifting the burden to the provinces. This generated greater restrictions in the functioning of the education system, with negative effects on personnel salaries, on conflict with unions, and on the quality of services.

The Federal Educational Law aimed to resolve the sector's main structural problems: low retention and high dropout rates (particularly for secondary education); deficiencies in quality; social and geographical inequalities; and institutional fragmentation. To these ends, new guidelines were developed for the system's functioning: changes in the structure and length of the cycle of obligatory education, which was extended to ten years;[13] ratification of the principle of free public education; renovation of curricular content; creation of a national quality evaluation system; compensatory programmes to address social inequalities in the system. In respect to financing, the Law established concrete goals for increases in public spending on education which should be done in a five-year term: the most favourable option between duplicating in absolute values (20 per cent minimum) the resources budgeted in 1993, or an increase of 50 per cent in relation to the GDP of the base year. In real terms, this represented an increase from 4 to 6 per cent of GDP.

### Results

Ten years after the reforms, progress has been uneven regarding both general objectives and the situation in the various jurisdictions. Specific results include the following:

1. **Coverage:** the increase in school enrolment is often pointed to as an achievement of the reforms, due partly to the upward and downward extension of obligatory education. However, at the same time, there was an important increase in enrolment in higher education. This process seems to be fuelled by families' demands. Thus, evidence shows that this tendency toward expansion in coverage is not exclusive to the 1990s, since it had already manifested itself with some intensity during the previous decade: according to the Population Census of 1980, the gross rate of school enrolment for ages 15–19 was 43 per cent; in the 1991 census that rate increased to 54 per cent, and in the 2001 census it reached 69 per cent (see Appendix, Table 4.A2).
2. **Education Spending:** Although public spending on education increased during the early 1990s, this growth must be evaluated in light of accumulated decreases during previous years and the increase in the school population (see Appendix, Table 4.A2). The goals for increased public spending established in the Federal Education Law were not met. Consequently, investment per student continues to be low, especially in secondary and higher education: in 2001, the average educational spending per high school student was 1.6 times that of kindergarten and primary school children, and 2.3 times that of higher education (Morduchowicz 2002: 24). This problem has its direct reflect on lower quality of educational services.
3. **Teachers:** The principal budget-cutting mechanism was a reduction of salaries in public administration.[14] In 2000 the basic teacher's salary was only 40 per cent of the average salary in the economy. Furthermore, 11.6 per cent of primary school teachers and 4.2 per cent of high school teachers live in households with even lower incomes.[15] The situation of the teachers contains other factors of tension and conflict, such as gaps between their training and the requirements introduced by pedagogical and curricular changes, or permanent government pressures to modify the statute that regulates working conditions. Regarding the former, although training schemes have been implemented, teachers have rated them poorly.
4. **Geographical Disparities:** National evaluation campaigns show the existence of great disparities in the quality of educational services and between the provinces, and a high dropout rate, especially at the secondary level. For the entire country, more than 12 per cent of the students that began primary school did not complete it. In provinces such as Misiones, Chaco, Corrientes and Santiago del Estero, the percentage of dropouts varied between 25 and 30 percent.

5. **Social Disparities**: The most relevant point is the profound gap between the poor and the non-poor, less in terms of access to the system than in their ability to complete the various cycles, especially high school: in 2002, only two out of every ten 'poor' youth finished or went beyond high school, composed to five out of every ten 'non-poor' youth (Judengloben *et al.* 2003). A critical subgroup of youth between 15 and 17 years of age, most of them from poor households, abandoned the educational system without completing even minimal schooling. Their vulnerability and risk of exclusion have increased: While in 1995 only 11 per cent of dropouts had not finished primary school, in 2002 this percentage grew to 24.8 per cent. Finally, the disparity in access to higher education for youth aged 18 to 24 in different socioeconomic groups also grew significantly (Judengloben *et al.* 2003).
6. **Circuits of Differentiated Quality**: Studies on the job placement of high school graduates reveal what Daniel Filmus calls 'circuits of differentiated quality' inside the educational system. This term refers to vicious circles in which a child's initial educational and social disadvantages lead to continued educational deficits. The causes of this differentiation are multiple. Some are associated with the socioeconomic origin of the youths' families. Others are the consequence of having attended institutions of inferior educational quality – 'Poor schools in poor neighbourhoods for poor children' is an expression that well summarizes the problem. Disparities in educational preparation impact significantly on students' track records and job placement possibilities (Filmus and Moragues 2003). Nearly 20 per cent of the youth that completed high school are neither in work nor in further study, which demonstrates that an education credential is insufficient either to find work or to access higher education. Education policy's goal of equality is weakened, and in current conditions, tends actually to in exacerbate original social and cultural differences.

In this context, if the expectation of achieving some degree of upward social mobility rests upon higher education, the consequence – and a highly undesirable one – is that only well-off students (with the potential to access and complete higher education) attend high school.

In sum, an educational system which presumed to homogenize groups with heterogeneous sociocultural backgrounds has given way to an aggregate of heterogeneous institutions with a notable tendency toward segregating homogenous populations (Tiramonti 2003).

## Social security reform

Law 24.241 of 1994[16] brought wide-ranging reforms to the social security system in keeping with the diagnosis and arguments of the so-called New Social Security Orthodoxy (NSSO).[17] In short, a public 'pay-as-you-go' regime was replaced by a 'mixed' system that combines a publicly administered 'pay-as-you-go' regime and a private fully funded regime managed by the *Administradoras de Fondos de Jubilaciones y Pensiones* (AFJP, Administrators of Pensions and Retirement Funds).[18] At the same time, the minimum retirement age was raised from 55 to 60 for women and from 60 to 65 for men. The minimum number of years of employee contributions for eligibility to access payments was increased to 30.

For those who contribute to an AFJP and meet the above-mentioned requirements, payment is composed of a 'defined' portion financed by the state and an 'undefined and uncertain' portion that depends on the actuarial value of the accumulated savings (net of deductions for commissions) in each individual account at the moment of retirement.[19] Those who opt to remain within the state-run regime and meet those requirements have the right to an entirely state-financed, 'defined' payment with three components: a uniform basic payment; a payment linked to the history of contributions up to the reform; and another linked to the period between the reform and the date of retirement.[20]

### Results

After nearly a decade, the principal results of the social security reform are grouped as follows:

1. **Coverage**: The reform had a negative impact on coverage. A decrease in the number of contributors (which has fallen dramatically since the end of 2001) and the remarkable fall in the coverage of the EAP are the most worrisome aspects of the system's current situation.[21] In addition, coverage of persons at retirement age fell (in fact, there has been a quite unprecedented decrease in the absolute number of beneficiaries) (see Appendix, Table 4.A3).
2. **Evasion**: The reform was supposed to diminish the evasion of employee contributions due to the incentives inherent in individually fully funded pension schemes. In reality, the reverse occurred and evasion increased, particularly among the self-employed. This reversal was affected by increases in open employment, underemployment, unregistered employment and a fall in wages. However, the ineffectiveness of incentives is demonstrated by other factors: the majority of contributors chose not to exercise the option of deciding between a payment or capitalization regime, nor did they choose which AFJP would receive their contributions.
3. **Disparities**: In a labour market such as that in Argentina, the contribution regime ends up covering only a reduced group of workers with the sustained capacity to make regular contributions during their entire working life. In this context, a 'social assistance' benefit becomes the norm. In Argentina, the system clearly excluded those who lacked regular and high level incomes.[22]

4. **AFJPs**: From the beginning of the new system, the market of AFJPs suffered a significant concentration. Today, the majority of the AFJPs (and the largest ones) belong to financial holdings that offer this service as a complement to their portfolio of products. In addition, competition between AFJPs led to elevated marketing costs rather than differential costs and profitability. In fact, the cost of administration is high and has greatly reduced the amount contributed by members. Finally, the financial crisis that shook the Argentine economy in 2001 affected the AFJPs' investment portfolios, causing heavy losses and uncertainty about future benefits.
5. **Economic-Financial Equation**: Because of the reform, the public system lost capital due to the shift of employee contributions to individually funded accounts. Currently, the majority of the resources used for social security payments come not from employer and employee contributions, but rather from general taxes. In the short run, the system was financed by extraordinary funds (privatizations, external debt, etc.). However, the situation became unsustainable and the social security system became an appendix to short-term macroeconomic policy, which included the squandering of savings from capitalization funds (see Appendix, Table 4.A4).

## Reform of social assistance policies, job promotion and protection against unemployment

The formal reform of policies related to the remunerated labour market began with the 1991 National Employment Law. This statute established unemployment insurance and created different, unstable modes of contracting labour, promoted by decreases in or the elimination of employment benefits and of job programmes for so-called 'special groups of workers'.

At the same time, the government introduced successive measures of 'labour flexibility', ostensibly to improve competitiveness and promote growth: lower costs and the greater ease of firing workers; greater decentralization of collective bargaining; extension and variability of the working day; and a freezing of the minimum wage (Beccaria and Galín 2002). In reality, work productivity increased, but salaries did not; unemployment increased and jobs became more precarious.

In response to the deeper and broader deterioration in working conditions and incomes, various targeted assistance programmes and actively promoted by international financial institutions, were introduced. In each case programmes have been relatively small-scale, fragmented and aimed at overlapping groups of beneficiaries.

Finally, after the economic, social and political crisis exploded in December 2001, the new interim government launched a massive income transfer programme: the *Programa Jefes y Jefas de Hogar Desocupados* (*PJJHD* – Programme for Unemployed [Female and Male] Heads of Households).

Presented as a 'family right to social inclusion', this programme maintains the traditional logic of previous social assistance programmes.[23] The PJJHD consists of a monetary payment of $150 (roughly US$50) per month to those who present a sworn statement that they qualify as an unemployed head of household with dependent children under 18 (or proof of pregnancy). Their children must be in school and comply with certain requirements regarding health care. As well, beneficiaries must accept on obligatory, part-time job.

The most significant change introduced by this programme is one of scale: it provides two million subsidies and uses resources equivalent to 0.8 per cent of GDP. Financing comes from diverse sources: the national treasury, the reassignment and unification of funding for previous social programmes, a portion of taxes collected on post-devaluation exports, and a loan from the World Bank.

Although the core of unemployment is found in the EAP above 40 years of age, 65 per cent of PJJHD beneficiaries are younger than 40. Two-thirds are women, even though this proportion is not reflected in the female unemployment rate. According to available information, 70 per cent of the beneficiaries comply with the work requirement, mostly in the public sector in unskilled, part-time jobs (approximately 20 hours per week), and a high percentage of the beneficiaries seek other work. Still, there are doubts about the effectiveness of these work commitments and the procedures utilized for the selection of beneficiaries.

Despite the scale of the programme, its effects on unemployment rates and poverty have been negligible. In October 2002, the urban unemployment rate stood at 17.8 per cent, and the figure would have been 23.6 per cent if plan beneficiaries were not considered as 'employed'. At the same time, the number of households in the Buenos Aires metropolitan area with incomes below the poverty line had dropped marginally – from 42.6 to 42.3 per cent – as a result of PJJHD.

Currently, the government is attempting to reformulate PJJHD in two directions. First, in order to strengthen it as an income maintenance programme, the government plans to limit PJJHD to elderly persons with no pension and young people without children. Secondly, to emphasize its nature as an employment programme, it will provide subsidies to private employers, incorporate beneficiaries into public works, and provide small loans for micro-enterprises.

### Results

Policies implemented over the last decade failed to alleviate and, to some degree, actually worsened the socioeconomic insecurity resulting from imbalances in the labour market – including the persistent fall and instability in incomes, the expansion of unregistered salaried work, the underutilization of the workforce, etc. In this context, pretended compensatory actions towards labour insecurity did not build a minimal social protection income network either for individuals or for families. We summarize below the main weaknesses and problems:

1. **Unemployment Insurance**: The nature of contributions and the precarious labour situation led to low levels of coverage (between 5 and 7 per cent) of open unemployment. Furthermore, the rate of replacement wage for employed workers decreased systematically.
2. **Temporary Employment Programmes**: The failure of these programmes is demonstrated by their continual changes. Furthermore, they have been implemented on a reduced scale and with little efficiency, without specialized and geographically distributed employment agencies. The selection of beneficiaries has been predominantly favour-for-vote.
3. **Job Promotion Programmes**: These programmes have focused primarily on employer exemptions from social security contributions and other tax incentives. Their coverage and fiscal cost are both unknown. Weak controls lead one to believe that they have little effect on the net creation of jobs, and that they favour tax fraud as well as the substitution and rotation of workers.
4. **Programme for Unemployed Heads of Households (PJJHD)**: The most positive aspect of this programme is the expanded scale of operation and the intention to intervene with compensatory measures in a context of grave social crisis. Still, this programme has notable weaknesses as an income maintenance scheme and also as an employment programme, including, first, its emergency-response nature in addressing a structural, long-term problem. Secondly, this programme makes reparations (ex post) and is not preventive (ex ante). Thirdly, it reproduces the same shortcomings present in the targeted programmes implemented during the 1990s, such as favour-for-vote and lack of autonomy. Fourthly, this programme encourages fraud as well as changes in family arrangements that promote the precarious incorporation of women in the workforce. Fifthly, by providing a fixed benefit independent of the number of children in the household, it has little effect on poverty, especially since poor households are characterized by a greater number of children. Finally, this programme fails to address the situation of low-wage workers.

## Guidelines for (re-)constructing the social protection system

The picture described above illustrates the failure of the reform experiment carried out in Argentina during the 1990s.

The macroeconomic context defined by the convertibility rule (of one peso to one dollar) started to change when a new recessionary phase began in mid-1998 (see Appendix, Figure 4.A3).[24] At the beginning of 2001, the situation was already extremely critical: while recession and fiscal imbalances were worsening, capital flight was on the increase, as was the loss of deposits from financial institutions. In December 2001, the government imposed restrictions on cash withdrawals from banks (known as '*el corralito*', or 'little playpen') and on cash transfers out of the country.

An explosion of social protest precipitated the resignations of the economy minister, Domingo Cavallo, and President Fernando de la Rúa. In the final days of December, Argentina announced it was defaulting on its public debt, and, shortly afterwards, the peso was devalued, finally ending convertibility.

The end of the fixed exchange rate regime took place in an environment of extreme political fragility and disjointed, even contradictory, economic measures (Lo Vuolo 2003). The first stage of the crisis was administered with the same sources of financing as during convertibility: increases in public debt and wage repression.[25]

New public debt (largely compulsory) was aimed primarily at sustaining the financial system. This increased the stock of existing public debt contracted in foreign currency, whose value exploded because of the devaluation (see Appendix, Table 4.A1). The ratio of debt to GDP reached 124 per cent in 2003.

Between May 2001 and May 2003, the average level of salaries in real terms dropped by 19 per cent, unemployment and poverty rates rose strongly, while global private consumption and gross fixed internal investment fell by 16.9 per cent and 33.2 per cent, respectively (see Appendix Figures 4.A1–3). Domestic adjustment corresponds to the external sector adjustment: the trade balance changed from negative to positive on a scale equivalent to nine points of GDP, which allowed for the financing of transfers of resources out of the country (see Appendix Table 4.A5).

Several factors contributed to the improvement of the fiscal and external accounts during 2003. These factors included: the reconstruction of political authority after the presidential elections of May 2003; limits on the payments of the public debt; the devaluation and changes in the exchange rate regime; the high international prices of primary exports; and the implementation of export taxes on these goods. Economic reactivation was the result of inflation controls following the devaluation, policies aimed at improving the private sector's minimum wage and the short-term agreement with the IMF of January 2003 among others. As a result, GDP growth for 2003 is estimated to be 6 per cent.[26]

The deepening and maintenance in time of the fledgling economic recovery depends upon how two key conflicts are confronted and resolved. On the one hand, there is the conflict on the external front related to the restructuring of public external debt currently in default. The way in which this issue is solved will, for the most part, define future flows of foreign exchange transfers abroad, as well as the ability to dispose of national income for domestic spending. The recent agreement with the IMF has imposed an exacting primary fiscal surplus (excluding debt service) commitment of 3 per cent of GDP for 2004.

On the other hand, it should be stressed that public debt restructuring in terms of maturity, levels, and interest rates compatible with the maintenance of the actual economic recovery is a necessary, but not a sufficient condition to achieve a process of economic growth and equity that will be sustainable over time. For this to occur, an integrated capital accumulation and income distribution strategy is required. In this sense, there are some important lessons from Argentina's recent experience that should be taken into account.

The principal lesson to be learned from the Argentine case is that a 'compensatory' vision of social policy is inefficient in a context of the permanent deterioration of indicators of employment and income distribution, which feeds a cumulative and expansive spiral of deterioration in labour and social conditions.

Adopting an alternative vision of current social protection regime in Argentina requires simultaneously an economic policy based on alternative principles. In this sense, the first social policy should be economic policy. In particular, for social policy to be effective in sustaining and improving life opportunities and socioeconomic security, political economy should be focused on: (i) a progressive change in the pattern of wealth and income distribution; (ii) a new strategy for generating employment in productive sectors; and (iii) employment relationships that favour greater cooperation between capital and labour.

## Guidelines for education policy

The principal questions derived from the evolution of the education system and the reforms of the 1990s can be summarized as follows:

- How can we sustain and intensify the expansion of school enrolment?
- How can we make that expansion as universal as possible, reducing geographical and socioeconomic differences?
- How can we repair and promote the quality of educational services?
- How can we undo the 'circuits of differential quality' that operate in the educational system, especially in secondary education?
- How can we improve training for teachers, and their work and life conditions?

1. **Coverage**: The principal challenge is to reduce the dropout rate, especially in high school. The principal cause is external to the education system and has its origins in the deterioration of family income. Here, the answers may lie in children-based income maintenance policies linked to their school attendance. In addition, schools must have improved infrastructure, equipment, and functioning to equalize the performance of different social groups.

2. **Quality Improvement**: This implies extending the length of time children spend in school (i.e. increasing the number of institutions that offer a full school day) and changes in the systems of teaching and of training for teachers. The role of personnel is key and requires a new collective commitment that redefines the incentive scheme, including salary recovery and systems to promote a professional career structure and path. This commitment also requires greater participation of teachers in education management and in the design of training programs.
3. **Reduction of Regional Disparities**: Due to the operative decentralization of the system, a new Federal Education Pact is required. This pact must assign reciprocal responsibilities between the federal government and the provinces based on concrete goals for increasing enrolment, commitments regarding funding and school infrastructure improvement, etc.
4. **Financing**: Any federal pact to implement the guidelines outlined above imply access to additional resources, even under a strategy of gradual implementation. The possibilities for resolving this problem are subject to additional issues, such as the future behaviour of the Argentine economy, the renegotiation of the public debt, but also, and especially, on the future agreements with international organizations, national and provincial tax reforms.

### Guidelines for the social security system

The social security reforms of 1994 had negative effects on the system's current and future assets. Clearly a new, integral reform is needed that should address three basic objectives, whose order and priority will determine the characteristics of the final design:

1. **Coverage**: Increase effective and direct coverage to the working and non-working population.
2. **Income**: Decrease uncertainty with respect to future benefits, distribute risks among all affiliated groups and assure the subsistence of all elderly persons.
3. **Sustainability**: Guarantee a sustainable economic-financial regime, differentiating between contributive and non-contributive components.

In the current Argentininian context, the construction of a new social security system should address the heterogeneities and instabilities in the labour market, be as unified and simple as possible, have defined criteria for controls, and be coordinated with other social protection schemes and taxes. Based on these elements, the application of so-called 'multi-pillar' systems seems to be the most advisable option.

A first pillar should assure the payment of a certain basic level of benefit.[27] For a labour market as unstable as Argentina's, the best option could be to guarantee universal coverage for all elderly persons,[28] consisting of a uniform sum of money paid monthly to all (male and female) citizens of retirement age with no additional eligibility requirements.[29]

The reformed system should include a second, obligatory pillar and a third, voluntary pillar for those who wish to increase their contributions. The design of this system will require the resolution of several questions:

1. How can we guarantee compliance with the mandatory nature of the system? To this end, the system should be simple, accessible and easy to monitor, especially for self-employed workers, the most difficult group to incorporate.
2. Should the system be 'pay-as-you-go' or an individual fully funded scheme? Most likely, the option that best overcomes this dichotomy is that of the so-called 'notional accounts'.[30] The advantages of this option are that contributions are defined and payments come from an explicit actuarial calculation (which is more predictable). In addition, payment of a worker's benefits would more directly reflect his or her lifetime employment income, at the same time that intergenerational solidarity is maintained as current workers support current retirees.
3. How can we resolve the coexistence of the 'pay-as-you-go' and individually fully funded schemes? Discussion on this issue has been ample. Here we suggest only that it is not helpful to continue with two competing public obligatory regimes. It would be much more rational to have one integrated system that distributes risks.
4. What are the possibilities for financing and sustainability? There are several imaginable lines of action for the financing of the growth in coverage (a basic, universal pillar) and improvement in current minimal payments: (i) recovering fiscal resources from the personal contributions that today flow totally into the system of individually fully-funded pensions; (ii) a more universal and progressive tax reform; and (iii) stronger incentives to contribute and greater control over evasion.

**Guidelines for income policies**

In present-day Argentina employment income is extremely unstable and, for the majority of people, critically insufficient. As a result, consumption of essential goods and services is also both insufficient and volatile. The current design of policies that transfer monetary income do not allow for reparation, let alone prevention, of the damages and human suffering that result. Construction of a policy that guarantees basic levels of income security seems an essential objective for controlling emerging social problems and poverty.

Argentina must create institutions and implement policies that modify the current pattern of distribution of wealth and income and amplify basic socioeconomic security. One must analyse the political and ideological support that such actions might generate. Data from a recent survey show a positive predisposition towards such policies: more than 50 per cent of the population believes that there should be some type of maximum limit to personal income and 23 per cent supports the idea of guaranteeing a minimum income (Barbeito and Lo Vuolo 2001).

In this context, the idea of implementing some variant of the '*ingreso ciudadano*' or basic citizen income seems feasible. This proposal recognizes the citizens' right to receive a universal and unconditional monetary income that operates as a complement to personal income from the labour market or other sources. Arguments in favour of this policy highlight its preventive nature as opposed to an ex-post reparation. This policy avoids favour-for-vote and increases the level of personal autonomy. It does not stigmatize nor discriminate regarding family arrangements. It does not promote the traps of unemployment and poverty. The arguments against this policy are primarily about the ethical value of work, with the consequent claim for any kind of labour requirement for the benefits and about the budgetary restrictions for its financing.[31]

In the case of Argentina, and probably other Latin American countries, a strategy for the progressive implementation of this policy could begin by guaranteeing a citizen income for the most dependent socioeconomic groups: infants and older adults – especially as the poverty rate is much higher for these sections of the population.

## Conclusion

Throughout history the relationship between the development of the system of social protection in Argentina and the political and economic regimes has not been a linear one. The foundations of the modern welfare state laid between 1945 and 1950 were sustained practically through to the end of the 1980s. During this prolonged period, democratic governments (more or less restricted) were interspersed with dictatorships. On the economic front, important changes resulted from the crisis of the ISI model. However, until the hyperinflation of 1989–90, institutional changes always respected the principles of the traditional welfare state, with increasing contradictions resulting from changes in the economic regime.

The crisis of social integration resulting from hyperinflation provided opportunities for reforms in the organizational principles of the majority of Argentina's social and economic policies. In this sense, Argentina was an extreme example of economic liberalization and the retraction of the welfare state's institutions, whose results are expressed in an unprecedented deterioration in welfare indicators and in the distribution of wealth and income.

The social, political, and economic collapse at the end of 2001 highlighted the contradictions and the weaknesses of the economic and social regime installed in the 1990s. A profound economic depression initiated in 1998, cumulative macroeconomic imbalances, and the inconsistency between new operative rules of the institutional reforms and economic imperatives all resulted in chaos. The most evident expressions of this chaos were a brusque devaluation, the freezing of bank deposits, and the conversion of dollar-denominated bank accounts into pesos, a fall in incomes, and an increase in public debt and in poverty levels.

The manner in which this crisis was administered did not change the foundations of the economic and social regime constructed under the convertibility regime. The principal sources of financing continued to be a regressive distribution of income and an increase in public debt – with no apparent definition of an alternative development strategy or a substantive change in the logic of the functioning of social policy.

The future of the social protection system depends upon the design of an alternative development strategy for Argentina. In our opinion, the driving force behind this strategy must be a gradual, but sustained modification in the pattern of distribution of income and wealth. This is not achieved with 'shock' policies, or with temporary, emergency, or isolated measures. On the contrary, what is needed is an ample and integrated series of consistent policies that reciprocally increase their potential and operate on all relevant fronts: macroeconomic policies that stimulate effective demand, labour market policies, income maintenance policies, tax policy, reprogramming of the public debt, and so on; what could also be described as the evolution of a new LADWS model.

In this sense, Argentina's experience over the last few years suggests some very clear lessons concerning the links that must necessarily occur between social and economic policies. First, Argentina has shown the failure of the 'compensatory' vision of social policy during a generalized deterioration of employment and income distribution. Secondly, reducing labour costs or weakening protective labour norms does not achieve improvements in productivity and competitiveness. Rather, such improvements are the result of systemic medium- and long-term processes based on the incorporation of innovations in capital investment, including human capital. Thirdly, distributive regression does not promote savings and capital accumulation; rather, it contracts the internal market, employment, and fiscal income. Fourthly, orthodox fiscal and monetary policies are inconsistent for managing the economic cycle: they worsen recessive tendencies and lead to cuts in social services at the precise point when the population's life conditions are most affected.

The design of a new social protection system in Argentina must consider these factors. The social problems are massive and require attention from institutions that offer more universal coverage and, at the same time, allow for the basic conditions of integration and social cohesion. This implies changing the operative rules of social policy institutions, but, more importantly, economic policy, and the way in which these two areas of public policy are connected. Argentina must define a new social and economic development strategy that is gradual, consistent, and sustainable over a long period. This seems to be the central question of our times.

## Notes

1. Three laws passed during Perón's first presidency were critical to the predominance of professional and union interests: the Law of Professional Associations, the Law of Collective Bargaining and the Law of Obras Sociales. However, the system of corporatist groups is not limited to these associations, but rather includes a complex network of actors linked to each area of state activity, be they contractors, input providers, subsidized institutions, technical consultants, etc. In the social policies system, a group of professionals and technicians defined a system of norms and customs that many times changed in practice the original intention of the norms in question (Murillo 1997).
2. According to the 1914 census only 3 per cent of the population had completed high school (Tenti Fanfani 1989: 212).
3. By the end of the 1980s, nearly all primary education services had been transferred to the provinces.
4. In Argentina, private primary and secondary education is financed in large part by government subsidies. At the end of the 1980s, the government subsidized 90 per cent of private institutions, of which 80 per cent paid their entire teaching staff with public funds.
5. The practical effect of this measure is to reduce the cost of labour via a subsidy that is financed in the long term by the workers since it reduces the basic contributions used to calculate retirement income.
6. At the beginning of the 1990s this debt was estimated at nearly US$8 billion, which was approximately equal to the total annual distributions of the entire NSSS.
7. Two indicators illustrate the path toward the crisis of systemic integration of the regime in question: inflation and the fiscal deficit. The central explanation of these problems is found in the contradictions in the functioning of the domestic economy.
8. As indicated by Habermas (1973), crises in social systems are not produced by accidental changes in the environment, but rather by systemic imperatives inherent in the structure of the system in question. These imperatives are incompatible and cannot be hierarchically integrated.
9. The measures demanded were part of a nucleus of policies called for historically by these sectors, by virtue of their traditional ideological orientation. What changed in the second half of the 1980s is, perhaps, these groups' support for democratic institutions and their intention to establish themselves as privileged interlocutors of the government elite, as a means of achieving their objectives? See Beltrán (1999).
10. The central points of the economic reforms were: trade and finance liberalization, privatization, labour reform, and a fixed exchange rate system that made the peso fully convertible by pegging it to the dollar. For a detailed analysis, see Lo Vuolo (2001).

11. According to an ESS-OIT/Ciepp 2001 survey, only 6 per cent of workers believe that unions represent them adequately.
12. The policy of decreasing employers' contributions relative to salaries sought to recover part of the competitiveness affected by the overvalued currency; from here on they are known as 'fiscal devaluations'.
13. The previous educational structure consisted of a seven-year cycle of obligatory primary school followed by a five-year cycle of high school. The post-reform structure established one year of obligatory pre-school (kindergarten) followed by three cycles of three years each, also obligatory. The new structure also established a three-year 'polymodal' cycle, which is not obligatory.
14. In this context, and given the high level of conflict in this sector, the government that took power in 1999 created a Teacher Incentive Fund, financed initially with a special tax on vehicle registration. Since then, this salary complement has had a complex history of non-fulfilment and delays of more than a year.
15. IIPE (2000).
16. The reform project was presented in June 1992, and was modified considerably during the negotiations between legislators and union leaders. For example, in order to achieve union support, the bill incorporated the possibility that unions could form private retirement investment funds known as AFJPs.
17. Arguments for the NSSO are outlined in Lo Vuolo (1996) and Müller (2002).
18. For many, the Argentinian reform looks like a 'mixed' system which attempts to find an intermediate route between the 'totally private' Chilean system of individual fully-funded schemes and contributions and a 'totally public' system of payments. In reality, the Argentinian system was born as a disconnected hybrid and as the first stage in a strategy aimed at achieving a system like Chile's, which would be arrived at gradually as the result of the progressive de-legitimization of the public component.
19. Emission of public debt to finance the budget deficit – generated largely by social security reform – led to a systematic increase in the proportion of public bonds in the portfolios of the various retirement funds (which are today in default). This makes the 'undefined' value of the benefit from capitalized contributions even more uncertain.
20. For an analysis of the functioning of the new system and its modifications see Lo Vuolo and Goldberg (2002).
21. Given the demands of the new system, more than 50 per cent of workers and two thirds of the current EAP have a high probability of receiving no pension in the future, or one that is merely symbolic.
22. In the context of greater inequality in the distribution of income, the average salary of contributors is higher than the average salary in the economy. In addition, there exists a great disparity among contributors.
23. For a detailed explanation of PJJDH, see MTEySS (MTEySS 2003) and Pautassi (2003).
24. The variation in GDP was negative from then until 2003: −3.4 per cent in 1999; −0.8 per cent in 2000 and −4.4 per cent in 2001.
25. The sale of the public patrimony had already been totally exhausted during the 1990s.
26. It is important to remember that GDP had shrunk by almost 11 per cent during 2002 and 20 per cent between 1998 and 2002.
27. On this point the discussion fluctuates between: (i) assistance benefit, substantially inferior to the 'minimum pension' and available to those who are not

eligible to access the normal benefit (normally at a lower age) and frequently restricted to those who lack any other source of income; and (ii) a universal benefit independent of the system of contributions and financed by general profits.
28. For this proposal see Lo Vuolo *et al.* (1999).
29. The official reform proposal (Social Security Secretariat 2003: 179) fails to consider the variable of a universal and uniform pillar, although this modality is recognized in many varied experiences such as those of New Zealand, the Scandinavian countries, Barbados, and South Africa. It is also considered in works published by the International Labour Organization, such as Standing (1999).
30. 'Notional accounts' register individual contributions but 'notional' contributions are calculated on the basis of a reference rate of return (growth in the average national salary, the rate of growth of GDP, etc.) that allows for monitoring the evolution of the system's financial equilibrium.
31. For a broad discussion of the citizen income proposal and the main points of debate surrounding it, see Lo Vuolo (Lo Vuolo *et al.* 1995, 1999), and van der Veen (van der Veen *et al.*, 2002).

## References

Alonso, G. (2000). *Política y seguridad social en la Argentina de los 90'*. Buenos Aires: Miño y Dávila Editores.

Barbeito, A. and Lo Vuolo, R. (2001). *Encuesta de Seguridad Socioeconómica. Argentina.* Buenos Aires: Infocus Programme Socio-Economic Security – OIT.

Barbeito, A. and Lo Vuolo, R. (1998). *La nueva oscuridad de la política social. Del estado populista al neoconservador.* Buenos Aires: Ciepp/Miñoy Dávila.

Barbeito, A. and Vuolo, R. (1992). *La modernización excluyente. Transformación económica y Estado de Bienestar en Argentina.* Buenos Aires: Unicef/Ciepp/Losada.

Beccaria, L. and Galin, P. (2002). *Regulaciones labourales en Argentina. Evaluación y propuestas.* Colección diagnósticos y propuestas. Buenos Aires: OSDE-CIEPP.

Beltrán, G. (1999). 'La crisis de fines de los ochenta bajo la mirada de los sectores dominantes. Justificación e inicio del proceso de reformas estructurales de los años noventa'. *Revista Epoca de economía política* 1.

Di Gropello, E. (1999). 'Los modelos de descentralización educativa en América Latina'. *Revista de la Cepal* 68, 153–70.

Filmus, D. (1998). 'La Descentralización Educativa en el Centro del Debate', in E. Isuani and D. Filmus (eds), *La Argentina que viene: análisis y propuestas para una sociedad en transición.* Buenos Aires: Unicef – Flacso – Grupo Editorial Norma.

Filmus, D. and Moragues, M. (2003). *Para qué universalizar la educación media?* Mimeo, Buenos Aires.

Fiszbein, A. (2001). 'Instituciones, provisión de servicios y exclusión social. Estudio de caso del sector educación en Buenos Aires'. *Revista Desarrollo Económico* 41 (162), 235–59.

Habermas, J. (1973). *Problemas de legitimación en el capitalismo tardío.* Buenos Aires: Amorrortu Editores.

IIPE (2000). *Los docentes y los desafíos de la profesionalización.* Buenos Aires: UNESCO.

Judengloben, M., Arrieta, M. and Falcone, J. (2003). *Brechas educativas y sociales: un problema viejo y vigente.* Ministerio de Educación, Ciencia y Tecnología, Secretaría de Educación, Subsecretaría de Calidad y Equidad. Buenos Aires: Dirección Nacional de Información y Evaluación de la Calidad Educativa.

Lo Vuolo, R. (2001). *Alternativas: La economía como cuestión social*. Buenos Aires: Grupo Editor Altamira.

Lo Vuolo, R. (1996). 'Reformas estructurales, mercados de trabajo y exclusión social en Argentina'. *Investigación económica* 217, 49–84.

Lo Vuolo, R. (ed.) (1995). *Contra la Exclusión. La propuesta del ingreso ciudadano*. Buenos Aires: CIEPP-Miño and Dávila.

Lo Vuolo, R. and Goldberg, L. (2002). *Un diagnóstico preliminar de la evolución y actual situación del sistema previsional*. Documento de Trabajo 35. Buenos Aires: CIEPP-Miño and Dávila Editores.

Lo Vuolo, R., Barbeito, R., Pautassi, L. and Rodríguez, C. (1999). *La pobreza... de las políticas contra la pobreza*. Buenos Aires: CIEPP-Miño and Dávila Editores.

Monza, A. and Giacometti, C. (2003). *Los beneficiarios del Plan Jefes y Jefas de hogar*. Mimeo, Documento de trabajo. Buenos Aires: OIT.

Morduchowicz, A. (2002). *El financiamiento educativo en Argentina: Problemas estructurales, soluciones coyunturales*. Buenos Aires: IIPE-UNESCO.

Müller, K. (2002). *La economía política de las reformas previsionales en Europa Centro-Oriental*. Buenos Aires: CIEPP-Miño and Dávila.

Murillo, M. V. (1997). 'La adaptacíon del sindicalismo argentina a las reformas de Mercado en la primera presidencia de Menem', *Desarollo Económico* 37(147).

MTEySS (2003). *Plan jefas y jefes de hogar desocupados. Un año de gestión: mayo 2002–mayo 2003*. Buenos Aires: MTEySS.

O'Donnell, G. (1977). 'Estadoy Alianzas de clases en Argentina, 1956–1976', *Desarollo Económico*, 16(64).

Offe, C. (1984). *Contradictions of the Welfare State*. Cambridge, MA: The MIT Press.

Pautassi, L. (2003). *Plan Jefes y Jefas: derecho social o beneficio sin derechos?* Buenos Aires: CELS.

Pierson, P. (1995). *Dismantling the Welfare State? Reagan, Thatcher, and the Politics of Retrenchment*. Cambridge: Cambridge University Press.

Porto, A. (2000). *Reforma fiscal para el financiamiento de la educación pública básica*. La Plata: Universidad Nacional de La Plata.

Repetto et al (2001). 'Transferencia educativa hacia las provincias en los años '90: un estudio comparado'. Centro de Estudios para el Desarrollo Institucional. Documento 57. Buenos Aires: CELS.

Roca, E. (2001). *'La seguridad social en un contexto de precariedad laboural'*. Taller 'Precariedad laboural, vulnerabilidad social y seguridad socio-económica'. Buenos Aires: CIEPP.

Rodríguez C. (2001). *Inseguridad socio-económica en Argentina: una aproximación de género a la zona de vulnerabilidad laboural*. Buenos Aires: CIEPP.

Secretaría de Seguridad Social (2003). *Libro blanco de la previsión social*. Buenos Aires: MTEySS.

Sidicaro, R. (2001). *La crisis del Estado*. Buenos Aires: Libros del Rojas.

Standing, G. (1999). *Global Labour Flexibility: Seeking Distributive Justice*. London: Macmillan.

Tedesco, J. C. and Tenti, E. (2001). *La reforma educativa en Argentina: semejanzas y particularidades*. Buenos Aires: Ministerio de Educación de la Nación.

Tenti Fanfani, E. (1989). *Estado y Pobreza: estrategias tipicas de intervención*. Buenos Aires: CEAL.

Tenti Fanfani, E. (2003). *La educación media en la Argentina: desafíos de la universalización*. Buenos Aires, Mimeo.

Tiramonti, G. (2003). *Estado, educación y sociedad civil: una relación cambiante*. Buenos Aires, Mimeo.

Torrado, S. (2003). *Historia de la familia en la Argentina Moderna (1879–2000)*. Buenos Aires: Ediciones de la Flor.

Turull, F. (2001). *La matrícula de Educación Común: Análisis de su evolución en los primeros años de implementación de la Ley Federal (1996–2000)*. Buenos Aires: IDECE.

Van der Veen, R., Groot, L. and Lo Vuolo, R. (2002). *La renta básica en la agenda: Objetivos y posibilidades del ingreso ciudadano*. Buenos Aires: Colección Políticas Públicas, Miño y Dávila-CIEPP.

# Appendix 4.A: Tables and Figures

*Table 4.A1* Federal public sector debt (US$ million)*

| *Year* | *Amount* |
|---|---|
| IVQ-93 | 69.626 |
| IVQ-94 | 80.679 |
| IVQ-95 | 87.091 |
| IVQ-96 | 97.105 |
| IVQ-97 | 101.101 |
| IVQ-98 | 109.062 |
| IVQ-99 | 117.703 |
| IVQ-00 | 122.910 |
| IVQ-01 | 137.707 |
| IVQ-02 | 124.240 |
| IVQ-03 | 145.504 |

* Exchange rate at the end of each period.
*Source*: Ministry of Economy.

*Table 4.A2* Educational system indicators (annual variation rates)

| *Indicator* | *1980–2000* | *1980–1991* | *1991–2000* | *1996–2000* |
|---|---|---|---|---|
| Total | 2.64 | 3.02 | 2.19 | 2.54 |
| Initial | 4.91 | 6.72 | 2.74 | 3.30 |
| Primary | 1.48 | 1.87 | 1.00 | 1.09 |
| Secondary | 3.89 | 3.96 | 3.81 | 4.49 |
| Higher | 8.25 | 9.42 | 6.84 | 6.44 |
| *Public Expenditure* | | | | |
| Total | 3.13 | 0.26 | 6.75 | 6.28 |
| Basic | 2.89 | 0.34 | 6.09 | 6.77 |
| Higher | 4.09 | −0.14 | 9.50 | 4.64 |

*Source*: Authors' elaboration on data of the Ministry of Education.

*Table 4.A3* Coverage of the social security system in year 2000

| | *Female* | *Male* | *Total* |
|---|---|---|---|
| Pension benefits Population over 65 years old | 34.6 | 69.8 | 49.0 |

*Source*: Authors' elaboration on data of Secretaria de Seguridad Social and population census.

*Table 4.A4* Resources of the public social security system

| *Period* | *Payroll taxes (%)* | *General taxes* | *Other sources* |
|---|---|---|---|
| 1991 | 76.6 | 15.9 | 7.5 |
| 1992 | 76.3 | 16.3 | 7.4 |
| 1993 | 63.3 | 24.5 | 12.2 |
| 1994 | 65.9 | 29.2 | 5 |
| 1995 | 53.6 | 40.3 | 6.1 |
| 1996 | 39.8 | 56.2 | 4.1 |
| 1997 | 37.2 | 58.2 | 4.6 |
| 1998 | 36.0 | 61.4 | 2.6 |
| 1999 | 31.3 | 67.3 | 1.6 |
| 2000 | 30.1 | 68.1 | 1.9 |
| 2001 | 29.6 | 70.2 | 0.2 |
| 2002 | 37.9 | 61.8 | 0.3 |

*Source*: Secretaria de Seguridad Social.

*Table 4.A5* External trade 1993–2002 (US$ million)

| *Years* | *Exports* | *Imports* | *Balance* |
|---|---|---|---|
| 1883 | 13,118 | 16,783 | −3,666 |
| 1994 | 15,839 | 21,543 | −5,703 |
| 1995 | 20,963 | 20,122 | 841 |
| 1996 | 23,766 | 23,712 | 54 |
| 1997 | 26,430 | 30,450 | −4,020 |
| 1998 | 26,441 | 31,404 | −4,964 |
| 1999 | 23,333 | 25,508 | −2,175 |
| 2000 | 26,410 | 25,243 | 1,167 |
| 2001 | 26,610 | 20,321 | 6,289 |
| 2002 | 25,410 | 8,988 | 16,422 |

* Provisional figure.
*Source*: *INDEC*.

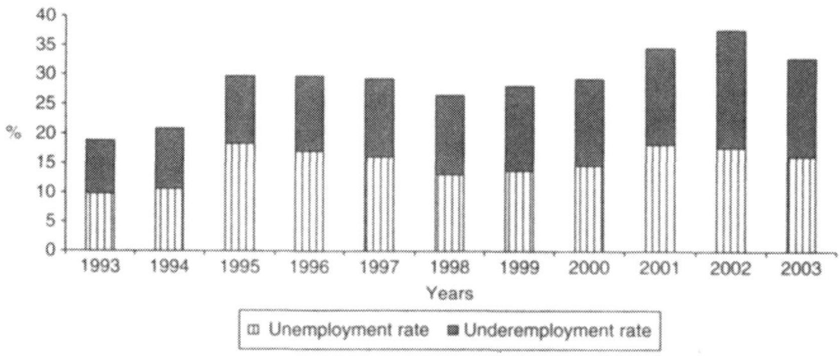


*Figure 4.A1* Labour market indicators 1993–2003
*Source*: EPH.

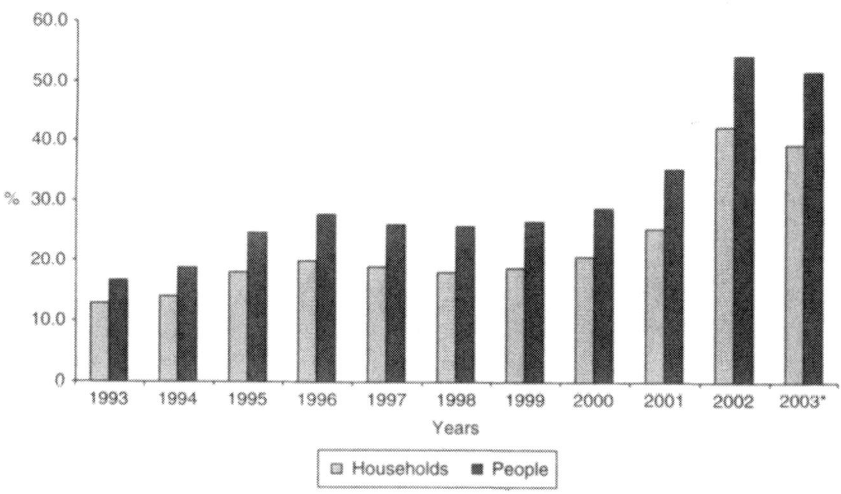


*Figure 4.A2* Poverty rate 1993–2003: Larger Buenos Aires
*Note*: * May
*Source*: EPH .

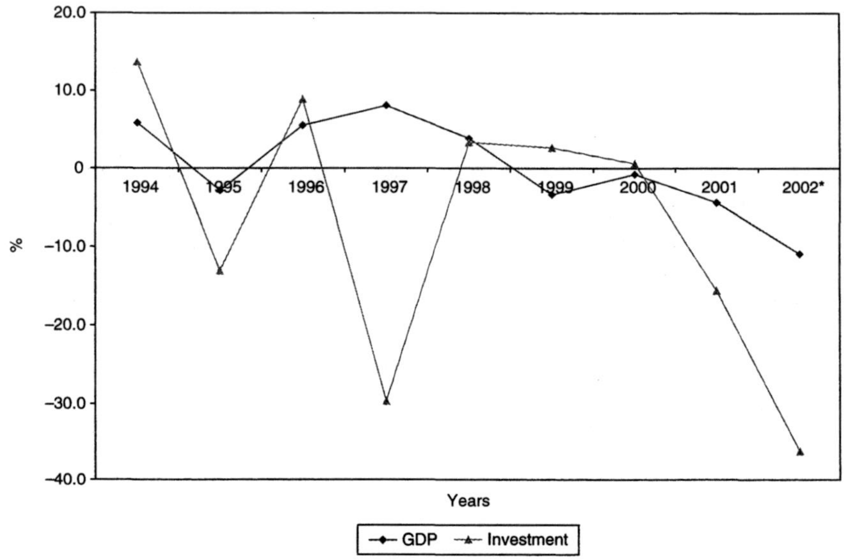


*Figure 4.A3* Economic activity growth rates
*Source*: Ministry of Economy.

# 5

# Uruguay's Social and Economic Challenges and Its Policy Responses

*Maria Bonino, Huck-ju Kwon and Alexander Peyre Dutrey*

Uruguay has been described as Latin America's first 'welfare state', not only because its introduction of social programmes occured earlier than in other countries, but also because the system offered comprehensive social protection in the early development of social policy. In recent years, however, the welfare state in Uruguay has faced considerable challenges. This chapter will examine social policy in Uruguay and analyse the problems it is experiencing. In doing so, it will identify the political and economic dynamics of the Uruguayan welfare state.

The chapter will also describe the Uruguayan reaction to the economic crisis of 2001–02 and the economic and political transition that followed in its aftermath. This crisis not only threw Uruguay into its deepest crisis since the return of democracy in the 1980s, but also became the initiation of a political reform that is still in progress. The chapter will pay particular attention to some of the structural problems of the Uruguayan labour market, such as an ageing population, unemployment and public sector reforms. These problems are serious challenges to Uruguay, not only in terms of social protection but also for its economic development. As we will illustrate, unless these challenges are tackled effectively, they could have a negative effect on the social and economic prospects for Uruguay. Finally, we will present a brief overview of the new social policy and reforms that have been initiated by the new government of Tabaré Vásquez. Are social policy responses to these challenges adequate and effective? Are they economically developmental and socially inclusive? These are the questions that this chapter will try to answer through an examination of Uruguay's social policy, focusing on employment policies and policies against poverty. In the concluding remarks we will briefly summarize the findings and suggest policy options for the future.

## Development of social policy in Uruguay

Uruguay was one of the pioneers in the development of the welfare state in Latin America. Early in the twentieth century, Uruguay introduced social programmes in the areas of education, social security and employment.

Programmes against poverty were also implemented during this period. With respect to pensions, for example, Uruguay first introduced the civil servant pension programme in 1838. In 1904, a new civil servant pension programme, *Caja Civil*, was implemented after the previous programme was abolished due to its financial difficulties. In 1919, a pension fund for private employees, *Caja de Indústria y Comercio*, was created. In the same year, non-contributory old-age pension benefits were introduced. In the area of education 5 per cent of total public expenditure was spent on public education in 1904, and school enrolment increased rapidly as public expenditure increased in the following years. By 1930 76 per cent of children aged between five and 14 were able to read. Infrastructure for university education was also considerably improved.

Uruguay was also a frontrunner in terms of labour legislation. By 1920, eight-hour working-day legislation and child and woman labour protection had been instituted. Minimum wage legislation was also introduced during this period. Such progress in labour protection had much to do with the long tradition of labour movements in Uruguay. There were many examples of labour rights struggles. In 1895, the bricklayers and masons in Montevideo achieved an eight-hour working day after a long strike, while graphic workers achieved an eight-hour shift (and a seven-hour night shift) in the same year. In 1906, when the government submitted a bill on the eight-hour working day rule to the Parliament, many workplaces where unions were strong already had the system in place (Rama 1956).

In contrast to its early achievements (Mesa-Lago 1985; Pendle 1963) in later decades the Uruguayan welfare state has been in steady decline. The welfare model has also been subject to a host of criticism. Some commentators have pointed to the inefficiency of social policy spending, saying that the better off have been the main recipients, while others in need have not been protected effectively. There are, however, two important concerns regarding the future of the Uruguayan welfare state. First, as Katzman, Filgueria and Furtado point out, the economic recession in Uruguay has, to date, prevented the economy from creating new jobs, which has made it difficult to reduce unemployment. In consequence, the long-term unemployed withdraw from the formal labour market after searching for jobs for some time, which in turn places a heavy burden on the social protection system while reducing state revenues from taxation (Katzman and Filgueira 2000). The second challenge facing the welfare state in Uruguay is related to its demographic structure. In contrast to most other countries in Latin America, Uruguay is an ageing society (Ferreira-Coimbra and Forteza 2004). With a shrinking labour force, it will be a challenge for the Uruguayan economy to fully overcome its economic stagnation. In short, Uruguay's long-term developmental potential is constrained by its ageing population.

Much of the historic economic growth that Uruguay has enjoyed took place in the first part of the twentieth century. This was due to the fact that

Uruguay, being a large exporter of meat and agricultural products, benefited from the increased demand in the international market created by the First and Second World Wars and the Korean War. Uruguay was a competitive producer well able to take advantage of such opportunities. During the second half of the century, in contrast, the international market for agricultural products became depressed as a result of the introduction of protectionist policies in Europe, North America and Japan. Domestic conflicts such as political upheavals and military clashes in the 1960s prevented Uruguay from producing an effective economic strategy to reform its economy and its relations with the international market. Since the 1970s Uruguay, Argentina and Brazil have tried to integrate their economies in order to compete in the world market. Uruguay signed the CAUCE (Convenio Argentino-Uruguayo de Cooperación Económica) agreement with Argentina and the PEC (Protocolo de Expansión Comercial) with Brazil in 1975. In 1985 these agreements were extended, and in 1991 Uruguay participated in the founding of the MERCOSUR whose headquarters is in Montevideo. Uruguay is also a founding member of the Latin American Integration Association (LAIA). Although it remains to be seen whether or not this international economic integration will bring positive effects to Uruguay, other signs are not encouraging. For example, the manufacturing sector has not grown much since the 1990s (UNIDO 2003), and capital investment decreased over the last decade. In terms of GDP growth, the performance of the Uruguayan economy was below the average of the Latin American countries during the 1990s and the beginning of this millennium.

## The socioeconomic impact of the crisis and its aftermath

In 1999, the Uruguayan economy was affected by a sharp recession, to a large extent a spillover effect from the crises in Brazil and Argentina. Starting with the devaluation of the Brazilian real in 1999, the peak of the Uruguayan crisis occurred in 2001 when Argentina defaulted on its public debt and devalued its currency to one-third of its previous value. The massive Argentine withdrawals in mid-2002 from offshore accounts in Uruguayan banks started a domino effect, generating a bank run and a financial crisis that seriously threatened the Uruguayan economy. GDP fell by about 11 per cent in 2002 alone. In total, household income fell more than one-fifth in the period 1998–2002 (see Table 5.1). The crisis dramatically raised unemployment, peaking at 17 per cent of the workforce, and aggravated the country's social problems. Poverty increased from 18 per cent to 31 per cent of the population between 2000 and 2003, while extreme poverty doubled during the period to around 2.8 per cent of the population. A recent study by Pellegrino and Vigorito on the migration impact of the crisis estimates that around 100,000 Uruguayans, about 3 per cent of the population, emigrated between 1999 and 2002. Most of these were young and highly educated, something that

*Figure 5.1* Real wage index development in Uruguay
*Source*: Instituto Nacional de Estadística 2005.

affects the demographic situation, as it has become a serious brain drain of highly educated people (El País 2004).

The acute crisis was only resolved by massive borrowing from international financial institutions. Emergency loans from the IMF with the support of the IADB limited the damage and allowed the economy to avoid crashing in the same way as in Argentina. These loans were among the largest (as percentage of GDP) ever granted by the IMF (World Bank 2005). In addition, the heavy debt burden – 102.5 per cent of GDP – that the loans generated created huge sustainability problems. In 2003 Uruguay managed to restructure some of its debt, which alleviated the country's amortization burden substantially and restored public confidence. The country debt is, however, still very high representing 90 per cent of GDP in 2004, from a level of 29.1 per cent in 1994 (World Bank 2005). The sustainability of the public debt has therefore been an issue of concern, both in Uruguay and internationally. A recent publication by the Inter-American Development Bank has, for example, analysed debt sustainability in several scenarios. The conclusion is that Uruguay needs to maintain a strict monetary and fiscal policy to manage the debt. The country is also dependent on a continuous positive national and regional economic development to improve the debt situation (Ardana *et al.* 2005).

2004 was to a large extent a year of recovery (see Table 5.2). The Uruguayan economy grew 12.6 per cent in 2004 as a result of a combination of factors:

high commodity prices for exports, the weakness of the dollar against the euro, general growth in the region (and, in particular, the strong economic recovery in Argentina and Brazil), low international interest rates, and greater export competitiveness. The forecast for 2005 is a 6 per cent growth of the economy. Unemployment that had peaked at 17 per cent in 2003 fell to 13.1 per cent in 2004 and fell still further in 2005. Most macroeconomic indicators were back to numbers seen before the crisis in late 2004.

The year was a year not only of economic transition but also of political change. In the elections of 2004, Tabaré Vásquez and the left-wing coalition of *Frente Amplio-Encuentro Progresista-Nueva Mayoria (FA-EP-NM)* won, ending more than 170 years of alternating dominance by the two traditional parties *Blancos* and *Colorados*. The coalition came to power with a political programme emphasizing investments in social programmes and infrastructure, while maintaining the continuity of the macroeconomic policies of the previous governments.

The new government launched its programme of transition, *El gobierno del cambio: la transición responsable*, which was divided in six distinct areas: *Uruguay Productivo*, enhancing economic productivity, developing capital markets and a more progressive tax reform; *Uruguay Social*, with the objective of enhancing social development and achieving universal protection;

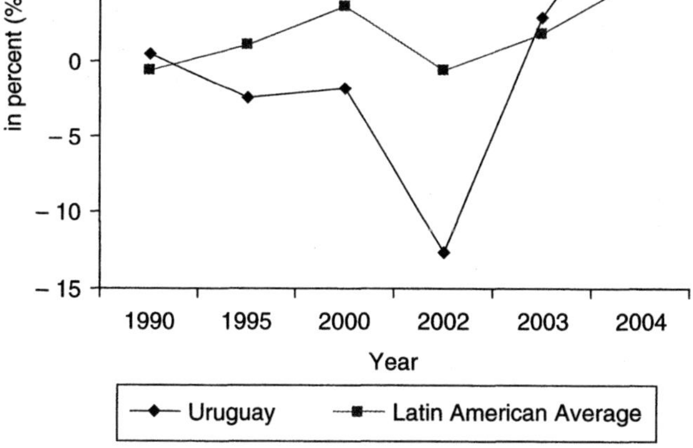


*Figure 5.2* Performance of the Uruguayan economy (GDP growth rate)
*Source*: ECLAC, *Annual Statistics of Latin America and Caribbean, 2004* (2004).

*Uruguay Innovador*, enhancing scientific and technological progress in key areas such as the agro-industry, IT and communication, manufacturing and tourism; *Uruguay Democrático*, strengthening democracy and democratic participation; *Uruguay Integrado*, enhancing rural and regional integration; and *Uruguay Cultural*, strengthening cultural identity and social inclusion (Presidencia de la República Oriental del Uruguay 2005).

## Structural problems of the labour market

### Pensions and an ageing population

The proportion of public social expenditure (PSE) in Uruguay is the highest in Latin America. It was 23.5 per cent in 2001 in Uruguay, higher than in Argentina and Brazil and much higher than the rest of Latin America (ECLAC 2002). As Table 5.1 shows, much of the high level of social spending is accounted for by social security pensions. It is necessary, however, to give a more detailed explanation of the trend in public spending and pensions in the following three aspects.

The first aspect is the politics of pensions. In 1972, public social expenditure (PSE) reached 16.7 per cent of GDP. In the following years, under the dictatorship, PSE dropped by three points as the government tried to reduce social spending. Later, following the return of democracy in 1985, PSE increased steadily, reaching 23.5 per cent in 2001. The same is true of the sub-areas of social spending such as education, health and social security. However, after the 1985 democratization, the government placed more emphasis on education and health. Table 5.1 shows that there were big increases in education and health, while social security spending remained at the same level. This was due to the fact that the level of pensions was not satisfactorily indexed to wage increases. In 1989 social organizations for pensioners passed a referendum that forced the government to adjust the level of pensions in line with the Average Wage Index (AWI) instead of the Minimum Wage Index (MWI). The result was a surge in expenditure on social security, which jumped from 11.1 per cent to 16.3 per cent.

*Table 5.1* Public social expenditure in Uruguay (percentage of GDP)[1]

| | *1972* | *1975* | *1980* | *1984* | *1990* | *1998* | *2000* | *2001* | *2002* | *2003* |
|---|---|---|---|---|---|---|---|---|---|---|
| Education | 2.3 | 2.6 | 1.9 | 1.4 | 2.5 | 3.2 | 3.1 | 3.3 | 3.3 | 3.2 |
| Health | 1.1 | 0.9 | 1.1 | 0.8 | 2.9 | 2.8 | 3.1 | 3.0 | 3.0 | 2.8 |
| Social Security | 12.8 | 10.4 | 10.6 | 11.1 | 11.1 | 16.3 | 16.9 | 16.9 | 15.9 | 13.8 |
| Others | 0.5 | 0.2 | 0.4 | 0.3 | 0.3 | 0.5 | 0.5 | 0.4 | 0.5 | 0.5 |
| Total | 16.7 | 14.1 | 14.0 | 13.6 | 16.8 | 22.8 | 23.5 | 23.5 | 22.7 | 20.3 |

*Source*: ECLAC 2002; Oficina de Planeamiento y Presupuesto 2004.

Secondly, there is also an important structural aspect in the increase of social spending on pensions. The demographic structure of Uruguay has already witnessed the ageing process. In 2000, the population aged over 65 is 12.9 per cent, and this figure will be 17.2 per cent in 2020 while the average of Latin America and the Caribbean will be 8.1 per cent. The population aging has necessarily put the pressure on public spending.

The third aspect is the decreasing number of active contributors to the public pension programmes. In Uruguay there are six main pension programmes. Table 5.2 details those six programmes, and the numbers of active contributors and beneficiaries. With respect to the ratio of contributors to beneficiaries in Table 5.2, except the Professional Fund and Notary Fund, which are relatively small, all pension funds manifest very low ratio levels. In the case of the Military Fund, the number of beneficiaries exceeds that of contributors, which is obviously an unsustainable situation.

On top of this, the ratio is in a decreasing trend. With respect to the *Banco de Previsión Social* (BPS), which accounts for 89 per cent of contributors to the public pension programmes, the ratio has steadily decreased – from 1.33 in 1994 to 1.20 in 2002. This decrease can be attributed to four main trends. First, the falling numbers of people entering the labour market. Secondly, a large number of working-age people have migrated to other countries. Thirdly, people evaded the system, choosing not to pay, especially during the periods of economic recession. Finally, an increasing number of workers have left the formal labour market for the informal, which places them outside the pension programmes.

In summary, it is clear that the public pension programmes are facing an increasingly difficult situation, which seems unsustainable unless there are serious reforms. Various measures should be taken. First, the BPS needs to develop policies that will incorporate informal sector workers. Secondly, the BPS also needs to find measures that can prevent people from evading their contributions to the pension system.

*Table 5.2* Public pension programmes in Uruguay

| *Programmes* | *Contributors (A)* | *Beneficiaries (B)* | *Ratio (B/A)* |
|---|---|---|---|
| *Banco de Previsión Social* | 899,075 | 717,572 | 1.25 |
| Bank Fund | 15,929 | 15,000 | 1.06 |
| Professional Fund | 34,078 | 9,876 | 3.45 |
| Notary Fund | 6,613 | 1,772 | 3.73 |
| Military Fund | 31,005 | 43,268 | 0.72 |
| Police Fund | 25,371 | 24,749 | 1.03 |
| Total | 1,012,071 | 812,237 | 1.25 |

*Source*: Instituto Nacional de Estadística (INE), Uruguay en cifras 2003, www.ine.gub.uy.

## The labour market and unemployment

Since the 1970s, when the military government introduced neoliberal policies in the labour market, the employment situation in Uruguay has been increasingly precarious. In the 1990s, such policy was reinforced through trade liberalization, and the formal labour market was further weakened in its capacity to absorb the working population. In 1998, for example, when the Uruguayan economy was experiencing growth, the unemployment rate quickly rose significantly – to 10.1 per cent. Figure 5.3 shows that the unemployment rate subsequently rose to 17 per cent in the first half of 2003, although following the recovery from the crisis in 2004 it fell back to 13 per cent.

According to the study by Bucheli and Casacuberta (2003), the profile of the unemployed was strongly influenced by age. During the period 1991 to 2002, the unemployment rate among those aged between 18 and 24 was three times higher than that of the age group 25 to 35. However, the unemployment rate of the latter group was higher than that of the age group 35 to 44. With respect to gender, unemployment hits female workers harder than their male counterparts. Bucheli and Casacuberta (2003) estimated that there was a 4 per cent difference between male and female unemployment during the period 1991 to 2002. This can be partly attributed to gender discrimination in the labour market. Education is another relevant variable explaining unemployment risks. In the 1990s, those who had higher education were less likely to be unemployed than those with less education. Since

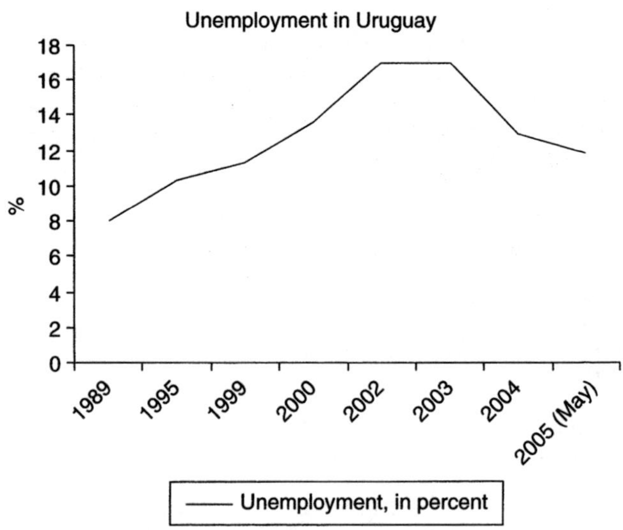


*Figure 5.3* Unemployment rate in Uruguay
*Source*: Instituto Nacional de Estadística (2003, 2005).

2000, however, the unemployment rate has increased regardless of the level of education.

There are other worrying phenomena observed in the labour market. As Bucheli and Casacuberta (2003) noted, since 1995 there has been a tendency for a growing number of unemployed people to remain unemployed for longer than six months. In the early 1990s, the long-term unemployed accounted for only one-third of the unemployed, but in 2002 46 per cent of the unemployed are characterized as long-term in nature.

Even when they do find employment, many Uruguayans have experienced a deterioration in the quality of their employment conditions. Bucheli and Furtado's study (2001) shows that workers who had been unemployed suffered losses of income for three main reasons: (i) those who became self-employed were likely to have a lower income than before; (ii) many of those who found a job experienced a reduction in their working hours, which in turn led to a loss of income; and (iii) those who resumed full-time work were likely to see reductions in their wages. It is also worth noting that the wage reduction was greater in the second half of the 1990s than in the first half.

In addition to the decline in wages, an increasing number of Uruguayan workers have to work without any social security. The proportion of people without social protection such as unemployment insurance, health insurance and family allowance has risen since the 1990s. While the percentage of people without any social protection was 33.5 per cent of the employed workers in 1998, the figure had reached 37.2 per cent by 2002. Considering that the Uruguayan labour market has traditionally been dominated by formal sector workers protected by social security, this transformation marked a dramatic change.

### Reduction of public and industrial sector jobs

The high level of unemployment in Uruguay in recent years and the precarious nature of the labour market cannot be understood without taking into account two factors which took place simultaneously in the years of crisis: (i) the stagnation of the growth in the public sector and (ii) the reduction in the number of jobs in the private sector. This meant that vacancies in the public sector remained unfilled, while many private firms continue to lay off workers.

In an international comparison, the ratio of civil servants to the total population is no higher in Uruguay than in her Mercosur neighbours. Compared to some of the OECD countries, the civil servant ratio in Uruguay was below the average, only being higher than that in Italy and Spain. The underlying reason for the attempt to reduce the size of the public sector is, apart from economic reasons, related to the historical legacy of the public sector rather than the number of civil servants as such. Civil servants were often hired through political connections instead of an institutionalized meritocratic process. Human resource management was not in place, which resulted in personnel policies that had been seen as arbitrary, even corrupt. Inevitably, productivity in the public sector was relatively poor in relation to that observed in the private sector.

Such an inefficient management of the public sector was, to some extent, related to the policy that used public sector employment as a macroeconomic measure for employment in the past. This has not been the case since the late 1990s. There are two main reasons that underlie this policy change. First, the state had to exercise tight control over public expenditure because of the fiscal crisis. Secondly, public sector reform to improve efficiency prevented the government from creating new positions in the public sector. This was couched in Neoliberal terms, which has a strong bias against the public sector (King 1987). The law 16.736, passed in 1995, blocked all new recruitment of public employees until 2005 (Ardana *et al.* 2005). Between August 1995 and June 2001, the number of civil servants dropped from 244,151 to 218,111, that is, a fall of 10 per cent. The reduction in public sector jobs had not only a great impact on national employment itself, but also gave a signal that private employers can lay off their employees whenever necessary without strong objections from the government.

Uruguay also suffered from a continuous stream of job losses in the industrial sector. What has been particularly worrying in the case of Uruguay is that the number of jobs in industry has steadily declined over the past 15 years with a small, but not sufficient compensation in other 'new' sectors of the economy. Furthermore, many of the jobs that were created in new sectors (such as, for example tourism and financing) were often unsuitable for those thrown out of industrial jobs. More important is that the quality of many of the new jobs (in terms of employment security, wages and benefits) has been lower and with a strong tendency to become jobs in the informal sector. Figure 5.4 shows that jobs in the manufacturing sector declined steadily during the 1990s. The number of manufacturing jobs in 2001 was less than a half of that of 1989.

This decline even continued when the Uruguayan economy recorded positive growth rates (1989–98), and not just during the period when the economy was in crisis (1998–2002). Here it is necessary to be cautious in interpreting those numbers in Figure 5.4 since the drop does not necessarily mean the disappearance of as many jobs as it might imply. A large part of the decline in jobs was accounted for by the restructuring that firms have carried out since the 1990s. In particular, manufacturing firms began to contract out a range of domestic services for workers – such as cleaning, security, maintenance and catering services. Many jobs, which had earlier been counted as manufacturing jobs, are now counted as service sector jobs. In reality, however, these people disappear in the statistics because they become informal sector workers. What it means in practice is that their wages and related welfare entitlements have often been dramatically reduced.

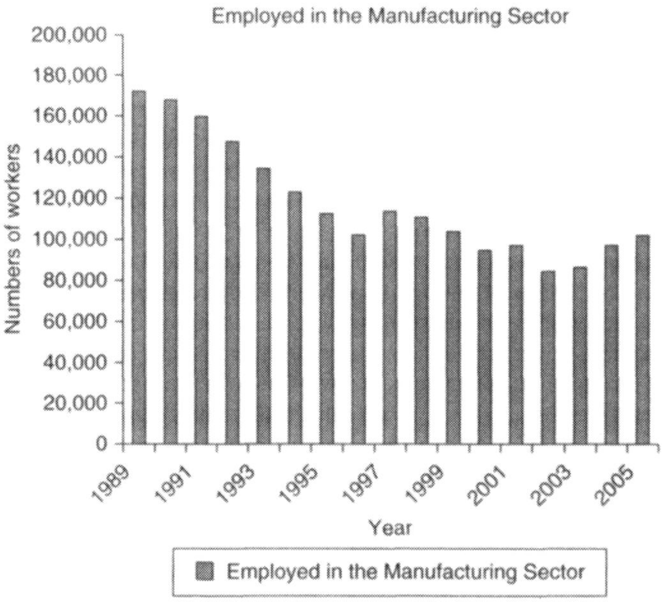


*Figure 5.4* Employment in the manufacturing sector* in Uruguay
*Note*: *Companies with more than five employees.
*Source*: Instituto Nacional de Estadística (1989–2005, 1989–2005b).

Of course, there are other important factors that have influenced such a fall in the number of industrial jobs. The second factor is the trade liberalization that took place during the 1990s. In addition to joining the World Trade Organization and MERCOSUR, the Uruguayan government also maintained a fixed exchange rate that overvalued its currency. All of these policies led to the introduction of stiff competition for Uruguayan companies. Furthermore, the Uruguayan government did not manage to apply effective anti-dumping regulations to imported goods, despite complaints from many Uruguayan companies. Economic technocrats in the government argued that trade liberalization would lead to a compensatory productivity increase in Uruguay, something that has not, in fact, happened. On the contrary, with the exception of a few Uruguayan enterprises that experienced positive productivity, many industries found it very difficult, if not impossible, to compete in the new highly competitive environment. The industrial sector's share of the total GDP was 25.9 per cent in 1990, but it fell to 20.2 per cent in 1995, and 16.0 per cent in 2001. The reduction in industrial output coincided, therefore, with the reduction of employment in the sector.

## Social policy responses

### Employment policy

In general, employment policies can be divided into active and passive labour market policies (Standing 1999). Over the last two decades, the Uruguayan government has implemented both active and passive policies to tackle unemployment. This section will examine employment policy in Uruguay according to this categorization.

Unemployment insurance, which can be regarded as a passive policy, was introduced in 1958, and revised on a number of occasions. Workers who lost their jobs are eligible to unemployment benefits for up to six months. In certain circumstances where unemployment increased, such benefits can be extended for up to another year. However, workers must be registered in the social security system, which means that the unemployment insurance only covers workers in the formal sector. During the economic downturn of 1999, the government extended the benefit period an additional six months, since unemployed people found it difficult to secure new jobs. Such measures can be very effective in providing social protection during shorter recessions. In the case of the unemployment insurance it benefits only a limited number of formal sector workers, and it cannot do much in helping people finding a job.

The active labour market policy aims to provide the unemployed with those skills needed for the modern technology-oriented industries. It also provides specific skills to certain categories of people who have disadvantages in the labour market, such as women, the elderly and people with low levels of education. Although the active labour market policy itself does not create jobs it improves the probability of finding a job by enhancing the skills of the unemployed. Since the 1990s, the National Employment Office and National Board of Employment have carried out various active labour market policies for the unemployed as well as employed workers who need further training to retain their jobs. Training was financed by the Labour Training Fund, to which each of 0.25 per cent of workers' income was contributed by workers and employers. There are also programmes for micro-enterprises and self-employment.

During the second half of the 1990s, two instruments were introduced to improve labour market conditions and promote employment stability. The first, created by the 1996 law, allows enterprises to deduct employee-training expenses from the Industrial and Commercial Income Tax (*IRIC*) payments. Training expenses, which can be posted as costs, increased up to one and a half times, and expenses related to technological research programmes, which in a similar way can be posted as costs, doubled. The following year, in 1997, a new law creates incentives through different modalities for firms that hire young people. Through this, firms can even benefit from absolution of employer contributions to social security.

The Municipality of Montevideo, *Intendencia Municipal de Montevideo* (IMM), has established an initiative to promote employment for young people. Through the programme, firms can receive the reimbursement of municipal taxes such as real estate taxes, general taxes, and vehicle license taxes, if they hire young people between 16 and 24 years of age, for 12 months and with a remuneration of no less than three minimum salaries. Young people must complete training programmes offered by certain institutions recognized by the IMM.

## Outcome of employment policies

The number of workers who resorted to unemployment insurance increased steadily during the second half of the 1990s, an evident consequence of the increase in the level of unemployment. The total amount of subsidiaries more than doubled between 1997 and 2003, from 17,100 beneficiaries in 1997 to 37,302 in 2003 (Banco de Previsión Social 2005).

In spite of its limitations, unemployment insurance proved to be a useful instrument of social protection for those unemployed who used to work in the formal sector, and who had contributed insurance premiums (see Figure 5.5). However, there are a number of critical weaknesses in this programme. First, it only covers those workers in the formal sector who have contributed during the last 12 months before unemployment, and it cannot provide help for those made unemployed in the informal sector, the numbers of which have been growing quickly since the 1990s. Secondly, there is a critique that unemployment benefits do not give incentives the unemployed to return to work. However, this critique has been contested. Rodriguez (2003) points

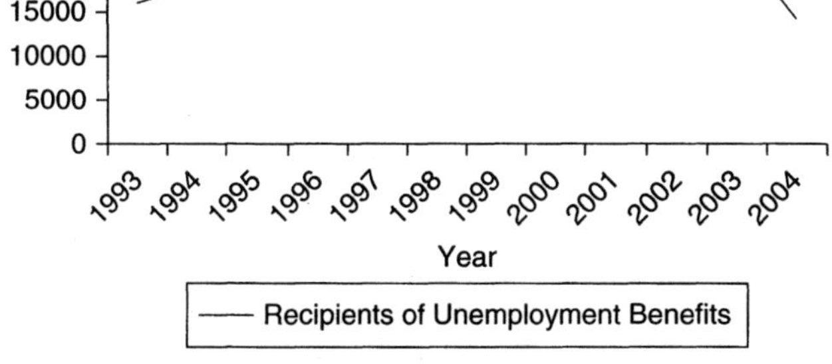


*Figure 5.5* Uruguay: recipients of unemployment benefits
*Source*: Banco de Previsión Social 2005.

out that in Uruguay unemployed people receive payments between 50 to 70 per cent of the previous wage, which is not a very high income. Also, since the period covered is six months, it is difficult to believe that it produces a negative incentive.

Lastly, a serious problem has been the large number of workers that are excluded from the system. Since the unemployment benefit is currently only available to workers who have contributed insurance premiums to the BPS and many fail to do so, it is only a minority of the workers that are covered. This was made clear in the first crisis of 1999 when unemployment benefits covered only 17 per cent of the unemployed (World Bank 2005).

The introduction of active employment policies seems to be a positive step. During the last decade, various programmes were applied, which could be considered useful for their beneficiaries. However, some important limitations have been pointed out (Rodriguez 2003). First there is a lack of coordination between *Banco de Previsión Social – BPS* (Social Security Bank), which is responsible for the passive policies and the Ministry of Labour, which operates the active labour market policies. Secondly, there have been doubts about the effective outcomes of active labour market policies. Some evaluations carried out – although scarce– indicate that active labour market policies have not always had positive results. Rodriguez points out that the most recent evaluation of the *Programa de Calificación Laboral – PROCAL* (Labour Qualification Programme), which absorbs most of the resources, shows no positive results. In spite of the limitations of the evaluation, this result is still compatible with evaluations of similar programmes in other countries (Rodriguez 2003). These evaluations recommend a better focus on target populations.

### Policies against poverty and social exclusion

Poverty incidence has risen sharply since the 1999 recession, in line with the rise in unemployment. The increase of the poor also coincided with other social challenges such as malnutrition of children, and homelessness (Severi 2002). Although poverty is one of the main causes of social exclusion, there are many other factors causing social exclusion. In Uruguay, prolonged unemployment and underemployment has led to a significant growth of peripheral neighbourhoods and precarious settlements. This generates territorial segregation, which in turn increases social segregation. This segregation affects the quality of education, health, recreation, and cultural services. People in these segregated areas often have poor levels of education and difficult family situations, which in turn leads to unemployment, high levels of teenage pregnancy, low self-esteem and difficulties in entering the labour market. All of these disadvantages create a chronic cycle of poverty. In response, the Uruguayan government introduced a number of social policies to fight poverty and social exclusion.

*Family allowances*

Family allowances constitute a transfer to those families with children below a certain level of income. Since 1995, when the programme was modified, it gives different allowances to families with children according to their levels of income. Families with incomes of up to 60 per cent of Minimum National Salaries (MNS) receive an allowance per child of up to 16 per cent of the MNS; families with incomes between 60 and 100 per cent of MNS receive an allowance per child of 8 per cent of the MNS. Targeting introduced through the 1995 reform has been criticized because it has resulted in a reduction in the number of beneficiaries. According to *BPS* figures, in 1994, there were 413,000 family allowance beneficiaries and in 2001, there were only 367,000. This decrease seems surprising at a time when there was a sharp increase in the level of poverty in Uruguay. It has also been said that the allowance is very small – 8 to 16 per cent of the MNS which is approximately 43 dollars – and that it is of very little help for the benefiting households. There have been attempts to correct the undercoverage in targeting. A new reform in 2000 extended the benefits to the unemployed, to women who were heads of households, and to pregnant women, even though they did not contribute to social security and were not incorporated in the formal system. This second reform recognized that the population with most shortages is precisely that which is most affected by informality and unemployment.

*Care for children between 0 and 4 years of age*

*Instituto Nacional del Menor* (the National Institute for Minors) is the organization concerned with social protection of children and has historically accomplished the task of caring for those children without access to regular family care. In 2003, the institution was responsible for 42,000 children, 33,000 of them through agreements with NGOs through different modalities (Katzman and Filgueira 2001). Half of the latter are cared for through the *Centro de Atención a la Infancia y la Familia – CAIF* (Children and Family Care Centre) programme, where the state and civil society organizations are working closely to offer integral care for children between the ages of one and four. Through the existence of 200 such centres in the country, 25 per cent of the targeted population received social care. The challenge for these institutions is not only to extend the coverage, but also to persuade those mothers who are very unwilling to participate or to send their children to this type of service. Some of them are those who need it the most.

*Pre-primary and primary schooling*

The educational reforms started in 1995 initiated two programmes which focused on the poorer sections of the population: pre-school education for children of 4 and 5 years of age and full-time schooling for children over 6 years of age in areas where the population is considered more vulnerable. Pre-school education covers 70 per cent of the population and its priority apparently is to reach those parts of the population with lower incomes. In contrast, only 20 per cent of children of the poor families receive full-time schooling, although the programme plans to extend its coverage. Through different pedagogic methodologies and instruments, these schools have been able to retain the children in the educational system and to improve their levels of learning. Since the number of children begging on the streets has increased in recent years it is necessary to develop new strategies to keep them in school.

*Education and employment support for young people from poor families*

Two of the main reasons why many young people from poor families fall into social exclusion are (i) lack of education and (ii) employment opportunities. Some of these young people do not finish primary schools, which makes it impossible for them to go on to attend secondary schools. Even among those going into secondary schools 50 per cent of them drop out. In Uruguay 25 per cent of 14-year-olds do not continue study, compared to figures of 4 per cent in Chile, and 5 per cent in Argentina. Those between the ages of 15 and 24 account for 46 per cent of total unemployment, but among the unemployed youth only 2 per cent receive some sort of training (and only 4 per cent receive unemployment insurance) (World Bank 2005).

Ten programmes implemented by the Ministry of Interior, and sponsored by the Inter-American Development Bank, provided young school dropouts with basic skills (reading, writing, and arithmetic) and basic social skills (teamwork, problem solving and self-esteem). Among those programmes *Instituto Nacional de la Juventud* (the National Youth Institute) was carried out in collaboration with enterprises, and was very successful. 50 per cent of the trainees found jobs or actively searched for them, demonstrating that these young people from very poor families can do well in the labour market.

The IMM's programmes with which NGOs have collaborated closely are also considered as having been successful in youth training. Thousands of young people have received training and their first work experience through these programmes. Some of the trade unions, however, criticized these programmes, arguing that those jobs that the trainees obtained were previously covered by municipal workers.

*Women's employment programmes*

Along with young people, women have a high risk of unemployment. They are often employed in precarious and low-paid positions. Considering that poor women tend to have more children and also tend to be unemployed, women's employment programmes are vital in fighting poverty and social exclusion. It is also worth noting that the incomes earned by women are more likely than those of men to be shared by the rest of the family. In other words, increasing women's incomes is likely to be more effective in relieving the hardship of poor families.

The Ministry of Labour, with support from the ILO, has carried out a pilot programme focusing on female workers who have difficulties in finding work. This programme pays particular attention to the areas where women can easily find work, such as childcare and domestic work. The IMM, in conjunction with collaborating NGOs, also has employment programmes for women similar to youth work experience programmes. The results have been positive since many women found work after participating in the programmes. Both programmes are especially concerned with promoting non-traditional gender roles in the labour market. The male–female wage gap increased significantly between 1990 and 2000 and there is now a wage differential of 14 per cent between male and female wages (World Bank 2005). In order to evaluate these programmes in a systematic manner, further research is necessary.

### *Uruguay Social* – a new social policy in development

One of the main points in the agenda of the new Uruguayan government has been its increased focus on social policy, formulated in the political manifesto *Uruguay Social*. One of the first actions in the social arena has been the foundation of the new Ministry of Social Development. This ministry is now responsible for the new social emergency programme *PANES* (Plan de Asistencia Nacional a la Emergencia Social), the objective of which is to attend to the worst-off in society, those living in extreme poverty or close to it and who currently include about 6 per cent of the population. The ministry's budget at present is around 0.5 per cent of GDP. It includes cross-coordinated social programmes in the areas of food security, health, housing, education and employment. The programme includes a temporary labour subprogramme *Trabajo por Uruguay* (Work for Uruguay) with the objective of strengthening the capabilities of those participating and reintegrating them in the formal labour market and another parallel programme *Ingreso Ciudadano* (with the double meaning Citizen Income and Citizen Enrolment) which consists of a monetary transfer to families in extreme poverty that in return must send children and young sons and daughters to schooling and health control (Arismendi, Mirza, and Melenez 2005).

The government has recently initiated the first step of reforms of the social and educational programmes, public sector and a fiscal sector reform supported by the economic situation and new loans from the World Bank and the Inter-American Development Bank. The new social policy also includes a reform of the education system, increasing funding to schools and universities, with the goal of universal and compulsory primary and secondary education. The government has also declared as a major goal to create a harmonized and universal national health insurance to ensure more equitable access to health care and reduce the financial burden and fragmentation of the system (Presidencia de la República Oriental del Uruguay 2005; World Bank 2005).

## Concluding remarks

Uruguay was one of the pioneering welfare states in Latin America, with social protection for workers and women developing earlier than in its Latin American neighbours. This also means that the Uruguayan welfare state has a lot of experience in areas such as pensions, education, health and social protection. As this chapter has shown, spending on social security and pensions accounts for the largest share in social expenditure. The ageing of the population also puts pressure on those that are of working age, a process that will accelerate in the future. At the same time, the Uruguayan economy has not created more jobs in the last decade, but has lost many existing jobs. The manufacturing sector has been in recession, and capital investment did not rise throughout the 'lost decade' of the 1990s to the level required to enhance competitiveness. With the crisis, the unemployment rate rise to its highest level while the number of jobs in the public sector and industry fell. As a result of this, a growing number of people who used to work in the formal sector now work in the informal sector, where the levels of income are low and there is no social protection. The recession culminating in the crisis of 2002, and with the structural problems of the labour market, are signs that the challenges are serious not only in terms of social protection, but also for the future economic development of Uruguay.

This chapter has examined social policy responses to these challenges, focusing on employment. Given the context of the structural problems, it is clear that social policy responses should be socially inclusive and economically developmental. Enhancing productivity and inclusion in the formal economy is a necessary policy focus in order to defend and develop Uruguay's welfare achievements. Uruguay has carried out a number of active labour market programmes that aim to enhance employment through the provision of training. The National Employment Office and the *Intendencia Municipal de Montevideo* (IMM) have been very active in running these programmes. This chapter has also shown that Uruguay places a particular emphasis on youth and women: income support, education and training. These programmes can be very effective in terms of social protection and economic development since youth and women are the two social groups in Uruguay who are socially vulnerable and at the same time offer the potential for the future development of the economy. So far the evaluations of these programmes have been tentative and the outcomes are not yet clearly visible.

With the so-called transition, initiated by the new leftist government under Tabaré Vásquez, the new government seems committed to carrying on and reinforcing social programmes such as those detailed above, linking the themes of social inclusion to economic development. The broad support for these reforms, both nationally and from large international financial institutions, such as the World Bank and the IADB, is positive and will be helpful for the government in the difficult challenges that await them in the reform of social policy and institutions. However, although the new government might have the will and broad national and international support for its reform policies, the room for political manoeuvre is restricted by the very large debt, a dark memory of the recent crisis. Whatever the economic performance over the next few years, the debt will consume a considerable amount of the government's resources. It is therefore difficult to predict if the reforms and aspirations that are currently expressed will be successful. At least social policy responses currently seem to be moving in the right direction and it will be an imperative for Uruguay to enhance the coverage and effectiveness of its new social programmes over the next few years.

## Note

1. These figures do not include expenditure on housing, which during the past few years has been around 2 per cent of GDP.

## References

Ardana, D., Bour, J., Catena, M. and Navajas, F. (2005). *Sostenibilidad fiscal y de la deuda pública en Uruguay*. Montevideo: Banco Interamericano de Desarollo.

Arismendi, M., Mirza, C. and Melenez, L. (2005). 'Informe sobre Ingreso Ciudadano-Construyendo Rutas de Salida', in *Conferencia de prensa*. Montevideo: Presidencia de la Republica Oriental del Uruguay.

Banco de Previsión Social (2005). *Prestaciones de Actividad*. Montevideo: Banco de Previsión Social.

Bucheli, M. and Casacuberta, C. (2003). *El desempleo y características de los desocupados en Uruguay*. Montevideo: ILO.

Bucheli, M. and Furtado, M. (2001). *Impacto del desempleo sobre el salario: una estimación de la perdida salarial para Uruguay*. Santiago: ECLAC.

ECLAC (2004). *Preliminary Overview of the Economies of Latin America and the Carribean 2004*. Santiago: ECLAC.

ECLAC (2002). *Social Panorama of Latin America*. Santiago: ECLAC.

*El País* (2004). 'Expatriados poseen un nivel educativo más alto que el uruguayo medio' in *El País* 29749.

Ferreira-Coimbra, N. and Forteza, A. (2004). *Protección Social en Uruguay: Financiamiento, Cobertura y Desempeño 1990–2002*. Geneva: International Labour Office.

Instituto Nacional de Estadística (2005a). *Encuesta Industrial Anual*. Montevideo: Instituto Nacional de Estadística.

Instituto Nacional de Estadística (2005b). *Encuesta Industrial Mensual*. Montevideo: Instituto Nacional de Estadística.

Instituto Nacional de Estadística (2005c). *Índice de Salario Real*. Montevideo: Instituto Nacional de Estadística.

Instituto Nacional de Estadística (2005d). *Tasa de actividad, empleo y desempleo*. Montevideo: Instituto Nacional de Estadística.

Instituto Nacional de Estadística (2003). *Uruguay en cifras 2003*. Montevideo: Instituto Nacional de Estadística.
Katzman, R. and Filgueira, F. (2000). 'Nuevos desafíos para la equidad en el Uruguay', (New Challenges for Equity in Uruguay). *ECLAC Magazine*. Santiago: ECLAC.
Katzman, R. and Filguiesa, F. (2001). *Panorama de la Infancia y a la Familia en el Uruguay*. Montevideo: Catholic University.
King, D. S. (1987). *The New Right: Politics, Markets and Citizenship*. Basingstoke: Macmillan Education.
Mesa-Lago, C. (1985). *La Política Social en América Latina y el Caribe*. Santiago: CEPAL.
Oficina de Planeamiento y Presupuesto (2004). *El gasto público en el Uruguay (1999–2003)*. Montevideo: Oficina de Planeamiento y Presupuesto.
Pendle, G. (1963). *Uruguay: Latin America's First Welfare State*. London: Oxford University Press.
Presidencia de la República Oriental del Uruguay (2005a). *El gobierno del cambio: la transición responsable*. Montevideo: Presidencia de la República Oriental del Uruguay.
Presidencia de la República Orienta del Uruguay (2005b). *Noticas del PANES*. Montevideo: Presidencia de la República Oriental del Uruguay.
Rama, C. (1956). 'Battle and the Social and Labour Movements', in C. Rama (ed.), *Battle: His Life and Works*. Montevideo: Editorial Acción.
Rodriguez, J. (2003). *Coordinación entre políticas activas y positivas de empleo*. Montevideo: DIANE-UNDP.
Severi, M. C. (2002). *Impactos de las crisis en la alimentación de los uruguayos*. Montevideo: CLAEH-PNUD.
Standing, G. (1999). *Global Labour Flexiblity: Seeking Distributive Justice*. New York: St Martin's Press.
UNIDO (2003). 'UNIDO Country Data'. Vienna: UNIDO. Available online at www.unido.org/data/geostatcfmcc=Uruguay.
World Bank (2005a). *Country Assistance Strategy for the Oriental Republic of Uruguay 2005–2010*. Washington DC: World Bank.
World Bank (2005b). *Uruguay at a Glance*. Washington, DC: World Bank.

# Part IV

# In the Imperial Immensities, and the Revolutionary Island, of Former American Slavery

# 6
# The Brazilian Developmental Welfare State: Rise, Decline and Perspectives

*Sônia M. Draibe*

> Despite huge obstacles we were making progress, but when those great years of prosperity arrived and we allowed ourselves to be blinded by the centres, the search for our own path was broken off.
>
> (Raúl Prebisch, UNCTAD Conference, 1982)

> We do not ignore that the historical time accelerates and counts against us. The question is to know if we have a future as a nation that matters in the construction of the human future. Or if will prevail the forces that fight in order to interrupt our historic process of Nation and State building.
>
> (Celso Furtado, 1992)

## Introduction

In line with the analytical proposals underpinning this book, this chapter examines the Brazilian social policy system in order to identify the challenges and possibilities of a new pattern of social and economic development. The main objective has been to review the historic process of construction and development of the twentieth-century Brazilian Development Welfare State. This review has emphasized the institutional and political legacies that may, in the future, either favour or limit the achievement of a new social contract, and the creation of a new democratic, and inclusive, model of development – one in which social protection interacts with the economic sphere, fostering economic growth, as well as greater social equality among its citizens.

Throughout the twentieth century, and especially in the period from 1930 to 1980, Brazil has constituted itself as a modern economy and society with an urban, industrial base, abandoning its agrarian past, founded on primary exports, which had predominated until the first decades of the century. In this transition, the country has followed a path that is similar to that of many LA countries, standing out among those that have advanced the furthest in the industrialization process, together with Mexico, Argentina,

Chile, and Uruguay. This achievement seems greater when the particular characteristics of Brazil are taken into account, such as the huge size of the country and its population, the spatial fragmentation of its old agro-export economy, together with the recent abolition of slavery, which occurred only after 1888, and the late constitution of state republican structures, initiated only by the end of the empire, in 1891.

Economic modernization, sustained by strong increases in urban employment, has resulted in social advances, albeit modest ones when compared to similar processes in Uruguay, Argentina, Chile, and even Mexico in many respects. Poverty was significantly and constantly reduced until the 1980s, but has stayed persistently high ever since. Improvements in overall social indicators and better access to basic social services have been more persistent and stable.

Nevertheless, growth and modernization have certainly been contradictory, partial, and unbalanced, in both their movement and their results. They took place under republican institutions, albeit hardly democratic ones. Moreover, over half of the time the process has been led by two military regimes – the Vargas regime from 1930 to 1945, and the military dictatorship that governed from 1964 to 1985. Economic growth has been very strong, but has been concentrated mainly in the Southeast and South regions. Regarding income distribution, Brazil has always shown a quite absurd pattern of concentration, which classifies the country among those with the worst indicators in this respect. In these aspects, Brazil's transition to modernity has only partially fulfilled its promises of progress and well-being.

The last two decades of the preceding century registered economic stagnation, and, for the first time, a reversal in the secular growth patterns. Slightly later than its neighbours and in a much less radical fashion, Brazil has undergone a severe fiscal adjustment during the 1990s, together with institutional reforms, an opening of commercial markets, privatization, deregulation, and so-called enhanced flexibility, all within a rigid macroeconomic policy. Restructuring of the private sector has been deep, and especially painful in manufacturing. Nevertheless, some industries, and particularly commodity-producing agribusiness, have taken advantage of the opening up to international markets, especially in the Mercosur region. However, over the course of the last quarter century, the country seems to be increasingly a prisoner of a financial vicious circle, strapped with debt, and experiencing slow growth, high unemployment, inequity, and poverty.

The political system has been showing better signs, however. This period of economic crises has coincided with the democratization of the country, in both its social relations and its political institutions. The new century opens with even deeper changes in these respect, with the election of President Lula, a former labour leader and head of a leftist party, with the support of a wide developmentalist coalition.

This is the complex and challenging environment within which the future chances and alternatives for Brazil are being explored. First, the analyst is confronted with the two classic questions of studies on development: the 'external' question, that is, the possibilities and limits of the international integration of the country; and the question of leadership or direction of the developmental process, especially relevant in *latecomers* such as Brazil, which did not experience a classical bourgeois revolution.

Brazilian development was always associated with the cyclical movement of central capitalism, benefiting from windows of opportunity, as well as internalizing in a more acute form its general tendencies (Tavares 2003). During the old primary-export economy centred on coffee, Brazil integrated with a certain precariousness into the gold standard, supported by external debt, and reproducing internally, in an extreme form, the crisis and instabilities of those times. From the 1930s, and especially during the post-Second World War period, Brazil took advantage of the possibilities that opened in the wake of the 1929 crisis, which widened during the 'golden age' of capitalism. During this period, Brazil industrialized, experiencing much higher growth rates than those observed in industrialized countries. In later decades, Brazil followed the vicissitudes of globalization, experiencing more acutely than in the centre the tendencies to stagnation, high unemployment, and deep levels of secular inequity. The international integration process is precarious, difficult and, as yet, rather ill defined. This chapter questions itself over the alternatives of such international insertion that may favour a new expansive cycle of the Brazilian economy, which may run parallel to social progress.

Which actors may lead such a process? It is a well-known fact that the structural transformation experienced by the country during the past century has little or nothing to do with a 'natural' process, and neither may it be reduced to being a consequence of international crisis or cycles. On the contrary, the modernization movement has been the result of an explicit national development project, led by a particular form of state. Furthermore, leading and stimulating this process, by itself the state created the economic and institutional basis that made the transition possible.

No doubt, such a process was favoured by the Keynesian orientation in the central world economies, as well as by new ideas that favoured and legitimized national development and industrialization strategies that also promoted social change. Really, the so-called *developmentalist doctrine* and *Developmentalist State* that then predominated in LA were born out of the same process that generated Keynesianism and welfare states in the central countries. Different historical constructions, the LA Developmental State and the European Welfare State, have both been part of a wider international experience, forged in the miseries and misfortunes generated by capitalism during the 1920s and 1930s, and especially in the wake of the Great Depression. The new intellectual and political milieu of the decades after the 1930s, conferred legitimacy, and centrality, to states that provided themselves with structures and instruments that were efficient and capable of lifting their countries out of depression. Furthermore, it was able to lead this process of technological modernization and industrialization, or to build and develop them from scratch in countries where industry was hitherto insignificant, such as Brazil and LA in general.

Perhaps one of the advantages of coming late to modernity and industrialization in countries such as Brazil was that they took place under the strong leadership of the state, and implied building the material and financial basis for industrialization, but simultaneously confronting the so-called *social question*. This meant bringing large masses of peasants into urban market economies in a short period of time. Thus, phenomena that took place spontaneously and separated by centuries in the early developers of Europe and North America, were in turn brought together into a common process, with a certain degree of rational guidance, in latecomers. Regardless of how incomplete and insufficient they may have been, and they certainly were, nevertheless it was through the modern social protection institutions put in place by these states during this period that Brazil and other latecomers began to address new social demands generated and widened by rapid urbanization and industrialization. The state that channelled this process was simultaneously a developmentalist state and a welfare state. The concept of the Brazilian Developmental Welfare State (BDWS), which follows the approach advanced in the introduction and first chapter of this book, tries to cope with this particular and bivalent historical construction.

The analysis in this essay has a double purpose. On the one hand, to capture its main determinants and particular ways of evolving, in order to identify the instruments and capacities and institutions through which, in the past, it managed to attain its purposes. On the other hand, the purpose is to review its later changes, to identify its legacy for the future.

## The Brazilian Developmental Welfare State: architecture and dimensions

Brazil is one of that family of Latin American countries that, since the 1930s, advanced towards an urban and industrial economy, in the same movement that had modernized and extended the state's regulation and intervention mechanisms. In this process, in common with all *capitalismo tardio* countries[1] (Cardoso de Mello, 1982), the state played a decisive role of coordinating and providing incentives to the market, itself becoming a capitalist producer, with a presence in strategic sectors of the economy.

The construction of the *Brazilian Developmental Welfare State* (hereafter, BDWS) has been one of the dimensions of this movement. Between 1930 and roughly 1980, the country has constructed a *corporatist* or *conservative* type of welfare state (Titmuss 1958; Esping-Andersen 1990; Draibe and Aureliano, 1989). Characteristics of the *Developmental* Welfare State type may also be found in the Brazilian system, due to the mutually dynamic effects between economic and social policy (Gough, 1999, 2001; Kuhnle, 2002; Kwon, 2002, 2003).

As expected, the evolution of this social protection system has mainly concerned the relations between capital and labour, to which it has contributed to conform, regulate, and reproduce. Nevertheless, in contrast with most of the international experiences, especially the European one, this state form has paid little attention to social rights and citizenship. Certainly, as in other similar processes, the construction of its modern social protection system has been the political and institutional answer to the *social question* posed by capitalist development in Brazil. However, in the absence of a classical bourgeois revolution, that answer has been a specific one, in fact a dimension, among others, of the *conservative path* or the *modernization from above*, processes through which the capitalistic material basis and life-styles were completed in the country (Draibe, 1985).

From a morphological view, it could be said that BDWS is organized according to three pillars, each one corresponding to an aspect of social provision: (i) The *universal public provision*, covering the universal programmes of health, and education as well as the social assistance and other targeted programmes designed for poor people; (ii) The *contributory and subsidized programmes* (the social security programme and some other funds supported by mandatory social contributions); and (iii) the *private sector*. Families, philanthropy and the modern *third sector*, mainly the NGOs, also share social provision. The oldest communitarian forms of social protection, typical of the traditional non-urban world, are likely to survive in a very restricted way.

Such morphology must be completed with a brief reference to the federalist structure of the Brazilian state, since this strongly shapes the social programmes, particularly the public ones. Despite the social policy system's high degree of centralization, some social programmes have always had a 'naturally' decentralized form, as is the case with primary and secondary education, corresponding to states and municipalities' constitutional responsibility in the social field. Given the accented autonomy of the subnational governments, in public social provision, Brazilian federalism tends to be competitive rather than collaborative, leading to the creation of overlaps and distortions (Draibe, 1998; Arretche, 2000).

## The challenge of the great numbers

*Timing* and *dimension* are two remarkable characteristics of the system's evolution, concerning the rapidity of the institutional construction as well as the gigantic dimensions of *clienteles* (Draibe, 2002b). Dealing with a population of about 180 million people, the BDWS encompasses mass programmes, such as public education, for instance, covering about 55 million students and roughly two million teachers, or the students' food programme, delivering

35 million meals a day. Needless to say, enormous institutional and funding challenges are generated by social demands of such dimensions.

Social spending ranks Brazil among the higher-spending Latin American countries, which also includes Uruguay, Argentine, Chile, and Mexico. Public social expenditure has been estimated to be about 18.8 per cent of GDP, in the period 2000–01. More than half of the expenditure goes to social security (11.8 per cent), while education received 3.8 per cent; health 3.0 per cent, and housing and training programmes one per cent. The per capita social public spending has been estimated at US$936, in the same period (ECLAC, 2004). A distinctive feature is the double origin of the resources, the fiscal and the contributory ones, the second being channelled to so-called *social funds*,[2] funding by quasi-fiscal resources amounting to around 80 per cent of total public social spending. Employment in the public social arena predominates in all government employment. It is worth mentioning that Brazil is ranked among the lowest positions among 64 compared countries, in respect of the size of employment in the public sector (spending 5.5 per cent of the GDP on salaries in the public sector), public employment participation in the total employment (11.5 per cent) and public employment participation in population (5.1 per cent) (OECD, 1994).[3]

## Public social provision

Education and health systems, constructed in very different historical conditions, constitute the core of the Brazilian DWS. The educational system, since the first Republican Constitution (1891), is nationally regulated but strongly decentralized, in terms of both funding[4] and provision,[5] into state and municipal levels. Primary education is compulsory and free, while secondary education is free but not mandatory. In Brazil, educational provision is predominantly public at pre-school, and also at primary and secondary levels (respectively 73 per cent, 91 per cent and 86 per cent of all enrolments) and predominantly private in higher education (67 per cent of all enrolment).

Public education spending is about 3.8 per cent of GDP; one-half of this goes to the union, the other half to the states and to municipalities. However, it is little short of astonishing that educational outcomes have ranked Brazil towards the bottom of Latin American countries. Effective universal access to primary education – about 97 per cent of the age group – has been reached only during the second half of the 1990s, yet the coverage of the secondary education is a little over 25 per cent, and only 9 per cent in higher school, in line with other poor indicators.[6]

Despite the fact that the performance of the educational system has improved in recent years and a successful reform concerning the funding system of primary education was undertaken during the second half of the 1990s (Draibe, 2004), education still remains a matter of debate on the national public agenda. Increasing concern over the state of educational outcomes seems also to reflect the greater perception of the middle and working classes that good education is perceived as the only mechanism for upward social mobility.

On a different path, the national health system was only created in the late 1980s, until then evolving through a very fragmented, not systemic, nor nationwide structure. Led by a nationwide coalition of expert activists, deeply rooted in social movements, it occupied a central place in the democratic agenda and acquired a definite form in the 1988 Constitution, with the creation of the public Integrated Health System (*Sistema Unificado de Saúde – SUS*), one of universal entitlement.

The private health market shares the Brazilian health system through three different sectors. The *complementary sector*, constituted by private health care providers, contracted by the public sector in order to complete the public provision.[7] The *supplementary health care system*, in which either people or enterprises have their own voluntary private health insurance plans, and the *private market of health care provision*, in which people buy some of their own health care services (Arretche, 2004).

The current target population is approximately 140 million citizens, while private health markets cover more than 40 million people. Public health spending is estimated to be around 3.0 per cent of GDP, and if we add families spending – about 1.9 per cent of GDP in 1997 – the aggregate expenditure totals around 4.9 per cent of GDP.

Under the reformist wave of the second half of the 1990s, corrective and improvement measures were introduced in the health system, aiming to reinforce its financial base,[8] to improve its distributive impact[9] and to strengthen the public regulatory capacity on private sectors. Improvement in health indicators has been highlighted by researchers, mainly in infant and child health, probably because of the decentralization of primary health care. However, the improvement has been strongly unequal, among social groups and regions (Medici, 2002; Arretche, 2004).

Until now, the SUS implementation has been faced by enormous difficulties, even greater than those during the 1990s, through intense pressures for austerity. Nevertheless, the construction of the Brazilian national health system, founded on a principle of universal entitlement, has undoubtedly shifted the BDWS towards a more inclusive pattern of social protection.

*Social assistance and pro-poor programmes*, in the public sector, have changed substantially over the last decade. Differences are especially sharp regarding the huge *clientelistic* legacy of the 1930–85 period.[10] A national system of social assistance has been created by the new 1988 Constitution, with two main distinctive features: strong institutions and a participatory design, supported by social councils created in almost all of the Brazilian municipalities. In the 1990s, other innovations in pro-poor policies, such as job and training programmes, as well as popular funding loans, have accented the *productivist* drive of the system.

Perhaps the most significant change has been the recent introduction of programmes providing cash benefits to poor families. This shift in the

Brazilian social assistance model, which was traditionally opposed to such programmes, started during Fernando Henrique Cardoso's second term (1998–2002), supported by the Poverty Fund, created in 2000,[11] and strengthened during the first year of President Lula's government (2003–06).

## Contributory and subsidized programmes: the social security system and housing policy

The Brazilian social security system covers 30 million contributors and has almost 22 million beneficiaries. Social security spending has reached 11.5 per cent of GDP and approximately half of total public social expenditure. In 2002, the system deficit reached 5.5 per cent of GDP (4.2 per cent in the public sector). Only 42.3 per cent of the economically active population contributes regularly, therefore roughly 55 million workers, most of them in the informal labour market, are not covered by any pension insurance system.

The system is public, nationwide, and centralized, organized according to mandatory affiliation and the typical rules of the categorized or corporatist systems.[12] Benefits are income-related, supported by a 'pay-as-you-go' regime, and funded by social contributions, 95 per cent going to employee and employer.[13] It is worth noting that rural workers, who have been incorporated gradually since the 1970s, are exempted from making contributions, this being perhaps one of the most important redistributive aspects of the system. A complementary sector, private and voluntary, operates according to a capitalization scheme (Draibe and Matijascic, 2001).[14] Inequality among the schemes and benefits is great, a 'natural' characteristic of a corporatist and categorized system such as the Brazilian one. However, the systems concerning the salaried workers of the private sector were highly homogenized through reforms introduced by the military regime of 1964–85.

Created seventy years ago, at a time of comparatively low levels of industrialization and urbanization, the Brazilian social security system seems to have answered adequately the new social demands, but only in a limited way. Since the second half of the 1990s, it has faced increasing unbalances, because of the rising value of benefits, the ageing of the population and mostly because of the explosion of unemployment rate during the last five to seven years.

Social security reform has been at the centre of the social agenda since the early 1990s. Deemed responsible for the unbalanced public accounts and a condition in negotiations with the IMF and other multilateral agencies, it became a source of contention in the social arena, leading to intense debates and strong resistance, especially on the part of public employees. Two recent reforms have partially changed the system, the first in 1998, during the first term of President Fernando Henrique Cardoso, and the 2003 reform, in the first year of President Lula's government. The first reform, dealing mainly with workers and retirees in the private sector, has introduced the principle of linked contributions, new eligibility criteria and norms for calculating pensions,[15] while the second one has mainly affected the civil servants.[16] The fiscal goal has been clear in both cases. Despite the fact that the system has not been changed in nature and structural principles, a certain *market principle* has been introduced.

Among the social programmes supported by the aforementioned social funds, *housing policy* has been one of the most significant, undertaken through an enormous system created in 1964. In spite of the fact that the access to individual housing assistance was originally aimed at low-income families, the system later diverted resources from the popular sectors and reinforced those for the middle class, which guaranteed the best investment return.[17] Since the abolition of this system in 1986, Brazil no longer has a national housing policy.

Taking the range of public social sector programmes as a whole, it is easy to verify the unequal distribution of resources among them: 29 per cent goes to universal and pro-poor programmes; 70 per cent to social security and the other contributory programmes, and only one per cent goes to subsidized programmes, such as housing.

### Market social provision

The market sector shares social provision in a significant way, through a wide range of schemes, among them the express participation of the contracted private sector as a provider within the universal public programmes, as in the health care system. This feature is not a recent one, since participation has undergone steady growth from the 1970s onwards, pushed by state incentives – both the guaranteed public demand and the subsidized funding – and also by the new consumption patterns of the affluent middle-class and high-wage workers, two social groups that demand better and more diversified social services.

How was Brazil able to face the challenges of building the complex institutions of such extended national systems of social protection, in the short span of five or six decades, and, furthermore, in such a big, heterogeneous, and unequal country? The following sections explore the background of social policy development, according to different economic and political contexts as well prevailing social development strategies.

## Strong and incomplete development: economic contexts and long-term trends in social transformation

Two moments may be identified in Brazilian modernization during the twentieth century, which are similar to those identified in other LA countries. The first goes from the 1930s up to 1985, and a second one, during the last two decades of the century and up to year 2002. Some economic indicators give a clear account of the differences between both periods.

Industrialization, urbanization and social structure modernization constituted the main contents of the first period (roughly the period from 1930 to 1985) pushed by the *Estado Desenvolvimentista* and encouraged by the broad national project pursued during that time. Under the import substitution model (IS), the industrialization process has evolved through the phases of 'restricted industrialization' (1933–56)[18] and 'heavy industrialization' (1956–59),[19] the last one corresponding to the moment when the dynamic of the capitalistic accumulation was finally internalized in the country (Cardoso de Mello, 1982). Economic growth performed well during the period. However, the acceleration of inflation, starting in 1958, and the sharp decline in growth rates, combined with a deep political crisis, in the early 1960s, evolving into the military coup of 1964 and, with it, the end of the *Varguista State* (1930–64),[20] that first form of the *Brazilian Developmental Welfare State.*

Nevertheless, during this time developmental strategies were continued and even strengthened, being pursued by the new military dictatorship regime that lasted until 1985.[21] After an initial period of economic stabilization (1964–67), the Brazilian economy resumed at even higher rates its fast growth pattern, advancing into the so-called *economic miracle* period, from 1968 to the mid-1970s. However, from the second half of the 1970s onwards, the economic boom faded gradually, under the successive impacts of increasing debt interest, the drastic reduction of Brazilian reserves, the oil crisis, and, beginning in the 1980s, the debt crisis.

The new critical phase, from 1985, has evolved in line with political liberalization and the process of political transition towards democracy.[22] Governments of different orientations have succeeded during these two decades, but perhaps it could be stated that economic development was no longer the predominant goal pursued by the Brazilian state. From the 1980s onwards, the new public agenda has been strongly dominated by two major concerns – how to stabilize the economy and, at the political level, how to enhance and consolidate democracy.

Throughout the 1980s, after the deep recession of 1981–83, when GDP declined by 6.3 per cent, the Brazilian economy evolved at slow and oscillating growth rates, although higher than the Latin American average. Oscillating growth rates and increasing inflation, in line with growing poverty and unemployment levels, characterized the new democratic period, under the first civil government of José Sarney (1985–90).[23] Starting with the 1986 heterodox *Plano Cruzado* (Cruzado Plan), three nonconventional stabilization plans were attempted. Nevertheless, they failed and inflation grew fast, reaching about 80 per cent a month in 1990.

President Collor de Mello (1990–93) inaugurated Neoliberal-inspired economic policy reforms, introduced in a partial way, through a radical and chaotic stabilization plan, in line with a rapid opening up of the economy and quite ineffective administrative reforms. The results were that economic instability reached an almost hyperinflationary situation, while a deep political crisis evolved into the presidential impeachment, in the second half of 1993.[24]

The 1994 Plano Real signalled a new approach, started by President Itamar Franco (1993–94), and evolved by the double mandate of President Fernando Henrique Cardoso (1995–98 and 1999–2002). Stability was achieved,[25] supported by an overvalued currency and extremely high interest rates, as well as pro-market structural reforms that were undertaken.[26] However, in line with the international crisis, the Brazilian economy faced successive financial crises, finally addressed by a currency devaluation of around 80 per cent in January 1999, a few weeks after Cardoso's second term inauguration.[27] Dramatic changes in the economic structure characterized this period: besides the privatization of the bigger state companies, deep industrial restructuring has promoted participation by multinational companies, changes in productivity and managerial standards, and sharp sector retrenchment.[28] Economy grew at low rates, mainly from 1999 onwards; despite the reduction from 40 to 30 per cent in the poverty rate, the unemployment rate grew very quickly, and the income of middle and popular sectors fell strongly.[29]

These are tendencies that still persist in the country, even though it would be reasonable to expect changes in the new political scenery, following the election of the government of President Lula and the Party of the Workers (PT) (2003–06). Lula's goverment has shown continuity in respect of Cardoso's economic policy – rigid goals of stabilization, high interest rates and the fiscal generation of a surplus of the order of 4.75 per cent of GDP has oriented macroeconomic policy in the first two years of the new government. Successes in those plans have been responsible for the significant extension of the national and international credibility of the government. Nevertheless, the severe recession in 2003 has not allowed the orthodoxy of economic policy go unnoticed: GDP growth has been negative (–0.2 per cent), unemployment rates have risen, and household average income has fallen about 13 per cent in one year.

The recent interruption of the secular tendency of growth has been a dramatic experience for Brazilian society. Nevertheless, this does not mean the interruption of the strong social changes initiated during the first decades of industrialization. On the contrary, Brazilian society has changed rapidly and profoundly in periods of both fast and slow economic growth. In the recent period, in addition, it has experienced the deepest and most stable process of democratization of its social and political institutions in the whole of its recent history.

The next section provides some basic information concerning these long-term trends of change.

## Contradictory modernization

By far the most salient changes have been the demographic ones, with rapid increases in both the total population growth and also the percentage living in urban areas. Between 1940 and 2003, the Brazilian population grew from about 40 million to 180 million people; however, in recent years this rate of growth has slowed. The mean annual growth rate of 2.6 per cent from 1950 to 1980 dropped to 1.6 per cent in 2000, an impressive fall indicating that Brazil's population has already entered a transitional phase.

The urbanization process has also rapidly transformed the country from one in which, in 1940, 70 per cent of the population were peasants, into another one, in which, in the year 2000, more than 80 per cent of the population live in cities. No doubt, the underlying process has been a savage rural modernization, that is, an intense process of capitalist expansion in agriculture, led by large landowners and later by agribusiness, without any extensive land reform. The exodus from the rural areas has been vertiginous: in the short span of three decades nearly 40 million people have migrated towards the cities, 24 per cent of whole population in the 1950s, 36 per cent in the 1960s and 40 per cent in the 1970s (Cardoso de Mello and Novaes, 1998: 581).

Rapid growth has also been a feature of the Brazilian economy until the 1980s[30] (IBGE, 2003), when a rupture seems to occur in the long process, leading the modern Brazilian economy to its current situation of prolonged low growth, stagnation and noticeable financial fragility. Under the BDWS, during both the Varguista Era and the military dictatorship, the Brazilian economy grew at an impressive rate, maintaining annual average growth rates between 6.5 per cent and 10.3 per cent.[31] By contrast, in the new economic scenario, growth rates fell to an average of 3.3 per cent in the 1980s and 1.8 per cent in the 1990s (Gordon, 2001; IBGE, 2003).[32]

Industrialization and (de)industrialization processes are clearly illustrated by the rise and decline of the manufacturing sector's participation in Brazilian GDP: 19 per cent in 1940, 34 per cent in 1980, and 27.7 per cent in 2000. Agriculture has displayed the opposite trend, dropping from 30 per cent in 1940 to 9.8 per cent in 1980, although it subsequently rose to 11 per cent in 2000 (IBGE, 2003). Service sector participation grew during both periods.

Labour markets reflected these economic changes. During the fast growth phase, urban employment grew at a remarkable rate, as did the participation rate, while the participation rate of women has grown in a significant way, albeit with some variation, since the 1970s.[33] In the second period, parallel to economic stagnation and pro-market reforms, predominant trends were the strong growth of both unemployment, reaching about 13 per cent of the working EAP today, and the informal labour market, reaching 58 per cent of the EAP.

**An uneven and unequal development**

What kind of social progress was generated in Brazil, in the second half of the twentieth century? Nobody could deny that economic and social changes have generated enormous improvements in the material living standards of the Brazilian population – surprisingly in both fast and low growth periods – as shown by some indicators of household public services and consumption items.[34] Social conditions have also improved, as is reflected in education and health long time series indicators. The poverty rate declined slowly but continuously from the 1940s until the late 1970s, a long-term trend that was partly reversed in the 1980s.[35] The Brazilian Human Development Index has improved, shifting the country from the 76th position in 1991 to 65th in 2003.

Yet, Brazil arrives in the twenty-first century showing one of the world's most unequal patterns of income distribution. With a Gini index maintained at around 0.60 for over forty years,[36] Brazil ranks in the sixth lowest position among 154 countries (IBGE, 2003; World Bank, 2004). Besides income, other hard and durable inequalities have always characterized Brazilian society. Racial inequalities are by far the most persistent: in the case of education, for example, even though all groups experience better results, the distance between black and white remain the same (Henriques, 2001).[37] Regional inequalities were secularly deep, dividing the country between the poorer Northeast/North regions and the richer Southeast/South/Centre-West regions. Many complex factors could explain the notorious and durable high levels of inequality in Brazil. In the approach of this study, it seems important to stress at least two of them, the pattern of social mobility, resulting from the deep trends of structural changes, and the pattern of economic growth pursued during the period of fast development.

In line with industrialization and urbanization, three other processes have affected the dynamics of the Brazilian social structure in an important way: strong migratory movements, both internal and external,[38] a widening agricultural open frontier,[39] and strong social mobility, both upward and downward, at least until the 1980s. Considered together, these social processes configure many types of social mobility, in space, in sector, as well as in social terms. However, as these types of social mobility are contradictory, the level of global inequality continued to grow (Tavares, 2003), configuring a special pattern of development, one that Furtado (2003) has recently labelled *deformed development*. In a different way from what has been classically described by the 'duality' thesis (the 'two' Brazils, the rural–urban, Northwest–Southwest, Belgium–India, rich–poor people and so on), argues Furtado, the movement has been one of increasing structural heterogeneity, surprisingly during periods of both growth and stagnation.

Inequalities are also related to the pattern of economic growth advanced by the *Brazilian Developmental Welfare State*. Economic growth, in particular during the military regime (1964–85), has been led by a *concentrated and excluding model of development*, in fact, a pattern of high growth and a macroeconomic regime supported by

> a stable but chronic rate of inflation, a high indexed rate of exchange and an under indexed minimum wage. Thus our 'golden age' of economic growth was accompanied by high rural poverty, intense migratory flux, permanent increases in food prices, declining minimum wages and labour class political repression in the big cities. In this context the wages paid to skilled labour, the rate of profits in modern industry and land rents in rural and urban propriety shaped a high concentrated income distribution. (Medeiros, 2002: 4)

Therefore, as with the god Janus, such a development pattern would have had two heads. The first one, as noted, has continuously generated social exclusion and low-paid workers. The second one, contrarily, would have promoted the emergence of a new affluent, more educated, and high-earning middle classes and salaried workers. In fact, it could be said that such sectors were directly connected to the prevailing economic pattern through the twofold role they should fulfil in the economic system. On the one hand, as a source of highly qualified manpower, able to respond to the requirements of the modern labour market structures, as well as the carrier patterns. On the other hand, as a new market for the consumption of higher-priced durables, such as houses or cars, as well as high value-added products and services. Some scholars have identified one of the roots of what they called the *Americanization process of the Brazilian society* precisely in such a high-value-added-based adjustment between mass production and mass consumption, one of an indisputable pro-income concentration drive.

Deeply embedded in those social and economic processes, Brazilian society has become more heterogeneous and diversified, as widespread social differentiation has accelerated from the 1970s onwards. Among the more remarkable changes we could note the enhancing of the aforementioned new middle classes, more educated and economically powerful, related to services and the administration of large enterprises. In addition, there is the new salaried and wage-earning working class, part of which is in white-collar employment, and most of them connected to large industrial and internationalized enterprises. In addition, there are the new civil servants, many of them linked to the indirect state administration or to state-owned companies. Obviously these modern economic sectors also follow a spatially concentrated pattern, another factor contributing to the widening of social and regional inequality in Brazil.

The emergency of the more affluent salaried sectors brought together new and enhanced demands for better and more diversified social services. A new kind of social pressure over BDWS, still in its formation period, promoting, among others, two important effects. On the one hand, increasing pressures on social expenditure, as such high-earning sectors own power and 'voice'. On the other hand, in the same measure as social public programmes have expanded and faced growing quality challenges, as in the 1970s, these new social sectors have manifested increasing dissatisfaction with public social services, 'exiting' the system, towards the private market of social provision. Bearing in mind the socioeconomic background detailed above, the next section summarizes the historic process of formation and evolution of the BDWS, from the viewpoint of social actors and state developmental strategies.

## Ways to modernity during times of developmentalism

The *Brazilian Developmental Welfare State* could be seen as the creature of the *Estado Desenvolvimentista* (1930–85), in both historical forms it has assumed, the Varguista State (1930–64) and the Military Developmentist State (1964–85). Focusing on the political regime, four configurations could been identified from 1930 to 1985: the authoritarian regime (1930–37), and the open dictatorship (1937–45) of the *Estado Novo* (New State), led by Getúlio Vargas; the period of restricted democracy, known as the Populist State (1945–64), and the authoritarian and technocratic military rule (1964–85).[40]

### The Vargas Era: socioeconomic strategies under the *Estado Varguista*

Until 1930, social policies had only a modest and localized impact in Brazil. In cultural terms, it is interesting to note that the great legacy of the Colonial and Imperial times was twofold: the patriarchal family tradition and the slavery legacy. The first one constituted the predominant model, firstly transported from Europe and adapted or transformed according to the highly diversified social structure over which it developed, from Colonial times onwards[41] (Dessen and Torres, 2002). Only in the Northern region was it possible to find elements of indigenous tradition, within the extractive populations. Regarding the legacy of slavery, the emphasis is less on family structure, and more on the authoritarian and vertical pattern of domination, disseminated in an impressive form throughout Brazilian culture.[42]

In terms of social policy, limited social measures had been introduced during the Empire (1822–89), mainly in the educational field, and in a more elaborate and institutionalized way during the Old Republic (1889–1930).[43] Indeed, it could be admitted that the departure point of the new social policy system has been localized in the social tissue of the economic phase previous to 1930, corresponding to the coffee-based export economy (1880–1930). Even if supported by predominantly agrarian, traditional, social relations, that economy also expanded in the urban sector, where the financial and commercial services associated with export activities were localized, as was the the industrial production of wage-consumption goods and the small capital goods industry. In the cities, such social division of labour generated a relatively differentiated urban social structure. It included, in addition to the small industrial bourgeoisie, the emergent industrial working force, constituted mainly by European immigrants. In addition, middle-class sectors linked to urban services, bureaucratic strata and, already in a significant proportion, urban poor people, those 'poor free men' as literature has labelled former slaves and their families, emigrated but did not integrate into the urban economy, after the abolition of slavery in 1888. Although these heterogeneous urban sectors would not play leading roles, they would nevertheless become distinctive forces supporting the modernizing process, and the new governing elites who emerged following with the 1930 Revolution.

The crisis of 1929, which decisively affected the coffee-based, export economy, also had a political manifestation in Brazil, the Revolution of 1930, an anti-oligarchic movement that broke with the Oligarchic State and the First Republic (1889–1930). Led by Getúlio Vargas, the armed movement was supported by young military officers, the *tenentes*, who, since the 1920s, through a series of rebellions and uprisings, had expressed the frustrations of the aforementioned middle and popular urban sectors, whose social and political demands had been continually ignored by the conservative and oligarchic ruling elites of the *Ancien Régime*.[44] The revolutionary movement evolved in 1937, through a new *coup d'état*, into Vargas' open dictatorship, which lasted until 1945. This particular moment in Brazil's modern history has had strong implications, among them the acceleration of the process of formation of the national state.

Brazilian political science studies generally concur about the specific power structure that underlined the Developmentalist State. The new 1930s regime emerged during the crisis of the Oligarchic State as a result of the long agrarian crisis and the hegemonic incapacity of its dominant groups, regional oligarchies as well as the industrial bourgeoisie; however it was also stimulated by increasing pressure from the urban popular and middle-class sectors. In such a hegemonic crisis, the New State saw the possibility of acting as an arbitrator among heterogeneous social interests, rooting its source of legitimacy in a direct, not institutionalized relationship with the masses (Weffort, 1968; Draibe, 1985). This new power arrangement would have generated the autonomous strategies of both the state's political nucleus and the modern economic bureaucracy, anchored in the new state apparatus created from the 1930s onwards, encouraged by the strong state-building trends carried out in the new institutional context. In a similar way to other processes of welfare state formation, the expansion of social programmes has been a favoured political activity, contributing greatly to both the Varguista state-building project and the regime's political legitimacy.

The overthrow of Vargas marks the beginning of the limited democratic regime of 1945–64. Given the theme of this book, it is important to underline the central role played by the fledgling social protection system in the new power structure. This structure was supported by a centre-right coalition structured around the two political parties created by Vargas, the Social Democratic Party (PSD) and the Labour Party (PTB), whose purpose was to accommodate and resolve the differences between the interests of the agrarian elites, the first, and middle classes and unionized urban workers, the second.[45]

Rapid economic growth, the building of the modern and strong state capabilities and the nation's modernization were the true ingredients of the twentieth-century Brazilian DWS, oriented by the ideological compounds of nationalism, statism, and developmentalism. In the Vargas Era, this development project has had two specific goals: to drive economic development through a policy of heavy industrialization, on the one hand, and to promote the controlled incorporation of the new contingents of urban salaried workers, on the other hand.

In common with many Latin American countries in the 1930s, Brazilian policies to combat the economic crisis had dynamic effects on the whole economy, sustaining effective demand, offering minimal protection to the export sector, and promoting the import-substitution process. However, in a different way, the Varguista industrialization plan was not limited to the protection of pre-existing industry, its true ambition being the implantation of the infrastructure and the large industrial sectors.

To reach this goal, the crucial obstacles were how to obtain funding and how to access updated technology.[46] These challenges were finally addressed, in the second half of the 1950s, by the winning industrialization strategy led by President Juscelino Kubistchek, the *associated strategy*, one organized on a tripartite arrangement between foreign capital, domestic private capital and state capital – the last in the form of the state-owned firms.[47] Under the slogan '50 years in 5' of the Juscelino Kubistchek administration, it could be said that the industrialization cycle was successfully achieved (Lessa, 1978; Cardoso de Mello, 1982; Draibe, 1985). In addition to the accelerated speed of the process, the Varguista State has also been able to build domestic economic capacity and, no less important, it took advantage of the windows of opportunity opened in international markets in postwar times.

Another distinctive axis of the Varguista strategy, the social integration of the urban wage and salaried workers, was supported by four core new institutions: the nationwide labour union structure, the social security system, labour regulations, and the imposition of a national minimum salary.

Union structure was organized according to the corporatist model, founded on restrictive legislation and barriers to both entry and free representation.[48] Notwithstanding these restrictive and controlling features, both the union system and labour legislation were maintained, practically unchanged, from the 1940s to the present day, perhaps a clear manifestation of its strength and political efficacy. Pensions systems were, specifically, conceived as a national and centrally controlled system, however decentralized by economic sector, each one regulated by a specific state agency, providing differentiated security benefits according to the funding capacity of each one. Unions controlled security agencies funding, as well as the distribution of benefits.

The new social security institutions were designed only for the urban workers in the formal labour market, and limited to unionized categories recognized by the state. As a consequence, the expansion of social rights was dependent upon, first, a group's participation in the productive structure, and, secondly, the relative political weight of the corresponding professional category. This limited and controlled form of social incorporation was labelled 'regulated citizenship' (Santos, 1979).

However limited and partial they may have been, it has been under these social institutions that social rights have been inaugurated in Brazil: the right to regulated jobs, unions, and minimum wage.[49] It is true that, during the Vargas Era, social rights were far from being generalized, and this is still the case in Brazil. Yet few would deny that the introduction of those new social policies has had the effect of being almost a social revolution, at a time when there is still a low degree of political development and in a society that is widely permeated by the authoritarian relationship pattern inherited from its heritage of slavery. Not by chance have historians mentioned this moment, in Brazilian political history, as one in which, for the first time, 'people have entered into the history'. In the social imaginary, even today Vargas is considered the 'father of the poor'.

Indeed, the Varguista social policy strategy has been conceived and implemented in a limited form. First, the predominance of the industrialization goals has limited the emergent social protection system to the urban salaried workers. Excluded from the new pension system, as well from much labour and union regulations, peasants and rural workers – that is, the great majority of the population until roughly the 1970s – were viewed as the 'forgotten class' throughout most of the Vargas Era. In the absence of land reforms and due to the state omission to address its social demands, it could be said that, during the period of modernization, for Brazilian peasants the future would likely be reduced to little more than two alternatives – to remain prisoner of the traditional and authoritarian agrarian relations, in conditions of extreme poverty, or to be expelled from the countryside, migrating themselves to cities which were unprepared to receive them. Agrarian movements of a certain weight have emerged later, at the end of the 1950s, led by some local and weak organizations. At the end of the Varguista period, limited labour and union regulations were introduced, but agrarian reform has remained a non-negotiable issue for the conservative elites. The social incorporation of rural workers through social protection policies was begun, in a limited and slow manner, only in the 1970s, under the military regime. The decisive shift, if it is allowed to say that, has been done in the new democratic period, starting in 1985.

The same 'industry bias' seems to have magnified the place of social security policy in the whole Brazilian welfare state, leaving little or no room for all other social policies. Although the reformist wave of 1930 had affected practically all social areas, through new national codes and a copious legislation, evidence shows that social policies such as education and, still more, health policy have not occupied a central place in the governmental social agenda, nor in the successive development plans from 1930 until 1964.

In spite of the discourse and some institutional measures, whose goals perhaps were mainly political, it seems that the Varguista social strategy has been only marginally concerned with Brazil's enormous social differences. The new system of social protection does not seem to have succeeded as a mechanism that could correct them. In those conditions, the only mechanism of income redistribution was likely to be the minimum national salary; despite its undoubted positive effects, it has not been capable of changing the growing trend in income concentration.

In sum, during the Vargas Era, the rising system of social protection has been an effective answer to the new challenges of the rapid social transformation of the country, while it has also constituted a powerful mechanism of political legitimation and social control. However, as far as such strategy has privileged economic goals, rather than social ones, it has limited, in this manner, the distributive and equality capacity of the new social policies system. In the new stage of the BDWS, under the military dictatorship of 1964, this pattern of social protection was taken to its limits.

## 1964–85: the Brazilian Developmental Welfare State under military rule

The military coup of 1964 ended the political cycle which began in 1930. Its starting point has been the critical political conjuncture, 1961–64, a widespread institutional crisis that undermined the governance capability and legitimacy of the last civil government of the democratic period.

From the theoretical perspective we observe throughout this book, the crisis of the Varguista State, often referred as the 'populist crisis', could be identified as the first crisis of the BDWS, a consequence of its own success. That is, as a consequence of the industrialization progress and from the rapid transformation of the agriculture at the end of the Vargas Era, the economic and social structure had changed in such way that its own 'modern' institutions, those created during the 1930s, became obsolete, as new and updated rules and institutions were now required. In the first years of the 1960s, the political movement known as *Reformas de Base* (basic reforms), beyond the financial, tax, administrative and agrarian reforms, also demanded social reform. The strong politicization of the conservative sector and the political mobilization of the new middle sectors against reforms, stimulated and supported the military coup that overthrew President Jango Goulart in 1964 (Draibe, 1985).

Practically, all of those policy reforms were implemented by military dictatorships, in an elitist and authoritarian vein, but not exactly in accordance with the more traditional and backward social sectors. Perhaps one of the distinctive features of the Brazilian military dictatorship of 1964–85 could be found here: its authoritarian but modern economic orientation, that is, a non-agrarian economic orientation, rather than the one hoped for by most of the conservative forces. Parallel to the elimination and even the savage purging of the democratic opposition groups, the military rulers were concerned to promote industrial economic growth, conceived in the broader context of the nation integration and of the international projection of Brazil as a Great Power, in the classical military vision of national power.

Immediately after the 1964 coup, alongside the monetary stabilization measures, policy reforms such as *tax, monetary, financial, and administrative* were also implemented. A new expansive cycle started in 1968, pushed by strong governmental incentives, and foreign investments grew significantly; export-based agriculture modernized rapidly, while the infrastructural and private capital goods sectors also expanded strongly. A financing and investment programme network, managed by public agencies and official banks, was activated, while state companies broadened their spectrum of activities based on the expansion of foreign debt (MRE, 2004). Under the term of President Geisel (1975–79), an ambitious IS new cycle plan was undertaken. Simultaneously, economic growth began to decline, under the impact of the oil crisis and, later, the debt crisis.

In spite of repressive controls, the authoritarian regime relied upon the support of society at large, mainly the business elites and the quite extended middle-class segments, who came to have a quite positive response to the regime's capacity to adopt expansive economic policies, mainly during the 1967–74 period (Diniz, 1994).

In a strongly centralized decision-making process, the military–technocracy alliance, a tradition started with the *Estado Novo*, was enhanced; however it no longer operated according to the previous corporatist approach. In fact, the new authoritarian regime privileged the co-optation of individuals and private interests, rather than interest associations. Cardoso (1974) has coined the term 'bureaucratic rings' to describe this pattern of relationship between state and civil society. The political power of state bureaucratic agencies grew, gaining increasing autonomous control over policies and over co-optation of business interests, in a context of complete closure of old participatory channels. In addition, efforts in state-building directions strengthened the nationwide scope of policies.

It does not seem heretical to suggest that BDWS assumed its purest form under the military rule of the period 1964–85. The complex system of public social intervention was established and consolidated. The state was equipped with powerful new mechanisms and instruments of economic regulation and intervention, capable of promoting private investment and simultaneously extending the state's economic participation. Economic policy was oriented in an almost aggressive form, in order to take advantage of the favourable international conditions, at least until the oil crisis. Social funds were successfully used with economic goals (Draibe, 1994).[50]

At the same time, the Brazilian social policies system became fully developed, institutionalized and significantly modernized, according to authoritarian and technocratic orientations, and in an extremely centralized way, with a clear reduction in the autonomy of states and municipalities. In addition to educational and social security reforms, urban labour legislation was changed in a restrictive way; however, it was also paradoxically extended to rural workers. Consolidating the complex system of social intervention, the period 1974–80 was characterized by a huge expansion of the state structures and social spending, in line with rapid economic growth. The access and coverage of social programmes have been expanded; however, the most prominent feature of the military regime in the social field was perhaps the incorporation, albeit in a very limited way, of new social groups to the social protection system: this involved mainly the rural workers, but also domestic workers and the self-employed. Given the restrictions or the suspension of civil and political rights, some analysts explained such expansion of social policies as an attempt by military rulers to enhance the regime's legitimacy (Andrade 1982; Carvalho, 2000).

Nevertheless, social privation and inequity grew strongly during the period, as is widely recognized. In general, the shape of the social protection system negatively conditioned the outcomes, as the abolition of all forms of social participation in the decision-making processes contributed to a deeper penetration of the authoritarian style into the field of social policies. Subordinated to the imperatives of economic goals, social policy decisions were becoming a restricted technocratic decision, insulated from competitive politics, but also from any social or public control. The multiplication of autonomous public entities, state enterprises and foundations, resulted in an enormous, fragmented, and heterogeneous system, characterized by overlapping activities, crossed by countless channels of interest articulation, making governmental institutions remarkably porous to the entreaties of interest groups. In addition to the deficiencies in the regulatory framework of the private systems, politics also entered by another door, as clientelism and patronage grew in the same proportion as social benefits were used in order to increase the regime's chances of electoral success.

Not surprisingly, the outcomes of the social policies of the military regime have registered all kinds of insufficiencies and distortions, among them the so-called mistargeting of Brazilian social programmes – that is, that they would have tended to favour those social groups in less need. Dissatisfaction with the authoritarian model of social policies, already explicit at the end of the 1970s, achieved critical dimensions, even among the regime's supporters, as economic difficulties advanced. As expected, the *social question* would occupy a central place in the democratization agenda, during the early 1980s.

### 1985–2003: reforming BDWS in difficult and exciting times

The Brazilian social policy system has shown substantial changes during the last twenty years. Before summarizing such changes, it seems important to identify the social and political context in which they occurred.

## Democratizing Brazil: new patterns of state–society relations

Some moments of Brazil's modern history have been marked by remarkable changes, representing a kind of historical concentration of comprehensive social change, affecting bigger schemes, for instance the cognitive or value matrix, as well as social and political behaviour, even the 'habits of the heart', in Tocqueville's words. Surely, the revolutionary 1930s decade was one of these moments. Late in the 1950s, the *JK Years*, the period of the presidency of Juscelino Kubistchek (1956–59), was another magic moment in national culture.[51]

Indeed, the 1980s were another of these turbulent and exciting times. One of the first signals of social changes was the extraordinary growth of civil society. Immediately following political liberalization, initiated by military rulers at the end of the 1970s, the public sphere expanded rapidly, occupied by a flourishing civil society, which was manifest at all levels by increasing numbers of diversified social organizations.[52] The energetic civic and political movement pushed for the restoration of civil and political rights and democratic elections, as well as the improvement of social conditions (Jardim Pinto, 2004; Power and Doctor, 2002; Leite Cardoso, 1983; Jacobi, 1989). The remarkable characteristics of this movement seemed to reveal deep changes in Brazilian society, evolved and accumulated from the 1960s on, however not yet fully perceived. The new unionism, of which President Lula has been the outstanding leader since the early 1970s, has been a notable feature of the 1980s, as well as producing a political party, the Workers' Party or *Partido dos Trabalhadores* (PT), which was founded in 1980. As emphasized by much of the literature, such new unionism was rooted in two social strands – the new working class emerging from the 1960s on, as well as the new working-middle class, as disscussed above.

Regarding workers in the private sector, it appears that same sort of rupture with the past has occurred, as new unionism pointed towards new patterns of social demands as well as new forms of political behaviour. With respect to the first issue, besides higher salaries, it also demanded issues such as adequate housing, education, health, social security – in brief, better social protection. That is, the classical agenda of *social inclusion*, the project of workers' social integration through social policies. In other terms, the social agenda of new unionism, although motivated by solidarity values, has also been motivated by values of social incorporation and citizenship. Concerning political behaviour, an eminent feature of new unionism has been the independence or autonomy regarding the state, in contrast to the old union–state relationship and the corporatist tenets of labour regulation, as shaped by the Varguista State. A political incarnation of this grassroots unionism, PT also rejected the old historical worker-based parties, such as the Labour Party and the Communist Party (Power and Doctor, 2002).

Entrepreneurial elites, which had reaped great benefits during the previous period of rapid economic growth, also evolved according to a more independent path. In the late 1970s, facing the first signals of the economic crisis, they expressed growing dissatisfaction with the strong state presence in the productive sector, through a movement known as the 'Campaign for De-estatization'. In this way they joined with other social groups in the common claim to free society from excessive state intervention and control (Tavares de Almeida, 1998). On the other hand, starting in the 1970s, new and non-corporatist mechanisms of interest representation also became manifest. Diniz and Boschi (2002) stressed the changing behaviour of business associations, in the 1980s, improving performance and moving away from their exclusive focus on the Executive to also include Congress in their lobbying activities. From the mid-1980s onwards, the adherence of large segments of business elites to the anti-statism and market-friendly orientations in economic policy, mainly after the failure of Sarney's stabilization plans, also became apparent.

The 1980s have also revealed new patterns of political mobilization by the middle and popular sectors, bringing together new and distinctive features such as major independence regarding the elites and the control of political parties, greater participation of young people, big street demonstrations and long periods of demobilization. The early 1980s social mobilization claiming for direct elections (*Diretas Já*) or the 1990s movement *Ethics in Politics*, pushing President Collor's impeachment provide good examples of these new social patterns.[53]

Another crucial feature has been the dramatic change in the weight of social actors in Brazil shifting towards mass democracy, with the inclusion, for the first time, of broad masses of the population in the electorate, since the new Constitution of 1988 widened the franchise to illiterate people. Armijo (2003) argued that, besides the fantastic growth of the electorate, which exceeded 100 million voters in the first half of the 1990s, the average Brazilian voter, for the first time, has typically been a poor person – a change of incalculable political effects.

What would these signs appear to indicate? It could be said that the Brazilian society emerging from the authoritarian regime was more fragmented and heterogeneous. Doubtless, it is more complex, more pluralist, also a more organized society, from trade unions to middle-class associations. Brazil is now a society that seems to value freedom and independence (from the state), as much as other modalities of social relationship, rooted in horizontal, rather than hierarchical relations, other forms of collective action, politicized but not persistent nor necessarily partisan. Individualism and consumerism did not seem to be absent from this new form of capitalist sociality (Cardoso de Mello and Novais, 1998). However, as argued by many, it already seemed to hold new modalities of solidarity and social commitment, rooted in the organizations of civil society, mobilized less to exert pressure on the state, than to take action on their own account.

### A conservative transition through democracy

Why has Brazil been one of the last countries in the region to turn to market reforms? Is it true and, if so, why do the so-called Neoliberal reforms in Brazil seem to have been, as argued, not so reformist, so Neoliberal, so severe or anti-statism, as they have been in other Latin American countries? How can we explain the remarkable event of the 2002 election of Lula da Silva, a former unionist and founder of the grassroots Workers' Party, as president of Brazil? Furthermore, how can we explain the relative continuity between the PT economic policy and that of the previous regime, of Fernando Henrique Cardoso's government, one said to embrace market reforms lumped under the label Neoliberalism?

A range of academic literature has explored these and other questions, from the economic view[54] (Kingstone 1998), as well as from the perspective of the power structure and the ruling coalitions, along the transition process from authoritarian regime toward democratic rule (Sallum and Kugelmas, 2003; Sallum, 2003a; Avritzer, 2003). Under the approach of this chapter, it seems indispensable to outline, albeit briefly, the main trends of the country's political evolution in the last twenty years.

Brazil's political transition to civilian rule has been a conservative and negotiated one, an outstanding feature to be accounted in order to explain why the deep movements of Brazilian society's democratization have not always been openly manifested in the outcomes of the political process. Perhaps the fate of the huge 1982–84 popular movements clamouring for direct elections could provide considerable insight on the theme. As is generally argued, the conservative sectors, through the oppositionist PMDB (Party of the Brazilian Democratic Movement) and the dissident PFL (Party of the Liberal Front),[55] gained control of the movement, and the indirect election was negotiated as a solution with the military regime. Besides the survival of old institutions, conservative politicians brought to the new period most of the former domination practices, chiefly patronage and clientelism, as viewed in the *Plano Cruzado* episode[56] (Power and Doctor, 2002).

Scholars strongly concur that the Brazilian party system is fragmented; parties are weak, and politicians notoriously non-ideological, often moving from one party to another, motivated mainly by access to patronage and services to their parochial constituencies. Under such conditions, the construction of stable coalitions has always been difficult. From Sarney to Lula, the construction of all governmental coalitions inexorably followed such a pattern. The other side of this intensive process of majority building has been the absence of opposition forces, with the exception of PT while in opposition. Between the mid-1980s and mid-1990s, certain trends shaped the Brazilian political system in a quite interesting manner. Briefly, the political decline of the former *Developmentalist coalition*, from the late 1980s onwards, despite the *liberal Developmentalist group* shared President Cardoso's government (Sallum, 2003a).[57] In addition, the declining political position of rightist forces and its leading party, PFL, converted into the pole of the Neoliberal strand[58] (Avritzer, 2003) and the declining position of PMDB, despite the role of *great elector* it fulfilled from the 1980s until nowadays.

Left-wing forces also moved strongly, the PT certainly showing the most dramatic changes. As many argued, the institutional evolution of the PT, between the 1980s and the 1990s, has been remarkable. Having developed as a mass party, strongly structured, vertically commanded, and well integrated in the Brazilian party system, the PT has accumulated considerable experience in ruling and managerial activities through the growing number of municipal and states governments it commanded during the period. In line with such an evolution, changes have affected several parties' dimensions, mainly the internal balance between the founding forces – the unionists, the progressive Catholic Church and the social movements – in favour of the former. In addition, there has been an absorption of latecomer members, mainly arising from PT's municipal and state bureaucracies; also, the growing risk of the party's oligarchization and the isolation of its leadership from the base; and, finally, the changing policy of political alliances, varying according to electoral interests.

The set of changing processes thus schematically presented, perhaps allows us to understand the fast fading of the optimism with which Brazilian society mobilized to fight against military rule, and to protest about inflation. By the mid-1990s, after almost 15 years of low growth, high inflation, near hyperinflation, and a strong continuity of the secular mechanisms of patronage and corruption, a wave of pessimism was disseminating widely through society. These events brought together risky elements of mistrust among economic agents, a lack of faith in both politicians and political institutions, and declining confidence in the future.

Fernando Henrique Cardoso in 1995 – promising sustainable stabilization and structural reforms aiming to 'modernizing Brazil' – and Lula da Silva, in 2002 – promising economic recovery, mass job creation, and social inclusion – both winner candidates had benefited strongly from these feelings and expectations, converting pessimism and tiredness into hope and confidence, and into votes. They were different candidates, supported by distinct social bases. Nevertheless, both of them were rooted in common grounds: the recognition that Brazilian society wanted to bring changes to the spheres of economic relations as well as political institutions. In addition, there was the knowledge that ordinary people – now the average Brazilian voter – valued and wanted currency stabilization.

No doubt, broad and heterogeneous social groups supported President Cardoso's reformist agenda, while the reform process generated a considerable political constituency. Decisively supported by the media, the issues of the stabilization and reform policies fed the population's hopes, allowing the re-election of the president in 1998, despite negative outcomes from the macroeconomic policy pursued during his first term. Nevertheless, in the second government, pragmatic flexibility of economic policy, the failure in resuming economic growth, in addition to the rise in unemployment and the fall in incomes of the middle classes became the Achilles' heel of Cardoso's rule, the main factors that probably explain the electoral failure of its candidate, in the Presidential election of 2002. Inversely, they have permitted the astonishing victory of Lula, with over 60 per cent of votes cast.

Even his opponents agree that Lula's electoral victory marked a watershed in Brazilian political history, signalling the triumph of political democracy, that is, the maturity of democratic institutions, able to absorb the ascent of popular sectors to the top of the political structure, furthermore an early metalworker and unionist as president. Perhaps it would be permissible to suggest that the true novelty of 2002 has been less Lula's non-elitist social origin, than the fact that Lula, as well as PT commanders in general, are leaders not co-opted by the elites. This is new. Scholars on Brazilian political history had taught that the secular pattern of political change, in Brazil, had been the *elites conciliation*, the pacts among dominant sectors and, whenever elites had fear of some threat, the co-optation of subordinate classes. In electing Lula, it seems that hopeless Brazilian society has ushered in an outsider from the mainstream, the possibility to begin a new age.

President Lula was elected by a pro-growth coalition, of wide and heterogeneous social spectrum, not merely popular, since the electorate covered strands of the biggest industrial sectors as well as part of the affluent middle-class sector, clearly motivated by the disaffection from current hardships, perceived as the result of the neo-liberal reformist policies. However, the broad electorate had already made clear its preference for economic stabilization, a mood that PT has captured as a lesson of its failure in the 1998 elections. From this time on, as stressed by scholars, the PT has been sharply moving right, toward the centre, toward positions closer to the establishment's values and interests. (Sallum and Kugelmas, 2003).[59]

The electoral strategy[60] and then the government strategy took into account the conflicting objectives of a fast renewal in growth, on the one side, and on the other, the maintenance and deepening of the previous macroeconomic model. These strategies also resulted in conflicting results.

The short duration of the new government and the expected difficulties it confronted immediately suggest cautiousness at the time of evaluation. Nevertheless, among its successes it should be noted that Lula's government, elected with very wide support, managed to maintain credibility among international investors.[61] Even bigger successes have been obtained in foreign policy; where alongside traditional Brazilian stances have been complemented with the new government's trademark that tends to reinforce South–South relations, especially in relation to LA and Mercosur. In internal policy, the government has managed to build a remarkably wide coalition in Congress, which has provided the government with large majorities in key legislation.

Two dimensions stand out in the negative and rather problematic side of this strategy of dual conflicting objectives. On the one hand, the economic depression,[62] and on the other hand, the use of traditional political mechanisms and the manoeuvres of clientelism and patronage.[63] Therefore, Lula had already lost popularity during his first year, together with a certain increase in discredit, in addition to conflicts within his own party and certain ruptures in the leftist front that put him in power. In terms of this chapter, it should be noted that there has been a certain political retrenchment of the middle classes, a return of a certain pessimism regarding economic growth and, consequently, fractures in the developmentalist coalition supporting Lula.

Further on this chapter will return to present economic perspectives, but before this, it seems necessary to offer a brief review of the recent evolution of the Brazilian social protection system, through a consideration of the reforms and restructuring it has experienced during the last decades.

## The Brazilian Developmental Welfare State (DWS): two waves of reforms

Since 1985, the Brazilian DWS has changed profoundly as a result of two reform cycles (Draibe, 2002c). First came the democratization cycle, implemented in the second half of the 1980s, in a context of re-democratization and economic instability. This was followed by the (social) liberal cycle, undertaken during President Fernando Henrique Cardoso's government (1995–2002), and driven by the complex agenda of stabilization, market-friendly reforms, and the consolidation of democracy.

Early in the 1980s, the agenda of democratic transition conferred undeniable centrality on the social issue and the new Brazilian Constitution of 1988, to a large degree, reaffirmed the principles and content of the intended reforms.[64] Among the innovations, we should acknowledge the more comprehensive scope of the social protection system, by means both of the reinforcement of universal entitlements – as in health policy – and a relative slackening of the contributions link. In addition to the former, there was the establishment of a minimum value for benefits and the expansion of social rights to new groups, mainly rural workers. Decentralization has been an outstanding orientation. The social rights of some professional categories and mainly the civil servants have been strengthened at the same time.

However, the results of such reformist waves were contradictory. Although the new policies shifted the Brazilian DWS towards a more inclusive model, the egalitarian, universal concerns have proved incapable of challenging the corporative resilience to reduce or change special benefits. Mesa-Lago (1988) has labelled this *vertical massive expansion*, a pattern that extends social benefits to groups already protected and benefited. It could be said that such a pattern has oriented the described first reformist cycle, although some trends of *horizontal massive expansion* have also been observed. Perhaps here we can find one of the main limits of that reformist path, one that intended democratizing the social welfare system without changing the previous benefits distribution among different social categories. During the next decade, a period of declining resources and increasing demands, the strong expansion of social security expenditures, not exclusively but largely a consequence of the 1988 reforms, has shown the severe limits of such a strategy.

The *second reformist cycle*, the reform strategy of Cardoso's administration, focused on three broad and articulated purposes: to strengthen and improve the social impact of *universal public social services* (social security, health, education, welfare, housing and sanitation); to introduce, as a priority, *work, employment and income programmes*; and, thirdly, the *programme against poverty*. Main innovations and policy changes, mentioned earlier, have observed a quite homogeneous orientation, according to some strategic principles, mainly the articulation of universal and targeted programmes within universal parameters, the decentralization and the participatory decision making. Yet, the period registers an enormous affirmation of the social rights, in accordance with trends initiated in the preceding decade.

Notwithstanding the fact that authors disagree strongly on this evaluation (Sallum, 1999, 2003), accumulated evidences permit to say that, to some extent, the set of social policy changes of the 1990s have moved BDWS a little more towards a more inclusive trend. Clearly, the Neoliberal model of social reform, experimented with more or less in other Latin American countries, has not oriented the referred changes. In contrast to privatization trends, the social public programmes have been institutionally strengthened, meanwhile public social spending grew during the period, supported mainly by increasing fiscal pressures.[65] Therefore, the period cannot be considered being as a reaction to the reformist and democratizing movement of the 1980s (Draibe, 2002a, 2002b, 2003b).

Nevertheless, one cannot deny the negative effects of liberal economic policy on the institutions and capacities of the BDWS, through some well-known processes. The social costs of low growth, high rates of unemployment and poverty, on the one hand, and the weakening of state capacities, not only by the fiscal constraints, but also mainly for the lack of investments designed to maintain and expand social services. During its first 12 months, President Lula's government has not introduced significant changes in social policies it inherited from the previous government. As said, the 2003 reform of social security has continued the 1998 reforms, concentrating instead on polemic aspects set aside in the previous reforms.[66] Maybe there is a change in style, centralizing more decisions at the federal level. However, the greatest change has certainly been the centrality assigned to the focalized, pro-poor programmes, mainly cash benefits, led by the *Fome Zero* and *Bolsa Familia* programmes.[67]

In fact, writing in the third year of Lula's term, we could say that social policy has been reduced mainly to these programmes. *Bolsa Familia* registered a remarkable growth, reaching about nine million families, even supplanting the Fome Zero Program, which practically disappeared because of the government agenda.

## Conclusions and perspectives

Brazil is living through difficult, but exciting times. Once again, Brazilian society seems to have been placed in a juncture of possibilities, on a terrain of choices, whose central challenge is to resume economic growth, under a new democratic and socially inclusive pattern. Will it still have time for such a choice? Would conditions exist, allowing the country to choose such a development path? These times are particularly interesting in Brazil because, for the first time, the country has not only the economic conditions, but also the political chance for the creation of a new model of social policies, embedded in a developmental context.

As suggested in this chapter, Brazil may be considered a successful case of *late capitalist* development, under the aegis of that particular historic product, named here, following the insights of the essay, the *Twentieth Century Brazilian Developmentalist Welfare State model*. One that has successfully promoted the social incorporation of new social actors pushed by the industrialization, urbanization and modernization processes, during the last century – the urban wage-earning workers and middle-class sectors. A quite remarkable success has also been achieved in the plan of the social policies institutions. At the onset of the 1980s, the BDWS has been already nationwide completed, covering enormous clienteles, with social public spending reaching about 18 per cent of GDP.

Yet this chapter stressed the strong limits shown by the twentieth-century BDWS. As an intrinsic part of the *Estado Desenvolvimentista*, and developed under two dictatorial regimes, it has fulfilled social objectives, however, under the imperatives of economic growth. Mainly limited to the urban salaried sectors, the BDWS was neither democratic nor socially inclusive. In other terms, it has never been very effective in its capacity to promote equity. Not by chance, Brazil has arrived in the twenty-first century with one of the world's most unequal patterns of income distribution.

Perhaps this is the first lesson of this study of the past: that a new paradigm of development that associates growth, social cohesion and democracy, has to be defined from the start as growth with redistribution.

Economic growth is a possibility. Favourable conditions for a renewal of growth have been noted by many analysts, among them the fact that most of the industrial sector has not only withstood trade opening but has also adjusted, gaining in efficiency and competitiveness and redirecting itself towards exports. The conquest of relevant positions in the world market by Brazilian agribusiness has also been remarkable. On the other hand, because of more pragmatic and negotiating stances adopted during the second Cardoso and Lula governments, the fiscal situation now seems more comfortable.[68] Human capital has developed significantly as well, over the noted limitations.[69]

Thus, Brazil has been gradually taking advantage of windows of opportunity in the international markets and also of dynamic circuits of investment.[70] Such a process seems to be effectively supported by Brazilian foreign policy, which since the 1990s, through different orientations and inflexions, has tried to reinforce the stance of the country in the new international geometry, combining bilateral agreements with bloc accords such as Mercosur.

It is clearly in the political area that better conditions may be found for the implementation of a new model of growth with social inclusion. As stated above, the ongoing democratization process is deep and affects all institutions, as well as society as a whole. Already the expression of social demands affect the political and decision-making process, and this has led, moreover, to the election of President Lula and the wide popular movement that still supports his government. As Celso Furtado (2003) has said, the new developmental alternative depends less on the solution to economic problems through abstract models, and less on a special tolerance of the global centres of power, than on that foundation 'with popular roots, social roots . . . that democratically rooted public opinion . . . that will allow . . . for the transformation of Brazil based on the social rather than on economic forces' (Furtado, 2003: 1).

It seems unnecessary to stress that there are no automatic shortcuts on the path to a new development paradigm. There are projects and choices, which must be followed in the midst of difficult conditions, as emphasized in the text. On the other hand, it is well known that historical opportunities may be lost, over omissions or bad choices. Present times are exciting exactly because the possibilities are still open.

## Notes

1. *Capitalismo Tardio* refers to the industrialization pattern characterized by a double determination: the *starting point* – the insertion of the country in the international labour division as colonies and, after, as export-oriented economies – and the industrialization take-off moment – the monopolistic stage of international capitalism. It is different, therefore, from both the *original industrialization* and the *late industrializations* (economies with a feudal past, whose industrialization process is undertaken during the competitive stage of capitalism).
2. Social funds mean some special resources generated by mean of a special tax or social contribution, created explicitly to funding a specific sector of social provision. Funds can be classified according to three types: social security fund; workers' asset funds, as the Fundo de Garantia de Tempo de Serviço (FGTS), supporting the policy housing, or the patrimonial funds (PIS/PASEP) and the Fundo de Apoio do Trabalhador (FAT), supporting unemployment-insurance and training programmes; and, thirdly, contributions linked to specific social programmes, such as the FINSOCIAL or the Education Salary.
3. Spending on public salaries ranks Brazil at 58th out of among 64 compared countries, according to OECD figures. Brazilian public employment participation in total employment is the lowest, apart from Japan (7.3 per cent), while it is 37.6 per cent in Norway, 20.1 per cent in Canada, 18.9 per cent in the United Kingdom, 17.7 per cent in Spain, 16 per cent in USA and 8.4 per cent in Colombia. Brazilian public employment in percentage terms of the whole population is higher than Greece (4.7 per cent), Mexico (4.3 per cent), Turkey (3.9 per cent), and Japan (3.6 per cent) only (OECD, 1994).
4. Beside taxes, the resources come also from the Education Salary, a compulsory contribution of 2.5 per cent on payroll. Spending in education is mandatory as a proportion of resources, varying from to 18 per cent to Union to 25 per cent for states and municipalities.
5. States and municipalities share the responsibility for primary and secondary schooling, and municipalities are the main providers of pre-school education
6. Adult schooling is, on average, less than six years. The rate of primary education completion is low, about 50 per cent of students that have initiated the primary cycle. Bad quality it seems to be the Achilles' heel within the educational system.
7. Since the 1970, under contract, the private providers share the *public provision of health services* in a significant way, mainly in hospital facilities, where its participation is about 70 per cent of all services.
8. A new and specific tax was created in 1996, and a constitutional amendment, in 2000, has enforced a minimum expenditure of 17 per cent of income in all state and municipal governments.
9. In 1998 the *Family Health Program* (*PSF – Programa de Saúde da Família*) was created, a strategy to implement community health care. It also introduced the per capita as the new criteria for resource allocation.
10. Social assistance programmes started as a nationwide and institutionalized form in the early 1940s, marked by centralized decision-making, fragmented actions, glaring ineffectiveness and, above all, strong levels of clientelism and patronage.
11. Curiously, during Cardoso's term, the law that created the Poverty Fund was an initiative of the opposition forces led by the conservative former senator Antonio Carlos Magalhães, with the support of the Workers' Party. Until then, President Cardoso's administration had deliberately resisted the emergency

fund and social network model for fighting poverty, which had been widely disseminated in Latin America in the 1980s.

12. The urban benefits plan covers all of the classic risks. Unemployment insurance was created only in 1988. Pensions ages vary between gender (65 years for men, 60 for women). Public civil servants have their own pension schemes and until the 2003 reform, the reposition rate was about 100 per cent; cumulative pensions are allowed in some special cases and legislation is permissive regarding retired labour activity.
13. Contributions vary between 8 and 11 per cent of employees' salary (20 per cent for the self-employed) and 22 per cent over the total payroll for employers, in the urban sector. Rural workers are exempt, while rural employers are taxed at 2.5 per cent on the amount of the first harvest sale. In 2000, rural social security covered 7.2 million retirees.
14. There are two main forms of complementary funds: 'Closed' Private Pension Funds and 'Open' Private Pension Funds. In 1997, the beneficiaries of both systems amounted to 10.7 per cent of the total number of beneficiaries of public schemes, while its contributors represented only 6.8 per cent of all those insured.
15. End of the length-of-service criteria; of proportional pensions (5 years before retirement age, with up to 30 per cent reduction of full pension benefits) and of special pensions for certain occupations, except for basic and secondary education teachers. Special pensions for occupations involving risk activities remain, as well as the social security factor to calculate pensions in the private sector. Although signs were given that rules would follow market criteria and individual responsibility for risks, the public system of uniform sharing was maintained.
16. The more controversial measure has been the extension of mandatory social contribution to retirees.
17. Between 1965 and 1986, the BNH system produced about 4.5 million housing units, of which only about 20 per cent were designed for low-income families.
18. The restriction refers overall to the strong external constraints and critical bottlenecks, notably in transportation and energy supplies.
19. Corresponding to voluminous and timing-concentrated investments undertaken during the presidency of Juscelino Kubistchek.
20. In the democratic period of 1945–1965, Brazilian rulers were the following: Marechal Eurico Dutra (1945–1949); Getúlio Vargas (1951–1954); Juscelino Kubistchek (1955–1959); Jânio Quadros (1960–1961) and Jango Goulart (1961–1964). Elected through free elections, in 1950, Vargas did not complete its term, as he committed suicide in 1954, President Jânio Quadros resigned before completing the term and the vice-president Jango Goulart was overthrown by a military coup in 1964.
21. During the periods of the military dictatorship, Brazil has been governed by General Humberto Castelo Branco (1964–67); General Arthur da Costa e Silva (1967–69); General Emílio Garrastazu Médici (1969–74); General Ernesto Geisel (1974–79) and General Joâo B. Figueiredo (1979–85).
22. In the democratic period, Brazilian civil presidents were the following: José Sarney (1985–1990); Collor de Mello (1990–1992); Itamar Franco (1992–1994); Fernando Henrique Cardoso (1995–1998, 1999–2002) and Luiz Ignácio *Lula* da Silva (2003–2006).
23. In 1985, the first year of the first post-authoritarian civil government, the economy grew at a rate of 8.3 per cent, but inflation surpassed the monthly average of 45 per cent.

24. Collor de Mello, a charismatic political outsider from a dominant family in a rural Northeast state, resigned to avoid being impeached for corruption after serving only two years of his four-year term.
25. Inflation fell from an annual rate of 10,445 per cent to about 6 per cent, in the first year of the Plans Real.
26. Economic reforms included commercial opening, private bank restructuring, the privatization of larger state-based companies (mainly in the sectors of steel and ironworks, telecommunications and electricity), the (de)monopolization of state oil production, administrative reforms, as well a partial reform of social security. In addition, some flexibility measurers were introduced in labour regulations.
27. Agreeing the FMI, the Brazilian state has faced the rapid growth of the external public debt by running an annual average 3.6 per cent of primary fiscal surplus (the fiscal surplus before debt service payments) between 1999 and 2002.
28. The sharp (de)industrialization process could be indicated by the loss of about two million jobs in the manufacturing sector, between 1990 and 2000.
29. Between 1996 and 2002, the average real income of the workers has fallen by 12.3 per cent.
30. Between 1880 and 1980, no country other than Japan has grown more than Brazil. During the twentieth century, Brazilian GDP increased a hundred old, while population grew less than 10 times. In the period 1901–2000, the per capita GDP has increased 12 times, comparable only in international terms to Japan, Thailand, Finland, Norway and Korea. By contrast, the recent period of low growth has ranked Brazil lower than countries it was previously out performing. For instance, while in, 1980 the Korean per capita income corresponded to 63 per cent of the Brazilian one, in 2000 it was 2.55 times higher.
31. The annual average growth rates, by periods, were the followings: 7.6 per cent in 1945–50; 6.7 per cent in 1950–55; 8.1 per cent in both the periods 1955–60 and 1965–1970 and 10.3 per cent in 1970–1975. In the postwar period, the lower growth rate, of 4.3 per cent, corresponded to the period 1960–1965. In the period 1968–1973, industry's growth rates varied, according to sector, between 12 and 18 per cent.
32. The per capita GDP growth rate has been positive but modest in the years 2000 (2.99 per cent), 2001 (0.10 per cent) and 2002 (0.60 per cent) and negative in the years 1998 (−1.21 per cent), 1999 (−0.52 per cent), and 2003 (−1.5 per cent).
33. Between the 1950s and 1970s, urban employment has grown about 12 per cent annually while the unemployment rate followed its historical level, between 2 and 3 per cent of working labour.
34. In figures from 2001, about 85 per cent of households owned colour TVs and refrigerators, while roughly 62 per cent owned telephones. Household public services have evolved slowly, the water public system reaching about 80 per cent of household, while the public sewage system reached only around 50 per cent.
35. The poverty rate grew from about 20 to 30 per cent between the 1980s and the mid-1990s, before dropping bach to today's figure of around 20 per cent of the population.
36. The 0.50 Gini index of 1960 climbs to 0.58, 0.59, 0.63, and 0.59, respectively, in the years 1970, 1980, 1990, and 2000. In 1960, the income of the richest 10 per cent of the population was 34 times higher that of the income of the poorest 10 per cent, and in 1991, 60 times higher. In the year 2001, while the poorest 20 per cent shared 2 per cent of the income, the richest 10 per cent shared 46.7 per cent.

37. While a 25-year-old young black person has an average of 6.1 years of schooling, a young white of the same age has, on average, 8.4 years of schooling. This difference of 2.3 years is practically the same as existed between his parents and grandparents.
38. Since the late nineteenth century – in order to substitute the former slaves in coffee plantations – until roughly the 1960s, external immigration has been such a decisive demographic process in the country, pushed by the state policy to populate and develop rural areas and certain regions, mainly the South and Southeast. Internal migration started around in the 1930s, and there has been an increasing population movement since then, in three main directions: from the poorer Northeast/North to Southeast/South richer regions, from countryside to urban areas and into new areas of agriculture.
39. Since the 1940s, three main agricultural frontier expansions have attracted enormous number of peoples: coffee plantation in the far Southeast region (Paraná), between 1940 and 1960; the Amazonian frontier, open until now; and the Centre-East frontier, corresponding to the export-driven soybean plantations as well as the 'cerrado' agriculture exploration.
40. Although there is no general consensus about meanings and periods, it could be said that *Estado Novo* refers to both the new state form that has followed the Oligarchic State (1891–1930) and also the authoritarian and after the dictatorial Vargas both regimes (1930–1937 and 1937–1945). Concerning the broad period 1930–1985, the concept of *Estado Desenvolvimentista* is a more general one, corresponding to the special type of state that has led, pursued and implementing economic and social development strategies in most Latin American countries under different political regimes and ideological orientations. More ambiguously, the concept of Populism would be simultaneously concerned attached to a political regime, or a political ideology or yet a type of state, the common understanding would being the clientelistic–patronage–corporatist relationship, the key political mechanism operating in a semi-or non-institutionalized political system and restricted democratic regimes. Brazilian political science studies apply the term *populist democracy* to the limited democratic regime from 1945 to the military coup of 1964. In this chapter, we use the term *Vargas Era* to refer to the broad populist period from 1930 to 1964.
41. Authors emphasized five types of cultures and the respective family structure. In the Northeast and North regions, the 'crioula' (developed by the colonial patriachal family and the slave families) and the 'cabloca' (in the North region, formed by indigeneous natives and non-voluntary immigrants like the African slaves). Both of these sub-cultures, 'cabloca' and 'crioula,' are characterized by an authoritarian and patriarchal social system emphasizing group norms and group loyalty, in a vertical-collectivist cultural pattern. In Southeast and South regions, the 'caipira' and the 'gaucha' cultures, formed by descendants of the large European immigration of the seventeenth and eighteenth centuries, especially Italians and Germans. The first sub-culture, 'caipira', was devoted to coffee farms in the nineteenth century and has subsequently become modern, urban and industrialized, while the second, 'gaúcha', continues to be devoted to cattle production. In both types, a vertical-individualist cultural pattern, which does not sanction but recognizes and accepts the prevalent inequality. The 'sertaneja' culture flourished in the inland part of the Northeast as well as in the savannas of central Brazil (Dessen and Torres, 2002: 2).

42. The racial question is an enormous and disputed one, shaped by several myths, one of them, widely disseminated, is that of racial brotherhood, linked to the benevolent tradition of the Portuguese colonizers, thought to be immune to racial prejudice as they intermingled freely with Indians and blacks.
43. Local governments in the larger cities provided intermittent and insufficient public assistance to the poor and indigent sectors of the population. The primary education system of the *Old Republic* (1889–1930) was more consistent, but its implementation was the responsibility of state governments, each with a high degree of autonomy to define its educational policy. Some elements of such a health policy could eventually be found; however, they were limited to hygienist and preventive public health measures and to some large cities in the export-oriented regions. In the social insurance arena, the first initiatives, in the 1910s, take place outside of the state, led by mutual-aid associations according the anarchist tradition brought by immigrants. Incipient and highly limited legislation in the 1920s regulated the so-called *Caixas de Aposentadorias e Pensões* (Retirement Agencies).
44. The *tenentismo* began in the early 1920s and played a significant role in the 1930 Revolution. Widely understood as the expression of the urban middle classes dissatisfaction with the Oligarchic State, the *tenentismo* provided the *Estado Novo* with their main values orientation with respect to its state and nationalist ideology. Luiz Carlos Prestes, the Brazilian Communist Party leader, has been a *tenente* in the 1920s, having led one of the more prolonged revolts of that time.
45. Representing the interests of local and regional conservative sectors, the Social Democratic Party (PSD) has been effective in organizing 'coronelismo', that is to say, the system of patronage that channels votes for the government and at the same time permitted the access of rural chieftains (the typical 'coroneles'), to governmental benefits. A similar structure of co-optation was developed in the urban areas, through the Labour Party (PTB), to which Vargas affiliated himself. His instrument of political control was the Ministry of Labour and the trade unions, which were politically and financially dependent upon the government (Schwartzman, 1973)
46. That is to say, in the industrialization first phase (1933–56), the intensive use of incentives, subsidies and state controls over the exchange rate have been important in order to protect domestic industry However, in order to address the investments in infrastructure, in steel, oil, energy, transportation and other fields, large amounts of capital and modern technology were indispensable
47. Although foreign-capital-friendly, in the JK *associated strategy* the space for the future expansion of large and medium domestic capital has been relatively preserved, as has the leading role of state companies, mainly in the infrastructure sectors.
48. The union structure was organized according the following principles: the *unicidade sindical*, that is, only one union per category of worker in a given territory; the institutional *verticalidade*, meaning a vertical and hierarchical structure, ranging from the local union (municipal) through state federations and national confederations; and the *imposto sindical*, that is, a mandatory union tax on earnings, collected directly by companies, after being channelled to unions by the state.
49. Until the 1930s, social rights were, in practice, limited to primary education.
50. Good examples of such strategies are the large economic complexes created around the Housing Finance System (*Sistema Financeiro Habitacional – SFH*) and

the Health Insurance/Social Security Complex (*Complexo Médico-Previdenciário*). Through a dense articulation between private companies and state resources, very well articulated by an intense and entrenched network of interest groups and bureaucracies, funding required by the private sector have became available, in such a volume that it made possible the creation of Brazilian civil construction industry as well as the medical-pharmaceutical one.

51. The JK years are renowned for the optimism and euphoria generated by economic growth, the new investments either in industrial plants or highways, the construction of Brasília, and, over all, the new cultural avant-garde, from Bossa Nova to the Cinema Novo. The consumption pattern of the high middle sectors was likely to reach a turning point, pushed by the key consurption items, cars and televisions.
52. During the 1980s, it has been an exponential growth of social movements, grass-roots organizations, NGOs, neighbourhood and self-help organizations, middle-class professional associations, as well as the new labour unions, such as the Central Workers Union (*Central Única dos Trabalhadores* or *CUT*, pushed by the PT) and the General Workers Union (*Central General dos Trabalhadores* or *CGT*).
53. Starting in 1983, the *Diretas Já* campaign has been a mass movement against military rule, demanding the restoration of direct elections, which was, however, not achieved. In 1992, the *Movement for Ethics in Politics* has mobilized the whole of the country through street demonstrations in favour of the impeachment of President Collor de Mello.
54. As argued, market-friendly reforms could be delayed due to the success of the Brazilian IS process; a not well-defined constituency of economic reforms until the late 1980s; Brazil's sophisticated system of indexing inflation, allowing considerable protection for all society's groups, except the poorer and less organized ones; and difficulties in implementing reform policy due to Brazil's chaotic political system.
55. The military regime was support by the PDS – Democratic Social Party (before ARENA, Alliance for the National Renovation), while the oppositionist forces integrated the PMDB (before, the MDB). In 1984 dissidents of the PDS created the PFL. The PMDB was, in fact, a great political front shared by conservative as well progressive forces, encompassing social movements, intellectual and technical activists and so on. Since the liberalization process was initiated, successive groups and movements have separated from the PMDB, originating other parties, among them the Workers' Party, President Lula's PT, created in 1980, and President Cardoso's PSDB (Party of Brazilian Social Democracy), created in 1986.
56. *Plano Cruzado* was broadly supported by a highly mobilized society. Over nine months, activist groups were committed with daily verification of the *frozen* prices, however they were 'unfrozen' immediately after the elections, in a clear political manipulation of the electorate.
57. Sharing the ruling party PMDB during President José Sarney's administration (1985–89), the Developmentist coalition has became each time weaker after the failures of the successive heterodox stabilization plans, starting with the *Plano Cruzado* in 1986. Cardoso's candidate in the 2002 elections, José Serra, its former Planning, and Health Minister, was an outstanding leader of the liberal Developmentalist group, known for its open disagreement with the economic authorities. Not surprisingly, only few and secondary differences could be found between Lulay's and Serra's electoral programs.

58. Although participating in all governmental alliances until 2002, the PFL has lost confidence as a consequence of both the disastrous President Collor government it has supported and its failure to indicating the governing alliance's candidate to the presidential elections of 2002.
59. An inclination that had become clear through the choosing of both the vice-president, coming from a conservative party, and the economic ministries and authorities, recruited mainly from financial community.
60. Under the media image of Lula, Peace and Love, the PT presidential campaign tried to reconcile strong criticism of the Cardoso government with a discourse that was not in the least radical, nor statism, together with and emphasis in values of *good governance* (such as efficient and responsible management), as well as the tolerance and conciliation of interests.
61. The imminent victory of Lula, as may be remembered, launched a serious speculative attack against Brazil in the two months precededing his election. This has accelerated a new agreement with IMF, signed by the Cardoso government with the support of all the then presidential candidates.
62. Growth has only recently started to accelerate. In fact, rigid inflationary targets, mounting interest rates, and the (voluntary) increase in fiscal surplus, precipitated the 2003 recession, along with a severe lowering in incomes for middle and salaried segments of the population. In addition to the 2003 reform of social security motivated especially by fiscal reasons, public expenditures stayed in very low levels, compromising public investments and affecting especially the social sectors.
63. Notorious in the effort to widen the ruling coalition, as well as in the 'pragmatic' policy of alliances with which PT has confronted municipal elections of 2004.
64. Strong social mobilization has accompanied the Constitutional Assembly works, encompassing opinion groups, social professional categories, stakeholders, and also the bureaucratic strata related to social areas,
65. The fiscal burden grew from 25 per cent of GDP, in the mid-1990s, to 32.9 per cent in 2000, reaching 35.8 per cent in 2002.
66. Especially the restrictions in the system of public functionaries, and the introduction of compulsory contributions of retirees.
67. *Fome Zero* has been the key programme of the electoral campaign and the first six months of President Lula' s government. The programme brings together a wide range of programmes addressed to the needs of the poor, mainly those involving food distribution. Its success is undeniable as far as an international trademark of the government that continues to use it even though the programme itself has been overcome in practical terms. The *Bolsa Familiaon* is a wide-ranging cash benefit distribution programme, for poor families, and has resulted from the unification of several already existing ones, inherited from the previous government, such as *Bolsa Escola*.
68. As indicated in the reduction of the debt to GDP ratio from 58 per cent in 2002 to 53 per cent in 2004.
69. During the 1980s and 1990s human capital grew 3.7 and 1.5 times faster than GDP. Since the 1970s, the percentage of the population with eight or more years schooling has jumped from 8 per cent up to 35 per cent.
70. With regard to internationalized services, some areas of Brazil, especially around the metropolitan region of Sao Paulo, seem to have been transformed into, an offshoring zone for multinational corporations.

## References


Andrade, R. C. (1982). 'Política social e normalização institucional no Brasil', in Maira, L. de Souza, J.H., Andrade, R.C., Portantiero J.C. and Barraza (eds). *América Latina: Novas Estratégias de Dominação*. Vozes/São Paulo/Cedec, Petrópolis.

Armijo, L. (2003). *Mass Democracy: The Real Reason that Brazil Ended Inflation?* http://www.mindspring.com/~leslie.armijo/03massdemoc.pdf.

Arretche, M. (2004). 'The Politics of Health Care Reform in Brazil', in R. Kauffman and J. Nelson (eds), *Crucial Needs, Weak Incentives: Social Sector Reform, Democratization, and Globalization in Latin America*. Washington: Wilson Center Press.

Arretche, M. (2000). *Estado federativo e políticas sociais*. Rio de Janeiro: Editora Revan.

Avritzer, L. (2003). *Can President Lula Redeem Democracy in Latin America?*, http://www.bostonreview.net/BR28.3/avritzer.html.

Cardoso, F. H. (1974). *Autoritarismo e democratização*. Rio de Janeiro: Editora Paz e Terra.

Cardoso de Mello, J. M. (1982). *O Capitalismo Tardio*. São Paulo: Ed. Brasiliense.

Cardoso de Mello, J. M. and Novais F. (1998). 'Capitalismo Tardio e Sociabilidade Moderna', in L.M. Schwarcz (ed.), *História da Vida Privada no Brasil*. São Paulo: Cia. das Letras Editora.

Carvalho, J. M. (2000). *The Strugle for Democracy in Brazil: Some Lessons to Nigeria*. http://www.iisg.nl/~sephis/pdf/murilo.pdf.

Dessen, M. A. and Torres C. (2002). 'Family and Socialization Factors in Brazil: An Overview'. *Online Readings in Psychology and Culture*. Center for Cross-Cultural Research, Western Washington University, Bellingham, Washington. http://www.wwu.edu/~culture.

Diniz, E. (1994). 'Empresariado, regime autoritário e modernização capitalista: 1964–1985', in Soares G. and D'Araújo C. (eds). *21 anos de Regime Militar: balanços e perspectivas*. Rio de Janeiro: Fundação Getúlio Vargas.

Diniz, E. and Boschi R. (2002). *Strategies and Concerns of Brazilian Entrepreneurial Elites: Domestic and Multinational Interests*. Paper presented at the workshop *'Changing Nature of Business–State Relations in Brazil: Strategies of Foreign and Domestic Capital'*, Centre for Brazilian Studies, Oxford University.

Draibe, S. M. (2004). 'Federal Leverage in a Decentralized System: Education Reform in Brazil', in R. Kauffman and J. Nelson (eds), *Crucial Needs, Weak Incentives: Social Sector Reform, Democratization, and Globalization in Latin America*. Washington: Wilson Center Press.

Draibe, S. M. (2003). 'A política social do governo FHC e o sistema de proteção social'. *Revista Tempo Social*, 15, 2. Dossiê Fernando Henrique Cardoso (1999–2002). November 2003, USP, São Paulo. pp. 64–101.

Draibe, S. M. (2002a). *Brasil 1980–2000: proteção e insegurança sociais em tempos difíceis*. Paper presented at the Taller Inter-Regional Protección Social en una Era Insegura: Un Intercambio Sur-Sur sobre Políticas Sociales Alternativas en Respuesta a la Globalización. Santiago de Chile, PNUD/ Cenda, 13–14 May. http://videos.cep.cl:16080/sw2002/Informe_Brasil/SW2002_Brasil_Informe.doc

Draibe, S. M. (2002b). 'The Brazilian Welfare State in Perspective: Old Issues, new Possibilities', in J. P. Dixon and R. Scheurell (eds), *The State of Social Welfare: The Twentieth Century in Cross-National Review*. London: Praeger Publishers.

Draibe, S. M. (2002c). 'Social policies in the Nineties', in Renato Baumann (ed.), *Brazil in the 1990s – An Economy in Transition*. St Antony's Series. New York: Palgrave.

Draibe, S. M. (1998). 'La reciente descentralización de la política brasileña de enseñanza básica y de salud', in R. Cominnetti and E. Di Gropello (eds), *La descentralización de la educación y de la salud: un análisis comparativo de la experiencia latinoamericana.* Santiago de Chile: CEPAL/ECLAC.

Draibe, S. M. (1994). 'As políticas sociais do regime militar brasileiro,' in G. Soares and C. D'Araújo (eds), *21 anos de Regime Militar: balanços e perspectivas.* Rio de Janeiro: Fundação Getúlio Vargas.

Draibe, S. M. (1985). *Rumos e Metamorfoses. Um estudo sobre a constituição do Estado e as alternativas da Industrialização no Brasil 1930–1960.* Rio de Janeiro: Ed. Paz e Terra.

Draibe, S. M. and Aureliano L. (1989). *A especifidade do Welfare State brasileiro. Economia e Desenvolvimento 3.* Brasília: CEPAL.

Draibe, S. M. and Matijascic M. (2001). 'The Market Orientation of Social Security: The Brazilian Case', in J. Dixon and M. Hyde (eds), *The Marketization of Social Security.* New York: Quorum Books.

ECLAC (2004). *Statistical Yearbook.* http://www.cepal.cl.

Esping-Andersen, G. (1990). *The Three Worlds of Welfare Capitalism.* Princeton: Princeton University Press.

Furtado, C. (2003).'Entrevista Explosiva'. *Caros Amigos no. 71.* São Paulo, February.

Furtado, C.(1982). *Brazil – A construção interrompida.* Rio de Janeiro: Ed. Paz e Terra.

Gordon, L. (2001). *Brazil's Second Chance.* Washington: Brookings Institute Press.

Gough, I. (1999). *Welfare Regimes: On Adapting the Framework to Developing Countries.* Global Social Policy Programme. Working Paper 1. Bath: University of Bath.http://www.bath.ac.uk/Faculties/HumSocSci/IFIPA/GSP/.

Gough, I. (2001). 'Globalization and Regional Welfare Regimes: the East Asian Case'. *Global Social Policy,* 1, 163–89.

Henriques, R. (2001). *A cor da (in)justiça social.* http:// www.consciencia.net/ cidadania/ arquivo01/ negros2.html.

Intituto Brasileiro de Geografia e Estatística (IBGE). (2003). *Estatísticas do Século 20.* Rio de Janeiro: IBGE.

Jacobi, P. (1989). *Movimentos Sociais e Políticas Públicas.* São Paulo: Cortez Editora.

Jardim Pinto, C. R. (2004). *Neo populism in Brazilian Politics: the rapid exhaustion of a model; Núcleo de Pesquisa e Documentação da Política Rio-Grandense.* http://www.tche.br/nupergs/celi.html.

Kingstone, P. R. (1998). *Political Continuity versus Social Change: The Sustainability of Neoliberal Reform in Brazil.* Nafta: Law and Business Review of the Americas. April http://vm.uconn.edu/~kingston/Sust.html.

Kuhnle, S. (2002). *Productive Welfare in Korea: Moving Towards a European Welfare State Type?* Paper. Torino: ECPR Joint Sessions of Workshops.

Kwon, H.-j. (2003). *Transforming the Developmental Welfare State: A Comparative Study of the East Asian Countries.* Project Proposal. Geneva: UNRISD.

Kwon, H.-j. (2002). *The Economic Crisis and the Politics of Welfare Reform in Korea.* Background paper for the UNRISD Proyect Social Policy in a Development Context. Geneva: UNRISD.

Leite Cardoso, R. (1983). 'Movimentos Sociais Urbanos: Balanço Crítico', in M. H. Tavares and B. Sorg (eds), *Sociedade e Política no Brazil Pós – 64.* São Paulo: Editora Brasiliense.

Lessa, C. F. (1978). *A estratégia de Desenvolvimento 1974–1976. Sonho e Fracasso.* Doctoral Thesis presented at the Federal University of Rio de Janeiro, Rio de Janeiro.

Medeiros, C. (2002). *Economic Growth, Poverty and Income Distribution in Brazil.* Paper presented at the Conference 'New Ideas on Development Economics Growth and Distribution Under Financial Globalization'. Rio de Janeiro, 28–29, January. http:// www.networkideas.org/ themes/ inequality/ jan2002/ print/ prnt280102_Brazil.htm.

Medici, A. (2002). *El Desafío de la Descentralización: Financiamiento Público de la Salud en Brasil.* Working paper. Washington: BID.

MRE (2004). Ministério das Relações Exteriores. *Foreign Economic Connexions.* http://www.mre.gov.br/acs/diplomacia/ingles/h_diplom/gm017i.htm.

OECD (1994). *Sources statistiques sur l'emploi dans le secteur public – 1994.* Paris: Les Editions de l'OCDE.

Power, T. and Doctor, M. (2002). *The Resilience of Corporatism: Continuity and Change in Brazilian Corporatist Structures.* Working Papers Series. Centre for Brazilian Studies. Oxford: University of Oxford.

Sallum, B. (2003a). 'Metamorfosoes do Estado Brasileiro no final do Século 20'. *Revista Brasileira de Ciências Sociais* 18(52) 35–54.

Sallum, B. (ed.). (2003b). *Revista Tempo Social.* Dossiê Fernando Henrique Cardoso 1999–2002, 15, 2. November. São Paulo: USP.

Sallum, B. (ed.). (1999). *Revista Tempo Social.* Dossiê Fernando Henrique Cardoso 1995–1998, 11, 2. São Paulo: USP.

Sallum, B. and Kugelmas E. (2003).*Governo Lula – continuidade, avanço ou regressão?* La Insignia, July 2003. http://www.lainsignia.org/2003/julio/ibe_019.htm.

Santos, W. G. (1979). *Cidadania e justiça.* Rio de Janeiro: Editora Campus.

Schwartzman, S. (1973). 'Twenty Years of Representative Democracy in Brazil, 1945–1964', in H. Alker, K. Deutsch and A. Stoetzel (eds), *Mathematical Approaches to Politics.* Amsterdam: Elsevier Scientific Publishing Co.

Tavares de Almeida, M. H. (1998). *Negociando a reforma: a privatização de empresas públicas no Brasil.* Paper presented at the 21st Congress of ANPOCS. 22–25 October. Caxambu, Brazil.

Tavares, M. C. (2003). *O século XX Brasileiro.* Folha de São Paulo. 12 October.

Tavares, M. C. (1972). *Da substituição de importações ao Capitalismo Financeiro.* Rio de Janeiro: Zahar Ed.

Titmuss, R. (1958). *Essays on the Welfare State.* London: Allen and Unwin.

Weffort, F. (1968). 'O populismo na política Brasileira', in C. Furtado (ed.), *Brasil, tempos modernos.* Rio de Janeiro: Editora Paz e Terra.

World Bank. (2004). *Partners in Development: Progress in the Fight against Poverty.* Washington DC: World Bank.

# Appendix 6.A: Tables

*Table 6.A1* Brazil: demographic indicators, 1940–2003

| *Years* | *1940* | *1950* | *1960* | *1970* | *1980* | *1991* | *2000* | *2003* |
|---|---|---|---|---|---|---|---|---|
| Population (in millions) | 41.2 | 51.9 | 70.0 | 93.1 | 119.0 | 146.8 | 169.8 | 178.0* |
| Population Growth annual average rate | 1.49 | 2.39 | 2.99 | 2.89 | 2.48 | 1.93 | 1.63 | |
| % urban population | 31.2 | 36.16 | 44.67 | 55.92 | 67.59 | 75.59 | 81.25 | |

*Source*: IBGE (2003). *projection

*Table 6.A2* Brazil: GDP annual growth rate, 1980–2003

| | | | | | | | | | | |
|---|---|---|---|---|---|---|---|---|---|---|
| *Year* | *1980* | *1981* | *1982* | *1983* | *1984* | *1985* | *1986* | *1987* | *1988* | *1989* |
| Tax | 9.2 | (4.25) | 0.83 | (2.93) | 5.4 | 7.85 | 7.49 | 3.53 | 0.06 | 3.16 |
| *Year* | *1990* | *1991* | *1992* | *1993* | *1994* | *1995* | *1996* | *1997* | *1998* | *1999* |
| Tax | (4.35) | 1.03 | (0.54) | 4.92 | 5.85 | 4.22 | 2.66 | 3.27 | 0.13 | 0.81 |
| *Year* | *2000* | *2001* | *2002* | *2003* | | | | | | |
| Tax | 4.36 | 2.25 | 1.93 | −0.2 | | | | | | |

*Source*: IBGE (2003).

*Table 6.A3* Brazil: some labour market indicators, 1990–2002

| *Indicators* | *1990* | *1991* | *1992* | *1993* | *1994* | *1995* | *1996* | *1997* | *1998* | *1999* | *2000* | *2001* | *2002* |
|---|---|---|---|---|---|---|---|---|---|---|---|---|---|
| Earnings in GDP % | 45 | 42 | 44 | 45 | 40 | 38 | 39 | 37 | 38 | 37 | | | |
| Unemployment tax | 4.3 | 4.8 | 5.7 | 5.3 | 5.1 | 4.6 | 5.4 | 5.7 | 7.6 | 7.6 | 7.1 | 6.2 | 7.5 |
| Salaried workers as % of EAP | 48.8 | 49.0 | 48.2 | — | 40.7 | 40.4 | — | 40.5 | — | 40.4 | 40.3 | 39.3 | — |

*Source*: IBGE (2003).

*Table 6.A4* Brazil: household goods and public facilities, 1960–2002

| *Household/Years* | *1960* | *1970* | *1980* | *1991* | *2001/2* |
|---|---|---|---|---|---|
| % public sewage system | 13.9 | 17.5 | 27.7 | 35.3 | 50 |
| % water public system | 21.0 | 32.8 | 54.9 | 70.7 | 77.6 |
| Colour TV | | | | 46.7 | 83.0 |
| Refrigerator | | | | 71.3 | 85.1 |
| Fixed telephone | | | | 19 | 61.6 |
| Cell phone | | | | | 31 |

*Source*: IBGE (2003).

# 7
# Social Policies in Cuba within the Context of Development (1902–2002)

*Dr Julio A. Díaz Vázquez and Dr Julio Carranza Valdés*

## Introduction

On 20 May 1902, the Republic of Cuba was officially and internationally acknowledged and recognized as a state. It had been the last Spanish colony in America to gain independence and had to establish its republican institutions based on a heritage of four centuries of slave work. The new Republic had first to overcome the destruction wrought by the war of independence (1895–98) in order to reorganize the national economy and implement and assimilate the political practices related to the social order constituted with the Republic.

Thus, for Cuba the beginning of the twentieth century turned out to be a unique historical, economic, and social experience. The newborn Republic also had to accept the growing hegemonic policies of the United States in this hemisphere. In political terms, the Cuban Constitution of 1901 had to admit the right of intervention by the US (until 1934) whenever that country deemed it necessary, and it also had to agree not to apply for foreign loans that would put the capacity of the national budget at risk. In economic terms, with the Treaty of Commercial Reciprocity (1902–34), the island's market became tied to the US market as initiatives to implement policies for industrializing the country were totally blocked.

Over the course of the twentieth century the Cuban economy has suffered three great upheavals. The first occurred when the sugar industry, the only important production sector in the economy, collapsed between 1926 and 1933. The second happened, in 1959, when the triumph of the revolution brought about political, economic and social changes aimed at the creation and strengthening of new relations of social production and human coexistence. The third was triggered by the collapse of the Eastern European socialist bloc and the disappearance of the former Soviet Union (1989–91). When this happened the island lost what had been its main international economic partner for more than 30 years. These events revealed the inefficiencies in the use of production resources, which, together with the tightening of the blockade by the United States, led to the deepest and most complex economic crisis in the last 50 years.

Within the context of the different alternatives of economic development and social policies implemented in the whole twentieth century in Cuba, two great periods are readily identifiable. During the first phase social policies implemented by governments were characterized by private property, predominantly mercantile economy, including private health care services, education and social security. Under this regime, the social policies implemented were insufficient, both in quantity and in quality, and at the same time they were subject to administrative corruption.

By contrast, the Revolutionary Government led to a second stage, where private, mercantile activity disappears from all major social services, and an integrated free and universal system for educational, health care and social security services was established.

Taking as a starting point the previous attempts of economic development and the implementation of corresponding social policies, we have divided this chapter into six chronological periods between 1902 and 2002. We start with a brief summary of the colonial period and the US intervention in the island. Second, for the period 1926–33 we consider the implementation of political, military, and economic instruments that shaped the colonial model. The period 1934–58 was devoted to overcoming economic stagnation and pursuing policies of agricultural and industrial diversification. Social policies were implemented throughout these periods.

The period starting in 1959 is divided into three stages. Between 1959 and 1970 deep socioeconomic changes took place, the most important among them being the two acts of agrarian reform, the nationalization of the main means of production and, especially, a strategy aimed at economic development mostly in the agricultural sector and other related industries, with a paricular emphasis on the sugar industry. During this stage, a new system of free social services and social security was introduced, along with active policies to try and tackle the problem of unemployment.

Between 1971 and 1989, the changes that occurred in the society and the economy gave momentum to industrial development within the context of Cuba's participation and inclusion in the integrated socialist economic community. Finally, our analysis of the last decade of the past century and the beginning of the new millennium (1990–2002) will consider the challenges the island faces at present in economic and social sectors. However, even during the most critical moments, the top priority has always been placed on social development. The major economic and social achievements are explained through statistical tables and charts.

## Colonial legacy and US intervention 1899–1902

On 1 January 1899, Spanish rule in Cuba officially came to an end, after more than 400 years. The Treaty of Paris, signed on December 10, 1898, which had ended the Spanish–Cuban–US War, by decreed that Spain should renounce its sovereignty and all properties on the island. At the same time, Cuba was closing a stage that had begun at the turn of the nineteenth century.

The last War of Independence, started by Cubans on 24 February 1895, attracted US attention to the island. The US had tried several ways, even purchase, to take possession of the island, to no avail. The US government, which had never acknowledged the belligerency of the *Mambises*, now lobbied to obtain unilateral advantages. The Congress of the Union finally approved the so-called Joint Resolution (Pichardo 1973–80: vol. I, 508–11) signed by President William McKinley on April 20, 1898 and thus the US entered the war. Once hostilities were declared, the struggle for independence became the Spanish–Cuban–US War. For Spain, this war ended in the debacle of 1898, but for the Cubans it signalled the thwarting of 30 years of hard struggle to obtain national independence.

In January 1899, when the US occupied the country, it was divided into six provinces and 131 municipalities. The Intervention Government eliminated some 30 municipalities – those either destroyed or abandoned by the population because of the *Reconcentration*.[1] Existing first- and second-class roads amounted to 207 and 95 kilometres respectively, while 1,515 kilometres of railroads connected Havana with the provincial capitals of Pinar del Río and Santa Clara.

A number of measures aimed at assisting the population were adopted. These included, for example, the distribution of 50,000 rations of food per day, as well as medicine and other essential goods for those who had been evicted from their rural homes. Sanitation projects in the most important urban areas were also undertaken, with the creation of sewage networks, aqueducts and the paving of streets. In Havana, the project for public works resulted in the modernizing of the *Paseo del Prado*, construction of buildings especially for schools and other important social issues as well as the construction of the *Malecón* and other buildings.

The neglect of education that had prevailed for centuries was reflected in the 1897 census, the last one carried out by the colonial government: 72 per cent of the population was illiterate, that is, 1,179,357 illiterates. According to the information compiled by the census, 65 per cent of the white population and 87 per cent of the black population was illiterate.

The University of Havana, founded in 1728, operated on sixteenth-century lines rather than according to an eighteenth-century model. Around the same time (1722) the Catholic Seminaries of San Basilio el Magno, in Santiago de Cuba and San Ambrosio in Havana were created, both under the control of Jesuit priests. When the Jesuit Order was evicted from Cuba in 1767 and all its properties were confiscated, the Seminary of San Carlos and San Ambrosio was founded, which provided a more comprehensive and progressive training.

There were no teachers' training schools until 1890, and in 1898, the one active school had only four students. The 541 public schools in 1899, were in practice in the hands of inexperienced staff, with more goodwill than preparation to cope with the task of teaching to read and write and the rules of arithmetic. Preparatory courses for university were taught by a few, albeit excellent private schools. In 1878, the Secondary Institutes were created, one in each province, but in them, 'a few things were taught, and practically nothing was learned' (Figueras, 1907: 313–40).

The picture starts to change significantly following the end of Spanish rule. In the sector of elementary education, in August 1900, 3,313 new schools were opened. Intermediate-level education was reorganized, and priority was given to the urgent preparation of local professors and teachers, as well as to the construction of adequate buildings for teaching. In addition, the existing literacy textbooks were improved.

In 1900, the Varona (Enrique José) Project was implemented for higher education. Under this scheme, the university was to become 'the scientific laboratory of the country' (*Historia de la Nación Cubana* 7, 379–97) so its structure was changed, and the number of professors, which was excessive, was reduced; the programmes taught were modernized. However, the final objectives of the US Governor and the social reformer could somehow differ, in the end the country benefited from all this (*Historia de Cuba*, pp. 11–41).

In 1899 a census for population and resources was carried out, which yielded quite interesting results. The census showed a population of 1,572,797 inhabitants, 68,800 people fewer than the census of 1887. Therefore, if we take into account the likely natural increase of the population at this time, it can be estimated the war had caused some 200,000–300,000 deaths. Of the people interviewed in the census, 172,535 (11 per cent) were foreigners. Of the 1,004,884 national citizens, 64 per cent were illiterate. There were 280,905 whites of voting age, of whom 94,301 were illiterate (51 per cent), and 78,297 black voters, 74 per cent of them illiterate. There were 19,157 university graduates, only 1.2 per cent of the population. There were no women professionals and only three blacks among them; 1,406 were lawyers, of whom 172 (12 per cent) were foreigners; 1,223 were physicians, of which 217 (18 per cent) were foreigners; 162 were architects, of whom 68 (42 per cent) were foreigners. As for non-professional occupations, immigrants were predominant, except in the area of agriculture (Guerra Sánchez).

In March 1902, Order 62 regulated the demarcation and division of the remaining undivided lands (*hatos* and *corrales*) from colonial times. It was a particularly important issue for the acquisition of lands, particularly in the eastern part of the country, as it favoured the concentration of large amounts of land in the hands of US companies. When US troops occupied Santiago de Cuba in 1898 some customs reforms were issued. The first was to eliminate the so-called four-column tariff.[2] Then, duties were also reduced, falling from 35 per cent to 22 per cent *ad valorem*. In short, everything was aimed at eliminating Spanish privileges.

The war had affected agricultural production of the most significant items – sugar and tobacco. Recovery of the agricultural sector was therefore important, as 53 per cent of the population lived in rural areas or in towns of less than 1,000 inhabitants. In 1899, almost 58 per cent of the arable land was occupied by sugar cane and tobacco. In 1895 sugar production was more than one million tons, and the profits over 45 million pesos. By 1901, sugar production had decreased to 600,000 tons and profits to 19 million pesos (Moreno Fraginals, 1978: vol. III, 38). Tobacco production also fell, from 180,000 tons in 1896 to only 42,000 in 1897. By 1900, the tobacco sector was showing signs of recovery: production had surpassed that of 1896, and was close to the 280,000 tons produced in 1895.

The mining industry, however, with the exception of the few deposits being exploited in the Oriente province, become almost paralyzed during the war. By 1899, the industry had started recovering and expanding, and in 1902, exports of manganese and iron ore were more than 500,000 tons (Le Riverend 1974: 502–3).

Of the works carried out during the 1899–1902 period, the most significant was the construction of the railroad from Santa Clara to Santiago de Cuba. In barely three years, the two cities, separated by 500 km, were connected by railway. This gave the island a transportation infrastructure that connected the western and eastern areas of the country, and that at the same time facilitated the overall plan for the expansion and development of the sugar industry over the following 20 years (*Historia de Cuba*, pp. 12–13; Figueras 1907: 130; Zanetti 1989).

Minor crops, the basic direct food supply for most of the population, suffered a dramatic reduction during the 1895–98 period, because whole areas were completely destroyed, either by the war itself or by the *Reconcentration*. In 1899, the number of horses and mules amounted to 106,475, which were mainly used in urban transportation. Bovine cattle amounted to only 376,650 heads. Farming tools and animals were also very scarce (Guerra, 1948: 426–7).

The ruinous condition of the Cuban economy following three years of war (1895–98) had affected foreign trade and the general balance of the economy. For several years, the fall in sugar prices added another burden. The commercial balance was therefore unfavourable for the country. The value of tobacco exports was higher than the value of sugar exports, though US and British investments seemed to have compensated the Cuban balance of payments.

US intervention (1899–1902) also established the future economic policy of the country. However, alongside the recovery of the economy, the political intentions of the United States became evident: to submit Cuba to Washington's interests. Once the possibility of annexing was discarded, other methods would have to be applied, and the solution was given by a new policy: neocolonialism.

## Boom and crisis of the neocolonial model, 1902–33

Even though officially acknowledged as a free state since 1902, Cuba began its life as a republic chained to political, economic, and military mechanisms that made possible its submission to the US economy. From the political point of view, an amendment was imposed to its Constitution known as the Platt Amendment. Among other stipulations, this included the right of the United States to intervene in the island whenever the Americans considered it necessary.

In 1903 and 1904 two new agreements were signed, the *Treaty of Commercial Reciprocity* and the *Permanent Treaty*, to regulate commercial relationships and other issues between the two countries. According to the *Permanent Treaty*, Cuba would also lease a section of the Guantánamo Bay for a naval station and other territories supposedly for carbon stations, and the Isle of Pines would be eliminated from the boundaries of the Cuban archipelago (Pichardo, 1973–80: vol. II, pp. 69, 149, 212, 217).

The juridical platform opened the doors to foreign investment, facilitating the purchasing of lands, the construction of sugar mills (75), services, and other economic benefits, on the part of capitalists from the US and other countries. This process strengthened the one-crop system of sugar production based on landowning (for sugar cane and cattle raising), a productive specialization that also strengthened further the colonial characteristics of the economic structure. This model, which determined the Cuban economic profile in the twentieth century, went through three stages: consolidation (1902–15), boom (1916–25), and crisis (1926–33).

Meanwhile, through the so-called commercial reciprocity and in exchange for customs preferential rates (20 per cent reduction) for Cuban sugar, tobacco and other items in the northern market, Cuba would also import with preferential rates (20–40 per cent reduction) almost 500 items from the US. The agreement had two main results: first, it favoured US domination over imports and exports in the Cuban market; and secondly, it curtailed all incentives to diversify agriculture and industry. Tables 7.1 and 7.2 show the evolution of foreign trade in Cuba, its concentration, and structure.

The model required the employment of huge amounts of manual labour for the sugar cane harvest, which the normal growth of the population, even considering the relatively high levels of unemployment in urban areas and the expropriation of small agricultural producers, was unable to provide.

*Table 7.1* Structure of Cuban exports, 1902–58 (thousands of pesos; proportions)

| *Years* | *Sugar and subproducts* | % | *Tobacco and manufactures* | % | *Other items* | % | *Total value* |
|---|---|---|---|---|---|---|---|
| 1902–1906 | 260,122 | 58 | 138,728 | 31 | 45,842 | 11 | 444,692 |
| 1907–1911 | 388,964 | 65 | 151,780 | 25 | 56,511 | 10 | 597,255 |
| 1912–1916 | 844,599 | 79 | 144,500 | 14 | 80,548 | 7 | 1,069,647 |
| 1917–1921 | 2,126,630 | 88 | 195,756 | 8 | 90,960 | 4 | 2,413,346 |
| 1922–1926 | 1,580,815 | 86 | 189,146 | 10 | 70,847 | 4 | 1,840,808 |
| 1927–1931 | 922,148 | 79 | 169,975 | 15 | 69,032 | 6 | 1,161,155 |
| 1932–1936 | 432,437 | 78 | 69,827 | 13 | 53,414 | 9 | 555,678 |
| 1937–1941 | 640,355 | 78 | 68,835 | 8 | 106,031 | 13 | 815,221 |
| 1942–1646 | 1,393,315 | 75 | 201,511 | 11 | 257,005 | 14 | 1,851,831 |
| 1947–1951 | 3,059,482 | 89 | 167,404 | 5 | 216,074 | 6 | 3,442,960 |
| 1952–1956 | 2,541,599 | 82 | 210,650 | 6 | 362,846 | 12 | 3,115,095 |
| 1957–1958 | 1,249,822 | 81 | 98,433 | 6 | 193,109 | 13 | 1,541,364 |

*Source*: Compiled from: data *Cuban Sugar Annuary*, 1946 and 1959. Quoted by Oscar Zanetti Lecuona, *The Captives of the Reciprocity*. Havana: ENPES, Editorial, 1989, Frame II.

*Table 7.2* Cuban exports by areas, 1902–58 (thousands of pesos; proportions)

| *Years* | *United States* | % | *America remainder* | % | *United Kingdom* | % | *World remainder* | % | *Totals* |
|---|---|---|---|---|---|---|---|---|---|
| 1902–06 | 367,559 | 83 | 8,866 | 2 | 29,996 | 7 | 38,254 | 8 | 444,675 |
| 1907–11 | 515,141 | 86 | 14,453 | 2 | 30,690 | 5 | 36,978 | 7 | 597,262 |
| 1912–16 | 860,566 | 80 | 21,073 | 2 | 131,524 | 12 | 56,484 | 6 | 1,069,647 |
| 1917–21 | 1,834,379 | 76 | 59,652 | 2 | 376,122 | 15 | 143,066 | 7 | 2,413,219 |
| 1922–26 | 1,497,302 | 81 | 52,901 | 3 | 197,178 | 11 | 94,408 | 5 | 1,841,789 |
| 1927–31 | 872,580 | 75 | 45,567 | 4 | 154,219 | 13 | 88,789 | 8 | 1,161,155 |
| 1932–36 | 419,121 | 75 | 12,684 | 2 | 77,128 | 14 | 46,745 | 8 | 555,678 |
| 1937–41 | 655,820 | 80 | 20,222 | 2 | 84,336 | 10 | 54,843 | 7 | 815,221 |
| 1942–46 | 1,389,847 | 75 | 107,650 | 6 | 162,373 | 9 | 191,961 | 10 | 1,851,831 |
| 1947–51 | 2,032,184 | 59 | 147,157 | 4 | 498,361 | 14 | 765,258 | 22 | 3,442,960 |
| 1952–56 | 1,997,696 | 64 | 155,250 | 5 | 190,234 | 6 | 771,915 | 25 | 3,115,095 |
| 1957–58 | 941,382 | 61 | 61,600 | 4 | 86,581 | 6 | 451,801 | 29 | 1,541,364 |

*Source*: Compiled from data in '*Treasury Ministry, Selected Statistics Résumés*', pp. 23–4. Quoted by Oscar Zanetti Lecuona, *The Captives of the Reciprocity*, Havana: ENPES, Editorial, 1989, Frames III–V.

Immigrants from Haiti, Jamaica, and other countries provided the labour force required to cope with continuous increases in production (Table 7.3). This immigration, however, had a downward impact on the levels of salaries and a negative impact on the living standard of the population in general.

From 1903 to 1913, US investments increased from $108 million to $215 million (Pino 1973: 31); colonial productive specialization was also

*Table 7.3* Immigrants arriving in Cuba, 1902–34

| *Period* | *Immigrants* | *Origins of immigrants (1902–1934)* | *Immigrants* |
|---|---|---|---|
| 1902–03 | 30,040 | Spain | 734,454 |
| 1904–08 | 178,326 | Jamaica, Haiti, Puerto Rico | 323,264 |
| 1909–13 | 188,906 | United States | 60,774 |
| 1914–18 | 108,245 | China | 10,344 |
| 1919–23 | 415,111 | Other Countries | 64,222 |
| 1924–28 | 232,189 | | |
| 1929–34 | 40,241 | | |
| Totals | 1,193,058 | | 1,193,058 |

*Source*: Republic de Cuba. Treasury secretary, *Immigration and Mobility of Passengers* (Report from years 1902–1934). Quoted by Rolando García Quiñones, *The Cuban Case: A Long Data Phenomenon*, chapters from SELA, number 65, May–August 2002, Caracas, Venezuela, pp. 199–210.

pronounced, concentrated in sugar and tobacco. The First World War (1914–18) initiated a sugar boom that reached its peak in 1925, with a production of 5.4 million metric tons of crude sugar, while the neocolonial model exhibited its maximum splendour.

In 1926, there was a limitation of sugar production, and the lowest point was reached during the world economic crisis of 1929–33, when the neocolonial model tested in Cuba (1902–33) showed its dark side, and its limitations in relation to the social and economic development of the country. During the first six decades of the twentieth century, problems created by the hypertrophy of the sugar industry sharpened the political, social, and economic contradictions in the country.

Nevertheless, during the first quarter of the twentieth century Cuba achieved a level of economic development that was strong in comparison with its Latin American neighbours. It received an influx of foreign capital unparalleled in the region, and its growth in exports were even higher than those in the US. For example, the per capita sugar production in 1925 was 1.6 tons; the country also had a railroad network unequalled in the continent at the time. Though the agricultural sector was ostensibly weak due to its one-crop scheme, on the other hand in 1927 the country had 1.4 head of cattle per inhabitant and a good number of horses, mules and donkeys. Nevertheless, the non-sugar-related industry was of practically no importance in economic terms. The island also became an immigration attraction for the Latin American continent in general, during those years.

In 1902, by virtue of the 1901 Constitution, Cuba adopted a political regime of two legislative bodies and a president. Early on, both legislative bodies, by means of Acts and Decrees, established regulations and controls that influenced three areas of public interest, namely education, public health, and social security. The new republic, based on economic liberalism, also granted a space in the market to organize profitable activities within the social arena.

In education, the School Act was passed in 1909. Later, more than a dozen Acts and Presidential Decrees (to 1927) introduced a new order in elementary education (urban and rural), and in secondary and university education, establishing the corresponding administrative bodies.

At the elementary level, between 1902 and 1932, the number of classrooms had also increased, to 7,389. The lack of teachers for the elementary level was addressed by the recruitment of rapidly, trained personnel who, through periodic examinations, received the certificate as teachers for First, Second and Third Grades. In addition, there was some upgrading, through summer courses, for complementary teaching and pedagogy. Later, the Teacher's Training Schools (for boys and girls) were created in all provinces as well as the Higher Elementary Schools (for grades 7 to 9), High Schools (granting Bachelors' degrees) and other specialized schools, to complete the system of education up to university level.

Table 7.4 provides information on the enrolment by province in elementary-level education (1932). By that time, out of a population of 3,962,344 inhabitants (1931) more than 50 per cent of school-age children did not attend school; only one out of every 20 teenagers had the opportunity to obtain an intermediate-level education and the situation was even worse in rural areas. The budget for education was supposed to distribute 14 pesos for every enrolled student. There were very few classrooms and most of these were not adequate for educational purposes. The average number of children per teacher was 45, and teaching was characterized by formal teaching, particularly at the higher levels (*Problemas*, pp. 142–73).

*Table 7.4* Students registered in primary schools (public and private) by provinces, population proportion, 1932

| *Province* | *Population* | *Students in primary schools* | *Percentage of population* |
|---|---|---|---|
| Pinar del Río | 345,638 | 39,890 | 12 |
| La Habana | 987,212 | 129,171 | 13 |
| Matanzas | 340,267 | 52,555 | 13 |
| Santa Clara | 822,198 | 84,845 | 10 |
| Camagüey | 411,382 | 25,560 | 6 |
| Oriente | 1,082,011 | 94,687 | 10 |
| Totals | 3,988,708 | 426,708 | 11 |

*Source*: *Problems of the New Cuba*. New York: Foreign Policy Association, 1935, p. 148.

At the same time, private schools, religious schools, and schools sponsored by cultural mutuality societies and patriotic groups, in a very modest way, compensated for the lack of public schools. However, enrolment in private schools was never more than 20–25,000 students (1933), which indicates the relatively small number of people who could devote part of their family income to the education of children.

Higher education was available only at the University of Havana, where most of the students were enrolled in the Law School, the Humanities and Medicine. Between 1925 and 1930 of the 2,830 graduates, only 14 per cent were engineers. In 1933, the university was declared an Autonomous or Independent Institution and was assigned 2 per cent of the State Budget.

When the republic was inaugurated, the Secretariat of Health and Welfare continued its role and improved the works implemented during the US intervention. Thanks to research carried out by Dr Carlos J. Finlay, yellow fever was controlled and eliminated. Between 1920 and the 1930s the main causes of death in children were malaria, tuberculosis, typhoid fever, and diarrhoea. Syphilis was also extensive across the island. Parasitism was endemic in rural areas, but leprosy was gradually disappearing. In 1933 the level of infant mortality of children under one year old was 112 per 1,000 live births across in the whole island. This was not a bad rate for the time, although it was 50 per cent higher than in many countries.

In 1934, the country had, around 2,500 physicians, one for every 1,345 inhabitants. The distribution of doctors per province is shown in Table 7.5, and Table 7.6 summarizes the number of free hospital services and the number of beds per inhabitant. Outside the city of Havana, the state employed around 200 doctors for the consultation of poor people. Havana had a total of 3,000 hospital beds and 1,200 doctors – that is, more beds and almost the same number of doctors as the rest of the country. The expenses

*Table 7.5* Amount of doctors per provinces in 1934

| *Province* | *Population* | *Doctors* | *Inhabitants per Doctor* |
|---|---|---|---|
| Pinar del Río | 343,820 | 130 | 2,645 |
| La Habana | 1,035,500 | 1,416 | 731 |
| Matanzas | 337,119 | 164 | 2,056 |
| Santa Clara | 815,412 | 317 | 2,572 |
| Camagüey | 408,076 | 175 | 2,332 |
| Oriente | 1,072,757 | 340 | 3,115 |
| Totals | 4,012,684 | 2,542 | 1,580 |

*Source*: Data from 'The Medical Trouble and Mutualist Assistance in Cuba', Dechamp and Troncoso, Havana, June 1934. Quoted in *Problems of the New Cuba* New York: Foreign Policy Association, 1935, p. 130.

*Table 7.6* State and municipal hospital services in 1934

| *Province* | *Hospitals* | *Doctors* | *Beds* | *Population* | *Inhabitants per bed* |
|---|---|---|---|---|---|
| Pinar del Río | 3 | 6 | 380 | 343,820 | 2,642 |
| La Habana | 4 | 11 | 113 | 443,000 | 3,850 |
| Matanzas | 5 | 19 | 329 | 337,119 | 1,025 |
| Las Villas | 7 | 19 | 589 | 815,412 | 1,384 |
| Camagüey | 2 | 6 | 222 | 408,076 | 1,838 |
| Oriente | 9 | 18 | 454 | 1,072,757 | 2,363 |
| Totals | 30 | 79 | 2089 | 3,420,184 | 1,637 |

*Do not include Havana City and Insanes National Hospital (Author' note).
*Source*: 'The Medical Trouble and Mutualist Assistance in Cuba', C. Dechamp and M. Poblete Troncoso, Havana, June 1934. Quoted in *Problems of the New Cuba*. New York: Foreign Policy Association, p. 131.

of the state in 1933 in health services were barely 22 cents per inhabitant (*Problemas*, 119 and 131).

Medical and hospital care were being improved through the services rendered by mutual societies, most of which were Spanish. Under these schemes, by making a modest monthly outlay of two pesos, the associate would receive some of the best medical care in the country. The main limitation on the scheme was its concentration, like that the other the health care services, in the capital.

For the rest, the picture of health care in the country remained largely unchanged. In 1934, though it was admitted that the state trained more doctors than were actually required, it was also true that the distribution of medical care professionals did not meet the real and most pressing needs of the population. The opportunities for private practice, professional, social and economic development of doctors, plus the presence of scientific societies, libraries, stimulating professional relationships, etc., drew most doctor to Havana, to the detriment of those areas in which the services were most needed (*Problemas*, 128–35).

Social security issues claimed the attention of Cuban legislators at an early stage, both in the labour arena and also in respect of the protection of workers. From 1916, the Act of Social Security in case of working accidents covered all salaried workers. Employers were forced to buy a policy from an insurance company, or workers had to insure themselves. In 1933, the benefits of this law were extended, adding protection against professional diseases, and incorporating agricultural workers; however, it did not cover domestic service workers, the self-employed, relatives with no monetary compensation or temporary workers (Mesa-Lago, 2002b: 239).

Social prevention through retirement funds appears for the first time among the groups of civil servants, and extends afterwards to the private and professional sectors. Between 1913 and 1933, 13 new social security projects were implemented (Table 7.7). Insurance policies were also declared non-transferable, meaning that, when the employee moved from one job to another, the beneficiary could not transfer the contributions he had made

*Table 7.7* Introduction of insurance and social security programmes in Cuba, 1902–33

| *Year* | *Risk* | *Branch* | *Sector* |
|---|---|---|---|
| 1913 | P | Armed Forces | Public |
| 1915 | P | Communication | Public |
| 1916 | A | All Wage Earners | Public–Private |
| 1917 | P | Judicial Power | Public |
| 1919 | P | Officers And Employees | Public |
| 1920 | P | Police | Public |
| 1921–23 | P | Telephones, Railroads And Street Cars | Private |
| 1927 | P | Maritime | Private |
| 1929 | P | Notary: Register of the Property | Professional |
| 1933 | SI | Wage Earner Workers | Public–Private |
| 1934 | M | Wage Earners | Public–Private |
| 1935 | P | Journalism | Professional |
| 1938 | P | Banking | Private |
| 1939 | P | Mercantile Register | Professional |
| 1941 | P | Sugar – Industrial and Agriculture | Private |
| 1943 | P | Doctor | Professional |
| 1945 | P | Lawyer, Textile And Henequen | Professional–Private |
| 1946 | P | Barber Shops and Hair Dress Shops, tobacco: Industrial and Agriculture; Attorneys; State, Province and County Workers | Public–Private |
| 1947 | P | Printing Shops; Pharmaceutical | Private–Professional |
| 1948 | P | Electricity, Gas and Water: Custom Brokers | Private–Professional |
| 1949 | P | Dentists, Veterinarians, Architects, Bakeries and Commerce | Professional–Private |
| 1950 | P | Hotels and Restaurants; Legislative Power | Private–Public |
| 1951 | P | Petroleum and Radio | Private |
| 1952 | P | Insurance and Finances; Nurses | Private–Professional |
| 1953 | P | Breweries | Private |
| 1954 | P | Stenographers, Civil Engineers, Maternity Insurance Employees, Building Cattle; Shoes, Leathers | Professional–Public–Private |
| 1955 | P | County Courts, Sciences and Philosophy Doctors, Agriculture Engineers, Pedagogue, Private School Teachers | Public–Professional |
| 1956 | P | Governors and Mayors and Their Employees | Public |
| 1957 | P | Drivers | Private |

*Note*: M = Maternity; P = Pension; W = Work Accident; SI = Sickness Insurance.
*Source*: Made with data of CERP, 1964; Mesa-Lago 1985. Quoted in *The Social Security, Encuentro magazine*, Madrid, 2002, pp. 240–1.

up until that moment. Besides, the conflicts that had arisen between the different projects because of affiliation, and the absence of coverage for employees or workers that were not protected by the scheme, remained unsolved for a long time.

The worst problem in this area of social regulation was the lack of adequate funding, a limitation that became more critical in the private sector than in the state sector. The fiscal contribution varied considerably between different collective retirement funds. In some cases, the state was the key supplier, while others had no support at all. Certain groups received a fixed amount, or a percentage of the worker's wage, and the national lottery contributed funds to some others. The professionals created their own taxes related to their profession, which covered half of their contributions (Mesa-Lago, 2002b: 242).

In relation to labour legislation, the 1888 Act was extended, grouping guilds and unions by occupational sectors. In 1909, a new Act banned the payment of wages by means of bonds or chips, though this was certainly not always enforced. Working hours were limited to 10 in drug stores and pharmacies, eight for labourers and mechanics employed by the government and 12 hours for sugar industry workers. In 1933, the eight-hour working day was officially established throughout the whole country. Curiously, in 1913 data were compiled to draft a Labour Code, which would contain thirteen chapters (*Historia de la Nación*, vol. IX, 403–4).

The first Labour Courts were created in 1924. The *Intelligence Committees of the Ports* would settle disputes between workers and employers in the maritime sector. Their remit covered labour contracts, salaries, maximum working hours, vacations and free days, strikes, and in general anything that could affect working conditions. At the same time, in 1927 the country ratified 16 agreements of the international labour convention that had been passed during the first nine International Labour Conferences.

The worst problem suffered by the island's workers in the labour arena was unemployment, especially between 1929 and 1933. For the next 25 years this period would become known as the 'dead time', a period when the phenomenon would become chronic in the Cuban economy.

## Recurring economic crisis or latent stagnation: 1934–58

The fall of Gerardo Machado's government in August 1933 heralded a revolutionary stage that lasted until January 1934, and was marked by the nationalism of heterogeneous political groups. After a tempestuous conservative stage, the Constitution passed in 1940 included many of the achievements launched in the USA by F. D. Roosevelt in 1933, aimed at modifying the juridical status that had tied Cuba – both politically and economically – to the United States, in view of the social unrest that raged across the island.

From the political point of view, on 29 May 1934, the *Treaty of Relationships* was again signed between Cuba and the United States. This agreement derogated the right of the US to intervene in Cuba that had been established by virtue of the Platt Amendment, and left the issue of leasing for the naval station in Guantánamo to future agreements between both governments. In the economy, 1934 also marks the signing of another *Treaty of Commercial Reciprocity*. In exchange for a quota of Cuban sugar (28.6 per cent) in the market of the northern country, Cuba granted several tariff preferential rates (20–60 per cent) to around 490 US products. The treaty, modified in 1939 and then again in 1941, remained in force until 1947, when it was supersed by the General Agreement on Tariffs and Trades (GATT) (Pichardo, 1973–80: vol. IV, 416–63; Pino Sants, 1973: 48–53).

The 1934 Treaty helped to arrest the decline in Cuban crude sugar exports to the US market, which had been increasingly threatened by imports from the Philippines, a country which did not pay tariffs in the US. Sugar prices were therefore reduced to 0.90 cents a pound, plus the difference between the general tariff (0.975) and the tariff effectively paid (1.875) in favour of the Cuban vendor. In reciprocal arrangements, Cuba agreed: (a) not to modify any of the clauses of the agreement without US approval; (b) not to impose import tariffs on US products; and (c) not to tax any imported article from the US without imposing the same tax on a similar Cuban product. Thus, the agreement became a very rigid commercial instrument and hindered negotiations with other countries, giving much more priority to US products in the Cuban market, and leaving most of the national production without adequate protection.

At the same time, the US imposed quotas on Cuban sugar, but also on other products like tobacco, fruit, vegetables and other exports from the island. In addition, custom tariffs imposed on Cuban products could be modified, or internal taxes imposed on articles sold in Cuba, that did not have to be paid by similar US products also sold in the island (Torras, 1984–85 vol. I, pp. 198–206). To the problems generated by the Treaty in terms of trade activity with the United States, was added the loss of European markets for Cuban sugar between 1939 and 1941. Once the US entered the Second World War, the production of crude sugar grew, apart from a brief hiatus in the period 1943–45, from 3.5 million in 1942, to 7.2 million TM in 1952 (Table 7.8).

The war had several distinct consequences for the Cuban economy. Among the most significant were: (a) an increase in the hard currency income due to the increase in exports; (b) an increase in non-sugar-related industrial production, mainly consumer, non-luxury goods, and also due to the diversification of agricultural production both for exports and for the domestic market. Likewise, imports suffered a contraction due to limitations in maritime transportation and because at that time US industry was oriented towards the war. In 1948, Cuba had the largest reserve of hard currency (US $860 million) in Latin America (Conference, 1949: 308).

*Table 7.8* Cuban foreign commerce, 1932–58

| *Years* | *Exports* | *Imports* | *Remnant* | *Average Population* | *Average Exports* | *Average Imports* |
|---|---|---|---|---|---|---|
| 1932–36 | 555,678 | 365,483 | 190,195 | 4,028.7 | 27 | 18 |
| 1937–41 | 815,221 | 579,191 | 236,030 | 4,252.6 | 38 | 27 |
| 1942–46 | 1,852,792 | 1,071,985 | 780,807 | 4,816.7 | 76 | 44 |
| 1947–51 | 3,442,960 | 2,654,021 | 788,938 | 5,315.9 | 130 | 100 |
| 1952–56 | 3,115,094 | 2,870,067 | 295,027 | 5,948.6 | 105 | 95 |
| 1957–58 | 1,541,199 | 1,549,948 | −8,749* | 6,457.5 | 119 | 119 |

*Note*: *In 1958 the remnant was of : −43, 575 thousand pesos. In 1957 the remnant was of +34, 826 thousand pesos.
*Source*: Data from *Cuban Sugar Annuary*, 1959. Quoted by Oscar Zanetti Lecuona, *The Captives of the Reciprocity*. Havana: ENPES Editorial, 1989, frame I.

On the other hand, during the war the relatively weak non-sugar-related bourgeoisie tried to strengthen their economic positions. In 1948 the National Association of Cuban Industrialists sponsored the Conference for the Progress of the National Economy; and shortly after, in 1950, a Technical Mission of the World Bank carried out a study, at the request of the Government, on the socioeconomic situation in the country, known as the Truslow Report. Both proposals were attempts to introduce changes in the structure of the Cuban economy.

The opposition of the Cuban sugar oligarchy and the merchants, the lack of political will on the part of the government in power at the time, together with the increase in demand of sugar as a result of the Korean War, dampened down all the claims in favour of the diversification of agriculture and the national industry. Positive elements at this stage were the creation of two monetary-financial institutions: the National Bank (1948) and the Bank for the Agricultural and Industrial Development of Cuba (1950). The breaking of the institutional order with Fulgencio Batista's dictatorship (1952–58) precipitated a traumatic chapter in the economic development of the country.

The contraction of the sugar industry that damaged the Cuban economy between 1953 and 1955 was mitigated by an economic policy of compensatory expenditures. Such policy was based on: (a) an expansion of public expenses; (b) an increase in public and private credit; and (c) fiscal incentives for agricultural and industrial development. In 1955, the first Plan for the Economic and Social Development of Cuba was implemented.

The results of the development plan could not have been worse. Public debt skyrocketed to unprecedented levels. Investments were concentrated in non-productive works and less in agriculture and industry. Investments made were inflated to around 30–50 per cent above their real value, and the difference created opportunities for speculation and theft. There was also a contraction in the production of crude sugar, and a decrease in sugar exports, and therefore income from external sources, and so, the negative balance evaporated the reserves of hard currency. The political climate in the country (1958) also encouraged the drain of capital. Compensatory actions were not implemented in the sugar industry, and as a result, the living standards in the countryside deteriorated still further. The plan failed to reduce unemployment, which in 1958 stood at around 25–30 per cent of the labour force (Rodríguez, 1978: 52–69).

Meanwhile, direct investments from the US in Cuba suffered a significant change during the 1936–58 period. Essentially, investments moved away from the agricultural sugar sector and into other more profitable branches of the economy, such as mining, oil, manufacturing, and so on. Most Spanish investments, on the other hand, then became national investments as investors obtained Cuban citizenship.

Economic performance in the period 1934–58 did not have very promising results in the social sector. In education, by the mid-1950s 44 per cent of children between 6 and 14 years of age did not attend school, only 17 per cent of children between 15 and 19 years of age were receiving some kind of education and the average educational level of the population over 15 years of age was 3rd grade. Statistics reveal the condition of education in Cuba by 1958: over one million illiterates, over one million semi-illiterates, 800 children without schools, and 10,000 unemployed teachers.

The educational picture was even bleaker in the areas of technical and professional education, taking into account the limited number of specialized schools and the fact that teaching conditions in the schools were also inadequate. In 1958, education was allocated a budget of 79.4 million pesos, amounting to around 12 pesos per capita. However, for several decades, the funds supposedly devoted to education had been object of a systematic plundering by successive ruling governments.

Higher studies in public schools could be obtained at three universities: the University of Havana, the University of Oriente, and the Central University of Las Villas. In 1957, all three together had a total of 15,600 students, and only 12 per cent of them were studying any technological or engineering specialiy (Díaz Vázquez 1986: 89–96). Again, public education was complemented by private schools, which developed during this period. The number of authorized private elementary and secondary schools at some point reached 3,000 schools, with an enrolment of more than 140,000 students. Of these, some 40,000 students attended 162 religious schools and one university. Private education was subject to state supervision (Friguls; p. 20; *Historia de la Nación*, T, X: p. 55–144).

In the area of public health, there was a widening of the gap between health care services in the city of Havana and those in the rest of the country. In 1958, the public and private network of hospitals and clinics (mutuality and cooperatives) counted for 90 hospitals, 40 clinics and 200 emergency centres; the number of beds was around 28,000 – that is, 421 inhabitants per bed – and there were 6,250 doctors, which gave a mean of 1,040 inhabitants per doctor. There was, however, an excess of health care services concentrated in the capital. Here the number of beds amounted to some 16,000, some 60 per cent of the national total, which amounted to an average of one bed for each 130 inhabitants. In Havana, where 20 per cent of the country's population lived at the time, there were some 3,700 doctors, that is, one per 310 inhabitants (Torras, 1984–85: vol. II, 333–61; Mesa-Lago, 2002b: 244; Castro Ruz, 1975: 133–6).

The budget allocated for health care in 1958 was around 24 million pesos, or around 37 pesos per head of population. The main causes of death were tuberculosis, malaria, gastroenteritis, diphtheria, poliomyelitis, and tetanus. Infant mortality per thousand live births was more than 60 and life expectancy was 64 years (Mesa-Lago 2002b: 246).

In 1958, there were 51 social security programmes, 20 of them public, 11 private and 20 professionals. Of these schemes, 38 had been implemented between 1934 and 1958. In 1934, a maternity security programme was implemented for working women in both the private and public sectors, which extended its coverage to agricultural workers in 1951–52. The percentage of the salary to be paid for health was raised and more maternity hospitals were built. In 1950, the law granted workers in the private sector a paid leave of absence for sickness, but this was limited to only three days in a month and nine days in any one year.

Between 1934 and 1950, Cuba passed advanced labour legislation. This included, among other things, the creation of a state agency (the Ministry of Labour) to make decisions on labour conflicts, with legal authority to intervene in company disputes in order to enforce the Ministry's regulations. It established minimum salaries, compensations for industrial accidents and diseases, compensated, or paid vacations, and the right to strike. It also provided payment of 48 hours for every 44 hours completed, regulation of female and child work, including night work. It also prohibited working hours both night and day without interruption, in commerce and industry, among other provisions.

In spite of advances regarding social-labour policy made by the country, in 1957 a moderate labour organization carried out research into the living standards of the agricultural workers, highlighting the severe poverty that could be observed there. The situation of the 2.5 million inhabitants living in the countryside, and particularly that of agricultural workers, was characterized, for example, by a daily consumption of 2,500 calories or less. Only 4 per cent of persons interviewed mentioned meat as part of their diet, less than one per cent had fish in their diet, less than 2 per cent included eggs and only 11 per cent included milk. In the health care sector, only 8 per cent of agricultural workers had received public medical care, 14 per cent had suffered tuberculosis, 13 per cent typhoid fever, 3 per cent malaria, and 36 suffered parasitism. In addition, 44 per cent of agricultural labourers had never attended school and 90 per cent used kerosene lamps. Residents in rural areas represented 34 per cent of the population, but the 350,000 agricultural workers received only 10 per cent of the national income (Encuesta, pp. 188–212).

In summary, after more than half a century of political independence (1902–58), there was still a heavy colonial burden on the shoulders of the country. The consolidation of a better and more prosperous republic, with more social justice, was still a goal to achieve.

## Social and economic transformations, 1959–70

For Cuba the triumph of the Revolution in 1959 meant the beginning of a new era in its history. The revolution was ostensibly the result of the political struggle that began after the Batista coup of 10 March 1952, and the first declared objective of the revolutionary movement was the ousting of the dictatorship. Early on, however, Fidel Castro, leader of the revolutionary movement, presented a political programme that intended to implement important transformations in the country, with a particular emphasis on the social sector (Castro 1953).

Based on this, in the two-year period 1959–60, the first Act of Agrarian Reform was passed, limiting land tenancy to only 30 *caballerías* or 402 hectares, and also the Housing Reform Act, which reduced rents by 50 per cent and eliminated the property of house owners or landlords. In addition, the prices of electricity, phone calls, and medicines were reduced. At the same time, salaries, retirement pensions and pensions in general, were increased and all retirement pension funds in the country were unified. Public services were also extended during this period, including education and health care, creating the preliminary conditions for establishing a system of free universal coverage for these two important social sectors. In addition, laws and decrees for the confiscation of funds misappropriated during the previous period were adopted.

This process of rapid social and economic change led to a worsening of the situation for US interests in the island, because of the popular measures adopted by the Revolutionary Government. This confrontation, as is well known, finally led to the imposition by the US government of a strict blockade against Cuba, and, on the Cuban side, to the expropriation of those US companies established on its national territory. Two key moments in this confrontation were the Bay of Pigs invasion, in April 1961, and the Missile Crisis, in October 1962.

The political contradictions and the escalation of the conflict with the US led to a radicalization of the measures adopted by the government and to the establishment of closer relationships with the Eastern European socialist countries, led by the then Soviet Union. In July 1960, all of the

US companies established in the country were nationalized, and in October of the same year all of the large foreign and national companies, including banks, were nationalized. Also nationalized were 105 sugar mills and 383 large companies. In April 1961, the socialist character of the revolution was officially proclaimed. In 1963, the Second Agrarian Reform was established; this was much more radical than the first, as it expropriated farms larger than five *caballerías* or 67 hectares.

The strategies for economic development during the first five years after the revolution were industrialization, aimed at the substitution of imports, and the diversification of foreign economic relations and agricultural production, aimed at reducing the country's dependency on sugar. As a result, the lands devoted to sugar production were reduced and nine sugar mills were closed down. Investment in industry increased at the same time investments in agriculture were reduced.

During this period, the market continued to be the main mechanism of resource allocation, but at the same time a new structure of government institutions was articulated for the centralized management of the economy, which included the National Institute of the Agrarian Reform, the National Bank of Cuba, the new Ministries of the Treasury, of Labour, and of Foreign Trade. By 1963 the system of centralized planning had been implemented in the state sector, but not for the private sector, which continues to play an important role within the national economy: 30 per cent in agriculture and 25 per cent of the retail trade.

The results obtained between 1959 and 1963 were much better in the social sector than in the economic sector. Immediately, there was a more equitable distribution of income and an expansion of public services. However, economic development was not stable, showing a moderate growth between 1959 and 1961 and a decrease in both 1962 and 1963.

Capital formation was reduced, but between 1961 and 1963, and an attempt at recovery was made by increasing the investment rate and reducing the level of consumption. A policy of rationing the consumption of goods was implemented during this period. The reduction in sugar production, which was recorded as 28 per cent in 1962 and 21 per cent in 1963, was undertaken in the absence of other economic sectors that could substitute the income generated by sugar. This affected the general functioning of the economy and led to a commercial deficit. The situation became even worse when Hurricane Flora hit the island in 1963.

In March 1963 the new Act of Social Security was passed, ensuring protection for all workers and their families in situations of disease, maternity, work accidents, industrial diseases, old age, and death. The overall protection guaranteed to the family included education, health, food, and housing. The act also ensured monetary payments for any risk, as well as other payments or services. The legislation equally recognized, for the purposes of social security, the years worked by the person in any working activity, at any time (Gutiérrez-Peñate, 2000). The right to retirement was established at the age of 60 for men and of 55 for women, and retirement pensions were to be set at equal to 50 per cent of annual salary during 25 years of work and a one per cent increase for every extra year worked. Child labour was eliminated and special plans were created for the improvement of living conditions of children and for the financial support of families with children.

Education was nationalized in 1961, when it was established as a free right under the responsibility of the state. The national system of education was thus established, with a comprehensive programme of scholarships at the different levels of education, as well as programmes for teacher training. In addition, in 1961, a national campaign against illiteracy was carried out, with the result that the rate of illiteracy was reduced from 23.1 per cent to only 3.9 per cent. Since 1962, the campaign has been complemented with follow-up and upgrading courses for workers. Also in that year university reforms were implemented, which, among other things, considerably extended the access to higher studies. Likewise, there was a significant effort in the training and upgrading of the labour force, in different sectors of the economy.

In 1961, every important hospital in the country was nationalized, and in 1963, a national system was also established for health care, with free and universal coverage. The system integrated medical care at different territorial and specialization levels. National vaccination campaigns took place that, together with stricter epidemiological control, managed to eradicate poliomyelitis in 1963, malaria in 1968, diphtheria in 1981, and tuberculosis in 1981. New hospitals were built and doctors and dentists were sent to rural areas in the country in mandatory rural service for two years, a period which was later extended to three years. An intensive programme for the preparation of medical and paramedical personnel was implemented, overcoming the deficit left by the massive exodus of doctors to the US, which accounted for half of the doctors accounted for in 1959. In 1965, the first class of those doctors who had been trained completely after the Revolution graduated. In 1963, the pharmaceutical industry was also nationalized.

In 1962, 35.7 per cent of the national budget was allocated to social services: education, health care, social security, housing, sports, and recreation. Since that date, this indicator has always remained above 30 per cent.

From the very beginning of the revolution, several housing construction projects were also implemented, with the aim of eliminating poverty areas, and through these projects, many families became the owners of their own houses or apartments. However, the housing problem was not solved, and it was even aggravated in later years.

The economic results of the previous period led to a revision of the strategy for economic development. Import-substitution industrialization continued to be the strategic objective, but it was now seen over a longer period. It was also understood in relation to a more gradual reduction of dependency on the production and export of sugar, which was now seen as an essential factor in the generation of hard currency, to allow for the necessary imports, and, in turn, future industrialization. This new strategy was the basis of the first agreements signed with the socialist bloc. By 1970, 52 per cent of foreign trade was being carried out with the Soviet Union.

The sugar industry received considerable investment, so that with a solid infrastructure, qualified personnel, and the necessary technical equipment, it consolidated its role as the main source of funding and income generation for the rest of the economy. For the 1970 sugar harvest, the goal was to produce 10 million tons of sugar – the best harvest ever before this had been in 1952, when 7.2 million tons had been produced. Those areas with better soils were planted with sugar cane; over 1.5 million hectares in all, and 700,000 sugar cane cutters and other labourers were mobilized. The level of mechanization was low, so large groups of workers from the city were mobilized to the countryside in order to support the harvest.

At the same time, there were also projects to develop cattle herds and to improve their genetic quality, and to improve efficiency in the agricultural sector in general. Projects for the promotion of the fishing industry and nickel extraction were also implemented. The period was also characterized by a high rate of accumulation, as well as contraction of consumption.

During that period, new systems of direction and organization of the economy were adopted, but a few years later, these were dismissed as too idealistic and self-willed (Castro 1975). The system of incentives was essentially based on moral and ideological factors, and so the monetary-mercantile relations were reduced to a minimum. In 1968, small private property was finally nationalized or eliminated, and as a result, only one-fifth of transportation means and 2 per cent of agriculture were left in private hands (Table 7.9). State enterprises were merged into 300 huge conglomerates and accounting controls were eliminated, while at the same time the so-called special plans proliferated.

In the end, the economic result of the period was stagnation. Only 8.5 million tons of sugar was harvested, out of the 10 million planned. The results in cattle-raising plans were also modest, though the production of eggs was considerably higher, as was the production of nickel. The non-sugar industrial sector and tourism decreased dramatically. These economic results, together with the lack of correspondence between production and salaries, generated strong inflationary pressures, scarcity of products, and a growth of the black market.

However, in spite of the period of economic stagnation, following the policy of full employment, the level of employment and subemployment remained very high. In 1971, the Act Against Vagrancy was passed. Unemployment fell from 12.5 per cent in 1958 to 9 per cent in 1962 and further to 1.3 per cent in 1970 (Table 7.10). Another important issue was the increase

*Table 7.9* Evolution of state social property in Cuba, 1961–77 (percentage)

| *Sectors* | *1961* | *1963* | *1968* | *1977* |
|---|---|---|---|---|
| Agriculture | 37 | 70 | 70 | 79 |
| Industry | 85 | 95 | 100 | 100 |
| Construction | 80 | 98 | 100 | 100 |
| Transport | 92 | 95 | 98 | 98 |
| Retail trade | 52 | 75 | 100 | 100 |
| Foreign and wholesale trade | 100 | 100 | 100 | 100 |
| Bank | 100 | 100 | 100 | 100 |
| Education | 100 | 100 | 100 | 100 |

*Source*: Mesa-Lago, *La Economía en Cuba Socialista*. edit Univ. Nvo México, 1983.

*Table 7.10* Structure of employment by type

| *Concept* | *1970(α)* | *1981(α)* | *1995* | *1998* | *2001* |
|---|---|---|---|---|---|
| Total of occupied | 100.0 | 100.0 | 100.0 | 100.0 | 100.0 |
| State agencies | 86.3 | 91.8 | 77.9 | 75.0 | 71.4 |
| Cooperatives | | 1.1 | 9.7 | 8.8 | 8.0 |
| Joint ventures and mercantile societies | | | 2.4 | 4.1 | 4.9 |
| Political, mass and social organizations | | | 0.9 | 1.0 | 1.0 |
| National private | 12.5 | 5.5 | 5.2 | 8.1 | 10.9 |
| Self-employed | 1.2 | 1.6 | 3.9 | 3.0 | 3.8 |

*Source*: *Censos de Población de 1970 y 1981*; and *Cuba en Cifras 1997 y 1998*. ONE 1998 y 1999. *Anuario Estadístico 2001*.

in the level of female employment. The difficult economic situation had not affected the priority given by the government to social sectors, and these continued to receive a substantial proportion of the state budget and government's efforts. In general, during this period social indicators showed some improvement.

By the end of the 1960s and the beginning of the 1970s, the distribution of income in Cuba was already the most equitable in the whole of Latin America. The poorest groups increased their income during the first few years of the revolution, then the intermediate-income groups benefited, while the higher-income groups were adversely affected (Mesa-Lago 1983). The difference between the maximum salary and the minimum salary was 10 to 1, compared to a ratio of about 1,000 to 1 in 1959. In 1963, a new system of payment of salaries was introduced.

## Economic integration into the socialist bloc: 1971–89

When the plan to produce 10 million tons of sugar in 1970 was not achieved, and the impact of the economic results of the period was analysed, the government decided to make a critical analysis of the economic mechanisms that had been implemented during the last few years. This review led to important decisions being taken. In the first place, it was considered necessary to change the mechanisms for planning and directing the economy; the country was also restructured, using the European socialist countries' model as a reference, and entering the system of socialist economic integration (COMECOM). In 1976, therefore, a new political-administrative division was implemented in the country.

The strategy for economic development continued to be the same, that is, import-substitution industrialization, reinforcing the production of sugar as a source of external financing and investing in the sector in order to increase the level of mechanization. The production of sugar cane by-products was also included in the plans, along with the production of agricultural machinery. At the same time, new production programmes were implemented and others, such as nickel, citrus fruit, and fishing, among others, were reinforced.

Integration to COMECOM in 1972 and the signing of more agreements with the USSR, offered the country more economic stability, and access to considerable external resources. In addition to preferential prices, it received credits, technology transfers, military aid, and other benefits. The production of sugar for the socialist market at preferential prices was one of the pillars of the relationships between Cuba and the socialist countries.

The new economic system implemented in the country established self-financing at the level of enterprises and central state planning as the ruling mechanism of the economy, by means of five-year plans. Accounting and administrative management were also re-established, and the 300 existing state conglomerates were split into 3,000 enterprises. Peasants' cooperatives were organized, and by the end of the 1970s, 10.2 per cent of the land was organized into cooperatives. Markets were opened for agricultural products and for artisans.

Mercantile-monetary relationships operated again among different economic actors and new forms of payment to the labour force were introduced, that bore some relation to the performance of workers. This led to differentiation in the levels of income that was favourable to those members of the labour force with higher qualifications and those holding more responsible jobs. The system of incentives was now based on material factors, the level of self-employment increased, and the amount of voluntary work fell. Payment of copyrights was reinstalled after being abolished back in the 1960s.

The system for rationing industrial and food products was also modified. Rationed products continued to be subsidized, but a small increase in their prices achieved a better financial balance. Rationing was complemented by parallel markets offering produce at prices that were three to eight times higher. However, the black market did not disappear, and it its prices were still significantly higher, but with a differentiated offer.

Plans for social development continued to exist, but their relative importance or weight within the economy diminished, as investments in production and infrastructure were given more emphasis.

During this period, new schools in the countryside were built, both for secondary education and for higher intermediate education, in which students combined study with agricultural work, assuming this form of education as a fundamental issue in the education of new generations. These schools were under the regime of boarding schools, where the students received free of charge all school materials and books, uniforms and clothing to work in the country, as well as shoes, meals and medical care. In addition, during this period, the training of professors for intermediate and higher-level education was intensified.

The number of doctors and dentists per inhabitant continued to grow with massive graduations. The budget allocated to the public health sector increased 18 times from 1959 to 1980, though most of it was concentrated in the first decade of that period (Mesa-Lago 1983). Health indicators for the population continued to improve during this period.

In 1979, a new Social Security Act was passed, as a result of which social security was declared a system ensuring the protection for workers and their families, with the widest coverage possible; as well as for that part of the population whose essential needs were not covered for reasons of their living or health conditions. Such new acts gave way therefore to a two-sided system: social security and social welfare (Gutiérrez-Peñate, 2000). The Constitution of 1976 had established that social security was a responsibility of the Cuban state.

The level of employment during the period was still high, though subemployment acquired an increased importance. The 1981 census records unemployment of 3.4 per cent. Workers who were unemployed received 70 per cent of their salaries, paid directly from the national budget. The average salaries between 1970 and 1980 increased by an average of 2.9 per cent a year. By the end of the 1980s, more than 14,000 disabled people were unemployed. Another important issue was the raising of the level of qualifications among the general labour force: by the end of the 1980s, eight out of 10 workers had a university degree, and 13 out of every 100 workers had professional technical training. The minimum level of education for the whole population was first raised to 6th grade and a few years later to 9th grade.

In 1982, another general reform of salaries was implemented, establishing new higher salaries and payment of premium bonuses and an extra for risk or for special conditions of the job in priority sectors (such as health, education, and the sciences). The reform established a 25 per cent increase in the fund for salaries. The minimum salary was established at 100 pesos, reducing the difference between the minimum and the maximum salary to 4.5 times.

In 1984, a new Housing Act was passed, which gradually transferred the property of all houses to their occupants, and rents were thus considered to be part of the payment for the value of the house, which should not be more than 10 per cent of family income. At the beginning of the 1970s, the so-called 'micro brigades' were created, a scheme under which a worker who would need a house or an apartment would join a group of construction workers to which the state gave construction materials, a piece of land and a project or design for the construction of apartment blocks. The worker continued to receive his or her salary, and a colleague at the office did his work. During the 1970s, micro brigades built approximately 100,000 houses. Later, the number of housing projects in this system was reduced considerably as it was considered economically inefficient and the construction of houses by the person's owns resources was favoured. Micro brigades were re-established during the second half of the 1980s, much more strongly this time, to be reduced again with the crisis in the 1990s. Housing needs, as stated earlier, have not been covered effectively during any period.

The 1971–85 period was characterized by considerable economic growth, averaging over 5.3 per cent per annum. Sugar production increased, as well as industrial production and tourism, as well as the physical infrastructure, which achieved an important growth rate. The percentage of investment in the Global Social Product (GSP) grew from 9.6 per cent in 1970 to 16.8 per cent in 1985. Productivity of work also increased at a 4.2 per cent annual rate. Circulating money diminished, leading to a more balanced financial structure and commercial deficit was reduced. However, the commercial dependency on the USSR and the COMECOM increased considerably, as did the dependency on sugar production (see Table 7.11), and there was a contraction of some of the social indicators by the end of the period, such as construction of houses, nursery schools, construction, and maintenance of schools and of hospitals, while an emphasis was placed on productive investment. Outstanding failures were also detected in the

*Table 7.11* Structure of Cuban exports (percentage)

| | *Sugar* | *Tobacco* | *Minerals* | *Other* | *Total* |
|---|---|---|---|---|---|
| 1958 | 78 | 6 | 6 | 10 | 100 |
| 1960 | 80 | 10 | 1 | 9 | 100 |
| 1965 | 86 | 5 | 6 | 3 | 100 |
| 1970 | 77 | 3 | 17 | 3 | 100 |
| 1978 | 87 | 2 | 5 | 6 | 100 |

*Source*: Mesa-Lago (1983).

system of direction of the economy, such as false profitability in enterprises, excess of employees, payment of unjustified salaries and premiums, uniformity of designs, copying of methods applied in other socialist countries, among others.

The increase in subemployment was an interesting phenomenon during this period, and one of the most criticized since 1986. This phenomenon was the result of an employment policy based more on social objectives than on economic efficiency criteria, which resulted in low levels of productivity. In spite of the critical treatment to the problem, the contradiction has not been overcome by the Cuban economy even nowadays.

The years 1984 and 1985 were of economic stagnation, due to internal problems in the economy, the increase of the external debt with the West and the Paris Club's refusal to renegotiate the debt. The existing problems and stagnation of the economy led the government to make a very critical analysis of the entire situation, and to admit that distortions were carrying the country far away from the construction of socialism. Blame was placed on the excessive use of monetary-mercantile relationships, as well as on the unjustified use of material incentives, and insufficient attention being paid to important social needs. A rectification process was then started, in order to solve the problems found.

However, the problems of the Cuban economy seemed to be larger and more complex than simply the insufficiencies of the system of direction and planning in the economy. Between 1970 and 1985, the advantageous relationships with the socialist bloc had allowed the country to maintain a higher level of surplus to finance both a higher level of investment and an expanding social expense. Nevertheless, this growth proved to be both excessive and inefficient (Monreal, Carranza 2000), as it was based on an ever increasing dependency on foreign aid and resources. By 1985, the exhaustion of economic resources seemed quite apparent, and therefore the need to implement a more efficient model of intensive growth. These limitations had not yet been overcome, and the events that would follow would make them more complex.

Between 1986 and 1987, taking into account all the above-mentioned elements, the government implemented yet another programme of rectification of errors and negative tendencies. In practice, this meant a critical revision of the decisions adopted during the 1970s that had impelled Cuba to adopt economic, political, and ideological concepts and ways of organization similar to those seen in European socialism.

In the economic aspect, rectification meant the introduction of more centralized mechanisms of economic management, monetary-mercantile relationships were again reduced, agricultural and produce markets as well as artisans' markets were closed, and parallel markets almost disappeared. Self-employment was also dramatically reduced, and new ways of organizing the labour force were created, aimed at tackling the priorities of the revolution. These task forces were granted special working conditions and an important level of recognition by society in general. Micro brigades were also re-established for housing construction projects and material incentives were reduced, while at the same time moral incentives were again adopted. Investments in social works such as schools, hospitals, nursery schools, etc. were also increased during this time. From 1985 to 1988, investment in social works grew from 17.7 per cent to 21.8 per cent of the total level of investment in the country. Another priority sector was food production, though the results in this area have been limited (Table 7.12).

In general, the development strategy continued to be the same as during the previous period, with the characteristic of new programmes being implemented, which in a few years would become of great importance, such as tourism and biotechnology.

The critique of socialist countries, explicit in the process of rectification, did not bring about a reduction in trade with those countries. Trade with the socialist bloc rose to 86.7 per cent of total trade in 1988. The refusal of the Club of Paris to accept any renegotiation of the foreign debt forced the suspension of payments to settle the debt, which in turn led to the suspension of credit by capitalist countries and a greater concentration of trade with socialist countries which seemed to be the only alternative. This event helps to better understand the impact that the collapse of the socialist bloc would have on the Cuban economy a few years later. It must also be remembered that the relationship between Cuba and the socialist countries, principally with the USSR, was not only a trade relationship. It also included preferential prices, compensations and credits, technical assistance, transfers of technology, coordination of economic plans, military aid, etc, all of which, apart from the resources, offered a considerable level of certainty to our economy, even though these relationships had always been accompanied by several contradictions.

From an economic point of view, the period was one of stagnation. The annual average growth of GDP between 1986 and 1989 was only 0.2 per cent.

*Table 7.12* Distribution of arable lands according to use (in thousand ha.)

| | *1959* | *%* | *1970* | *%* | *1992* | *%* |
|---|---|---|---|---|---|---|
| Agricultural area | 7,000 | 100 | 6,800 | 100 | 6,775 | 100 |
| Of it: cultivated | 2,300 | 32.9 | 3,900 | 57.3 | 4,437 | 65.4 |
| Sugar cane | 1,300 | 18.6 | 1,700 | 25.0 | 1,916 | 28.2 |
| Other export crops | 100 | 1.4 | 200 | 2.9 | 340 | 5.0 |
| Grasses | 300 | 4.3 | 1,300 | 19.1 | 1,079 | 15.4 |
| Food crops | 600 | 8.6 | 700 | 10.3 | 1,102 | 16.3 |
| Natural grasses | 3,700 | 52.9 | 1,600 | 23.5 | 1,879 | 27.7 |

*Source*: A. González, *et al.*, *Cuba: el sector agropecuario y las políticas agrícolas ante los nuevos retos.* Havana, 2000.

The level of foreign debt in hard currency grew rapidly because of the accumulation of interest, while work productivity and efficiency in the use of capital decreased. Sugar production remained at around 7.6 million tons per year and tourism grew. Infrastructure in social works was improved and special plans, like the family doctor and nurse project, were implemented, and improved with the construction of special places for doctors' consultations, with adequate equipment for an average of 110 families. As has been explained before, during this period the highest priority was given to the social sector, and the infrastructures in the educational and health care sectors were expanded and improved.

In the middle of this period, the European socialist bloc collapsed, leading to the disappearance of the COMECOM and the USSR. These events had a catastrophic impact on the Cuban economy, and led to the crisis of the 1990s, called the Special Period. To the structural problems of the Cuban economy and the closing of credits by western countries, were now added the disappearance of the country's most important economic partners and the tightening of the US blockade with the Torricelli (1991) and Helms–Burton (1996) Acts.

## The Special Period: 1990–2002

This difficult situation led to a policy of resistance, with the main objective of keeping the Revolutionary Government in power in a scenario of crisis, uncertainty, and international pressures. Obviously, the inevitable crisis in the economy would create a contraction in the standards of living of the population, and would make it difficult to maintain the social consensus and the work of the government. The country's leadership insisted on the need to resist, preserving the sovereignty of the nation and the social conquerors of the revolution.

In the midst of a situation like this, it was very difficult to identify a clear strategy for economic development because all of the measures adopted were emergency measures whose purposes were primarily political. Sugar production continued to be a priority, directly monitored by the government, as well as the expansion of other export sectors within the economy, such as tourism and biotechnology. Oil exploration began, as well as a new policy of openness to foreign investment, whose presence in Cuba had been much reduced during the previous decades by a decision of the Revolutionary government. Centralized planning was practically eliminated and increased autonomy was granted to enterprises to establish direct international economic relations.

In 1992, a constitutional reform modified the fundamentals of the Constitution of 1976, linking them more to national tradition and culture, than to the European socialist model which had influenced it previously. It also created the juridical bases for the changes that would be implemented a year later that presupposed higher levels of economic decentralization.

The most difficult years were from 1990 to 1993. During those years, the accumulated fall in GDP was more than 35 per cent and the contraction of imports was more than 88 per cent. Consumption also contracted, including food, and transportation, where extensive use of bicycles was encouraged, among other measures. At the beginning of the crisis, the purpose of the Revolutionary government was to hold income distribution as equitable as possible. With this aim in mind, three important measures were adopted: available products were distributed through a generalized system of rationing, while freezing prices to prevent inflation; all enterprises with economic losses – that is, most of them – were subsidized, thus preventing massive and uncontrolled growth of unemployment; and the priority of social sectors such as education, health care and social security was maintained. The state budget devoted to the social sector grew constantly during the years of the crisis, at an annual average of 2.6 per cent (Tables 7.13 and 7.14).

The first impact of the crisis was tackled by the measures adopted, but by mid-1993 the need for new measures was becoming evident. Production, including sugar production, continued to decline, and only tourism managed to maintain reasonable growth rates. Food production also contracted to a considerable degree, and, between 1989 and 1995, there was a strong reduction in the distribution of calories as well as proteins and fats to the population. The decline of production and imports and the increase of money in the economy because of the subsidizing policies generated a large imbalance in internal finances. The budget deficit rose to

*Table 7.13* Social expenses in the budget (millions of pesos)

| *Concept* | *1990* | *1996* | *1997* | *1998* | *2001* |
|---|---|---|---|---|---|
| Total expenses | 14,213.1 | 12,813.5 | 12,662.6 | 13,061.7 | 15,761.0 |
| Social expenses | 4,517.0 | 5,115.3 | 5,264.0 | 5,565.3 | 7,336.8 |
| Education | 1,619.5 | 1,421.3 | 1,453.9 | 1,509.7 | 2,368.6 |
| Public health | 937.4 | 1,190.3 | 1,265.2 | 1,344.9 | 1,796.6 |
| Social security | 1,164.1 | 1,630.2 | 1,635.9 | 1,705.1 | 1,870.3 |
| Housing and community service | 382.7 | 462.4 | 487.6 | 565.5 | 827.2 |
| Culture and arts | 200.6 | 165.2 | 164.7 | 168.8 | 310.7 |
| Sports | 117.1 | 117.5 | 121.5 | 125.9 | 163.4 |
| Percentage of total expenses | 31.8 | 39.9 | 41.5 | 42.6 | 46.6 |
| Subsidies due to price differences | 736.8 | 867.3 | 757.9 | 1,352.0 | 1,900.2 |

*Source*: *Anuario Estadístico de Cuba 1996, 1998, 2001; Cuba en Cifras 1997*. ONE, 1998.

*Table 7.14* Social security expenses[1] (α) (millions of pesos)

| *Concept* | *1990* | *1995* | *1997* | *1998* |
|---|---|---|---|---|
| *Total* | 1352.3 | 1741.2 | 1846.4 | 1900.8 |
| Social security services | 1314.3 | 1701.1 | 1794.6 | 1848.5 |
| Pensions for age, disablement and death | 1102.3 | 1471.5 | 1500.8 | 1557.7 |
| Subsidies for sickness, accident and maternity | 191.8 | 196.6 | 264.7 | 261.1 |
| Pensions for partial disablement | 14.6 | 21.9 | 18.3 | 17.7 |
| Complementary | 4.3 | 2.2 | 1.5 | 1.5 |
| Of them: Resolution No. 8/92 | 0.3 | 0.7 | 0.3 | 0.3 |
| Others | 1.1 | 8.9 | 9.3 | 10.5 |
| Social assistance services | 38.2 | 40.1 | 51.8 | 52.3 |

[1]Civil sector.
*Source*: Ministry of Labour and Social Security. In *Cuba en Cifras 1997*.

almost 30 per cent of GDP (Table 7.15). A highly inflationary black market flourished, and the value of the national currency on the black market was devalued, from eight pesos per dollar in 1989 to 150 pesos per dollar in 1993.

*Table 7.15* Selected economic indicators, 1994–99

| *Selected indicators* | *1994* | *1995* | *1996* | *1997* | *1998* | *1999* | *2000* |
|---|---|---|---|---|---|---|---|
| GDP (millions of pesos) (at 1981 prices) | 12,868 | 13,185 | 14,218 | 14,572 | 14,754 | 15,674 | 16,556.4 |
| Yearly average growth of GDP | 0.7 | 2.5 | 7.8 | 2.5 | 1.2 | 6.2 | 5.6 |
| Fiscal deficit (millions of pesos) | -1,421 | -766 | -571 | -459 | -559 | -611 | -672 |
| Fiscal deficit/ GDP (in %) | 7.4 | 3.5 | 2.5 | 2.0 | 2.3 | 2.4 | 2.4 |
| Liquidity of the population (in thousand millions pesos) | 9.9 | 9.2 | 9.5 | 9.4 | 9.7 | 9.9 | 10.5 |

*Source*: ONE, *Estadísticas seleccionadas de Cuba, 1996,* April, 1997. ONE, *Cuba en Cifras,* several years, *Anuario Estadístico 2001*.

This situation created a clear separation between salaries and the economy. The average salary of 200 pesos could cover the basic goods distributed by the rationing system, which at the same time were insufficient to meet a family's needs. However, such a level of salary was not enough to pay black market prices. This situation created a spiral of speculation and increased the level of social tensions. On top of everything else, the opening up to foreign investment and tourism created an emerging sector that operated by different regulations to those applied in the rest of the economy. This created a strong tendency, among the most qualified in the labour force, to move towards the emerging tourism-related sector, where they could obtain dollars, and thereby access to privileged markets. On the other hand, it was difficult to obtain hard currency so that the economy could move forward. This scenario prompted the government to implement deeper economic changes, a process that began in the summer of 1993.

In August 1993, the first changes would be implemented, opening a new era of important modifications in Cuban economy and society. The use of foreign currency by the Cuban population became legal. Greater possibilities for self-employment were also allowed. The *Unidades Básicas de Producción Cooperativa* (UBPC) or basic units for cooperative production were created. The last was a significant change in achieving the restructuring and the better functioning of the Cuban economy, because it favoured a noteworthy modification in the forms of agricultural production. The majority of the state farms implemented cooperative forms of production, which differed from previously existing cooperative ways of production in that the latter received the land in usufruct, rather than in property. Nevertheless, its members become owners of means of production other than land, of production itself, and of income.

Such measures were introduced with the intention of tackling the deep economic crisis the country was suffering. The use of hard currency by the population legalized a de facto situation. Tourism, foreign investment, and family remittances increased rapidly during these years, up to 800,000 thousand and one billion dollars per year. These added to the proliferation of dollar stores and other hard currency services originally intended for tourism, and now at the disposal of the general population. It also led to a growing use of foreign currency by large sectors of the population. On the one hand, this measure stimulated family remittances from abroad, mainly from South Florida, which became an important inflow of external resources. With time it also favoured the revival of several important productive sectors now again in high demand (Monreal 2000). Self-employment became a source of employment, and a very important one, with more than 205,000 registered as self-employed, at a time when potential unemployment was very high (Table 7.16). New cooperatives would increase the production of food produce and export products, when it was very difficult to sustain large-scale agricultural production, typical of large state enterprises, which depended upon large quantities of fuel, machinery, chemicals, and other imports.

*Table 7.16* Workers occupied in the national economy (thousands of workers)

| *Year* | *No. of occupied* | *Employment (%)* |
|---|---|---|
| 1991 | 4,888.2 | 100.0 |
| 1995 | 3,591.0 | 92.3 |
| 1997 | 3,746.8 | 96.3 |
| 1998 | 3,753.6 | 96.5 |

*Source*: *Cuba en Cifras 1997 y 1998*. ONE 1998 and 1999, respectively.

In May 1994, after a heated national debate, other measures – aimed at re-establishing the internal economic balance and reducing the amount of money in circulation – were adopted. These measures included: increasing the price of non-priority goods, while maintaining subsidies on basic goods and products; the elimination of gratuities such as water and sewage services, tickets to sports events, etc.; an increase in tariffs, new tax laws for all income, except for salary and family remittances; and the reduction of subsidies to enterprises. The latter was important, because the level of the enterprise subsidies accounted for a larger part of the budget deficit than social expenses did.

In October 1994, the free market was opened again for produce and artisans, a measure aimed at complementing the transformations of the agricultural sector in order to encourage the production of food. That year it was quite evident that the lack of food was the worst aspect of the crisis, even posing a threat to national security. It must be taken into account that US policy at this time was trying to exacerbate the general contradictions generated by the crisis. In the summer of 1994, for example, the rafter's crisis took place.

Other significant changes followed, such as a reduction in the apparatus of the state, greater autonomy for enterprises, changes in the traditional conception of planning, which was now to be based more firmly on financial indicators; banking reform, the establishment of money exchange for national currency with a freely floating rate, and the beginning of enterprise reform.

It should be pointed out that the Cuban economy operates with two different exchange rates: one of them is determined by demand and supply generated by the population; the other exchange rate artificially maintains the parity between peso and dollar, and is applied in all of the economic operations and transactions between enterprises and the international economy. This situation leads to distortions in the calculation of costs, and in the establishment of relative prices, which stimulates imports, and adversely affects exports. Economists view this as a complex problem affecting the Cuban economy.

The strategy for economic development at this stage emphasized tourism, with annual growth rates higher than 15 per cent, and foreign investment in the nickel and tobacco industries. It also tried to obtain profitable production of sugar, though sugar production from the second half of the 1990s has been the lowest in modern history. Oil production increased, from less than one million tons in 1990 to over 3.5 million tons in 2002. The idea of substitution of imports was preserved.

Decentralizing measures and new external financial influences such as foreign investment, tourism, nickel exports, and family remittances, favoured the recovery of the economy, albeit at a slower pace. Though GDP has grown since 1994, the production levels of the 1980s have not yet been matched. The economic structure of the country is now different; mechanisms of direction of the economy as well as many economic actors are new. In addition, the international economic arena is different.

The impacts of the crisis and economic changes have generated social inequalities and reintroduced problems that had been apparently overcome in previous decades. Disparities of income have risen, dependent upon the access to hard currency. There have been increases in a number of social problems: low birth weight and size of children in some regions: elderly people in precarious situations; and situations of marginality, prostitution, and procuring associated with tourism. In addition, there has been a deterioration in the condition of the housing stock, an increase in the crime rate and various forms of corruption. The Cuban authorities have acknowledged the situation and in 1999 they announced a number of projects in order to try and eliminate them.

Several regulations have attempted to address the process of differentiation in the population, but inequalities have increased nevertheless, and are quite visible in many expressions; the worst being those derived from the excluding dollar market or services, particularly the development of tourist resorts that veto the participation, and sometimes even the presence of Cubans (Valdés Paz 1999).

The national currency experienced a relative recovery. In 1993, one dollar was equal to 150 Cuban pesos, while in 2003 the free market rate was 1 to 26. However, in spite of the relative recovery of the national currency, there was no coherent relationship between the average salary and the level of prices in free markets, either in pesos or in dollars. Although nominal salaries in 1997 were an average of 214 pesos, an increase of 13.2 per cent over the whole period of the crisis, the increase in consumer prices reduced the real salary from 131 pesos in 1989 to 76 pesos in 1997 – a fall of 42 per cent (Togores, 1998). Such a situation not only creates social tensions, but also de-stimulates formal work and affects productivity and intensity of work.

Nevertheless, the relative recovery of food supplies, free markets and subsidies to basic supplies, have favoured a slow improvement of the population's levels of nutrition, particularly in its most vulnerable groups. However, the availability of foodstuffs has not covered the basic needs (Ferriol, 1998).

In public health care, the greatest problem has been the lack of medicine. However, organizational measures and a greater emphasis in preventive medicine have also sustained the essential quality of services. In fact, except for the appearance of new pathologies like polyneuritis and the discreet increase of some morbidity indicators in the first years of the decade, the group of health indicators has either been the same or improved at the end of the 1990s. For example, infant mortality, hospital and community services, life expectancy, and other indicators have continued to improve (Valdés Paz 1999) (Tables 7.17–7.20).

In education, apart from an accumulated deterioration of facilities and school materials, the main consequence of the crisis was the reduction in the numbers of teaching staff, mainly in intermediate-level and higher-level education. However, the measures adopted allowed the maintenance of educational coverage. In fact, in 1999 one of every five inhabitants was within the system of education. However, the number of graduates diminished dramatically – around 40 per cent – in intermediate and higher education, and the teaching staff had diminished by 28 per cent and 13 per cent for both educational levels, respectively, by the end of the decade. These

*Table 7.17* Indicators of public health services

| *Concept* | *1990* | *1995* | *1997* | *2001* |
|---|---|---|---|---|
| Total of doctors | 38,690 | 56,836 | 62,624 | 67,128 |
| Inhabitants per doctor | 275 | 193 | 176 | |
| Total of beds in hospitals | 78,164 | 81,364 | 82,037 | 70,927 |
| Total of inpatients per hospital | 1,652,205 | 1,477,787 | 1,493,214 | 1,351,144 |
| Total of outpatient consultations | 48,079,149 | 56,915,855 | 57,786,423 | 58,156,000 |
| Total of emergency consultations | 20,122,071 | 18,213,646 | 21,087,302 | 19,777,000 |
| Total of inoculations against basic diseases | 2,668,642 | 2,437,375 | 2,879,485 | 2,126,881 |

*Source: Cuba en Cifras 1997. ONE.* Havana 1998.

*Table 7.18* Trends in life expectancy at birth

| *Life expectancy at birth* | *1960–65* | *1970–75* | *1980–85* | *1985–90* | *1990–96* | *1995–2000* |
|---|---|---|---|---|---|---|
| Both sexes | 65.1 | 70.9 | 73.6 | 74.5 | 74.7 | 75.7 |

*Sources:* Cuba, National Action Program, December, 1991, p. 10; ONE, *Indicadores sociales y demográficos de Cuba*, several years.

*Table 7.19* Evolution of health indicators

| *Selected indicators* | *1960* | *1980* | *1985* | *1990* | *1991* | *1993* | *1995* | *1999* | *2000* | *2001* | *2002* |
|---|---|---|---|---|---|---|---|---|---|---|---|
| Infant mortality rate (per thousand births) | 42.0 | 19.6 | 16.5 | 10.7 | 10.7 | 9.4 | 9.4 | 6.5 | 7.2 | 6.2 | 6.5 |
| Mortality rate in children under 5 years (per thousand births) | 42.4[1] | 24.3 | 19.7 | 13.2 | 13.4 | 12.2 | 12.5 | 8.4 | 11.1[2] | 8.0 | |
| Low weight at birth (in %) | | 9.7 | 8.2 | 7.6 | 7.8 | 9.0 | 7.9 | 6.5 | 6.1[2] | | 5.9 |
| Maternity mortality rate (per thousand births) | 120.1 | 52.6 | 30.8 | 31.6 | 36.2 | 26.9 | 47.6 | 43.8 | 40.4 | 33.9 | 41.8 |
| Births in hospitals (%) | 63.0 | 98.5 | 98.8 | 99.8 | 99.8 | 99.8 | 99.8 | 99.9 | 99.9 | | |
| Inhabitants per doctor | | 641 | 439 | 274 | 251 | 214 | 193 | 172 | 170 | 167 | |
| Inhabitants per dentist | | 2,682 | 1,885 | 1,524 | 1,423 | 1,280 | 1,200 | 1,125 | 1,129 | 1,137 | |

*Notes*:
[1]Data from 1965.
[2]Provisional data.
*Source*: Figures supplied by the National Office of Statistics (ONE). 'Food for All.' Cuba's report to the World Summit on Food, Havana, November 1996. Cuba, National Program of Action, Reports 1 to 5. *Anuario Estadístico 2001*.

*Table 7.20* Budget expenses in health care

| *Year* | *Expenses in health care (millions of pesos)* | *% of the total expenses of the budget* |
|---|---|---|
| 1990 | 937.4 | 6.6 |
| 1991 | 924.9 | 6.3 |
| 1992 | 938.3 | 6.6 |
| 1993 | 1,076.6 | 7.4 |
| 1994 | 1,061.1 | 7.5 |
| 1995 | 1,108.0 | 8.0 |
| 1996 | 1,190.0 | 9.3 |
| 1997 | 1,265.2 | 10.0 |
| 1998 | 1,344.9 | 10.3 |
| 1999 | 1,553.1 | 11.1 |
| 2000 | 1,683.8 | 10.8 |
| 2001 | 1,796.6 | 11.4 |

*Source*: Anuarios Estadísticos de Cuba 2000, 2001.

indicators would recover when new programmes were implemented in the sector from 1999 (Tables 7.21–7.23).

Though the crisis did not reduce the level of expenditure on social security – in fact, it increased between 1990 and 1997 by 36 per cent in nominal terms – it did affect the real value of services and payments because of the inflation that began in 1991. Such devaluation has been compensated in part by the relative revaluation of the national currency, and the increase in pensions paid to lower-income sectors of the population. Another important problem, with future consequences, was that high levels of growth in social security expenses impose severe tensions on the state budget, while the population gets older as life expectancy increases (Valdés Paz, 1999; Gutiérrez-Peñate, 2000).

*Table 7.21* Budget expenses in education

| *Years* | *Millions of pesos* | *% of the total budgetary expenses* |
|---|---|---|
| 1959 | 76.5 | |
| 1970 | 351.1 | |
| 1985 | 1,587.8 | |
| 1989 | 1,650.6 | |
| 1998 | 1,509.7 | 11.6 |
| 1999 | 1,829.6 | 13.1 |
| 2000 | 2,094.6 | 13.4 |
| 2001 | 2,368.6 | 15.1 |

*Source*: Ministry of Finances and Prices, *Anuario Estadístico 2001*.

*Table 7.22* Levels of enrolment in relation to population of school age (in percentage)

| *Level of education* | *1953* | *1981* | *1999* |
|---|---|---|---|
| Grade school (6 to 11 years) | 55.1 | 97.7 | 99.1 |
| Enseñanza Secundaria Básica (12 to 14 years) | 56.5 | 92.4 | 96.3 |
| Elementary education (6 to 14 years) | 55.6 | 95.8 | 98.2 |

*Source*: Census from 1953 and 1981; ONE, *Anuario Estadístico de Cuba.*

*Table 7.23* Network of educational centres

| *Centre* | *Course 1958–59* | *Course 1999–00* |
|---|---|---|
| Nursery schools | – | 1,118 |
| Grade schools | 7,567 | 9,360 |
| Of which, rural | – | 7,099 |
| Junior high school | 6 | 1,003 |
| Pre-university schools | 21 | 274 |
| Polytechnic institutes | 40 | 647 |
| Special schools | 15 | 444 |
| Higher education centres | 3 | 48 |

*Source*: ONE, *Anuario Estadístico de Cuba 1999.*

Community services have also been affected by the crisis and, with the abovementioned levels of budget deficits, affecting the drinking water and sewage infrastructure (Table 7.24). These problems have produced a lowering of the living standards of the average Cuban, and everyday life has become more difficult. Recovery in this area, though considerable in some cases, such as in electric power supply, was still insufficient and insecure.

*Table 7.24* Coverage for drinking water and sewage at the end of 1999 (percentage)

| *Population* | *Drinking water* | | | | *Sewage* | | |
|---|---|---|---|---|---|---|---|
| | *Total population served* | *Facilities installed at home* | *Public service* | *Easy access* | *Total population served* | *Sewage* | *Pits and latrines* |
| Urban | 97.8 | 84.9 | 4.1 | 8.8 | 96.3 | 47.9 | 48.4 |
| Rural | 86.3 | 40.4 | 16.2 | 29.8 | 8.3 | 8.3 | 74.1 |
| Total | 95.0 | 73.8 | 7.2 | 14.0 | 92.8 | 38.1 | 54.7 |

*Source*: Cuba, *Informe Nacional sobre el Seguimiento al Acuerdo de Lima en el Marco de la Cumbre Mundial a favor de la Infancia*, Havana, August, 2000.

The crisis also had an impact on employment. The levels of almost full employment achieved in previous decades came to an end, because of the sharp contraction of the economy, mainly in the industrial and construction sector. Emergency policies, and later on some economic recovery, have alleviated this problem somewhat in latter years. Among the measures aimed at the protection of employment were the conservation of superfluous jobs, temporary subsidized employment, transfers between sectors of the economy, agricultural transformations and the authorization of self-employment. Because of these measures, by end of the decade, employment had reached 96.5 per cent of the 1991 level, and there was an annual average growth of one per cent (Valdés Paz, 1999).

The final years of the decade show a sustained creation of jobs, although this has been insufficient because of the fall in investment (Table 7.16). Therefore, the unemployment rate could be higher in the next few years because of the increase in working-age population, and of the rationalization of sub-employment. If the enterprise reform currently being implemented continues to advance, the number of potentially affected sub-employees in production activities is estimated to be up to 80,000. In this sense, several specialists advocate the expansion of small and medium-sized enterprise, private, cooperative, and state-owned, as the only alternative for the creation of productive employment in the medium and long term (Carranza, Gutiérrez and Monreal, 1996).

During this period, the commercial deficit persisted, as well as the deficit in the balance of payments and foreign debts, because of the high cost of short-term loans. Nonetheless, the budget deficit had been reduced from 30 per cent of GDP in 1994, to only 3 per cent in 2002. However, the level of debt among different enterprises in the country has increased (Carranza 2002).

It should be pointed out that, in spite of tensions, uncertainties and contradictions during this period, the priority of social policies was maintained, to protect the most vulnerable sectors in the country. As stated above, social expenses increased throughout these years, from 4,517 million in 1990 to 5,565 million in 1998 (Valdés Paz, 1997) (Tables 7.13, 7.20 and 7.21). At the same time, special plans for health care and education were considerably extended in the 1999–2003 period.

Finally, the 1999–2003 period was interesting because of two conditions that might seem contradictory, but which, in a way, were paradigmatic of the concepts that have historically characterized the Cuban process over recent decades. Since 1999 the recovery of the economy has been slower, and there has been less access to external resources; at the same time plans for social development in the sectors of education, health, culture and ideology have been extended and reprioritized.

Several hostile factors have also had an impact on the recovery of the economy. Sugar prices in international markets fell to their lowest level in history. The persistence of this situation has made sugar production unprofitable, and led, in 2001, to the closing of almost half of the existing sugar mills, so that the land and the resources available could be put to other productive uses. The productive base of the last 200 years has thus been radically modified, and this affects not only exports, but also inter-sectoral relationships, and the international criteria for the granting of loans and credits. The prices of nickel also suffered from a fall that lasted several years, though it has lately been recovering. Cooperation relationships with Europe have been suspended. The impact of September 11, 2001 on tourism and family remittances has also been considerable. Finally, between 2004 and 2005, three strong hurricanes hit Cuba in the space of less than a year.

At the same time, and since 1999, a group of programmes have been created or reinforced for the development of the social sector as part of what in Cuba has been called *The Battle of Ideas*. In education, emphasis has been placed on the maintenance, repair, and construction of new schools, the reduction of the number of students per class to 20 in grade school and to less than 15 in secondary and pre-university education. In addition, programmes for the emergency training of teachers, the revision of the syllabus and the teacher–student relationship have been put in place, based more on the inculcation of values and knowledge than on simple instruction. A new educational TV channel only for educational programmes has been created, equipping all of the schools in the country with TV and VCR, and solar energy panels have been installed in schools in the mountains so that they can receive TV signals. Special education has been strengthened, bringing university professors and courses to municipalities (Tables 7.22–7.23).

In the health sector, more attention is now being paid to the family doctor project, to repair works in hospitals, pharmacies, and the opening of drug stores. In addition, specialized medical services in the territories, and the training of more medical and paramedical personnel are now also offered (Table 7.19). In the area of culture, new schools for art instructors are being opened and cultural institutions are being repaired. In sports, better attention to sportsmen in the country and new facilities for training are being opened. An anti-doping lab is also being constructed.

In the social arena, three large schools for the training of social workers have been opened. This is a response to the idea that Cuba's problems need to be well identified in order to be properly addressed. In addition, there has been an increase in cooperation with other Third World countries, based on grants and scholarships, mainly in the sectors of medicine and sport. Medical brigades were sent to these countries, including doctors and nurses, as well as teachers and professors, and sports trainers.

It can be stated that the policies for social development have been a priority throughout all of the economic strategies adopted and implemented by the Cuban Government since 1959 (Table 7.13). Even during economic crises, this priority has prevailed. The emphasis on social policy has allowed universal and free access of all the population to all social services that provide them with a basic level of welfare and sovereignty (Valdés Paz, 1998). In this respect, therefore, the development pattern of Cuba does differ substantially from other LADWS.

However, it is important to bear in mind the stress of the present situation, suffered by an economy that is not able to grow at the levels necessary to overcome stagnation. It is affected by low levels of efficiency, subject to a strict blockade by the US, with a lack of natural resources, or with even the minimum level of productive investment required. In this situation, the economy seems ill prepared both for its own development, and also to maintain the growth and dynamics of social programmes.

Probably the highest strategic value of the social investment of the revolution, apart from the health indicators, is the high level of professional qualifications and potential for learning acquired by the labour force through its education system. This potential represents a great advantage for the country, when designing an economic strategy based on the intensive use of such resources, even in the difficult conditions of globalization (Monreal and Carranza 2003). This would give a more solid foundation for the sustenance and expansion of social policies in the long term, which is one of the main challenges for the future.

## Notes

1. On 21 October 1896 the Captain General of the Island, Valeriano Weyler ordered all residents in rural areas or outside the protected fortified urban settlements to settle in towns and other population centres. The order was first implemented in Pinar del Río; successive orders enforced it in the rest of the country. It was in force until Weyler was removed from his position in October 1897. According to conservative figures, casualties in the war were between 200–300,000 (20 per cent of the population).
2. The differences in tariff depending upon the ship's flag in maritime traffic were established in 1820. For example, wheatflour, in general, paid 2 pesos in tariff per barrel when being Spanish wheat on a Spanish ship; 6 pesos when Spanish wheat on a foreign ship; 8.50 pesos when foreign wheat on a Spanish ship; and 9.50 pesos when foreign wheat on a foreign ship. This system was termed the *four-column tariff* (Note from the authors).

## References

Carranza Valdés, J. (2002). *La economía cubana: Balance breve de una década crítica.* Revista Temas No. 30. Havana.

Carranza Valdés, J. (1998). *La viabilidad y adaptabilidad de los sistemas sociales.* Inédito. Havana.

Carranza, Valdés, J. (1998). *Las finanzas externas y los límites del crecimiento.* Revista Economía y Desarrollo No. 2. Havana.

Carranza Valdés, J., Gutiérrez Urdaneta, L. and Monreal González, P. (1996). *Cuba, La reestructuración de la economía: Una propuesta para el debate*. Caracas: Edit Nueva Sociedad.

Castro Ruz, F. (1975). *Primer Congreso del Partido Comunista de Cuba*. Havana: Informe Central.

CEPAL-INIE (2003) *Las políticas y la evolución social y económica de Cuba en el quinquenio 1998–2002*. Santiago: CEPAL.

Céspedes G. M. and. Manuel, C. (1996) *Promoción Humana, realidad cubana y perspectivas. Honrad*. Caracas: Adenauer Stifung.

CIEM-PNUD (1999). *Investigación sobre el desarrollo humano y equidad en Cuba*. Havana: UNDP.

Conferencia para el Progreso de la Economía Nacional (1949). Havana, Cuba.

Díaz Vázquez, J. A. (1986). *Cuba: integración económica socialista y especialización de la producción*. Havana: Editorial Pueblo y Educación.

Documentos (1972). *Encuesta de la Agrupación Católica Universitaria*, Rev. Economía y Desarrollo, 12, Havana.

Domínguez, M. I (1995). *Generaciones y procesos sociales en Cuba*, Rev. Contracorrientes, 1, Havana.

El Programa Económico de Cuba (1955) *Publicaciones del Consejo Nacional de Economía*. Havana.

Espina, Mayra, (1996) *Cuba: Reforma económica, cambios en la estructura social y desigualdad*. Havana: CIPS.

Ferriol, A. (1998) *La Pobreza en condiciones de reforma económica: el reto a la equidad en Cuba. 1998*. Investigación económica Año1. Havana.

Figueras, F. (1907). *Cuba y su Evolución Colonial, Imprenta el Avisor Comercial*. Havana.

Guerra Sánchez, R. (1970). *Azúcar y Población en las Antillas*. Havana: Edit Ciencias Sociales.

Guerra S. (1948). *Valores Espirituales del Trabajo y del Adelanto Material de Cuba*, Havana: Rev. Trimestre, II, 4, 403–44.

Gutiérrez, G. (1950). *Presente y futuro de la economía cubana*, Havana: Publicaciones de la Junta Nacional de Economía.

Gutiérrez Urdaneta, L. and Peñate, O. (2000). *La reforma de los sistemas de pensiones en América Latina*, La alternativa cubana. Havana: Edit Ciencias Sociales.

Hernández, R. (1998) *¿Hacia una nueva sociedad socialista*? Rev. Nueva Sociedad No 157. Caracas.

Historia de Cuba (1998) *La Neocolonia, organización y crisis, desde 1899 hasta 1940*. Havana: Edit Política.

Historia de la Nación Cubana (1952) *Editorial Historia de la Nación Cubana*, Tomos III–VII–IX–X. Havana: S. A.

Informe Ministerio de Hacienda del Gobierno Revolucionario (1959). Havana.

Le Riverend, J. (1974). *Historia Económica de Cuba*. Havana: Edit. Revolucionaria.

Mesa-Lago, C. (2002a) *Buscando un modelo económico en América Latina. ¿Mercado, Socialista o mixto? Chile, Cuba y Costa Rica*. Edit Nueva Sociedad.

Mesa-Lago, C. (2002b). 'La seguridad Social', *Rev. Encuentro*, 24. Madrid, pp. 248–9.

Monreal G. P. and Carranza Valdés, J. (2003) *Los desafíos de la globalización en el Caribe: Hacia una nueva estrategia de desarrollo en Cuba*. Mexico: Edit Siglo XXI.

Monreal, G. P. and Carranza, Valdés (1997) *Mitos y retos del desarrollo*. Rev. Temas No. La Habana.

Moreno Fraginals, M. (1978). 'El Ingenio', Tomo III,*Edit. de Ciencias Sociales*, Havana.

OXFAM (2002). *Cuba: Social Policy at the Crossroads*. USA: OXFAM-América.

Pardeiro, F. A. (1967). *Penetración de la Oligarquía financiera yanqui en la economía de Cuba capitalista*, Rev. Universidad de La Habana, July–December.
Pichardo, H. (1973–1980). *Documentos para la historia de Cuba, Tomo, I–II–III–IV*. Havana: Edit. Ciencias Sociales.
Pino Santos, O. (1973). *El imperialismo norteamericano en la economía de Cuba*. Havana: Edit Ciencias Sociales.
*Problemas de la Nueva Cuba* (1935). New York: Foreign Policy Association.
Rodríguez, C. R. (1978). *Cuba en el tránsito al socialismo*. Mexico: Editorial Siglo XXI.
Rodríguez García, J. L. and Carriazo Moreno, G (1987). *La erradicación de la pobreza*. Havana: Edit Ciencias Sociales.
Togores V. (1998) *Cuba: efectos sociales de la crisis y el ajuste económico de los 90s, en Balance de la economía cubana a fines de los 90s*. Havana:CEE, UH.
Torras, J. (1984–1985) *Obras Escogidas, Tomo I–II*. Havana: Edit Política.
Truslow, F. A. (1951). *Report on Cuba: Findings and Recommendations of and Economic and Technical Mission*. Baltimore: Johns Hopkins University Press.
Valdés Paz, J. (1997). *Procesos agrarios en Cuba, 1959–1995*. Havana: Edit Ciencias Sociales.
Valdés Paz, J. (1999). *Un examen de los cambios en curso y de su impacto en la sociedad cubana de los noventa*, inédito. Havana.
Zanetti Lecuona, O. (1989). *Los cautivos de la reciprocidad*. Havana: Edit ENPES.

# Part V

# On the Meagre Fringes of Early American Settlers

# 8

# Social Policy and Social Reform 'Costa Rican Style': A Paradigmatic Case of Heterodoxy in the Context of a Peripheral Economy

*Manuel Barahona, Ludwig Güendel and Carlos Castro**

> If development is recognized as an expansion of basic capabilities, there is little doubt that Costa Rica has one of the most outstanding histories of recent decades.
>
> Amartya Sen and Jean Drèze (1989)

## Introduction

Costa Rica is a small country located on a segment of the Central American isthmus between the Caribbean Sea and the Pacific Ocean, with a surface area of 31,758 square miles (51,100 square kilometres). Its population exceeds four million inhabitants. It is a country in full demographic transition, whose territory is organized administratively into seven provinces, 81 cantons and six planning regions.

Costa Rica was known as the poorest and most backward colony assigned to the Captaincy General of Guatemala. Until 1920, it was the next to last Central American economy in terms of the size of GDP. By the middle of the twentieth century, Costa Rica was among the world's medium-income countries, making it an exception in Central America. By the 1990s, the Costa Rican economy had surpassed all others in the region: its GDP was 20 per cent higher than El Salvador's and 70 per cent higher than Guatemala's. In 2002, its GDP per capita was 2.1 times that

* The authors wish to express their acknowledgement to Ana Victoria Soto for her careful translation to English from the Spanish version and also for her support in the revision's of style in both languages.

of El Salvador, 2.3 times that of Guatemala, 5.2 times that of Honduras and 7.4 times that of Nicaragua.

By 2003, Costa Rica was ranked 42nd according to the Human Development Index (HDI) of the United Nations Development Program (UNDP), placing it in the group of those countries with high human development levels. It was surpassed in Latin America only by Argentina (34th place) and Uruguay (40th place), with the rest of the Central American countries being ranked as having medium human development levels(Table 8.A1).

These aspects make Costa Rica an interesting case study, a laboratory perhaps, for considering the effects of social investment and development. In this sense, the present chapter intends to contribute to:

- Systematizing the Costa Rican experience as a paradigmatic case of a nation of high social and human development levels, despite sharing characteristics and economic insufficiencies with other peripheral countries.
- Establishing the specifics of its development style that have determined that outcome.
- Examining the social reforms underway while also highlighting their impacts and the challenges that they raise.

This chapter is structured into six sections. The next section carefully reviews the process that led the Costa Rican state to a decisive involvement in the fulfillment of social needs. Then, the principal milestones in development and social policy in the nation's developmental stage from the beginning of the 1950s until the beginning of the 1980s are discussed. In that later decade, the country was shaken by a deep crisis whose social consequences are detailed in the fourth section. The fifth section, which constitutes the main body of the chapter, explores the relationships between economic transformations associated with the establishment of a new development model, and the experiences of designing and implementing social policy. The sixth section presents the most important findings of our research. The work concludes with the bibliography and a statistical annex, which is a selection of tables and graphics capable, *per se*, of providing a general view of the country and of the changes experienced in its major social and economic indicators over the medium and long term. It should be noted that an article by Barahona, Sauma and Trejos published in 1999 (see Bibliography) was used as a basis to develop this study, and was subject to revision and expansion in its relevant aspects.

## Genesis of the *Estado Social de Derecho* (Welfare State)[1]

The importance of attending to the basic needs of the population grew as the Costa Rican state became consolidated as a modern state. In 1824, the

Governmental Board formulated the principle that 'public instruction is the basis and main foundation of human happiness and common prosperity'. Later, in 1886, when the liberal project took form and shaped the country's journey into modernity, primary education was established by law as being gratuitous and compulsory, thereby setting in motion the population's literacy process.[2] This led Rama to state that Costa Rica 'is the only society in Latin America which, being fundamentally agricultural and rural, made literacy and primary education widespread'[3] (IADB, 1994: 33).

At the beginning of the twentieth century, the state continued to promote some social initiatives – although in an isolated and unsystematic fashion. In the area of public health, programmes aimed at tackling contagious infectious diseases like hookworms and tuberculosis were organized, leading to the creation of the Secretariat of Public Health. In the area of education, the Secretariat of Education that created the so-called 'Normal School' (for the preparation of teachers) was founded and this in turn established schools and secondary education institutes. During the 1920s, this precocious insertion into the social realm was complemented with other measures, such as the establishment of a job-risk insurance scheme (Banco Nacional de Seguros or the National Insurance Bank, currently the Instituto Nacional de Seguros or National Insurance Institute, 1924); the regulation of labour relations (Secretaría de Trabajo y Previsión Social or Secretariat of Labor and Welfare, 1928); the creation of a Bismarckian model of social security – which in the end could not be institutionally materialized; and the protection of abandoned children (Patronato Nacional de la Infancia or National Children's Bureau, 1930).

These actions unfolded in the context of the emergence of the first urban social movements, anarchist and socialist political parties, as a loss of political influence by the military, and also an intense ideological and social discussion that confronted various political projects. It should be emphasized, nonetheless, that there was an interesting agreement among all those forces and actors about the importance of strengthening social issues, as well as on the view of liberal democracy as a national aspiration.

One of these proposals for harmonizing/complementing social vindications with the classical institutions of representative democracy arose very forcefully during the 1940s. During this time, the Catholic Church, the Communist Party and certain sectors within the ruling class that ascribed to Social Christianity combined to forge an alliance that helped them obtain to achieve success on two occasions. This proposal centred on four fundamental milestones: the creation of the University of Costa Rica (1940); the incorporation of a chapter on Social Guarantees in the country's Political Constitution (1942); the approval of a Labor Code (1943); and the creation of the Caja Costarricense de Seguro Social or Costa Rican Social Security System (1943). Under the leadership of the Ministry of Labor, a legal vision on the subject prevailed during this phase of social policy. The actions carried out had select coverage (with the target population being the urban wage-earning population)[4] and did not correspond to a comprehensive concept of human development. However, important advances were made in the quality of life of the population owing to breakthroughs adopted in the area of sanitation technology. Among these, an average gain of nine years in life expectancy at birth stands out, along with a significant reduction in infant mortality, which dropped from more than 100 per 1,000 live births in 1950 (Trejos, 1991: 76).

## Social policy in a developmental context: from the 1950s to the dawn of the 1980s

The discussion that had been taking place throughout this half-century among the different social and political groups was settled with the 1948 civil war, which set into confrontation Communists and Social Democrats allied with different factions of the ruling class. The so-called Second Republic emerged from this, synthesizing the views of the latter as the winners. It had the particularity of preserving not just the social institutions created during the 1940s, as well as building a more comprehensive, integrated vision of the development process that combined economic reform,[5] social reform and political reform[6] into a unique perspective. From this moment on, the state assumed a leading role in promoting development and, in short, institutionalized social policy, which stopped being a formal and unsystematic activity as it had been conceived in the liberal era, and became an outcome of the recognition of social rights. In this regard, Garnier and Hidalgo (1991: 25) stated that

> if there is anything that distinguishes the transformation attained by Costa Rica beginning in the 1940s, it was the privileged role conceded to social matters. Never before in the history of the country had such a sustained, systematic and comprehensive effort been carried out to use the State as the principal promoter – directly and indirectly – of social development.

Thus, the state presence in education and health was consolidated, social security was expanded, and a process of state involvement began in new areas such as professional training, the supply of electricity and drinking water, and housing construction and land distribution. Consequently, a series of institutions dedicated to attending to the needs of the population were created, and existing ones were strengthened. In terms of specific programmes, timely allocation of budgetary resources and the universal nature of their implementation stood out, thereby impregnating the process with a sense of equality.

During their initial stages, reforms focused on strengthening the more traditional social areas related to ensuring the survival and development of workforce productivity, with the result that strengthening the infrastructure for basic services was made a state priority. In this context, a number of important institutions were created. In particular, it is worth pointing out the Dirección General de Asistencia Médico-Social or General Directorate of Medical and Social Services (1950), the Consejo Superior de Educación or Higher Council of Education (1951) and the Instituto Nacional de Vivienda y Urbanismo or National Institute of Housing and Urban Planning (1954). In 1957 the Ley Fundamental de Educación or Fundamental Education Act – still in force today – was passed, which defined the aims of Costa Rican education. This was followed by the Ley Orgánica del Ministerio de Educación Pública or Organic Law of the Ministry of Public Education. These actions responded to changes proposed in the 1949 Political Constitution, where education was defined as a right of every Costa Rican citizen, and set the foundation for the development of an integrated educational system whose cycles are all correlated from pre-school through to university level. To make these reforms viable, relevant provisions were made for the system's financing with public funds.

Other actions were promoted, such as the nationalization of the banking system in 1948; the nationalization of the Instituto de Defensa del Café or Institute for Coffee Advocacy (subsequently renamed as the Oficina del Café or Coffee Bureau); and the creation of the Consejo Nacional de Producción or National Production Council and the Instituto Costarricense de Electricidad or Costa Rican Electricity Institute in 1949. Although such measures were focused primarily on regulating economic relations and did not strictly constitute social policies, they did set the foundations for a modernization and diversification of the economy, territorial integration and mobility of social sectors and emerging production groups.

In 1963, secondary education reform was launched, aimed mainly at expanding the coverage of public high schools (Figure 8.A3).[7] The expansion of primary schooling (especially in rural areas), pre-schooling and adult education continued during the 1970s. The impact of these measures is reflected in educational indicators, which show a significant reduction in illiteracy rates (both urban and rural), as well as increases in schooling rates and in the average number of years of study by the overall population, and therefore an improvement in the educational level of the economically active population. In this regard, a relevant milestone was the creation in 1965 of the Instituto Nacional de Aprendizaje or National Training Institute, a public institution offering job training in the face of a development model more complex than the agricultural exports model.

During the 1960s the state entered new areas of social work, undertaking the creation of six institutions: the Instituto Costarricense de Acueductos y Alcantarillados or Costa Rican Water Works Institute (1961, originally Servicio Nacional de Acueductos y Alcantarillados or National Water and Drain Service); the Instituto de Desarrollo Agrario or Agrarian Development Institute (1961, originally Instituto de Tierras y Colonización or Institute of

Lands and Human Settlements); the Patronato Nacional de Rehabilitación or National Bureau of Rehabilitation (1965); the Dirección Nacional de Desarrollo de la Comunidad or National Directorate of Community Development (1967); the Escuela Normal Superior or Higher Normal School (1967), created based on the Normal School of Heredia (1915); and the Escuela Centro Americana de Ganadería or Central American School of Stockbreeding (1969).

Throughout the following decade the country consolidated the social reforms launched in the 1940s by providing universal access to social services – particularly health and education – and developing an area devoted to social services. This process took place during a period of strengthening of democratic/liberal institutions and an unprecedented expansion of the state apparatus, which even involved incursions into the production field.[8]

Regarding the health sector, the spheres of action of both the Ministry of Health and the Costa Rican Social Security System (CCSS) were more precisely established, with primary health care being entrusted to the former and all aspects concerning secondary and tertiary levels of health care being entrusted to the latter. In 1973, the Ministry of Health began implementing a primary health care programme in rural areas, with the aim of expanding the coverage of services to those sections of the population lacking access to the health services network, and who up until that point were receiving occasional and limited attention through the Mobile Medical Units Programme. Infrastructure created for the control and prevention of malaria in previous decades was initially used for this experience, along with the mobile units. In subsequent years a large number of health care posts and centres were built. In 1976 the programme was extended to urban areas. Similarly, thanks to an ingenious modernizing strategy proposed during the previous decade, the Social Security System achieved universal coverage of medical services. This expansion also encompassed the pension system for disability, age and death, which even included a programme for the poor with state funding. In 1980 the CCSS's illness and maternity scheme came to cover 75.7 per cent of the population, whereas 30 years before it covered barely 8 per cent[9] (Figure 8.A2).

In the area of education significant progress was made in secondary education, especially in technical fields, and an unprecedented boom occurred in higher education with the creation of three new universities and three public para-university institutions for higher education. In addition, the first private university was established during the second half of the 1970s.

Another important characteristic of this period was a greater concern for equality and for tackling poverty. This was mainly a result of the first symptoms of a social decay brought about by the effects of the oil crisis, as well as the industrialization and urbanization process that had started two decades before. Urban social movements were strengthened, social conflict in rural areas worsened – mainly in banana plantation zones – and discussion of the nation's social issues intensified. All of this occurred in a context where the social and political situation in Central America was becoming difficult and was beginning to impact on Costa Rican society.

This concern for the social and political effects of the new manifestations of poverty – particularly in the city – led to the creation of the Instituto Mixto de Ayuda Social or Mixed Institute for Social Services in 1971, and the Fondo de Desarrollo Social y Asignaciones Familiares or Social Development and Family Allowance Fund (FODESAF) in 1974. A pioneer type of fund in Latin America, FODESAF was set up to finance complementary food programmes for students and other groups, rural health (including the construction of rural aqueducts), and the granting of non-contributory pensions to poor families and others. Both institutions, together with certain health care and education programmes and certain production programmes like the National Production Council and the Agrarian Development Institute, shaped a policy of attention to the poor that complemented existing universal attention services and an expansive policy of credit and salaries, leading to an integrated development policy.

Though this did not compensate for the growing inequalities caused by a greater concentration of wealth in both rural and urban areas, it did lessen such inequalities, encouraging the development of a society with a strengthened middle class. In addition, it contributed to shape a more integrated nation from a social and political standpoint, as compared with the rest of Latin American countries.

In fact, the strengthening of the state in general and of social policy in particular led to an expansion of the middle class, which by 1970 accounted for 22 per cent of the social structure as seen from an occupational viewpoint, thereby doubling their relative share with respect to 20 years before (Trejos, 1991: 79). There was also a significant expansion of the lower strata in urban areas (39 per cent), whose relative share of the social structure was increased by 11 percentage points between 1950 and 1970 as a result of the nation's processes of industrialization, modernization and urbanization. The idea of Costa Rica as a middle-class nation took root in the collective Costa Rican imaginary. The growth of the middle class and urban manual workers continued throughout the 1970s, though at a slower pace (by the beginning of the 1980s they accounted for 26 per cent and 43 per cent of the social structure, respectively), with an emphasis on service-related activities. This was an indication of an expansion of the micro-enterprise sector and some growth of the urban informal economy.

As a result, by the end of the 1970s the country had witnessed significant improvements in the areas of social development, owing to the accumulated successes of its continued health and education programmes, the expansion of social areas with state involvement, and the programmes to fight against poverty established during that decade, all within a context of the suitable allocation of budgetary resources[10] and great equality. Thus, the promotional and universal emphasis of social policies prevailed, in efforts to cover the entire population with social services. The 1970s may therefore be described as the 'golden decade' of social policy.

Developments in the major social indicators between 1950 and 1980 made plain the progress achieved: an increase in life expectancy at birth, a reduction in infant mortality rates, an increase in the percentage of medically attended births, a reduction in malnutrition rates, an increase in access to services for drinking water and sewage elimination, a growth in coverage of the education, health care and pension systems, an increase in schooling rates, a reduction in illiteracy rates, and rising general education and workforce education averages, among others. A selected group of indicators is presented in the Annex (Tables 8.A1–5 and Figures 8.A1–10) that shows some of the major advances in Costa Rican human development.

On the other hand, there was a significant reduction in poverty as measured by income: it dropped from an estimated 50 per cent at the beginning of the 1960s, to 39 per cent at the beginning of the 1970s, and 25 per cent at the end of that decade.[11] This improvement in living standards for the bulk of the population in a favourable economic context allowed for an expansion of citizenship and social integration, and brought about significant upward social mobility.

In short, it may be said that from 1950 to 1980 Costa Rica laid the foundations for a style of social development sustained by a broadening of public intervention. Its axis was the provision of education and health services as being fundamental to the entire population, as well as active state involvement in the provision of these and other relevant services with the aim of both directly and indirectly improving the quality of life of the population (e.g. electricity and drinking water). Additionally, during the final years of the period support was provided to the poorest sectors as a result of an explicit policy of the redistribution of wealth, which was made possible by the economic growth achieved in previous years.[12]

Now, then, three aspects should be taken into account to explain for the scope and limitations of this evolution of the Costa Rican social model. On the one hand is the prevailing economic situation of that period, characterized by high growth rates in national production and employment, low inflation levels, rising minimum wages, low unemployment levels, and – especially in recent years – access to external resources through indebtedness. While this economic context helped finance a high and growing social expenditure – in terms of GDP – it proved unsustainable by virtue of the weaknesses inherent to the country's production structure, which became apparent with an unusual intensity at the beginning of the 1980s.

On the other hand, social policy encouraged the creation of social institutions with specific competencies, although, in some cases, there was little coordination between them, and even some duplication of tasks. From this point of view, it would be erroneous to speak of a social development model that was neatly preconceived in its practical form (it is clear that the form was defined depending on both the role assigned to the public sector and the agenda of priorities), although all were guided by the higher objective related to the common good and welfare of the majority. It should also be highlighted that, to a significant extent, the success achieved in terms of social development was due to the consolidation of a body of experts and professionals within the relevant institutions, who knew how to promote the policies beyond the special circumstances leading to their emergence, thereby facilitating the sustainability of their actions and outcomes.

## The crisis of the import-substitution model: its social consequences

Various factors converged in the economic crisis that became apparent by 1979 and peaked in 1982. First were the internal imbalances caused by a development scheme in which domestic consumption and fiscal expenditure systematically exceeded export capacity and fiscal revenues. This led to a loss of dynamism and strangled the economy, something that was reflected in external and fiscal imbalances. Among external causes, the following should be mentioned: a deterioration in the terms of exchange, which fell abruptly in two years after showing a gradual deterioration (in the 1950–79 period); an international recession that stalled exports in 1981 and reduced them significantly in 1982; the international financial system's behaviour which, after a readiness to assume growing risks in Costa Rica, cut back on the resources available and raised interest rates, precipitating the debt crisis; and, finally, the Central American economic and political crisis that resulted in a reduction of trade and of foreign and local investment. In the domestic arena, this difficult external situation was not countered with a timely and coherent economic policy, thereby hastening the crisis and magnifying its consequences. Attempts were made to evade the adjustment through an increasingly onerous external and internal financing. This stepped up inflation and control was lost over key policy instruments such as exchange rate and interest rates.

The macroeconomic effects of such an adjustment may be summarized in a 10 per cent drop in GDP per capita over a two-year period, a 20 per cent drop in per capita private consumption, a doubling of open unemployment and underemployment rates in 1982, as well as a loss of wages' purchasing power of the order of 22 per cent per year, on average, for the years of the period.[13] Prices more than doubled and the exchange rate increased more than threefold. The strong impact on the labour market led to a significant rise in poverty, affecting more than half the country's households in 1982. In the case of social policy, a lack of mechanisms capable of consistently generating funding for social investment resulted in a poor state of public finances which – in the context of the country's fiscal crisis – forced a significant reduction in public expenditure. This impacted on the social sector, although, as will be seen later, this was not the most badly affected sector. Institutions were forced to cut the budgets of their programmes, resulting in a loss of coverage in some of them, and a decline in the quality of many. Additionally, investments were substantially reduced: the construction of new buildings and new equipment purchases were halted and even basic equipment was not repaired and infrastructure works deteriorated from a lack of minimum maintenance.

In a series of data on social public expenditure for 1980–96, Sauma and Trejos (1999) show that in 1981 and 1982 public expenditure in Costa Rica fell sharply, by over 30 per cent of total social expenditure, and by almost 40 per cent of social expenditure per capita. With respect to the GDP, social expenditure decreased from 20.7 per cent in 1980 to 15.2 per cent in 1982 – a 25 per cent drop over a period of just two years.

It is worth emphasizing that during this period social expenditure remained a fiscal priority, even in a scenario of contracting expenditure. Thus, social expenditure as a percentage of the GDP was reduced by only five points from 1980 to 1982, as compared to a loss of ten points of the total expenditure, and its share within the latter rose from 66 per cent in 1980 to 72 per cent in 1982. Investment in infrastructure was most seriously sacrificed, along with the payment of debt interest (Sauma and Trejos, 1999).

The economic crisis meant a point of inflexion that forced policy makers to rethink the place that 'the social realm' would have in the country's development. The nature of the crisis, and especially the way in which it was handled, inevitably led to a redefining of social policy priorities, as well as a reformulation of approaches and redesigning of institutions.

There is a clear explanation for such changes: the economic crisis was not solely the result of external variables associated with economic changes in global finances; it was also an expression of an exhaustion of the social pact on which the welfare apparatus was based. By the mid-1970s and just coinciding with the golden period, proposals were raised suggesting a reshaping of the state and a strengthening of the private sector. The crisis provided an opportunity for many of these proposals to be regarded as legitimate, and take shape in the way of more perfected technical formulations, rather than the initial mere denunciations and external criticisms. Such formulae crystallized in an instinctive rejection of state interventionism, which was justified with newly revived arguments advanced by the Neoliberal Asociación Nacional de Fomento Económico or National Association of Economic Promotion (ANFE) calling for a reduction in the size of the state to its minimum expression. The 1980s were then the scenario of constant and systematic criticism of state institutions.

This exhaustion, however, did not result in a state reduction, or in cuts in expenditure on social policy areas. Privatization and the closure of public entities focused strictly on the dismantling of CODESA's companies – then the axis of the entrepreneurial state.[14] Political institutions were sufficiently firm to withstand this first blow. Neoliberal prescriptions were filtered and limited in their scope, with a resulting mixture that has been called a heterodox and gradualist adjustment. Certain external factors contributed decisively in promoting this approach, for example the United States' continuous and significant financial assistance as a result of the Central American crisis, and, later on, an increase in the international prices of the country's major agricultural exports.

## Social reform and social policy in the transition to a new style of development

### Changes in social policy during the stabilization phase

It fell to the Monge Administration (1982–86) to develop an economic stabilization policy and to start a reorientation of the production model. Basically, this administration managed to re-establish the macroeconomic balances that complemented a political process of supporting impoverished sectors, in order to help reactivate the production apparatus, improve employment conditions, recover the purchasing power of wages and introduce an indexation mechanism for wage adjustment.

During this phase, the emphasis on social aspects was placed on designing and implementing social compensation actions, providing privileged attention to sectors directly affected by the crisis and the stabilization processes. The country had begun to implement a policy to address poverty at the beginning of the 1970s, but the new crisis context and the perspective of changes on the style of development posed new and complex challenges.

In tune with such orientations, from 1983, a Social Compensation Plan was imposed, using resources from the Social Development and Family Allowance Fund and from international cooperation agencies. Through this plan, resources were allocated to finance an employment programme, temporary food support, and other subsidies to support production aimed at poorer sections of the population in both urban and rural areas (Villasuso, 1992).

In addition to increased material deprivation, the impoverishment resulting from the crisis at the beginning of the 1980s had other consequences. As Trejos points out, it also produced a kind of poverty with exclusion and the emergence of previously unknown 'social pathologies', as well as the strengthening of other pathologies that had no significant impact on the collective life of the population, such as family violence. This led authorities to reinforce direct assistance to the poor, and to abandon the more integrated approach against poverty that sought to articulate economic policy – especially production policy – with social policy.

At an organizational level, the interventions for confronting poverty required a greater level of coordination on social matters. This led the Monge Administration – using a platform of sectoral planning – to establish a Social Council or Social Cabinet long before international agencies proposed this themselves, as a measure for improving the state's capabilities to respond the growing demand for social services in Latin America.

Stabilization of the economy allowed the country to begin recovering its levels of social investment, as well as to financially bolster key institutions such as the CCSS, INA, and FODESAF. This helped to minimize the social cost of adjustment programmes and turned the Costa Rican experience into a paradigm within Latin America, where various countries underwent serious social commotion and turbulence in the application of orthodox adjustment programmes. As was well stated by the International Labour Organization's Regional Employment Program for Latin America and the Caribbean (PREALC, 1990: 57): 'The crisis of the 1980s has helped clearly establish the importance of a group of Costa Rican State institutions that differentiate it from the other countries of the region, and which allowed it to carry out a rapid and profound economic stabilization at minimum social cost that was equitably distributed among the country's main social groups . . . ' With respect to education, the crisis, the subsequent changes in the economic model and its effects on labour opportunities all had negative effects on this sector. There was an significant drop in secondary education coverage during much of the 1980s, and the sector did not recover from this until the end of the following decade (Figure 8.A4).

## Social policy after the structural adjustment

The 1990s were a point of inflection of social policy reform. It is not possible to speak of reform in the strict sense of the term during the 1980s, if understood as a thought-through process aimed at effecting institutional and conceptual changes with precise objectives. Rather, this was a time when progress in many social indicators either slowed down or stagnated.

Policies implemented by the Arias Administration (1986–90) materialized the structural adjustment process in order to promote a change in economic direction, favouring the promotion of exports beyond the Central American region. In terms of social policy, the government defined three fundamental priorities. In the foreground was attention to the housing problem, an area in which the country had built up a large social debt. The government established goal of building 80,000 housing units per year. To make this goal viable, the Sistema Financiero Nacional para la Vivienda (National Financial System for Housing) was created and a Family Housing Bonus – a subsidy intended to help meet family needs like decent roofing for the poor – was instituted.

Secondly, interest focused on the quality of education in the face of a marked reversal in education indicators, although there was little progress in respect of coverage – the most important post-crisis problem (Sanguinetty, 1988b). A series of measures were advanced that included the incorporation of computer studies into school curricula, the re-establishment of the baccalaureate exams for secondary education, and the application of a comprehensive test at the end of the sixth grade in primary education.

Thirdly, regarding labour matters the government continued to provide an employment subsidy and to promote programmes to support the micro and small business sector. The Arias Administration had a cautious wage policy, and even though agreements were attained to effect wage adjustments any time inflation was higher than 7 per cent as measured by variations in the consumer price index, wages tended to fall in real terms (Barahona, 1997a).

Furthermore, in the health area a process of demonstrative experiences was started with a view to implementing the so-called English Model, which was crystallized into various modalities of health care that initially included turning two peripheral clinics into cooperatives.[15] Initial efforts for reorganizing and integrating the public health system were also promoted. All of these elements were the background of a health sector reform launched in 1994 (Güendel, 1987).

The Calderón Fournier Administration (1990–94) accelerated economic reform and sought more forcefully to introduce a social policy approach based on focusing help and on a subsidiary role for the state. Its management was characterized by a search for mechanisms to focus expenditure and transform actions for fighting poverty, resorting to transfers and subsidies as central elements of its strategy. Specifically, the Family Housing Bonus was turned into a free subsidy, and two other instruments were created – the food bonus and the school bonus. In its beginnings, the administration maintained a moderate wage policy, although high increases were later passed on, especially for public sector wages. Moreover, the Sistema de Selección de Beneficiarios de la Política Social (System of Social Policy Beneficiary Selection – SISBEN) was designed and was to be under the charge of the Mixed Institute for Social Services. A set of analytical instruments developed in Chile were thus transferred to Costa Rica in a non-critical fashion, though operation of this mechanism did not materialize during this governmental term.

In the educational area, progress was made on expanding the educational system's coverage and starting the implementation of a Program for the Qualitative Improvement of Costa Rican Education, although the promotion of computing studies in schools was weakened due to controversies with the Fundación Omar Dengo – the programme's executing entity (Barahona, 1997b).

In the area of sanitation, while progress was made on the technical design of a project to reform the sector, primary attention programmes actually declined due to prevailing restrictive fiscal policies – which translated into a deficit of 500 primary health care experts who quit under a job mobility scheme – reappearance of illnesses that had been eradicated in the country, declines in vaccination coverage, among others (Ministerio de Salud, 1995: 43).

The Figueres Administration (1994–98) developed a more integrated and explicit vision of social policy reform, as it sought to recover the promotional role of the institutions in charge of social services, based on a rejection of the previous administration's emphasis on targeted intervention. It became the aim to harmonize universal-coverage programmes (mostly education and health) and selective programmes to fight poverty (family housing bonus, training for poor female household heads, etc.).

In this context, social policy began to be reviewed based on objectives focusing on the search for equity, solidarity and efficiency. At the same time, it was assigned a role in improving productivity, which was seen as a means for a more advantageous reinsertion into the global market. Some of the main reforms were maintained to a certain extent in later governments, which helped to give social policies a perspective of continuity.

Social policy focused on three areas: the programme to tackle poverty, reform in social sectors with a universal coverage, and reform in pension plans.

Attention to the policy on poverty took shape as a National Plan to Combat Poverty. Among its main characteristics are its efforts to articulate universal-coverage and selective programmes in order to provide an integrated attention to the most vulnerable members of society: women, children and adolescents, and the elderly. The plan put an end to the restrictive targeting of the previous government, and encouraged the granting of priority to those areas with the highest concentrations of poverty. Nevertheless, it continued with efforts to identify beneficiaries, and maintained some of direct subsidy programmes implemented by that government.

Reform in the universal-coverage social sectors, on the other hand, involved two efforts with dissimilar results.

The first was the reform of the health sector. A Project for Health Sector Reform was implemented by the Figueres Olsen Administration. The project was designed by the Calderón Fournier Administration with financing from loans from the World Bank, the IADB, and cooperation funds from the Pan-American Health Organization. It incorporated most of the discussions and demonstrative experiences formulated since the end of the 1970s, when concerns for redefining health policies began, especially medical attention policies. The focus of the reform was based on three changes. First was a conceptual change revolving around a more social and comprehensive health perspective that did not renounce the system's remedial dimension (still viewed as necessary), and organized through the Equipos Básicos de Atención Integral or Basic Teams for Integrated Attention (EBAIS),[16] which are bodies/units charged with organizing and monitoring community health. The second change was an organizational one, and involved a separation between the leadership and the provision of health care. This crystallized in a transfer of people/patient attention to the CCSS, and a strengthened Ministry of Health as the governing body. Thirdly, there was a change in the management of the CCSS in order to separate the provision of services and its financing, with the aim of breaking with the health care establishment's historic budgets, defining theoretical prices (quasi-markets) and encouraging a style of management and administration based on results (Güendel, 1987; Castro and Sáenz, 1998).

With a combination of the preceding models of health services administration by cooperatives – and more recently by private associations of medical services and the University of Costa Rica – and the recent EBAIS experience, a population of 441,799 has come to be covered (11 per cent of the country's inhabitants), providing an idea of the impact of the health sector reforms (Table 8.A16). Furthermore, all of the EBAIS together cover a little over 90 per cent of the country's population.

The results in education are contradictory. While a so-called Education Toward the 21st Century Policy was promoted that sought to articulate and strengthen a set of innovative programmes such as those of computing for schools and the teaching of a second language in primary education, legislative reform – the EDU-2005 bill – was not passed. The EDU-2005 bill was promoted as a broad educational reform aimed at streamlining education to conform to the principle of equity, the latest constructivist and humanist approaches, and to demands in terms of quality improvements.

The bill was not passed by the Legislative Assembly because it encountered strong opposition from the educational community. However, the Political Constitution was amended to establish a minimum basic of 6 per cent of public expenditure for state education including universities, and pre-school education was made compulsory. In addition, a series of programmes were promoted within the framework of an Education Policy approved by the Higher Education Council, and regarded as a state policy intended to transcend governmental terms. These programmes included: (a) teaching a second language in primary schools, with a 50 per cent coverage of the total enrollment and which sought to reduce the social gap between public and private education; (b) strengthening the programme of computing for schools – which had stagnated during the previous government – by expanding its coverage and updating its technology;[17] (c) expanding and reforming social programmes aimed at improving the level of student retention in the school system and preventing dropouts;[18] and (d) extending the school year from 181 to 200 days. This involved arduous negotiations with teacher associations and trade unions; (e) preparing and distributing a new textbook series entitled 'Hacia el Siglo XXI' ('Toward the 21st Century'); and (f) strengthening secondary education through the opening of 72 new high schools to expand coverage and the design of new study plans (MIDEPLAN, 1998a: 159–90).

Finally, a bill to reform pension plans was promoted that aimed to rationalize the special plans allocated in the National Budget. A law was also passed on the private complementary pension system (Law No. 7523) that paved the way for approval of the Ley de Protección al Trabajador (Workers' Protection Law) that was promoted and passed by the following administration, and reforms were introduced to the teachers' pension system due to its impact on the fiscal deficit (MIDEPLAN, 1998a: 230–2).

The next two governments continued with the initiatives outlined during this presidential term, adding special emphasis to some areas, although without significant changes. In the Rodríguez Administration (1998–2002) the profile of social policy appeared to be weakened in two wide-ranging aspects: (a) the social governing authority was deactivated; and (b) there was a return to an assistential approach and to focalized social investment. Realization of a national census of the poor population through the Sistema de Información de Población Objetivo or Target Population Information System (SIPO) was proposed. Over the medium term, it would be used as the basis for allocating resources from the Social Development and Family Allowance Fund aimed at fighting poverty. Otherwise, the sectoral reform processes in health and education remained in force, largely as a result of the inertia resulting from their external funding.

In the social arena, the main legacy of the Rodríguez Administration was expressed in the approval of the Workers' Protection Law (Law No. 7983 of 2000). This law was aimed at establishing a 'multi-pillar' pensions system[19] and providing for additional sources of resources to make non-contributory pensions universally available for the poor, while also making reform to the Ley de Cesantía or Severance Pay Act a reality – a long-postponed social democrat aspiration. Furthermore, this law capped the agreements reached at the Foro de Concertación Nacional or National Reconciliation Forum (1998) on the issue of pensions, in fact the only topic addressed by the forum that was sanctioned by Congress. Approval of the Ley de Paternidad Responsable or Responsible Paternity Law (Law No. 8101) was another important milestone,[20] making a courageous appeal for a behavioural and cultural change on this regard.

Regarding the policy of tackling poverty, during the last two administrations transverse programmes such as the Rodriguez Administration's Triángulo de Solidaridad (Solidarity Triangle) were developed, which added elements of negotiation and the harmonization of investment plans at the local level. However, this effort could be institutionalized and was suppressed by the new government, even though both administrations were headed by the same political party. Meanwhile, the current government's Plan Vida Nueva or New Life Plan (Pacheco de la Espriella Administration 2002–06) is an attempt to develop integrated local and regional plans for addressing poverty. Furthermore, the last two administrations have strengthened beneficiary records systems, with the aim of improving the allocation of subsidies to the poor.

Specifically, the New Life Plan has the following main objectives:

- To foster a new period of social mobility based on an articulation of the advantages of economic growth, with a public policy focusing on the creation of opportunities and capacities for people.

- To work to create a positive and creative relationship between economic growth and the overcoming of poverty.
- To encourage an encounter of economic and social policies around the creation and strengthening of opportunities for the less favored population.
- To contribute to the full expression of people's capabilities and potentialities. (IMAS, 2002)

In the area of health sector reform, decentralization was promoted through the creation of health areas managed by providers other than the CCSS. Boards of Health were established with the aim of ensuring citizen involvement in hospital management, along with a superintendency charged with protecting the insured population's rights to health. Lastly, in the area of education concerns about coverage have arisen – especially in secondary education – in light of corroborations that one of out every three adolescents is outside the educational system.

Adoption of the human rights approach[21] is another important reform intended to reorient discourse and practices of social policy in the last fifteen years. This topic was especially well developed by the Rodríguez Administration, although efforts to achieve settlement's between different political and social sectors were already underway during the Figueres Administration. Regarding women's empowerment, this issue was first addressed in the mid-1980s. The human rights approach involved two dimensions: a juridical dimension, including reforms to define the rights of children and adolescents, youth, women, the elderly and disabled persons; and an institutional dimension, involving incipient efforts to achieve institutional reform in the social sector. It has also meant establishing coordination and governance entities such as the Instituto Nacional de las Mujeres or National Women's Institute, the Consejo Nacional de la Niñez y de la Adolescencia or National Council for Children and Adolescents, the Consejo de Persona Joven or Youth Council, and the Consejo Nacional de la Población Adulta Mayor or National Council for the Elderly.

The vital importance of having these sectors represented in major decision-making fora, such as the Government Council and the Social Council, has also led to the appointment of women as Ministers for the Condition of Children and Adolescents, and for Women's condition respectively – signalling a change of course in social policy from macro-social themes with an emphasis in the population, to themes associated with specific subjects. In contrast with economic policy, which has guided transformation in the style of development, centred on very specific aspects such as fiscal balance, a monetary regime harmonious with the competitiveness of export products, and a production policy aimed at ensuring foreign investment and the country's integration into international markets, Costa Rican social policy has lacked harmonious discourse and, as may be observed, has been affected by discontinuities and unsystematic efforts.

Despite the programmes to tackle poverty that have been developed over the last few decades, the incidence of poverty remained steady from 1994 to 2002,[22] affecting around one-quarter of Costa Rican households (Table 8.A13). Deterioration in the distribution of income starting in 1994 (Table 8.A12) and an increase in open unemployment and visible underemployment rates since 2000 (Table 8.A10) also stand out as discouraging trends. Coverage of the illness and maternity scheme – one of the main universal-coverage social programmes together with public education – has remained almost stagnant over the last 10 years without attaining effective universalization (Table 8.A2). The Costa Rican state also experiences recurring fiscal deficits (5.4 per cent of GDP in 2002, Figure 8.A7) and an enormous internal debt (27.6 per cent of GDP in 2001, Figure 8.A8), making investment in infrastructure suitable and hindering the sustainability of many social programmes.

While social expenditure has tended to recover since 1993 in respect of its relationship with GDP (Table 8.A14), it shows fluctuations determined by the circumstances and, in the case of education, it has failed to meet the constitutional principle of allocating 6 per cent of GDP, and instead has been set at some 5.5 per cent (Table 8.A15).

### Social authority and inter-institutional coordination

The institutional structure created by Costa Rican society is rather complex and has presented various problems with the passage of time, especially in terms of juxtaposing competencies and effectiveness in governance and coordination. Thus, the Monge Administration created a Social Council of Government through an Executive Decree. The council operates as a social authority that favours the defining of priorities, as well as intersectoral coordination and the overseeing and evaluation of actions undertaken. An important task of such social authority has been to bargain with the economic authority in order to ensure the financial resources required to achieve the desired functionality of social sectors for governmental action, a task by no means exempt from difficulties in light of current fiscal restrictions.

The Arias and Calderón Administrations used a similar scheme, assigning the office of the Second Vice-President with coordination of the Social Council. The Figueres Administration formulated an alternative proposal with five large areas of governmental action/coordination (social, economic, environmental, governance, and institutional renewal), but it quickly changed course in their operational scheme, and moved toward the more classic division between an Economic Council and a Social Council.

To make these councils operational, *ad hoc* technical/executive structures have been established that have therefore lacked continuity, thereby impeding that the issue of social authority and inter-institutional coordination become a question of state – that is, beyond any administration in particular.

In terms of the formation of a Social Authority, the decision of the Rodríguez Administration (1998–2002) not to institute a Social Council – and to that extent not to maintain the legal concept of a social authority – constituted a reversal. Alternatively, this administration proposed to strengthen the Government Council as such, as well as a new coordination mechanism that involved an active presence of the state, municipal governments, and the communities by means of the aforementioned Triangle of Solidarity. This decision was again reversed by the Pacheco Administration, as well as by Executive Decree No. 30493-MP-PLAN-MCAS, whereby the Social Council was re-established and a Coordinating Minister was designated. These duties ultimately fell to the Vice-President of the Republic and the Minister of National Planning and Economic Policy.

Despite prevailing difficulties, the state's social realm was able to generate, or rather be nourished with, innovative proposals, capable of repositioning topics that are strategic for national development and promoting actions to integrate the social and economic realms. In this regard, it is worth mentioning the introduction in 1987 of the Computing for Schools Program, which is intended to prepare the new generations to be proficient in computing. An outstanding feature of this programme is that far from aiming for computer literacy (for example, through learning about software packages), it is set up for students to create high-level cognitive structures, develop creative thinking, and be able to use new technologies intelligently.

Therefore, the programme aims to make simultaneous impacts on educational, economic and social fronts, as it contributes learning tools and opportunities for improving future insertion into job markets, and to a social life in the broad sense of the term. A set of innovative experiences relevant for their possibilities for articulation with other economic and social policy actions and actions to tackle poverty are the following: (i) creation of Equipos Básicos de Atención Integral de la Salud or Basic Teams of Integrated Health Attention (EBAIS), with an initial emphasis in rural areas; (ii) introduction of a second language in primary education starting in 1995, and of computing studies for schools at the end of the 1980s – both of them key aspects for cultural development in times of globalization; (iii) creation of a Plan Nacional de Combate a la Pobreza or National Plan to Combat Poverty (PNCP), with an explicit commitment to articulating universal-coverage and selective programmes to facilitate incorporation of poor sectors into mainstream development, and whose axes and components have marked the work carried out on these matters since 1994 – although each administration's own variations; (iv) creation of a programme for poor female household heads in the context of the Plan's women axis, which to this date has also been maintained, although with changes in name and emphasis; (v) promotion of a rights approach in social policy; (vi) emergence of new mechanisms for the coordination of inter-institutional and inter-sectoral action (e.g. the aforementioned National Council for Children and Adolescents, the National Council for the Elderly and the Youth

Council). These innovations vary in terms of their scope and degree of institutionalization.

## Lessons and challenges for the future: by way of conclusions

Since the mid-twentieth century, Costa Rica has had a rich tradition of social policies aimed at offering opportunities to the population in a systematic fashion, although their roots go back to the first stages of the country's republican life. To a great extent, this concern for social development accounts for the results achieved by the country over the long term in terms of human development, despite sharing many of the typical disadvantages of a peripheral economy.

On an international scale, the Costa Rican case has become paradigmatic since the 1950s, when the nation experienced remarkable progress in terms of social progress (reduction of child mortality, and increases in life expectancy and schooling rates, and so on). This progress was then halted by the economic crisis experienced by the country at the beginning of the 1980s.

Even though this crisis led to the design and implementation of economic stabilization and structural adjustment policies guided by the search for a new model of development, framed within the ascent of Neoliberal thinking and conforming to the so-called Washington Consensus, such policies had the particularity of avoiding the adoption of shock economic measures such as downsizing or the privatization of social institutions. Thus, it could be said that social investment – a key element for explaining such notable results in terms of human development – was protected.

But the transformation in the development model has resulted in a need to rethink social policy and foster successive chapters of institutional and sectoral reform, considering both their achievements and their shortcomings.

These reforms have impacted upon social sectors with a universal coverage (specifically health and education) where the traditional provision of social services by the state has added to a growing involvement of the private sector, putting to test the public sector's regulatory capabilities, along with the social security system, and actions aimed at fighting poverty.

Reform in the health care area appears more consolidated, especially as a result of transformations in the primary attention model. In the educational sector, reform has covered various aspects (curricular, administration, financing), although it has suffered from discontinuity and difficulties in consolidating itself through firm public policy. Regarding social security, the country achieved significant progress with approval of the Workers' Protection Law, ending a long period of conflict. This put the topic back on track towards the shaping of a multi-pillar system suited to Costa Rican reality.

Regarding the fight against poverty, three national plans have been formulated and implemented since 1994. Nonetheless, as yet, no qualitative leap has been observed either in the models of institutional intervention, or in articulation and inter-institutional coordination efforts, so that the issue of the social authority remains highly relevant and is clearly a pending reform.

In the area of social policy, Costa Rica is faced with several profound challenges: (i) confronting the transformations associated with the demographic transition process – in 2002 the country reached the replacement fertility level, which is used to determine the population's tendency to ageing. These developments are likely to put pressure on services on various sectors of the population pyramid; (ii) striking ailments such as the incidence of poverty, social asymmetries and the tendency to a broadening of social inequalities, through a combination of economic growth and suitable social policies; (iii) consolidating sectoral reforms in health and education, and increasing governance and regulation capabilities in social institutions charged with these competencies; (iv) enhancing the impact of social investment; (v) overcoming the fragmentation and 'routinization' of social programmes, advancing towards the adoption of models of integral and integrated intervention; and (vi) advancing towards the shaping of a social authority.

## Notes

1. The term *Estado Social de Derecho* refers to a model of state organization that encompasses the Rule of Law, while also aiming to meet the requirements for social development, with a view to ensuring the population's well-being. While keeping the necessary distance and using the term loosely, it may be likened to the concept of the welfare state. It is interesting to note how the historical trend of social policy and the current discussion on social policy reform touches upon the issue of how best to address the state's functions on issues relating to development, redistribution and welfare, as will be seen throughout this chapter.
2. This process has been documented by various researchers, among them Seligson *et al.* (1996) and Fischel (1993).
3. In 1882, some 70 per cent of the country's population was illiterate (Dengo and María, 1995: 112). This figure was reduced to 21.2 per cent in 1953, 14.3 per cent in 1963, 10.2 per cent in 1973, 6.9 per cent in 1984, and 4.8 per cent in 2000 (census data, Table 8.A5).
4. At the beginning, the social security system only covered wage-earning workers who worked more than 180 days per year (thus excluding seasonal agricultural workers) who resided in the main cities within the Central Valley (Rojas Bolanos, 1980: 52).
5. In the economic arena, a transformation and diversification of the production began, emphasizing industrial development within the framework of an import substitution model that was complementary to the prevailing model of agricultural exports.

6. Universal suffrage was strengthened with the inclusion of women and of the principle of transparency in political-electoral contests, and the separation of state branches. A decentralized state sector was also created.
7. The gross rate of coverage of secondary education increased from 17.4 per cent in 1957 to 36.4 per cent in 1970, to 60.6 per cent in 1980. Primary education coverage was already relatively high (91.5 per cent) in 1957 and reached 100 per cent by the mid-1960s (MEP – Statistics Department. *La educación en cifras 1884–2000*).
8. The *Corporación Costarricense de Desarrollo* or Costa Rican Corporation Development Corporation (CODESA) was created in 1972. It became involved in entrepreneurial activities that competed with private businesses, such as, among others, the production of sugar, cement, fertilizers and aluminum. In 1984 it had 15 subsidiary firms and it partnered with 21 other firms (Sojo, 1991: 68–9).
9. http://www.mideplan.go.cr/Sides/social/05-01.htm (IADB, 1994: 159).
10. Public social expenditure went up from roughly 9 per cent of GDP in 1950 to just over 20 per cent at the end of the 1970s (Garnier *et al.*, 1997). Such expenditure was usually funded with specific taxes to reduce their vulnerability. However, overall public finances were always in deficit, which, finally, led to a fiscal adjustment at the beginning of the 1980s.
11. The first figure is for 1961 and is from Piñera (1978), and the other two are estimates from IICE (1988) for 1971 and 1977.
12. Based on an inventory of support programmes for the poor carried out by Trejos *et al.* (1996), the authors found that three out of every five programmes were established before the 1980s, most of them actually during the 1970s. This reveals the importance of this period's legacy to Costa Rican social development in subsequent years, as well as the difficulties for advancing the renewal of the programmes in force.
13. The drop in average wages amounted to 40 per cent between 1980 and 1982 (−4.1 per cent in 1980, −10.9 per cent in 1981 and −29.0 per cent in 1982). Unemployment rose from an average of 5.1 per cent in 1976–1979 to 8.7 per cent in 1981 and 9.4 per cent in 1982. Inflation of 7.8 per cent for 1976–1979 increased to 17.8 per cent in 1980, 65.1 per cent in 1981 and 81.8 per cent in 1982. External public debt rose 3.7 times from 1979 to 1983. The public sector's deficit reached 13.7 per cent of the GDP in 1981 (Rovira Mas, 1980: 44).
14. CODESA's companies that were in deficit were closed, others were shifted to the public sector, and its two most successful firms (*Cementos del Pacífico* and *Fertilizantes de Centroamérica*) were privatized through a democratization scheme (they were sold to cooperatives), although they were ultimately bought by transnational companies (Villasuso, 2000: 30).
15. These cooperatives were established in two CCSS clinics from the Metropolitan Area's communities of Pavas and Tibás. Additionally, a training model was implemented in Barva de Heredia that was subsequently extended to two more communities in Heredia and Alajuela (Muñoz and Scrimshaw, 1995: 166–7).
16. A total of 427 EBAIS were set up between 1995 and 1997 to cover a target population of 1.6 million inhabitants (Castro, 1998: 21). In April 2002, at the end of the following administration, a total of 808 EBAIS covered 3.5 million inhabitants – 92 per cent of the national population (CCSS, 2002: 18–19).
17. Coverage of the computing for schools programme increased from 30 per cent to 50 per cent in primary education. In secondary education, a 30 per cent coverage

was attained in its academic modality, and a 100 per cent coverage was attained in its technical/vocational modality.

18. These are mainly the *Programa de Mejoramiento de las Escuelas Urbano Marginales* or Program for Improving Marginal-Urban Schools (PROMECUM) created in 1994; the *Programa Integral de Mejoramiento de las Escuelas Unidocentes* or Integrated Program for Improving Single-Teacher Schools located in rural zones with a dispersed population; and other more specific social programmes such as the one aimed at providing basic school supplies and uniforms to poor children (replacing the cash school bonus from the previous administration), student transport, scholarships for primary and secondary school students, among others (MIDEPLAN, 1998a: 169–72).
19. The pension system is structured upon three fundamental pillars: (i) the public contributive and non-contributory systems managed by the CCSS; (ii) a compulsory complementary pension system managed by either public or private pension fund operators; and (iii) a complementary voluntary savings scheme also managed by pension operators (Arguedas, 2002: 8).
20. This law was drafted because of a high and growing incidence of children born without a recognized father. In fact, according to official statistics one-third of the total births for 2000 corresponded to the category 'father unknown'.
21. The human rights approach refers to a stating of the rights of various groups subject to exclusion such as women, children and adolescents, indigenous communities, and so on. It underscores the importance of explicitly acknowledging their political and social citizenship both in public policy and within the culture than runs society as a whole, so that democracy may expand from the public sphere to private spheres as the family. But, in addition, it refers to the promotion of a proactive and reflexive approach towards the former, aimed at enabling people to participate in policy making and monitoring. Within the human rights approach, the concept of citizenship embraces all three dimensions – cultural, social and political.
22. Official data for 2003 disclosed at the beginning of November, showed a reduction in the percentage of poor households – from 20.6 per cent to 18.5 per cent. To analyse the nature of this change, additional data from the Household Survey would be required that is still unavailable – for example, on the size of the section of the population vulnerable to poverty. Likewise, a methodological discussion has started about the basket of goods and services used to determine the poverty line, and also involving the fixing of the line itself. The backdrop of this discussion is the need to update the parameters from an already obsolete 1988 Household Survey on Income and Expenses.

## References

Arguedas, C. (2002). *Reforma al sistema de pensiones en Costa Rica: evaluación de la nueva organización*. Estudio de Caso No. 62. Masters thesis (summarized version). http://www.mgpp.cl. Accessed in March 2003.

Barahona, M. (1997a). 'El desarrollo social', in J. R. Quesada *et al.* (ed.), *Costa Rica contemporánea: raíces del Estado de la Nación*. Proyecto Estado de la Nación, Chapter 2, San José, Costa Rica, pp. 141–84.

Barahona, M. (1997b). *La informática educativa en el contexto de la política social: las experiencias de Chile y Costa Rica*. San José: MIDEPLAN-FLACSO (Chile Program), (Unpublished).

Barahona, M., Sauma, P. and Trejos J. D. (1999). 'La política social costarricense y las reformas económicas 1983–1997', in C. Conejo, H. Mora and J. R. Vargas (eds); *Costa Rica hacia el siglo XXI: balance de las reformas económicas 1983–1998*. Costa Rica: Editorial Fundación UNA, Heredia.

Bulmer-Thomas, V. (1989). *La economía política de Centroamérica desde 1920,* 1st edition. San José: Central American Bank of Economic Integration (BCIE).

Bustelo, E. and Minujín, A. (1997). 'La política social esquiva', in R. Menjívar *et al.* (eds), *Pobreza, exclusión y política social.* San José: FLACSO, pp. 113–54.

Castro Valverde, Carlos and Luis Bernardo Sáenz. (1998). *La reforma del sistema nacional de salud.* Colección Tiempos de cambio. San José: MIDEPLAN.

CCSS (2002). *Memoria comprensiva mayo 1998 – abril 2002.* Caja Costarricense de Seguro Social (CCSS), http://modsjoweb01.ccss.sa.cr:81/down.asp. Accessed in November 2003.

Consejo del Sector Social (1996). *Plan Nacional de Combate a la Pobreza.* San José: Master Litho S.A.

Dengo O. and María E. (1995). *Educación costarricense.* San José: Editorial Universidad Estatal a Distancia (EUNED).

ECLAC (2003). *Anuario Estadístico de América Latina y el Caribe 2002.* Santiago: Economic Commission for Latin America and the Caribbean (ECLAC).

ECLAC (2002). *Panorama social de América Latina 2001–2002.* Santiago: Economic Commission for Latin America and the Caribbean (ECLAC).

ECLAC (2000a). *La Brecha de la Equidad: Una segunda evaluación.* Santiago: Economic Commission for Latin America and the Caribbean (ECLAC).

ECLAC (2000b). *Equidad, desarrollo y ciudadanía.* Santiago: Economic Commission for Latin America and the Caribbean (ECLAC).

ECLAC (2000c). *Panorama Social de América Latina: 1999–2000.* Santiago: Economic Commission for Latin America and the Caribbean (ECLAC).

ECLAC (1997). *La brecha de la equidad.* Santiago: Economic Commission for Latin America and the Caribbean (ECLAC).

ECLAC (1996). *Panorama Social 1996.* Santiago: Economic Commission for Latin America and the Caribbean (ECLAC).

ECLAC (1992). *Equidad y transformación productiva: Un enfoque integrado.* Santiago: Economic Commission for Latin America and the Caribbean (ECLAC).

ECLAC (1990). *Transformación productiva con equidad: La tarea prioritaria del desarrollo de América Latina y el Caribe en los años noventa.* Santiago: Economic Commission for Latin America and the Caribbean (ECLAC).

Franco, R. (1997). 'Paradigmas de la política social en América Latina', in R. Menjívar *et al.* (eds), *Pobreza, exclusión y política social.* San José: FLACSO, pp. 35–58.

Franco, R. and León, A. (1984). 'Estilos de desarrollo, papel del Estado y estructura social en Costa Rica'. *Pensamiento Iberoamericano,* 6, July–December.

Garnier, L. (1999). *Función de coordinación de planes y políticas.* Paper presented during the High-Level Seminar on the Functions of Planning, organized by ECLAC and ILPES in Santiago, Chile, 7–8 October.

Garnier, L. (1997). 'La política social en tiempos de ajuste'. *Revista Economía y Sociedad,* 5, September–December, Heredia, Costa Rica.

Garnier, L. and Roberto H. (1991). 'El Estado necesario y la política de desarrollo', in L. Garnier *et al.* (eds), *Costa Rica entre la ilusión y la desesperanza: una alternativa para el desarrollo.* San José: Ediciones Guayacán, pp. 7–72.

Garnier, L., *et al.* (1997). 'Costa Rica: Social Development and Heterodox Adjustment', in Mehrotra and Jolly (eds), *Development with a Human Face: Experiences in Social Achievement and Economic Growth.* New York and Oxford: Clarendon Press.

Garnier, L. *et al.* (1996). 'Cuando el desarrollo se hace posible en un país pobre: el caso de Costa Rica'. MIDEPLAN, *Cumbre Mundial sobre Desarrollo Social (selección de documentos relativos a la posición costarricense).* San José: Costa Rican Ministry of Planning and Economic Policy (MIDEPLAN), pp. 11– 57.

Garnier, L. *et al.* (1991). *Costa Rica entre la ilusión y la desesperanza.* San José: Ediciones Guayacán.

Grynspan, R. (1997). 'La pobreza en América Latina y estrategias para superarla', in R. Menjívar, D. Kruijt and L. van Vucht Tijssen (eds), *Pobreza, Exclusión y Política Social.* San José: Latin American School of Social Sciences (Costa Rican campus), The Netherlands Utrecht University, and UNESCO.

Grynspan, R. and Meléndez, D. (1999). *El factor institucional en reformas a la política de vivienda de interés social: la experiencia reciente de Costa Rica.* Serie Financiamiento del Desarrollo No. 81. Santiago: Economic Commission for Latin America and the Caribbean (ECLAC).

Güendel, L. (2000). 'La política pública y la ciudadanía desde el enfoque de los Derechos Humanos. La búsqueda de una nueva utopía', in S. Reuben (ed.), *Política social: vínculo entre Estado y Sociedad.* San José: Editorial de la Universidad de Costa Rica.

Güendel, L. (1987). 'Las políticas de salud: entre la sostenibilidad y el estancamiento'. UNICEF-Ministerio de Salud. *Las políticas de salud en el umbral de la reforma.* Serie de políticas sociales, No. 1. San José: UNICEF.

Güendel, L. and Trejos, J.D. (1994). *Reformas recientes en el sector salud de Costa Rica.* Santiago: ECLAC.

Gutiérrez, S. and Vargas Cullell A. J. (1996). *Costa Rica. Una revisión de las políticas de vivienda aplicadas a partir de 1986.* Consultancy Report for ECLAC. Santiago: ECLAC.

Herrero, F. and Durán F. (2001). *El sector privado en el sistema de salud de Costa Rica.* Financing for Development Series, No. 109. Santiago: ECLAC.

Inter-American Development Bank (IADB) (1984). *A la búsqueda del Siglo XXI: Nuevos caminos de desarrollo en Costa Rica.* Report by the Mission of IADB's Social Reform Program, Group on Social Agenda, November 1994.

IADB/UNDP (1993). *Reforma social y pobreza: hacia una agenda integrada de desarrollo.* Trabajos del Foro sobre Reforma social y pobreza. Washington: IADB.

IICE (1988). *Evolución de la crisis económica en Costa Rica y su impacto sobre el nivel de pobreza.* San José: Instituto de Investigaciones en Ciencias Económicas de la Universidad de Costa Rica (IICE). Informe final (unpublished).

Instituto Mixto de Ayuda Social (IMAS) (2002). *Plan Vida Nueva para la Superación de la Pobreza y el Desarrollo de las Capacidades Humanas 2002–2006.* San José: IMAS, electronic version.

Martínez, J. and Castro, M. (2000). *Reformas de salud en Costa Rica: ¿Está la reforma amenazando los principios de universalidad, equidad y solidaridad del sistema?.* Mimeographed paper, San José, Costa Rica.

MIDEPLAN (2002a). *La obra de todos. Cuatro años modernizando Costa Rica. Informe final 1998–2002.* San José: Costa Rican Ministry of Planning and Economic Policy (MIDEPLAN).

MIDEPLAN (2002b). *Plan Nacional de Desarrollo 'Víctor Manuel Sanabria' 2002–2006.* San José: Costa Rican Ministry of Planning and Economic Policy (MIDEPLAN). Electronic version.

MIDEPLAN (several years). *Panorama Nacional.* San José: Costa Rican Ministry of Planning and Economic Policy (MIDEPLAN), 1994–1997 editions.

MIDEPLAN (1998a). *Gobernando en tiempos de cambio.* San José: Costa Rican Ministry of Planning and Economic Policy (MIDEPLAN).

MIDEPLAN (1998b). *Principales indicadores de Costa Rica.* San José: Costa Rican Ministry of Planning and Economic Policy (MIDEPLAN).

MIDEPLAN (1998c). *Gobernando en tiempos de cambio: Administración Figueres Olsen.* San José: Costa Rican Ministry of Planning and Economic Policy (MIDEPLAN).

MIDEPLAN (1998d). *Panorama Nacional. Balance social, económico y ambiental.* San José: Costa Rican Ministry of Planning and Economic Policy (MIDEPLAN).

MIDEPLAN (1998e). *Principales indicadores de Costa Rica.* System of Indicators on Sustainable Development (SIDES). San José: Costa Rican Ministry of Planning and Economic Policy (MIDEPLAN).

MIDEPLAN (1998f). *Plan Nacional de Desarrollo Humano 1998–2002.* Chapter entitled 'La solución de todos'. San José: Costa Rican Ministry of Planning and Economic Policy (MIDEPLAN).

MIDEPLAN (1997). *Principales indicadores sociales de Costa Rica.* San José: Costa Rican Ministry of Planning and Economic Policy (MIDEPLAN), System of Indicators on Sustainable Development (SIDES). Documento MIDEPLAN/SIDES No. 2.

MIDEPLAN (1994). *Plan Nacional de Desarrollo Francisco J. Orlich 1994–1998.* San José: Costa Rican Ministry of Planning and Economic Policy (MIDEPLAN).

MIDEPLAN (1993a). *Balance del ajuste estructural en Costa Rica.* 1985–1991. San José: Costa Rican Ministry of Planning and Economic Policy (MIDEPLAN).

MIDEPLAN (1993b). *Documentos fundamentales del Tercer Programa de Ajuste Estructural (PAE III).* San José: Costa Rican Ministry of Planning and Economic Policy (MIDEPLAN).

MIDEPLAN (1991). *Plan Nacional de Desarrollo 'Desarrollo Sostenido con Justicia Social' 1990–1994.* San José: Costa Rican Ministry of Planning and Economic Policy (MIDEPLAN).

Ministerio de Salud (1995). *Memoria anual, 1994.* San José: Costa Rican Ministry of Health.

Miranda, G. (1994). *La Seguridad Social y el desarrollo en Costa Rica,* 2nd edn. San José: EDNASSS-CCSS.

Montero, S. and Barahona, M. (2003). *La estrategia de lucha contra la pobreza en Costa Rica 1994–2003. Institucionalidad – Financiamiento – Políticas – Programas.* Social Policy Series No. 77. Santiago: ECLAC.

Morley, S. and Alvarez. C. (1992). *Poverty and Adjustment in Costa Rica.* Work Document No. 123. Washington: Inter-American Development Bank.

Muñoz, C. and Scrimshaw, N. S. (1995). *La transición de la nutrición y la salud de Costa Rica democrática.* INFDC – Instituto de Nutrición de Centro América y Panamá (INCAP/OPS). http://www.unu.edu/unupress/food2/UIN06S/uin06s00.htm#Contents. Accessed in November 2003. Guatemala: International Foundation for Developing Countries.

Nowalsky, J. *et al.* (2003). *Asimetrías económicas, sociales y políticas en Costa Rica. Hacia una calidad de vida digna.* San José: Centro Internacional para el Desarrollo Humano (CIDH).

Piñera, S. (1978). *Cómo medir el progreso de los países?* Santiago: ECLAC. Mimeographed version.

PREALC. (1990). *La deuda social en Costa Rica.* San José: Programa Mundial de Empleo de la OIT.

Presidencia de la República (1998). *Plan de Solidaridad, 1998–2002.* San José: Office of the President of the Republic.

Proyecto Estado de la Nación (2003). *Informe sobre el Estado de la Nación en Desarrollo Humano Sostenible.* San José, Costa Rica.

Proyecto Estado de la Nación (several years). *Informe sobre el Estado de la Nación en Desarrollo Humano Sostenible.* 1st–8th Reports, 1994–2001, San José, Costa Rica.
Rojas Bolaños, M. (1980). *Lucha social y guerra civil en Costa Rica 1940–1948,* 2nd edn. San José: Editorial Porvenir.
Romero, C. M. (1983). *Estado y políticas sociales en Costa Rica.* Thesis to attain a Master's Degree at the Programa de la Maestría Centroamericana en Sociología, Universidad de Costa Rica, San José, Costa Rica.
Rovira Mas, J. (ed.) (2001). *La democracia de Costa Rica ante el Siglo XXI.* Editorial de la Universidad de Costa Rica, 1st edition, San José, Costa Rica.
Rovira Mas, J. (1995). *La actual coyuntura política nacional: notas para su comprensión.* San José: Universidad de Costa Rica, Instituto de Investigaciones Sociales, Contribuciones No. 22.
Rovira Mas, J. (1988) *Costa Rica en los años 80,* 2nd edn. San José: Editorial Porvenir.
Rovira Mas, J. (1982). *Estado y política económica en Costa Rica. 1948–1970.* San José: Editorial Porvenir.
Rovira Mas, J. (1980). 'Costa Rica, economía y Estado. Notas sobre su evolución reciente y el momento actual'. *Estudios Sociales Centroamericanos,* año IX, 26, May–August 1980, San José, Costa Rica.
Sancho, A. (1992). *Programas sociales financiados por el fondo de desarrollo social y asignaciones familiares.* Washington, DC: World Bank.
Sanguinetty, J. A. (1989). *El Sector de Asistencia Social en Costa Rica. La crisis y sus posibles soluciones.* San José: Development Technologies, Inc.
Sanguinetty, J. A. (1988a). *La Educación General en Costa Rica. La crisis y sus posibles soluciones.* San José: Development Technologies, Inc.
Sanguinetty, J. A. (1988b). *La Salud y el Seguro Social en Costa Rica.* San José: Development Technologies, Inc. and Pragma Cooperation.
Sauma, P. (2003). *Mercado de trabajo, distribución del ingreso y pobreza.* Ponencia al Noveno Informe Estado de la Nación en Desarrollo Humano Sostenible (2002), San José, Costa Rica. http://www.estadonacion.or.cr/Info2003/nacion9/ponencias.html. Accessed in November 2003.
Sauma, P. (2002). 'Pobreza, distribución del ingreso, mercado de trabajo e inversión social'. Ponencia al *Octavo Informe Estado de la Nación.* San José, Costa Rica, June 2002. http://www.estadonacion.or.cr/info2002/nacion8/frame-estnacion.html. Accessed in November 2003.
Sauma, P. (1999). *Liberalización de la balanza de pagos: efectos en el empleo, el crecimiento económico, la distribución del ingreso y la pobreza. El caso de Costa Rica.* Final Report of a study conducted within the framework of the regional project entitled the same and sponsored by UNDP, IADB, and ECLAC. San José, Costa Rica.
Sauma, P. (1990). *Evolución reciente de la distribución del ingreso en Costa Rica. 1977–1986.* Instituto de Investigaciones en Ciencias Económicas de la Universidad de Costa Rica (IICE), Documento de trabajo No. 132, San José, Costa Rica.
Sauma, P. and Leonardo, G. (1998). 'Efecto de las políticas macroeconómicas y sociales sobre la pobreza en Costa Rica', in E. Ganuza, T. Lance, and S. Morley (eds), *Políticas macroeconómicas y pobreza en América Latina y el Caribe.* Madrid: Mundi-Prensa Libros S.A., United Nations Development Program, ECLAC, and Inter-American Development Bank.
Sauma, P. and Trejos, J. D. (1999). 'El gasto público y los servicios sociales básicos en Costa Rica: un análisis en el marco de la iniciativa 20/20', in E. Ganuza, A. León and P. Sauma (eds), *Gasto Público en servicios sociales básicos en América Latina y el Caribe: análisis desde la perspectiva de la Iniciativa 20/20.* Santiago: UNDP/UNICEF/ECLAC.

Segunda Vicepresidencia (1994). *Plan Nacional de Combate a la Pobreza.* Office of the Second Vice-President of the Republic and Consejo Social de Gobierno, San José, Costa Rica.

Seligson, M., Martínez, J. and Trejos, J. D. (1997). 'Reducción de la pobreza en Costa Rica: El impacto de las políticas públicas', in José Zevallos (ed.), *Estrategias para reducir la pobreza en América Latina y el Caribe.* Quito: UNDP.

Seligson, M., Martínez, J. and Trejos, J. D. (1996). *Reducción de la pobreza en Costa Rica: el impacto de las políticas públicas.* Instituto de Investigaciones en Ciencias Económicas (IICE), Universidad de Costa Rica, Serie Divulgación Económica No. 51. San José, Costa Rica.

Sen, A. and Drèze, J. (1989). *Hunger and Public Action.* USA: Clarendon Press; Oxford: Oxford University Press.

Sojo, A. (2000). *Reformas de Gestión en Salud en América Latina: los cuasimercados de Colombia, Argentina, Chile y Costa Rica.* Social Policy Series No. 39. Santiago: ECLAC.

Sojo, A. (1991). *La utopía del Estado mínimo. Influencia de la AID en Costa Rica en los años ochenta.* Managua: CRIES.

Sojo, A. (1990). 'Naturaleza y selectividad de la Política Social'. *Revista de la CEPAL,* No. 41 January, Santiago: ECLAC.

Sojo, A. (1989). 'Las políticas sociales en Costa Rica'. *Revista de la CEPAL,* No. 38, August, Santiago: ECLAC.

Sojo, C. (1997). *Los de en medio.* San José: FLACSO.

Trejos, J. D. (2003). *La inversión social pública en Costa Rica.* Ponencia al Noveno Informe Estado de la Nación en Desarrollo Humano Sostenible (2002), San José, Costa Rica. http://www.estadonacion.or.cr/Info2003/nacion9/ponencias.html. Accessed in November 2003.

Trejos, J. D. (2001). *Elementos de una estrategia nacional para la superación de la pobreza en Costa Rica.* Study conducted for the United Nation's Development Program (UNDP) within the framework of Project COS/97/G51 entitled 'Agenda Nacional para la Superación de la Pobreza' (UNDP/MTSS/IMAS).

Trejos, J. D. (2000). *Reformas económicas y situación social en Costa Rica durante los años noventa.* Instituto de Investigaciones en Ciencias Económicas (IICE), Universidad de Costa Rica, Serie Divulgación Económica, No. 32, San José, Costa Rica.

Trejos, J. D. (1999). *Reformas económicas y distribución del ingreso en Costa Rica.* Economic Reform Series, No. 37. Santiago: ECLAC.

Trejos, J. D. (1994). *Estrategias para combatir la pobreza en Costa Rica: programas, instituciones y recursos.* Work Document No. 192. Washington: Inter-American Development Bank.

Trejos, J. D. (1991). 'La política social y la valorización de los recursos humanos', in L. Garnier *et al., Costa Rica entre la ilusión y la desesperanza: una alternativa para el desarrollo.* San José: Ediciones Guayacán, pp. 73–107.

UNDP (2003). *Informe sobre Desarrollo Humano 2003.* United Nations Development Program (UNDP). Mexico City: Ediciones Mundi-Prensa. http://www.undp.org/hdr2003/espanol/. Accessed in November 2003.

UNDP (several years). *Informe sobre el desarrollo humano.* 1990–1997 editions.

Universidad de Costa Rica (2002). *Hacia una solución integral en la lucha contra la pobreza: Una propuesta al país para el necesario ordenamiento conceptual y político institucional de la oferta gubernativa.* Rectoría Universidad de Costa Rica, San José, Costa Rica.

Vega, M. *et al.* (1994). *La medición empírica de las clases sociales en Costa Rica. Propuesta teórico-metodológica.* Instituto de Investigaciones Sociales, Universidad de Costa Rica, San José, Costa Rica.

Villasuso, J. M. (2000). *Reformas estructurales y política económica en Costa Rica*. ECLAC, Economic Reform Series No. 64, May, Santiago, Chile.

Villasuso, J. M. (1992). 'Fondos y programas sociales en Costa Rica durante los ochenta', in OPS - OMS (eds), *Fondos y Programas de Compensación Social. Experiencias en América Latina y El Caribe*. Washington: PAHO/WHO Program of Development of Health Policy.

# Appendix 8.A: Tables and Figures

*Table 8.A1* Costa Rica: Human Development Index 2003

| *Rating according to HDI (place and country)** | *Life expectancy at birth (Years) 2001* | *Adult literacy rate 2001*[1] | *Combined schooling/ enrolment rate*[2] | *GDP per capita PPP$*[3] *2001* | *Life expectancy index* | *Education index* | *GDP index* | *HDI value 2001*[4] | *Rating based on GDP per capita* |
|---|---|---|---|---|---|---|---|---|---|
| *High HDI* | | | | | | | | | |
| 34 Argentina | 73.9 | 96.9 | 89 | 11,320 | 0.81 | 0.94 | 0.79 | 0.849 | 11 |
| 40 Uruguay | 75.0 | 97.6 | 84 | 8,400 | 0.83 | 0.93 | 0.74 | 0.834 | 19 |
| 42 Costa Rica | 77.9 | 95.7 | 66 | 9,460 | 0.88 | 0.86 | 0.76 | 0.832 | 9 |
| 43 Chile | 75.8 | 95.9 | 76 | 9,190 | 0.85 | 0.89 | 0.75 | 0.831 | 10 |
| *Medium HDI* | | | | | | | | | |
| 59 Panama | 74.4 | 92.1 | 75 | 5,750 | 0.82 | 0.86 | 0.68 | 0.788 | 23 |
| 67 Belice | 71.7 | 93.4 | 76 | 5,690 | 0.78 | 0.88 | 0.67 | 0.776 | 16 |
| 105 El Salvador | 70.4 | 79.2 | 64 | 5,260 | 0.76 | 0.74 | 0.66 | 0.719 | −17 |
| 115 Honduras | 68.8 | 75.6 | 62 | 2,830 | 0.73 | 0.71 | 0.56 | 0.667 | 1 |
| 119 Guatemala | 65.3 | 69.2 | 57 | 4,400 | 0.67 | 0.65 | 0.63 | 0.652 | −22 |
| 121 Nicaragua | 69.1 | 66.8 | 65 | 2,450 | 0.73 | 0.66 | 0.53 | 0.643 | 2 |

*Notes*:
*The two Latin American countries with a higher HDI than Costa Rica are included for comparative purposes, along with the region's country that follows it immediately, and the remaining Central American countries.
1. Percentage of the population aged 15 and above.
2. Combined gross enrolment ratio for primary, secondary, and tertiary education, in percentages.
3. In United States Dollars and purchasing power parity exchange rates (PPP).
4. Human Development Index.

*Source*: UNDP. Informe de Desarrollo Humano 2003 (Human Development Report), Indicators Annex, Table 1.

*Table 8.A2* Costa Rica: basic demographic indicators, 1941–2002

| *Indicators* | *1941* | *1950* | *1960* | *1970* | *1980* | *1990* | *2000* | *2002* |
|---|---|---|---|---|---|---|---|---|
| Population | 664,086 | 831,358 | 1,171,441 | 1,758,042 | 2,301,984 | 3,050,556 | 3,925,331 | 4,087,124 |
| Natural growth | 2.62 | 3.31 | 4.22 | 2.55 | 2.69 | 2.34 | 1.63 | 1.39 |
| Gross birth rate | 43.4 | 44.8 | 50.80 | 32.90 | 31.10 | 27.20 | 20.10 | 17.60 |
| Gross mortality rate | 17.2 | 11.8 | 8.6 | 7.4 | 4.2 | 3.7 | 3.8 | 3.7 |
| Child mortality rate | 123.5 | 90.2 | 67.8 | 67.0 | 19.9 | 15.0 | 10.2 | 10.2 |
| Neonatal mortality rate | 32.3 | 26.1 | 23.0 | 26.1 | 11.5 | 8.6 | 7.1 | 7.7 |
| Overall fertility rate* | – | 7.0 | 7.3 | 5.0 | 3.7 | 3.2 | 2.4 | 2.1 |
| Life expectancy at birth | 46.9 | 55.6 | 62.6 | 65.7 | 74.3 | 76.8 | 77.7 | 78.5 |
| Unattended births* | – | 70.4 | 50.8 | 29.7 | 9.3 | 3.6 | 1.7 | 1.6 |

*Note*: *1955 data.
*Source*: Centro Centroamericano de Población (http://ccp.ucr.ac.cr/observa/CRindicadores/. Accessed in November 2003), based on official data from INEC.

*Table 8.A3* Costa Rica: child mortality per groups of causes, in percentages, 1970–2001

| *Indicator* | *1970* | *1980* | *1990* | *1995* | *1996* | *1997* | *1998* | *1999* | *2000* | *2001* |
|---|---|---|---|---|---|---|---|---|---|---|
| Child deaths | | | | | | | | | | |
| Total number of cases | 3.553 | 1.334 | 1.211 | 1.064 | 937 | 1.108 | 970 | 925 | 798 | 827 |
| % of overall mortality rate | 32.7 | 14.4 | 10.7 | 7.6 | 6.6 | 7.8 | 6.6 | 6.1 | 5.3 | 5.3 |
| Groups of causes (%) | | | | | | | | | | |
| *Total* | 100.0 | 100.0 | 100.0 | 100.0 | 100.0 | 100.0 | 100.0 | 100.0 | 100.0 | 100.0 |
| Infectious and parasitic diseases | 36.4 | 10.8 | 8.8 | 4.4 | 4.6 | 4.6 | 5.1 | 4.9 | 3.9 | 4.2 |
| Tumors | 0.3 | 0.2 | 0.6 | ... | 0.2 | 0.1 | 0.5 | 0.4 | 0.4 | 0.6 |
| Endocrine glands involved in nutrition | 2.1 | 2.4 | 1.6 | 1.0 | 1.0 | 0.9 | 1.2 | 1.0 | 1.1 | 0.4 |
| Blood | 0.6 | 0.3 | 0.2 | 0.1 | 0.1 | 0.3 | 0.3 | 0.4 | 0.4 | 0.4 |
| Nervous system | 1.9 | 2.0 | 2.0 | 2.3 | 1.4 | 1.2 | 2.6 | 1.8 | 1.5 | 1.6 |
| Circulatory system | 2.5 | 1.0 | 1.0 | 0.8 | 0.9 | 1.2 | 0.9 | 1.2 | 1.1 | 1.5 |
| Respiratory system | 18.5 | 12.9 | 12.1 | 10.2 | 12.5 | 11.2 | 12.6 | 8.4 | 8.8 | 6.9 |
| Digestive system | 7.0 | 0.8 | 1.0 | 0.6 | 0.6 | 0.6 | 0.7 | 0.1 | 0.6 | 0.5 |
| Urogenital system | 0.2 | 0.3 | 0.3 | 0.2 | 0.3 | 0.1 | 0.1 | 0.1 | 0.1 | 0.2 |
| Skin and cell tissue | 0.3 | 0.1 | 0.1 | 0.2 | 0.1 | 0.1 | 0.1 | 0.1 | 0.0 | 0.1 |
| Bone/Muscular system | ... | ... | 0.1 | 0.1 | 0.1 | 0.3 | 0.0 | 0.1 | 0.0 | 0.0 |
| Congenital abnormalities | 4.5 | 19.6 | 25.3 | 27.5 | 27.3 | 32.0 | 26.9 | 28.5 | 32.2 | 33.0 |
| Perinatal conditions | 17.9 | 40.5 | 41.2 | 49.0 | 49.9 | 45.7 | 47.2 | 50.8 | 48.2 | 49.6 |
| Traumatism and poisoning | 0.8 | 1.7 | 1.3 | 1.4 | 1.7 | 0.8 | 0.0 | 1.3 | 1.3 | 0.8 |
| Signs. symptoms and states...* | 12.7 | 7.2 | 4.5 | 2.3 | 1.3 | 1.1 | 0.9 | 0.9 | 0.4 | 0.7 |

... When the number is lower than one tenth.

* Poorly defined signs, symptoms or conditions of morbidity.

*Source:* MIDEPLAN / SIDES Webpage. Accessed in November 2003.

*Table 8.A4* Costa Rica: child malnutrition among school-age children, 1966–2000

| *Indicator* | *1966* | *1975* | *1980* | *1985* | *1996* | *2000* |
|---|---|---|---|---|---|---|
| National Nutrition Surveys[1] | | | | | | |
| Severe malnutrition | 1.5 | 1.1 | 0.5 | 0.3 | 0.4 | n.a.[2] |
| Moderate malnutrition | 12.2 | 11.2 | 8.5 | 6.0 | 4.7 | n.a. |
| Mild malnutrition | 43.7 | 40.9 | 36.8 | 24.6 | 17.3 | n.a. |
| Overweight | n.a. | 7.8 | 11.3 | 2.5 | 4.2 | n.a. |
| Childrend attended at CEN - CINAI[3] | | | | | | |
| Severe malnutrition | n.a. | n.a. | 0.1 | 0.0 | 0.3 | 0.2 |
| Moderate malnutrition | n.a. | n.a. | 5.0 | 3.1 | 3.9 | 3.0 |
| Mild malnutrition | n.a. | n.a. | 37.9 | 31.3 | 23.2 | 20.7 |
| Overweight | n.a. | n.a. | 7.1 | 10.8 | 3.1 | 3.5 |

*Notes:*

1. The 1980 data correspond to 1978, and the 1985 data correspond to 1982. Population under 6 years old was considered in 1982, while the population aged above 1 and under 7 years old was considered in 1996.
2. The last survey available is from 1996.
3. Centros de Educación y Nutrición or Education and Nutrition Centers (CEN) and Centros Infantiles de Atención Integral or Integrated Child Care Centers (CINAI). Data includes children under 6 years old.

*Source*: MIDEPLAN/SIDES Web site. Accessed in November 2003: http://www.mideplan.go.cr/sides/social/05-01.htm

*Table 8.A5* Costa Rica: indicators of the population's educational levels, in percentages, 1953–2000

| *Educational level* | *1953* | *1963* | *1973* | *1984* | *2000* |
|---|---|---|---|---|---|
| *Illiteracy*[1] | | | | | |
| *Total* | 21.2 | 14.3 | 10.2 | 6.9 | 4.7 |
| Men | 20.9 | 14.1 | 10.2 | 7.0 | 5.0 |
| Women | 21.5 | 14.5 | 10.3 | 6.9 | 4.5 |
| *Urban population* | 8.1 | 5.2 | 4.4 | 3.1 | 2.7 |
| Men | 6.5 | 4.0 | 3.7 | 2.7 | 2.7 |
| Women | 9.4 | 6.2 | 5.1 | 3.5 | 2.8 |
| *Rural population* | 28.5 | 19.7 | 14.7 | 10.2 | 7.9 |
| Men | 27.8 | 19.2 | 14.6 | 10.3 | 8.4 |
| Women | 29.2 | 20.1 | 14.8 | 10.0 | 7.4 |
| *Average years of schooling*[2] | 3.1 | 3.6 | 5.3 | 5.9 | 7.6* |
| Percentages of the EAP with: | | | | | |
| Primary studies completed | n.d. | n.d. | 27.4 | 31.7 | 30.8 |
| Secondary studies completed | n.d. | n.d. | 4.8 | 12.2 | 11.1 |
| Higher education[3] | n.d. | 3.7 | 6.7 | 11.2 | 20.2 |

*Notes*:

1. For population aged 10 and above.
2. For the 1954–1984 censuses, data correspond to the population aged 25 and above. Data for 2000 correspond to the average years of schooling of the population aged 15 and above, as taken from the Household Survey for Multiple Purposes (July 2002).
3. Includes the population with one or more years of university studies, as well as university graduates.

*Source*: MIDEPLAN/SIDES, based on census data and data from INEC's Household Survey. Website accessed in November 2003: http://www.mideplan.go.cr/sides/social/04-01.htm

*Table 8.A6* Costa Rica: economic indicators for the foreign sector, 1991–2002

| *Indicator* | *1991* | *1992* | *1993* | *1994* | *1995* | *1996* | *1997* | *1998* | *1999* | *2000* | *2001* | *2002* |
|---|---|---|---|---|---|---|---|---|---|---|---|---|
| Average exchange rate[1] | 122.5 | 134.5 | 142.2 | 157.1 | 179.7 | 207.7 | 232.6 | 257.2 | 285.7 | 308.2 | 328.9 | 359.8 |
| Exports, millions of dollars | 1,899 | 2,386 | 2,625 | 2,882 | 3,482 | 3,774 | 4,221 | 5,538 | 6,576 | 5,813 | 4,923 | 5,277 |
| Imports, millions of dollars | 2,147 | 2,730 | 3,275 | 3,506 | 3,804 | 4,023 | 4,718 | 5,937 | 5,996 | 6,025 | 5,745 | 6,825 |
| Current account | −285 | −412 | −679 | −517 | −357 | −264 | −481 | −521 | −681 | −707 | −737 | −946 |
| Foreign investment, millions of dollars[2] | 178 | 226 | 247 | 298 | 337 | 427 | 407 | 612 | 620 | 409 | 454 | 642 |
| Foreign investment as a % of GDP | 2.5 | 2.6 | 2.6 | 2.8 | 2.9 | 3.6 | 3.2 | 4.3 | 3.9 | 2.6 | 2.8 | 3.8 |

*Notes:*

1 Costa Rican Colones per US dollar.

2 Total direct foreign investment in millions of US dollars.

*Sources:* Based on BCCR and MIDEPLAN/ SIDES.

*Table 8.A7* Costa Rica: balance of public foreign debt and debt servicing, 1991–2002

| *Indicator* | *1991* | *1992* | *1993* | *1994* | *1995* | *1996* | *1997* | *1998* | *1999* | *2000* | *2001* | *2002* |
|---|---|---|---|---|---|---|---|---|---|---|---|---|
| Numbers in millions of US dollars | | | | | | | | | | | | |
| Balance of the Public Foreign Debt | 3266.9 | 3288.7 | 3158.4 | 3255.5 | 3258.6 | 2858.9 | 2640.2 | 2872.4 | 3056.5 | 3150.6 | 3242.5 | 3337.7 |
| Servicing effectively paid | 362.3 | 289.7 | 569.7 | 447.4 | 620.3 | 580.7 | 583.2 | 405.3 | 527.9 | 591.0 | 708.5 | 690.5 |
| Principal | 196.9 | 188.6 | 390.5 | 275.6 | 409.0 | 395.4 | 436.8 | 277.5 | 337.5 | 386.1 | 475.7 | 454.9 |
| Interests As a percentage of GDP | 165.4 | 101.1 | 179.2 | 171.8 | 211.3 | 185.3 | 146.4 | 127.8 | 190.4 | 204.9 | 232.8 | 235.6 |
| Foreign Public Debt Balance | 45.7 | 38.2 | 32.8 | 30.9 | 28.0 | 24.3 | 20.7 | 20.4 | 19.3 | 19.8 | 20.1 | 19.8 |
| Effective servicing | 5.1 | 3.4 | 5.9 | 4.2 | 5.3 | 5.0 | 4.5 | 2.9 | 3.3 | 3.7 | 4.4 | 4.1 |
| Principal | 2.8 | 2.2 | 4.0 | 2.6 | 3.5 | 3.4 | 3.4 | 2.0 | 2.1 | 2.4 | 2.9 | 2.7 |
| Interests | 2.3 | 1.2 | 1.9 | 1.6 | 1.8 | 1.6 | 1.1 | 0.9 | 1.2 | 1.3 | 1.4 | 1.4 |

*Source*: MIDEPLAN/ SIDES website (http://www.mideplan.go.cr/sides/economico/07-01.htm). Accessed in November 2003.

*Table 8.A8* Costa Rica: workforce participation rates, by sex, 1987–2002

| *Rate and sex* | *1987* | *1990* | *1995* | *1996* | *1997* | *1998* | *1999* | *2000* | *2001* | *2002* |
|---|---|---|---|---|---|---|---|---|---|---|
| Gross participation rate | 37.5 | 38.0 | 39.3 | 38.1 | 39.8 | 41.2 | 40.5 | 39.9 | 42.3 | 42.4 |
| Net participation rate | 53.9 | 53.5 | 53.9 | 52.2 | 53.8 | 55.3 | 54.8 | 53.4 | 55.8 | 55.4 |
| Employment rate | 50.8 | 51.1 | 51.1 | 49.0 | 50.7 | 52.2 | 51.5 | 50.6 | 52.4 | 51.8 |
| *Men* | | | | | | | | | | |
| Gross participation rate | 54.0 | 54.6 | 54.4 | 53.2 | 54.7 | 55.8 | 54.8 | 54.5 | 55.2 | 55.4 |
| Net participation rate | 78.8 | 77.0 | 75.9 | 73.7 | 74.5 | 75.6 | 75.1 | 73.5 | 73.7 | 73.2 |
| Employment rate | 75.1 | 73.8 | 72.5 | 69.7 | 70.9 | 72.3 | 71.4 | 70.3 | 69.8 | 69.1 |
| *Women* | | | | | | | | | | |
| Gross participation rate | 20.8 | 21.6 | 24.0 | 23.0 | 24.9 | 26.7 | 26.6 | 25.5 | 29.6 | 29.6 |
| Net participation rate | 29.4 | 30.3 | 32.4 | 31.1 | 33.5 | 35.6 | 35.5 | 33.8 | 38.6 | 38.2 |
| Employment rate | 27.1 | 28.6 | 30.3 | 28.5 | 31.0 | 32.7 | 32.6 | 31.5 | 35.7 | 35.2 |

*Notes*: Gross participation rate: Workforce as a percentage of the total population. Net participation rate: Workforce as a percentage of the population (in a working age) aged 12 and above. Employment rate: Working population as a percentage of the population aged 12 and above.
*Source*: INEC, Household Survey for Multiple Purposes, employment module (July of every year).

*Table 8.A9* Costa Rica: employed population per sector and area of activity, in percentages, 1987–2001

| *Sector and area of activity* | *1987* | *1990* | *1995* | *1996* | *1997* | *1998* | *1999* | *2000* | *2001** |
|---|---|---|---|---|---|---|---|---|---|
| Primary sector: agriculture | 28.1 | 25.9 | 21.6 | 21.6 | 20.6 | 20.1 | 19.7 | 17.3 | 15.6 |
| Secondary sector | 23.4 | 24.6 | 23.0 | 22.3 | 22.5 | 22.0 | 22.2 | 21.7 | 22.2 |
| Mines and quarries | 0.2 | 0.2 | 0.2 | 0.2 | 0.1 | 0.1 | 0.2 | 0.2 | 0.1 |
| Manufacturing industry | 17.3 | 18.0 | 16.5 | 16.5 | 15.6 | 15.7 | 15.7 | 14.8 | 15.4 |
| Construction | 5.9 | 6.5 | 6.3 | 5.6 | 6.8 | 6.2 | 6.4 | 6.7 | 6.7 |
| Tertiary sector | 47.6 | 48.7 | 54.6 | 55.1 | 56.2 | 57.1 | 57.5 | 60.4 | 61.8 |
| Electricity, water, and gas | 1.2 | 1.2 | 1.1 | 1.0 | 1.1 | 1.0 | 1.0 | 0.8 | 1.3 |
| Trade, restaurants, hotels | 15.7 | 15.7 | 19.3 | 19.6 | 19.1 | 19.4 | 20.7 | 21.3 | 21.3 |
| Transportation, storage and communications | 4.2 | 3.9 | 5.3 | 5.1 | 5.4 | 5.6 | 5.7 | 6.2 | 5.7 |
| Financial establishments, insurance | 3.0 | 3.3 | 4.3 | 4.4 | 5.1 | 5.4 | 5.0 | 5.4 | 6.0 |
| Social and personal services | 23.5 | 24.6 | 24.6 | 25.0 | 25.6 | 25.7 | 25.1 | 26.7 | 27.5 |
| N.S.A.** | 0.9 | 0.7 | 0.8 | 0.9 | 0.7 | 0.8 | 0.5 | 0.7 | 0.3 |
| TOTAL | 100.0 | 100.0 | 100.0 | 100.0 | 100.0 | 100.0 | 100.0 | 100.0 | 100.0 |

*Note*: *Includes data up until 1991. In 2002 INEC discontinued this classification for areas of activity, and at present it only uses the new classification.
**Non-specified activities.
*Source*: INEC. Household Survey, Employment module (every year in July).

*Table 8.A10* Costa Rica: rates of open unemployment, underemployment and workforce total under-utilization, 1990–2002

| *Rate* | *1990* | *1991* | *1992* | *1993* | *1994* | *1995* | *1996* | *1997* | *1998* | *1999* | *2000* | *2001* | *2002* |
|---|---|---|---|---|---|---|---|---|---|---|---|---|---|
| Open unemployment | 4.6 | 5.5 | 4.1 | 4.1 | 4.2 | 5.2 | 6.2 | 5.7 | 5.6 | 6.0 | 5.2 | 6.1 | 6.4 |
| Visible underemployment | 3.4 | 4.0 | 2.8 | 2.6 | 3.5 | 3.7 | 4.4 | 4.2 | 4.8 | 4.8 | 3.8 | 4.3 | 4.9 |
| Invisible underemployment | 2.7 | 2.6 | 3.6 | 2.0 | 2.4 | 2.1 | 3.3 | 3.2 | 2.7 | 3.0 | 3.0 | 3.3 | 3.3 |
| Total under-utilization | 10.7 | 12.1 | 10.5 | 8.7 | 10.1 | 11.0 | 13.9 | 13.1 | 13.1 | 13.8 | 12.0 | 13.7 | 14.6 |

*Source*: INEC, Household Survey for Multiple Purposes (every year in July).

*Table 8.A11* Costa Rica: indicators of evolution of the monthly minimum wages and average monthly income, nominal and real rates, 1991–2002

| *Years* | *1991* | *1992* | 1993 | *1994* | 1995 | *1996* | 1997 | *1998* | 1999 | *2000* | 2001 | *2002* |
|---|---|---|---|---|---|---|---|---|---|---|---|---|
| Colones in nominal value[1] | | | | | | | | | | | | |
| Minimum wage | 16,523 | 20,826 | 22,078 | 24,859 | 29,485 | 37,646 | 45,240 | 51,584 | 57,460 | 63,544 | 71,968 | 77,584 |
| Average income[2] | 25,839 | 32,475 | 40,236 | 48,830 | 57,882 | 66,992 | 76,231 | 91,361 | 101,482 | 111,233 | 135,447 | 145,264 |
| In US Dollars | | | | | | | | | | | | |
| Minimum wage | 135 | 155 | 155 | 158 | 164 | 181 | 194 | 201 | 201 | 206 | 219 | 216 |
| Average wage | 211 | 241 | 283 | 311 | 322 | 323 | 328 | 355 | 355 | 361 | 412 | 404 |
| Colones in nominal value[3] | | | | | | | | | | | | |
| Minimum wage | 28,276 | 29,432 | 28,403 | 28,597 | 27,523 | 29,608 | 31,410 | 32,064 | 32,748 | 32,430 | 33,007 | 32,653 |
| Average income | 44,218 | 45,894 | 51,763 | 56,172 | 54,030 | 52,688 | 52,927 | 56,788 | 57,838 | 56,769 | 62,120 | 61,138 |
| Real annual variation rate[4] | | | | | | | | | | | | |
| Minimum wage | – | 4.1 | –3.5 | 0.7 | –3.8 | 7.6 | 6.1 | 2.1 | 2.1 | –1.0 | 1.8 | –1.1 |
| Average income | – | 3.8 | 12.8 | 8.5 | –3.8 | –2.5 | 0.5 | 7.3 | 1.8 | –1.8 | 9.4 | –1.6 |

*Notes*:

1. Numbers through the month of July.
2. Monthly income for the total population employed (including wage earners and self-employed workers).
3. In 1995 colones, based on the Consumer Price Index for 1995 = 100.
4. Real rates calculated based on numbers in colones according to their nominal value.

*Source*: Based on numbers from Informe Estado de la Nación No. 8, Compendio Estadístico; Decree on Minimum Wages (July 0202); and MIDEPLAN/ SIDES.

*Table 8.A12* Costa Rica: indicators for distribution of household income by decils and quintiles of per capita income, 1990–2002

| *Indicator* | *1990* | *1991* | *1992* | *1993* | *1994* | *1995* | *1996* | *1997* | *1998* | *1999* | *2000* | *2001* | *2002* |
|---|---|---|---|---|---|---|---|---|---|---|---|---|---|
| Ratio X decil / I decil | 17.4 | 19.9 | 17.0 | 16.4 | 17.0 | 16.1 | 18.6 | 15.5 | 16.5 | 19.5 | 19.6 | 23.3 | 20.3 |
| Ratio V quintil / I quintil | 8.2 | 9.1 | 8.1 | 7.8 | 8.5 | 7.9 | 8.8 | 8.0 | 8.5 | 9.1 | 9.7 | 11.2 | 10.8 |
| Gini coefficient | 0.374 | 0.391 | 0.378 | 0.378 | 0.387 | 0.377 | 0.393 | 0.380 | 0.389 | 0.400 | 0.412 | 0.433 | 0.430 |

*Source:* Sauma (2003: 3; Based on Household Survey data).

*Table 8.A13* Costa Rica: poor household percentages by poverty level, 1990–2002

| *Poverty level** | *1990* | *1991* | *1992* | *1993* | *1994* | *1995* | *1996* | *1997* | *1998* | *1999* | *2000* | *2001* | *2002* |
|---|---|---|---|---|---|---|---|---|---|---|---|---|---|
| Total poor population | 27.4 | 31.9 | 29.4 | 23.2 | 20.0 | 20.4 | 21.5 | 20.7 | 19.7 | 20.6 | 20.6 | 20.3 | 20.6 |
| Basic poverty | 18.3 | 20.2 | 20.0 | 16.3 | 14.2 | 14.1 | 14.6 | 15.0 | 14.4 | 13.9 | 14.5 | 14.4 | 14.9 |
| Extreme poverty | 9.1 | 11.7 | 9.3 | 6.9 | 5.8 | 6.2 | 6.9 | 5.7 | 5.3 | 6.7 | 6.1 | 5.9 | 5.7 |

*Note*: *Percentage of the total households with a known income.
*Source*: INEC, Household Surveys July 1990–2002.

*Table 8.A14* Costa Rica: indicators of consolidated social public expenditure, 1991–2002

| *Indicators* | *1991* | *1992* | *1993* | *1994* | *1995* | *1996* | *1997* | *1998* | *1999* | *2000* | *2001* | *2002** |
|---|---|---|---|---|---|---|---|---|---|---|---|---|
| SE per capita (in thousands)[1] | 249.2 | 264.5 | 271.6 | 268.9 | 247.1 | 263.1 | 280.9 | 280.6 | 272.7 | 277.4 | 281.7 | 292.2 |
| 1990 Index =100 | 103.0 | 109.3 | 112.2 | 111.1 | 102.1 | 108.7 | 116.0 | 115.9 | 112.7 | 114.6 | 116.4 | 120.7 |
| Variation in percentage terms | 3.0 | 6.1 | 2.7 | −1.0 | −8.1 | 6.4 | 6.8 | −0.1 | −2.8 | 1.7 | 1.5 | 3.7 |
| Priority of social spending | | | | | | | | | | | | |
| Macroeconomic (% GDP) | 15.0 | 14.7 | 15.6 | 16.4 | 15.2 | 16.6 | 17.0 | 16.9 | 15.9 | 17.3 | 19.0 | 19.7 |
| Fiscal (% GGG)[2] | 68.7 | 71.0 | 73.5 | 65.5 | 66.1 | 68.3 | 74.1 | 75.6 | 70.7 | 74.9 | 74.2 | 74.9 |
| *Composition of social expenditure* | | | | | | | | | | | | |
| Total social expenditure | 100.0 | 100.0 | 100.0 | 100.0 | 100.0 | 100.0 | 100.0 | 100.0 | 100.0 | 100.0 | 100.0 | 100.0 |
| Health | 32.3 | 30.0 | 29.4 | 29.2 | 30.1 | 28.9 | 27.3 | 28.3 | 29.7 | 29.0 | 28.8 | 29.0 |
| Education | 24.4 | 26.5 | 26.1 | 26.0 | 24.9 | 26.3 | 25.8 | 26.5 | 25.8 | 27.2 | 27.6 | 28.1 |
| Social security | 30.6 | 30.8 | 31.3 | 32.4 | 33.5 | 32.2 | 36.1 | 34.9 | 34.5 | 34.4 | 33.7 | 32.8 |
| Housing and land | 11.7 | 11.7 | 12.0 | 11.0 | 10.5 | 11.5 | 9.6 | 9.3 | 9.1 | 8.6 | 8.9 | 9.2 |
| Culture and recreation | 1.1 | 1.0 | 1.3 | 1.4 | 1.0 | 1.0 | 1.2 | 1.1 | 0.9 | 0.8 | 1.0 | 0.9 |

*Notes*: *Preliminary data. Data of 2002 are not strictly comparable with the previous series due to methodological changes.
1. Per capita social expenditure in thousands of Costa Rican colones of 2002.
2. General government percentages.
*Source*: Trejos, Juan Diego (2003: 30).

*Table 8.A15* Costa Rica: social expenditure by sector as a percentage of GDP, 1991–2002

| *Indicators* | *1991* | *1992* | *1993* | *1994* | *1995* | *1996* | *1997* | *1998* | *1999* | *2000* | *2001* | *2002* |
|---|---|---|---|---|---|---|---|---|---|---|---|---|
| Education | 3.7 | 3.9 | 4.1 | 4.3 | 3.8 | 4.4 | 4.4 | 4.5 | 4.1 | 4.7 | 5.2 | 5.5 |
| Health | 4.8 | 4.4 | 4.6 | 4.8 | 4.6 | 4.8 | 4.6 | 4.8 | 4.7 | 5.0 | 5.4 | 5.6 |
| Social services | 4.6 | 4.5 | 4.9 | 5.3 | 5.1 | 5.4 | 6.1 | 5.9 | 5.5 | 6.0 | 6.3 | 5.9 |
| Housing | 1.8 | 1.7 | 1.9 | 1.8 | 1.6 | 1.9 | 1.6 | 1.6 | 1.5 | 1.5 | 1.7 | 1.7 |
| Others[1] | 0.2 | 0.1 | 0.2 | 0.2 | 0.2 | 0.2 | 0.2 | 0.2 | 0.1 | 0.1 | 0.2 | 0.2 |

*Source*: MIDEPLAN/ SIDES Website (http://www.mideplan.go.cr/sides/social/03-03.htm). Accessed in November 2003.

*Table 8.A16* Costa Rica: alternative management models in health care services, 2001

| *Healthcare* | *Number of EBAIS*[1] | *Population covered* |
|---|---|---|
| Barva[2] | 8 | 34,368 |
| San Pablo[2] | 5 | 19,453 |
| Montes de Oca[3] | 13 | 65,021 |
| San Pedro[3] | 12 | 59,384 |
| Pavas[2] | 11 | 82,266 |
| Tibás[2] | 16 | 59,910 |
| Escazú area[4] | 8 | 49,078 |
| Santa Ana[4] | 6 | 36,319 |
| León XIII and Carpio[4] health areas | 7 | 36,000 |
| Total | 86 | 441,799 |

*Notes*:

1. Equipos Básicos de Atención Integral de Salud or Basic Teams of Integrated Healthcare Attention (EBAIS)
2. Cooperatives.
3. University of Costa Rica.
4. Medical Services Associations.

*Source*: CCSS (2002: 20).

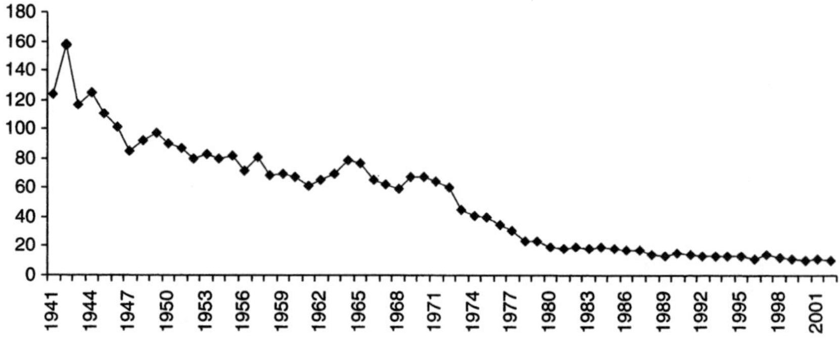


*Figure 8.A1* Costa Rica: child mortality rate, 1941–2002 (per 1,000 live births)
*Source*: Centro Centroamericano de Población (http://ccp.ucr.ac.cr/observa/CRindicadores/Accesed in November 2003), based on official data from INEC.

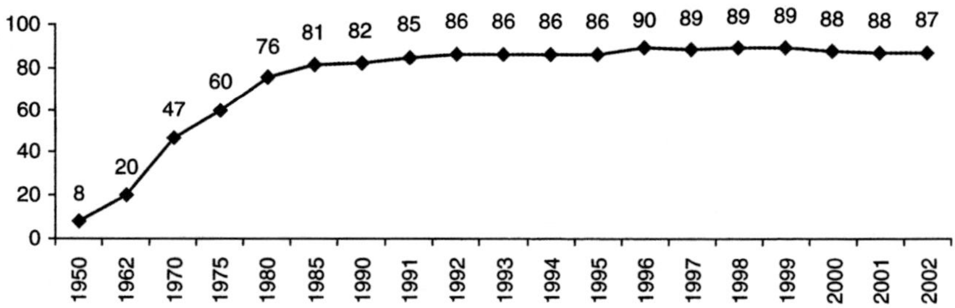


*Figure 8.A2* Costa Rica: coverage of the social security system and maternity scheme,* 1950–2002
*Régimen de Enfermedad y Maternidad or Illness and Maternity Scheme, Costa Rican Social Security System.
*Source:* IADB (1994: 159) and MIDEPLAN/SIDES website. Accesed in November 2003: http://www.mideplan.go.cr/sides/social/05-01.htm.

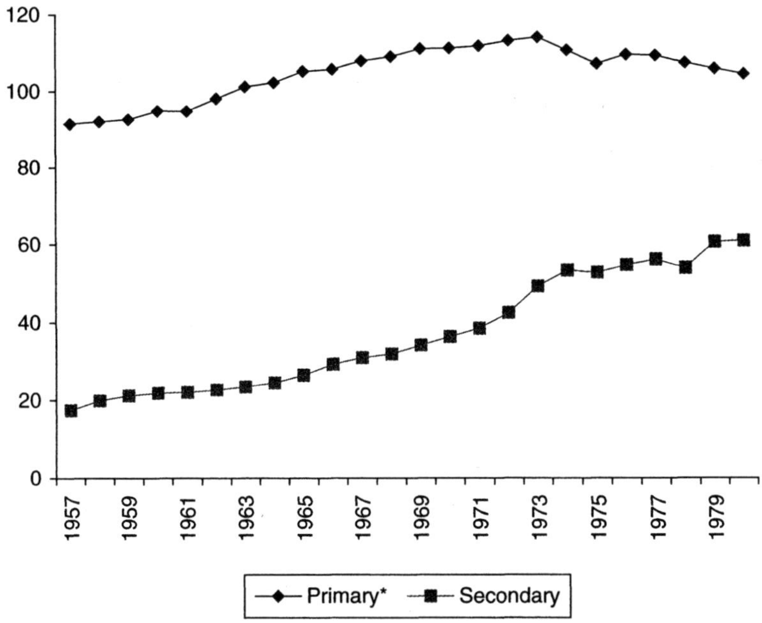


*Figure 8.A3* Costa Rica: primary and secondary education, gross coverage rate, 1957–80

*The numbers for primary education amount to more than 100 because of lagging students.

*Source:* MEP (Ministry of Public Education) Statistics Department, La educación en cifras 1884–2000.

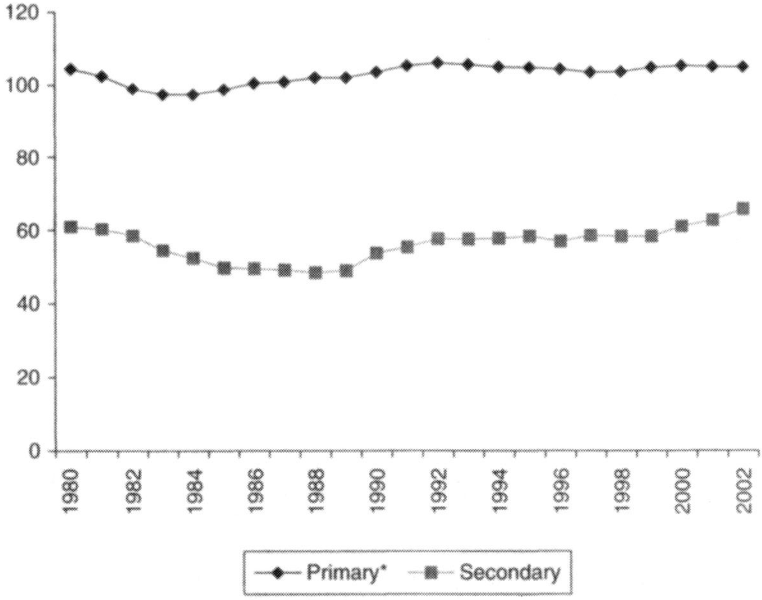


*Figure 8.A4* Costa Rica: primary and secondary education, gross rate of coverage, 1980–2002

* The numbers from primary education exceed 100 due to students lagging behind.

*Source*: Statistics Department, MEP (Costa Rican Ministry of Public Education), *La educación en cifras 1884–2000* (1980–1989 numbers.)

MEP, Statistics Deparment, *La expansión del sistema educativo costarricense 2002* (1990–2002 data).

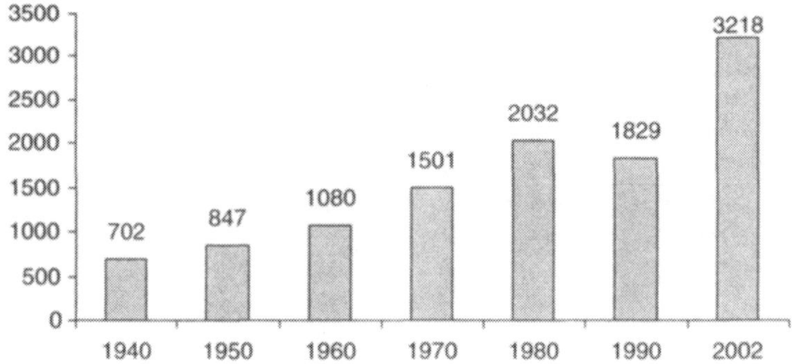


*Figure 8.A5* Costa Rica: GDP per capita in US dollars, 1940–2002

*Source:* Proyecto Estado de la Nación, 2003: 438.

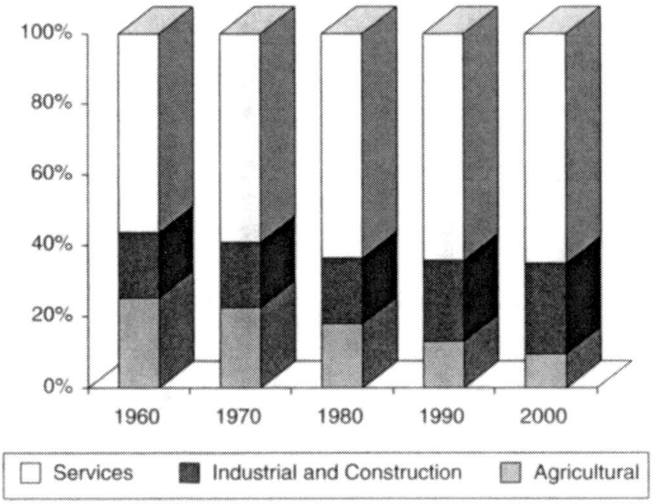


*Figure 8.A6* Costa Rica: domestic production structure per sector of the economy, in percentages, 1960–2000
*Source:* Based on data from MIDEPLAN and BCCR.

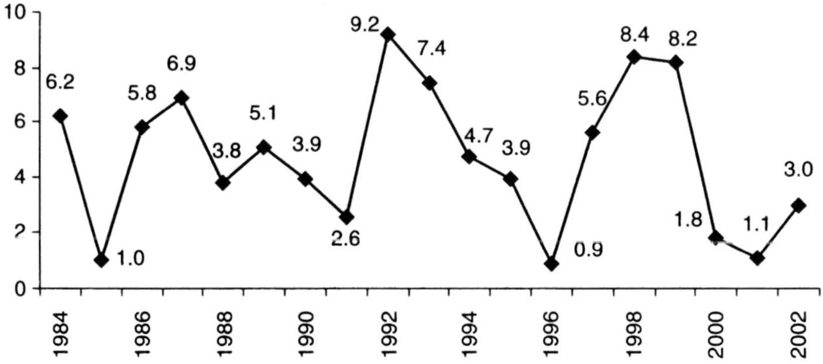


*Figure 8.A7* Costa Rica: GDP real annual variation rate, 1984–2002
*Source:* Based on numbers from BCCR.

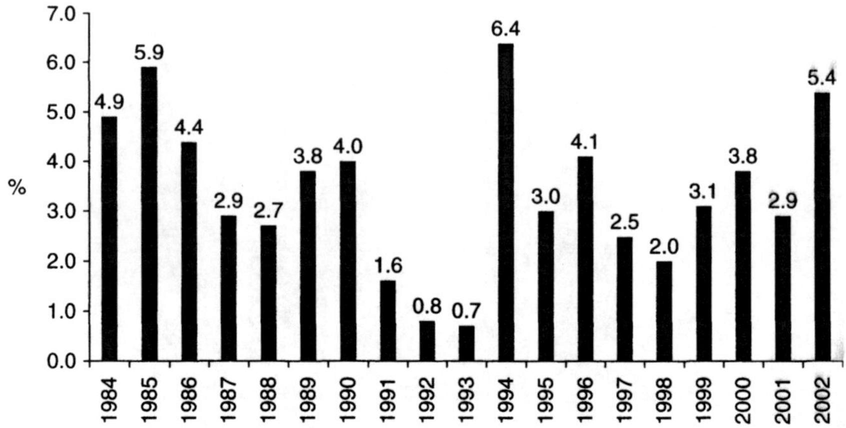


*Figure 8.A8* Costa Rica: public sector consolidated deficit as a percentage of GDP, 1984–2002
*Source:* BCCR and MIDEPLAN.

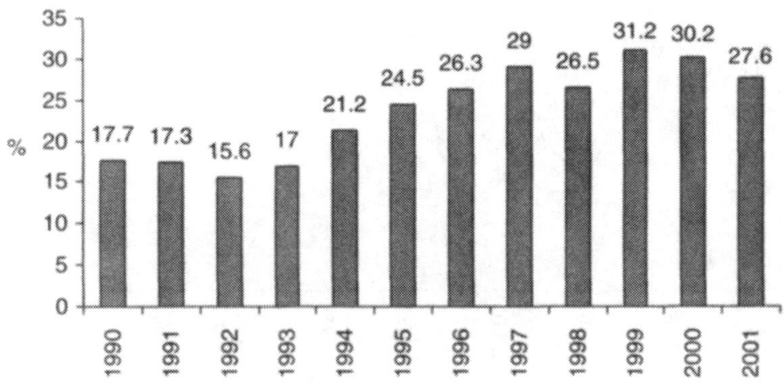


*Figure 8.A9* Costa Rica: internal public debt as a percentage of GDP, 1990–2001
*Source:* MIDEPLAN/SIDES Website http://www.mideplan.go.cr/sides/break economico/05-16.htm Accessed in November 2003.

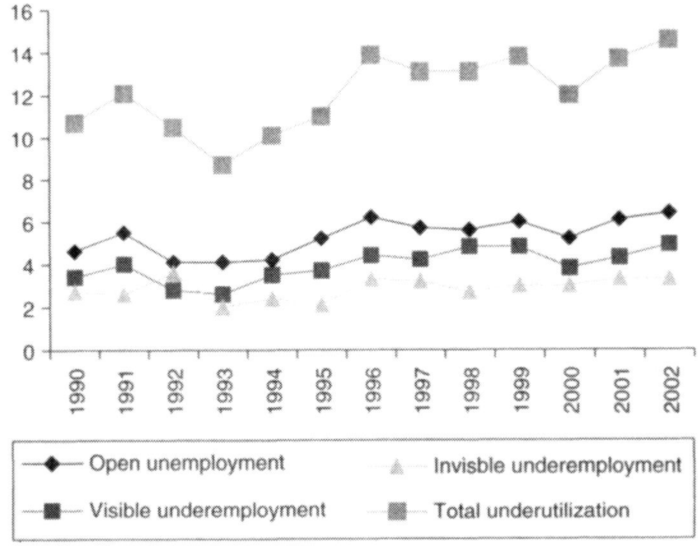


*Figure 8.A10* Costa Rica: workforce under-utilization rates, 1990–2002
*Source:* INEC, Household Surveys 1990–2002.

# 9
# Developmentalism and Social Change in Chile

*María Angélica Illanes and Manuel Riesco*

## Introduction

This chapter explores social policy in Chile, within the context of the UNRISD project 'Social Policy in a Development Context'. The chapter tries to address the project's general questions about the relation between social policy, economic development, and democracy, in the context of the historical evolution of social policies in Chile.

As emphasized in this book's analysis, the history of Chile in the twentieth century occurs against the backdrop of the country's quite fast and turbulent transition from an overwhelmingly rural, traditional agrarian, society, to a contemporary, modern kind of socioeconomic structure. During the twentieth century, rural population remained stagnant in Chile, inching up from 1.6 million in 1900 to 2.2 million in 1995. Meanwhile, Chile's urban population multiplied more than nine times, from 1.3 million in 1900 to 11.7 million in 1995 (Figure 9.A.1 in Appendix at the end of this chapter). This means that the whole of the rural population growth during the century, which accounts for a major part of the overall population growth, migrated to the cities. In addition, 8 out of 9 of the present urban dwellers are no older than third generation, and most of them are the daughters and sons of parents who were born peasants. Almost all of the overall increase in population in Chile, which multiplied more than five times over during the century up to the present 16 million (2005), is due to the increase in urban population. The proportion of rural inhabitants has fallen from nearly 60 per cent of the total population during the first decade of the century, to less than 15 per cent in the last, and it is still falling very fast, as will be shown below. The percentage of rural workers within the economically active population (EAP) also fell dramatically (Figure 9.A1).[1]

This chapter makes extensive use of the central concept introduced in this book as the *Latin American Developmental Welfare State (LADWS)*. As presented in the book's introduction and first chapter, this concept tries to capture the character of the central political institution that presided over

LA development throughout most of the twentieth century. Emerging in the 1920s throughout most of the region, it assumes *development*, both economic and social, to be a central concern of the state, and creates the institutions necessary to promote it. It is presented in the book as a particular form of the twentieth-century welfare state that evolved in late-developing countries. Its central determination is precisely the fact that the socioeconomic structure at the time was mainly pre-modern and agrarian – a majority of the population were in fact traditional peasantry, in a major part subordinated to *latifundia*, in most countries, throughout a good part of the twentieth century. Within that environment, the state assumed the dual challenge of promoting both economic development and social change. The state had to build by itself most of the main landmarks of economic development – infrastructure projects, industrial complexes, universities, etc. – because the dominant actors in civil society at the time proved largely unable to take on these tasks. This economic aspect has been extensively documented in the history of LA *Developmentalism*. Nevertheless, in parallel, the strategy promotes social change, nurturing, educating, and protecting, both the nascent modern entrepreneurs and salaried classes. This book and chapter stress this final aspect, as an integral and central part of the LADWS concept.

This chapter adds evidence to the argument presented in the initial chapters of this book, that the LADWS crisis by the end of the century, and also its replacement as a central development paradigm by the *Washington Consensus*, were both, in a certain sense, a result of the success of the former, in modernizing the social structure. In particular, this chapter considers how its revolutionary climax in Chile, and its violent termination by the 1973 military coup, became central determinations over the subsequent periods, regarding both the extreme character of the policies adopted, and also the dynamic overall economic results.

The chapter makes a critical assessment of the Neoliberal social and economic policies that replaced LADWS after the 1973 coup in Chile, underlining their main problems at present. Nevertheless, the chapter links these policies to the previous LADWS period, as two connected phases in the overall process of Chilean historical transition that proceeds throughout the whole century, and, moreover, both periods have mutually determining effects on the country's present reality.

Finally, the chapter turns to the book's concluding questions about an approaching point of inflexion regarding the development paradigm that has been hegemonic during the last three decades. The chapter adds evidence from Chile in support of the book's thesis, and it advances the idea that, in the case of Chile, a new development paradigm may now be emerging, which would be built on the overall achievements of the preceding phases.

The chapter draws heavily on a background historical paper on Chilean social policies, prepared for this purpose by co-author Maria Angelica Illanes

(Illanes 2003), and from a paper prepared by co-author Manuel Riesco for UNDP (UNDP 2002b), as well as from long-term data series compiled and published by Pontificia Universidad Católica de Chile[2] (PUC 2000).

## In pursuit of economic and social progress

Chilean experience of Developmentalism spans from 11 September 1924 up to 11 September 1973, starting with a progressive military movement and ending with a brutal counterrevolutionary coup. After the Great Depression, it presided over four decades of accelerating growth rates that follows a relatively smooth path, with no major economic crisis, which would last until the early 1970s (Figure 9.A2). During this period, the country moved away from its past existence as a predominantly rural society, as the proportion of peasants in the population fell dramatically. At the same time, state institutions were established and developed rapidly over this long period. Fiscal expenditures as a whole, which had been very small at the beginning of the century, in both absolute and relative terms, began to grow by the mid-1920s, and especially in the wake of the Great Depression, to peak at record levels during the early 1970s, as the period reached its climatic end (Figure 9.A2).

Social policy has formed an integral part of *Developmentalism* in Chile since its beginning during the mid-1920s, as will be shown below. Considering the overall picture, and as social policies may be represented by public social expenditures, the period witnessed a rapid increase in public social expenditure, especially after the Great Depression, and particular during the period's culmination, in the late 1960s and early 1970s (Figure 9.A3). However, even at its peak, at less than 14 per cent of GDP, it was not a very high figure. That level has already been surpassed in Chile at the beginning of the 2000s, as overall public social expenditure is now over 16 per cent of GDP, which is still low even by modest LA standards (Tables A1–A5 in Appendix to Chapter 1). Nevertheless, as will be explained below, more than 41 per cent of the present public social expenditure is dedicated to financing the transition to the private pension system. In contrast, at the beginning of the 1970s most public social expenditure was dedicated to education, health and housing. By the end of the period, during the early 1970s, these items attained levels that have not been achieved in Chile since that time, even after the intense efforts made during the 1990s, to restore public social expenditure from the severe cutbacks suffered during the Pinochet dictatorship (Figures 9.A3, 9.A7 and 9.A8).

The evolution of LADWS in Chile, as presented in this chapter, is divided into two main phases. The early phase (1924–50) was the period when the main institutions are formed, but their scope is still quite limited, although they represent a large increase in relation to the previous periods (Figure 9.A3, 9.A5 and 9.A6). During this phase state efforts are limited to relatively localized and nascent economic and social institutions, and a few development projects, while social policy addressed only a relatively minor part of the population, excluding most of the peasantry. Public social expenditures, although increased, still remained relatively low during this period (Figure 9.A3). Social change, as represented by the rate of rural migration, doubled during this phase in relation to the previous period, although it remains within relatively moderate levels in relation to the following periods (Figure 9.A4). Two shorter periods are distinguished within this first phase: the first period includes the military dictatorship headed by general Carlos Ibáñez (1924–31), during which the basic institutions were created, the ensuing period of instability (1931–32) and the second Alessandri Palma government (1932–38). The second period includes the *Popular Front* governments: Pedro Aguirre Cerda (1938–41), Juan Antonio Ríos (1941–46), and Gabriel González Videla (1946–52). Two long economic cycles may also be identified during this early period: the first spans from 1918 to 1929, and the second, which includes the Great Depression, from 1929 to 1946. Within the long cycles, there are also some minor economic peaks, for example, in 1920 and 1925 (Figures 9.A2 and 9.A4).

The strategy became increasingly universal during the second phase (1950–73), both in the scope of its economic development projects, and in the coverage of social policies over the population as a whole, particularly peasants. Social change accelerates dramatically, especially towards the end of the period, as rural migration triples in relation to the previous phase, which was already fast (Figure 9.A4). At the beginning of this period, General Carlos Ibáñez won a second presidential term, this time through elections (1952–58), to be followed by conservative president Jorge Alessandri Rodriguez (1958–64), the son of President Alessandri Palma. President Eduardo Frei Montalva, a Christian democrat, was elected in 1964, and followed by the socialist president Salvador Allende (1970–73). Two major economic cycles take place during this second phase – one from 1946 to 1958 – and another from 1958 to 1971, with minor peaks in 1953 and 1964, among others (Figures 9.A2 and 9.A4). LADWS reaches its climax in Chile during the last two governments of this phase. They presided over the most advanced reforms, and the revolutionary process – where peasants, workers, students and the middle classes, among other popular sectors, together with state bureaucracy, supported by the military until right before the coup, become leading political actors – that quite completely and irreversibly changed the social landscape of the country during the late 1960s and early 1970s.

## Early years (1924–50)

The 1920s mark a critical point of inflexion in Chilean history. The 1930 census measures two landmarks: for the first time the Chilean population passed four million inhabitants and, also for the first time, urban dwellers outnumber peasants, albeit by only a small margin (Figure 9.A1), while rural migration to the cities is beginning to grow (Figure 9.A4). The 1920s also witnessed both the highest point and the cataclysm of the basic pillars of the Chilean economy during the previous period: nitrates and agricultural exports. The decade coincides with a long economic cycle that started in 1918 and experienced oscillating, export-led growth that averaged slightly less than 4 per cent a year over the decade, to end in the 1929 crisis (Figures 9.A2 and 9.A4).

*Birth: manu militari*

At that time, according to the authors of the new social legislation, 'Chile showed the highest mortality rate in the world because of deteriorated living standards in the lower classes' (Illanes 2003), which began to evidence increasing discontent – echoing similar developments around the world after the First World War and the Russian Revolution. At the same time, the existing network of private social assistance organizations – created by the initiatives of socially conscious members of the upper classes allied to nascent worker organizations – became saturated as peasant migration started to gain in significance. In addition, the failure of the first government of President Arturo Alessandri Palma (1920–24) to deliver an ambitious programme, which included promises of social legislation, led to a crisis. In such circumstances, the first military coup in Chile during the twentieth century took place on 11 September 1924, which installed a military junta. The junta's first measures included the establishment of income taxes and social legislation, two Alessandri projects that had been delayed for years by a parliament that was dominated by the landed oligarchy. The labour legislation – which established the eight-hour workday, among other measures – and the obligatory social insurance, which became law by force under the junta, constitute two basic pillars of the social legislation that marked a new phase in Chilean history. In parallel, the new Constitution promulgated in 1925 also under military pressure, established that public health had become a primary interest for the state (Illanes 2003).

At this seminal political moment, a power alliance was established between the military and a social policy advocacy coalition of enlightened professionals, most of them medical doctors. Their main achievement was the reform of the character of the *oligarchic-liberal* state that had prevailed until then, and the establishment of the *social assistance* state, as was explicitly stated in the project that Dr Alejandro del Río presented to the military junta. The rationale of the project was welfare developmentalism, because it stated that the absence of a healthy population was a hindrance both to national defence and to a productive economy. In 1924, they created a social ministry, initially headed by Dr del Río, which included Health, Social Assistance, Social Provision, and Labour. Attached to this ministry, they created a semi-autonomous *Caja del Seguro Obrero Obligatorio* (Obligatory Social Insurance Fund), which would manage social contributions, which were to be fixed at

6 per cent of wages, contributed by the employer (3 per cent), the worker (2 per cent) and the state (1 per cent). In addition, they created the *Escuela de Servicio Social* (the Social Assistance School) to educate the professionals that would form the new public, professional, social service (Illanes 2003).

Educational policy was the centrepiece of the new *Assistance* state. The Ministry of Education was created in 1927, and an educational reform was initiated, which emphasized the development of national values of 'race, fatherland, and nation'. Health care and the nutrition of pupils in public schools were entrusted to school inspectors (Illanes 2003). The increased importance assigned to education is shown in the surge of state expenditure in primary, secondary and, especially, in tertiary education, while illiteracy levels began to fall and school enrolment began to increase, as it would at a faster pace as LADWS advanced in Chile, and the public Universidad de Chile received a substantial boost (Illanes 2003; Figure 9.A6).

These institutions and their offspring established the foundations of social policy during the whole period in Chile (1924–73), and, although in a different form, they remain key institutions that even today address the social policy needs for the vast majority of the population.

In a sense, what marked the difference from previous conceptions of state responsibilities was precisely the introduction of public social policy. Economic developmentalism also became a central state matter after 1924, but it was not a new function, as the Chilean state had completed a nationwide railroad system as early as the first decade of the twentieth century. Railroads were the first large developmentalist project engaged by the Chilean state, and quite a remarkable feat indeed, considering the length of the country – over 3,000 kilometres in the area spanned by the railroad – and its remarkably rugged surface all along. Nevertheless, it was not until the Ibáñez government that the properly developmentalist state economic institutions were also created, which, together with the social policy institutions, would form the basis of the Chilean version of LADWS (Illanes 2003).[3]

Ibáñez governed *manu militari*, imposing all of these measures in the face of the opposition from the landed oligarchy,[4] and even the initial resistance of the workers' movement who saw their own role in social assistance and their class independence eroded by the state's new social policies (Illanes, 2003). Nevertheless, it is worth noting that the Ibáñez dictatorship (1924–31), together with the Aguirre Cerda (1938–41) and Allende (1970–73) presidential periods, were the only governments of Chile during the twentieth century during which no worker massacres took place (PCCh 2000).[5]

*In the wake of the Great Depression*

The 1930s Great Depression marked a turning point in Chile, as elsewhere in the world. Social and economic transition was accelerated greatly by the crisis, and the governments that followed implemented a new economic development paradigm that was state-led and internal market driven, where social policy played an increasingly important role. Since 1938, LADWS paradigm became explicit state policy in Chile, after the election of the *Popular Front* governments, an alliance headed by Radicales, with the participation of Socialists and other progressive parties, including Communists until 1948 (Illanes 2003).

The Great Depression had a dramatic effect on the Chilean economy and people. Between 1929 and 1932, GDP fell 44.1 per cent and exports fell 73.1 per cent by volume, and 86.2 per cent in value. Real wages fell 51.8 per cent during the same period (Figure 9.A2, PUC 2000). Tonnage shipped through ports, which had grown at a rate of 12 per cent during the 1920–29 economic cycle, fell so dramatically during the 1929–32 crisis, that even after recovering during the following years, still averaged a 6 per cent net annual decrease rate during the 1929–46 economic cycle. GDP growth, which had averaged 4 per cent a year during the 1920–29 economic cycle, halved to around 2 per cent a year during the 1929–46 cycle, including GDP being slashed almost by half during the crisis itself, as stated above. Export-oriented agriculture actually fell during the following economic cycle. Mining, which had grown at 2 per cent a year during the 1920–29 cycle, averaged a net loss of 3 per cent a year during the following economic cycle (Figure 9.A4; PUC 2000).

Before the crash, the nitrate mining industry, located in the northern deserts of Chile, was by far the largest concentration of workers in the country, employing 59,900 workers at its peak in 1928. However, by 1932 that number had been sharply reduced – to 8,711 workers and 8,394 in 1933, before recovering slightly to 14,777 in 1934 (Ortiz 1982).[6] The displaced workers migrated back south, to the cities in the centre of the country, mainly Santiago. A significant number of them also returned to the countryside from where years before they had been *enganchados (snatcheds)* to be ferried thousand of kilometres north into the middle of the desert. This process generated, for the first time in Chile, the appearance of masses of workers freely available for hire by private entrepreneurs, two groups of social actors who were to become increasingly important in Chile throughout the twentieth century. This two-stage process seems to have been the main process through which the process by which peasants abandon the land to constitute the modern *salariat* started in Chile – as is well known, the same process has taken place during the transition to modernity in every country, but has occurred in very different historical forms and moments. First, during the end of the nineteenth and the first decades of the twentieth century, the *enganche* of peasants to the northern desert mining *campamentos*, which reproduced the same labour relation prevailing in *latifundia*, in very many respects.[7] This was then followed by their return to the cities, and in part to the countryside, in the centre of the country after the Great Depression. After decades extracting fabulous riches under the desert sun and cold nights, they took back despairingly few possessions with themselves, save abundant lice, and, of course, their new ability to read and write and to organize their labour, acquired during their years of common struggle in *campamentos*.[8] Rural migration also doubled its speed during the 1929–46 economic cycle in relation to the previous cycle (Figure 9.A4).

As a result of this process, the manufacturing workforce multiplied more than four times over, increasing from 84,991 in 1926 up to 287,872 in 1940 and 389,700 in 1949, becoming a social base both for the new widened social policies, and internal market-driven development strategy, that would come of age by the mid-century (Illanes 2003). The great fall in export markets prompted what was later to be conceptualized by ECLAC and others as the *import substitution* or *inward* development model, which was based heavily upon manufacturing. Productivity in this sector increased its growth rates from around one per cent a year during the 1920–29 cycle to 2 per cent during the 1929–46 cycle, to 4 per cent a year during the 1946–58 economic cycle, to culminate in yearly growth rates of over 5 per cent during the 1958–71 economic cycle. Meanwhile, export-oriented agriculture, which had recorded 4 per cent increases in productivity during the 1920–29 economic cycle, fell during the next cycle, and stabilized at 2–3 per cent yearly growth rates during the rest of the LADWS period. Agriculture now became oriented towards the internal market, as the country become a net importer of agricultural products (Figure 9.A4; PUC 2000).

After the crisis, the state started to build the national electricity network (Figure 9.A4), mainly through the efforts of the national electricity company ENDESA, formed in 1939. The *Corporación de Fomento* (*CORFO*), created in the same year, was to play an important role in the industrialization of the country over the following decades, and even now continues to play a relevant role in industrial policy. Petroleum was discovered in 1945, and the state oil company, ENAP, was created soon after, among many other relevant economic development projects.

Nevertheless, their scope was rather limited during their nascent stage, and it was not until after the mid-century that their full impact would be felt. Regardless of the advances in social policy since 1924, the Chilean population was still quite destitute, which prompted the state to adopt new social policy initiatives. In 1939, there were more than one million illiterates, about one-quarter of the population at the time. Low levels of school coverage excluded around 42 per cent of the population from primary school, while only 13 per cent of the pupils completed this educational level. Following his campaign slogan 'governing is educating', Pedro Aguirre Cerda, the first president elected by the *Popular Front* (1938–41), increased the educational budget, built new schools, and improved education as a whole, although still within the rather narrow limits of social policy in general during this period (Illanes 2003; figure 9.A3 and 9.A6). In 1947, a new state university, *Universidad Técnica del Estado*, was formed, as well as one of the leading private universities, Universidad Federico Santa María.[9]

In 1937, the health minister of the second Alessandri Palma government, Dr Eduardo Cruz-Coke, presented the new Preventive Health Law (Ley de Medicina Preventiva), which recognized the insufficient results of previous health policies, created new institutions, and funded them with an additional contribution of one per cent of wages, among other measures. Within the new developmental ideology, for example, the funds accumulated in the *Caja del Seguro Obrero Obligatorio* were now considered to be a strategic 'workers' accumulation fund', to be used in developmental projects as well as workers' well-being. These funds should produce the 'slow although inevitable transformation of most of private capitals, because of social insurance regimes, into authentic social capital', as formulated in 1939 by the young minister of health in the first *Popular Front* government, Salvador Allende (Illanes 2003).

Public social expenditure, which had been quite negligible and dedicated almost entirely to education until 1924, now began its long growth trajectory, which would peak at the end of the LADWS period in 1973, as stated earlier. Health expenditure becomes relevant only after the mid-1930s. Meanwhile, public expenditure in education continued to grow, again fastest at the tertiary level, which illustrates the special attention governments then dedicated to the national development strategy, which included developing highly-qualified professional and scientific skills (Figure 9.A3 and 9.A6).[10]

### Blooming years (1950–73)

The 1950s mark another point of inflexion in Chile regarding social policies in a development context. At this time there was growing awareness of the limitations of social policies applied to that date, especially regarding the exclusion of a good part of the population, mainly the peasantry. After the Second World War, socialism and a new international model for social policies in the western countries, the welfare state, were establishing themselves as new development paradigms across the world. The Cuban revolution in 1959 opened a new historical period in LA, where *developmentalism* and *social change* were to be recognized as the main directions to be followed on the way out of backwardness, by a wide spectrum of social and political actors. Dr Raúl Prebisch was one of the main authors of the new paradigm at a conceptual level, and ECLAC became one of its most effective promoters. Even the US government started supporting this kind of policies in the times of Kennedy's *Alliance for Progress* (Illanes 2003).

In addition, social agitation and organization started to grow again in Chile after some years of repression as, in the framework of a nascent Cold War, the last of the governments elected by *Popular Front* had turned against, and outlawed, part of its own supporters, namely the Communist Party. President Gabriel González Videla, who had recently declared 'there is no power on earth that can separate me from the communist party', justified the measure explaining that a Third World War was about to start, and

Chile could be aligned with the Soviet Union. A national labour union, the *Central Unica de Trabajadores (CUT)*, was created in 1953 and was to play a relevant role in the years to come. Meanwhile, poor city dwellers started the occupation of vacant urban lands, in a movement called *tomas* (takeovers), which would reach massive proportions in years to come, shaping a good part of the present popular urban map in the main Chilean cities (Illanes 2003). The ratio of days on strike to days worked, for example, grew by more than 8 per cent a year on average throughout this period (Figure 9.A6). Popular mobilization would continue to rise throughout the whole period, up to its widespread involvement in politics during the revolutionary climax in the early 1970s (Illanes 2003).

In 1950, Dr Francisco Mardones, the Minister of Health in the last *Popular Front* government, presented parliament with a bill that created a National Health Service, measures which had been drafted a decade before by Dr Salvador Allende when he was the Health Minister under President Aguirre Cerda. Now Dr Allende, as president of the Senate, achieved unanimous parliamentary approval for this project. As a result, the coverage of the *Servicio de Seguro Social* (social security fund) grew from one to three million beneficiaries, out of an overall population of 5.2 million at the time, which would be attended by the new *Servicio Nacional de Salud Pública (SNS)*. 'I have the intimate conviction' – said Allende – 'that we are not able to appreciate the transcendence of these initiatives in all their magnitude. Time will give them the projections that in my view they have, in defence of the race, in the protection of human capital, and in what they mean to avoid the tremendous injustices which derive out of the existence in our country of different social stratus' (Illanes 2003).

In March 1962, the *Conference on Education and Socio Economic Development for LA*, held in Santiago, in *Universidad Técnica del Estado,* and organized by the UN, UNESCO, ECLAC, FAO, ILO and OAS, formulated the discourse of this period, saying:

> We recognize these are times of urgency, times of efforts and sowing. They are also times of challenges and dangers. There is an imperious need to wage battle against the inevitable allies of insufficient economic development: acute poverty, ignorance, and desperation. There is an urgent need to include millions of our continent's inhabitants as soon as possible to the benefits and opportunities offered by the education, culture, and technological development of the 20th century. Peoples can wait no longer and their dissatisfaction may no longer be ignored.

In this way, developmentalism, inclusiveness, and democracy were embedded into the intention of social policy as LADWS entered the period where it would develop in full, in Chile (Illanes 2003).

This period witnessed the most rapid social change in Chile. Rural migration more than tripled again during the 1946–58 economic cycle, with respect to the already increased rate experienced during the previous economic cycle, to reach peak levels that would not abate until the 1981–95 economic cycle (Figure 9.A4).

The economy surged throughout two main economic cycles during this period – 1946–58 and 1958–71 – peaking at a record growth rate of more than 4.1 per cent a year achieved during the second cycle (Figures 9.A2 and 9.A4). Manufacturing was again the economy's locomotive, as productivity in this sector grew at 4 per cent a year, and over 5 per cent a year, during the first and second cycles, respectively. In addition, exports other than agriculture recovered during this period from their post-depression crash, as tonnage shipped picked up again at a rate of 6.5 per cent a year during the first cycle and 3 per cent a year during the second cycle. Mining lowered its productivity during the first cycle because of falling prices during the Korean War, but recovered rapidly during the second economic cycle of this period (Figure 9.A4).

Economic growth accelerated as LADWS approached its climax. In the different political periods considered here, the economy grew at 1.5 per cent a year from 1924 to 1938, because this period included the Great Depression. It rose to 3.5 per cent a year from 1938 to 1950, and reached an average of 3.9 per cent a year from 1950 to 1973. Manufacturing led economic growth since the 1930s, as said (Figure 9.A5). During the LADWS period as a whole, from 1925 to 1973, GDP grew by 3.2 per cent a year on average, even including the years of the Great Depression (PUC 2000).

During the period 1950–73, state-led industrialization and economic developmentalism reached their peak. Those state companies and economic development institutions created during the previous period matured to become large, nationwide systems. In addition, many new state companies and landmark economic development institutions were also formed during this period.[11]

Social policies assumed centre stage during this phase, and public social expenditures grew rapidly. From the 1960s, housing became an important item in public social expenditure, together with increased expenditure in education and health. Expenditure in the mentioned items and others, as said, peaked at record and still unsurpassed levels in the early 1970s, during the climax of the LADWS period (Figures 9.A3, A7 and A8). Illiteracy rate fell five times faster during this period than in the previous 1938–50 period, and ten times faster than during the 1924–38 period. School enrolment reached record – and still unparalleled – growth rates of over 5 per cent a year during this period (Figure 9.A6).

The period opened with the election of General Carlos Ibáñez as president for a second term (1952–58), by a large majority. Perceiving the need for new social policy institutions, he quickly pushed a law though parliament that created *Juntas de Auxilio Escolar*, institutions that would deliver meals to pupils in the educational system, in addition to many other social policy initiatives (Illanes 2003). Nevertheless, the 1954 economic recession seriously affected the levels of public social spending, as well as other governmental programmes implemented during the second Ibánez administration. In fact, public social spending took a dip during these years, only to recover by the end of the Ibáñez government, in 1957–58 (Figure 9.A2 and A3).

The conservative government of Jorge Alessandri (1958–64), who narrowly defeated Allende in the 1958 elections, vowed to develop an educational plan that would be in accordance with economic development, and in full agreement with LADWS principles. Under pressure from the teachers' union, Alessandri approved a law that enhanced some of the above-mentioned social policy institutions, creating the *Junta Nacional de Auxilio Escolar y Becas* (*JUNAEB*). Even today, this institution, after being greatly enhanced towards the end of the LADWS period, delivers meals to millions of pupils throughout the educational system. Public social expenditure was affected by the 1958 economic depression, but soon recovered and grew at a vigorous pace during the Alessandri government overall (Figure 9.A3).

Ibáñez had ended his period by revoking the outlawing of the Communist Party and enacting a new democratic election law (1957), which put an end to the extended practice of electoral bribery, and thus seriously undermined the political power of traditional landowners. For his part, Alessandri, under pressure from the US, passed the first agrarian reform law which, however limited – it was dubbed the 'flowerpot agrarian reform' – cleared the way for more advanced reforms in the future.

Developmentalism entered its culminating phase with the election of President Eduardo Frei Montalva (1964–70), who offered a 'revolution in liberty', as an alternative to the socialist programme of Allende, who was again runner-up in the 1964 election. The Frei government immediately engaged into a sweeping educational reform, which rapidly increased both school enrolment[12] and the provision of school meals. In addition, the reform overhauled the educational system, raising the basic level of education to eight years, introducing a new option that led towards a technical education, and creating a new admission test for universities, among other significant achievements. Universities were shaken by a student-led reform movement that began in 1967, which achieved a complete renovation and a large increase in enrolment in the tertiary level of education (Illanes 2003). This process would be completed during the government of Salvador Allende, when the growth of school enrolment, while maintaining high overall rates, peaked in the tertiary level, where it achieved unparallel yearly increases of more than 17 per cent (UNDP 2002b). In this manner, the LADWS period culminated its remarkable achievement regarding education. School enrolment raised 1.2 per cent a year during the period 1923–38, 2.6 per cent a year during the period 1938–50, and 5.3 per cent a year during the period 1950–73. Such growth rates were not to be achieved again during the following periods when, quite to the contrary, school enrolment would grow at a slower rate, and even decrease during the years following the coup, especially in universities (Figure 9.A6).[13]

The previously mentioned health care law that created SNS in 1950 was complemented in 1952 by a law of preventive medicine, and in 1968 by the *Servicio Médico Nacional de Empleados* (SERMENA), a health system addressed to the needs of white-collar employees. Finally, the Allende government unified these services into a *Servicio Unico de Salud*. At this point, the state had built a national network of hospitals and first-level medical centres, which were able to provide almost universal coverage to the population in vaccination and other sanitary campaigns, as well as certain areas such as maternity and birth, for example. In 1971, President Allende's first measure was to distribute half a litre of milk a day to every child in the country through this same network, and even today, all Chilean children are entitled to this benefit (Illanes, 2000).[14]

The pension system was overhauled in 1952 by the creation of the *Servicio de Seguro Social (SSS)*. Pension benefits were subsequently improved and widened, as new groups of workers were included in the system through the successive widening of the SSS coverage, or the creation or improvement of their respective pension funds. This process culminated in 1973, when the Allende government extended SSS coverage to informal workers, including peasants, transforming it in effect into a universal entitlement system. The Allende reform was never to be put in practice, however, because the military dictatorship made severe cutbacks to social programmes after the 1973 coup (Figure 9.A3).

In addition to its engagement into economic development and social policies, the Chilean form of LADWS became increasingly confrontational in its relations with traditional oligarchies and foreign capital. It actively and explicitly pursued social change – 'change in socioeconomic structures' as it was termed. At the same time, it nurtured, educated, protected, and promoted both the nascent salaried workforce, and the new entrepreneurs. These groups, in turn, provided the main political base for the strategy, together with the peasants, who became increasingly politically aware, as the century advanced into its second half.

Milestones in this process included the agrarian reform law and the law of peasant labour unions, approved in 1967 under President Frei Montalva. In addition, the nationalization of copper and other minerals was approved unanimously by the Chilean parliament on 11 August 1971, during President Allende's government (Illanes, 2003). These laws permitted the legal nationalization of almost all the usable land, and all the large mines in the country, in just two to three years at the end of the Frei government and during the Allende presidency. Small farms and mines, owned by peasants or small miners, were not expropriated. It is not widely known that these laws continued to be respected in large part even after the military coup headed by Pinochet. Moreover, as will be argued, these momentous social transformations realized by the reformist and revolutionary regimes of the 1960s and 1970s laid, in no small part, the foundations for the rapid development of capitalism in Chile during the following decades.

In addition to the above-mentioned measures, the Allende government nationalized the whole of the banking system and a good part of the largest industrial complexes, which had formerly been in private hands. Some of his extremist supporters also managed to take control of some medium-sized and even small private companies, including some peasant farms. However, these latter actions were quickly overturned in the wake of the 1973 coup. In addition, the latter were, in no small part, responsible for the serious deterioration in Allende's support among the middle classes by the end of his government. Moreover, the Allende government showed itself to be indecisive in addressing the increasingly urgent demand for ensuring a certain degree of public order. This demand became widespread once the main feats of his government, which were widely supported by the Chilean population, had been achieved (Haslam 2004).

Nevertheless, the radical character of the Chilean LADWS experience with respect to social change will perhaps be regarded eventually as its most lasting feature, in addition to its general legacy regarding economic and social development, because of the huge impact such radical measures had on the future modernization of the country, as is argued below. On the other hand, the violent end of the Chilean LADWS experience in 1973 was to have enduring consequences regarding the economic and social policies adopted during the following years. Because of these political occurrences, the emerging Neoliberal development paradigm was also to be pioneered in Chile in quite a radical form. In short, the revolutionary climax of LADWS in Chile was to have long-lasting historical effects.

## An extreme Neoliberal experience

The turbulent climax and violent end of LADWS in Chile would be followed by a long dictatorship in which political liberties were repressed and human rights severely violated. This was, in turn, followed by a conservative and still incomplete transition to democracy, which has been going on for as long as the dictatorship it replaced. Non-military state institutions built over a century – especially social policy institutions – were to be seriously damaged by the dictatorship, and then recuperated in part by ensuing governments, which still show the considerable influence of state-dismantling ideology. At the same time, the military were elevated to the constitutional category of 'upholders of the nation' up to the 2000s, even though their actual influence declined rapidly after Pinochet was detained in London in 1998. In addition, in accordance to the emergent development paradigm, optimal short-term economic conditions would be established for business – including a drastic reduction of salaries, and weakened labour legislation. All of this happened in the general framework of an enthusiastic opening up of the country to foreign trade and investment, in time to meet an advancing globalization process.

### Pinochet and the 'Chicago Boys' (1973–89)

The military assumed power in Chile in a political climate that favoured extreme rightist positions, since the main imperative of the new government was to suppress a socialist-inspired revolutionary movement. The government they overthrew, and the president they led to suicide, had been the subject of ferocious attacks, coming from powerful opponents both in Chile and abroad, during the course of the revolution over which they had presided. Within the Chilean upper classes, which had been affected by years of reform and revolution, the desire of reprisal against those who had directly supported Allende was widespread. The fury of the upper classes was also directed against those whom they considered to be their accomplices, those guilty of making room for the changes. The latter included the Christian Democrats, even though by the time of the coup they were mostly opposed to Allende. Large sections of the middle classes also shared this feeling of rage, although for different reasons, mainly as a result of their distress and insecurity because of the increasingly chaotic events that resulted from the acute political confrontation that had been happening in Chile for some years, and which the Allende government had been incapable of dealing with.

To put it simply, hatred was quite widespread in Chile among those opposed to the Allende government as the military took over in 1973. It was directed against socialist, revolutionary, or even mildly progressive ideas – and during this period LADWS ideology was justly considered in Chile to be quite socialist and revolutionary – as well as against the political and social actors who had supported them.

In such a political climate, it is no wonder that those willing to act in the most brutal manner against Allende and his followers – headed by Pinochet – easily imposed themselves within the military. Neither is it strange that the new military rulers were no longer sympathetic to LADWS ideas, as had been the case within the Chilean military since General Ibánez and up to General Prats, Pinochet's predecessor at the head of the Chilean army,[15] as well as within the military throughout LA.

Instead, the new military rulers lent their ears to a group of young rightist economists who presented them with a complete alternative development programme.[16] They had been working on this programme since the Frei Montalva years, and it was mainly addressed against the LADWS paradigm. The leaders of this group were sons of old landowners who had been formed in the University of Chicago, under the influence of Arnold Harberger and

Milton Friedman, whose ideas they immediately embraced with instinctive fervour. They had received their scholarships in the framework of an agreement that the University of Chicago had signed with Pontificia Universidad Católica de Chile (PUC) back in the mid-1950s They were to become the renowned 'Chicago boys' of Pinochet.

Nevertheless, even in this heated political climate, the alternative programme would not have stood a chance for long, had it dared to question, let alone try to reverse, the main achievements of the previous period; principally, the agrarian reform[17] and the nationalization of natural resources, especially copper mining.[18] These landmark achievements, as stated, were respected in general terms after the coup. In addition, the basic lines of the Chicago Boys programme – being business-friendly and open to foreign trade and investments – proved broadly adequate to address the needs of the new socioeconomic structure that was the result of the LADWS experience in Chile as a whole. Finally, such basic lines proved to be well synchronized with the emerging international economic environment.

The three above-mentioned conditions were fulfilled in part by the new development programme, especially the latter two, which it embraced enthusiastically, as it reluctantly accepted the first condition. A more advanced socioeconomic structure had already evolved in Chile, quite radically as the old agrarian model had been forcefully terminated. The resulting socioeconomic structure proved fertile soil for the new, business- and globalization-friendly economic policies. The more affluent among the emerging social actors, on the other hand, provided a long-term political base for the new development paradigm that was to replace LADWS (Therborn *et al.* 1999).

The new entrepreneurial elite that was bred in conditions such as those described above provided lasting support for the new development model, embracing the new Neoliberal-inspired economic model with an almost religious zeal. This does not seem to be the case in other LA countries, such as Brazil, for example, where business elites have remained quite attached to the LADWS model, which in turn was presided over mainly by military regimes, who were often conservative-leaning (Therborn *et al.* 1999; see also Chapter 6 in this book).

In part, key features of the new economic paradigm, such as the lowering of tariffs for example, capable of being introduced early on in Chile, in good part because the conservative social forces that managed to successfully resist such measures in other LA countries at the time, had been all but wiped out in Chile by the preceding revolution. The spectre of those times, in turn, made the new entrepreneurs quite willing to accept the considerable hardships that such measures meant for themselves, at least initially. For their part, the upper echelons of the new salaried middle classes also provided enthusiastic and lasting support for the new model, which soon offered them a wider variety of better-quality products and services – including social services, as will be mentioned below – which for their part they could well afford to buy (Therborn *et al.* 1999).

The LADWS experience and its violent termination by the military coup that brought an end to revolution in 1973 imposed relevant determinations over future economic and social policies. In this sense, it may be asserted that the main determinants of the Neoliberal experience were laid down over the successfulness of the previous strategy in radically changing the country's traditional socioeconomic structure.

For its part, the international economic environment became increasingly supportive of such ideas, as is well known. Soon, Thatcherism and Reaganism would become hegemonic over a good part of development theory, and increasingly over development practice, including social policies – especially within the realms of the influential Bretton Woods institutions, from where they were forcefully expanded worldwide.

Based on the conditions inherited from the previous period, the dictatorship that sprung from the military coup, and even the democratic governments that followed it, pioneered the economic reforms that configured the renowned Chilean 'economic miracle'. During the 1970s, the 1980s and most of the 1990s, Neoliberal-inspired policies were was put into place in Chile, both as a new development strategy and a new social policy paradigm. As has been noted by commentators, Chile introduced 'the most radical example of the Neoliberal market model, particularly under the Pinochet regime (1973–90)' (Mesa-Lago 2002: 3).

The favourable pro-business environment and the early opening up of the economy to foreign trade and investment established by the dictatorship accelerated the economic transformation of the country, but not without problems. The cyclical behaviour of the Chilean economy became increasingly pronounced, as two deep economic crises occurred during this period, which reached to their bottom in 1975 and 1982 respectively, followed by rapid recoveries (Figure 9.A2). The first economic cycle, 1971–81, shows one of the worst overall results since the Great Depression cycle of 1929–46. During this period, GDP growth halved from the previous 1958–71 economic cycle, to slightly over 2 per cent a year, and worker productivity in fact fell significantly during this cycle. All industries suffered, specially manufacturing, which experienced a significant net loss during the 1971–81 cycle. Even tonnage shipped through ports fell drastically during this cycle (Figures 9.A2 and 9.A4). The 1982 crisis was so severe (Figure 9.A2) that even after the rapid recovery experienced since 1985, the Pinochet years as a whole shows much lower average economic results than the previous LADWS period (Figure 9.A5). GDP growth during the dictatorship averaged slightly over 2 per cent and worker productivity suffered a net loss across the whole period. Growth was now based mainly on export-oriented agriculture, and mining, while manufacturing productivity growth dropped to one-fifth of the previous period (Figure 9.A5).

There were deep reductions in salary and a steep rise in unemployment during the Pinochet years (Figures 9.A9 and 9.A10), as well as increased job instability resulting from acute economic cycles and relatively slow average growth during the overall period (Figures 9.A4, 9.A5 and 9.A9). Labour unions were drastically repressed, as may be appreciated by the plummeting number of workers' strikes (Figure 9.A6).

At the same time, the ongoing social changes continued, and even accelerated during these years, as rural migration continued at peak rates, at least until the 1980s (Figures 9.A4 and 9.A5), and the number of workers grew very rapidly (Figure 9.A9). Additionally, this time, the process nurtured a young and aggressive entrepreneurial class, which was furthermore enriched by the privatization of state companies and activities, which took place during the period (Therborn *et al.* 1999). More will be said below about the resulting social structure.

The Pinochet dictatorship (1973–89) implemented severe cutbacks in social and overall state expenditures (Figure 9.A3, 9.A5 and 9.A6). Public social expenditure other than pensions, as said, once being slashed by half after the 1973 coup, in the midst of a massive state reduction and stabilization programme, was sustained at very low levels until the end of the dictatorship in 1989 (Figures 9.A3, 9.A7, and 9.A8).[19] The deterioration of public social services and the general hardships endured by the population during this period may be assessed by the fact that there were fewer pupils enrolled in the entire educational system in 1982 than there were in 1974, and that by 1987 about half the population was below the poverty line (UNDP 2002b).

The opposite stance, regarding social public expenditure, was adopted by the Chilean military regime concerning pension deficits, after the pension reform of 1981.[20] The privatization of the pension system generated considerable pressure on fiscal accounts, as all contributions were channelled to the AFP system, while the public system continued to provide most, if not all the pension benefits (Figure 9.A3). Even today, 41 per cent of the government's social budget, almost one-third of the overall government budget, and over 6 per cent of GDP, goes to fund the pension system deficit. The load is so large that it has more than offset the impact of the private system over savings (Mesa-Lago 2002) and the redistributive impact of the remaining social spending is offset by pension expenditure, most of which goes to the higher-income pensioners, including those in the military (ECLAC 2002; UNDP 2002b; INP 2005).

Nevertheless, new social policies were also implemented during this period. These emphasized the privatization of social services and the development of a social services industry capable of delivering differentiated services to the upper-income segments of the population. At the same time, a diminished public social expenditure was targeted on the poorest segments of the population, providing them with a social safety net.[21]

Pensions were almost completely privatized, under a widely known scheme, which most of the workforce have been forced to join since 1981.[22]

Education was privatized almost in half,[23] and a national private health insurance scheme was instituted, which presently cares for one-fifth of the population belonging to the higher-income brackets. A social 'safety net', conformed by a non-contributory minimum welfare scheme was also put in place, but then, only for the poorest.[24] Meanwhile, and as will be emphasized below, the majority of the population, remains largely unprotected (UNDP 2002b; INP 2004, 2005).

At the same time, levels of insecurity increased significantly, because of internal social transformation, enhanced by the country's early opening to the globalization process, which was evolving at around the same time. This phenomenon may be clearly appreciated in the above-mentioned steep increase in the cyclical behaviour of the economy as a whole (Figure 9.A2), and particularly regarding employment and salaries (Figures 9.A9 and A10). In the case of Chilean teachers, for example, almost half of them have migrated from relatively secure jobs in the public system to the new subsidized private, or outright private, sectors of education, which is characterized by part-time, temporary and, in general, insecure conditions. The reform of the public SP system as well, due to decentralization to local governments, has created less secure working conditions, both in health and in education (UNDP 2002b).

In a sense, as had been the case during the LADWS period, Neoliberal social policy continued to be an integral part of an overall economic development strategy. It has already been noted how, in a negative way, the drastic reduction of social spending was instrumental in the stabilization programmes of the 1970s. It has also been mentioned that the privatization of pensions, although not relevant in increasing the overall savings rate because of the accompanying public pension deficit, has nonetheless deepened the financial markets, no small achievement in itself (Mkandawire 2000). In addition, reforms drastically reduced the employers' contributions, transferring them almost completely to the employees. Even though this reform is probably minor in relation to overall salary-related costs, because gross salaries were raised more or less in the same proportion,[25] nonetheless it may have had an important psychological impact regarding general investment conditions. Last, but not least, the liberal reforms have resulted, as stated, in the rise of an important private social protection industry that sells services previously provided by the government at no charge. As a result of this, the same activities, say, the services of no less than half of the teachers, an important proportion of doctors and other health personnel, social security administrators and clerical personnel, etc. were previously realized by public servants and delivered for free. Now, instead, they appear adding value to the national accounts, as part of an increased private services sector.

## Democracy, justice, and equality, 'In so far as possible' (1990–2005)

The Pinochet dictatorship ended in 1989, and since then four democratic governments have been elected.[26] This time, however, and in stark contrast to the violent end of the LADWS period – or, perhaps, in part precisely because of that – the political transition to democracy has been very slow and remarkably peaceful. The transition process started after Pinochet lost a plebiscite in 1988. The preceding years, on the contrary, were marked by widespread political upheavals that were violently repressed, called *protestas nacionales*.[27] The unrest had started in 1983 in the midst of a deep economic crisis (Figure 9.A2) and culminated in 1986 with massive demonstrations that paralysed the country for days at a time. Massive *protestas* were accompanied by increasing guerrilla activity that peaked in 1986 with a highly sophisticated attempt to kill Pinochet, who barely escaped with his life. At that point, and under intense pressure from the US, Pinochet and part of the democratic opposition, agreed upon a transitional process that cleared the way to the above-mentioned plebiscite. This agreement included maintaining Pinochet as commander in chief of the army for a number of years even after a new president was elected, as well as most of the constitution Pinochet had imposed in 1980.[28] This constitution includes numerous provisions that endow the armed forces, and the rightist parties that have consistently supported the Neoliberal model, with an effective veto power over most relevant matters.[29] In this way, the incoming governments have been formally constrained in their reform purposes to what the rightist parties may approve. This prompted President Aylwin (1990–94) to famously declare that democracy, economic and social policy, and even justice in Chile, were to advance 'in so far as possible', which during most of the 1990s was not very far at all.

Nevertheless, even the most carefully crafted transitional design would not had been enough to ensure the maintenance of the Neoliberal model, had not this model been adequate to the current developmental requirements of Chile, at least to a certain extent. In addition, the 1990s witnessed the peak of this development strategy all over the world, as the Washington Consensus established in 1989 (Williamson 2002). This kind of thinking, which became known as *pensamiento único* because of its overwhelming dominance,was hegemonic in Chile at the time as well within the academic and professional elites, including the new government cadres.

Because of this, and despite its limitations, the above-described transitional arrangements have been supported consistently, even though increasingly unwillingly, by a large majority of the Chilean population. This reaction is unsurprising, because the main benefits of all of the overall historical processes that have been described in this chapter, which covered most of the twentieth century, began to be reaped during the 1990s, when the

Chilean economy grew at a very fast pace, and all social indicators improved accordingly.

In this manner, the basic lines of economic and social policy during the previous period were in large part maintained during the transition to democracy. No major changes were introduced in the overall economic development strategy, which continued to emphasize business-friendly policies, within a framework of increasingly opening up to foreign trade and investment.

In fact, many of these policies gave their fruits and were enhanced during the 1990s, as direct foreign investment that had failed to materialize during the 1970s and 1980s started inflowing at record rates during the 1990s. At the same time, several free trade agreements (FTA) were signed during the late 1990s and early 2000s, including FTA with the USA and the EU, among many others.

A long economic growth cycle started after the 1982 crisis which, following a slight pause in 1990, did not stop until 1998, when the crisis that began in Asia struck the Chilean economy (Figure 9.A2; PUC 2000; ECLAC 2003). During the 1990s, the growth rate of the Chilean economy was double the LA average, and topped all other LA countries, as it grew at a record 6.5 per cent a year, which means GDP roughly doubled in size during this period (Table 1.A1–1.A2 in Appendix to Chapter 1). Agriculture, once again export oriented, recovered a growth rate unseen since the 1920s, and new industries related to natural resources grew up from nothing to become major world players – such as salmon farming and other cultivated sea food, for example. Mining again grew very rapidly – copper production tripled during the decade, although manufacturing was still stagnant during the 1981–97 economic cycle as a whole (Figure 9.A4). Moreover, during the shorter 1990–97 cycle economic growth was quite spectacular, reaching 8 per cent a year as a whole, and peaking at previously unseen levels in all sectors, including manufacturing (Figure 9.A5).

Some new regulations were established during the early 1990s, such as the renowned control over short-term capital inflows known as *encaje*,[30] and a modest tax increase was then passed through parliament. In addition, a significant policy shift took place as democratic governments implemented a rapid recovery of overall public expenditure, and especially social expenditure (Figures 9.A2, A3, A5, A7 and A8). Overall, fiscal expenditure recovered briskly during the 1990s, roughly doubling itself as well, and increasing from 22.2 per cent of GDP in 1989 to 24 per cent in 2000 (Figure 9.A2 and 9.A5; UNDP 2002b). Government projects have included the re-building of the national road and highway network into a modern, mostly paved, system, the recovery of part of the national railroad network after decades of neglect, and tripling the subway lines in Santiago, among other major, multi-billion dollar economic development programmes. Most of these programmes, however, were financed and built through private concessions. In addition, a major part of the recovered government spending went into social policies, which raised their participation in the government budget from 64.8 per cent in 1989, to 70.5 per cent in 2000 (UNDP 2002b).

Public expenditure in health more than doubled, and public expenditure in education more than tripled during the 1990s, in absolute terms, although these items have yet to recover to their pre-coup levels as relative to GDP (Figures 9.A3, 9.A6, 9.A7 and 9.A8; UNDP 2002b). Nevertheless, by Latin American (LA) standards, Chilean public social expenditure is still moderate, as it stands at 16 per cent of GDP. This is not far from the LA average of 14.8 per cent, and lower than the continent leaders in this matter – Cuba, Panama, Uruguay, and Argentina – all of whom spend more than 20 per cent of GDP on social items. The Chilean figure is also lower than for Brazil and Costa Rica, whose public social expenditure amounts to 18.8 per cent and 18.2 per cent of GDP, respectively (2000–01) (Table A1.7 in Appendix to Chapter 1).

School enrolment increased significantly during the decade, reaching almost universal coverage in basic education, nearly 90 per cent in secondary education, and doubling the coverage in tertiary education – from 16 per cent of the respective age group in 1990 to over 33 per cent in 2002 (UNDP 2002b). Public expenditure per pupil recovered at record growth rates in the primary and secondary levels during the 1990s. Nevertheless, as mainly private universities and institutes absorbed the considerable increase in enrolment in tertiary education, expenditure per pupil continued to decrease in this level during the decade (Figure 9.A6; UNDP 2002b). Over two-thirds of the considerable increase in school enrolment in primary and secondary levels was also absorbed by private schools, but in this case over 92 per cent of the pupils receive a state subsidy which covers most of their fee (UNDP 2002b).

A partial system of unemployment insurance, as well as a partial reform of the health system, has been introduced in recent years, although both reforms still rely heavily on liberal schemes, but the former proved completely ineffectual during the 1998–2003 recession (UNDP 2002b).[31]

Wages also increased significantly during the 1990s (Figure 9.A10), along with union activity, as manifested in the number of strikes (Figure 9.A6). Nevertheless, in the cautious transitional political environment, labour unions exerted considerable self-restraint, and it was not until 1999 that real, inflation-adjusted wages recovered their pre-coup levels (Figure 9.A10). Wages of teachers and public employees in general are still below that level (UNDP 2002b). During the decade labour productivity grew significantly faster than wages (CENDA 2004e).

One of the results of economic growth was the reduction of poverty by more than half during the 1990s. Poverty decreased from 48 per cent of the population in 1987, to 20.6 per cent in 2000, and 18.8 per cent in 2003, as poverty reduction has continued, although at a slower pace, even during the recession that started in 1998. Extreme poverty has been reduced accordingly and at the time of writing stands at 4.7 per cent (UNDP 2002b; CENDA 2004a: 20/08/2004).

As a result, the country climbed several positions in the human development index (HDI), according to which it ranks second in LA together with Costa Rica, although still some way behind Argentina, the continental leader (Tables 1.A1–1.A6 in Appendix to Chapter 1).

On the other hand, despite the fact that strategies like the targeting of a diminished level of public social spending on the poorest fifth of the population have resulted in improvements in general quality of life indicators, as said, the growing differences in income have resulted in persistent and even increasing equity gaps. The distribution of income in Chile remains one of the most inequitable in the world, and within LA, it is second only to Brazil, scarcely beating Colombia, who comes third on this indicator. In the three countries, the upper 10 per cent receive over 40 per cent of total income (2002) (Tables 1.A1–1.A10 in Appendix to Chapter 1). Inequity has been increasing rapidly during the 1990s if social spending is not taken into account. On the other hand, if consideration is made of the targeted social spending, the large inequity breach has more or less stabilized over this period.[32] However, if non-targeted public social expenditure is included, namely expenditure in pensions that is the major part of overall public social expenditure, then public social expenditure as a whole becomes more regressive, as said (ECLAC 2003; INP 2005). Moreover, the privatization of social services has also increased the equity gap as only the upper income segments of the population benefit out of differentiated social services provided by the privatized SP industry (UNDP 2002b).[33]

In the background, social change in Chile continues to be rapid. Rural migration has halved from the peak rates achieved during the previous decades, but is still a noticeable phenomenon; with the decrease in the percentage of rural population, approaching 0.7 per cent of the total population per year, as it rapidly approaches the 10 per cent milestone (Figures 9.A1, A2, A4, A5 and A6). That means that over the last decade over 7 per cent of the population has abandoned their way of life in rural areas, to take their chances on the uncertainties of modern life in the rapidly expanding Chilean cities and towns (Table 1.A1 in Appendix to Chapter 1). In addition, Chilean cities are also changing. This may be appreciated by anyone who visits Santiago or other cities in Chile from time to time, and even by those who live in these cities and sometimes have trouble in finding their way around, as so many changes take place so rapidly that the city skyline alters continuously.

Continued reforms of SP during the 1990s in Chile, even if still within the Neoliberal framework, have followed a more diverse path than in the 1980s, as said, and the differences seem to stem largely from the fact that such reforms were now introduced not by a dictatorship, but by the ensuing democratic governments. In addition, there was an increased awareness during the 1990s of the importance of social policy, not just as a moral issue but also as contribution to the economic (and political) future of the countries. As a result, in LA in general, the reforms of the 1990s rode over a wave of rapidly increasing social spending, about 50 per cent on average on a per capita basis (UNDP 2002a; Figure 9.A7).

The objectives of SP reforms in the 1990s have been tilted more towards the objectives of greater efficiency through partial privatization, rather than to outright reduction, privatization, and replacement of the public social services, as had been the case in Chile under Pinochet, although the latter objectives were present and predominant in many cases, as well (UNDP 2002b). The previous 'imbalance has been gradually corrected by the three successive democratic administrations (1990 onwards) which, although maintaining the essence of the previous economic model, have placed higher accent on social policy under the more balanced approach' (Mesa-Lago 2002: 3). During the last decade, a substantial effort has been made in Chile regarding the recovery of the undermined and underfunded welfare institutions. However, and despite the above-mentioned efforts, the fact remains that public social spending excluding pensions – as per capita or related to GDP – has not yet returned, as said, to the levels that it used to have (Figures 9.A3, 9.A7 and 9.A8). This is still probably the main problem of the sector and its workers, even considering the need for a modernization of the public social protection institutions (UNDP 2002b).

## A new development strategy?

The Chilean Neoliberal model is beginning to be seriously questioned at home for the first time, three decades after it replaced LADWS as a development paradigm. The world economic crisis and a long depressive phase in the internal economic cycle, the awakening of the internal democratization process, new political and developmental trends in LA, and changing tides against Neoliberalism worldwide, seem to underlie this process.

Criticism of the present model is now concentrating in some of its already quite evident limitations regarding continued economic and social development, as well as its persistent equity gap. Some alternative policies, which have previously been the subject of severe criticism, are now flowing into the mainstream political agenda, at least in the areas of natural resources and social policies.

This process is in full development as this chapter is being written, and its outcome is, of course, quite uncertain.

### An inflexion point?

Two significant events took place in Chile in 1998. The long, high-growth economic cycle that had been going on since the 1980s came to an abrupt end. On the other hand, ex-dictator Pinochet, who had recently exchanged his position at the head of the army for the more comfortable chair of senator-for-life, was unexpectedly detained in London, following a requirement from Spanish judge Baltazar Garzón. Both events and their aftermath may finally prove to be the beginning of the end of the long political cycle that started in Chile in the wake of the 1973 military coup. At the same time, similar processes seem to be occurring in LA, and even worldwide, in the wake of the world economic crisis that started in Asia in 1997. As a result, the hegemony of Neoliberal development paradigm would be seriously questioned in Chile for the first time.

Towards the end of the decade, the economic crisis that started in 1998 diminished mean per capita economic growth almost to a halt. GDP growth fell from 6.6 per cent in 1997 to 3.2 per cent in 1998, took an actual dip of −0.76 per cent in 1999, followed by recoveries of 4.5 per cent, 3.4 per cent, 2.2 per cent, and 3.3 per cent the following years up to 2003, an average of 2.6 per cent a year over the period, whih is clearly disappointing by previous standards (BC 2004). Not until 2004 and 2005 has the Chilean economy recovered to growth rates above 6 per cent. Unemployment, which had descended to figures around 6.1–8 per cent during the booming 1990s, rose again to reach 8.5–10 per cent during the recession years 1998–2004 (BC 2004), and is proving so resilient that there is an ongoing discussion among some economists about a structural rise in unemployment.[34]

Meanwhile, democratic power has been consolidating slowly and more rapidly after the detention in London of the ex-dictator. Since he was sent back to Chile on the grounds of bad health, Pinochet has endured a relentless series of judicial processes over human rights violations. Recently, a new flank has opened for the ageing dictator, as a US Senate investigation on Riggs Bank in Washington DC uncovered millions of dollars in accounts owned by Pinochet and his family. It is probably difficult for someone who has not lived through the experience to assess the importance that these authoritarian political figures may acquire, and how determinant their personal fate may become for the overall political process in their countries. Even now, when the ex-dictator has been reduced to a diminished and pathetic figure, Pinochet still concentrates the energies of the Chilean political events in the manner of a lightning rod. Because of this, his political, physical, moral, and judicial, demise has been the key to the awakening experienced by the Chilean democratization process since 1998.

Democratization has consolidated in the judiciary, which has been the battlefield where Pinochet has fought – and lost – all of his final battles. It has also advanced fast even in the military, which are mostly now quite subordinated to civilian power, and the constitutional prerogatives they were still entitled to had become largely ineffectual long before they were eliminated from the constitution in 2005. Serious reforms of the 1980 constitution had been discussed in parliament for years, with the rightist parties now agreeing to most of them – except for the electoral mechanism, which continues to favour them greatly. Futhermore everybody knows that these electoral reforms are also inevitable.[35] Democratization has advanced even faster in realms other than the political system, as the press and media are becoming more independent, and a generalized liberal attitude is becoming widespread in the Chilean citizenry.[36] This has permitted, for example, to finally approve a divorce law in 2004. The general climate of widening democratization was reinforced by two national elections; one at a local level in late 2004, and in 2005, a Chile's first woman president was elected, together with the renewal of most of parliament, where the right reduced its presence significantly.

The development model has become subject to increasing internal criticism, as some of its extreme anti-state, pro-business, and pro-globalization features have been blamed for the relentlessness of the economic recession and high unemployment (ECLAC 2002; Ffrench-Davis 2001a,b; Fazio 2001, 2003, 2004). Specific problems have surfaced because of excessive permissiveness in the mining industry, as well as in other natural resources related industries (Riesco *et al.* 2004; CENDA 2004c). In addition, parallel to signing free trade agreements with the US, the European Union, and many other countries, Chile has began to suffer from certain isolation in its neighbourhood (CENDA 2004d).

Some of the alternative proposals have started to become absorbed into the mainstream political agenda. During 2005, for example, the government backtracked on its avowed decision not to make changes in legislation regarding taxation, and introduced a bill that establishes a small mining royalty. This measure has been long demanded by critics, as the mining industry not only now receives its raw materials free, but has also managed to avoid paying any income taxes, with one or two exceptions. It is significant that the government bill re-establishes ground rent doctrine into the economic model, a matter that had been long neglected by Neoliberal ideologues (Riesco *et al.* 2004; CENDA 2004c). In addition, there is growing pressure on the government, to initiate a major pension reform before the end of its mandate (CENDA 2004b). During the recent election, candidates from all sides – notoriously from the right – competed in their criticisms of the Neoliberal model, or at least of its consequences. A presidential debate that was aired live by CNN to the whole of LA and the Spanish-speaking audience in the US astonished millions when all of the presidential candidates agreed that the famed Chilean pension system was not working, and needed reform.

### New social policies?

There is an increasing awareness of limitations of liberal social protection schemes. After 20 years of experiments with liberal social protection schemes in Chile, the virtues and, especially, the serious weaknesses and shortcomings of such schemes have now become quite clear.

Broadly speaking, the main disadvantage of the private Neoliberal social protection schemes seems to be that they have remitted their benefits to the upper-income quarter of the population (UNDP 2002b). However, not even these segments of the population are quite satisfied with them, and they now demand a curb on raising the costs of health, education, and pension administration, as well as other regulations.

On the other hand, the amount of resources targeted on the lower-income segments of the population, in poverty alleviation programmes and other measures, although effective both in improving social indicators and in alleviating the condition of the poorest have proved insufficient. 'They are barely enough for the last quintile, but insufficient to attend those immediately above them, who are also horribly poor', as the Chilean finance minister has declared (UNDP 2002b).

Meanwhile, such schemes have proven to be quite ineffectual regarding the vast majority of the population, which is now largely unprotected, or has returned to state social protection systems where it is allowed to do so, such as in health care (UNDP 2002b).

The renowned Chilean AFP pension system seems to be a good example of this assertion. A quarter-century on, it seems clear that by itself the system will not benefit more than the upper-income quarter of the workforce, if that. Only that segment is contributing to the system with both the level of salaries and the regularity required, in order that their savings alone may ensure that they will receive pensions larger than the state-guaranteed 'minimum pension'. Even those who will receive benefits out of the system are quite dissatisfied with aspects of the scheme, and mostly derived from shortcomings in the regulatory framework. Administration fees charged by the AFPs are very high; so much indeed, that even though sales costs and other expenses of the AFPs are quite high, their net income has achieved record levels even during recession years (INP 2004).[37]

The salaries of the next fifth or so of the workforce are too low for their savings in the AFP system to be able to fund a 'minimum pension', but as they will satisfy the regularity condition[38] required to reclaim the guaranteed minimum, the state will subsidize them for the difference. The other more than half of the workforce will not even be entitled to this benefit, because they do not satisfy either of the two conditions. Only the poorest may request and stand in line for the government means-tested 'assistance pension' programme.[39] In conclusion, roughly half of the workforce is not entitled to any pension whatsoever out of the present AFP system, except withdrawing their meagre savings in the system when they reach pension age (INP 2004).

In addition, transition to the AFP system has created problems that are also important, including the so-called 'previsional damage' that presently affects at least half of the state employees, and about one-sixth of the workforce, who were forced to change to the new system back in 1981. Due to extremely low wages during the 1980s and early 1990s, and low contributions by the state during the 1980s in the case of state employees, they are now receiving pensions that are 60 per cent lower than their fellow employees of similar characteristics who remained in the old 'pay as you go' system (CENDA 2004b).

It seems worthwhile to mention that in this middle segment of the population resides most of the new modern *salariat* that, as mentioned earlier, has been emerging in huge numbers out of the social transformations that have shaken Chile throughout the last three or four decades. In this manner, the rapid social transformations are creating a powerful demand for enhanced social protection in Chile, mainly from this modern salaried middle class. The Neoliberal-inspired reforms have largely ignored it, as said, focusing mainly on satisfying the SP demands of the high-income brackets of the population and, in parallel, targeting public social expenditure in the lower-income segments. The same policies, as mentioned, have usually deteriorated, in some cases quite dramatically, the SP systems of the salaried middle class, or their main demands have been postponed. Unemployment protection in Chile, for example, is the worst-off area within the social protection components (UNDP 2002b).[40] Because of the above, dissatisfaction with the system is so widespread that the private pension and health systems usually occupy the last places in public satisfaction polls (UNDP 2002b; INP 2004; CENDA 2004).

Nevertheless, proposals for a reform of the pension system, which are presently the subject of widespread public discussion in Chile, do not suggest a return to the old 'pay-as-you-go' system, except perhaps in the case of those with the so-called 'previsional damage'. These proposals, in turn, show that the Chilean pension system is not really a privately administered, individual account-based, fixed contribution, etc. system, but instead a mixed, public–private system. A major part of the workforce depends today, and will rely in the future, on the non-contributory, state-financed, public pension pillar of the system, for the majority of their pensions. Some proposals suggest establishing a universal entitlement to basic pensions, somewhere in between the present 'assistance pension' and a 'minimum pension'. This universal entitlement, the proposal continues, could be supplemented with the savings on the individual accounts administered by the AFP system – both the obligatory, fixed contributions, as well as voluntary contributions. The proposals show that the high level of fiscal expenditures dedicated to pensions today, is roughly enough to finance the proposed universal basic pension in the future (Figure 9.A3; CENDA 2004b).[41]

The pension proposal mentioned above is perhaps a good example of one of the main conclusions of this chapter, regarding social policies in Chile, in a development context. As shown, the proposal for a new pension system is built upon the quite significant remnants of the old 'pay as you go' pension system that was created during the LADWS period. Most of the present pensioners still depend upon this system and most will depend upon it in the future, as stated. The AFP system, one of the main achievements of the Neoliberal period according to its own supporters, has in the end resulted only in the provision of differentiated pensions for the upper-income segment of the population. Nevertheless, the AFP system may well become quite useful for everybody, if inserted as a second, complementary, tier, on top of an overhauled and universally extended public first tier in a reformed, public–private pension system. In this way everybody would have real incentives to save in the AFP system, which is not the case now for at least three-quarters of the workforce. In other words, a decent pension system for all Chilean citizens may be well built upon the main achievements of both the LADWS and the Neoliberal period, with relative ease in this case, as huge public expenditures are already being dedicated to this item.

It seems possible to extend the above conclusion in a more general manner to the problems tackled in this chapter. Chilean social policies and institutions are the result of a long period of socioeconomic transition that has been going on for a good part of the last century. The basic political and economic institutions of a modern society, state and markets among them, have been built in Chile during this process. Presently, as democracy extends throughout the country, it seems possible such institutions could be overhauled and reorganized in order to benefit the majority of modern Chilean citizenship. In the final analysis, this modern citizenry – where masses of modern, urban, salaried middle classes prevail – is the main result of the overall historical process the country has lived through. This modern citizenry is providing the political pressure for a change in the present development model, and may also provide the political base for a new model that is developmental, but more inclusive and democratic than the present one.

In conclusion, the Chilean case seems to support the view, suggested in this book, that the country seems to be approaching a point of inflexion regarding the overall development paradigm that has been hegemonic during the last three decades. Against the backdrop of the political trends that seem to be emerging in LA, and even worldwide, in this same direction, there seems to be a reasonable case in support of a not overly pessimistic stance regarding the possible outcomes.

## Notes

1. This may be appreciated in the 'new data series' of workers in agriculture versus total workforce, shown in Figure 9.A1, which is available from the mid-1980s onwards. This series shows an even steeper decline in this variable than the old series, and may be projected backwards to better appreciate this phenomenon.
2. The data series (PUC 2000) was compiled at *Facultad de Ciencias Económicas y Administrativas* (FACEA), at Pontificia Universidad Católica de Chile (PUC), by

a team headed by Rolf Lüders, who was Minister of Economics and Minister of Finance during the Pinochet regime (1982). This long-term data time series span from 1810 up to 1995, and include demographic, economic, fiscal, social, and other data. The evolution of the data for some variables relevant to this study has been parsed according to the political cycles here considered (figures in Appendix to this chapter). Economic cycles are also considered, as they occurred, and the evolution of the data within each economic cycle is measured from peak to peak. The start and end dates of the political periods are adjusted to the nearest peak in economic cycle for measuring the economic performance within each political period.

3. Central Bank (Banco Central), Air Force, National Airlines (Línea Aerea Nacional, LAN), National Police Force (Cuerpo de Carabineros), National Treasury (Tesorería General), Superintendence of Insurance and Public Companies (Superintendencia de Seguros y Sociedades Anónimas), Superintendence of Nitrate and Iodine (Superintencdencia del Salitre y Yodo), National Accounting Office (Contraloría General de la República), Mining Loan Fund (Caja de Crédito Minero), Agricultural Loan Fund (Caja de Crédito Agrícola), Industrial Loan Fund (Instituto de Crédito Industrial), Coal Loan Fund (Caja de Fomento Carbonero), Agricultural Export Panel (Junta de Exportación Agrícola), Colonization Fund (Caja de Colonización) and the Ministry of Agriculture (Illanes 2003).
4. The initial military movement in 1924 became known as 'Ruido de Sables' ('Sabre Rattle'), because a group of young military officers led by Ibáñez, assisted to a parliament session where some social laws were being voted, and rattled their sabers to mark their presence. The laws were approved.
5. Nevertheless, more than 25 workers were killed in different protests during the second, democratically elected, Ibáñez government (1952–58) (PCCh 2000).
6. The number of workers employed in nitrate mines during the Great Depression years were: 1928: 59,900 persons; 1929: 58,700; 1930: 44,100; 1931: 16,563; 1932: 8,711; 1933: 8,394; 1934: 14,777 (Ortiz 1982).
7. The *Oficina* provided everything to the worker, including housing in *campamentos*, food and clothing, even prostitutes. Salaries were paid in significant part not in money but in *fichas* (tokens), which were only accepted in the company-run *pulpería* (octopussery, meaning a place where one is sucked out, the term remains as in Chile an exploiter is called a *pulpo* (octopus)).
8. Significantly, the Chilean Communist Party, which had been founded in 1912 in the nitrate mines in the northern desert, became a national political organization after the return south of the miners, in the wake of the Great Depression.
9. Founded by a financing, mining and industrial tycoon, who enriched himself enormously by speculating on the world sugar markets.
10. By contrast, as shown later, universities were particularly hit by the Pinochet dictatorship, and public expenditure per pupil at the tertiary level still has not recovered to the dollar amount attained before the 1973 coup.
11. For example: state steel company, *CAP* (1950), state commercial bank, *Banco del Estado* (1953), state sugar company, *IANSA* (1955), state telecommunications company, *ENTEL* (1967), state television company, *TVN* (1968), state cellulose company, *CELARAUCO-CONSTITUCION* (1971), state cement company, *INACESA* (1971), among many others.
12. In a very intelligent measure, the Frei government inaugurated two shifts in public schools, thus duplicating school capacity almost instantly.

13. Certainly, school enrolment growth tends to decrease and stop as full coverage is approached and attained. In Chile, this is the case with enrolment at the primary level during the 1980s and secondary enrolment during the 1990s. Nevertheless, enrolment at all levels actually decreased from 1974 to 1982, and then increased slowly at all levels during the 1980s, even though coverage in secondary and especially tertiary was still far from complete. During the 1990s, although enrolment at secondary level rose again, it slowed down as it approached full coverage. Tertiary enrolment rose fast, but never at the rate reached during LADWS.
14. Even though cow milk was briefly replaced by soya-based milk during the Pinochet years, in order to reduce costs. Hernán Buchi, who was later to become the chief economic architect of the dictatorship, was in charge of health policies when this replacement was made.
15. General Prats was sent into exile after the coup and murdered in Buenos Aires together with his wife, by DINA, the dictatorship's secret police, acting under direct orders from Pinochet, as has now been established by the Argentinean justices. The complete corps of generals in the Chilean army, with very few exceptions, had been replaced by Pinochet within one year of the coup, as they were considered to be 'soft' against Allende's supporters.
16. Called by them *el ladrillo* (the brick) because of the weight of the book that contained their outline for Neoliberalism in Chile. The leader of the group was Sergio de Castro, an economist formed in Chicago who would be the chief economic architect and finance minister of the Pinochet government during the 1970s and early 1980s. He would be fired during the 1982 crisis under pressure to devaluate – a measure which he had adamantly opposed as he had pegged the peso to the dollar.
17. After the coup, roughly one-third of the expropriated land was returned to the old landowners, or rather to their sons, in the form of *reservas* (reservations) established under the agrarian reform law. *Reservas* had a relatively limited small extension (40 'basic' hectares), which was completely inadequate to reinstall the traditional agrarian system, but quite enough to become modern, capitalist, farms. Nonetheless, about 40 per cent of the land was in effect delivered to peasants in the form of small farms, as established in the agrarian reform law, and even though many of the peasants sold their farms shortly after wards, most of them still own them, and many have also prospered. The thriving Chilean export-oriented agribusiness has based itself upon all these small and medium-sized farms, which predominate in the Chilean countryside even today. Finally, approximately another one-third of the nationalized lands, mainly mountain regions, was auctioned to large forestry companies, which in this manner amassed the giant landholdings they own today. Certainly, those peasants who had actively supported agrarian reform, as well as the Frei and Allende governments did not receive any land at all, even though they deserved the land the most. The names of their leaders are a majority in the list of those assassinated by the military in the wake of the coup, which is engraved in a monument in the cemetery of Santiago. Thousands of others were thrown off the land and even the huts they had inhabited during generations after the coup. Behind those displaced from the nitrate mines in the wake of the Great Depression, these peasants were to become the second largest mass of dispossessed manpower to swell the nascent modern Chilean working class (Therborn *et al.* 1999).
18. Some mines were privatized during the Pinochet dictatorship, such as iron and nitrate, for example, and even some of the medium-sized copper mines such

as Disputada which was purchased by Exxon in 1978. Nevertheless, the largest copper mines nationalized by Allende were kept as 100 per cent state-owned companies, although their previous owners, US companies, were paid a token compensation in the wake of the coup. These mines were merged in 1976 into CODELCO, the giant state copper company, which doubled in size during the Pinochet dictatorship and produced 90 per cent of copper exports in 1989. Today, CODELCO is still the largest copper company in the world and owns most of the copper reserves in the country. State ownership of all minerals was respected in the constitution dictated by Pinochet in 1980, which is still in force and retains even the exact wording of the Nationalization Act of 1971. However, in the early 1980s, starved of foreign investment, the dictatorship enacted legislation that made it possible to lease state-owned minerals to private firms – at no charge at all. Using this legislation, massive amounts of foreign investment flowed into copper mining during the 1990s, under democratic governments, and they now account for two-thirds of Chilean copper exports (Therborn *et al.* 1999). Recently, the Chilean government presented parliament with a bill to charge a mining royalty to these firms, which is being discussed as this chapter is being written.

19. It was only in the mid-1990s, and after a strong increase in social spending by the democratic governments, that public spending in education and health recovered the real, inflation-adjusted levels it had reached at the beginning of the 1970s (Figure 9.A8 and A9; UNDP 2002b).
20. Before 1976, social security was not accounted as public expenditures, because it was managed by semi-autonomous 'Cajas de previsión,' which generally ran at a surplus. Beginning in that year, the PUC series includes all social security expenses in the public budget, as well as the (larger) revenue of social security contributions. This purely accounting scheme, classified as 'other' by PUC (grey area in Figure 9.A3), turned into a real public expenditure since 1981, when almost all revenue from social security contributions was redirected to the new AFP system, meanwhile all pensions started to be paid directly from the public budget (red area in Figure 9.A3).
21. These facts may be suggestive about the relation between development and social policy, in the absence of democratic institutions. In the context of a complete absence of democratic opposition, back in the 1970s, the Chilean military dictatorship, for example, was able to subordinate social policy completely to its stabilization and privatization objectives, even to the extent of reducing its funding by half. Moreover, when pressed by the widespread popular *protestas* that stemmed out of the crisis of the 1980s, several 'safety net' programmes were introduced, including a wide 'minimum employment' programme (see footnote). On the other hand, when interested in transferring the mass of pension funds and contributions to the private capital markets, the dictatorship seemingly had no trouble in assigning a huge portion of the total governmental budget – part of it subtracted from health and education budgets – to cover the resulting deficit.
22. Under the Chilean pension system, 10 per cent of wages are deposited in individual accounts, administered by private, specialized firms, called AFPs, which charge an additional 2.5 per cent (approximately) of wages, for fees and disability insurance. Since 1981 this system has been obligatory for all new hired workers, as well as for most of the then occupied workforce, who have changed to the new system. Only some 4 per cent of the workforce, belonging to the armed forces, or those who managed to resist pressures to change to the new system back in 1981, continue in the old 'pay as you go' pension system. Most of the ongoing

pensions are also paid by the old system, as the new system's pensioners have only recently been growing in number (UNDP 2002b).

23. The national public school system, at the basic and secondary levels, was decentralized to local government level, funding, which continued to support most of the cost of education for 90 per cent of the students at those levels, is distributed in a national 'voucher' scheme, according to class assistance, both to public schools – which have been reduced to 53 per cent of the enrolment – and to 'subsidized' private ones – which now enroll 38 per cent of the students (2000); the rest of the students in those levels attend private nonsubsidized schools. At the higher educational level, public funding to the public and other traditional universities (including the Catholic universities and others), which still account for half the enrolment in this level, has been reduced to approximately one-third of their budgets, while they have been encouraged to charge student fees and to rely on services rendered for the rest of their finances. The other half of the enrolment at the higher level is attended by a rapidly growing sector of private universities and other higher education institutes (UNDP 2002b).
24. The 'safety net' consists mainly of a means-tested 'assistance pension', that is currently half the US$100 a month 'minimum pension' that is guaranteed by the state to those affiliates of the AFP system that complete 20 years of contributions to that system. It also includes 'family allowances' and included a particularly massive 'minimum employment' programme that applied to 10 per cent of the workforce, in the worst moments of the deep economic crisis the country suffered in the 1980s and during which one in every three persons in the workforce were unemployed (UNDP 2002b).
25. Initially, salaries were raised proportionately and, as contributions decreased overall, liquid salaries were raised marginally for those who changed to the new system.
26. Chile's first woman president, Michelle Bachelet, a socialist whose father, general, was killed by Pinochet after the coup, and she was herself a victim of torture, has been elected as this chapter goes into press.
27. Over 60 people killed in just one night in Santiago during 1984 gives some idea of the extensive nature of *protestas*, and the violence of military repression,
28. Under pressure from both the US Southern Command and the Chilean military, the agreement also included the political exclusion of the Chilean Communist Party, which had played a key role during the long struggle against the dictatorship, and had organized much of the armed resistance.
29. The electoral system, which elects two members of parliament (MP) in each district, ensures that a minority, if larger than approximately a quarter, elects about half of parliament. On the other hand, the districts have been tailored in such a way as to give disproportionate representation to regions where the right ensures electing at least one of the two MPS. Finally, the constitution requires large majorities to modify its own disposition, larger than two-thirds in many cases. For their part, the armed forces retain control of their budget, their commanders in chief cannot be changed at least without the support of a large majority of parliament where the right holds effective power of veto, and, finally, they have been assigned the role to 'warrant the constitution'.
30. Part of the financial investments coming into Chile had to be deposited in the central bank at no interest. Initially this part – called *encaje* – was fixed at one-third of the investment, a proportion that was lowered after the 1998 crisis and is

presently zero. In addition, financial investments could not be withdrawn during the first year.

31. The unemployment insurance system works on contributions by employees to individual savings accounts, where employers also deposit their corresponding severance provisions. The unemployed worker is entitled to withdraw the savings if he has been previously employed for at least one year. Nevertheless, the statistics from this same system have shown that 90 per cent of contracts last less than one year, so, in practice, very few of the unemployed during the recession could enjoy even the limited benefits of this scheme.
32. In 1990, the relation between the autonomous money income of the upper-income 5 per cent of the population and the lower-income 5 per cent was 1:130. A decade later, in 2000, the same relation was 1:209. That is, the breach in autonomous income derived from salaries mainly in the lower strata had almost doubled during the decade. If the figure is adjusted to take into account the increase in monetary subsidies given by the state, the breach stabilized at 1:90 during the whole decade. It is worth mentioning that the breach between the upper 5 per cent and the next 5 per cent is 1:2.8 – in other words, the upper 5 per cent earns 2.8 times more than the next 5 per cent (UNDP 2002b).
33. In health, for example, mean per capita expenses in the private segment are four times as large as in the public system, and in education, expenses per child are twice as large in the private sector as in the subsidized system that applies to 90 per cent of children.
34. One of the co-authors of this chapter has participated in the discussion, arguing that unemployment should eventually diminish as the current economic cycle accelerates during the following years. He has argued that employment–growth elasticity has proved to be highly cyclical itself during previous economic cycles, usually diminishing during the early recovery years of each cycle, only to grow as the cycle gains speed. The evolution of employment in 2004 and 2005 seem to prove this point, as jobs, mainly salaried, are growing at a record pace. Nevertheless, unemployment is still over pre-recession levels, and jobs are very short term, less than four months in more than half of contracts.
35. Bachelet, the new president-elect, has promised the communist party that the electoral system – which has let them out of parliament during the transition – will be democratized during her government. In exchange for this and other compromises, including pension reform, the communists voted for Bachelet in the second round the presidential election, in early 2006, these by ensuring her victory.
36. The most notorious expression of this was the massive assembly of people to pose naked for photographer Spencer Tunic on a freezing winter morning. After the end of the session, thousands of naked Chileans of all ages and conditions flooded into downtown Santiago, running happily for hours.
37. In the case of the private health system, only one-fifth of the population is presently using it. In education, as has been mentioned, only the upper-income 9 per cent of the population attends the private nonsubsidized system at the basic and medium levels, although 38 per cent attends private subsidized schools. Only at the higher educational level do private universities and institutes serve 50 per cent of the students but, from the Mid-2000s, up to 50 per cent of them will receive government-subsidized study loans (UNDP 200; UNDP 2002b).
38. Presently, 20 years (or 240 monthly contributions) are required to be entitled to the minimum pension, which is now fixed slightly over US$100 a month.

39. Those who prove extreme poverty may apply to a US$50 a month 'assistance pension'. Nevertheless, as funds for this benefit are limited, there are tens of thousands waiting in line to receive it.
40. The public resources allocated to traditional unemployment protection schemes have been negligible even during the present economic crisis, where, in addition, more stringent eligibility criteria have been put in place. On the other hand, new private unemployment insurance schemes have introduced some improvements with respect to the traditional time-related ones, as well as some elements of solidarity. However, the private unemployment schemes are not designed to be effective enough in periods of massive unemployment, and have certainly been completely ineffective during the current crisis, because it was only activated in 2002 (UNDP 2002b).
41. The present Chilean pension system is really a mixed, public–private system. It is a two- or three-tier system. The first tier of the Chilean pension system is not private, but public. It is not financed by the individual capitalization of fixed contributions, but is instead non-contributory and paid out of general taxation. This first tier presently provides some kind of assistance pension to nearly 90 per cent of advanced-age population (those more than 75 years of age), and pays for most of the present pensions overall. The amount of public resources presently dedicated to finance the public tier of the pension system is huge, as said, and amounts to more than 41 per cent of the public social budget and around 6–7 per cent of GDP. If divided evenly among the population who are over retiring age at present – 1.7 million people who are over 60 years in the case of women, and 65 years in the case of men – the present public expenditure results in over US$250 per month per person. That is, more than 2.5 times the amount of the present minimum pension. In other words, Chile is presently expending an amount of public resources in pensions that is enough to finance a decent – by albeit very modest Chilean standards – universal minimum pension for all those who reach retirement age. In other words, if Chile maintains into the future the 7 per cent of GDP that it presently earmarks for pensions out of the government budget, it will be able to provide this universal basic pension entitlement for all its citizens, as the number of people over retirement age will increase at a slower rate than GDP. CELADE estimates the growth of the number of people over retirement age at 3 per cent a year, up to 2025. GDP, of course, has recorded higher historical growth rates. This significant amount of resources is presently spent mainly on military pensions (about one-fifth); on pensions of the old 'pay as you go' system, mostly in the better pensions offered by that system (about two-fifths); in transfers to the AFP system benefiting the persons who changed form the old system back in 1981 (one-fifth); and, finally, in 'safety net' pensions (one-fifth). Of these items, the first four are due to diminish gradually and finally disappear, as the beneficiaries die off. The last item would be completely replaced by the universal basic pension proposed (CENDA 2004b).

## References

Banco Central de Chile (BC) (2004). *Base de Datos Estadística*. http://www.bcentral.cl. Santiago: BC.

Barbeito, A. (2002). 'Social Insecurity as Public Policy.' Report to the UNDP on 'Social Protection in an Insecure Area: A South–South Exchange on Alternative Social Policies Responses to Globalization'. Inter-Regional Workshop, Santiago,

Chile, 14–17 May 2002. http://videos.cep.cl/sw2002/Informe_Final/SW2002_Final _Report.html. Accessed on 17 November 2004.

CENDA (2004a). *Centro de Estudios Nacionales de Desarrollo Alternativo. Base de Datos Cuadernos de Información Económica de Prensa.* Santiago: CENDA.

CENDA (2004b). 'Propuesta para una Nueva Política de Integración Regional'. http://cep.cl/CENDA/Proyectos/Minsegpres/Propuesta_Integracion.doc. Accessed on 17 November 2004.

CENDA (2004c). 'Propuesta para una Reforma del Sistema de AFP'. http://cep.cl/ CENDA/Cen_Documentos/Indice_AFP_CENDA/Varios_CENDA_AFP/Propuesta_ Reforma.doc. Accessed on 17 November 2004.

CENDA (2004d). 'Propuesta para un Nuevo Esquema de Royalty e Impuestos para la Minería'. http://cep.cl/CENDA/Cen_Documentos/Cobre/Impuestos_Mineria _0408.doc. Accessed on 17 November 2004.

Draibe, S. M. (2002). 'Brasil 1980–2000: Proteção e insegurança sociais em tempos difíceis' in 'Social Protection in an Insecure Era: A South–South Exchange on Alternative Social Policy Responses to Globalization', Draft Report on the SU/TCDC, UNDP Inter-Regional Workshop. Santiago: UNDP. http://videos.cep.cl/sw2002. Accessed on 17 November 2004.

ECLAC (2004a). *Panorama Económico Social 2004.* Santiago: ECLAC.

ECLAC (2004b). *Statistical Yearbook.* Santiago: ECLAC.

ECLAC (2000). *Mas allá del Consenso de Washington.* Santiago: ECLAC.

Fazio, H. (2004). *Cartas Económicas.* http://cep.cl/CENDA/Cen_Documentos/Cartas_ Economicas. Accessed on 17 November 2004.

Fazio, H. (2003). *Quienes Gobiernan America Latina?* Santiago: LOM Ediciones.

Fazio, H. (2000). *La transnacionalización de la economía chilena: Mapa de la extrema riqueza al año 2000.* Santiago: LOM Ediciones.

Ffrench-Davis, R. (2003). Press clippings in CENDA Cuadernos de Información Económica de Prensa and interventions in panels in CENDA. http://www.cenda.cep.cl.

Ffrench-Davis, R. (2002). *Economic Reforms in Chile from Dictatorship to Democracy.* Michigan: Michigan University Press.

Ffrench-Davis R. (ed.) (2001). *Financial Crises in 'Successful' Emerging Economies.* Washington DC: Brookings Institution Press/ECLAC.

Haslam, J. (2004). 'The Death of Allende's Chile: A Case of Assisted Suicide'. Manuscript. London: Verso.

Illanes, M. A. (2003). 'Política social y modelos de desarrollo: puntos de saturación histórica. Chile, 1924–2003'. Santiago: CEPAL., http://cep.cl/UNRISD/Papers/ Chile/Chile_MAIllanes_Final.doc.

INP (Instituto de Normalización Provisional) (2004). 'Chile: Proyección Previsional de la Población Afiliada y Cotizante a las AFP'. Santiago: INP. http://cep.cl/Cenda/Proyectos/INP/INP.htm.

INP (2005). *Factibiidad de una Pensión Básica Universal.* Santiago: CEPAL. http://www.cep.cl/Cenda/Proyectos/INP/INP_2005/INP_2005.doc.

Kwon, H.-j. (2003). *Social Policy in a Development Context.* Draft. Geneva: UNRISD.

Kwon, H.-j. (2002). 'Transforming the Developmental Welfare State: A Comparative Study of the East Asian countries'. A Project within the UNRISD Research Area 'Social Policy in a Development Context'. Geneva: UNRISD. http://cep.cl/CENDA/Proyectos/UNRISD/References/Project_Proposal_Kwon.doc.

Mesa-Lago, C. (2002). 'Models of Development, Social Policy and Reform in Latin America'. Background paper for the UNRISD Project 'Social Policy in a Development Context'. Geneva: UNRISD.

Mkandawire, T. (2002). 'Courrier de la Planète: Développement, environnement, les défis d'un monde solidaire'. Draft country papers on Social Policy in LA in a Development Context 67 (1).

Mkandawire, T. (2001). *Social Policy in a Development Context.* Geneva: UNRISD.

Mkandawire, T. and Virginia, R. (2000). 'Globalization and Social Development after Copenhagen: Premises, Promises and Policies'. Project entitled 'Geneva 2000: The Next Step in Social Development'. Geneva: UNRISD. http://www.unrisd.org/unrisd/website/document.nsf/(httpPublications)/DEA5491C2B61C47980256B67005B74CB?OpenDocument.

Ortiz, E. (1982). *La gran depresión y su impacto en Chile, 1929–1933.* Santiago: Vector.

Partido Comunista de Chile (PCCh) (2000). 'Historia del Partido comunista de Chile'. http://personales.com/chile/santiago/partidocomunista/anexoiii.html.

PT (Partido dos Trabalhadores) (2002). 'Programa de Governo'. http://www.pt.org.br/.

Quijano, J. M. (2002). 'La Protección Social en Uruguay'. Report to the UNDP on 'Social Protection in an Insecure Area: A South–South Exchange on Alternative Social Policies Responses to Globalization'. Inter-Regional Workshop, Santiago, Chile, 14–17 May. http://videos.cep.cl/sw2002/Informe_Final/SW2002_Final_Report.html. Accessed on 17 November 2004.

Riesco, M. (2004). 'Pay Your Taxes! Corporate Social Responsibility in the Mining Industry in Chile'. Paper prepared for UNRISD. http://cep.cl/UNRISD/UNRISD_CSR/Mining_CSR_Chile.doc.

Riesco, M. (2002). 'Chile: 20 Years of Liberal Experiences in Social Protection'. Brief of the Report to UNDP Inter-Regional Workshop, Santiago, Chile, 14–17 May. http://videos.cep.cl/sw2002/Informe_Chile/SW2002_Chile_Brief.html. Accessed on 17 November 2004.

Stallings, B. (2002). 'Social Protection in an Insecure Area: A South–South Exchange on Alternative Social Policies Responses to Globalization'. Inter-Regional Workshop, Santiago, Chile, 14–17 May 2002. http://videos.cep.cl/sw2002/SW2002_Movies.html. Accessed on 17 November 2004.

Standing, G. (2002). 'Globalisation: The Eight Crises of Social Protection'. UNDP Inter-Regional Workshop, Santiago, Chile, 14–17 May.

Stiglitz, R. (2003). Press clippings in CENDA Cuadernos de Información Económica de Prensa. http://cenda.cep.cl.

*The Economist* (2002). 'Brazil's Presidential Election: The Meaning of Lula for Latin American Democracy. How Good for Brazil?', 5 October.

Therborn, G. (ed.) (1999). *Globalizations and Modernities.* Stockholm: FRN.

UNDP (2002). 'Social Protection in an Insecure Area: A South–South Exchange on Alternative Social Policies Responses to Globalization'. Final Report. Inter-Regional Workshop, Santiago, Chile, 14–17 May 2002. http://videos.cep.cl/sw2002/Informe_Final/SW2002_Final_Report.html. Accessed on 17 November 2004.

Universidad Católica de Chile (PUC) (2000). *Economia Chilena 1810–1995.* Estadísticas Históricas. Instituto de Economía. Santiago: PUC.

UNRISD (2003). 'Late Industrializers and the Development of the Welfare State'. Draft paper. Geneva: UNRISD.

UNRISD (2002). 'Social Policy in a Development Context: East Asia, Latin America and Sub-Saharan Africa'. Project Proposal. Ford Foundation. http://cep.cl/UNRISD/References/unrisd_ford.doc.

Williamson, J. (2002). 'Did the Washington Consensus Fail? Institute for International Economics'. Outline of remarks at the Center for Strategic & International Studies, 6 November.

# Appendix 9.A: Tables and Figures

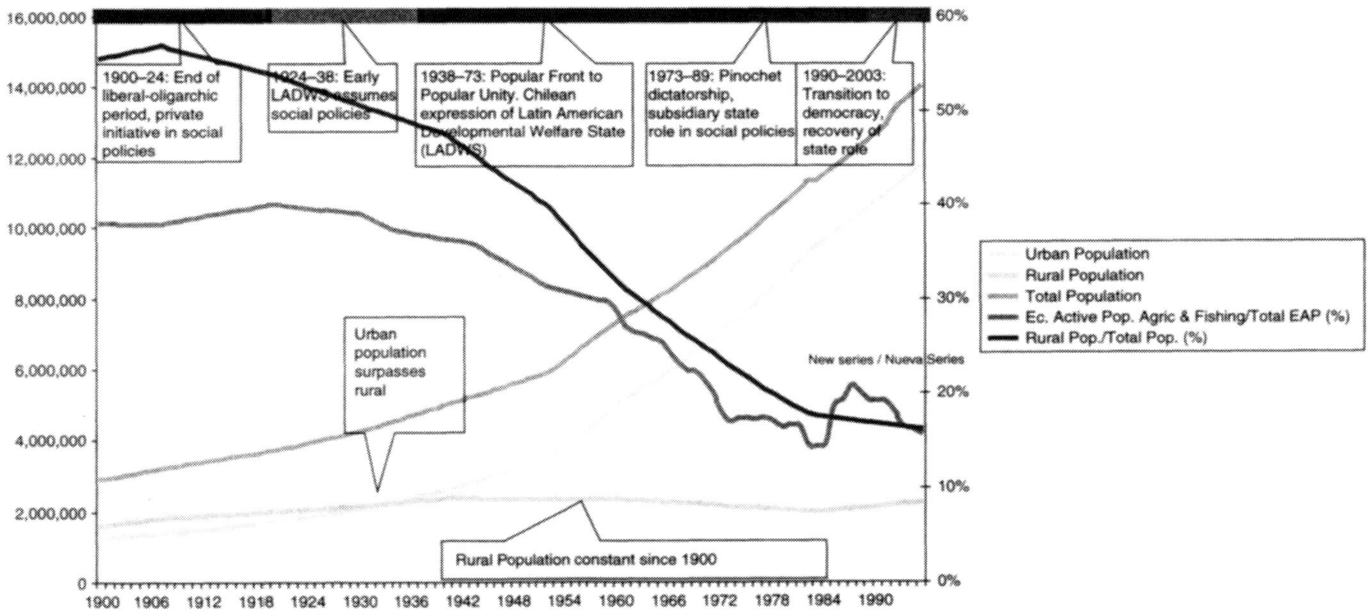


*Figure 9.A1* Chile: social and political change, 1900–1995
*Source:* Universidad Católica (2000).

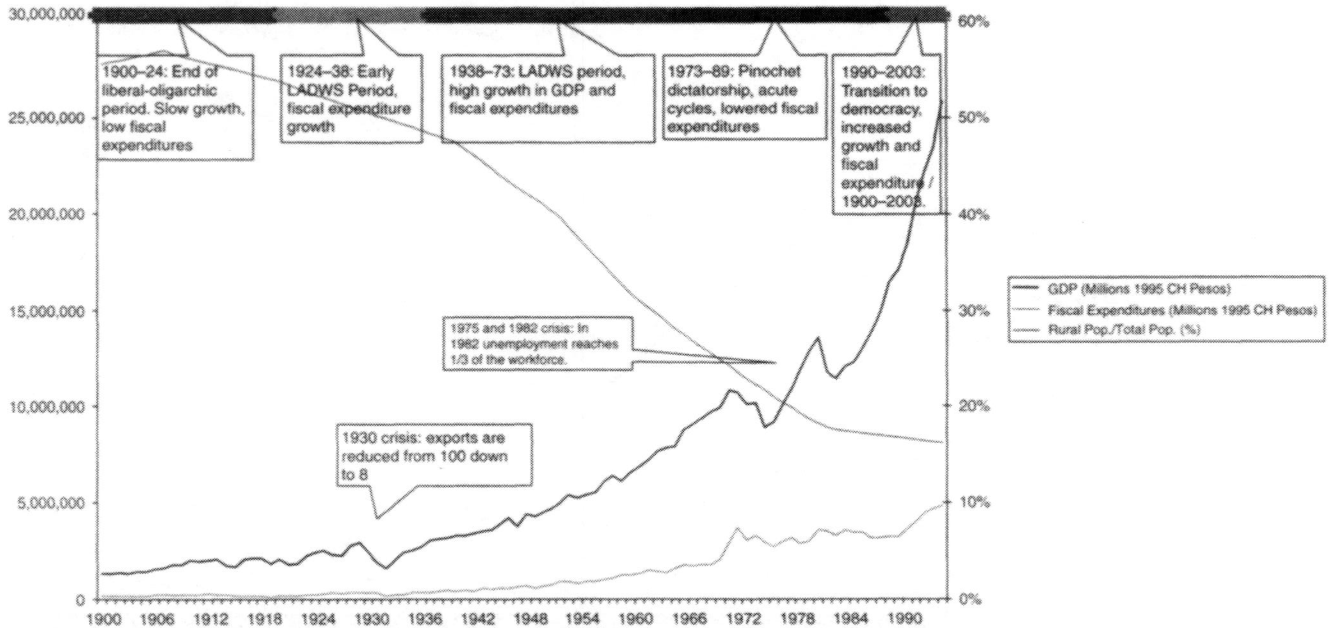


*Figure 9.A2* Chile: GDP and fiscal expenditure (million pesos at the 1995 rate)
*Source:* Universidad Católica (2000).

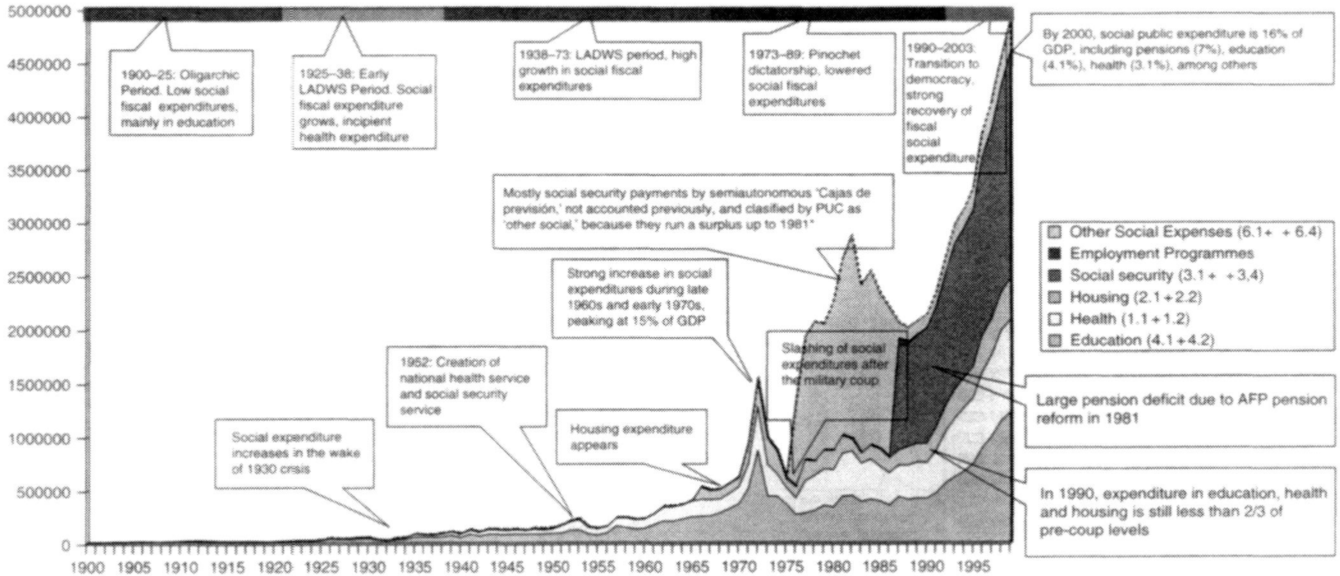


*Figure 9.A3* Chile: social fiscal expenditures, 1900–1999 (millions 1995 CH$)

* Before 1976, social security was not accounted as public expenditures, because it was managed by semi-autonomous 'Cajas de previsión', which run at a surplus in general. Starting that year, the PUC series includes all social security expenses in the public budget, as well as the (larger) revenue of social security contributions. This purely accounting scheme, clasified as 'other' by PUC (grey area), turned into a real public expenditure since 1981, when almost all revenue from social security contributions was redirected to the new AFP system, meanwhile all pensions started to be paid by the public budget (red area).

*Source*: Pontificia Universidad Católica (2000).

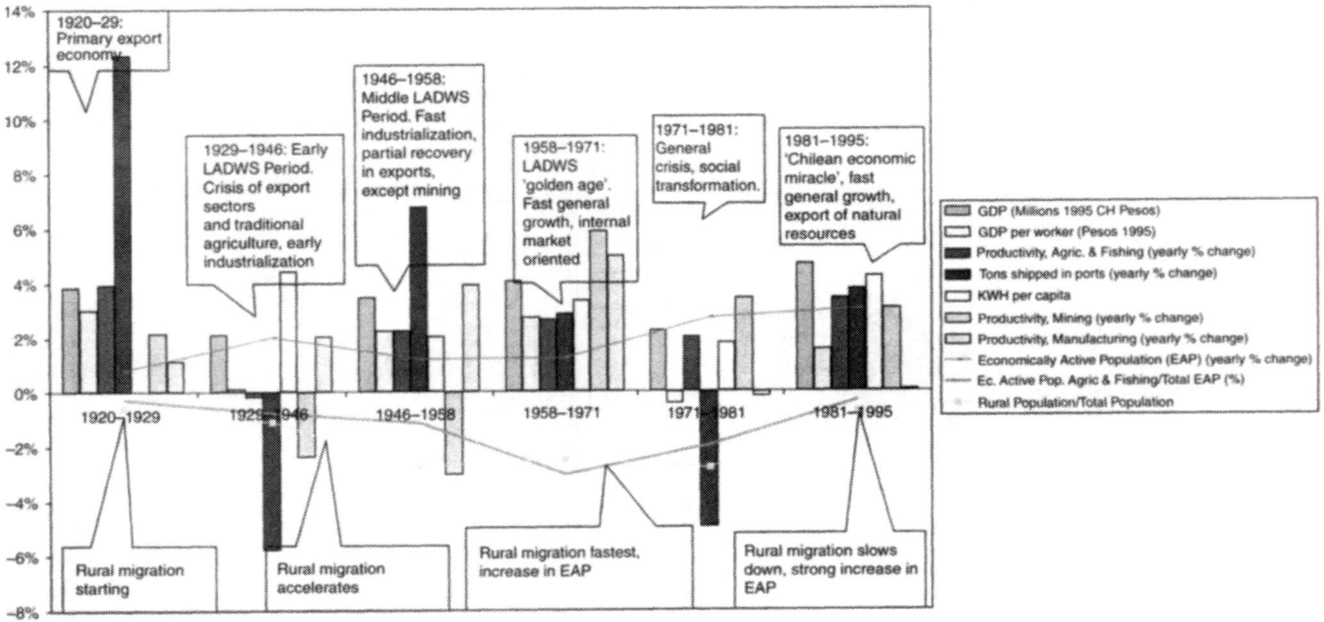


*Figure 9.A4* Chile: main economic cycles (peaks) (yearly % change)
*Source*: Universidad Católica (2000).

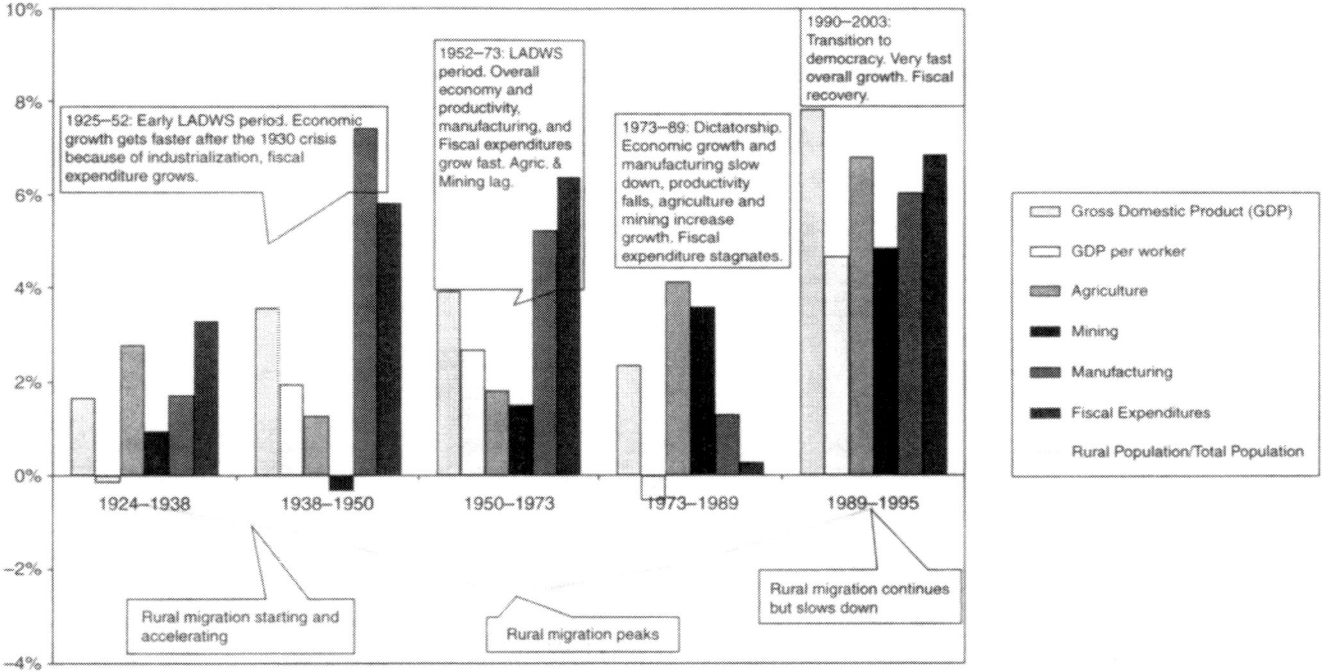


*Figure 9.A5* Chile: growth during main political cycles (average % yearly change)

*Note*: For economic data, start and end years of each cycle have been moved to the nearest peak in the corresponding economic cycle.

*Source*: Universidad Católica (2000).

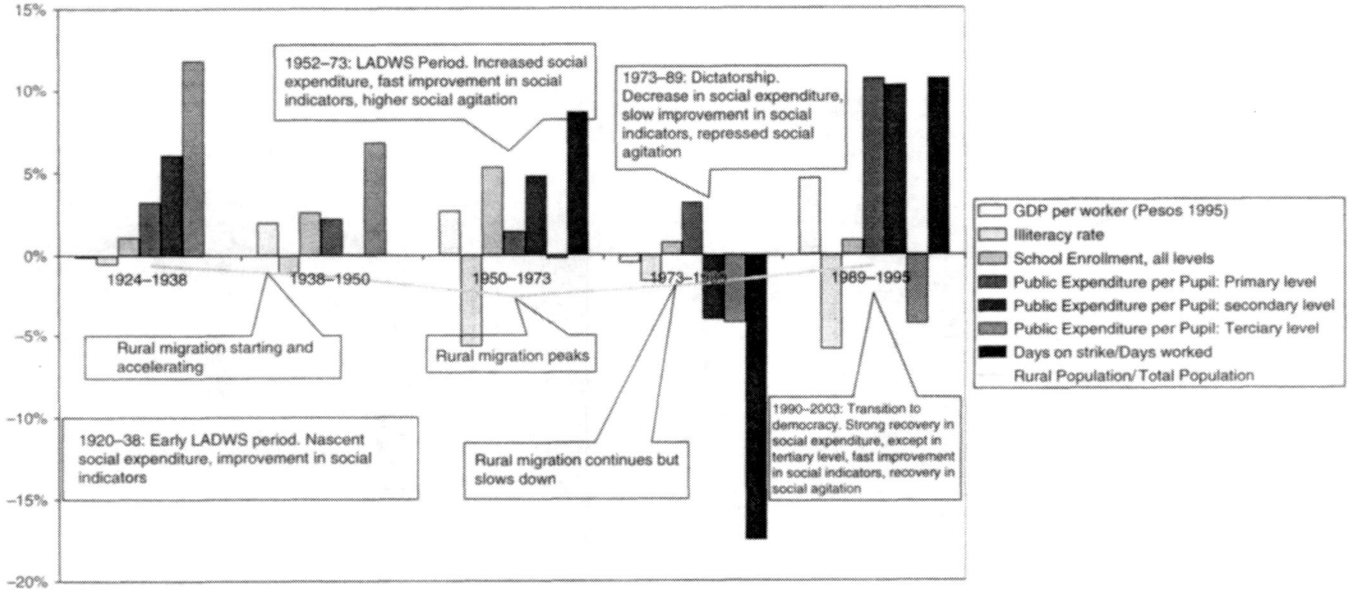


*Figure 9.A6* Chile: social indicators and political cycles (average yearly % change)
*Note*: For economic data, start and end years of each cycle have been moved to the nearest peak in the corresponding economic cylce.
*Source*: Universidad Católica (2000).

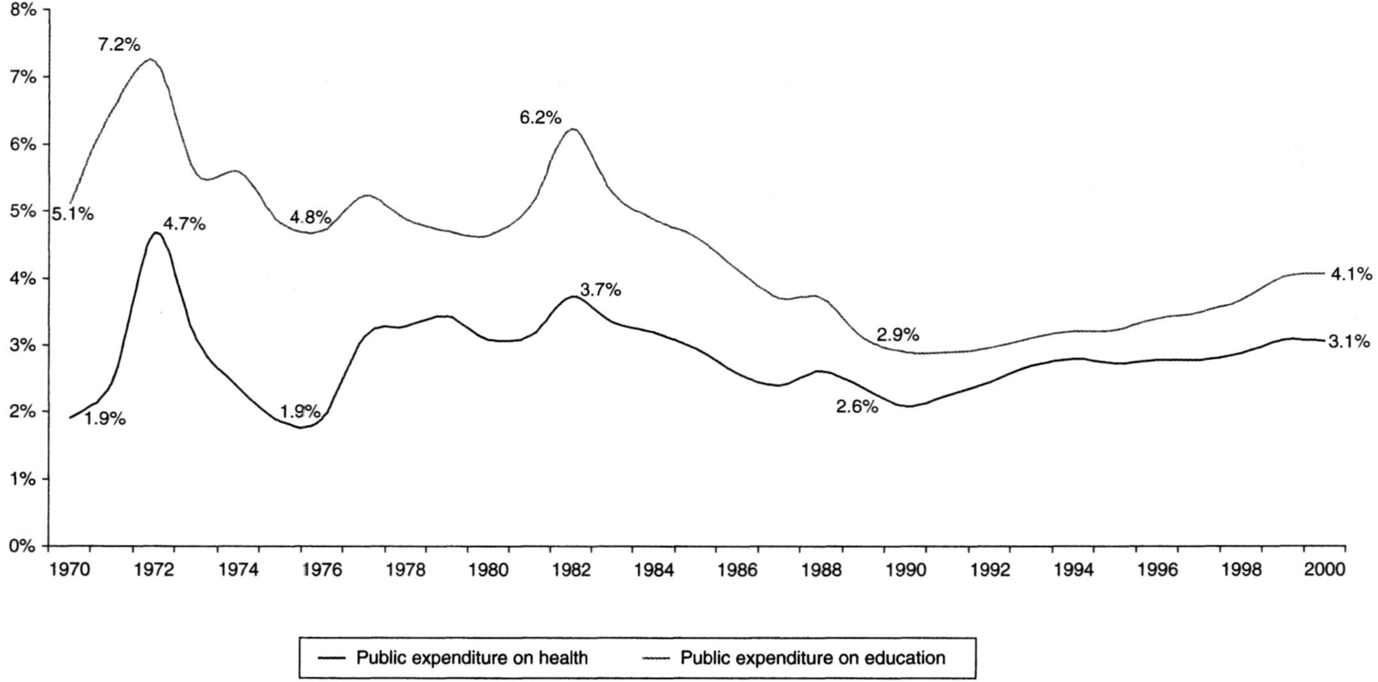


*Figure 9.A7* Chile: public expenditure on education and health (% GDP)
*Source:* UNDP (2002b).

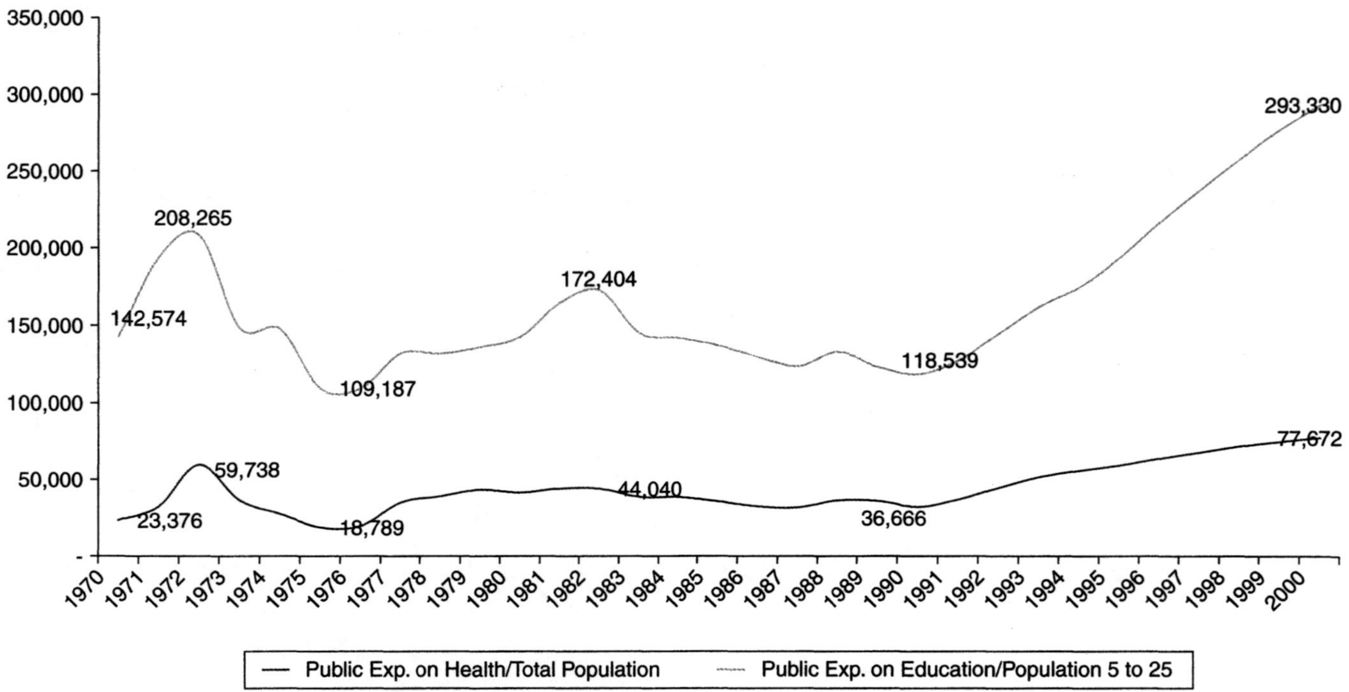


*Figure 9.A8* Chile: per capita public expenditure on education and health, 1970–2000 ($2,000/person-year)

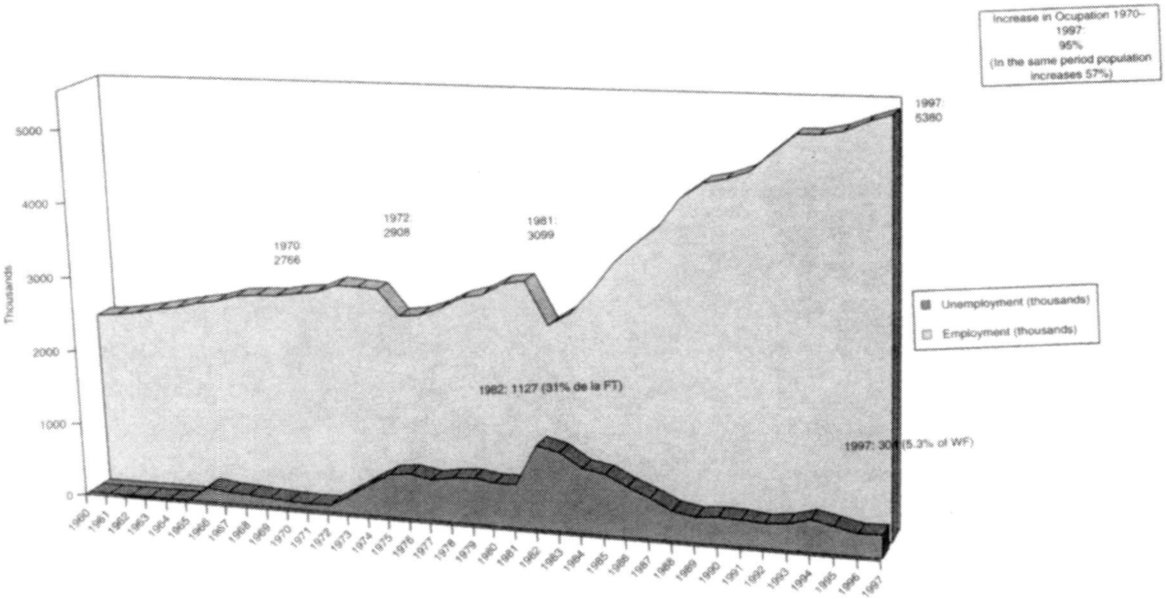


*Figure 9.A9* Chile: occupied and unemployed workforce, 1960–1997
*No unemployment data before 1965.

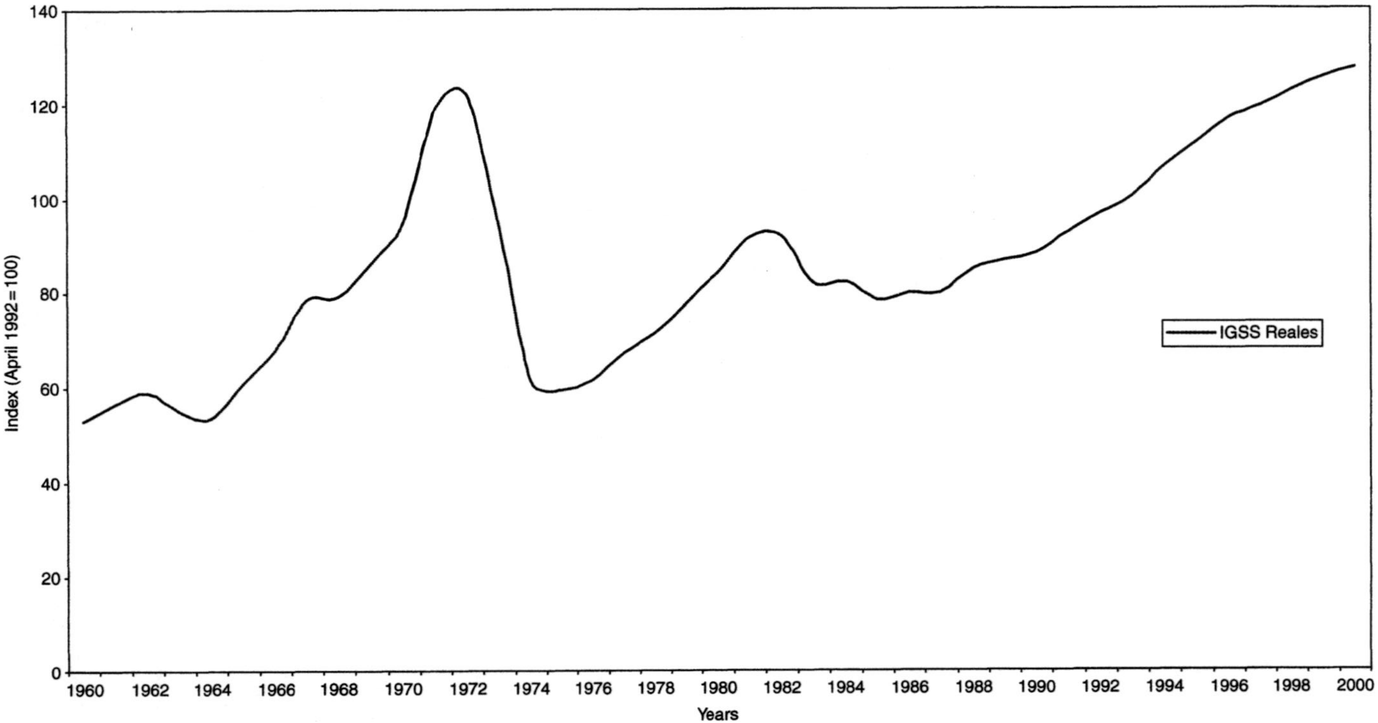


*Figure 9.A10* Chile: wages adjusted by inflation, 1960–2000*

*Note*: *'IGSS Real' stands for real, inflation-adjusted general index of salaries and wages.

# Index


Africa 2
Agenda: PERU 150
agriculture
  see Latin America; *individual countries*
*Alcabala* taxes 121
Allende, Salvador 381, 386, 389, 390, 391, 392
*Alliance for Progress* 386
American Popular Revolutionary Party (APRA) 155, 156
anti-dumping regulations 226
Argentina 1, 23, 26, 45, 54–5, 187–216, 219, 239, 244, 328, 399
  1991 National Employment Law 199
  *Administradoras de Fondos de Jubilaciones y Pensiones* (AFJP) 198, 199
  development strategies 187
  economic crisis 199, 206–7
  economic growth 188
  economic policy 188–9, 193
  economic recovery 202
  economic stabilization plan 193
  education 188, 189–91
  educational reforms 195–7, 203–4
  employment policies 192–3
  exchange rate 201
  Federal Education Law 195
  government expenditure 203
  hyperinflation 206
  income policies 205–6
  income taxes 192
  labour flexibility 199
  labour market 194
    instability 200–1, 205–6
  Menem regime 193
  National Education System 189–91
  National Social Security System (NSSS) 191–2
  *obras sociales* 188, 194
  pension programmes 188, 192, 198
  Perónism 188, 189
  *Programa Alimentario Nacional* 192
  *Programa Jefes y Jefas de Hogar Desocupados (PJJHD)* 200
  social actors 188
  social mobility 190
  social protection system 187, 188, 191–2, 201–6, 206–7
  social protest 202
  social security reforms 197–9, 204–5
  social spending 188
  structural reforms 193
  unemployment rates 194, 200
  Washington Consensus 193
  welfare state 187, 189, 193–5
Asian crisis 9, 69
Asian 'Tigers' 31
Australia 31, 69
Authoritarianism 11
Aylwin, President 397

Belaúnde, Fernando 158, 159, 160, 162
Bolivia 34
Brazil 1, 23, 25, 31, 35–6, 45, 53–4, 148, 219, 239–81, 393, 400
  agriculture 250, 258, 268
  agro-export 240, 241
  benefits 246
  *Bolsa Familia* 266
  Brazilian Development Welfare State 239, 242–7, 248, 254, 257, 258, 260, 267
  business interests 258
  capital 255
  *capitalismo tardio* 242, 269
  clientelism 264
  coffee production 241, 254, 258
  Constitution (1988) 265
  contributory and subsidized programmes 243, 246–7
  deindustrialization 250
  democratization 240, 248, 254–5, 260, 262–5
  development
    economic 239
    social 239
  *Developmentalist coalition* 263
  *Diretes Já* (direct elections) 261
  Economic crisis 255

Brazil – *continued*
economic growth 240, 255, 264
economic policy 243
economic restructuring 240
economic stabilization 264
education and 244, 251
*Estado Desenvolvimentista* 248, 253, 267
*Ethics in Politics* 261
health system 245
'heavy industrialization' 248
housing policy 247
Human Development Index 251
hyperinflation 264
income distribution 240
industrialization 239, 242, 250, 251, 255, 257, 266, 267
inequity 259
inflation 263, 264
labour legislation 259
military regimes 250, 253, 257–8
modernization 240, 253, 264, 267
oligarchic state 254
*Partido de Trabalhadores* (PT) 260, 263
*Plano Cruzado* 248, 262
Plano Real 248
policy reforms 258
political mobilization 261
population growth 250
Portuguese influence 35–6
private sector manufacturing 240
pro-poor programmes 245, 247, 266
*Reformas de Base* 257
reformist cycle 266
reformist wave 257
'restricted industrialization' 248
rural migration 250
slavery and 240
social contract 239
social indicators 240
social policy 239, 242, 253, 259
social security system 246, 255, 256, 259
social services 240
social spending 244
state–society relations 260–5
structural reforms 248
technology 242
trade liberalization 268
unemployment 240
universal public provision 243
urban base 239, 254
urbanization 250, 251, 254, 267
Vargas regime 240, 250, 253, 254, 255, 256
*Varguista State* 248, 253, 255, 261
workers 267
Bretton Woods institutions (BWI) 8, 9, 47, 60, 394
BRIC countries 31
Bush, George H. 63
Bustamante, José Luis 155

Canada 31
Camacho, Avilà 125, 126
Cardoso, Fernando Henrique 246, 263, 264, 265
Caribbean 23
Castro, Fidel 37, 299
Central America 23, 34, 45
Chávez, Hugo 59
Chicago, University of 392–3
Chile 1, 23, 38, 69, 152, 155, 240, 244, 378–424
AFP pension system 404, 406
agrarian society 378, 390, 393, 398
agricultural sector 382, 388, 390, 398
and globalization 403
and Neoliberalism 391–6, 397, 400, 401, 402, 405
and the 'Chicago Boys' 49, 392–6
and the Great Depression 383–6
Assistance state 383
banking system, nationalization of 391
*campamentos* 385
capital inflows 398
*Central Unica de Trabajadores* (CUT) 387
copper industry, nationalization of 390
*Corporacion de Fomento* (CORFO) 385
democratization 378, 402, 403, 406
judiciary and 402–3
developmentalism 378, 379, 380, 382, 383, 386, 401
economic and social progress 380
economic cycles 381, 384, 387, 388, 394, 398
economic development 378

economic growth 388, 402
economic institutions 406
'economic miracle' 394
education 383, 386, 389–90, 396, 399
electricity 385
ENDESA 385
foreign investment 398
free trade agreements 398
health system 382, 386, 391, 399
housing 388
human development index (HDI) 400
income distribution 400
infrastructure 398
*Junta Nacional de Auxilio Escolar y Becas (JUNAEB)* 389
*Juntas de Auxilio Escolar* 388
labour legislation 382
*latifundia* 379, 384
*manu militari* 382–3
manufacturing 385, 388
military coup 391, 402
Neoliberal policies 391–6
nitrate industry 384
*oligarchic-liberal* state 382, 383
'pay as you go' pension system 405–6
pension funds 386, 395
pension system 391, 395, 404–5
  privatization of 395
Pinochet regime 391–6
*Popular Front* 381, 384, 386, 387
population growth 378, 381
poverty 399–400
Preventive Health Law (Ley de Medicina Preventiva) 386
privatization 401
*protestas nacionales* 397
public expenditure 386, 395, 398, 399
rural migration 382, 385, 387, 400
*Servicio de Seguro Social* (SSS) 387, 390
*social assistance* state 382
social change 378, 380, 400
social expenditure 380, 400
social policy 378, 397, 401, 403–5, 406
state, dismantling of 391
unemployment 394
unemployment insurance 399
urbanization 378, 382
  welfare state 379
  workforce 395
China 31, 148
CODESA 335, 348
Collor de Mello, President 248, 261
Colombia 23, 400
COMECOM 304, 306, 309
Confederation of Mexican Workers (CTM) 125
Copenhagen Summit on Social Development 3
*Corporacion de Fomento* 385
Costa Rica 1, 37–8, 152, 327–77, 400
  Arias Administration 338, 344
  banking system 331
  Calderon Fournier Administration 339, 344
  Catholic Church 329
  child mortality 358, 372
  coffee industry, nationalization 331
  consumption 335
  Costa Rican Social Security System (CCSS) 332, 338, 348, 349
  debt 362, 376
  democracy 329
  demographic indicators 357
  development theory 330
  economic growth 327, 361
  economic reforms 330, 345, 346
  education 329, 331, 332, 338, 339, 341, 344, 345, 346, 360, 373, 374
  Education Toward the 21st Century policy 341
  *Estado Social de Derecho* 328
  exchange rates 335
  Family Allowance Fund (FODESAF) 333, 338
  Figueres Administration 339–40, 343
  health 329, 332, 338, 339, 340–1, 343, 346, 371
  housing 338
  import-substitution model 335–7
  income distribution 344, 366, 367
  infrastructure 331
  Human Development Index (HDI) 328, 356
  human rights approach 343
  labour 339, 363, 364, 365, 377
  life expectancy 334
  malnutrition 359

Costa Rica – *continued*
Ministry of Health 332, 3400
Monge Administation 337
National Plan to Combat Poverty (PNCP) 345
pension system 341
Plan Vida Nueva (New Life Plan) 342–3
public expenditure 335, 369, 370
poverty 327, 332–3, 339, 344, 347, 368
Rodriguez Administration 341, 342, 343, 345
Second Republic 330
Secretariat of Education 329
Secretariat of Public Health 329
Social Compensation Plan 337
social reforms 332, 333, 346, 347
state involvement 330, 347
structural adjustment 338
universal-coverage programmes 340, 344
water and sewage 333, 339
Workers' Protection Law 341–2, 346
Cuba 1, 23, 36, 45, 282–323, 399
1959 revolution 299
Act of Agrarian Reform 299
agriculture 283, 285, 286, 289, 295, 296, 298–9
cattle raising 302
nickel industry 320
sugar industry 283, 285, 289, 295, 296, 300, 302, 304, 310, 319
tobacco industry 285, 289
and Spain 282, 284
and the US 283, 284, 285–7, 296
balance of payments 319
capital formation 300
Castro, Fidel 299
Constitution (1901) 282, 289
community services 318
cooperatives 304
currency devaluation 311–12
customs reforms 286
Batista 296
Bay of Pigs 299
debt 296–7
disease 291, 298
economic conditions 285
economic crisis 289
economic development 289
economic stagnation 302
education 284, 290–1, 296, 301, 305, 315, 317, 320
employment 305, 319
female 303
industrial and construction sector 319
exports 288
family doctor project 320
foreign investment 287–8
health care 297, 298, 301, 315, 317, 320
health indicators 306, 315–17
beds 315
doctors 291–2
hospitals 306
hospitals, nationalization of 301
housing 301, 306
Housing Act 306
housing reform 299
Housing Reform Act 299
immigration 288
import quotes 295
income distribution 303
industrialization 300
infant mortality 291
insurance policies 293
investment 289
foreign 314
labour legislation 294, 298
life expectancy 315
micro brigades 306, 308
mining industry 285, 286
Missile Crisis 299
mutual societies 292–4
nationalization of enterprises 299–300
neocolonial model 287–94
nickel industries 320
oil exploration 309
population 285
railroad 285
rationing 304–5
*Reconcentration* 284, 285
retirement funds 294
retirement policies 301
Revolutionary Government 283, 299, 309
School Act (1909) 290

slavery 282
social development 305
social policies 283, 298
Social Security Act 300, 305
social security programmes 298, 305
Soviet Union and 282, 299, 304, 306
subemployment 307, 319
subsidies 313
sugar industry 282, 296, 302, 306, 310, 319–20
tariffs 313
teacher training 285
tourism 309, 312
Treaty of Commercial Reciprocity 282, 295
Treaty of Relationships 295
Treaty of Paris 284
unemployment 302
war of independence 282
customs duties 286

del Rio, Dr Alejandro 382
development theory 148, 330, 378
developmentalism 9, 10, 21, 263, 380, 387, 389
Diaz, Porfirio 121
dictatorships
*see individual countries*

East Asia 2, 69
*East Asian Development Welfare State* 2
Eastern Europe 299
Economic Commission for Latin America and the Caribbean (ECLAC) 9, 39, 158, 171, 385, 386
economic development 2, 4, 6, 25, 49, 390
economic growth 25, 48, 399
economic policies 8, 42, 206–7
economically active population (EAP) 26, 191, 194, 200
Ecuador 34, 68
education 122, 138, 195–7, 203–4, 383
*see individual countries*
El Salvador 327
Esping-Andersen, G. 4, 5, 12
European Union 4, 62, 68, 242

families of nations 5
Fox, Vicente 136

France 117
Free Trade Area of the Americas (FTAA) 62–3
free trade areas (FTAs) 56, 62
Frei Montalva, President Eduardo 381, 390, 392
Friedman, Milton 393
Fujimori, President 60, 149, 163, 165

General Agreement on Tariffs and Trade (GATT) 295
G6 countries 32
Germany 117
Global Social Product 306
globalization 1, 7, 10, 396, 403
Great Depression 155, 241, 380, 383–6, 387, 388
Guatemala 34, 327

Harberger, Arnold 392
health policy 53–4, 122, 298, 386
*see under individual countries*
Honduras 328
housing
*see under individual countries*
Huerta, Victoriano 123
human development 3, 49
Human Development Index (HDI) 37, 328, 356

import-substitution industrialization 158, 188, 301–2
inclusion 3
India 31
industrialization 10, 118, 239, 242, 250, 251
*see under individual countries*
inflation
*see under individual countries*
Inter-American Development Bank (IADB) 220, 231, 234
International Labour Organization (ILO) 233, 338
International Monetary Fund (IMF) 131, 203, 246
Italy 117, 225

Japan 31, 219
*Jumbo* supermarket chain 64

Keynesian virtuous circle 3
Keynesianism 9, 241
Korea 69
Kubistchek, President Juscelino 255, 260

labour creation schemes
  *see under individual countries*
late industrializers 1
*latifundia* 33, 379
Latin America 1, 2, 4, 10, 11, 21–113
  aerospace industry 64
  affluent elites 58
  bureaucratic elites 45
  Catholic Church 33, 41
  colonial period 32–8
    classical colonial 33
    slavery 35–6
  demography 24–6
  developmentalism 21, 37, 46–7, 49, 64
  early developers 42
  economic development 45
  economic policies 42
  energy agreements 63–4
  entrepreneurial classes 44–5, 56
  foreign capital 67
  free trade areas 62–4
  GDP per capita 25
  globalization 51
  ground rent 66–7
  health 43
  historical background 32
  human development 28–31
  Human Development Index 28, 31
  hyperinflation 48
  infrastructure 42
  job instability 57
  landowning elites 45, 55–6
  natural resources 66–7
  Neoliberalism 21, 48–9, 49–57
  'New Deal' 61
  oligarchies 45
  *pampas húmedas* 35
  political actors 38
  poverty reduction 52–3
  privatization 56, 57
  public expenditure 26–8, 41, 55, 69
  *seignori* 38
  self-employment 57
  social actors 40
  social legislation 42
  social policies 26–8, 38–9, 42–4, 45, 49, 50–1, 52–3, 67, 70
  socioeconomic structures 31–2
  state employment 45
  state-led development 21, 45
  transition 26–8, 29, 31–2
  urbanization 26–7, 34–5, 56
  'young giant' 61–2
  *see also individual countries*
Latin American Development Welfare State (LADWS) 1, 2, 4, 10, 11, 22, 38–47, 59, 179, 207, 241, 321, 378, 379, 380–1, 383, 385, 387, 396, 397, 401, 406
  *see also under individual countries;* Neo-LADWS
Latin American Integration Association (LAIA) 219
Lopez Portillo, José 129, 131
Lula da Silva, President 59, 246, 262, 263, 264, 266, 268

Machado, Gerardo 294
macroeconomic populism 48
McKinley, President William 284
Mediterranean Welfare State 5
Mercosur 62–4, 68, 219, 225, 226, 227, 240, 264, 265
Mexican Social Security Institute (IMSS) 126
Mexico 1, 25, 41, 45, 117–47, 240, 244
  1857 Constitution 123
  1910 Revolution 140
  and Catholic Church 119, 123–4
  and NAFTA 133, 136
  and pensions 132
  *campesinos* 123, 125, 130
  COPLAMAR 130, 131, 133
  de la Madrid government 132
  democracy 123
  Echeverría era 129, 130
  education 119–20, 123, 124, 130
  health policy 122, 126, 138, 139
  health reform programme 134–5
  housing policy 130
  Independence 118–20
  labour unions 124
  land reform 125

literacy 122
National Action Party (PAN) 132
National Solidarity Programme (PRONASOL) 133, 139
pension system 134
Porfiriato 118, 121–2
PROGRESA 136, 139
Reforma 118–20
Republic 118–20
rural poverty 139
SAM 130–1
social expenditure 131
social insurance 123, 126–7, 134–5
Social Security Law (NLSS) 136
welfare state 118, 124–31
Zedillo regime 134–6
Middle East 2
Mkandawire, Thandika 70
modernization 13, 250
Modernization Theory 6, 7, 13

NAFTA 62, 133
National Institute for Community Development (Indeco) 128, 139
National Worker Housing Fund (INFONAVIT) 128, 129, 138
Neo-Latin American Development Welfare State (Neo-LADWS) 59, 68, 69
Neoliberalism 1, 7–9, 10–11, 21, 46, 52–3, 55–6, 58, 59, 60, 65, 67–9, 224, 226, 248, 262, 263, 285, 266, 335, 346, 379, 391, 394, 396, 400, 401, 402, 404, 405, 406
New Zealand 31, 69
Nicaragua 328
non-governmental organizations (NGOs) 12, 232, 243
north-western Europe 2, 117
North Africa 2
North America 219, 242

Odrìa, General Manuel 156
OECD 225

Panama 37, 399
Paris Club 307, 308
Perón, Juan Domingo 191
Peru 1, 23, 148–84
agricultural sector 157
*Convivencia* 157
*Cooperacion Popular* (COOPOP) 160, 161
democratization 152, 162
demographic changes 176–7
Departmental Development Corporations (CORDES) 158, 160, 161
economic crisis 163
economic development 167–70
economic dualism 162
economic growth 149, 157
economic reforms 162
education 152, 153, 161, 172–3
employment generation 174–5
*Fondacion Nacional de Desarrollo Economico* (FNDE) 158
*Fondo de Compensacion Social y Desarrollo* (FONCODES) 164–5
funding 154
GDP per capita 150–1
government spending 156, 159, 161, 166
health 152, 160, 161, 173
housing 158, 159, 173
income 160
*indigenismo* 156
industrialization 159
inflation 162, 163
investment programmes 163–4
labour markets
land reform 161
literacy 160
living standards 171
Ministry of Production and Public Works 158
'modern' sector 155, 157
National Plan of Development 161
Neoliberal policies 149
pension system 173–4
political rights 161
poverty reduction 174
private sector 178
privatization process 164
*Pueblos Jovenes* 149
regional development 177–8
rural poverty 155
'Shining Path' 162
social deficit 171
social insurance

Peru – *continued*
social policy 149–50, 152–3, 154, 157–8, 163–6, 175–9
social programmes 159–60
stabilization programm 163–4
state–society relationship 2, 156–8
structural problems 150, 153, 166
trade 155, 157
trade unions 155
urban poor 149, 158
urbanization 160
wages 163
pensions 43
Philippines 295
Pinochet, General 391, 392, 393, 401
Platt Amendment 295
Pontifica Universidad Catolicà de Chile 393
poverty 51, 120, 121, 130, 138, 219, 230, 333, 344
Prado, Manuel 155, 156, 157
Prebisch, Raùl 158, 239, 386
private sector 69
privatization 68, 240, 336
pro-market reforms 1
productivism 12
public sector 69, 225
Puerto Rico 23, 37

Reaganism 394
Revolutionary Institutional Party (PRI) 60, 125
Rio de la Plata region 34–5
Rockefeller Foundation 156
Roosevelt, President F.D.R. 61, 294
Russia 31

Salinas de Gortari, Carlos 132
Sen, Amartya 148
September 11, 2001 320
slavery 36
Slim, Carlos 64
social Darwinism 121
social development 3, 4, 49, 333, 379
social legislation 117, 118, 129, 191, 218, 228
social policy 8, 10, 11, 26–8, 32, 39–40, 41, 43–4, 47, 50–1, 53, 121, 128, 187, 193, 204–5, 217, 233, 235, 243, 283, 328, 330, 334–5, 337, 338–40, 342, 378, 379, 381, 395, 396, 398, 401, 403–6
social protection 1, 192, 199, 201–2, 229, 231, 243, 244, 246, 247, 292–3, 403–4
social reforms 123, 192, 197–9, 294, 332
socialism 307
South Korea 148
Southern Europe 5
Southern Model of Welfare 5
Soviet Union
and Cuba 302
Spain 117, 118, 225
and Mexico 118
Spanish–Cuban–US War 284
structural adjustment policies 148
sustainable human development 148

Taiwan 69
Thatcherism 394
trade liberalization 226
trade unions 155
transition 23–5, 28, 31–2, 34, 38, 50, 93–113, 220–1, 262
Turkey 148

UNCTAD 239
UNDP 31, 148, 328
UNESCO 172
United Kingdom 117, 148
United States 148
*see also individual countries*
Universidad de Chile 383
University of Havana 284, 291
UN Latin American Demographics Centre (CELADE) 23
UNRISD 2, 10, 14, 21, 39, 378
urbanization
Uruguay 1, 23, 26, 51, 152, 217–36, 240, 244, 328, 399
ageing population 217, 222
and Mercosur 225
*Banco de Prevision Social* 223, 229, 230
*Caja Civil* 218
*Caja de Industria y Comercio* 218
children 230–1
debt 220
economic crisis 217, 218, 219–22

economic growth 226
education 217–18, 223, 231–2
emigration 219
employment 217, 225
employment policies 228–30
financial crisis 219, 220
health 223
Industrial and Commercial Income Tax (IRIC) 228
*Instituto Nacional del Menor* 231
*Intendencia Municipal de Montevideo* (IMM) 229, 234
labour market 222–3, 244–7
  informal sector 226
labour movements 218
Minimum National Salaries (MNS) 231
National Employment Office 234
pension fund 218, 223, 224
poverty, alleviation of 148, 230–2
public pension programmes 223
social policy 217–19, 228–33
social insurance 225,
social protection 234
structural problems 217
tax reforms 221
unemployment 217, 219, 224–7, 228, 229, 234
  female 224
  industrial sector 225
  insurance 228
  male 224
  public sector 225
*Uruguay Cultural* 222
*Uruguay Democratico* 222
*Uruguay Innovador* 222
*Uruguay Integrado* 222
*Uruguay Productivo* 221
*Uruguay Social* 221
welfare state 218, 234
women's employment 232–3
US companies
USSR 308, 309

Vásquez, Tabaré 59, 217, 221, 234
Velasco Alvarado, General Juan 149, 158, 161, 162

Washington Consensus 9, 22, 49, 50, 51, 52, 58, 59, 65, 346, 379, 397
welfare capitalism 4
welfare programmes 117
'welfare regimes approach' 5, 13
welfare state 10, 117, 131, 140, 187, 328
welfare state models 241
welfare state regimes 3, 13
Western Europe 5, 12, 13
World Development Report 148
World Bank 135, 148, 234, 296
World Trade Organization 226

CPSIA information can be obtained at www.ICGtesting.com
Printed in the USA
LVOW070225200412
278412LV00007B/21/P

9 780230 007888